Council for Standards for Human Service Education (CSHSE) National Standards (2013) Covered in This Text

Standards and Specifications	Ch 1: Introduction to Human Services	Ch 2: History of Social Welfare	Ch 3: Ethics & Values	Ch 4: Generalist Skills	Ch 5: Child Welfare	Ch 6: Adolescent Services	Ch 7: Gerontology Older Adults	Ch 8: Mental Illness	Ch 9: Homelessness	Ch 10: Medical, Health Care, Hospice	Ch 11: Public Schools	Ch 12: Religion, Spirituality	Ch 13: Violence, Victim Advocacy	Ch 14: Rural Human Services	Ch 15: International Human Services

Knowledge, Theory, Skills, and Values

1. History

Context: The history of human services provides the context in which the profession evolved, a foundation for assessment of present conditions in the field, and a framework for projecting and shaping trends and outcomes. Thus, human services professionals must have knowledge of how different human services emerged and the various forces that influenced their development.

Standard 11: The curriculum shall include the historical development of human services.

Specifications for Standard 11

Demonstrate how the knowledge, theory, and skills for each of the following specifications are included, analyzed, and applied in the curriculum:

Specification	Ch 1	Ch 2	Ch 3	Ch 4	Ch 5	Ch 6	Ch 7	Ch 8	Ch 9	Ch 10	Ch 11	Ch 12	Ch 13	Ch 14	Ch 15
a. The historical roots of human services.		✓			✓	✓	✓	✓	✓	✓	✓				
b. The creation of the human services profession.	✓	✓		✓	✓			✓			✓				
c. Historical and current legislation affecting services delivery.		✓			✓	✓		✓	✓	✓	✓	✓	✓	✓	
d. How public and private attitudes influence legislation and the interpretation of policies related to human services.	✓	✓	✓	✓	✓	✓	✓	✓	✓	✓			✓		
e. Differences between systems of governance and economics.	✓	✓												✓	✓
f. Exposure to a spectrum of political ideologies.	✓	✓													✓
g. Skills to analyze and interpret historical data for application in advocacy and social change.	✓	✓													✓

Standards and Specifications	Knowledge, Theory, Skills, and Values														
	Chapter 1: Introduction to Human Services	Chapter 2: History of Social Welfare	Chapter 3: Ethics & Values	Chapter 4: Generalist Skills	Chapter 5: Child Welfare	Chapter 6: Adolescent Services	Chapter 7: Gerontology Older Adults	Chapter 8: Mental Illness	Chapter 9: Homelessness	Chapter 10: Medical, Health Care, Hospice	Chapter 11: Public Schools	Chapter 12: Religion, Spirituality	Chapter 13: Violence, Victim Advocacy	Chapter 14: Rural Human Services	Chapter 15: International Human Services

2. Human Systems

Context: The human services professional must have an understanding of the structure and dynamics of organizations, communities, and society, as well as the nature of individuals and groups. This understanding is prerequisite to the determination of appropriate responses to human needs.

Standard 12: The curriculum shall include knowledge and theory of the interaction of human systems including: individual, interpersonal, group, family, organizational, community, and societal.

Specifications for Standard 12

Demonstrate how the knowledge, theory, and skills for each of the following specifications are included, analyzed, and applied in the curriculum:

Specification	Ch1	Ch2	Ch3	Ch4	Ch5	Ch6	Ch7	Ch8	Ch9	Ch10	Ch11	Ch12	Ch13	Ch14	Ch15
a. Theories of human development.	✓	✓		✓	✓	✓	✓					✓		✓	
b. Small groups: 1. Overview of how small groups are used in human services settings, 2. Theories of group dynamics, and 3. Group facilitation skills.				✓											
c. Changing family structures and roles.		✓		✓	✓	✓	✓								
d. An introduction to the organizational structures of communities.	✓	✓	✓												
e. An understanding of the capacities, limitations, and resiliency of human systems.	✓	✓	✓	✓	✓							✓	✓	✓	✓
f. Emphasis on context and the role of diversity (including, but not limited to ethnicity, culture, gender, sexual orientation, learning styles, ability, and socioeconomic status) in determining and meeting human needs.	✓	✓	✓	✓	✓	✓	✓	✓	✓	✓	✓	✓	✓	✓	✓
g. Processes to effect social change through advocacy work at all levels of society including community development, community and grassroots organizing, and local and global activism.	✓	✓	✓	✓	✓	✓	✓	✓	✓	✓	✓	✓	✓	✓	✓
h. Processes to analyze, interpret, and effect policies and laws at local, state, and national levels that influence services delivery systems.		✓		✓				✓	✓						✓

Standards and Specifications	Knowledge, Theory, Skills, and Values														
	Chapter 1: Introduction to Human Services	Chapter 2: History of Social Welfare	Chapter 3: Ethics & Values	Chapter 4: Generalist Skills	Chapter 5: Child Welfare	Chapter 6: Adolescent Services	Chapter 7: Gerontology Older Adults	Chapter 8: Mental Illness	Chapter 9: Homelessness	Chapter 10: Medical, Health Care, Hospice	Chapter 11: Public Schools	Chapter 12: Religion, Spirituality	Chapter 13: Violence, Victim Advocacy	Chapter 14: Rural Human Services	Chapter 15: International Human Services

3. Human Services Delivery Systems

Context: The demand for services and the funding of educational programs has been closely related to identifiable human conditions including, among others, aging, delinquency, crime, poverty, mental illness, physical illness, chemical dependency, and developmental disabilities. The needs that arise in these conditions provide the focus for the human services profession.

Standard 13: The curriculum shall address the scope of conditions that promote or inhibit human functioning.

Specifications for Standard 13

Demonstrate how the knowledge, theory, and skills for each of the following specifications are included, analyzed, and applied in the curriculum:

	Ch1	Ch2	Ch3	Ch4	Ch5	Ch6	Ch7	Ch8	Ch9	Ch10	Ch11	Ch12	Ch13	Ch14	Ch15
a. The range and characteristics of human services delivery systems and organizations.	✓			✓	✓	✓	✓	✓	✓	✓	✓	✓	✓	✓	✓
b. The range of populations served and needs addressed by human services.	✓			✓	✓	✓	✓	✓	✓	✓	✓	✓	✓	✓	✓
c. The major models used to conceptualize and integrate prevention, maintenance, intervention, rehabilitation, and healthy functioning.				✓	✓	✓	✓	✓	✓	✓	✓	✓	✓	✓	✓
d. Economic and social class systems including systemic causes of poverty.	✓	✓		✓	✓				✓		✓				✓
e. Political and ideological aspects of human services.	✓	✓	✓	✓											✓
f. International and global influences on services delivery.															✓
g. Skills to effect and influence social policy.	✓	✓		✓	✓	✓	✓	✓	✓	✓	✓	✓	✓	✓	✓

Standards and Specifications	Knowledge, Theory, Skills, and Values														
	Chapter 1: Introduction to Human Services	Chapter 2: History of Social Welfare	Chapter 3: Ethics & Values	Chapter 4: Generalist Skills	Chapter 5: Child Welfare	Chapter 6: Adolescent Services	Chapter 7: Gerontology Older Adults	Chapter 8: Mental Illness	Chapter 9: Homelessness	Chapter 10: Medical, Health Care, Hospice	Chapter 11: Public Schools	Chapter 12: Religion, Spirituality	Chapter 13: Violence, Victim Advocacy	Chapter 14: Rural Human Services	Chapter 15: International Human Services

4. Information Management

Context: The delivery of human services depends on the appropriate integration and use of information such as client data, statistical information, and record keeping. Information management skills include obtaining, organizing, analyzing, evaluating, and disseminating information.

Standard 14: The curriculum shall provide knowledge and skills in information management.

Specifications for Standard 14

Demonstrate how the knowledge, theory, and skills for each of the following specifications are included, analyzed, and applied in the curriculum:

	1	2	3	4	5	6	7	8	9	10	11	12	13	14	15
a. Obtaining information through interviewing, active listening, consultation with others, library or other research, and the observation of clients and systems.				✓	✓	✓	✓	✓	✓	✓	✓	✓	✓	✓	✓
b. Recording, organizing, and assessing the relevance, adequacy, accuracy, and validity of information provided by others.				✓											
c. Compiling, synthesizing, and categorizing information.				✓											
d. Disseminating routine and critical information to clients, colleagues, or other members of the related services system that is: 1. Provided in written or oral form, and 2. Provided in a timely manner.				✓											
e. Maintaining client confidentiality and appropriately using client data.				✓											
f. Using technology for word processing, sending email, and locating and evaluating information.				✓											
g. Performing an elementary community-needs assessment.				✓											
h. Conducting a basic program evaluation.				✓											
i. Utilizing research findings and other information for community education and public relations.				✓											
j. Using technology to create and manage spreadsheets and databases.				✓											

Standards and Specifications	Knowledge, Theory, Skills, and Values														
	Chapter 1: Introduction to Human Services	Chapter 2: History of Social Welfare	Chapter 3: Ethics & Values	Chapter 4: Generalist Skills	Chapter 5: Child Welfare	Chapter 6: Adolescent Services	Chapter 7: Gerontology Older Adults	Chapter 8: Mental Illness	Chapter 9: Homelessness	Chapter 10: Medical, Health Care, Hospice	Chapter 11: Public Schools	Chapter 12: Religion, Spirituality	Chapter 13: Violence, Victim Advocacy	Chapter 14: Rural Human Services	Chapter 15: International Human Services

5. Planning and Evaluation

Context: A major component of the human services profession involves the assessment of the needs of clients and client groups and the planning of programs and interventions that will assist clients and client groups in promoting optimal functioning, growth, and goal attainment. At regular intervals, the outcomes must be evaluated and necessary adjustments made to the plan both at an individual client and program level.

Standard 15: The curriculum shall provide knowledge and skill development in systematic analysis of services needs; planning appropriate strategies, services, and implementation; and evaluation of outcomes.

Specifications for Standard 15

Demonstrate how the knowledge, theory, and skills for each of the following specifications are included, analyzed, and applied in the curriculum:

	Ch1	Ch2	Ch3	Ch4	Ch5	Ch6	Ch7	Ch8	Ch9	Ch10	Ch11	Ch12	Ch13	Ch14	Ch15
a. Knowledge and skills to analyze and assess the needs of clients or client groups.	✓	✓		✓	✓	✓	✓	✓	✓	✓	✓	✓	✓	✓	✓
b. Skills to develop goals, and design and implement a plan of action.	✓	✓		✓	✓	✓	✓	✓	✓	✓	✓	✓	✓	✓	✓
c. Skills to evaluate the outcomes of the plan and the impact on the client or client group.				✓				✓							
d. Program design.				✓											
e. Program implementation.				✓											
f. Program evaluation.				✓											

Standards and Specifications	Knowledge, Theory, Skills, and Values														
6. Interventions and Direct Services **Context:** Human services professionals function as change agents and must therefore attain and develop a core of knowledge, theory, and skills to provide direct services and interventions to clients and client groups. **Standard 16:** The curriculum shall provide knowledge and skills in direct service delivery and appropriate interventions.	Chapter 1: Introduction to Human Services	Chapter 2: History of Social Welfare	Chapter 3: Ethics & Values	Chapter 4: Generalist Skills	Chapter 5: Child Welfare	Chapter 6: Adolescent Services	Chapter 7: Gerontology Older Adults	Chapter 8: Mental Illness	Chapter 9: Homelessness	Chapter 10: Medical, Health Care, Hospice	Chapter 11: Public Schools	Chapter 12: Religion, Spirituality	Chapter 13: Violence, Victim Advocacy	Chapter 14: Rural Human Services	Chapter 15: International Human Services
Specifications for Standard 16															
Demonstrate how the knowledge, theory, and skills for each of the following specifications are included, analyzed, and applied in the curriculum:															
a. Theory and knowledge bases of prevention, intervention, and maintenance strategies to achieve maximum autonomy and functioning.	✓			✓	✓	✓	✓	✓	✓	✓	✓	✓	✓	✓	✓
b. Skills to facilitate appropriate direct services and interventions related to specific client or client group goals.				✓	✓			✓							
c. Knowledge and skill development in the following areas: 1. Case management, 2. Intake interviewing, 3. Individual counseling, 4. Group facilitation and counseling, 5. Location and use of appropriate resources and referrals, and 6. Use of consultation.				✓											

Standards and Specifications	Knowledge, Theory, Skills, and Values														
	Chapter 1: Introduction to Human Services	Chapter 2: History of Social Welfare	Chapter 3: Ethics & Values	Chapter 4: Generalist Skills	Chapter 5: Child Welfare	Chapter 6: Adolescent Services	Chapter 7: Gerontology Older Adults	Chapter 8: Mental Illness	Chapter 9: Homelessness	Chapter 10: Medical, Health Care, Hospice	Chapter 11: Public Schools	Chapter 12: Religion, Spirituality	Chapter 13: Violence, Victim Advocacy	Chapter 14: Rural Human Services	Chapter 15: International Human Services

7. Interpersonal Communication

Context: The ability to create genuine and empathic relationships with others is central to the human services profession. These skills are applicable to all levels of education, and a greater proficiency is expected at each progressively higher level.

Standard 17: Learning experiences shall be provided for the student to develop his or her interpersonal skills.

Specifications for Standard 17	1	2	3	4	5	6	7	8	9	10	11	12	13	14	15
Demonstrate how the knowledge, theory, and skills for each of the following specifications are included, analyzed, and applied in the curriculum:															
a. Clarifying expectations.			✓	✓				✓							
b. Dealing effectively with conflict.				✓											
c. Establishing rapport with clients.	✓		✓	✓	✓	✓	✓	✓	✓	✓	✓	✓	✓	✓	
d. Developing and sustaining behaviors that are congruent with the values and ethics of the profession.			✓	✓											

Standards and Specifications	Knowledge, Theory, Skills, and Values														
	Chapter 1: Introduction to Human Services	Chapter 2: History of Social Welfare	Chapter 3: Ethics & Values	Chapter 4: Generalist Skills	Chapter 5: Child Welfare	Chapter 6: Adolescent Services	Chapter 7: Gerontology Older Adults	Chapter 8: Mental Illness	Chapter 9: Homelessness	Chapter 10: Medical, Health Care, Hospice	Chapter 11: Public Schools	Chapter 12: Religion, Spirituality	Chapter 13: Violence, Victim Advocacy	Chapter 14: Rural Human Services	Chapter 15: International Human Services

8. Administrative

Context: A holistic approach to human services recognizes direct and indirect services as components of the same system. Administrative support (indirect service) is essential to the effective delivery of direct services to clients or client groups.

Standard 18: The curriculum shall provide knowledge, theory, and skills in the administrative aspects of the services delivery system.

Specifications for Standard 18

Demonstrate how the knowledge, theory, and skills for each of the following specifications are included, analyzed, and applied in the curriculum:

	Ch1	Ch2	Ch3	Ch4	Ch5	Ch6	Ch7	Ch8	Ch9	Ch10	Ch11	Ch12	Ch13	Ch14	Ch15
a. Managing organizations through leadership and strategic planning.	✓		✓	✓											
b. Supervision and human resource management.															
c. Planning and evaluating programs, services, and operational functions.															
d. Developing budgets and monitoring expenditures.															
e. Grant and contract negotiation.															
f. Legal and regulatory issues and risk management.															
g. Managing professional development of staff.															
h. Recruiting and managing volunteers.															
i. Constituency building and other advocacy techniques, such as lobbying, grassroots movements, and community development and organizing.				✓											✓

Standards and Specifications	Knowledge, Theory, Skills, and Values														
	Chapter 1: Introduction to Human Services	Chapter 2: History of Social Welfare	Chapter 3: Ethics & Values	Chapter 4: Generalist Skills	Chapter 5: Child Welfare	Chapter 6: Adolescent Services	Chapter 7: Gerontology Older Adults	Chapter 8: Mental Illness	Chapter 9: Homelessness	Chapter 10: Medical, Health Care, Hospice	Chapter 11: Public Schools	Chapter 12: Religion, Spirituality	Chapter 13: Violence, Victim Advocacy	Chapter 14: Rural Human Services	Chapter 15: International Human Services

9. Client-Related Values and Attitudes

Context: There are values and ethics intrinsic to the human services profession that have been agreed to as governing principles of professional practice.

Standard 19: The curriculum shall incorporate human services values and attitudes and promote understanding of human services ethics and their application in practice.

Specifications for Standard 19

Demonstrate how the knowledge, theory, and skills for each of the following specifications are included, analyzed, and applied in the curriculum:

Specification	Ch1	Ch2	Ch3	Ch4	Ch5	Ch6	Ch7	Ch8	Ch9	Ch10	Ch11	Ch12	Ch13	Ch14	Ch15
a. The least intrusive intervention in the least restrictive environment.				✓				✓			✓				
b. Client self-determination.	✓	✓	✓	✓		✓	✓	✓	✓	✓					
c. Confidentiality of information.			✓	✓	✓			✓			✓	✓			
d. The worth and uniqueness of individuals including culture, ethnicity, race, class, gender, religion, ability, sexual orientation, and other expressions of diversity.	✓	✓	✓	✓	✓	✓	✓	✓	✓	✓	✓	✓	✓	✓	✓
e. Belief that individuals, services systems, and society can change.	✓	✓		✓											✓
f. Interdisciplinary team approaches to problem solving.				✓								✓	✓		
g. Appropriate professional boundaries.	✓	✓	✓	✓	✓			✓	✓	✓	✓	✓		✓	
h. Integration of the ethical standards outlined by the National Organization for Human Services/Council for Standards in Human Service Education (available on NOHS website).			✓	✓	✓			✓			✓		✓	✓	

Standards and Specifications	Knowledge, Theory, Skills, and Values														
	Chapter 1: Introduction to Human Services	Chapter 2: History of Social Welfare	Chapter 3: Ethics & Values	Chapter 4: Generalist Skills	Chapter 5: Child Welfare	Chapter 6: Adolescent Services	Chapter 7: Gerontology Older Adults	Chapter 8: Mental Illness	Chapter 9: Homelessness	Chapter 10: Medical, Health Care, Hospice	Chapter 11: Public Schools	Chapter 12: Religion, Spirituality	Chapter 13: Violence, Victim Advocacy	Chapter 14: Rural Human Services	Chapter 15: International Human Services

10. Self-Development

Context: Human services professionals use their experience and knowledge for understanding and helping clients. This requires awareness of one's own values, cultural bias, philosophies, personality, and style in the effective use of the professional self. It also requires an understanding of how these personal characteristics affect clients.

Standard 20: The program shall provide experiences and support to enable students to develop awareness of their own values, personalities, reaction patterns, interpersonal styles, and limitations.

Specifications for Standard 20

Demonstrate how the knowledge, theory, and skills for each of the following specifications are included, analyzed, and applied in the curriculum:

Specification	C1	C2	C3	C4	C5	C6	C7	C8	C9	C10	C11	C12	C13	C14	C15
a. Conscious use of self.	✓			✓											
b. Clarification of personal and professional values.			✓												
c. Awareness of diversity.	✓	✓	✓	✓	✓	✓	✓	✓	✓	✓	✓	✓	✓	✓	✓
d. Strategies for self-care.				✓											
e. Reflection on professional self (e.g., journaling, development of a portfolio, or project demonstrating competency).				✓											

FOURTH EDITION

Introduction to Human Services

Through the Eyes of Practice Settings

Michelle E. Martin
California State University, Fullerton

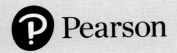

330 Hudson Street, NY, NY 10013

Director, Teacher Education & the Helping Professions: Kevin M. Davis
Portfolio Manager: Rebecca Fox-Gieg
Content Project Manager: Pamela D. Bennett
Portfolio Management Assistant: Anne McAlpine
Executive Field Marketing Manager: Krista Clark
Executive Product Marketing Manager: Christopher Barry
Procurement Specialist: Deidra Smith
Cover Designer: Melissa Welch
Cover Cover Photo: Getty Images/laurenepbath
Full-Service Project Management: Srinivasan Sundararajan, Lumina Datamatics, Inc.
Composition: Lumina Datamatics, Inc.
Printer/Binder: LSC Communications
Cover Printer: Phoenix Color
Text Font: DanteMTPro 10.5 pt.

Library of Congress Cataloging-in-Publication Data

Names: Martin, Michelle E., author.
Title: Introduction to human services : through the eyes of practice settings
    / Michelle E. Martin, California State University, Fullerton.
Description: Fourth edition. | New York, NY : Pearson, [2018] | Includes
    bibliographical references and index.
Identifiers: LCCN 2016049108 | ISBN 9780134461038 | ISBN 0134461037
Subjects: LCSH: Human services—Vocational guidance—United States.
Classification: LCC HV10.5 .M37 2018 | DDC 362.973023—dc23
LC record available at https://lccn.loc.gov/2016049108

3   18

 **Pearson**

ISBN-10:   0-13-446103-7
ISBN-13: 978-0-13-446103-8

Brief Contents

Contents

Preface

The fourth edition of *Introduction to Human Services: Through the Eyes of Practice Settings* includes many important updates and additions reflecting the many changes that have occurred in the world since the first edition was written. I began writing this book in 2003, the year MySpace was created and three years before Facebook was opened to the public. Social media wasn't even a thing back then, and I could never have imagined how much the Internet and social media in particular would change the human services profession and the world in general. Back in the early 2000s, most human service agencies had just one computer (called a CRT) for the entire staff. Fast forward to 2017, and most human service providers are now armed with laptops, iPads, and smartphones, enabling them in be in contact with their clients, colleagues, and service providers anywhere at almost any time. New technology hasn't just changed the world; it's altered the way we can effect change in the world as well. Do you want to start a social movement? Create a Facebook page and mobilize thousands of people globally, creating social awareness through the posting of status updates, online news articles, blogs, and YouTube videos.

I was inspired to write this text because as a human service provider who had a few decades of direct practice and community work under my belt, I wasn't satisfied with the way most texts were written. I was (and still am) convinced that it's impossible to truly understand the nature of human services without exploring the role and functions of human service providers within the context of their work in various practice settings, confronting a range of social problem that impact a diverse client population. I've worked with children in several different contexts—foster care, schools, and hospice, for instance—and the manifestation of issues that guides interventions and problems are very different. Sure, developmental dynamics are generally the same across the life course, but my point is that context matters, especially in the human services, a profession committed to confronting a range of social problems impacting the world's most vulnerable populations.

NEW TO THIS EDITION

The fourth edition of this text has involved a major rewriting for several reasons. First, the text needed a general "facelift," an overall updating, with fresh writing and newer perspectives. Second, because so much has happened in the world since this text was first published, updates throughout the entire text needed to be holistic and comprehensive. Virtually all of the research has been updated. Social media has been integrated throughout, wherever relevant, to illustrate how technology is impacting our lives (for good and not-so-good). Current events have been updated, as well as legislation impacting those in the human services and the populations they serve. I have made a distinct effort to incorporate suggestions from professors and students from around the country who use my text and were kind enough to take the time to reach out to me.

Here are some of the major updates in this text:

- A greater infusion of cultural competency content related to African Americans, Latinos, Native Americans, Native Alaskans, and Native Hawaiian and Pacific Islanders throughout the text, which will help students recognize the varied way social problems impact diverse populations.
- Added new content on the role of technology in social problems and intervention strategies, including new content on social media.
- Increased content on mandated child abuse reporting requirements with current legal reporting requirements.
- Increased infusion of issues related to LGBTQ+ populations, including content on the current climate related to a range of sexual and gender expressions.
- Updated content reflecting the DSM-5, which provides more accurate information on how mental disorders and illnesses are currently viewed and categorized.
- New content on military personnel and their family members, and veteran populations, which will better prepare students who wish to work with these populations and their growing needs.
- Added new content on the Affordable Care Act, which will assist students in better serving a range of populations relying on government-subsidized health care.
- In Chapter 12 on faith-based agencies, added new content on the mindfulness movement and contemplative practice, which will help students expand their knowledge of a range of religious and spiritual experiences.
- Updated content on interfamily violence and campus rapes to better reflect the current state of gender inequity and the state of rape culture.
- A new content on sexual assault, including rape on college campuses, will benefit students in expanding their knowledge on current trends and responses, while new content on the Violence Against Women Act will provide students with relevant information on the most recent reauthorization extending coverage to immigrants and Native American women.
- New content on immigrants and refugees will provide students with increased awareness about current dynamics surrounding global conflict and migration flow.
- A new chapter on rural human services was added, exploring dynamics and social problems impacting rural communities and rural enclaves, a generally newer practice setting that addresses the growing awareness of challenges facing many rural communities and rural enclaves, including economic challenges related to deindustrialization and a growing problem of opioid addiction, particularly among middle-aged women.
- Updated content on global human services provides students with increased global awareness necessary for an increasingly globalized world.
- Reflections on the political climate leading up to the 2016 presidential election and an updated epilogue addressing post-election dynamics have been added.

Pearson Enhanced eText

The fourth edition is available as an enhanced Pearson eText—a rich, interactive learning environment designed to improve the reader's mastery of content with the following multimedia features[1]:

- Design: The overall design fosters the reader's understanding, with learning outcomes, clear explanations, applications, and feedback.
- Videos: Our new digital format allows direct linking to videos illustrating and expanding on the human services issues presented in the text.
- Self-Checks: Embedded assessment questions align with learning outcomes and appear as a link at the end of each major chapter section in the Pearson eText. Using multiple-choice questions, the self-checks allow readers to assess how well they have mastered the content.
- Chapter Quizzes: At the end of each chapter, short-answer questions encourage readers to reflect on chapter concepts. We have provided feedback to support the development of thoughtful responses.

ACKNOWLEDGMENTS

I would like to thank several people who helped make this edition possible. First and foremost, I would like to thank my family—my son Xander, who was only 9 when I started writing this book, and is now 22 and a senior at Colorado University, Boulder. I'd like to thank Professor Joanne Little at the University of Hawai'i and her students, who provided valuable information on the nature of Native Hawaiians and Pacific Islanders, and Dr. Jo Ann Barley, chair of the human services program at the University of Alaska, for her valuable feedback on a range of issues, including Alaskan Natives.

I'd like to thank my friend and longtime colleague Kathy Clyburn, assistant dean at Dominican University in River Forest, Illinois, for her valuable feedback and support. I'd also like to thank my colleagues and MSW students at California State University, Fullerton, who sharpen my mind and give me new ways to think about this wonderful profession and the people whom we serve.

Finally, I would like to thank the reviewers who provided valuable input for revising this edition: Tommy Lopez, Central Piedmont Community College; Loretta Mooney, Rowan University and Rutgers University; James A. Myers, Genesee Community College; Frank Ridzi, Le Moyne College; and Tara J. Walk, Lincoln Land Community College.

---

[1]Please note that eText enhancements are only available in the Pearson eText and are not available in third-party eTexts such as VitalSource and Kindle.

1

Introduction to the Human Services Profession

Purpose, Preparation, Practice, and Theoretical Orientations

© BLAS / FOTOLIA

Sara works for a hospice agency and spends one hour twice a week with Steven, who has been diagnosed with terminal cancer of the liver. He has been told that he has approximately six months to live. He has been estranged from his adult daughter for four years, and Sara is helping him develop a plan for reunification. Sara helps Steve deal with his terminal diagnosis by encouraging him to talk through his feelings about being sick and dying. Steve talks a lot about his fear of being in pain and his overwhelming feelings of regret about many of the choices he has made in his life. Sara listens and also helps Steve develop a plan for saying all the things he needs to say before he dies. During their last meeting, Sara helped Steve write a list of things he would like to say to his daughter, his ex-wife, and other family members. Sara is also helping Steve make important end-of-life decisions, including planning his own funeral. Sara and

Steve will continue to meet weekly until his death, and if possible, she will be with him and his family when he passes away.

Gary works for a public middle school and meets with six seventh graders every Monday to talk about their feelings. Gary helps them learn better ways to explore feelings of anger and frustration. During their meetings, they sometimes do fun things like play basketball. They also play board games where they each take turns picking a "self-disclosure" card and answering a personal question. Gary uses the game to enter into discussions about healthy ways of coping with feelings, particularly frustration and anger. He also uses the game to get to know the students in a more personal manner, making it easier for them to open up to him. Gary spends one session per month discussing the students' progress in their classes. The goal for the group is to help the students learn how to better control their anger and to develop more prosocial behavior, such as empathy and respect for others.

Cynthia works for her county's district attorney's office and has spent every day this past week in criminal court with Kelly, a victim of felony home invasion, aggravated kidnapping, and aggravated battery. Cynthia provides Kelly with advocacy as well as counseling to help Kelly deal with the trauma of having a man barge through her back door searching for money, and threatening Kelly and her baby. Cynthia keeps Kelly apprised of all court proceedings and accompanies her to court, if Kelly chooses to assert her right to attend the proceedings. She also accompanies Kelly during all police interviews and helps her prepare for testifying. During these hearings, as well as during numerous telephone conversations, Cynthia helps Kelly understand and deal with her feelings, including her recent experience of repeatedly imagining the violent incident, her intense fear of being alone, and her guilt that she had not locked her back door. Lately, Kelly admitted that she has been crying a lot more and has had feelings of unrelenting sadness, so Cynthia has referred Kelly to a licensed professional counselor as well as to a support group for survivors of violent crime for Kelly and her husband.

Frank works for county social services, child welfare division, and is working with Lisa, who recently had her three young children removed from her home for physical and emotional neglect. Frank has arranged for Lisa to take parenting classes and receive individual counseling so that she can learn how to better manage her frustrations with her children. He has also arranged for her to enter a drug rehabilitation program to treat her addiction to alcohol and cocaine. Frank and Lisa meet once a week to talk about her progress toward her case goals. He also monitors her weekly visitation with her children. Frank is required to attend status updates in court once per month so that the judge assigned to the case can remain apprised of Lisa's progress in her parenting plan. Successful completion of this plan will enable Lisa to regain custody of her children. Frank will continue to monitor her progress, as well as the progress of the children, who are in foster care placement until a decision can be made about the custody of her children.

Allison is currently lobbying several state legislators in support of a bill that would increase funding for child abuse prevention and treatment. As a social policy advocate for a local grassroots organization, Allison is responsible for writing position statements and contacting local lawmakers to educate them on the importance of legislation aimed at reducing child abuse through prevention measures and other outreach efforts. Allison also writes grants for federal and private funding of the organization's various child advocacy programs, and is consistently called upon to provide opinions about a range of child abuse prevention measures.

What do all these professionals have in common? They are all working within the interdisciplinary field of human services, each possessing a broad range of generalist skills and having a wide range of responsibilities related to their respective roles in helping people overcome a variety of **social problems**. The National Organization for Human Services (NOHS), a national professional association of human services practitioners and educators, describes the human services profession as an interdisciplinary field that exists to meet the needs of clients through prevention efforts and direct practice, with the goal of significantly improving their lives. Human service professionals are also committed to improving the ways in which services are provided (service delivery systems), as well as improving the quality of those services (NOHS, n.d.).

WHAT IS HUMAN SERVICES?

Human services is a broad term covering a number of careers, all having one thing in common—helping people meet their basic needs that for whatever reason cannot be met without outside assistance, allowing people and communities to function at an optimum level. The human services field can include a variety of job titles, including caseworker, program coordinator, outreach counselor, crisis counselor, and victim advocate. However, increasingly those working in the human services fields with a degree in human services are identified as human service professionals, human service practitioners, or human service generalists.

The human services profession is relatively young, and thus is still developing a professional identity, which includes distinguishing human services from its close "cousin," social work. Many human service educational programs were developed in the 1970s by social workers, and thus there was considerable overlap with Bachelor of Social Work (BSW) programs (Topuzova, 2006). But in recent years, human service educational programs have become far more distinctive from social work programs, despite some overlap remaining.

With regard to similarities, both human services and social work disciplines are interdisciplinary in nature, and both focus on meeting the needs of marginalized and historically oppressed populations. Both are committed to social justice and advocacy on micro and macro levels. Additionally, both disciplines require a field component, which is perceived as a foundational component of the program's pedagogy.

Differences include the role of the professionals in psychology, counseling, and other mental health fields in further developing the human services profession from a practice perspective. Additionally, many human service programs tend to be more interdisciplinary in hiring practices, including hiring instructors from a variety of helping fields, whereas social work programs place an emphasis on hiring faculty with social work degrees from Council on Social Work Education (CSWE) accredited programs (Topuzova, 2006). Social workers also have state licensing requirements, whereas currently there are no state licensing requirements for human service graduates.

An important question then is, are the differences between human services and other helping professions solely educational ones or are there actual differences in the field? And if the former is true, why did the field of human services evolve at all as a specific discipline? The answers to these questions are complex, and while there remains no prevailing consensus, many believe that with regard to social work specifically, human services evolved to fill gaps left by social work's increasing professionalization. In other words, as the requirements to become a social worker continued to increase, professional social workers tended to move out of paraprofessional and/or grassroots roles and into more highly trained direct service and administration roles.

Prior to the professionalization of the social work discipline, anyone who worked with those in need could identify as a social worker. Yet, licensing requirements mean that only professionals who have a BSW or Master of Social Work (MSW), and hold a state license (Licensed Social Worker [LSW] or Licensed Clinical Social Worker [LCSW]), can refer to themselves as social workers. So what about everyone else? What about those professionals working in homeless or domestic violence shelters, those who are court advocates working with victims of violent crime, or those who manage the cases of recently arrived refugees? Well, if they have completed an associate, baccalaureate, or a master's program in human services, we call them *human service professionals, practitioners,* or *generalists.* Thus, human service professionals fill a very important role in society, and while there is some overlap with social work with regard to the professions' roots, educational philosophies, and professional missions, they are unique professions in their scope and in some respects, their focus.

Because of the overlap between human services and social work, I use the title *human service professional, practitioner,* or *generalist* to refer to all professionals working within the human services field; however if I use the term *social worker,* then I am referring to the legal definition and professional distinction of a licensed social worker, indicating either a BSW or MSW level of education. Also, I use the terms *human services* and *human service agency* rather than *social services* and *social service agency,* although these terms tend to be used interchangeably in the professional literature.

Why Is Human Services Needed?

All human beings have basic needs, such as the need for food, shelter, and safety. People also have social needs, such as the need for interpersonal connection, love, and community. People have psychological needs, such as the need to deal with trauma from past abuse, or the psychological ramifications of enduring a disaster, such as a tornado or hurricane. People can get their needs met in a variety of ways. For instance, family, friends, and places of worship can meet social and psychological needs. Needs related to food, shelter, and other more complicated needs such as health care needs can be met through employment, family assistance, and employer-sponsored health benefits. The path toward meeting many needs is education, which increases access to good jobs and increased consumer awareness.

But sometimes people experience crises that are beyond their ability to manage with their available resources. Examples include a natural disaster or a health care crisis. There are also many people in society who are unable to meet even their most basic needs. Perhaps they do not have a supportive family or have no family at all; they may have no friends or have friends who are either unsupportive or unable to provide assistance. They may have no social support network of any kind—no faith community, no family, no friends, no supportive neighbors. They may lack the skills or education to gain sufficient employment, and thus they may not have health insurance and may live paycheck-to-paycheck and not have a "rainy day" savings account. Perhaps they've spent the majority of their lives dealing with an abusive and chaotic childhood and are now suffering from the manifestation of that experience in the form of psychological problems and substance abuse, and as a consequence cannot focus on meeting their basic needs until they are able to deal with their childhood psychological trauma. Or perhaps they are older adults and their savings account and pension are exhausted.

People who have always had good support systems and have not experienced challenges requiring extensive resources may mistakenly believe that those who cannot meet their most basic needs of shelter, food, health care, and emotional and social needs must be doing something wrong. This belief is often incorrect because numerous barriers exist that prevent some people from meeting their needs. These barriers may or may not be apparent to others, but they often exist. Some of these barriers might be related to individual behavior, but more often the reasons people cannot meet their basic needs are quite complex and often lie in dynamics beyond an individual's control. Thus while some people have great families, wonderfully supportive friends, the benefit of a good education, and have not experienced oppression or marginalization, nor have had significant history of abuse or loss and may be self-sufficient in meeting their own needs, this does not mean that those who struggle to meet their basic needs are doing something wrong.

Many people experience challenges that push them beyond their level of self-sufficiency.

Essentially, human service agencies come into the picture when people find themselves confronting barriers to getting their basic needs met and their own resources for overcoming these obstacles are insufficient. Some of these barriers include the following:

- Lack of family (or supportive family)
- Lack of a healthy support system of friends
- Mental illness
- Poverty (particularly chronic poverty)
- **Social exclusion** (e.g., due to racial discrimination, gender bias)
- Racism
- Oppression (e.g., racial, gender, age, ability)
- Trauma
- Natural disasters
- Lack of education
- Lack of employment skills
- Unemployment/underemployment
- Economic recession
- Physical and/or intellectual disability

A tremendous amount of controversy surrounds how best to help people meet their basic needs. Various philosophies exist regarding what types of services effectively help those in need. For instance, some philosophies advocate that liberal social welfare programs foster dependence, and thus should be stigmatized to discourage overreliance. Other philosophies suggest that a solid safety net fosters self-sufficiency, and that what may appear to be dependence and entitlement on the part of recipients is really discouragement and resignation.

Regardless of what philosophy one adopts with regard to social welfare assistance, the primary goal of human services is to assist people in achieving self-sufficiency and reaching their optimal level of functioning. This means that human service professionals are committed to helping people develop the necessary skills to become self-sufficient

Watch this video on the aftermath of Hurricane Katrina in 2005. How many primary and secondary social problems can you identify in this video? How can human services help?

ENHANCEDetext *video example 1.1*

www.youtube.com/
watch?v=TnA_NvDul6M

and fully functioning (to the best of their ability), personally and within society. Thus, although an agency may subsidize a family's rent for a few months when they are in a crisis, human service professionals will then work with the family members to remove any barriers that may be keeping them from meeting their housing needs in the future. Examples of such barriers are substance abuse disorders, a lack of education or vocational skills, health problems, mental illness, or gaining self-advocacy skills necessary for combating prejudice and discrimination in the workplace, to the greatest extend possible.

Human service professionals are committed to working on a **micro level** and a **mezzo level** with a broad range of populations, including high-needs and **disenfranchised populations**, as well as members of **historically oppressed and marginalized groups**, and providing them with the necessary resources to get their basic needs met. Human service professionals are also committed to working on a **macro level** to remove barriers to optimal functioning that affect large groups of people. They do this by giving oppressed and marginalized populations a voice and extending them political and social power within society. For instance, by advocating for changes in laws and various policies, human service professionals have contributed to making great strides in confronting prejudice and discrimination based on race, gender, sexual orientation, socioeconomic status (SES), or any of a number of characterizations that may lead to marginalization within society.

ENHANCEDetext *self-check 1.1*

EDUCATIONAL REQUIREMENTS AND PROFESSIONAL STANDARDS FOR THE HELPING PROFESSIONS

Because of the interdisciplinary nature of the human service discipline, as well as the overlap with other helping professions, determining the required levels of education, specific degrees, and when and where a license is required for specific employment positions within the human services is often quite confusing. Understanding what degrees are needed to enter a particular career within the human services is made even more confusing because while there are educational programs specific to the human services discipline, professionals with other degrees (e.g., social work, psychology, public policy) may also be considered human service professionals if they work in practice settings focusing on social problems impacting marginalized and oppressed populations.

Thus, while many careers in the human services fields may require a BSW or MSW, many others do not. In fact, often careers engaging in grassroots work require a degree in human services (or a related field) at an associate's level (Associate of Arts [AA] or Associate of Science [AS]), bachelor's level (Bachelor of Arts [BA] or Bachelor of Science [BS]), or master's level (Master of Arts [MA] or Master of Science [MS]). Educational and licensing requirements depend in large part on specific state and federal legislation (particularly for highly regulated fields, such as in the educational and health care fields), industry-specific standards, agency preference, and community need (Gumpert & Saltman, 1998). For instance, a child protection services caseworker may need a Master of Social Work (MSW) in one state, but another state, with a high need for bilingual workers and a small workforce, may require caseworkers to have only a BSW or similar degree in a related field, such as human services.

So what does all of this mean? Essentially, it means that the human services field is generalist, which means it's broad, encompassing many different careers and professionals with a range of educational backgrounds. But it's also important to note that the human services field is a growing one and as such is experiencing increased professionalization and uniqueness. In response to this growth, human service degree programs have evolved considerably in the last two to three decades, as have practice requirements. Keeping in mind such variability within the human services fields, as well as differences among state licensing bodies, Table1.1 reflects a very general breakdown of degrees in

Table 1.1   Multiple Discipline Degree Requirements

Degree	Academic Area/Major	License/Credential	Possible Careers
BA/BS	Human Services	BS-BCP	Caseworker, youth worker, residential counselor, behavioral management aide, case management aide, alcohol counselor, adult day care worker, drug abuse counselor, life skills instructor, social service aide, probation officer, child advocate, gerontology aide, juvenile court liaison, group home worker, child abuse worker, crisis intervention counselor, community organizer, social work assistant, psychological aide
BA/BS	Psychology, Sociology	N/A	Same as above, depends on state requirements
BSW	Social Work (program accredited by CSWE)	Licensing (LSW, LCSW) depends on state requirements	Same as above, depends on state requirements
MA/MS 30–60 credit hours	Counseling Psychology	LCP (Licensed Clinical Professional—on graduation); LCPC (Licensed Clinical Professional Counselor—~3,000 postgrad supervised hours)	Private practice, some governmental and social service agencies
MSW 60 credit hours	Social Work (program accredited by CSWE)	LSW (on graduation, depending on state); LCSW (Licensed Clinical Social Worker—~3,200 postgrad supervised hours)	Private practice, not-for-profit social service agencies, for-profit agencies, governmental agencies (some requiring licensure)
PsyD 120 credit hours	Doctor of Psychology	PSY# (Licensed Clinical Psychologist—~3,500 postgrad supervised hours)	Private practice, many governmental and social service agencies, teaching in some higher education institutions
PhD (Psychology) 120 credit hours	Doctor of Philosophy in Psychology	PSY# (Licensed Clinical Psychologist—~3,500 postgrad supervised hours)	Private practice, many governmental and social service agencies, teaching in higher education institutions

the helping fields, their corresponding certifications and licenses, as well as commonly associated careers.

Human Service Educational Standards

The Council for Standards in Human Service Education (CSHSE) was established in 1979 for the purposes of ensuring excellence in human service education at the associate, baccalaureate, and master's levels, through the guidance and direction of educational programs offering degrees specifically in human services. The CSHSE developed a set of research-based national standards for curriculum and subject area competencies for human service education degree programs at colleges and universities, and provides guidance and oversight to educational programs during the accreditation process.

The CSHSE requires that curriculum in a human services program cover the following standard content areas: *knowledge* of the human services field through the understanding of relevant *theory, skills, and values* of the profession, within the context of the *history* of the profession; the interaction of *human systems*; the range and scope of *human service delivery systems*; *information management*; common *planning and evaluation* methods; appropriate *interventions and direct service delivery* systems; the development of students' skills in *interpersonal communication*; *client-related values and attitudes*; and students' *self-development*. The curriculum must also meet the minimum requirements for *field experience* in a human service agency, as well as illustrate that students are receiving appropriate *supervision* within their field placement sites (CSHSE, 2013). The CSHSE is the only organization that accredits human service educational programs and also offers continuing education opportunities for human service professionals and educators, networking opportunities, an informational website, and various professional publications.

Human Service Professional Certification

In 2010, the CSHSE and the NOHS in collaboration with the Center for Credentialing & Education (CCE) took a significant step toward the continuing professionalization of the human services profession by developing a voluntary professional certification called the Human Services Board Certified Practitioner (HS-BCP). In order to sit for the national certification exam, applicants must have earned at least a "technical certificate" in the human services discipline from a regionally accredited college or university and completed the required amount of post-graduate supervised hours in the human services field (1,500 hours with a master's degree, 3,000 hours with a bachelor's degree, 4,500 hours with an associate's degree, and 7,500 hours with a technical certificate).

Applicants who have earned degrees in non-CSHSE-approved programs, such as in counseling, social work, psychology, marriage and family therapy, or criminal justice, must complete coursework in several different content areas related to human services, such as "ethics in the helping professions," "interviewing and intervention skills," "social problems," "social welfare/public policy," and "case management." The implementation of the HS-BCP certification has moved both the discipline and the profession of human services toward increased professional identity and recognition within the larger area of helping professions by verifying human service practitioners' attainment of a high standard of education and practice knowledge. Credentials are maintained through a recertification process that requires 60 hours of continuing education every five years (CCE, n.d.).

ENHANCEDetext *self-check 1.2*

DUTIES AND FUNCTIONS OF A HUMAN SERVICE PROFESSIONAL

As the primary professional organization for human service students, educators, and practitioners, the NOHS provides a range of benefits to members, including opportunities for professional development as well as networking, advocacy of a human services agenda, and the promotion of professional and organizational identity (NOHS, n.d.). The NOHS has also been significantly influential in developing the scope and parameters of human service professional functions and competencies, some of which include:

- Understanding the nature of human systems, including individuals, groups, organizations, communities, and society, and how each system interacts with others.
- Understanding conditions that promote or limit optimal functioning of human systems.
- Selecting, implementing, and evaluating intervention strategies that promote growth and optimal functioning, and that are consistent with the values of the practitioner, client, agency, and human services profession.
- The development of process skills that enable human service professionals to plan and implement services, including the development of verbal and oral communication skills, interpersonal relationship skills, self-discipline, and time management skills.

The reason why these competencies are so important is because in the human services profession we, the human service practitioners, are the tools. Thus, we need to develop a comprehensive and **generalist skill set** that enables us to work with a wide range of clients, with diverse backgrounds, dealing with a wide range of challenges, within varying contexts. For instance, you may have one client who is a 40-year-old mother of two young girls who has recently left a violent relationship and is currently residing in a transitional housing shelter. You may have another client who is a retired veteran with an alcohol addiction who is grieving the recent death of his wife. And finally, you may have a client who is a young teen who recently ran away from home due to sexual and physical abuse, who is living on the streets and hasn't attended school in weeks, and is refusing to return home.

Each of these cases will require you to understand and assess the systems within which each client is operating, as well as how each system interacts with the others (e.g., individual, family, legal, school, government). These cases also will require you to understand and assess conditions that support or limit functioning, such as histories of trauma and abuse, mental and physical health status, educational and employment backgrounds, prior losses, coping styles, and available resources. They will require you to have an awareness of a range of intervention strategies, including the ability to evaluate

Watch this video produced by the National Organization for Human Services. What do you think about having a career in human services?
ENHANCEDetext *video example 1.2*

www.youtube.com/
watch?v=TNzvADts1NI

which interventions would be appropriate for client situations. They will require that you have the ability to use the interventions and engage in an ongoing evaluation of the selected interventions' effectiveness. Finally, you would need additional skills to pull all this off, such as good interpersonal skills that enable you to connect with clients who are likely very different from you, who may be resistant to change, or who are emotionally guarded. You will also need to have excellent writing skills so that you can succinctly write process notes and enter them on your agency's electronic records system using your excellent technical skills. Whew! If you can accomplish all of this, you'll be a true generalist human service professional!

Of course, you won't be flying by the seat of your pants and making things up as you go along. Rather, you will have a set of guiding principles, also called *theoretical orientations,* to guide your decision-making and interactions with client and client systems. The human services discipline is built upon a theoretical foundation that reflects the values of the profession. Understanding the underlying assumptions of any theoretical framework is important because such assumptions guide practice decisions about the people we work with and society as a whole. For instance, theoretical orientations and frameworks (also called *theoretical models*) make assumptions about human nature and what motivates people to behave in certain ways under certain conditions. We rely on theories every day when coming to conclusions about people and events, and we espouse views on why people behave as they do. So if you have ever expressed an opinion about why people don't work (they are lazy, or they don't have sufficient opportunities), or why some people commit crime (they are evil, or they are socialized during bad childhoods), you are espousing a theory and may not even realize it!

ENHANCEDetext *self-check 1.3*

THEORETICAL FRAMEWORKS AND APPROACHES USED IN HUMAN SERVICES

Theoretical frameworks can serve as the foundational underpinnings of a profession, reflecting its overarching values and guiding principles (such as human services' commitment to social justice and a belief in a person's natural capacity for growth). They can also extend into the clinical realm by outlining the most effective ways to help people become emotionally healthy based on some presumptions about what caused them to become emotionally unhealthy in the first place. For instance, if a practitioner embraces a psychoanalytic perspective that holds to the assumption that early childhood experiences influence adult motivation to behave in certain ways, then the counseling will likely focus on the client's childhood. But if the practitioner embraces a cognitive-behavioral approach, which focuses on behavioral reinforcements and thinking patterns, then the focus of counseling will likely be on how the client frames and interprets the various occurrences in his or her life.

All of this information about theoretical frameworks and approaches raises the question of which theories tend to be used the most in the human services discipline—both as theoretical foundations (or underpinnings) for the profession, as well as those that guide direct practice. When considering the various theories of human behavior and social dynamics, it is important to note that theories can be either descriptive (e.g., describing a range of child behaviors), or prescriptive (e.g., determining which behaviors in children are normative and healthy, and which ones are not). A theory may begin by merely describing certain phenomena related to how people think, feel, and behave, but in time, as the theory develops, it may become more prescriptive in the sense that certain determinations are made by the theorists with regard to what is normative and healthy versus what is maladaptive.

Yet, it is also important to remember that culture and history often affect what is considered normative thinking and behavior. For instance, 100 years ago if a woman chose to remain single and not have children so she could focus on her career goals, she may very well have been considered mentally ill. A common criticism of the major theories of human behavior is that they are based on Western cultural mores, and thus what behaviors are deemed normative and healthy are culturally prescribed and not necessarily representative or reflective of non-Western cultures. For instance, is it appropriate to apply Freud's psychoanalytic theory of human behavior, which was developed from his work with high-society women in the Victorian era, to individuals of a Masai tribe in Kenya? What about using a Western-based theory of parenting with parents from an indigenous culture in South America?

Theories of human behavior used in the human services must not only reflect the values and guiding principles of the profession but also the range of human experiences, and must permit the evaluation and assessment of clients *in context*. Important areas of context include personal characteristics, such as age, race and ethnicity, national origin, and sexual orientation and gender. Context involving social characteristics is important as well, such as the economy, political culture, various laws, the educational system, the health care system, racial oppression, privilege, gender bias, and any other broader social dynamic that may have an impact (even a distant one) on an individual's life. The theoretical frameworks and approaches most commonly used within the human service discipline evaluate and assess clients in the context of their various personal and environmental systems, while also considering the transactional relationship between the two.

Consider this case example:

> A woman in her forties is feeling rather depressed. She spends her first counseling session describing a fear that her children will be killed. She explains how she is so afraid of bullets coming through her walls that she doesn't allow her children to watch television in the living room. She never allows her children to play outside and worries constantly when they are at school. She admits that she has not slept well in weeks, and she has difficulty feeling anything other than sadness and despair.

Would you consider this woman mentally ill? Paranoid, perhaps? Correctly assessing her mental state does not depend solely on her thinking patterns and behavior, but on the *context* of her thinking and behavioral patterns, including her various experiences within her environment. If this woman lived in an extremely safe, gate-guarded community where no crimes had been reported in decades, then an assessment of some form of paranoia might be appropriate. But what if she lived in a high-crime neighborhood, where "drive-by" shootings were a daily event? What if you learned that her neighbor's children were recently shot and killed while watching television in their living room? What about her economic level, the dynamic between her, her neighborhood, and local law enforcement? What about the connection between her children and their school? Her thinking and behavioral patterns do not seem as bizarre when considered within the context of the various systems in which she is operating; rather, it appears as though she is responding and adapting to her various social systems in quite adaptive ways!

Frameworks Based on General Systems Theory

General systems theory is a foundational framework used in the human service discipline because it reflects these systemic interactions. General systems theory is based on the premise that various elements in an environment interact with one another, and that this interaction (or transaction) has an impact on all elements or components involved. This presumption has certain implications for the hard sciences such as ecology and physics, but when applied to the social environment, its implications involve the dynamic and interactive relationship between environmental elements (such as one's family, friends, neighborhood, and gender, as well as broader social elements, such as religion, culture, one's ethnic background, politics, and the economy) with an individual's thoughts, attitudes, beliefs, and behavior.

The systems within which we operate influence not just our thoughts, attitudes, beliefs, and behaviors, but our sense of identity as well. Consider how you might respond if someone asked you who you were. You might describe yourself as a female college student who is married, who has two high school–aged children, and who attends church on a regular basis. You might further describe yourself as having come from a large, Catholic, Italian family. On further questioning you might explain that your parents are older and you have been attempting to help them find alternate housing that can assist them with their extensive medical needs. You might describe the current problems you're having with your teenage daughter, who was recently caught with drugs by her high school's police officer and has been referred to drug court.

Whether you realize it or not, you have shared that you are interacting with the following environmental and social systems: family, friends, neighborhood, Italian-American culture, Catholicism, gender, marriage, adolescence, the medical community, the school system, and the criminal justice system. Your interaction with each of these systems is influenced by your expectations of these systems and their expectations of you. For instance, what are your expectations of your college professors? Your family? The Catholic Church? And what about what is expected of you as a college student? What is expected of you as a woman? As a wife? As a Catholic? What about the expectations of you as a married woman who is Catholic? What about the expectations of your family within the Italian-American Catholic community? As you attempt to focus on your academic studies, do these various systems offer stress or support? If you went to counseling, would it be helpful for the practitioner to understand what it means to be a member of a large, Catholic Italian-American family?

The focus on the transactional exchanges between individuals and their social environment is what distinguishes the field of human services from other fields such as psychology and psychiatry (which tend to take a more intrinsic view), although recently systems theory has gained increasing attention in these latter disciplines as well. Several theoretical frameworks and approaches have evolved in the last 100 years or so that are based on general systems theory and thus capture this reciprocal relationship between individuals and their social environment and broader social systems, including Bronfenbrenner's ecological systems theory, the ecosystems perspective, and a practice orientation called the person-in-environment approach.

Urie Bronfenbrenner (1979) developed the ecological systems theory, which conceptualizes an individual's environment as four expanding spheres, each with increasing levels of interaction with the individual. The microsystem includes one's family, the mesosystem (or mezzosystem) includes elements such as one's neighborhood and school, the exosystem includes elements such as the state government, and the macrosystem includes elements such as one's broader culture. The primary principle of Bronfenbrenner's theory is that individuals can best be understood when evaluated in the context of their relationships with the various systems in their lives, and understanding the nature of these reciprocal relationships will aid in understanding the individual holistically.

Similar to Bronfenbrenner's theory is the ecosystems theory, which conceptualizes an individual's various environmental systems as overlapping concentric circles, indicating the reciprocal exchange between a person and various environmental systems. Although there is no official recognition of varying levels of systems in ecosystems theory (from micro to macro), the basic concept is very similar to Bronfenbrenner's theory. Most who rely on the latter theory understand that there are varying levels of systems involved, each interacting in some manner, and thus impacting the individual in a variety of ways. It is up to the human service professional to strive to understand the transactional and reciprocal nature of these various systems (Meyer, 1988).

The person-in-environment (PIE) approach is often used as a basic orientation in practice because it encourages practitioners to evaluate individuals within the context of their environment (see Figure 1.1). Clients are evaluated on a micro level (i.e., intra- and interpersonal

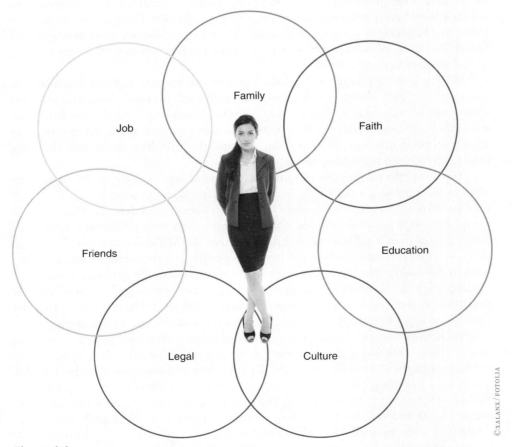

©XALANX/FOTOLIA

Figure 1.1
The person-in-environment approach encourages practitioners to evaluate individuals within the context of their environment

Maslow's Hierarchy of Needs

relationships and family dynamics) and on a macro (or societal) level (i.e., the client is an African American male youth who lives in an urban community with significant cultural oppression). It is important to note that these theories do not presume that individuals are necessarily aware of the various systems they operate within, even if they are actively interacting with them. In fact, effective human service professionals will help their clients increase their personal awareness of the existence of these systems and how they are currently operating within them (i.e., the nature of reciprocity). It is through this awareness that clients increase their level of empowerment within their environment and consequently in all aspects of their life.

Self-Actualization and Strengths-Based Frameworks

Other theories that can help human service professionals better understand why people behave as they do come from the positive psychology movement, which focuses on people's strengths rather than viewing people from a pathological perspective. Abraham Maslow (1954) developed a theoretical model focusing on needs motivation, theorizing that people self-actualize naturally, but are motivated to get their most basic physiological needs met first (e.g., food and oxygen) before they are motivated to meet their higher-level needs. According to Maslow, most people would find it difficult to focus on higher-level needs related to self-esteem if they were starving or had no place to sleep at night.

Maslow's theory suggests that thoughts of self-esteem and self-actualization quickly take a back seat to worries about mere survival. Maslow's hierarchy of needs theory can assist human service professionals in recognizing a client's need to prioritize more pressing needs over others, and can also explain why clients in crisis may appear to resist attempts to help them gain insight into their situations, choosing instead to focus on more basic needs.

The strengths perspective is another theoretical approach or model commonly used in the human services field because it encourages the practitioner to recognize and promote a client's strengths rather than focusing on deficits. The strengths perspective also presumes clients' ability to solve their own problems through the development of self-sufficiency skill development and self-determination. Although there are several contributors to the strengths perspective approach, Dennis Saleebey is often considered the primary theorist who contributed to the strengths-based practice approach in social work. Saleebey (1996) developed several guiding principles for practitioners that promote client empowerment. Sullivan (1992) was one of the first theorists to apply the strengths perspective to the area of chronic mental illness, where practitioners encourage clients to recognize and develop their own personal strengths and abilities. This was a revolutionary approach since the prevailing approach to working with the chronically mentally ill population was based on a medical model, involving a pathological approach to treatment where clients were viewed as sick. Sullivan claimed that by redefining the problem and focusing on a clients' existing strengths and abilities rather than on their deficits, treatment goals were more consistent with the goals of early mental health reformers who sought to remove treatment barriers by promoting respectful, compassionate, and comprehensive care of the mentally ill.

Watch this video produced by Resiliency Initiatives. How is conceptualizing clients using a strengths-based approach different than using a traditional model of helping?
ENHANCEDetext *video example 1.3*

www.youtube.com/
watch?v=eGaEAzqWeQQ

In the field of human services, using a strengths-based approach is empowering for both the human services professional as well as the client and client system because we aren't coming into their lives presuming we are the experts. Rather, we spend as much time looking for strengths as we do looking for problems. The strengths-based approach also enables us to partner with our clients in a way that encourages them to take more ownership over their journey toward increased self-sufficiency and more optimal functioning.

ENHANCEDetext *self-check 1.4*

CONCLUSION

Human service professionals practice in numerous settings, such as schools, hospitals, advocacy organizations, faith-based agencies, government agencies, hospices, prisons, and police departments, as well as in private practice if they have advanced degrees and required licensing. The nature of human service interventions is completely dependent on the specific practice setting delivering the services. In other words, intervention strategies and approaches are contextually driven. For instance, let's assume you work with children in a school setting and your colleague works with children in a hospice setting. Certainly there will be some overlap, particularly if the children are in a similar age range, but for the most part your jobs will be quite different, utilizing different skill sets and intervention strategies to deal with significantly different psychosocial issues.

It would be difficult to present an exhaustive list of categories of practice settings due to the broad and often very general nature of the human services profession. Sometimes practice settings target specific social issues (i.e., domestic violence, homelessness, child abuse), and sometimes a specific target population is the focus (i.e., older adults, the chronically mentally ill), and sometimes practice settings may target a specific area of specialty (i.e., grief and loss, marriage and family). Regardless of how we choose to categorize the various fields within human services, it is imperative that the nature of this career be examined and explored contextually in order to accurately explore the nature of the work performed by human service professionals, the range of psychosocial issues experienced among various client populations (including how these psychosocial issues most commonly manifest), and the career opportunities available to human service professionals, within each practice setting.

Some human services practice settings that offer micro, mezzo, and macro services include (but are not necessarily limited to) child and family services, including adoption agencies and child welfare and child protective service agencies; adolescent services, including group homes and residential facilities; geriatric services, including assisted-living facilities; mental health services, including outpatient mental health community centers; services for the homeless and those experiencing housing insecurity, including shelters and the government housing authority; faith-based services, including faith-based agencies and spiritually-based services; medical facilities, including hospitals and hospices; schools; victim advocacy agencies, including domestic violence, sexual assault, and victim–witness assistance programs; and social advocacy organizations, such as human rights and policy advocacy organization.

Regardless of the manner in which practice settings are categorized, there is bound to be overlap because one area of practice could conceivably be included within another field, and some practice settings provide comprehensive services. For instance, Christian hospices might provide medical, social work, and faith-based practice services, or human service professionals might work with both survivors of domestic violence (victim advocacy) and batterers (forensic human services), or they might work with homeless survivors of domestic violence and their children (homelessness and housing services, domestic violence, and child welfare).

For the purposes of this book, the roles, skills, and functions of human service professionals are explored in the context of particular practice settings, as well as areas of specialization within the generalist human services field—general enough to cover as many functions and settings as possible within the field of human services, but narrow enough to be descriptively meaningful. The role of the human service professional is examined by exploring the history of the practice setting, the range of clients served, the psychosocial issues most commonly encountered, the modes of service delivery, the nature of case management, the level of practice (e.g., micro, mezzo, or macro), and the most common generalist intervention strategies used within the following practice settings and areas of specializations: child welfare; adolescents; geriatric and aging; mental health; housing; health care and hospice; schools; faith-based agencies and spirituality; violence, victim advocacy and corrections; and international practice and human rights work.

SUMMARY

- A working definition of the human service professional is developed that identifies key reasons why people may need to use a human service professional. The nature of the human services profession was explored, providing comparisons and distinctive aspects of the human services profession compared to other helping fields. A range of social problems and individual challenges that may lead to people needing the services of a human service professional is explored. The nature of vulnerability and how social conditions often render some populations more at risk of needing assistance to overcome various challenges are also explored.
- The role of the Council on Standards for Human Service Education (CSHSE) and the National Organization for Human Services (NOHS) is described. The function and purpose of the professional organizations that monitor and support the human services profession, including educational standards, state licensure, and professional certification, are also explored.
- The rationale for the scope and parameters of human service professional functions and competencies is described. The roles, functions, and scope of human service professionals engaging in practice on micro and macro levels are described.
- Key theoretical frameworks used in the human services discipline to real scenarios are applied. The foundational theoretical approaches most often used in the human services discipline, including systems theory, self-actualizing, and strengths-based approaches, are explored.

Internet Resources

Conduct an Internet search for "What is Human Services?" on the National Organization for Human Services website.

Conduct an Internet search for the Council for Standards in Human Service Education and navigate the site to

learn more about the human service accreditation process.

Conduct an Internet search for the "Human Services Guide" on the Human Services Education website.

References

Bronfenbrenner, U. (1979). *The ecology of human development: Experiments by nature and design.* Cambridge, MA: Harvard University Press.

Center for Credentialing & Education [CCE]. (n.d.). Human Services–Board Certification Practitioner. Retrieved from http://www.cce-global.org/hsbcp

Council for Standards in Human Service Education [CSHSE]. (2013). National Standards. Retrieved from http://www.cshse.org/standards.html

Gumpert, J., & Saltman, J. E. (1998). Social group work practice in rural areas: The practitioners speak. *Social Work with Groups, 21*(3), 19–34.

Maslow, A. (1954). *Motivation and personality.* New York, NY: Harper.

Meyer, C. H. (1988). The eco-systems perspective. In R. A. Dorfman (Ed.), *Paradigms of clinical social work* (pp. 275–294). Philadelphia, PA: Brunner/ Mazel, Inc.

National Organization for Human Services [NOHS]. (n.d.). What is human services? Retrieved from http://www.nationalhumanservices.org/what-is-human-services

Saleebey, D. (1996). The strengths perspective in social work practice: Extensions and cautions. *Social Work, 41*(3), 296–305.

Sullivan, W. P. (1992). Reclaiming the community: The strengths perspective and deinstitutionalization. *Social Work, 37*(3), 204–209.

Topuzova, L. (2006). Community Colleges and the Preparation of the U.S. Human Services Workforce. Retrieved from http://www.cswe.org/File .aspx?id=16354

2

The History and Evolution of Social Welfare Policy

© EVERETT HISTORICAL/SHUTTERSTOCK

THE ROOTS OF THE AMERICAN SOCIAL WELFARE SYSTEM: POOR CARE IN ENGLAND

The practice of helping others in need can be traced back to ancient times, but the human services profession in its current context has historic roots dating back to at least the late 1800s. Since the United States was once a colony of England, many of the laws and systems in the United States can be traced back to its "mother country." Thus, in order to gain a comprehensive understanding of the U.S.

social welfare system, including its various influences, it is important to understand the evolution of poor care in England.

The Middle Ages: Feudalism in England and the Role of the Catholic Church: 1100 to 1550

A good place to begin this examination is the Middle Ages, from about the 11th to the 15th centuries, where a system called **feudalism** prevailed as England's primary method of caring for the poor. Under this elitist system, privileged and wealthy landowners would parcel off small sections of their land, which would then be worked by peasants or serfs. Many policy experts consider feudalism a governmentally imposed form of slavery or servitude because individuals became serfs through racial and economic discrimination.

Serfs were commonly born into serfdom with little hope of ever escaping, and as such they were considered the legal property of their landowner, or what was commonly called, a lord. Although lords were required to provide for the care and support of serfs in exchange for farming their land, the lords had complete control over their serfs and could sell them or give them away as they deemed fit (Stephenson, 1943; Trattner, 1998). Despite the seeming harshness of this system, it did provide insurance against many of the social hazards associated with being poor, a social condition considered an inescapable part of life, particularly for the lower classes. Many economic and environmental conditions led to the eventual decline of the feudal system from the mid-14th century through its legal abolition in 1660. Some of these conditions included several natural disasters that resulted in massive crop failures, the bubonic plague (also called Black Death), various political dynamics, social unrest, and urbanization due to the development of trade and towns.

Official poor relief during the Middle Ages was the responsibility of the Catholic Church, primarily facilitated through the monasteries and local parishes. Catholic Bishops administered poor care through the support of mandatory taxes or compulsory tithing. Poverty was not seen as a sin, and in fact, the poor were perceived as a necessary component of society, in that they gave the rich an opportunity to show their grace and goodwill through the giving of alms to the less fortunate. Thus, caring for the poor was perceived as a noble duty that rested on the shoulders of all those who were able-bodied. Almost in the same way that evil was required to highlight good, according to biblical scripture and Catholic theology, poverty was likewise necessary to highlight charity and goodwill as required by God (Duncan & Moore, 2003; Trattner, 1998).

The Poor Laws of England: 1500s to 1601

Mass urbanization, coupled with the decline of the feudal system, as well as the closing of most Catholic monasteries in 1530 (under King Henry III, who was a Protestant), led to a dramatic increase in poverty from the mid-1500s through the early part of the 1600s. In fact, during this time period about one-third of the English population was poor, prompting the need for a complete overhaul of the social welfare system

(Trattner, 1998). Increased demand for factory wage labor in the cities ultimately led to droves of people moving from rural communities to the city to work in factories. The creation of towns also created new urban problems associated with urban poverty, including begging, vagrancy, and crime.

England responded to these changing dynamics and the associated problems by passing several relief laws, called **Tudor Poor Laws**, between the mid-1500s and 1601. Tudor Poor Laws placed responsibility for dealing with the poor at the local level and reflected a complete intolerance of idleness. Local police scoured the cities in search of beggars and vagrants, and once found, a determination was made between those who could not work—the **worthy poor**, and those who were able-bodied but refused to work—the **unworthy poor**.

Legislative guidelines typically stipulated that only pregnant women, individuals who were extremely ill and unable to work, or any person over the age of 60 were justifiably poor. The worthy poor were treated more leniently, such as having government authorization to beg (typically in the form of a letter of authorization), or they were given other forms of sustenance, such as food assistance. If a person was found to be able-bodied and unemployed (the unworthy poor) they were often determined to be vagrant, which was punishable by whippings, naked parading through the streets, being returned to the town of birth, or incarceration. Repeat offenders were often subjected to having an ear cut off or even death (Beier, 1974; Birtles, 1999; Jones, 1969).

Clearly, there was no sympathy to be had for individuals, male or female, who were deemed capable of working but found themselves without a job or any means of support. Additionally, little consideration was given to social or economic dynamics or what is now referred to as the **cycle of poverty**. What's even more surprising is that little sympathy was extended even to children, particularly adolescents who were unparented and found begging in the streets. In fact, district officials often took these children into custody, placing them into apprenticeship programs or almshouses, and subjected them to what we would now consider to be child slavery (Trattner, 1998).

© CHIPPIX/SHUTTERSTOCK

Factory with child workers

The Elizabethan Poor Laws

The Tudor Poor Laws were replaced by the **Elizabethan Poor Laws of 1601**, a set of laws that established a system of poor relief for England and Wales. The Elizabethan Poor Laws of 1601 reflected an organized merging of England's earlier, sometimes conflicting and erratic, social welfare legislation. The Elizabethan Poor Laws of 1601 formalized many of the driving principles rooted in the Tudor Poor Laws, including the belief that the primary responsibility for provision of the poor resided with one's family, that poor relief should be handled at the local level, that vagrancy was a criminal offense, and that individuals should not be allowed to move to a new community if unable to provide for themselves financially.

It was quite common for community members to bring charges against others if it could be proven that they had moved into the district within the last 40 days and had no means to support themselves. Such individuals would be charged as vagrants by the local officials and returned to their home districts. The underlying notion was that local parishes didn't mind supporting individuals who had fallen on hard times after years of paying taxes and contributing to society, but they didn't want to be forced to support strangers who came to their district for the sole purpose of receiving aid. The Elizabethan Poor Laws of 1601 served as the foundation for social welfare legislation in colonial America, and elements of residency requirements can be found in current U.S. welfare policy.

During this time period in England there were generally two types of charitable provision: **indoor relief** and **outdoor relief**. Indoor relief was provided for the unworthy poor—those deemed able-bodied but who did not work (vagrants, indigents, and criminals). Indoor relief consisted of mandatory institutionalization in workhouses or poorhouses, where residents were forced to work. Workhouses were designed to be harsh, with the hope that they served as a deterrent for those individuals who either lacked the skill or desire to work and become self-sufficient. Outdoor relief consisted of money, clothing, food baskets, and medicine, provided in the homes of those who were considered the worthy poor, most often widows, the disabled, and the aged (Jones, 1969; Slack, 1990).

ENHANCEDetext *self-check 2.1*

THE HISTORY OF POOR CARE IN EARLY AMERICA

Life in colonial America not only offered tremendous economic opportunities but also presented significant hardship related to life on the frontier. Many immigrants were quite poor to begin with, and the long and difficult ocean voyage to the New World often left them unprepared for the rigors of life in America. Thus, even though colonial America offered many opportunities not available in the Old World, such as land ownership and numerous vocational opportunities, many of the social ills plaguing new immigrants in their homeland followed them to America.

Colonial America: 1607 to 1775

English and Scottish colonization of North America began in 1607 in Virginia and continued through most of the 1700s until independence. Because there was no existing infrastructure in the original 13 British colonies, poor relief consisted primarily of mutual kindness, family support, and distant help from England. Self-sufficiency was a must, and life was not easy on the frontier. There was a dramatic rise in the population between 1700, when there was an estimated population of about 250,000, and 1775 (just prior to the revolution and independence), when there was an estimated 2.5 million settlers (Lemon, 1990). As the population increased, so did the need for a more formal and organized system of poor care.

Although the prevailing assumption among many is that the United States was founded on a desire to be completely different than England, in reality, the overriding reasons for the American Revolution, although certainly complex, were based more on the desire for independence than solely on the desire for a completely different governmental structure. This presumption is evident in the development of many of the social customs, governmental infrastructures, and legislation, including the social welfare policy of the American colonies. Thus, the colonies adopted not only the social welfare legislation of England, but much of the perceptions of and attitudes about the poor and indigent as well.

Poor Care in the Industrial and Progressive Eras: 1776 to 1920s

After independence in 1776, poor care remained minimal, consisting primarily of free land grants, pensions for widows, and aid to disabled veterans. There was very little formal social welfare legislation passed at the state or federal levels until the early 1900s.

World War I veterans stand in front of a New York City post office to fill out applications for their long promised bonuses

And even those early laws provided minimally, primarily for some groups of children and the disabled on the state level. One of the first federal social welfare efforts was the Civil War Pension Program, passed in 1862, which provided aid to Civil War Veterans and their families. Unemployment benefits were offered in most states by about 1929, and a program offering veterans benefits, consisting primarily of medical aid, was instituted after World War I.

Essentially, prior to the Great Depression in 1929, which marked the first time that the federal government recognized the necessity of a national social welfare program, poor care was primarily handled by families, churches, and private charities. The nature of provision in the late-1800s and early 1900s was highly influenced by philosophical and religious belief systems that presumed to explain why poverty and other social ills existed, which in turn influenced how the leaders of early American society believed poverty should be addressed.

One such philosophical belief system was rooted in John Calvin's doctrine of predestination, which emanated from the Protestant Reformation in the 16th century. Calvin wrote about the nature of God's control over the world and how this control was exercised, primarily in the form of who God would allow into heaven (the elect) and who he would condemn to hell (the condemned). According to Calvin's doctrine, a person's salvation was predestined by God and based solely on God's grace, not by what people did in their lives (whether they were essentially good or bad). Thus even though all people were called to faith and repentance, not all people would be allowed into heaven.

Even though many Protestants rejected Calvin's concept of predestination, including Lutherans and Methodists, Calvin's doctrine became embedded into early American society in a number of ways. In his book *The Protestant Ethic and the Spirit of Capitalism,* Max Weber described in detail the vast influence of Calvin's doctrine on European and American society. According to Weber, Calvin theorized that since everyone deserved to go to hell anyway, that was the lot they should accept, and those who were saved from condemnation were blessed by the grace of God. Human action in an attempt to secure salvation (through works) was futile since one's eternal fate rested not on human goodness, but solely on God's mysterious desire and will (Weber, 1905/1958). Roman Catholic theology, which previously influenced poor care, recognized the omnipotence of God in matters of salvation, but also acknowledged that people had free will and choice, and could elect to walk with God and have everlasting life by following his commandments.

According to Weber, the Calvinists accepted the concept of predestination, but did not accept that there was no way to determine who was saved and who was condemned, since participation in society and privilege was based in large part on separating people into two categories: those who were Godly and those who were not. For instance, only God's faithful were allowed to become members of the church, receive communion, and enjoy other benefits of salvation, including societal respect. Determining that one was condemned to hell, not because of anything that person necessarily did, but because of God's mysterious determination, became a legitimate form of social exclusion.

In time particular behaviors and conditions became certain indicators—or signs—of one's eternal fate. For instance, hard work (what Weber referred to as the **Protestant work ethic**) and good moral conduct (the ability to deny worldly pleasures in pursuit of purity) became signs of the elect since it was believed that God blessed the elect by giving them a vocation, and only the elect were given the ability to be pure (Weber, 1905/1958,). In other words, those who could not work for any reason, even through no fault of their own, were considered condemned by God, because they were not bestowed a vocation. A "catch-22" with regard to living a pure life was that it was the privileged members of society who determined what was considered "pure." For instance, church attendance was a requirement of purity, but only members of the elect were permitted to join the church, and the remainder were excluded, which was then used as an indicator that they were not pure, and thus not a member of the elect. Even if the poor and suffering had a voice and could protest the paradoxical reasoning behind the signs, according to Calvin, everyone deserved to be condemned anyway, thus there was simply nothing to complain about (Hudson & Coukos, 2005; Weber, 1905/1958).

The influence of the Protestant work ethic and Calvin's doctrine of predestination on society as a whole, and specifically on the poor, were significant, extending well beyond that of the religious community (Kim, 1977). With hard work, material success, and good moral conduct serving as the best signs of election to salvation, it did not take long for poverty and presumed immoral behavior (remember, it was presumed that only the elect had the spiritual fortitude to behave morally) to become clear indications of one's condemnation (Chunn & Gavigan, 2004; Gettleman, 1963; Hudson & Coukos, 2005; Kim, 1977; Schram, Fordingy, & Sossz, 2008; Tropman, 1986; Weber, 1905/1958).

Social Darwinism was another philosophy that significantly influenced how poverty and the poor were perceived, as well as how they should be treated. Social Darwinism involved the application of Charles Darwin's theory of natural selection to the human social world. Darwin's theory, developed in the mid-19th century, was based on the belief that environmental competition—a process called natural selection—ensured that only the strongest and most fit organisms would survive (allowing the biologically fragile to perish), thus guaranteeing successful survival of a species (Darwin, 1859/2009).

Darwin's theory was focused primarily on the biological fitness of animals and plant life; yet, it appears that he applied his theory to humans as well, in an attempt to provide naturalistic explanations for various phenomena in human social life. Weikart (1998) describes written discussions between Darwin and a colleague, in which Darwin espoused a belief that humans were subject to natural law as well, and that economic competition was a necessary component of natural selection. Darwin argued that socioeconomic inequality was due to biological inequality, and thus those in society who suffered from poverty and other forms of misfortune were merely victims of their own biological inferiority, and their demise was necessary for the survival of society as a whole (Weikart, 1998). In other words, the poor should be allowed to perish, and attempts at intervention could harm society. By maximizing competition for economic resources, the weaker members of society would be weeded out. Thus, allowing the biologically (and mentally) superior to prevail, ensuring survival of the human species.

One of the most influential social Darwinists was Herbert Spencer, an English sociologist and philosopher who actually preceded Darwin in applying concepts of natural selection to the social world. Spencer coined the term **survival of the fittest** (a term often incorrectly attributed to Darwin) in reference to the importance of human competition for resources in securing the survival of what were considered the fittest members of society. Spencer was a fierce opponent of any form of government intervention or charity on behalf of the poor and disadvantaged, arguing that such interventions would interfere with the natural order, thus threatening society as a whole (Hofstadter, 1992). Although Spencer's theory of social superiority was developed in advance of Darwin's theory, his followers relied on Darwin's theory of natural selection for scientific validity of social Darwinism.

The fatalistic nature of the concept of predestination, the Protestant work ethic, and social Darwinism became deeply imbedded in U.S. religious and secular culture, and were used to justify a laissez-faire approach to charity throughout most of the 19th and 20th centuries (Duncan & Moore, 2003; Hofstadter, 1992). Although the specific tenets of these ideologies may have softened over the years, the significance of hard work, good fortune, material success, and living a socially acceptable life have remained associated with special favor and privilege in life, whereas poverty and disadvantage have remained associated with presumed weak character, laziness, and immoral behavior. Leaving the poor and disadvantaged to their own devices was perceived as nothing more than complying with God's (or nature's) grand plan (Duncan & Moore, 2003). Remnants of these doctrines and philosophies can still be seen in contemporary approaches to helping the poor and disadvantaged, and continue to influence the development of legislation in the United States, as well as people's attitudes about poverty and the poor (Chunn & Gavigan, 2004; Duncan & Moore, 2003; Gettleman, 1963; Hudson & Coukos, 2005; Kim, 1977; Schram et al., 2008; Tropman, 1986).

Charity Organization Societies: 1870 to 1893

The **Charity Organization Society** (COS), often considered one of the forerunners of the modern social services profession, marked one of the first organized efforts within the United States to provide charity to the poor. The COS movement began in England

Watch this video on Herbert Spencer and social Darwinism. Do you agree with Noam Chomsky about capitalism and social Darwinism? Why or why not?

ENHANCEDetext *video example 2.1*

www.youtube.com/
watch?v=RjermDZ1qfl

in 1869, in response to increased urbanization and immigration and common frustration with the current welfare system, which consisted primarily of disorganized and chaotic almsgiving. The COS movement was started by Rev. S. Humphreys Gurteen, who believed that it was the duty of good Christians to provide an organized and systematic way of addressing the plight of the poor in a manner that would increase self-sufficiency and personal responsibility. Gurteen and his colleagues strongly believed that giving alms indiscriminately, and without conditions, encouraged fraud and abuse, as well as encouraging laziness among those receiving the help.

The first COS was founded in Buffalo, New York, in 1877 and served as a sort of umbrella organization for other charities by assisting in the coordination and oversight of relief services to the poor (Schlabach, 1969). The COS concept of organized and systematic provision quickly spread to large cities across the nation, and in 1890 over 100 cities had at least one COS serving the community (Wahab, 2002). The COS philosophy focused on self-sufficiency and reducing dependence. Therefore, outdoor relief, such as cash assistance, was discouraged because it was considered harmful to the beneficiary based upon the belief that material relief would encourage dependence and laziness, thus ultimately increasing poverty (Gettleman, 1963; Kusmer, 1973). In this respect, the COS embraced many of the principles of social Darwinism, as well as the concepts of the unworthy and worthy poor.

A part of aid provision involved the evaluation of poor women's situations to determine whether they were worthy of aid. To accomplish this goal, the COS employed volunteer **friendly visitors**, primarily Christian women from the middle to upper classes, who visited the homes of those in need, and evaluated the root causes of their poverty. A case plan would then be written, detailing the visitor's assessment and recommendations (Trattner, 1998). Since material relief was discouraged, most friendly visitors offered only sympathy, encouragement, and guidance on how to seek employment, with perhaps minimal financial assistance (Wahab, 2002).

A social hierarchy was reflected in the philosophical motivation of COS leaders, often the community's wealthiest and most religious members, who agreed to provide charity to the poor as long as the poor remembered their proper place in society (Gettleman, 1963). Yet, even the deserving poor did not escape the influence of the Protestant work ethic or the fatalism of social Darwinism, both of which were deeply imbedded in COS culture. For example, friendly visitors often focused excessively on the sexual behavior of the women who they helped. The COS viewed immorality as the primary problem in most slums, believing that the women living in the slums (many of whom were single mothers) were weak and fallen, having succumbed to the charms and sexual advances of male suitors (Wahab, 2002). The friendly visitors often used the guise of friendship to connect to these women, hoping they could influence them through modeling the value of becoming a good Christian woman. Many COS visitors even went so far as to ask neighbors to monitor the younger women in the slums and report back on any male visitors (Wahab, 2002).

The principles of the Protestant work ethic and social Darwinism, with their focus on hard work, self-sufficiency, and natural selection, were clearly reflected in various speeches and writings of COS leaders. Common themes included arguments that even widows would become lazy if too much help was given and life was made too easy for them. Many COS leaders also argued that providing charity to the unemployed, able-bodied poor was actually immoral since, according to natural selection, they were destined to perish, and providing them charity only prolonged their suffering and was therefore in neither their nor society's best interest (Gettleman, 1963).

Mary Richmond, the general secretary of the Baltimore COS, had a far more compassionate attitude toward the poor. She was a fierce advocate for social justice and social reform, and believed that charities could employ good economics and compassionate giving at the same time. Richmond became well known for increasing public awareness of the COS movement and for her fundraising efforts. Richmond's compassion for the poor was likely due to her own experience with poverty as a child. Richmond was orphaned at the age of two and then later abandoned by her aunt, who left Richmond to fend for herself in New York when she was only 17 years old. Thus, Richmond no doubt understood the social components of poverty, and how factors outside of peoples' control could have a devastating impact on their lives. Richmond is credited for contributing to the development of the modern case management model through her conceptualization of **social diagnosis**, a process involving friendly visitors assessing clients and their environments. Social diagnoses enabled the visitor to identify sources of power and barriers to self-sufficiency (Kusmer, 1973; Richmond, 1917).

Despite the general success of the COS and the contributions the movement made to professionalizing the helping fields, its adherence to deterministic philosophies that negated social factors of poverty while pathologizing the poor deepened the belief that the poor were to blame for their lot in life. In retrospect, one can recognize the naivety of believing that poverty could be controlled merely through moral behavior. But, the country was about to learn a very hard collective lesson during the Depression era—one that immigrants, many ethnic minority groups and single mothers had known for years—that sometimes conditions exist that are beyond an individual's control and that create immovable barriers to economic self-sufficiency.

Jane Addams and the Settlement House Movement: 1889 to 1929

During the same time that the COS friendly visitors were addressing poverty in the slums by focusing on personal morality, Jane Addams was confronting poverty in a vastly different way—by focusing on social injustice. Addams was a social justice advocate and a social reformer who started the **settlement house movement** in the United States with the opening of the Hull House in Chicago. Addams considered the more religiously-oriented charity organizations rather heartless because they were more concerned with efficiency and controlling fraud than alleviating poverty (Schneiderhan, 2008). Addams used a relational model of poverty alleviation based on the belief that poverty and disadvantage were caused by problems within society, not idleness and moral deficiency (Lundblad, 1995). Addams advocated for changes within the social structure of society in order to remove barriers to self-sufficiency, which she viewed as an essential component of a democracy (Hamington, 2005; Martin, 2012). In fact, the opening of the Hull House, the first settlement house in the United States, was considered the beginning of one of the most significant social movements in U.S. history.

Addams was born in Cedarville, Illinois, in 1860. She was raised in an upper-class home where education and philanthropy were highly valued. Addams greatly admired her father, who encouraged her to pursue an education at a time when most women were destined to solely pursue marriage and motherhood. She graduated from Rockford Female Seminary in 1881, the same year her father died. After her father's death, Addams entered Woman's Medical College in Pennsylvania but dropped out because of chronic illness. Addams had become quite passionate about the plight of immigrants in the United States, but due to her poor health and the societal limitations placed on women during that era, she did not believe she had a role in social advocacy.

The United States experienced another significant wave of immigration between 1860 and 1910, with 23 million people emigrating from Europe, including Eastern Europe. Many of these immigrants were from non-English-speaking countries, such as Italy, Poland, Russia, and Serbia, thus did not speak English and were very poor. Unable to obtain work in the skilled labor force, many immigrants were forced to work in unsafe urban factories and live in subhuman conditions, crammed together with several other families in tenements. For instance, New York's Lower East Side had approximately 330,000 inhabitants per square mile (Trattner, 1998). With no labor laws for protection, racial discrimination and a variety of employment abuses were common, including extremely low wages, unsafe working conditions, and child labor. Poor families, particularly non-English-speaking families, had little recourse, and their mere survival depended on their coerced cooperation.

Addams was aware of these conditions because of her father's political involvement, but she was unsure of how she could help. Despondent about her father's death and her failure in medical school, as well as her ongoing health problems, Addams took an extended trip with friends to Europe, where among other activities she visited Toynbee Hall settlement house, England's response to poverty and other social problems. Toynbee Hall served as a neighborhood welfare institution in an urban slum area, where trained settlement house volunteers worked to improve social conditions by providing community services and promoting neighborly cooperation.

The concept of addressing poverty at the neighborhood level through social and economic reform was revolutionary. Rather than monitoring the behavior of the poor through intermittent visits, settlement house workers lived right alongside the immigrant families they endeavored to help. In addition to providing a safe, clean home, settlement houses also provided poor immigrants with comprehensive care, such as assistance with food, health care, English language lessons, child care, and general advocacy. The settlement house movement had a mission of no longer distinguishing between the worthy and unworthy poor, and instead recognizing the role that society played in the ongoing plight of the poor—a stance that was a departure from the traditional charity organizations.

Addams returned home convinced that it was her duty to do something similar in the United States, and with the donation of a building in Chicago, and the help of friend Ellen Gates Starr, the Hull House became America's first settlement house in 1889. Addams and her colleagues lived in the settlement house, in the middle of what was considered a bad neighborhood in Chicago,

Social worker Jane Addams (R) talking with a little girl in the Hull House nursery school

offering services targeting the underlying causes of poverty such as unfair labor practices, the exploitation of non-English-speaking immigrants, and child labor. The Hull House became the social center for all activities in the neighborhood and even offered residents an opportunity to socialize in the resident's café. From the late 1800s through the mid-1900s, up to 400 settlement houses were opened in the United States, primarily in low-income urban, immigrant neighborhoods.

Addams' influence on American social policy was significant, in that her work represented a shift away from the fatalistic perspectives of social Darwinism, as well as the religious perspectives of Reformed theology. Instead, Addams highlighted the need for social change so that barriers to upward mobility and optimal functioning could be removed (Martin, 2012). Addams and her colleagues were committed to viewing the poor as equal members of society, just as worthy of respect and dignity as anyone else. Addams clearly saw societal conditions and the hardship of immigration as the primary cause of poverty, not necessarily one's personal moral failing. Social inequality was perceived as the manifestation of exploitation, with social egalitarianism perceived as not just a desirable but achievable outcome (Lundblad, 1995; Martin, 2012). Addams' focus on social inequity was reflected in her tireless lobbying for the passage of child labor laws (despite fierce opposition by corporations and conservative politicians). Addams also advocated on a local and national level for labor laws that would protect the working-class poor, who were often exploited in factories with **sweatshop conditions**. She also worked alongside Ida B. Wells, an African American reformer, confronting racial inequality in the United States, such as the extrajudicial lynching of black men (Addams, 1909).

Although there are no working settlement houses today, the prevailing concept espoused by this movement, with its focus on social components of poverty and disadvantage, remains foundational to the human services and social work professions, and also serves as the roots of today's urban neighborhood centers. Yet, despite the overall success of the settlement house movement and the particular successes of Addams with regard to achieving social reform in a variety of arenas, the threads of moralistic and deterministic philosophies have remained strongly interwoven into American society, and have continued to influence perceptions of the poor and social welfare policy and legislation.

ENHANCEDetext *self-check 2.2*

THE NEW DEAL AND GREAT SOCIETY PROGRAMS

In 1929 the stock market crashed, leading to a series of economic crises such as the United States had never before experienced. For the first time in modern U.S. history, large segments of the middle-class population lost their jobs and all means of income. Within a very short time thousands of people who had once enjoyed financial security were suddenly without jobs and eventually without homes and food. This served as a wake-up call for social reformers, many of whom had abandoned their earlier commitment to social activism because of decades of a good economy. In response, many social reformers started pushing President Hoover to develop the country's first comprehensive system of social welfare on a federal level.

Hoover was resistant, though, fearing that a federal system of social welfare would create dependency and displace the role of private and local charities. Hoover wanted

Watch this video on the Great Depression and reflect on the precursors and consequences of this time of economic crisis. ENHANCEDetext *video example 2.2*

www.youtube.com/watch?v=f8k0jJdqKP0

to allow time for the economy to self-correct through the capitalist system and the market economy before intervening with national entitlement programs. But much of the country apparently did not agree with this plan. In 1933, Hoover lost his bid for reelection, and Franklin D. Roosevelt was elected as the country's 32nd president. Roosevelt immediately set about to create changes in federal policy with regard to social welfare, promising dramatic changes, including sweeping reforms in the form of comprehensive poverty alleviation programs.

From 1933 through 1938, Roosevelt instituted a series of legislative reforms and domestic programs collectively referred to as the **New Deal programs**. In his first 100 days in office, Roosevelt passed 13 acts, including one that created the Civil Works Administration (CWA), which provided over a million temporary jobs to the unemployed; the Federal Emergency Relief Act (FERA), which provided direct aid and food to the unemployed (and was replaced by the Works Progress Administration [WPA] in 1935), and one that created the Civilian Conservation Corp (CCC), which put thousands of young men ages 18 to 25 to work in reforestation and other conservation programs. Yet, as progressive as Roosevelt was, and as compassionate as the country had become toward the poor due to the realization that poverty could strike anyone, racism was still rampant, as illustrated by Roosevelt placing a 10 percent enrollment limit for black men in the CCC program (Trattner, 1998).

By far the most famous of all programs in the New Deal were those created in response to the Social Security Act of 1935, which among other things created old-age pension for all workers, unemployment compensation, Aid to Families with Dependent Children (AFDC), and aid to the blind and disabled. Programs such as the Federal Deposit Insurance Corporation (FDIC), which provided insurance for bank deposits, helped to instill a sense of renewed confidence in the banking system, and the development of the Securities and Exchange Commission (SEC), which regulates the stock market, helped to ensure that a crash similar to the one in 1929 would be unlikely to occur again. In total Roosevelt created 15 federal programs as a part of the New Deal, some of which remain today, and some of which were dismantled once the crisis of the Great Depression subsided. Although some claim that the New Deal was not good for the country in the long run, it did pull the country out of a severe economic decline, providing relief for millions of Americans who may have literally starved had the federal government not intervened.

The United States recovered from the Great Depression and has since experienced several periods of economic growth and decline, but never any as severe as that which was prompted by the 1929 stock market crash. This is likely because of federal programs such as the FDIC and creation of the SEC (and others). In later times though, the dismantling of some post–Depression financial regulations would contribute to yet another devastating economic downturn in 2007—perhaps not as severe as the Great Depression, but more serious and longlasting than any other recession experienced in the U.S. post–Depression era, particularly because of its global consequences.

The 1940s remained a time of general recovery and the 1950s was a relatively stable time, both economically and socially. Several laws were passed and agencies created that continued to advance the state of social welfare in the United States, including the creation of the U.S. Department of Health, Education, and Welfare (HEW) in 1953, and the passage of the U.S. Housing Act of 1954 (Ch. 649, 68 Stat. 590).

The 1960s was a time of civil unrest and increasing rates of poverty, which spawned a resurgence of interest in social problems, including poverty and social injustice, particularly related to many at-risk populations, such as ethnic minority populations, older adults, and the mentally ill. For instance, President John F. Kennedy signed into law the

Community Mental Health Centers Act (PL 88-164) on October 31, 1963, which transitioned the U.S. mental health system from one of institutionalization to a community health model. Kennedy was assassinated less than a month later, on November 22, 1963, and President Lyndon B. Johnson continued the Kennedy legacy with the introduction of the **Great Society programs**—a set of social welfare programs designed to eliminate poverty and racial injustice.

Policy areas within the Great Society programs included civil rights, education, and poverty (later popularly referred to as Johnson's **War on Poverty**). Examples of some of the social welfare legislation and programs included under the umbrella of the Great Society include the Economic Opportunity Act of 1964 (PL 88-452); the Civil Rights Act of 1964 (PL 88-352); the Food Stamp Act of 1964 (PL 88-525); Medicare, Medicaid and the Older Americans Act of 1965 (PL 89-73); the Elementary and Secondary Education Act of 1965 (PL 89-10); the U.S. Department of Housing and Urban Development (HUD); and the Voting Rights Act of 1965 (PL-89-110).

Whether the Great Society and the War on Poverty programs were successful in reducing poverty, racial discrimination and other social problems continue to be debated to this day. It's no surprise that conclusions tend to fall along party lines, with many conservatives complaining that Johnson's social experiment amounted to nothing more than throwing money at oversimplified problems with disastrous results, and liberals decrying just the opposite—that most of the programs had the potential to be successful, but were grossly underfunded (Zarefsky, 2005). Some point to racism as the reason why many Great Society programs were ultimately dismantled (Quadagno, 1994), while others pointed to the Vietnam War as the reason for government (and societal) shifting priorities (Zarefsky, 2005). Regardless, many of the programs remain and represent a time in history when there was increased recognition of structural barriers in society that can keep many people from functioning at their optimal level and achieving economic self-sufficiency.

ENHANCEDetext *self-check 2.3*

SOCIAL WELFARE IN CONTEMPORARY UNITED STATES

A Time of Recovery: 1970 to 1990

The 1970s and 1980s was a time of mixed reviews on welfare and welfare reform. There was considerable conservative backlash in response to what was considered a few decades of liberal social welfare legislation and entitlement programs, but despite President Nixon's opposition to welfare, existing programs continued to grow. The mid-1970s through the 1980s was a boom time economically in the United States, and boom times typically mean that people become less sympathetic toward the plight of the poor, and that's exactly what happened—there was a resurgence of earlier negative sentiments toward the poor beginning in the mid-1970s and peaking in the 1990s.

This increased negative attitude toward the poor was reflected in several studies and national public opinion surveys that indicated a general belief that the poor were to blame for their lot in life. For instance, a national survey conducted in 1975 found that the majority of those living in the United States attributed poverty to personal failures, such as having a poor work ethic, poor money management skills, a lack of any special talent that might translate into a positive contribution to society, and low personal moral values. Subjects ranked social forces, such as racism, poor schools, and the lack of sufficient employment opportunities, the lowest of all possible causes of poverty (Feagin, 1975).

Ronald Reagan capitalized on this negative sentiment toward the poor during the 1976 presidential campaign when he based his platform in large part on welfare reform. In several of Reagan's speeches he cited the story of the woman from the South Side of Chicago who was finally arrested after committing egregious welfare fraud. He asserted that she had 80 names, 30 addresses, and 12 Social Security cards, claiming that she was also collecting veteran's benefits on four husbands, none of whom were real. He also alleged that she was getting Social Security payments, Medicaid, and food stamps, and was collecting public assistance under all of her assumed identities (Zucchino, 1999). While Reagan never mentioned the woman's race, the context of the story as well as the reference to the South Side of Chicago (a primarily black community) made it clear that he was referring to an African American woman—thus playing on the common stereotype of welfare users (and abusers) as being black (Krugman, 2007). And with that, the enduring myth of the **welfare queen** was born.

Journalist David Zucchino attempted to debunk the myth of the welfare queen in his expose on the reality of being a mother on welfare, but stated in his book *The Myth of the Welfare Queen* that the image of the African American woman who drove a Cadillac while collecting welfare illegally from numerous false identities was so imbedded in American culture it was impossible to debunk the myth, even though the myth was not (and is not) supported by factual evidence (Zucchino, 1999). Krugman (2007) also cites how politicians and media pundits have used the myth of the welfare queen ever since in order to reduce sympathy for the poor and gain public support for welfare cuts, arguing that while covert, such images clearly play on negative racial stereotypes. They also play on the common belief in the United States that those who receive welfare benefits are poor because they are lazy, promiscuous, and generally immoral.

More recent surveys conducted in the mid-1990s revealed an increase in the tendency to blame the poor for their poverty (Weaver, Shapiro, & Jacobs, 1995), even though a considerable body of research points to social and structural dynamics as the primary cause of enduring poverty. Examples of structural causes of poverty include a shortage of affordable housing, recent shifts to a technologically based society requiring a significant increase in educational and training requirements, longstanding institutionalized oppression of and discrimination against certain racial and ethnic groups, and a general increase in the complexity of life (Martin, 2012; Wright, 2000).

The general public's perception of social welfare programs seems to be based in large part on this negative bias against the poor and the stigmas such bias creates. Surveys conducted in the 1980s and 1990s showed support for the general idea of helping the poor, but when asked about specific programs or policies, most respondents became critical of governmental policies, specific welfare programs, and welfare recipients in general. For instance, a 1987 national study found that 74 percent of those surveyed believed that most welfare recipients were dishonest and collected more benefits than they deserved (Kluegal, 1987).

Watch this video of former President Reagan addressing the nation of welfare reform. Note any negative stereotypes reflected in his speech. ENHANCEDetext *video example 2.3*

www.youtube.com/watch?v=MjnTQ8b6byY

Welfare Reform and the Emergence of Neoliberal Economic Policies: 1990 to Now

Political discourse in the mid-1990s reflected what is often referred to as economic **neoliberal philosophies**—a political movement embraced by most political conservatives, espousing a belief that capitalism and the free market economy were far better solutions to many social conditions, including poverty, than government programs, which were inefficient and poorly run. Advocates of neoliberalism pushed for social programs to be privatized based upon the belief that getting social welfare out of the hands of the government and into the hands of private enterprise, where market forces could work their magic, would increase efficiency and lower costs. Yet, research has consistently shown that social welfare services do not lend themselves well to free market theory due to the complexity of client issues, unknown outcomes, a highly trained workforce, the lack of competition among providers, and other dynamics that make social welfare services so unique (Nelson, 1992; Van Slyke, 2003).

During the 1994 U.S. Congressional campaign, the Republican Party released a document entitled *The New Contract with America,* which included a plan to dramatically reform welfare, and according to its authors, the poor would be reformed as well (Hudson & Coukos, 2005). *The New Contract with America* was introduced just a few weeks prior to Clinton's first mid-term election, and was signed by all but two of the Republican members of the House of Representatives, as well as all of the party's Congressional candidates. In addition to a renewed commitment to smaller government and lower taxes, the contract also pledged a complete overhaul of the welfare system to root out fraud and increase the poor's commitment to work and self-sufficiency.

Hudson and Coukos (2005) note the similarities between this political movement and the movement 100 years before, asserting that the Protestant work ethic served as the driving force behind both. Take, for instance, the common arguments for welfare reform (policies that reduce and restrict social welfare programs and services), which have often been predicated on the beliefs that (1) hardship is often the result of laziness; (2) providing assistance will increase laziness (and thus dependence), hence increasing hardship, not decreasing it; and (3) those in need often receive services at the expense of the working population. These arguments were cited during the COS era as reasons why material support was ill-advised. One of the more stark (and relatively recent) examples of this sentiment was expressed by Rep. John Mica, Congressman of Florida, when he stood in front of the U.S. House floor, holding a sign that read *Don't Feed the Alligators* while delivering an impassioned speech in support of welfare reform. During hearings on the state of public welfare in the United States Rep. Mica compared people on welfare to alligators in Florida, stating that the reason for such signs is because "unnatural feeding" leads to dependency and will cause the animal to lose its nature desire for self-sufficiency. Mica argued that welfare programs would do the same for people, creating another generation of enslavement and servitude (Lindsey, 2004).

While there may be some merit in debating the most effective way of structuring social welfare programs, arguments such as Mica's negate the complexity of poverty and economic disadvantage, particularly among historically marginalized populations. They also play into longstanding stigmas and negative stereotypes that portray the poor as a homogenous group with different natures and characters than mainstream working society. These types of narratives also reflect the *genderized* and *racialized* nature of poverty, contributing to institutionalized gender bias and racism.

Whether veiled or overt, negative bias, particularly that which is bestowed upon female public welfare recipients of color, negates the disparity in social problems experienced by African American women and other women of color (El-Bassel, Caldeira, Ruglass, & Gilbert, 2009; Martin, 2012; Siegel & Williams, 2003). Negative stereotypes and myths also provide a false picture of welfare recipient demographics by implying that the largest demographic of beneficiaries is African American single women with numerous children, which statistics do not support.

PRWORA of 1996, TANF, and Other Programs for Low-Income Families

Although a Republican Congress initiated welfare reform, it was passed by the Democratic Clinton administration in the form of the **Personal Responsibility and Work Opportunity Reconciliation Act** (PRWORA) of 1996, illustrating wide support for welfare reform as well as for the underlying philosophical beliefs about the causes of poverty and effective poverty alleviation methods.

The social welfare program authorized under PRWORA of 1996 is called the **Temporary Assistance for Needy Families** (TANF) program, which replaced the **Aid to Families with Dependent Children** (AFDC). TANF is operated at the state level through federal block grants as well as state funding. According to the PRWORA act, TANF has four primary goals: 1) to provide help to needy families and their children, 2) to promote job preparation, employment, and marriage so that families no longer need to depend on government assistance, 3) to reduce out-of-wedlock births, and 4) to encourage two-parent families.

Initially, TANF listed 12 different categories of acceptable work activities, but in 2008 the federal government provided additional clarity in terms of what activities would count toward TANF's work requirement in each category. Among the 12 categories, nine are considered "core," which means they directly count toward the required number of hours per week. Three of the categories are considered "non-core" and count only after the required hours for core activities are met. The nine core work activities include: unsubsidized work, subsidized work, work experience, on-the-job training, job searches, job readiness, community service, vocational education, and providing child care to anyone participating in community service. Non-core activities include employment-related education and job skills training and attendance at a high school or GED program.

TANF benefits include modest cash assistance for basic needs; transitional services focused on self-sufficiency, such as vocational training, rehabilitation, and child care; substance abuse, mental health, and domestic violence screening and referrals; medical assistance through a government funded health insurance program; and Supplemental Nutrition Assistance Program (SNAP) benefits (formerly called food stamps).

States have considerable latitude in how to meet the four goals of TANF as well as how to deliver the benefits, as long as their programs remain within federal guidelines. Guidelines include *time limits*, which are not to exceed 60 months of lifetime benefits (in most cases); eligibility requirements, which include barring all immigrants, including documented immigrants who have lived in the United States for less than five years; and work requirements of at least 30–35 hours per week for two-parent families and 20 hours per week for single parents with young children. Parents who fail to comply with the work requirement experience sanctions, such as the termination of all family

Racial Breakdown of 1,638,983 Families Receiving TANF in FY 2013

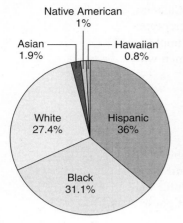

Figure 2.1
TANF Family Racial Demographics
Source: Based on "Administration for Children & Families, Office of Family Assistance," 2015 by U.S. Department of Health and Human Services.

TANF Benefits Received by FY 2013: 1,638,983 Families

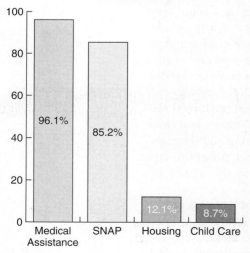

Figure 2.2
TANF Breakdown of Benefits Received FY 2013
Source: Based on "Administration for Children & Families, Office of Family Assistance," 2015 by U.S. Department of Health and Human Services.

benefits. Approved work activities include subsidized and unsubsidized work at a for-profit or not-for-profit organization, and can also include on-the-job training and vocational training (not to exceed 12 months). A significant area of concern among social justice advocates is that educational programs, including programs to assist recipients with earning their high school diplomas, are not included in approved work categories.

According to a 2015 U.S. Department of Health and Human Services report, in fiscal year 2013 there were just over 1.6 million families receiving TANF benefits, with the total individual TANF caseload of about 3.8 million individuals. About half of all caseloads consisted of small female head-of-household families with one or two children, with the other half consisting of child-only cases. With regard to the racial makeup of recipients, 36 percent were Hispanic, 31.1 percent were black, 27.4 percent were white, 1.9 percent were Asian, 1 percent were Native American, and .8 percent were Hawaiian (see Figure 2.1) (U.S. Department of Health and Human Services, 2015).

With regard to benefits received, 96.1 percent of TANF families received medical assistance, 85.2 percent received SNAP benefits, 12.1 percent received housing assistance, and 8.7 percent received subsidized child care (see Figure 2.2).

Many social welfare advocates believe that TANF is too punitive in nature because of its strict time limits for lifetime benefits, stringent work requirements, and other punitive measures designed to control the behavior of recipients. Supporters of welfare reform on old arguments, citing the need to control welfare fraud and welfare dependency. They cited a host of other behaviors exhibited by female welfare recipients, including perceived sexual promiscuity and out-of-wedlock childbearing, while focusing very little on the behaviors of the fathers, particularly those who abandon their children (Hudson & Coukos, 2005).

Some of the more powerful voices within the Republican Party that were highly supportive of welfare reform were members of the **Christian Right**—a group of individuals from conservative Christian denominations who espouse conservative family values, personal responsibility, and smaller government. Many conservative Christian organizations, such as the Christian Coalition, the Eagle Forum, and Focus on the Family (under James Dobson), have wielded considerable influence within the Republican Party beginning in the 1980s, becoming a fringe core of the party in the 1990s (Green, Rozell, & Wilcox, 2003; Guth & Green, 1986; Knuckey, 2005). These groups were instrumental in the call for welfare reform, voicing significant concerns about the moral decline of society and citing the need to defend and uphold traditional family values (Reese, 2007; Uluorta, 2008).

Uluorta (2008) points out though that far too often morality in the United States has been defined in very narrow terms, focusing on select groups of individuals and on very specific behaviors, such as sex and sexuality, marital status, and social standing (it is interesting to note that rarely do those criticizing the poor also frame behaviors such as greed or lacking compassion in moral terms).

While individual responsibility is certainly worth achieving, it can also be a code word for philosophies that scapegoat the poor, and minimize long-standing social inequalities. Such scapegoating is of great concern to many within the human services fields and others who recognize the wide range of ways that social problems and their causes can be framed, and the danger of focusing too heavily on perceived behavioral patterns of those who are struggling.

Similar political rhetoric often relies on American traditionalism and patriotism as the basis of arguments against social welfare programs, citing the "good old days" when people just worked hard and saved their money to get ahead. But many poverty experts assert that arguments such as these often reflect the experiences of the majority population only, many of whom have had the cumulative benefit of white privilege and do not reflect the experiences of historically marginalized populations, including many ethnic minority groups (Bullock, 2008; Pinterits, Poteat, & Spanierman, 2009). Additionally, continued attempts to cast TANF recipients as primarily people of color, particularly African Americans, with large families do not reflect the factual data. As previously referenced, the typical TANF family is small, and, for the most part, relatively evenly split among the three major racial groups in this country: Caucasian, African American, and Hispanic.

The Tea Party Movement

Another conservative social movement that appears to overlap at least to some extent with the Christian Right is the American Tea Party Movement, a social movement and a part of the Republican base, that advocates for smaller government, lower taxes (the name of the group is a reference to the Boston Tea Party), state rights, and the literal interpretation of the U.S. Constitution. The Tea Party movement has quickly gained a reputation for advocating on behalf of very conservative policies, similar in many ways to the Christian Right agenda. For instance, Michele Bachmann, a Tea Party member, former Minnesota Congresswoman, and 2012 presidential candidate, was heavily criticized for her position on social issues, many of which are based on her conservative Christian values. For example, in 2006 a speech to a Christian youth group, Bachmann asserted that religion was supposed to be a part of government, and that the notion of separation of church and state (contained in the First Amendment of the U.S. Constitution) was a myth (Turley, 2011).

Box 2-1

White privilege is a social phenomenon where Caucasian members of society enjoy a distinct advantage over members of other ethnic groups. White privilege is defined as the institutionalized unearned advantage and associated power of being white in a racially stratified society (Pinterits, Poteat, & Spanierman, 2009). It is something that most Caucasians do not necessarily acknowledge, leading many Caucasians to take personal credit for whatever they gain through white privilege (Neville, Worthington, & Spanierman, 2001). Unfortunately, this also means that many Caucasians may blame those from non-Caucasian groups for not being as successful as they are. Yet, due to various forms of racial discrimination, it has typically been the white man who has benefited most from white privilege—gaining access into the best educational systems (or being the only ones to obtain an education at all), the best jobs, and the best neighborhoods. Even if white privilege were to end, the cumulative benefit of years of advantage would continue well into the future, just as the negative consequences of years of social exclusion will continue to negatively impact diverse groups who have not benefited from white privilege.

A conservative Tea Party Express protest of big government and Obamacare in Dallas. Taken September 4, 2009.

There have also been allegations made against some members of the Tea Party movement for their stance on immigration and racial issues in general, which critics claim are based on negative racial stereotypes. The media has consistently highlighted the racially charged tone at some Tea Party political rallies, pointing out racial slurs on posters, many of which are directed at President Obama's ethnic background. Proponents of the Tea Party deny these allegations and complain that the media is exaggerating racist elements at the protests and rallies by seeking out and over-focusing on the more extremist fringe of the movement. Although "tea partiers" often deny racist or homophobic values, a relatively recent study showed that about 60 percent Tea Party opponents believed that the movement had strong racist and homophobic overtones (Gardner & Thompson, 2010). Currently the Tea Party is considered a part of the Republican base, but its existence appears to be creating some controversy within the Republican party, particularly among the more moderate base. Whether the Tea Party remains a part of the Republican Party or branches off into its own political party will depend on many factors, including whether it can maintain its current momentum and increase the number of its supporters.

The economic recession of 2007–2009 consisted of a dramatic and lengthy economic downturn not experienced since the Great Depression. The real estate market bubble burst, the stock market crashed, the banking industry seemed to implode, and many people lost their jobs and their houses as a result (Geithner, 2009). President Obama and the 111th Congress responded to the economic crisis with several policy and legislative actions, including the passage of the American Recovery and Reinvestment Act of 2009 (often referred to as the Stimulus bill [Pub. L. No. 111-5]). This economic stimulus package, worth over $787 billion, included a combination of federal tax cuts, various social welfare provisions, and increases in domestic spending, and was designed to stimulate the economy and assist Americans who were suffering economically.

As a part of the 2009 Recovery Act, Congress allotted five billion dollars in emergency funding to assist states with increased TANF caseloads (expired in September of 2010). TANF was reauthorized in 2009, and was up for reauthorization in 2015, but experienced several delays. The National Association of Social Workers (NASW) released a statement regarding reauthorization recommending several changes to the TANF program, some of which include:

- Increase the floor for TANF benefits to 100 percent of the federal poverty line. Currently, many states' benefits are 50 percent of the federal poverty line, while benefits in several states are only about 30 percent of the federal poverty line;
- Expand the definitions of employment to include higher education, English and literacy classes, and vocational training;
- Address common barriers to employment, such as physical illness, mental illness, disabilities, substance abuse, domestic violence, and sexual violence;
- Restore benefits for documented immigrants (NASW, 2015).

EMERGING ISSUES IN THE AREA OF SOCIAL JUSTICE REFORM

Ethnic minorities, women, and immigrants are not the only groups in U.S. society to be used as social or economic scapegoats. The gay community, typically referred to as the LGBTQ+ (lesbian, gay, bisexual, transgendered, and questioning and/or queer), has long been a marginalized group in the United States (as well as in most countries in the world). Members of the LGBTQ+ community are often victims of hate crimes, often solely because of their sexual orientation and/or gender expression. For years this community has been excluded from many of the social welfare laws designed to protect disenfranchised and socially excluded groups. Yet, in the last three decades, several LGBTQ+ advocacy organizations, such as the Gay & Lesbian Alliance Against Defamation (GLAAD), have become increasingly vocal about the right of the LGBTQ+ community to live openly and enjoy the same rights and protections as heterosexuals without fear of reprisal. Specific issues GLAAD has advocated for include the right to be included as a specially protected group in hate crimes legislation, the right to legal marriage (often referred to as marriage equality), and the right to serve openly in the military.

Despite strong opposition from social conservative groups, the LGBTQ+ community has experienced recent success in response to their efforts. In 2009 President Obama signed into law the Matthew Shepard and James Byrd Jr. Hate Crimes Prevention Act, which expanded existing hate crime legislation to include crimes committed against individuals based upon perceived gender, sexual orientation, and gender identity. Marriage equality—the right of same-sex couples to legally marry—has been a battle fought on both a federal and state level. In 1996 the Defense of Marriage Act was passed, which defined marriage on a federal level as a union between one man and one woman. Arguments for same-sex marriage are typically based on rights of equality. The GLAAD website lists several benefits and protections marriage offers, which includes:

- automatic inheritance
- child custody/parenting/adoption rights
- hospital visitation
- medical decision-making power
- standing to sue for wrongful death of a spouse
- divorce protections
- spousal/child support
- access to family insurance policies
- exemption from property tax upon death of a spouse
- immunity from being forced to testify against one's spouse
- domestic violence protections, and more (GLAAD, 2010, p. 7).

Arguments against same-sex marriages are often based on religious values that hold homosexuality as sinful and unnatural, and define traditional marriage as being between a man and a woman. There also appears to be a general fear that the normalization of homosexuality will lead to the lowering of moral standards in a variety of respects throughout society. Yet, advocates of same-sex marriage confront religious arguments by citing research that disputes allegations that same-sex marriage will somehow dilute traditional marriage or harm children. They also cite the increasing acceptance among U.S. citizens of same-sex marriage and of same-sex partnerships in general. For instance, according to a series of Gallup polls, in 2016, 61 percent of the U.S. population surveyed stated that they believed that same-sex couples should be able to marry, compared to 53 percent in 2011 and 42 percent in 2004. These results represent a steady increase since Gallup began polling on this issue in 1996 (when the percentage of those who agreed with same-sex marriage was 27 percent) (Gallup, 2016).

In June of 2015 the U.S. Supreme Court rendered a decision in the case of Obergefell v. Hodges, a case challenging Ohio's ban on same-sex marriage, that the right to marry was fundamental, and that under the 14th Amendment, same-sex couples could not be denied the right to marry. This landmark ruling granted legally married same-sex couples the same rights and privileges as heterosexual couples throughout the country, thus over-riding state laws that defined marriage as a union solely between a man and a woman.

Another area of success for the LGBTQ+ population involves the right to openly serve in the U.S. military. Historically, gays and lesbians were systematically discharged from the military if their sexual orientation was discovered. In December 1993, in response to mounting pressure to change this policy, the Clinton administration com-promised by implementing **Don't Ask, Don't Tell (DADT)**, an official policy of the U.S. government that prohibited the military from discriminating against gay and lesbian mil-itary personnel as long as they kept their sexual orientation a secret. In other words, military personnel could no longer investigate the sexual orientation of those serving in the military, but if a member of the military admitted to being a gay or lesbian, he or she could legally be discharged from armed service. DADT was repealed by Congress in December 2010 pending review by military leadership who were to determine the effect of open service on military readiness. But in July 2011 a federal court of appeals rul-ing barred further enforcement of the policy, and it was officially repealed by President Obama in September 2011.

ENHANCEDetext *self-check 2.5*

CONTRIBUTIONS OF AFRICAN AMERICAN REFORMERS IN THE FIGHT FOR SOCIAL JUSTICE

A review of the historical influences in the development of the human services field would be remiss without a discussion of the influences of reformers from ethnic minority populations from the latter part of the 19th century to current times. People of color, particularly African American women, have had a significant influence on the development of social justice and human services, often filling the vacuum left by a rac-ist social system that created harsh conditions for racially diverse populations.

Ida B. Wells was an African American reformer and social activist whose campaign against racial oppression and inequity established the foundation for the civil rights movement in the 1960s. Wells was born in 1862 to parents who were slaves in rural Mis-sissippi, and although her parents were ultimately freed, Wells's life was never free from the crushing effects of severe racial prejudice and discrimination. Wells was orphaned at the age of 16, and went on to raise her five younger siblings with little outside assistance.

This experience not only forced Wells to grow up quickly, but also seemed to serve as a springboard for her subsequent advocacy against racial injustice. In Wells's earlier advocacy career, she was the editor of the black newspaper *The Memphis Free Speech,* where she consistently wrote about matters of racial oppression and inequity, including recently passed segregation laws and a vast amount of socially sanctioned crimes committed against the black population, particularly black men (Hamington, 2005).

The indiscriminate lynching of black men was an example of such crimes, and was an issue that Wells became quite passionate about. Black men were commonly perceived as a threat on many levels and there was virtually no protection of their personal, political, or social rights. The black man's reputation as an angry rapist was endemic in white society, and many speeches were given and articles written by white community members (including clergy) about this alleged growing problem. An article published in *The Commercial,* a mainstream newspaper in the South, entitled *More Rapes, More Lynchings,* alleged the black man's penchant for raping white women, a trend the author attributed to the black man no longer being in awe of the white race since the end of slavery. The author justified the lynching of black men based on the argument that in the absence of white restraint inherent in the system of slavery, the black man was both unable and unwilling to control his animal instincts and lustful desires (Davidson, 2008).

Wells wrote extensively on the subject of the myth of the angry black man, challenging the growing sentiment in white communities that black men, as a race, were a threat due to their aggressiveness and lust of white women (Hamington, 2005). Wells believed these myths were prompted by racial tension rooted in the rising economic status of many in the black community, as well as the increasing number of biracial couples. In fact, Wells wrote articles accusing white women of pursuing romantic relationships with black men, which prompted white men to react by accusing the black men of rape. The response to Wells's articles was swift and harsh. A group of white men surrounded the building where her newspaper was located with the apparent intention of lynching her, but when she could not be found, they burned down the building instead (Davidson, 2008; Wells-Barnett, 1969).

In response to the destruction of her newspaper as well as increasing threats against her life, Wells moved initially to New York, and eventually to Chicago where she continued to wage a fight against racism, often coordinating efforts with Jane Addams (Hamington, 2005; Wells-Barnett, 1969). Wells and Addams coordinated their social justice advocacy efforts fighting for civil rights for the African American population. Together, they ran the Chicago branch of the *National Association for the Advancement of Colored People,* and worked collectively on a variety of projects, including fighting against racial segregation in schools (Martin, 2012; Munro, 1999).

Many other African Americans contributed to social reform efforts as well, particularly with regard to confronting the ongoing disenfranchisement of African Americans within U.S. society. African American social reformers operated as a tight community, developing close relationships with each other, even though many of these women were spread across the United States. Because African Americans were excluded from receiving many social welfare benefits and services, including educational opportunities and health services, many early social welfare reformers focused on these two areas, developing schools and health care facilities for members of the black community. One such reformer was Modjeska Simkins, who developed health care programs focusing on everything from infant mortality to tuberculosis. Another creative example of African American reformers working in the face of extreme opposition was the work of the

Watch this video about African American women and the right to vote. What are your thoughts on the government's efforts to exclude black women from becoming equal members of society?

ENHANCEDetext *video example 2.4*

black sorority Alpha Kappa Alpha, whose members were determined to provide health care services to sharecroppers in Mississippi. When the white community refused to rent them office space, they offered health services from cars (Gordon, 1991).

Other examples include Anna Cooper, an African American social reformer who pushed for increased educational opportunities for blacks, and Jane Hunter, who formed the first black Young Women's Christian Association (YWCA) (Gordon, 1991). Although often unreported and undervalued, African American social welfare reformers not only assisted their own communities but helped the broader community as well by modeling the power of networking and relentlessly pursuing social justice for all, particularly for those who are the subject of social oppression and discrimination.

ENHANCEDetext *self-check 2.6*

CONCLUSION

The United States is often referred to as a reluctant welfare state because throughout its history. A battle has been waged between reformers, who advocate for a compassionate, inclusive, less stigmatized social safety net, and opposing groups, who advocate for a system with less government involvement, more privatization, and increased work incentives. Currently it would be more accurate to describe the U.S. social welfare system as a piecemeal welfare-to-work system that focuses more on the behavior of the poor than on structural causes of poverty or the role of various social problems as the barriers to self-sufficiency, such as mental illness, domestic violence, and aging out of the foster care system. But it is also accurate to describe the U.S. social welfare system as ever-evolving, reflected in the relatively recent passage of the **Patient Protection and Affordable Care Act** (ACA), a comprehensive health care legislation essentially overhauling much of the U.S. health care system (explored in more detail in the chapter on health care). Other changes are on the horizon as well, but they will be highly influenced by political leadership and economic constraints.

SUMMARY

- The ways in which England's historic system of poor care influenced the development of social welfare policies in the United States is analyzed. England's early social welfare system, including the development of social welfare policy in the United States, is discussed, tracing aspects of social welfare provision from England's feudal system in the Middle Ages, to Elizabethan Poor Laws, to the development of the social welfare system in the New World.
- Movements and associated philosophical influences in poor care and social reform in early America are compared and contrasted. Various philosophical and religious movements that have influenced perceptions of the poor and social welfare policy, such as Calvin's Protestant work ethic and the concept of predestination, social Darwinism, and the settlement house movement, are discussed.
- The ways that the New Deal and Great Society programs alleviated poverty after the Great Depression are discussed. The successes and failures of the post–Depression New Deal programs on poverty alleviation in the United States are explored.
- Key debates surrounding TANF program goals, benefits, and eligibility requirements are identified. The nature of welfare reform in the United States from the mid-1990s through contemporary times, are explored, focusing on the

ongoing debate about the best way to provide a safety net in times of economic boom, recession, and recovery. Issues include whether the current program, Temporary Assistance for Needy Families (TANF), effectively addresses the source of poverty, or rather stigmatizes the behavior of recipients.

- The impact of increased rights on the social welfare of LBGT populations is analyzed. Contemporary social justice issues that have significantly impacted social welfare legislation in the United States, including the expanding rights for members of the LGBTQ+ population, particularly in the realm of same-sex marriage and military service, are explored.
- The impact of contributions made by key African American reformers in the area of social welfare and justice is described. The contributions of key African American social justice reformers to the social welfare landscape in the United States, including the contributions of Ida B. Wells, Modjeska Simkins, and Anna Cooper are explored.

Internet Sources

Conduct an Internet search for the "Hull House" on the National Women's History Museum.

Conduct an Internet search for "About Jane Addams" on the Jane Addams Hull House Museum website.

Conduct an Internet search for the "Social Security Act of 1935" on the Official Social Security website.

Conduct an Internet search for the "Milestones in the Development of Social Work and Social Welfare 1950s to Present" on the national NASW website.

Conduct an Internet search for "Lesbians and Gay Men in the U.S. Military: Historical Background" on the UC Davis website.

References

Addams, J. (1909). *The spirit of youth and the city streets* (Vol. 80). University of Illinois Press.

Beier, A. L. (1974). Vagrants and the social order in Elizabethan England. *The New England Quarterly, 43*(1), 59–78.

Birtles, S. (1999). Common land, poor relief and enclosure. *Past & Present [Great Britain]*, (165), 74–106.

Bullock, H. E. (2008). Justifying inequality: A social psychological analysis of beliefs about poverty and the poor. *The colors of poverty, 52*–75.

Chunn, D. E., & Gavigan, S. A. M. (2004). Welfare saw, welfare fraud, and the moral regulation of the 'Never Deserving' Poor. *Social & Legal Studies, 13*(2), 219–243.

Darwin, C. (2009). *The origin of species: By means of natural selection, or the preservation of favoured races in the struggle for life.* Boston, MA: Cambridge University Press. (Original work published in 1859.)

Davidson, J.W. (2008). *They say, Ida B. Wells and the reconstruction of race.* New York, NY: Oxford University Press.

Duncan, C. M., & Moore, D. B. (2003).Catholic and Protestant social discourse and the American Welfare State. *Journal of Poverty, 7*(3), 57–83.

El-Bassel, N., Caldeira, N. A., Ruglass, L. M., & Gilbert, L. (2009). Addressing the unique needs of African American women in HIV prevention. *American Journal of Public Health, 99*(6), 996–1001.

Feagin, J. R. (1975). *Subordinating the poor: Welfare and American beliefs.* Englewood Cliffs, NJ: Prentice Hall.

Gallup. (2016). "Do you think marriage between same-sex couples should or should not be recognized by the law as valid, with the same rights as traditional marriages?" [Survey Report]. Retrieved from http://www.gallup.com/poll/117328/marriage.aspx

Gardner, A., & Thompson, K. (2010). Tea Party group battles perceptions of racism. Washington Post-ABC News Poll. Retrieved from http://www.washingtonpost.com/wp-dyn/content/article/2010/05/04/AR2010050405168.html?hpid=moreheadlines

Geithner, T. F. (2009). Regulatory perspectives on the Obama administration's financial regulatory reform proposals-part two. House Financial Services Committee. Retrieved from http://www.house.gov/apps/list/hearing/financialsvcs_dem/geithner_-_treasury.pdf

Gettleman, M. E. (1963). Charity and social classes in the United States, 1874–1900. *American Journal of Economics & Sociology, 22*(2), 313–329.

GLAAD. (2010). GLAAD's Media Reference Guide: In Focus: Marriage. Retrieved November 12, 2011 from http://www.glaad.org/reference/marriage

Gordon, L. (1991). Black and white visions of welfare: Women's welfare activism, 1890–1945. *Journal of American History, 78*(2), 559–590.

Green, J. C., Rozell, M. J., & Wilcox, C. (2003). The Christian right in American politics: Marching to the millennium. Washington, DC: Georgetown University Press.

Guth, J., & Green, J. C. (1986). Faith and politics: Religion and ideology among political contributors. *American Politics Quarterly, 14*(3), 186–199.

Hamington, M. (2005). Public pragmatism: Jane Addams and Ida B. Wells on lynching. *Journal of Speculative Philosophy, 19*(2), 167–174.

Hofstadter, R. (1992). *Social Darwinism in American thought.* Boston, MA: Beacon Press.

Hudson, K., & Coukos, A. (2005, March). The dark side of the Protestant Ethic: A comparative analysis of welfare reform. *Sociological Theory, 23*(1), 1–24.

Jones, G. H. (1969). *History of the law of charity, 1532–1827.* CUP Archive.

Kim, H. C. (1977). The relationship of Protestant Ethic beliefs and values to achievement. *Journal for the Scientific Study of Religion, 16*(3), 252–262.

Kluegal, J. R. (1987). Macro-economic problems, beliefs about the poor and attitudes toward welfare spending. *Social Problems, 34*(1), 82–99.

Knuckey, J. (2005). A new front in the culture war? Moral traditionalism and voting behavior in U.S. House elections. *American Politics Research, 33,* 645–671.

Krugman, P. (2007). *Conscience of a liberal.* New York, NY: W.W. Norton & Co.

Kusmer, K. (1973). The functions of organized charities in the progressive era: Chicago as a case study. *Journal of American History, 60*(3), 657–678.

Lemon, J. T. (1990). Colonial America in the eighteenth century. *North America: Historical geography of a changing continent* (p. 2). Savage, MD: Rowman and Littlefield.

Lindsey, D. (1994). *The welfare of children.* Oxford University Press.

Lundblad, K. (1995, September). Jane Addams and social reform: A role model for the 1990s. *Social Work, 40*(5), 661–669.

Martin, M. E. (2012 January). Philosophical and religious influences on social welfare policy in the United States: The ongoing effect of Reformed theology and social Darwinism on attitudes toward the poor and social welfare policy and practice. *Journal of Social Work, 12*(1), 51–64.

Munro, P. (1999). *Political activism as teaching: Jane Addams and Ida B. Wells* (pp. 19–45). M. S. Crocco, P. Munro, & K. Weiler (Eds.). New York, NY: Teachers College Press.

National Association of Social Workers [NASW]. (2015). Temporary Assistance to Needy Families (TANF) Reauthorization. Retrieved http://www.naswdc.org/advocacy/issues/tanf/resources/GR-FL-10015.TANF-Flyer.pdf

Nelson, J. I. (1992). Social welfare and the market economy. *Social Science Quarterly, 73*(4), 815–828.

Neville, H., Worthington, R., & Spanierman, L. (2001). Race, power, and multicultural counseling psychology: Understanding white privilege and color blind racial attitudes. In J. Ponterotto, M. Casas, L. Suzuki, and C. Alexander (Eds.), *Handbook of multicultural counseling.* Thousand Oaks, CA: Sage.

Pinterits, E.J., Poteat, V.P., & Spanierman, L.B. (2009). The white privilege attitude scale: Development and initial validation. *Journal of Counseling Psychology, 56*(3), 417–429.

Quadagno, J. (1994). *The color of welfare: How racism undermined the war on poverty.* Oxford University Press.

Reese, E. (2007). The causes and consequences of U.S. welfare retrenchment. *Journal of Poverty, 11*(3), 47–63.

Richmond, M. E. (1917). Social diagnosis. New York, NY: Russell Sage Foundation.

Schlabach, T. (1969). *Rationality & welfare: Public discussion of poverty and social insurance in the United States 1875–1935.* Social Security Commission, Research Notes and Special Studies. Retrieved from http://www.ssa.gov/history/reports/schlabachpreface.html

Schneiderhan, E. (2008, July). *Jane Addams and the rise and fall of pragmatist social provision at Hull-House, 1871–1896.* Paper presented at the annual meeting of the American Sociological Association, Sheraton Boston, and the Boston Marriott Copley Place, Boston.

Schram, S. F., Fordingy, R. C., & Sossz, J. (2008). Neoliberal poverty governance: Race, place and the punitive turn in U.S. welfare policy. *Cambridge Journal of Regions, Economy and Society, 1,* 17–36.

Siegel, J., & Williams, L. (2003). The relationship between child sexual abuse and female delinquency and crime: A prospective study. *Journal of Research in Crime and Delinquency, 40*(1), 71–94.

Slack, P. (1990). *The English poor law, 1531–1782* (Vol. 9). Cambridge University Press.

Stephenson, C. (1943). Feudalism and its antecedents in England. *The American Historical Review, 48*(2), 245–265.

Trattner, W. (1998). *From poor law to welfare state* (6th ed.). New York, NY: Free Press.

Tropman, J. E. (1986). The "Catholic ethic" versus the "Protestant ethic": Catholic social service and the welfare state. *Social Thought, 12*(1), 13–22.

Turley, J. (2011). Separation of church and state? Not on the 2012 campaign trail. *The Washington Post.* Retrieved from https://www.washingtonpost.com/opinions/separation-of-church-and-state-not-on-the-2012-campaign-trail/2011/09/27/gIQA0vT8AL_story.html?utm_term=.4b69a993d4ef

Uluorta, H. M. (2008). Welcome to the "All-American" fun house: Hailing the disciplinary neo-liberal non-subject. *Millennium: Journal of International Studies, 36*(2), 51–75.

U.S. Department of Health and Human Services. (2015, July 24). Characteristics and Financial Circumstances of TANF Recipients, Fiscal Year 2013. Office of Family Assistance, Administration for Children & Families, Retrieved http://www.acf.hhs.gov/programs/ofa/resource/characteristics-and-financial-circumstances-of-tanf-recipients-fiscal-year-2013

Van Slyke, D. M. (2003). The mythology of privatisation in contracting for social services. *Public Administration Review, 63*(3), 296–315.

Wahab, S. (2002). For their own good: Sex work, social control and social workers, a historical perspective. *Journal of Sociology and Social Welfare, 29,* 39.

Weaver, R. K., Shapiro, R. Y., & Jacobs, L. R. (1995). The polls–trends: Welfare. *Public Opinion Quarterly, 59,* 606–627.

Weber, M. (1958). *The Protestant ethic and the spirit of capitalism* (T. Parsons, Trans.). New York, NY: Charles Scribner's Sons. (Original work published in 1905.)

Weikart, R. (1998). Laissez-faire social Darwinism and individualist competition in Darwin and Huxley. *The European Legacy, 3*(1), 17–30.

Wells-Barnett, I. B. (1969). *On Lynching: Southern horrors, a red record, mob rule in New Orleans.* New York, NY: Arno and the New York Times.

Wright, T. (2000). Resisting homelessness: Global, national and local solutions. *Contemporary Sociology, 29*(10), 27–43.

Zarefsky, D. (2005). *President Johnson's war on poverty: Rhetoric and history.* University of Alabama Press.

Zucchino, D. (1999). *The myth of the welfare queen: A Pulitzer-prize winning journalist's portrait of women on the line.* New York, NY: Touchstone.

Ethics and Values in Human Services

Ethics can be defined in many different ways, with most definitions including references to a set of guiding principles or moral values. In a professional context, ethics often refers to a set of standards that provide guidance to individuals within a particular discipline with the goal of assisting them in resolving **ethical dilemmas** they may face in the process of engaging in their business practices. A professional set of **ethical standards** is typically based on a set of **ethical values** that stipulate what behaviors and practices are considered acceptable and which are not and also provides general guidance in managing ethical dilemmas.

Now you might be asking yourself—I'm a good person, so why do I need a detailed set of ethical standards to tell me what to do? Don't good people behave "good" naturally? The answer may surprise you! Although it may be true that very few people wake up in the morning and say to themselves, "Hey, I think I'm going to lie, cheat, and steal today!" it is also true that many people become highly emotional in certain situations, which may impact their ability to see a situation in an unbiased and objective manner. People can also act in ways that reflect naiveté or ignorance, and in the process of being so very human, they may behave quite unethically as they make decisions based on their urges, desires, passions, personal biases, negative stereotypes, or uninformed opinions.

THE COMPLEX NATURE OF ETHICAL AND MORAL BEHAVIOR

It would be very convenient for many of us if there was one long list of rules in life, and all situations could be perceived in the same manner by everyone. But of course that is not how life works. Some people believe there are universal moral principles, particularly relating to issues such as murder and robbery. But even with these seemingly black-and-white situations, the gray seems to abound. Such is the case when someone kills in self-defense, or steals bread for a starving child. So, is **morality** universal or relative? Is there an absolute right and wrong in this world? Or, is the rightness and wrongness of a decision or action dependent on perspective, culture, or even one's own version of the truth?

This is an age-old debate and not one that I will attempt to answer definitively here. But, many moral theorists argue that both are true—there are **universal moral principles** that exist across almost all cultures (e.g., sexually abusing a child is always considered morally wrong) and there are **relative moral principles** where one must consider the appropriateness of a certain behavior within situational context (e.g., killing someone in self-defense) or one's culture—shared values among a community of people (e.g., burping in public or eating with one's hands). I want to address some of the issues that have the greatest potential of "muddying" the waters when it comes to determining how we know whether an action is moral or immoral, ethical or unethical, which in turn will help us determine how we can ensure we're making moral and ethical decisions not only in our personal lives, but also in our professional lives.

Watch this video on the nature of morality. Do you agree that babies are born with an innate sense of justice? If so, what are the implications of the studies highlighted in the video?
ENHANCEDetext *video example 3.1*

www.youtube.com/
watch?v=FRvVFW85IcU

Ethical Values versus Emotional Desires

When there is a breakdown in moral behavior, often it is because people get caught up in their emotions, which cloud their judgment. This does not mean that whenever we are emotional we're bound to behave immorally, but it is both normal and common to at times feel caught in a tug-of-war between our ethical standards (or sense of right and wrong) and our emotional desires or feelings. I used to have a counseling practice, and I often told my clients that feelings and emotions are like the interior design of a house—moving and poignant, even beautiful at times—but useful only if protected by the exterior and structure of the house—the walls and roof, which are the framework, like our ethical standards, values, and principles. Thus, although humans are by nature emotional beings, individuals with high character are not driven to act solely on the basis of their desires and passions.

Certainly there are times when emotions should lead, and we do not want to become rigid or heartless in our application of rules. When someone is driven to act solely on the basis of their values or rules, they are often deemed rigid and legalists. But when someone behaves in a manner that is solely driven by their feelings and desires, they are often deemed immature, volatile, and impulsive. This is not because their emotions are wrong, or inherently evil, but because their values and principles may not be sufficiently defined and/or developed to contain or regulate their emotions. So they act out impulsively—say things they don't mean, or behave in ways that are self-or-other destructive. For instance, an employee who has poor emotional regulation might become angry with his boss and punch him the face, even if he doesn't believe in violence, because he acts on his anger before thinking about the consequences. A person's ethical values can act as a rudder of behavior, and although there are certainly times when people will be influenced by their passions, typically their emotions should not drive their decision-making processes.

Another reason why it is important to understand the relationship between ethical values and emotions is that people often use their emotions to justify their unethical or immoral behavior: cheating on a test is wrong, unless the test is too hard and we hate our teacher; adultery is wrong, unless we're in a loveless marriage, and are extremely lonely, and fall hopelessly in love with someone else; lying is wrong, unless we need the day off from work and will only get paid if we're sick; violence is wrong, unless we're provoked; drinking too much alcohol is wrong, unless we've gone two weeks without and we've had a very bad day. One of the primary functions of ethical values is to keep us on a good moral track, particularly when we find our ethical values at odds with our emotional desires and urges.

When Our Values Collide

Behaving ethically may also be challenging if we experience conflicting values. Employees who shred documents to protect their employers may very well believe they were acting ethically based on their ethical value of loyalty to their employer. Yet, they may later be perceived as unethical, they may even be charged criminally for their actions. Perhaps in retrospect these employees will realize that their values were conflicting, which clouded their judgment, or they may forever believe that they were behaving ethically and were treated unfairly. So how do you make choices when your ethical values collide, and when you're on the front end of your decision and don't have the benefit of retrospect? How can you ensure that your behavior is ethical and consistent with your value system?

In 1945 Corrie ten Boom, a Christian woman living in occupied Holland, decided to hide Jews in her attic because she believed that was most consistent with her Christian values. But she also chose to lie to the Nazi officers who came to her door questioning her, even though she believed lying to be wrong (ten Boom, Sherrill, & Sherrill, 1974). Corrie's value of fighting injustice was in conflict with her value of honesty. In order to make the most ethical decision in the face of competing values, she had to choose the higher value—the more important value. What did she value more? Complete honesty at all costs? Obedience to authority? Personal safety? Or interceding in matters of inhumane cruelty and injustice at all costs? In light of what we now know about Nazi Germany and the Holocaust, Corrie and her family are lauded as heroes, behaving in the highest moral fashion, refusing to stand by and do nothing as an evil regime slaughtered millions of innocent people. We know that now, but did Corrie have the same confidence? Corrie took a risk, and although she paid dearly, history has proven that she was correct in her ethical decision-making.

Bodies of dead inmates fill the yard of Nordhausen, a Gestapo concentration camp. Photo was taken shortly after the camp's liberation by U.S. Army. April 12, 1945, Germany, World War II

Does this mean that those who did not hide Jews acted unethically? What if you had the opportunity to interview a family who refused to hide a Jewish neighbor? What if this family told you that Nazis used the practice of presenting as Jews and going door-to-door asking for refuge and that the punishment for harboring a Jew was imprisonment in a concentration camp and likely death? What if this family explained that they believed they behaved morally in not hiding Jews because their first responsibility was to protect their children? Would you still consider their behavior unethical? Or, what about the ruling authorities' perspective? Corrie ten Boom and her family broke the law. From the authorities' perspective, then, their behavior was unethical (and illegal).

What makes the ten Boom family's behavior ethical now? Our belief that the Nazis were evil? So does this mean that if you or I believe our government is evil that we'd be justified in disobeying its laws? Some divorced parents kidnap their children because they strongly believe the family courts will not protect the children from the other abusive parent. If this is true, is their decision to disappear with their children justified? Many African American men believe that if they are pulled over by the police, it is because they are being racially profiled, and they may be arrested for no legitimate reason. Does this justify an attempt to flee? Would their behavior be any more or less ethical than a slave who escaped prior to the Civil War? Why or why not?

I hope you are beginning to see that evaluating ethical behavior in retrospect, when we have the benefit of perspective and know all the facts, including the outcome, is a far easier task than determining what is truly ethical in the moment. In fact, the lens that we use to evaluate the ethical nature of a behavior is often determined *by* the outcome—something that we don't have the benefit of knowing (or any control over)—when making our decisions. This explains why some people who are initially perceived as highly unethical are later considered heroes, while other people, who authentically believe they are behaving ethically, end up going to prison.

The Development of Moral Reasoning Ability

Before adopting a set of ethical and moral values, it is important to understand how most of us develop the ability to think and reason morally. How do we grasp the nature of ethical behavior? How do we choose right from wrong? And does everyone have the same ability? Do adolescents have the same ability to understand the implication of behaving immorally or unethically as do adults? Do all adults have this same ability, or are there some people who, for whatever reason, have deficits in their ability to identity various choices and select the most ethical path by using their cognitive reasoning ability?

Obviously what people base their values on can vary dramatically. Value systems can be based on the values of one's family of origin, on one's culture, or on one's religious beliefs. But Lawrence Kohlberg (Gibbs, 2003) theorized that an individual's ability to reason morally relys on the ability to reason intellectually. In other words, in order for people to really grasp the nature of moral behavior, they needed to first have the cognitive capacity to do so. To test his theory, Kohlberg conducted interviews presenting subjects of all ages with what he called *moral dilemmas*, and asking for their opinions about the most moral course.

The Heinz dilemma, one of the more popular of Kohlberg's moral dilemmas, involved a woman who had cancer and was close to dying. The dilemma was that there was only one drug that could save her life and the local druggist, who discovered the drug, was charging 10 times what the drug costs him to make, making the drug beyond Heinz's financial ability to pay. Heinz was able to raise half the cost of the drug and pleaded with the druggist to either lower his cost or let him pay the other half later, explaining that his wife will die without the drug. The druggist refuses, citing his desire to make money from the drug. In order to save his wife, Heinz breaks into the laboratory, steals the drug, and saves his wife's life. Kohlberg would then ask the subjects whether Heinz's actions were moral or immoral and why.

Kohlberg discovered that those who had not developed sufficient cognitive reasoning ability (younger children and immature adults) had difficulty considering contextual factors when determining the most ethical course of action. As a result they often cited external factors, such as the negative consequences of a behavior, as their reasoning for why stealing the drug was morally wrong, but they had difficulty exploring the more nuanced nature of moral behavior. For instance, if you were to ask pre-adolescent children if hitting someone is wrong, they would likely say yes. When asked why, they would likely cite that hitting is wrong because they would get in trouble. They would also likely have difficulty identifying the impact of hitting on another's feelings, or even instances when hitting might be justified (e.g., in self-defense).

Adolescents and mature adults have developed abstract reasoning abilities and thus have the cognitive ability to grasp the various shades of gray involved in a moral dilemma. When confronted with the Heinz dilemma, these subjects could cite the moral nature of a situation, relying on internal references and contextual factors. For instance, they could cite examples of when stealing might reflect the highest level of moral behavior if it resulted in saving someone's life. Kohlberg also theorized that the capacity for moral reasoning did not necessarily mean that someone would behave morally. Thus someone may have the cognitive ability to apply moral reasoning but may still behave immorally.

ENHANCEDetext *self-check 3.1*

THE NATURE OF PROFESSIONAL ETHICAL STANDARDS AND CODES OF CONDUCT

Virtually all professions rely on some form of ethical standards to maintain integrity and trust within the profession. Numerous professions espouse basic ethical principles that serve as a foundation for their business practices, but a number of professions are also bound by legally enforced standards, or codes of conduct, which if violated can result in punitive consequences, ranging from professional or financial sanctions (such as license suspension or fines) to a wide range of criminal penalties (including incarceration).

Many professions operate under a professional organization or licensing entity that enforces their ethical codes in some form. Attorneys operate within certain legal ethical standards administered by the American Bar Association. Psychologists must abide by the professional standards set forth by the American Psychological Association (APA). Stockbrokers must abide by the legally binding ethical standards set forth by the Securities and Exchange Commission (SEC), which if violated can include both professional and financial sanctions, or in extreme cases, even a criminal indictment. And the

*"We have an agreement in principle.
The question is, do we all have the same principles?"*

© CARTOONRESOURCE / FOTOLIA

human services profession is bound by both a set of professional standards set forth by the National Organization for Human Services (NOHS), as well as applicable state and federal laws pertaining to specific practice settings, such as mental health, health care, school, and child care settings.

Professional codes of ethics are evolving and changing entities, never in final form, and always open for evaluation and debate. The ever-evolving state of professional codes of ethics enables a profession to remain current with contemporary ethical thinking, particularly with regard to matters of social justice and equity. Consider how far **Western society** has evolved from the time when the APA once considered homosexuality to be a mental disorder. The APA's historic stance on same-sex relationships would be considered highly unethical in today's culture. West (2002) discussed the importance of "ethical mindfulness" in evaluating the ethical nature of mental health practices, citing several real-world examples of questionable ethical practices, including the failure to inform clients of their rights, as well as the risks of engaging in the counseling process (informed consent), the use of real clients in therapist educational videotapes, and other ethical issues appropriate for discussion and evaluation.

Resolving Ethical Dilemmas

Watch this video about research on people's attitudes toward cheating. What are the implications of this research on professional ethical standards?

ENHANCEDetext *video example 3.2*

www.youtube.com/
watch?v=nUdsTizSxSl

Once a professional code of ethics has been adopted, the next challenge is to determine how to respond when an ethical breach is believed to have occurred, and if that is deemed to be the case, what action should be taken. Keeping Kohlberg in mind, what if a professional has been cited for breaching an ethical code. Then what? Do we presume that the professional is unethical and must be punished? Keeping Kohlberg's ethical dilemmas in mind, what if the higher moral ground requires the technical breaking of an ethical standard? How does a professional ethical board evaluate the ethical and moral nature of a professional's behavior without becoming neither moral relativists nor legalists?

Kitchener's (1984) model of ethical decision-making can help. Kitchener's model is based on five assumptions that Kitchener maintains need to be at the heart of any ethical evaluation. Kitchener's model can, in a sense, be used as a "litmus test" when attempting to determine whether a certain action or behavior is in fact unethical. The model's assumptions are that all ethical behaviors are presumed to be based on: (1) autonomy, (2) beneficence, (3) nonmaleficence, (4) justice, and (5) fidelity. When evaluating the ethical nature of actions and behaviors using Kitchener's model within the context of the helping professions, the evaluator would examine whether the professional permitted clients to act of their own free will (autonomy), whether the professional's actions were intended to benefit the client (beneficence), whether the professional's actions did harm to the client (nonmaleficence), whether the actions were carried out in a manner that respected the rights and dignity of all involved parties (justice), and whether the actions reflected loyalty and commitment to the client (fidelity).

Let's use the following vignette as an example of how to apply Kitchener's model of ethical decision-making to a common counseling situation:

Kate works for an adoption agency in the Chicago area. Although she has many responsibilities, her primary role is to counsel women experiencing an unplanned pregnancy and help them decide whether they want to place their babies for adoption. Kate counsels the parents (primarily the mothers) about all viable options, and if the parents select adoption, Kate helps to prepare them emotionally and practically for the adoption process. Kate also coordinates services with her co-worker, Sara, who is the caseworker for adoptive families. Kate and Sara work together to prepare both the birthmothers and adoptive parents, ensuring that both know their legal rights and are psychologically and emotionally prepared for what may occur. More specifically, the birthmothers need to be prepared to manage the grief they will experience after placing their babies for adoption, and the adoptive parents must be able to prepare for becoming parents, while understanding that the birthmother has the legal right to change her mind at any time until she signs the adoption papers (and in many states, even for a certain amount of time after that point). Kate and Sara have been working very hard lately to match a 16-year-old birthmother with an adoptive family. Kate is aware of the plight of this adoptive family, including numerous miscarriages and three failed adoption attempts, so she really hopes this one will work out for them. Kate is an adoptive parent herself, so she knows how emotionally devastating it is when a birthmother changes her mind at the last minute (even though Kate knows they have the legal right to do so). When the birthmother goes into labor, Kate cannot help but feel elation for the adoptive couple who has waited so long to have a baby. But then the birthmother starts expressing doubts, describing how she had no idea of the emotional connection she would feel for her baby once he was placed in her arms. Kate cannot help but feel conflicted by her client's seeming wavering. Kate does not believe her client has the emotional maturity or the resources necessary to be a good parent. The birthfather is not involved, nor is the birthmother's extended family. Also, the birthmother seems to think of her baby almost as if he were a puppy—something to love, something fun to play with. Kate cannot fathom having to break the news to the adoptive parents that they may not be taking this baby home. After some consideration, and based on Kate's belief that her client would likely not be a very good parent, Kate decides to place pressure on her to go through with the adoption. She does this by being very directive with her client, and by making her feel guilty and selfish for wanting to take her baby home. Kate concludes by telling her client that the best way she can show her love for her baby is by making a sacrifice and placing him with a family who can provide for all of his needs—something that a 16-year-old certainly cannot do. Although Kate knows that her client is emotionally vulnerable and very confused, she continues to push, reminding her client of incidences of abuse she disclosed during counseling sessions—"remember when you told me about how your own teen mother wasn't loving, and neglected you so often? Do you want to do that to your own child?" By the time Kate was done with the session, her client agreed to sign the adoption papers, effectively terminating her parental rights.

Were Kate's actions ethical or unethical? She was, after all, considering the best interest of the baby, wasn't she? Isn't it best that all babies to be raised in a two-parent, financially secure, and emotionally mature home? Do the ends justify Kate's means? Apply Kitchener's model of decision-making to this scenario (see Figure 3.1) and then you decide. Did Kate's actions (and motivations) support her client's right to act with *autonomy* and independence? Were Kate's actions *beneficent*; was she acting in a way that reflected altruism toward her client and all others involved? Did Kate's action harm her client, or was there *maleficence* involved? Were Kate's actions *just*? Did Kate consider the rights of her client, the birthmother, alongside the rights of the baby and adoptive parents? Could Kate's client, the birthmom trust that Kate had her best interest in mind, or did Kate violate her *fidelity* and commitment to her client?

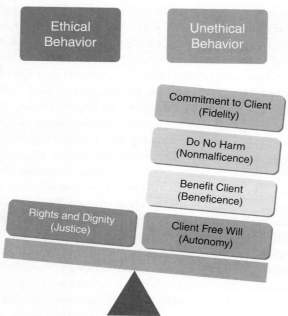

Figure 3.1
Applying Kitchener's Model of Ethical Decision-Making to Kate's Professional Actions

Can you see now how complicated ethical decision-making is, particularly in high-stakes cases? Which, let's face it, includes the majority of human services caseloads! While there may be some disagreement about the nature of Kate's actions, my evaluation of this case using Kitchener's model deemed Kate's behavior as unethical. Even though she may have been motivated by her desire to ensure the best interest of the child, I believe she was more motivated by her sympathy for the adoptive parents and their plight, and perhaps was even influenced by her own experiences as an adoptive parent.

Cultural Influences on the Perception of Ethical Behavior

Cultural context is another important variable to consider when evaluating the ethical nature of behavior since not all cultures evaluate behaviors in the same way (Garcia, Cartwright, Winston, & Borzuchowska, 2003). For instance, Garcia et al. note that not all cultures value autonomy equally—many cultures operate on a very interdependent basis, thus ensuring that clients making decisions completely independently may not be appropriate in some cultural contexts. The normative nature of behaviors is also perceived differently from culture to culture. Regardless of how one goes about determining what is ethical and how ethical decisions are made (or how unethical decisions are made), it is very important to be sensitive to various cultural influences, as well as characteristics such as gender and age cohort. As previously mentioned, it is also very important to remember that often what appears clearly unethical in retrospect may have seemed quite ethical when the decision was being made. Thus, taking the time to understand behavior from the actor's perspective is imperative, despite its challenging nature.

ENHANCEDetext *self-check 3.2*

ETHICAL STANDARDS IN HUMAN SERVICES

The ethical standards that govern the human services profession depend on different factors such as the human services professionals' level of education, professional license (including whether they have one), and the state in which they practice. The NOHS website states that its purpose is to connect educators, students, practitioners, and clients within the field of human services. Although it has no enforcement powers, NOHS members agree to abide by a set of ethical standards, which can be used as a guideline for resolving ethical dilemmas they face with clients and within the community-at-large (NOHS, 2015). Those who can use the NOHS code of ethics include human services professionals working in community agencies, researchers, administrators, students in academic programs focusing on human services, and faculty in human services programs.

The preamble of the NOHS *Ethical Standards for Human Service Professionals* states that its purpose is to provide human service professionals and educators with guidelines to help them manage ethical dilemmas effectively. The guidelines are broken down into two sections, with section one focusing on standards for human service professionals, and section two focusing on standards for human service educators. In the section on human service professionals, the standards are organized by categories pertaining to *responsibilities to clients, responsibilities to community and society, responsibilities to colleagues, responsibilities to the profession*, and *responsibilities to employers*. Overall, the general theme of these ethical standards centers on respect for the dignity of others, doing no harm, honoring the integrity of others, and avoiding exploitation of others, particularly clients and students, by recognizing power differentials within society. This is accomplished through maintaining self-awareness, engaging in all aspects of one's professional and personal life honestly and ethically, and developing an awareness of past and current global dynamics, particularly those involving the marginalization and oppression of others.

Watch this video about common ethical dilemmas in human services practice. How would you have handled this situation? ENHANCEDetext *video example 3.3*

Examples of a human service practitioner's duty to clients includes the recognition of the client's strengths (Standard 1); the right to confidentiality, except in cases where this right may be limited, such as in cases of harm to self or others (Standard 3); the obligation to avoid having sexual or romantic relationships with clients (Standard 6); avoiding imposing personal biases and values on clients (Standard 7); and the protection of client records and information electronically (Standard 9).

Examples of a human service practitioner's responsibility to the public and society include an obligation to provide services without discrimination or bias (Standard 10); the awareness of local, state, and federal laws and the advocacy for changes if such laws violate a client's or client group's rights (Standard 12); an awareness of social and political issues that impact clients of diversity (Standard 14); and the advocacy for social justice to eliminate oppression (Standard 16). Examples of a human service practitioner's responsibility to colleagues include avoiding the duplication of services (Standard 19) and responding to the unethical or problematic behavior of another human service professional (Standard 21).

Examples of a human service practitioner's responsibility to the profession include promoting cooperation among related disciplines (such as psychology and social work) (Standard 29) and the promotion of continuing professional development. An example of responsibility to self includes human service practitioners' awareness of their own cultural backgrounds, beliefs, and biases (Standard 34). And finally, a few examples of human service practitioners' commitment to students include high standards of scholarship and pedagogy, staying current in the field (Standard 39) and appropriately monitoring students' field placements (Standard 41).

ENHANCEDetext *self-check 3.3*

A FOCUS ON SOCIAL JUSTICE

Watch this video produced by the Love Alliance. What does social justice mean to you?

ENHANCEDetext *video example 3.4*

www.youtube.com/watch?
v=-VS20XrHivw&index=5&list=
PL6929BBACD76A3EB1

I began this chapter by discussing how many professional fields have adopted ethical codes of conduct. Virtually all the helping professions have such ethical codes mandating how practitioners should conduct themselves professionally. There are significant similarities among the ethical standards of the various helping professional organizations, such as the NOHS (2015), the APA (2010), the ACA (2014), and the NASW (2008). However, a review of each discipline's ethical standards reveals how the disciplines focusing on the human services (NOHS and NASW) tend to focus as much on macro responsibilities (communities and the broader society) as on the individual client. For instance, the human services and social work fields have the added responsibility to advocate for social justice—both on behalf of clients and on a societal level as a whole. *Ethical Principles of Psychologists and Code of Conduct* (APA, 2010), for instance, refers to justice in individual terms as it relates to every individual's right to benefit from the contributions of psychology, but there is no reference to advocacy for social justice on a societal level.

Since the human service profession is rooted in social justice movements, professionals focus as much on the role of society in the lives of clients and client groups as on personal behaviors and functioning levels. Thus, virtually all aspects of the helping relationship will include an evaluation not only of the client's personal dynamics (e.g., personal coping strategies, mental health, resilience, personal motivation, personality style), but also of societal dynamics that are potentially impacting the client and the client's environment (e.g., structural racism, historic oppression and marginalization, gender bias, poverty). The focus on social justice in a broader context is important because it highlights the macro focus of human services, with the recognition that society and its social structures play a significant role in the mental and physical health of its members.

ENHANCEDetext *self-check 3.4*

CONCLUSION

Ethical principles are an integral part of everyday life, enabling us to conduct business effectively and fairly both on a personal and professional level. Ethical standards in the human services field require that practitioners manage their practice in a respectful and safe manner, striving to respect the dignity of all persons, regardless of age, gender, race, sexual orientation, nationality status, and socioeconomic status (SES). Without ethical guidelines to help us navigate the various situations we will likely encounter in the helping professions, we're all at risk of the influence of personal biases, conflicting values, and emotional desires. Ethical principles in the human services profession are foundational to the continued development of this discipline that strives to objectively, professionally, and compassionately meet the complex needs of the most vulnerable members of society. Without such guidelines, we are at risk of exposing clients to potential harm and even revictimization.

SUMMARY

- *Ethics* and *morality* within a professional context are defined. The definitions of ethics and morality are discussed within a broader framework of what constitutes moral thinking and action, as well as how people know what is and is not moral or ethical behavior, both in the moment and in retrospect.
- The ways that professional ethical standards and codes of conduct can assist professionals in resolving ethical dilemmas are described. The purpose and nature of professional ethical standards, with a focus on the human services profession, are explored, including how professional ethical standards can help practitioners better understand and ultimately resolve ethical dilemmas.
- The ways that cultural diversity affects ethical perceptions and decision-making within the context of the human service profession are analyzed. The importance of human service practitioners being culturally sensitive when evaluating ethical behaviors is explored, with a particular focus on how culture plays a significant role in ethical decision-making.
- Key reasons are identified for why the human services and social work professions include statements regarding the obligation to advocate for social justice on a societal level in their professional ethical codes. The unique commitment to social justice and advocacy on a macro level within the human services field is explored.

Internet Resources

Conduct an Internet search for the article "The Different Ways People Handle Ethical Issues in the Workplace" on the Bloomberg Business website.

Conduct an Internet search for "Ethical Standards for Human Service Professionals" on the National Organization for Human Services website.

Conduct an Internet search for the "Code of Ethics" on the National Association of Social Workers website.

Conduct an Internet search for the "2014 American Counseling Association Code of Ethics" on the American Counseling Association website.

Conduct an Internet search for the article "Ethical use of social media: The responsibility of human services providers" on the husITa website.

References

American Counseling Association. (2014). *Code of ethics*. Alexander, VA: Author. Retrieved from www .counseling.org/resources/aca-code-of-ethics.pdf

American Psychological Association. (2010). *Ethical principles of psychologists and code of conduct*. Washington, DC: Author. Retrieved from http://www.apa.org/ethics/code/

Garcia, J. G., Cartwright, B., Winston, S. M., & Borzuchowska, B. (2003). A transcultural integrative model for ethical decision making in counseling. *Journal of Counseling & Development, 81*(3), 268–277.

Gibbs, J. (2003). *Moral development and reality: Beyond the theories of Kohlberg and Hoffman*. London: Sage Publications Ltd.

Kitchener, K. S. (1984). Intuition, critical evaluation, and ethical principles: The foundation for ethical decisions in counseling psychology. *The Counseling Psychologist, 12*, 43–55.

National Association of Social Workers. (2008). *Code of ethics of the National Association of Social Workers*. Washington, DC: Author. Retrieved from http://www.socialworkers.org/pubs/code/code.asp

National Organization for Human Services. (2015). *Ethical standards of human service professionals*. Washington, DC: Author. Retrieved from http://www .nationalhumanservices.org/index.php?option= com_content&view=article&id=43:ethics&catid= 19:site-content&Itemid=90

ten Boom, C., Sherrill, J., & Sherrill, S. (1974). *The hiding place*. New York, NY: Bantam Books.

West, W. (2002).Some ethical dilemmas in counseling and counseling research. *British Journal of Guidance & Counseling, 30*(3), 261–268.

4

Generalist Skills and Intervention Strategies

© MONKEY BUSINESS / FOTOLIA

Most professionals use tools to accomplish their job duties. A professional baseball player uses a bat, a ball, and a mitt. An accountant uses various computer programs; an airline pilot uses an airplane. What is unique about the human services field is that the professional *is* the tool. Human service practitioners use their instincts, their compassion, and their insights along with their interpersonal or people skills to affect meaningful change in the lives of their clients.

Most people who enter the field of human services already possess many of these skills, which is often what prompts them to pursue this career in the first place. One might question, then, why someone who is naturally inclined toward counseling needs a degree to become a human service professional. The answer is that while we can certainly help others by just being a good friend, or by volunteering for a charity or humanitarian organization, in order to work within a professional capacity, even the most naturally talented counselor needs training to learn theoretical foundations, models, and approaches; the underlying reasons why some people need assistance; the nature of the change process; how multicultural considerations impact people's lives and the helping relationship; and different intervention strategies and counseling methods that have been shown to be effective in research studies.

Because the human service practitioner is the primary tool for intervention, it is very important those working in the field to gain insight into their own values and belief systems, which influence how we perceive people and their experiences. Without gaining insight into what we believe and how our values evolved, we risk being biased against some people and for others. Gaining personal insights into one's own life experiences, whether one was raised with privilege or disadvantage, for instance, will help the human services professional consistently address and confront any personal biases in relation to certain groups of people, and social problems.

Throughout this chapter I use the words *counsel* and *counseling* in a general sense in reference to engaging in any type of direct practice with clients. This distinction is important because although most human service professionals engage in some level of counseling, in most states one must have at least a master's degree and hold a clinical license in order to provide clinical counseling services. In the human services field, though, many professionals, particularly those with Associate of Arts (AA) degrees and Bachelor of Arts (BA) or Bachelor of Science (BS) degree provide generalist counseling services.

Generalist counseling services may include case management, such as talking with clients about their feelings and experiences, interviewing clients during an intake process, facilitating a support group, and talking with people who call a crisis hotline. Generalist practice may also include more therapeutic counseling if the human service professional has a license to provide professional counseling services. Since the human services profession includes such a wide range of activities at so many levels of practice (from paraprofessional helpers to professional licensed counselors), the term *counseling* within this chapter should be interpreted rather broadly.

THE GENERALIST PRACTICE MODEL

According to the National Organization for Human Services (NOHS) the primary role of the human service practitioner is to help people function at their optimal level in the various areas of their life, such as interpersonally, within their family, friendships, work domain, and community. Human service practitioners also help communities function better in much the same way, but by using different techniques on a broader level. The term *generalist practice* refers to a model of working with people in a helping capacity that focuses on basic skills involved in the helping process.

Generalist practice is a theoretical approach used to helping individuals, families, groups, organizations, and communities. But before I describe the underpinnings of the generalist practice model, it will be useful to describe what generalist practice is not. Typically, when we reference generalist practice or a **generalist practice model**, we are not referring to specific theoretical modalities, such as psychoanalysis or Adlerian therapy. Rather, we are referring to basic skills and capacities that can be used with a broad range of clients and client systems.

A generalist practice model is based on certain assumptions about the nature of generalist practice. The first assumption is that generalist practice involves a basic skillset and goes beyond our natural inclinations and abilities (although certainly relies on them). The second assumption is the recognition that all interventions occur within an ethical framework based on adopted ethical guidelines and standards. The third assumption is that clients (individuals, families) and client systems (groups, organizations, and communities) operate within systems, and therefore certain assumptions can be made about the nature of a client's or client system's functioning within their respective environments. Finally, an assumption is that human service practitioners use problem-solving approaches and intervention strategies that are well researched, planned, and effective (Kirst-Ashman & Hull, 2015).

The National Organization for Human Services lists several generic human service professional competencies on its website. Some of these competencies include understanding the nature of human systems and their interactions; understanding conditions that promote or limit optimal functioning; and having skills that allow for the effective identification and selection of interventions that promote personal growth and the ability to reach personal goals and desired outcomes, and that are consistent with the values of the provider, client, the organization, and professional ethics of the profession. Other competencies include the ability to plan, implement, and evaluate chosen intervention strategies used with client and client systems, where the provider is considered the primary intervention tool and has a wide range of both interpersonal and generalist skills.

Informed Consent and Confidentiality

Prior to any discussion of generalist skills and competencies, the important topics of **informed consent**, confidentiality, and the **limits of confidentiality** must first be discussed. Informed consent involves disclosing to clients the nature and risks of the counseling relationship prior to their engaging in these services. According to the NOHS (2015), before beginning any formal relationship with a client, the client and the human service practitioner must first agree on the purpose, goals, and nature of the helping relationship—in other words, clients must have a clear understanding of what the helping relationship involves, including what it can and cannot do (i.e., the limitations of the helping relationship). Clients must also be informed that they have the right to terminate the helping relationship at any time they choose (with the exception of mandated clients).

The NOHS (2015) also mandates the client's right to privacy and confidentiality, which is an important aspect of the counselor–client relationship because it assures that whatever clients share with their counselors will not be shared with others. The commitment to maintain confidentiality of **privileged communication** is considered so vital to mental health treatment that confidentiality is a legal mandate in every state in the nation. Thus, most mental health professionals offering counseling services must by law maintain confidentiality or face professional sanctions that could include the loss of their professional license.

The importance of confidentiality is based on the premise that for trust to develop in the counseling relationship, clients must be assured that they have a safe place to discuss their most private thoughts, feelings, and experiences. Without such a guarantee, clients might not be willing to discuss their deepest feelings—their fears that they are not good parents, their intermittent desire to abandon their families because they are so overwhelmed in life, their histories of child sexual abuse, a recent extramarital affair, or a current struggle with drug abuse. Knowing that they have a safe place to share their deepest secrets with a person who is not personally affected, and who cannot disclose what they have shared, makes this exploration possible for many individuals, enabling them to become better parents, be less overwhelmed in their lives, be able to turn child-hood victimization into a survivor mentality, and to gain the strength and insight to work through difficult times in their lives.

There are occasions, though, when privileged communication is disclosed to others, either with or without the client's consent (voluntarily or involuntarily). Situations involving voluntary disclosure of privileged communication include the release of information at the request of the client to other treatment providers or insurance companies. In these cases, a client will sign an **authorization to release information**—a legal document that provides all relevant information about what information can be released, how it is to be released, and for what purpose it is being released.

Involuntary disclosure of privileged communication generally occurs in three types of situations: (1) when a client is legally mandated to receive mental health treatment and does not comply, (2) when clients pose a danger to themselves or others, and (3) in cases of suspected child abuse, maltreatment, and neglect. Situations involving the involuntary breaking of confidentiality highlight the limits of confidentiality—those difficult situations where a counselor (or other mental health professional) is legally required to break confidentiality.

Mandated Clients and Duty to Warn

Human service practitioners often have **mandated clients** on their caseload—those clients who are required by some legal requirement to seek mental health treatment. Individuals are often mandated to receive certain types of mental health treatment as a part of a criminal case. Examples include clients who are legally mandated to complete a batterers' intervention program, to complete a parenting class, or to attend a drug and alcohol treatment program. If a mental health provider works for an agency that has a contract to provide legally mandated services, they are typically required to submit periodic progress reports to the court, including whether the client has failed to comply with the requirements of the court.

When clients pose a danger to themselves or others, a counselor has a **duty-to-warn** and a **duty-to-protect**. For instance, if a client tells his counselor that he plans on leaving the office and killing himself, the counselor has the legal obligation to protect the client from himself by disclosing this information to the client's family or perhaps even law enforcement. If a client shares that she was recently fired from her job and plans to kill her former boss, the counselor has a legal obligation to warn her former employer, as well as report the disclosure to authorities.

Duty-to-warn laws have been greatly influenced by a tragic event that occurred on the University of California, Berkeley, campus when a student disclosed his intent to kill his girlfriend to a campus psychologist. Although the psychologist informed various individuals, including his supervisor and campus police, he did not inform the intended victim or her family. The client later killed the girlfriend, and the family of the victim sued

Watch this video on the case involving James Holmes, the Colorado theater shooter. Do you think the psychologist could have done more? What actions would professional ethical and legal obligations deem appropriate?

ENHANCEDetext *video example 4.1*

www.youtube.com/
watch?v=p6Bt0KnGLuo

the university based on the psychologist's failure to warn the victim. The case, *Tarasoff v. Regents of the University of California,* resulted in two decisions by the California Supreme Court in 1974 and 1976 (*Tarasoff I* and *II,* respectively). *Tarasoff I* found that a therapist has a duty to use reasonable care to give threatened persons a warning to prevent foreseeable danger. *Tarasoff II* was more specific in referencing the therapist's duty and obligation to warn intended victims, if necessary, to protect them from serious danger of violence. Virtually every state in the nation now uses the *Tarasoff* decisions as a foundation for duty-to-warn laws (Fulero, 1988).

It's not always so clear-cut when and if confidentiality should be broken. There are many occasions when counselors find themselves needing to use their clinical skills to determine whether breaking confidentiality is the appropriate course of action. For instance, consider the client who *may* be suicidal and who discloses a level of despair that *may* indicate suicidal ideation. Couple this with a disclosure that the client attempted suicide four months before and told no one, that he uses alcohol to make the pain go away, and that although he won't admit to a suicide plan, he doesn't always feel safe.

A client who shares this type of disclosure—denying any outright plan to commit suicide, but appearing to manifest many signs of suicidal behavior—can present quite a clinical challenge, because it requires that the counselor take a clinical risk. If the counselor takes no action, the client may indeed commit suicide; however, if the counselor breaks confidentiality and the client was not really at risk for suicide but just expressing feelings of temporary despair, then the counselor–client relationship might be seriously damaged. Because confidentiality laws in most states do not bar professional discussions among practitioners within the same agency, clinical dilemmas such as these are most appropriately explored in clinical supervision, where a team of counselors discusses the risks and benefits involved with each possible response.

Mandated Reporting of Child Abuse

Human service professionals are **mandated reporters**, and as such they are required by federal and state statute to report all cases of suspected child abuse, maltreatment, and neglect to the appropriate authorities. The requirement to report suspected child abuse is established by federal law, but the circumstances under which a report is made is stipulated by state law. Mandated reporters include any professional who comes into contact with children as a part of their professional duties. Some examples of mandated reporters are social workers, teachers (and other school personnel), health care workers, counselors, therapists, and all other mental health workers, childcare providers, church ministry personnel, and law enforcement officers (Child Welfare Information Gateway, 2016). Other people can certainly report suspected child abuse if they wish (and in most states they can do so anonymously), but they are not legally required to unless they are designated as a mandated reporter.

A counselor or other mental health provider needs not be certain that a child is being abused; rather if they have a reasonable suspicion of abuse, they are required to make a report, which in most states involves calling a toll-free child abuse hotline facilitated by a county or state child welfare agency. Decisions about whether a situation warrants a hotline call is difficult. A spanking that seems to the counselor to go beyond mere discipline, verbal abuse that might meet the criteria of child maltreatment, a child's disclosure that a babysitter or other supervising adult behaved in a way that made the child uncomfortable and may indicate potential sexual abuse, or any other indication that the child *may* be experiencing abuse at home may each warrant a hotline call.

Determining when the line has been crossed between appropriate caregiving and abuse is an issue best explored within clinical supervision, whenever possible, or even consultation with child protective services. It is important to note though that it is the counselor who is legally responsible for complying with child abuse reporting laws. It is the counselor's professional license that may be at risk if appropriate actions are not taken in response to cases where it would be reasonable to assume that child abuse, maltreatment, or neglect is likely. In some states a failure to report suspected child abuse can result in professional sanction, loss of the clinician's license, and even criminal charges in extreme cases. Thus, while clinical supervision can be very helpful in making these types of decisions, the counselor must make the final reporting decision.

Although clients are told about the limits of confidentiality in a written informed consent waiver, prior to receiving counseling they may forget or be confused about what would warrant the breaking of confidentiality. Clients who share deeply personal information with their counselor may feel betrayed by the counselor who informs them that a disclosure is going to be made to protect the client or others. Or, clients who disclose deeply personal information about unethical behavior (such as a shoplifting incident or infidelity) may worry unnecessarily that the counselor will disclose this information to law enforcement or a family member. It is vital that the topic of what can remain confidential and private, and what cannot, be fully discussed during the first counseling session and reiterated from time to time throughout the counseling relationship.

HIPAA Laws

According to federal legislation called the Health Insurance Portability and Accountability Act of 1996 or, more commonly, the **HIPAA Privacy Rule**, patients have the right to have their personally identifiable medical and mental health information remain confidential and protected. The HIPAA Privacy Rule stipulates how patients' electronic health information and records are to be kept private. Covered entities include insurance companies (including contractors and subcontractors), health care providers (including mental health care providers), and health care clearinghouses. Entities that are not covered under HIPAA include life insurers, employers, schools and school districts, and state agencies such as child protective service agencies and law enforcement agencies.

As mental health care providers, many of who work for state agencies (e.g., child protective services, law enforcement), human service professionals are bound by HIPAA; thus it is important for anyone entering the field of human service to understand HIPAA laws and how they impact work with clients. It's also important for human service professionals to know what information HIPAA laws protect, and what information is not protected. For instance, any information that is placed in a client's file is protected, as are conversations our clients have with us. Any information about clients that is in electronic form is protected, as well as any billing information.

HIPAA laws also stipulate how client information is to be protected. Human service professionals must employ safeguards to protect client records to ensure that protected information is not disclosed inappropriately or inadvertently. For instance, a file cannot be left unattended in a caseworker's car, but rather it must be contained in a locked filing cabinet. Agencies must make all necessary efforts to ensure electronic information is protected, including using secure and encrypted online sites and password-protected online access, where only necessary and appropriate employees have access to protected client information. Client protected information must also be shared with others only to the extent that is necessary. For instance, in clinical supervision meetings mental health care providers may elect to not share the names of the clients when discussing clinical situations and dilemmas unless such identifying information is absolutely necessary. Agencies are also required to train their employees on HIPAA laws, including what information is protected, and how to appropriately and effectively protect client information.

Covered entities are required to inform clients of their rights with regard to HIPAA laws. Notification is typically in written form and provides clients clear, concise, and easy-to-understand information about their rights under HIPAA legislation. There are many templates available for use by covered entities, including a range of acceptable options provided by the U.S. Department of Health and Human Services website. Essentially a HIPAA notification must inform clients that they have the right to see and obtain a copy of their health records, have corrections added to their health information, and receive a notice about how their protected information may be used and shared. Clients also have the right to decide whether to provide permission to providers prior to information being shared (for marketing purposes, for instance), receive a report on when and why protected information was shared, and how to file a complaint with a covered entity or the U.S. government if clients (or patients) believe their rights under HIPAA were violated.

HIPAA laws may appear relatively straightforward, but in the era of the Internet, this is not always the case. Consider the clinical intern who has a frustrating day and posts a status on Facebook without client names, but with enough information that someone may be able to deduce to whom the intern is referring. Or consider a counselor who responds to a client's email from a home computer, providing answers to personal questions that include protected information. Or consider a human service caseworker whose car is stolen when she inadvertently leaves it unlocked with a stack of client files piled on the backseat. All of these either are or could be HIPAA violations, depending on the circumstances and the nature of the information involved. Thus, it is very important for practitioners working as sole practitioners or with a covered entity to be educated and aware of HIPAA laws in all respects to avoid overt or inadvertent violations.

ENHANCEDetext *self-check 4.1*

GENERALIST PRACTICE COMPETENCIES AND SKILLS

Generalist practice is characterized as involving a wide range of competencies and skills that are used with a diverse population. Therefore, the competencies and skills referenced in this chapter will be general enough to be applied to a variety of situations and clients, while more specific competencies and skills used with particular intervention strategies will be discussed in successive chapters as they apply contextually to clients seeking services in particular practice settings. Despite the generalist nature of the human service profession, and the fact that in most (if not all) states human service professionals working on a bachelor's level will not be permitted to work in the capacity of a professional licensed mental health provider, some direct practice with clients will occur in various contexts. Thus, it is important for all human service professionals engaging in any type of direct work with clients to become familiar with some basic skills and counseling techniques as well as some of the foundational theories that guide generalist practice.

When referring to direct work with clients, we often use the term **micro practice**, which is defined as working with individuals. This is in contrast to **mezzo practice**, which involves working with groups, and **macro practice**, which involves working on a larger scale, with organizations, communities, and society in general. I will initially explore skills used in micro practice within the context of helping characteristics shared by effective human service providers, including the nature of effective communication skills, and intervention strategies that can be used within generalist practice. In the latter part of this chapter I will explore the nature of macro practice, including the focus and types of practice on a broader scale.

Watch this video on students' thoughts on effective practice. Which sentiments can you relate to?
ENHANCEDetext *video example 4.2*

Basic Helping Characteristics

Many of the foundational competencies and skills shared by effective human service professionals could be considered personality characteristics, and while many people who go into the helping fields may be naturally inclined toward empathy, compassion, and caring, these characteristics still need to be developed and honed. For instance, someone can be naturally empathic, compassionate, and caring, but such traits are learned, not necessarily innate, and must be further developed in a professional capacity. Helping characteristics are important to develop educationally and professionally because generalist skills, such as communication and intervention skills, emanate from foundational helping characteristics.

Empathy is an important and foundational skill. Empathy allows us to authentically walk in the shoes, and see the world through the eyes of, another. Empathy is not the same as sympathy though. This is an important distinction, particularly for human services professionals. Sympathy involves feeling sorrow or concern for another's welfare, whereas empathy involves being absorbed in the feelings of another (Escalas & Stern, 2003). Sympathy is not a difficult emotional response to muster, particularly when in response to those we believe are real victims, but empathy is far more challenging with unsympathetic clients such as batterers or child abusers (Greenberg, Elliot, Watson, & Bohart, 2001).

Empathy is also difficult when the issues clients are facing are frightening. Imagine watching the news and hearing about the plight of a young couple whose five-year-old child was recently abducted. Your immediate response would likely be to express feelings of sorrow for this family. You would likely express concern for the welfare of the parents as they search for their daughter, and you may feel very sorry for the little girl, who is no doubt feeling intense fear and who knows what else. But, you may stop short of allowing yourself to become absorbed in the parents' feelings of grief and fear because allowing yourself to immerse that deeply may hit too close to home, particularly if you have children of your own. In fact, you may feel compelled to distance yourself emotionally from their situation to resist putting yourself in their place.

Human service professionals do not have the luxury of shutting out the world of their clients in this way. They cannot limit their emotional responses to sympathy alone. To be effective counselors and advocates they must be willing to go on the emotional rollercoaster ride with their clients, extending their responses to empathetic ones, which in a counseling relationship involve the ability and willingness to experience a client's beliefs, thoughts, and feelings through their clients' personal lenses. Empathy requires emotional maturity, the ability to be honest with oneself, the capacity for immersing oneself in another's emotional crisis without getting lost in the experience, and being able to keep the focus solely on the client in the process. An empathetic response in a counseling relationship not only requires the counselor to have the emotional capacity to see the world through a client's eyes, but also to have the willingness to walk alongside the client through their difficult times.

This process can be emotionally exhausting. Consider the counselor working with a client who has been sexually assaulted. Counselors must be willing to understand the experience of being sexually violated as best they can, without having gone through the experience themselves. They must be able and willing to understand what it feels like to be traumatized, powerless, and humiliated, and what it feels like to be filled with shame, embarrassment, and stigmatized in response. While the idea of empathy might seem appealing on the surface, empathizing with clients is very challenging because it requires that clinicians search their own minds and hearts, to reflect on their own past hurts, and in this example, times in their lives where they have been humiliated, shamed, embarrassed, and stigmatized—experiences and feelings many may not be particularly inclined to experience.

The challenge of responding empathetically to clients who do not seem worthy is based at least in part on our perception of what they are or the things they have done. It is challenging for many within the helping fields, including the human services, to empathize with the feelings of those engaging in violent behaviors—batterers and child abusers, those who have sexually assaulted women, or those who have gotten intoxicated and crashed into a family on the freeway. Since human service practitioners often work with mandated clients, it is quite likely that they will be working with clients who are generally unsympathetic—parents who abuse their children, clients who have anger problems and have engaged in violent behavior, clients who are alcoholics and drug users. Looking at the world through the eyes of a domestic batterer or a chronic alcoholic might be the last thing any sane human being would want to do, but the willingness and ability to do so is a requirement for human service professionals, at least to some extent.

So how does one accomplish this feat, when the behavior of a client is often morally incomprehensible? The first step in developing the ability to empathize with unsympathetic clients is to understand that to empathize does not mean to condone. Consider the last motion picture that you watched. It is the director's job to help the viewer see the world through each of the characters' eyes. Considering the role of the director, although not a direct parallel, illustrates the concept of the human service professional essentially sitting alongside those they counsel and seeing the world through their eyes. You do not have to believe their perspective is accurate, and you certainly do not have to agree with their actions, but to be an effective human service professional you must be willing and able to understand what it feels like to be them.

For instance, many perpetrators of abuse were victimized themselves, and it is important that the counselor permit an unsympathetic client to share his or her own experiences of being a victim. While it might not make sense that a victim of abuse goes on to become the batterer, this dynamic does occur. The boy who was sexually abused *may* grow up to be a pedophile, the child who was beaten *may* grow up to beat her own children, and the boy who witnessed his father beat his mother *may* grow up to beat his own wife. The nature of this dynamic will be discussed in later chapters, but understanding that most abusive behavior is borne out of pain might help to see mandated clients not as monsters, but as broken human beings who have suffered greatly themselves.

Attorney John Fitzgibbons (seated-L) and Debra Lafave (R) speak to the media during a press conference after accepting a plea bargain to charges of having sex with a 14-year-old, March 21, 2006 in Marion County, Florida. Prosecutors there indicated that they did not want the 14-year-old on the witness stand. Lafave served 3 years house arrest and 7 years probation for molesting the boy, who was her student.

Setting Healthy Boundaries

Any discussion of empathy and the need for emotional immersion in another's problems must be considered in the context of boundary setting. Although the human services profession is not the sort of career one can leave at the office, it would be imprudent to become so immersed in a client's problems that practitioners cannot distinguish the difference between their problems and the problems of their clients. It is probably easier to discuss good boundary setting by giving examples of poor boundary setting. The practitioner who counsels a victim of domestic violence and spends the majority of the session talking about her own abusive relationships has poor boundaries. The practitioner who becomes so upset about a mother abusing her child that he takes the child home with him is not setting good boundaries. The practitioner who becomes so upset at a client who projects anger in the counseling session and yells back is not setting good boundaries. Finally, the practitioner who gets so immersed in his clients' problems that he becomes convinced his clients cannot survive without him is not setting good boundaries.

To help understand the nature of personal boundaries, they can be compared to physical boundaries, such as the property line around one's house—porous enough so that someone can enter the property, but solid enough that a neighbor knows not to set up a shed in another neighbor's yard (Cloud & Townsend, 1992). So too must human service professionals establish boundaries in their mental, physical, and emotional lives to determine what falls within their domain and responsibility and what does not.

In the human services field, some boundaries are determined by the ethical standards of the profession. For instance, having a sexual relationship with a client violates an ethical standard because this type of intimacy can exploit the practitioner–client relationship that grants the practitioner a significant measure of control—even authority—over the client. Violating the prohibition against having sexual relations with a client is so serious that it can result in suspension of one's professional license. Violating this ethical boundary might seem like an obviously bad idea to most people, but it occurs more often than one might suspect. Counseling someone of the opposite sex creates a sense of intimacy that can sometimes foster romantic feelings, particularly on the part of the client. Much like the child who develops a crush on a teacher, a client who is depressed and lonely may experience the counselor's comfort and guidance as intimate love. But a sexual relationship when one party possesses power and some level of control over another who is vulnerable and struggling will result in emotional and physical exploitation. A counselor who respects this boundary will recognize the clinical nature of the client's feelings and will help clients see that experiencing intimacy can be a positive experience without exploitation of their vulnerabilities. This is an example of a clearly marked boundary, and it is difficult to cross this boundary line without knowing one is in dangerous territory. However, other boundaries are not so clear and may be more readily violated (or at least somewhat trampled upon) by human service professionals, including myself.

My first job in human services was as an adolescent counselor at a locked residential facility. I was 23 years old, fresh out of college, and excited to finally be making a difference in people's lives. I became too involved in my clients' lives, though, and quickly began to overidentify with the teens on my caseload because I had also experienced a difficult adolescence. I was so flattered by my clients' expressed need for me that I was willing to work any hours necessary to make sure they knew how much I cared. If I worked a later shift, and one of the girls on my caseload told me that she needed me there in the morning, I would make sure I was there bright and early, even if it meant getting little sleep. If another counselor called me at home because a teen on my caseload was struggling, and was insisting that she would only talk to me and no other counselor, I dropped whatever I was doing and rushed down to the facility, feeling good that I was so needed.

This sort of behavior indicated several problems. First, it led to a situation where I almost left the field of human services altogether because after three years I was so burned out that I was no longer sure I could handle the pressure. My behavior also encouraged a sense of dependency among the girls on my caseload. Because it felt good to be needed, I neglected one of the fundamental values of the human services profession: empowering clients to be more self-sufficient. Setting healthy boundaries would not have been uncaring; rather, it would have encouraged my clients to develop positive relationships with other counselors, and it also would have taught them how to rely on themselves and their newly developed coping skills.

Since that point in my career I have developed some *rules for the road* for recognizing healthier boundaries with clients that better balance the need to be caring with the need to foster client self-sufficiency. One rule is that I try to avoid overfunctioning in the counseling relationship. If I start to feel exhausted and burned out, I ask myself if I am working harder than my client. This does not mean that I do not advocate for my clients, or that I do not assist my clients in performing various tasks, but what it does mean is that I recognize that I am not helping my clients if I am doing the work for them. Overfunctioning is often rooted in impatience and a need to see progress more quickly. However, clients have the right to self-determination, as well as the right to go as slowly as they wish or are able. So if I begin to feel exhausted and impatient with a particular client, I recognize these feelings as a sign that it may be time to step back a bit and give my clients more room to grow, and ultimately to decide the best course of action for themselves.

Our clients' lives and all that occurs within them are a part of *their* journey, not ours. We may believe we know what is best for them under certain circumstances, but that may not always be the case because ultimately they need to live their lives in the way they deem best. This conceptualization allows us to view ourselves as one of many individuals who will come alongside clients and help them at some point along their journeys, just as various people have helped and influenced us along our own life journeys. This conceptual framework helps to remind us that our clients have free will to make whatever choices they deem fit. This self-determination means that they can accept our assistance and suggestions, or they can reject them.

Another conceptualization that can help establish and maintain healthy boundaries in a counseling relationship is to recognize that people grow and change at varying rates and in their own unique ways. Thus, when we are working with clients early in their journeys we may be the *seed planter*. This is an important role, but it can also be frustrating if it appears as though nothing we are doing or saying is making a difference. Seed planters do just as it sounds—they plant the seeds of future growth—but oftentimes they do not have the benefit of seeing growth actually come to fruition. It is often this way when working with children and adolescents. Sometimes we see the manifestation of our work with them, but often we do not. We can trust that in most cases, years later, something we said, some kindness we showed, some reframing we did will result in healthy personal growth.

It is equally important to recognize the role of the *fertilizer* and the *harvester* in counseling relationships. These are the counselors who come into the lives of clients after the seeds have already been planted. The fertilizer is the practitioner who helps the client do the hard work, the productive work. This is no easy task, but the counselor often has the benefit of seeing the results of the seed planting and intervention strategies. The harvester is often the most gratifying role of a human service professional because the client is ready to make the necessary changes for a healthier life, recognizes past negative patterns in relationships and choices, can better navigate challenges they've experienced in their environment, and has the necessary insight and motivation to effect true change.

I recently had a client who was at this point in her life. Fortunately, I was able to recognize that I could not take full credit for helping her to make the significant realizations and changes she was making in counseling. She'd had several prior counseling experiences, and my role was to help her merge all that she had previously learned so that she could finally make the necessary permanent changes in herself and her approach to life. She was highly motivated to become a healthier, happier, and more productive individual, recognizing her own right to self-determination and dignity and her responsibilities to herself, her family, and her community. I did not take credit for all of her rapid progress. Instead, I appreciated the work of the previous counselors, recognizing that my client had the benefit of many talented counselors through the years, each of whom had contributed greatly to her personal growth and progress.

If you are working productively with a client but see little to no progress, you may very well be the seed planter. If you are working productively with a client but it seems as though change is still a long way off, then you are probably the fertilizer, and if you are reaping changes left and right with a client, then you may very well be the harvester. If you are all of these things with one client, the seed planter, the fertilizer, and the harvester, then you are fortunate to have a long-term client! Regardless, envisioning yourself operating as a part of a team, even though you may never actually meet the counselors who came before you (or those who may come after), helps to ease the sense of responsibility you may feel for a client's growth (and it helps us to resist the temptation to take full credit for the client's progress!). It is important for harvesters to recognize that other helpers have likely come before them. It is also possible that a counselor can serve in all three roles—seed planter, fertilizer, and harvester, particularly if the counselor and client have been working together for a long time.

ENHANCEDetext *self-check 4.2*

INTERVIEWING SKILLS AND ASSESSMENT TOOLS

After honing our basic helping competencies and skills, we are ready to move onto assessing a client's needs so that a good generalist counseling intervention strategy can be developed. While we continue to interview clients in some respects throughout the counseling relationship, effective interviewing skills are most often used during the assessment phase of a counseling relationship. Effective interviewing utilizes a combination of skills, such as **active listening skills**, **observation skills**, and the ability to ask **open-ended questions**, which includes reflecting back the client's answers while summarizing their concerns and needs, in a way that doesn't seem artificial or condescending.

Active listening skills involve good eye contact

Active listening skills involve the ability to attend to the speaker fully, without distraction, without preconceived notions of what the speaker is saying and without being distracted by thoughts of what one wants to say in response. Active listening in the counseling relationship also includes behaviors such as maintaining direct eye contact (if that is deemed culturally appropriate) and observing the client's body language and nonverbal cues. It also involves considering virtually everything that the client says as relevant. It is often the subtle offhand comment that yields the most information about the client's interpersonal dynamics.

Good observation skills are also an important part of the assessment process because individuals communicate as much through their bodies as they do through their words. Practitioners should observe their clients' eye contact, whether they are shifting uncomfortably in their seats when talking about certain subjects, crossing their arms self-protectively, or tapping their feet anxiously. All these behaviors can be clues or indicators of deeper dynamics. Employing good observation skills can also yield information about whether a client is being direct or evasive, genuine or masked, sincere or manipulative, open or guarded.

A good interviewer can obtain very specific information in a way that seems natural and conversational, while at the same time increasing a client's comfort level and openness. Counselors who are uncomfortable tend to appear contrived and too formal, which may make a client feel equally uncomfortable and therefore reluctant to share sensitive information. I recall a time when I was in college and seeking the services of a counselor. While the counselor was asking all of the right questions, he was awkward and too formal in his delivery, almost as if he were checking boxes off a list. When I began sharing something deeply personal, I shifted my glance, which allowed me to feel safer and more comfortable, and yet he was so determined to maintain eye contact that he moved his head in a way that dramatically and rather artificially attempted to reconnect. I found his insistence that I maintain eye contact intrusive and almost aggressive, and it shut me down emotionally. He also reflected back my answers in a way that seemed artificial:

Me: "Well, I suppose even though all of this occurred years ago, it is still quite painful."
Him: "It sounds like even though all of this occurred years ago, it is still quite painful."
Me: "Yes. This is exactly what I said."

Needless to say, I never went back.

Honing good interviewing skills that allow for us to actively listen, maintain appropriate eye contact, observe our clients holistically, ask open-ended questions, and reflect back and summarize what our clients have shared is difficult. Authenticity cannot be faked. Interest cannot be faked. Genuineness cannot be faked. If you are authentically interested in your client's story, and genuinely care, then this will shine through and compensate for any nervousness or awkwardness you may feel. Studying good interviewing skills and practicing them diligently is important, but so is having trust in oneself and a desire to really hear what clients share by showing genuine interest in and concern for their experiences.

Watch this video on the importance of eye contact when working with clients. Do you think maintaining eye contact is important? Could encouraging eye contact ever be detrimental to a client? If so, when and how?

ENHANCEDetext *video example 4.3*

The Psychosocial Assessment

The first session with a client is often spent conducting an intake interview for a **psychosocial assessment**—a report that includes comprehensive information about clients and their needs that will be relied upon when developing an intervention and treatment plan. Psychosocial assessments can take on many forms depending in large part on the types of services being offered and the client's needs, but generally they include basic demographic information about the client (e.g., age, marital status, number of children, and ethnicity), the nature of the identified problem(s), employment status, housing situation, physical health status, medications taken, history of substance abuse, criminal history, history of trauma, any history of mental health problems (including depression, suicidal thoughts, or other mental illness), and any history of mental health services.

Human services psychosocial evaluations use a **strengths-based approach** or perspective, which means that while clients' needs are identified, their strengths are as well. This practice perspective helps the counselor avoid seeing the client from a pathological perspective, focusing solely on their deficits, while viewing clients as having inherent strengths, such as resiliency (Saleebey, 2005). According to Saleebey (2005), the strengths-based approach can be used with other practice theories, particularly those that encourage self-determination and personal growth.

The specific focus of the psychosocial assessment will vary depending on the services being sought. For instance, clients who are seeking services from a domestic violence shelter will be asked more questions related to the clients' relationship histories, histories of family abuse, and levels of functioning, sufficiency, and safety. Clients seeking hospice services will be asked more health-related questions and questions pertaining to their feelings about dying. Finally, some agencies have very specific forms used for psychosocial evaluations, thus the human service professional won't have much latitude in the questions being asked, whereas in other agencies, the counselor will have much greater latitude, particularly if the services being provided are of a more general nature.

Even though the psychosocial assessment process will be concentrated in the first few sessions, it will continue to a certain extent throughout the counseling process. This is important because more often than not new information will continue to emerge long after the initial assessment period is over. If counselors assume the assessment is complete after the first few sessions, they might overlook important information about the client that emerges later in the counseling relationship.

I recall working with one female client for depression and parenting issues, who in response to my questions regarding her perception of the origin of her problems spent a considerable amount of time discussing her troubled marriage and her difficulty making friends. In a much later session she was sharing a particularly painful story about a difficult interaction with a friend, and in the process made a casual and joking comment about it reminding her of something hurtful her mother always said to her when she was a child. If I had not been actively listening, I could have missed the significance of her comment, but I also noticed her brief pause and a very subtle sadness in her eyes. The entire exchange lasted no more than a few seconds, but it completely turned the course of our counseling. In other words, she shared something months after the psychosocial assessment was completed that altered my assessment of her situation.

Patience, therefore, is imperative in conducting an effective assessment. One reason why people enter the field of human services is because they love to figure other people out, but a seasoned professional will not allow this passion to result in a rush to judgment. It is important to hold at bay the intense desire to exclaim "Aha!" too quickly. People are complex beings, with unique communication patterns and perspectives. Gaining a comprehensive picture of our clients' lives involves allowing their stories to emerge slowly and at the client's pace. We are not conducting a criminal investigation, which involves seeking the ultimate truth; rather, we are interested in our clients' perspectives and their version of their lives, which may or may not be completely accurate. Understanding this dynamic does not detract from counselors' advocacy role of their clients, but rather supports the counselor's ability to help clients reframe various incidences and situations in their lives, and to help them gain a healthier and more balanced perspective.

Generalist Practice Assessment Tools

In addition to conducting a clinical inventory, human service professionals often use assessment tools to evaluate their clients' mental health functioning and psychosocial needs. Assessment tools may consist of psychological inventories, such as Beck's Depression Scale or the Rosenberg Self-Esteem Scale, which can be facilitated by any mental health professional, or may involve the use of psychological testing, such as an IQ test, or the Minnesota Multiphasic Personality Inventory (MMPI), which must be facilitated by a licensed psychologist or psychiatrist.

Another type of assessment tool includes those based on a particular theory, such as a family genogram, developed by Dr. Murray Bowen and based on a theory he developed in 1978, called family systems theory (Bowen, 1978). Bowen's family systems theory postulates that individuals can best be understood within the context of their familial environments. A family system is composed of individuals operating as interdependent components that impact the other components. Patterns of behaving and functioning, including relational patterns with self and others, not only impact other members of the system but are also transmitted from one generation to the next.

Examples of intergenerational relational patterns include how feelings are managed (are anger and grief expressed openly?), how communication is handled (is open communication embraced or is it threatening to the family system?), how discipline is meted out to children (authoritarian? authoritative? permissive?), even whether families are generally open or closed systems (are outsiders, such as new partners, accepted with open arms, or are they treated with wariness and caution?). Relational styles also tend to be passed down from generation to generation, such as the types of behaviors that are most likely to result in alliances (and enmeshment) or estrangement from the family.

Having a client develop a **family genogram** is a very effective way of better understanding the big picture of the client's life. What are the intergenerational transmissions of communication styles, emotional regulation, and relational styles? What has the

Genogram emotional relationships legend

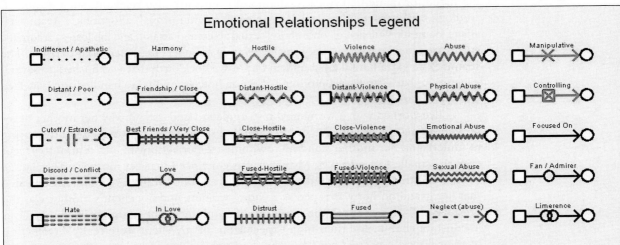

client taken for granted as normative functioning that was actually passed down from generation to generation? Bowen believes that in order for one to achieve positive wellbeing one must be able to have a healthy personal autonomy and individuation while maintaining appropriate closeness with one's family system. Those who are so close to their family system that they cannot make decisions without family approval (or risk being considered betrayers of the family), may be *enmeshed* with certain family members. Those who find it necessary to emotionally distance themselves to the point of estrangement to achieve independence are considered *cut off* from their family systems.

A family genogram can assist a client in developing a level of objectivity about their family systems, which can ultimately help them to see that they are not victims, but viable participants with choices about future behaviors. Thus, rather than fearing shame and disapproval from a parent, the client can recognize that shaming in response to increased autonomy is a relational style that has been passed down from generation to generation, perhaps in response to some trauma related to a loss experienced several generations back. And perhaps the seemingly negligent parent isn't being purposely distant and unloving, but is reacting to his own parent who was harsh and authoritarian.

Creating a family genogram takes considerable time and effort. Most people have some information about their parents, limited information about their grandparents, and oftentimes no information about their great-grandparents. They may have grown up hearing one-sided (and unquestioned) versions of family feuds or odd distant relatives. To gain accurate and valuable information about one's family system, information seeking must be intentional. This can be uncomfortable and may even ruffle the feathers of certain family members, because it is often the family members who have been cut off, or are considered the black sheep, who hold the family secrets that will unlock the hidden underlying dynamics of a family system. Poking around the skeleton closet may threaten families, particularly in closed family systems.

Genograms use a variety of symbols designed to indicate gender, the type of relationship (married, divorced, etc.), *and* the nature of the relationships (cut off or enmeshed). Traumatic events, such as deaths, divorces, and miscarriages, are noted, as are the family's responses to these events (e.g., losses are openly talked about, never discussed, or denied). Typically, shameful events are also relevant, such as out-of-wedlock births (particularly relevant in earlier generations), abortions, extramarital affairs, domestic violence, alcohol abuse, sexual abuse and assault, and job losses. Traumatic events are often kept secret, but can affect family members for generations to come. The shame of an extramarital affair and an out-of-wedlock birth that was hushed up several generations back can have a profound effect on how emotions are handled and how feelings are communicated.

I once worked with a woman who struggled to understand why her mother never seemed to accept or approve of her. She had spent years in counseling attempting to understand her mother's and her own intense perfectionism and refusal to accept even the smallest of mistakes. My client was convinced that her mother was ashamed of her, and this belief affected every area of her functioning. A genogram revealed that her grandmother was raped as a young woman, and my client's mother was the product of that rape. Both the grandmother and my client's mother lived their lives in constant shame, and their high expectations of my client were really a reflection of their desire to protect her from the shame they were forced to endure because of cultural restraints common in that era, not some statement of their disapproval of her.

It was through the development of a family genogram that my client was able to take a few emotional steps back and see herself and her family system with more clarity and objectivity.

A family genogram provides a structured way of obtaining a comprehensive family history so that the practitioner and client can develop a more complete understanding of the broad family dynamics that are affecting the client in ways perhaps never before recognized or acknowledged. It also provides for an objective and non-shaming way to gain a level of objective understanding of various issues within one's family system that can potentially pave the way for the clients to view relationships and various events in their own lives without personalizing hurtful experiences, including gaining an objective understanding of the nature of conflict-filled family relationships (Prest & Protinsky, 1993). No longer is the client blaming himself for his father's seeming disapproval or feeling hurt because his mother seemed emotionally distant and rejecting. Instead clients can develop a greater understanding of the broader picture and can see their family members as individual people who are as much a victim of circumstances as the client. A family genogram is an effective assessment tool, as well as a very effective intervention tool that can be used to address long-standing psychosocial issues that have potentially kept clients in emotional bondage for years.

The Nature of Clinical Diagnosing

Many human service practitioners working as paraprofessionals will not be formally diagnosing clients, but it is important that they understand the nature of mental health diagnosing since their clients may have one or more clinical diagnoses. Additionally, licensed human service professionals will likely be required to diagnose clients as a part of the assessment process depending on the nature of their work and the practice setting in which they are working.

There are many components to conducting a clinical diagnosis, including a comprehensive awareness of mental and emotional disorders. Mental health providers in the United States use the *Diagnostic and Statistical Manual of Mental Disorders*, fifth edition (*DSM-5*) to diagnose the mental and emotional disorders of their clients. The *DSM-5* is a classification system developed by the American Psychiatric Association (APA, 2013) that includes criteria for mental and emotional disorders, such as schizophrenia, depressive disorders, anxiety disorders, and personality disorders such as narcissistic personality disorder and antisocial personality disorder (sociopathy). The *DSM-5* shifted away from the *DSM-IV*'s multi-axial system toward a more dimensional approach. Disorders that used to be diagnosed on three different axes: Axis I (clinical disorders), Axis II (personality disorders and mental retardation), and Axis III (general medical conditions), are now recorded on one axis. Psychosocial and environmental stressors used to be recorded on Axis IV, but are now reflected in clinical descriptions. Axis V used to reflect the client's Global Assessment of Functioning (GAF). But, due to the overwhelming consensus among experts that an individual's level of function cannot be sufficiently captured with a single number, clinicians are now encouraged to evaluate a client's mental and psychosocial functioning within a separate assessment of the client's severity and disability.

Another important consideration when evaluating someone's level of functioning and mental-health status is to recognize that virtually all behaviors occur on a continuum. It is only when a particular behavior occurs frequently enough, and at an intensity level high enough to interfere with normal daily functioning for a significant amount of time, that it becomes the subject of clinical attention. All of us feel sad at times, but if we are so intensely sad that we stop eating and want to stay in bed all day, then we may be suffering from clinical depression. Similarly, many of us become concerned from time to time that our friends might be talking behind our backs or that one of our coworkers is trying to get us fired, but if we're convinced that everyone is out to get us, even people we've never met, then we may be suffering from some form of clinical paranoia.

The *DSM-5*

The *DSM-5* accounts for the continuum of mental health experiences by including criteria relating to frequency and intensity of psychological experiences in the diagnoses process. For instance, meeting the criteria for major depressive disorder requires that an individual not just be depressed, but also have a depressed mood nearly every day for at least a two-week period. An individual who meets the criteria for generalized anxiety disorder isn't someone who worries from time to time, but someone who worries *excessively,* more days than not, for at least six months.

Although the diagnostic criteria of the *DSM-5* relies significantly on professional peer consensus and review, and is backed by a large body of research, many professionals in the human services field have some concerns about the *DSM-5* because of its reliance on the medical model, which pathologizes what might just be a broader range of human thoughts and behaviors. Pathologizing normative behavior tends to create a stigma for those who are suffering from emotional problems. Consider someone who has recently been the victim of a violent crime. If he experiences mental flashbacks of the traumatic event, is he exhibiting behaviors that are adaptive and expected, perhaps even healthy? Or, in the alternative, is he suffering from post-traumatic stress disorder? Is the angry adolescent whose parents were just divorced exhibiting a normal grief response to this loss? Or does he have oppositional defiant disorder? Even if human service professionals do not inherently view human behavior from a disease perspective, using the *DSM-5* can influence practitioners to view their clients from a pathological perspective (Duffy, Gillig, Tureen, & Ybarra, 2002).

Yet, even if one believes that the medical or disease model is appropriate to use when evaluating psychological disorders, an important distinction between the diagnostic system used to diagnose medical conditions and the system used to diagnose mental disorders is that the *DSM-5* uses criteria based on symptoms, whereas medical conditions are diagnosed based on the etiology (cause or origin) of the disorder. Thus rather than diagnosing a patient with a stomachache, which could potentially have many causes, the medical diagnosis would be a virus, an ulcer, or cancer. Yet, when considering mental disorders, one is not diagnosed with a neurotransmitter disorder, negative thinking, or an abusive childhood, but with major depressive disorder based on the symptoms the client is experiencing (not on etiology).

Other criticisms of the *DSM-5* include questioning the process that determines what behaviors are deemed abnormal enough to be included in the *DSM-5* and which behaviors are not, and whether it is appropriate to categorize human behavior by pathologizing alternative understandings of the spectrum of human experiences (Duffy et al., 2002). Many human service professionals use the *DSM-5* but may rely on it less than other mental health disciplines because the human service profession is based on empowerment theory and a strengths-based approach, in which clients are encouraged to recognize that they have more control over their lives than they may have previously thought. Self-determination is a related concept and refers to the rights of all individuals to make choices they believe are in their own best interest.

In summary, the value of services provided depends on the effectiveness of the assessment. A good assessment defines problems that the client is experiencing, develops a needs assessment to determine where the client's strengths and deficits lie, ascertains the client's social support system, and develops an appropriate treatment plan. It is also important to reassess the client at various points in the counseling process to monitor new or previously masked issues, and to make sure that treatment goals are consistent with the assessment.

ENHANCEDetext *self-check 4.3*

INTERVENTION STRATEGIES FOR GENERALIST PRACTICE

Once the initial assessment is complete, a treatment plan is developed to address the client's identified issues. I will explore **direct practice** and counseling techniques appropriate for clients served in particular practice settings in more detail in subsequent chapters. However, there are basic techniques involved in generalist practice that apply in a broad way to most counseling and intervention situations that will be explored in this section. Effective intervention strategies are based on counselors' ability to build a positive alliances and mutual trust with their clients. They also are based on the counselors' having the freedom and space to state their observations about their clients and granting them this same freedom and space. These are all vitally important ingredients to effecting positive change in clients. We may use the most successful, theoretically-based strategies available, but if our clients don't trust us (and if we don't trust ourselves), and if our clients don't feel safe to share what they're thinking, then our work with them, regardless of the strategies we use, will not be successful.

Many individuals seeking services at a human service agency will need assistance with developing better coping skills. Regardless of whether the problems experienced by the client are pervasive or more limited, most clients can benefit from learning to manage high levels of stress, learning to prioritize the various problems in their lives, and learning how to manage the current crisis in a way that diminishes the possibility of a "domino effect" of crises. A crisis with one's child requiring a significant amount of time and attention can quickly result in a job loss, which can in turn result in the loss of housing. Confronting crises effectively, though, can have a positive impact on one's life, including an increase in self-esteem, the development of new and more effective coping skills, the gaining of wisdom, the development of new social skills, and the development of a better overall support system.

Most mental health experts recognize that one of the best opportunities for personal growth is a crisis, due to the possibility of shaking up long-standing and entrenched maladaptive patterns of behavior. Park and Fenster (2004) studied stress-related growth in a group of college students who experienced a stressful event and found that struggles involving a life crisis produced personal growth, but only for those who expend the necessary energy to work through their struggles in a positive way. Those in the study who remained negative and avoided dealing with the problems borne out of the crisis did not take advantage of the growth-producing opportunities and thus did not experience any significant personal growth. Those who worked hard to manage the stress resulting from their crisis and were able to see the crisis as an opportunity for growth often developed better personal mastery skills and developed a changed and healthier perspective. Recognizing this potential for personal growth provides the counselor with a framework for assisting clients in developing more effective coping skills that can better assist them in the management of concrete problems and can also help them to shift their entire perspective of life struggles in general. For instance, clients who once saw themselves as powerless victims can begin to see themselves as empowered survivors.

Case Management

Case management is likely one of the most common activities for human service professionals in their professional practice, often consuming more than 50 percent of their time (Whitaker, Weismiller, & Clark, 2006). Case management is defined as the coordination of services and advocacy for clients and involves human service professionals working with other professionals to coordinate an array of services for the client that diminishes fragmentation and service gaps (Barker, 2003).

There are numerous differences between case management and direct counseling services. Although both encompass a broad range of activities, they are distinctly different. Direct practice with clients is focused more on an individual's psychological growth and the development of emotional insight and personal growth, whereas case management involves coordinating services with other systems impacting the life of the client.

A case manager might coordinate services with a client's school social worker, the housing authority, the local rape crisis center, or even a court liaison, all in an attempt to meet the needs of the client who is interacting in some manner with each of these systems. The goal of the case manager is to assist the client in plugging in to necessary and supportive social services within the community and to learn how to improve the reciprocal relationship or transaction with each of these social systems. These efforts have many purposes and goals, but chief among them is the caseworker's proactive attempt to strengthen and broaden the client's social support network.

In the Human Services-Board Certified Practitioner Examination handbook that is provided to human service professionals in preparation for the HS-BCP examination, a description of case management includes the following tasks:

- Collaborate with professionals from other disciplines
- Identify community resources
- Utilize a social services directory
- Coordinate delivery of services
- Participate as a member of a multidisciplinary team
- Determine local access to services
- Maintain a social services directory
- Participate in case conferences

Watch this video produced by Portland Community College case manager, Carlos Ramos. How many of the tasks can you identify that Carol engages in that are on the HS-BCP list?

ENHANCEDetext *video example 4.4*

www.youtube.com/
watch?v=G7TqQtaBCM0

- Serve as a liaison to other agencies
- Coordinate service plan with other service providers (Center for Credentialing & Education [CCE], 2011).

The Task-Centered Approach

When most individuals are confronted with a crisis, panic sets in, and it becomes difficult to address the problem in a systematic way. Most of us can relate to feeling completely overwhelmed when facing a life crisis. We know there are things we need to do to manage the crisis, but all we see is a gigantic mountain looming before us. For some, this has a motivating effect, and they attack the mountain until every issue is resolved. But for some, particularly those with a history of crises, those with poor coping skills, or those suffering from emotional or psychological problems with diminished personal management skills, the mountain can seem virtually insurmountable, and their response is to shrink away with a feeling of despair and defeat.

A counseling technique called the Task-Centered Approach, an intervention strategy developed by the School of Social Services at the University of Chicago (Reid, 1975), works well with clients who feel paralyzed in response to the challenges of various psychosocial problems and crises. Treatment is typically short, lasting anywhere between two and four months, and is focused on problem solving. The client and counselor or caseworker define the problems together and develop mutually agreed-upon goals. Each problem is broken down into smaller and more easily manageable tasks. Goals can be as tangible as finding a new job or as intangible as learning how to more effectively manage frustration and anger. Rather than having one broad goal of obtaining a job, a client might have a Week 1 goal of doing nothing more than looking at job ads on a major online job board and a Week 2 goal of submitting a resume to one job posting. Dividing large goals into smaller stepping-stone goals diminishes the possibility that clients will allow their anxiety to overwhelm them. By focusing on specific problems and breaking them into bite-sized manageable pieces, clients not only learn effective problem-solving skills, but also gain insight into the nature of their problems, develop increased self-esteem as they experience successes rather than failures in response to meeting goal expectations and learn to manage their emotions, such as anxiety and depression, without allowing such states to overtake and overwhelm them.

The counselor or caseworker assists clients in meeting goal expectations through a variety of intervention strategies specific to the actual problem, but can include planning for obstacles, role-playing (where the client can actually act out difficult situations in the safety of the counselor's office as a way of practicing communication), and mental rehearsal—similar to role-playing but involving the client thinking or fantasizing about some specific situation, such as an upcoming job interview or a difficult confrontation (Reid, 1975). Revisiting original goals and evaluating client progress are also powerful tools in helping clients experience a sense of personal mastery and empowerment as they are helped to recognize and acknowledge their progress. Consider the following case study and then reflect on how you might use the Task-Centered Approach with a similar client.

Case Study 4.1   Case Example of Task-Centered Approach

Kara is the 34-year-old single parent of a 5-year-old boy. She has been living with her mother since her divorce three years ago. This is a negative situation because her mother is verbally abusive to Kara and her son, abuses alcohol, and smokes inside the home. In addition, their living space is small, and Kara and her son share a bedroom. Kara's original goal was to live with her mother for only six months, but whenever she considers moving out she becomes overwhelmed with the prospect of not only finding an appropriate apartment, but finding child care as well, because despite her mother's abusive behavior, Kara has been relying on her mother for before- and after-school child care while she works. Kara feels trapped but completely powerless to do anything about her situation. During Kara's intake interview she described her prior counseling experiences, sharing that she quit counseling because whenever she was faced with the prospect of finding an apartment, her fears would snowball into so many fears that she simply couldn't even bring herself to make the first phone call in search of housing. She ended up feeling embarrassed, as if she were letting the counselor down, and just decided she could not deal with any more failures, so she stopped going to counseling. Kara explained that throughout the past several years her mother has consistently reminded her that she would never make it on her own, that she would surely fail, and that she would end up destroying her life and the life of her son. Her mother also told Kara that if she moved out and ran out of money, she would not bail Kara out again and would instead force Kara and her son to go to a shelter. Going online to look for a rental advertisement resulted in a flood of worries and concerns for Kara—some specific and some she could not put into words. She worried about everything from whether she would know what to say when calling on an apartment manager to whether she would be able to support herself and her son. What if she was laid off from her job and could no longer afford her apartment and had to live in a shelter? What if she couldn't find a babysitter she could afford? What if she found an apartment and got a babysitter, but the babysitter ended up abusing her son worse than her mother did? She heard about such things all the time on the news, she reasoned. Or what if she found an apartment, but she had a financial emergency such as her car breaking down, and she started falling behind in her rent and was evicted? She couldn't fathom the thought of moving out and then having to move back in with her mother again, or worse what if her mother made good on her threat and refused to allow them to move back in with her? Once confronted with this slippery slope of catastrophizing, she would resist even taking the first step toward independence and could not bring herself to even look at online rental postings. Kara's mood became increasingly melancholy over the years, and after years of verbal abuse from her mother, her ex-husband, and now her mother again, she had no confidence in her ability to financially support her own son or even to manage her own life without her mother's assistance. Kara's caseworker reassured her that there was absolutely no rush in finding an apartment. In fact, she reminded Kara that she was in charge of her own life and could make the choices she thought were best for her and her son. During the first two sessions, Kara and her caseworker developed realistic goals for her, including securing an apartment when Kara had the funds to ensure financial security. Kara and her caseworker developed a detailed budget and determined that she would need three months' salary put away in a savings account to ensure against any realistic financial emergencies. By identifying possible obstacles to Kara achieving independence, decisions were made based on facts and realistic risks, not on undefined and generalized fear. Once goals were developed and obstacles identified, Kara and her caseworker agreed on tasks to be accomplished by the following week. Kara's task for the first week was to look through the newspaper and circle rental advertisements within her price range. She was not to call any of them though, even if she found one that seemed ideal. Kara came in the second week with printouts of rental postings. Kara and her caseworker spent the first portion of the session discussing how Kara felt while printing out these posts. Kara explained that her initial excitement was quickly followed by intense anxiety, but when she realized she could not call the apartments even if she had wanted to, she calmed down almost immediately.

(Continued)

The next portion of the session was spent on determining tasks for the following week. The first task included calling on two apartments for informational purposes only. Because Kara had a significant amount of anxiety about calling and talking to a stranger, Kara and her caseworker wrote a script and rehearsed it by doing a role-play with the caseworker playing the part of the potential landlord. Kara's additional task for the week was to talk to her boss to seek reassurance that her employment was secure. Kara returned the following week excited. She called on two apartments and followed the script on the first one, but the second call went so well she did not even need the script. Her discussion with her boss also went well, and he reassured her that her job was secure. Kara shared excitedly that her boss was pleased that Kara showed assertiveness in approaching him and offered her an opportunity to attend some training courses so that she could be promoted. For the next three months Kara's counseling proceeded in a similar fashion with weekly tasks that inched her along slowly enough that she did not become overwhelmed by unreasonable fears, but quickly enough that she gained confidence and courage with each successive step. Kara rented an apartment during her fourth month of counseling with three months' income safely tucked away in a savings account, a promotion with a raise, and reputable and affordable day care.

Perceptual Reframing, Emotional Regulation, Networking, and Advocacy

Another generalist intervention strategy involves perceptual reframing—reframing a client's perception of a situation, emphasizing the importance of viewing various events, relationships, and occurrences from a variety of possible perspectives. For some reason it seems easier to assume the negative in many situations, or consider the worst possible outcome. Whether considering the intentions of a boyfriend or the prospects of getting a better job, or even whether good things can happen to good people, many people tend to gravitate toward negative assumptions, particularly during times of crisis.

Many people in the midst of a physical or emotional crisis of any proportion will often resort to taking a somewhat polarized negative stance on an issue and would benefit from assistance in viewing situations and relationships from a different perspective. A client's perception that life is unfair and nothing good ever happens to her can be encouraged to see life struggles as normative and even good because they promote positive personal growth. Clients who feel shame because they were recently fired from a job they didn't really like in the first place can be encouraged to see this incident as a disguised blessing opening the door to find a career for which they are far better suited.

Additional generalist intervention goals include assisting clients with *emotional regulation,* teaching them how to effectively manage their emotions, particularly intense emotions, rather than acting on them in an unhealthy way. For instance, clients can be taught how to sit with their emotions, despite the discomfort this may involve, rather than getting angry and behaving in an impulsive manner. Developing a better social support network is another example of a generalist intervention goal. Health social support systems assist clients in becoming emotionally independent and self-reliant.

Cultural Competence and Diversity

Because human service professionals work with such a wide range of people across various cultures, socioeconomic levels, and backgrounds, it is vital that human service education and training be presented in a context of cultural competence and cultural sensitivity. **Cultural competence** is reflective of a counselor's ability to work effectively with people of color and ethnic minority populations by being sensitive to their needs and recognizing their unique experiences. Cultural competence is a required component of working in the human services field. For instance, the NOHS ethical standards specify the requirements and competencies human service professionals are required to maintain. Specifically, standards 17 through 21 deal with issues related to cultural competence, focusing in particular on anti-discrimination, cultural awareness, self-awareness relating to personal cultural bias, and requirements for ongoing training in the field of cultural competence.

The human services field is not the only discipline to require cultural training. Most professional organizations require that their mental health professionals obtain cultural competency training based on a foundation of respect for and sensitivity to cultural differences and diversity (Conner & Grote, 2008). Yet, cultural competency extends beyond that of ethnic differences. For instance, counselors who undergo cultural competency training will learn the importance of remaining sensitive to populations from different income levels, religions, physical and mental capacities, genders, ability levels, and sexual orientations. Therefore, they will learn the importance of avoiding what is commonly referred to as ethnocentrism—the tendency to perceive one's own background and associated values as being superior or more normal than others. In recent years, the issue of cultural or multicultural competence has become so important that training protocols have been developed with recommendations that all those who work in the helping fields engage in some form of cultural competency training.

Cultural competence is somewhat of a general term though and is often used synonymously with other terms such as cultural sensitivity. Despite the relatively universal belief among human services and mental health experts that cultural competence is a vital aspect of practice, very little consensus exists as to what constitutes cultural competency on a practice level (Fortier & Shaw-Taylor, 2000). Although broad themes of respect and sensitivity tend to be universally accepted as foundational to cultural competent practice, the concept of cultural competency has tended to remain a general philosophy that has not yet been operationalized in a concrete way.

For instance, Cunningham, Foster, and Henggeler (2002) surveyed counselors who considered themselves culturally competent and found a vast difference in terms of which counseling methods they believed were most effective with culturally diverse clients. This lack of consensus among experts on which specific counseling approaches and counselor responses constituted cultural competence makes it difficult, if not impossible, to determine what methods will have the greatest likelihood of having a positive outcome in counseling a particular ethnically diverse client group. Although recent research has attempted to develop what is called *evidence-based practice* with regard to cultural competence, to date there remains very little research on what constitutes cultural competent practice.

ENHANCEDetext *self-check 4.4*

EFFECTING CHANGE AT THE MACRO LEVEL

When students consider entering the field of human services, they often do so because they want to help people meet their basic needs by counseling them—helping them obtain much-needed services and teaching them to learn new ways of meeting their needs in the future. In other words, most students think of direct practice with individuals and families when considering a career in the human services profession. But many times the challenges clients encounter are caused by some external force—an injustice that is structural or systematic. Some of these external forces might be a school system that offers no bus service and therefore inadvertently contributes to low-income students' truancy rates, a government social welfare policy that inadvertently punishes single mothers who work part-time by cutting their benefits, or a **three-strikes law** that sends a young man to jail for 25 years for a third, yet relatively minor, offense. How do human service professionals combat harmful policies that punish when they should reward or unfair legislation that hurts certain segments of the population?

The human services profession is grounded in the notion that people are a part of larger systems and that to truly understand the individual one must understand the broader system this individual is operating within (e.g., ecological systems theory, person-in-environment). As such, there is a reciprocal dynamic involving both the individual and the system, where each has an impact on the other. Hence, an individual can be very motivated and respond well to direct intervention, but until structural deficiencies are addressed within society, they will likely continue to experience difficulty in some manner.

It is important, then, for human service professionals to recognize that people can be helped best by approaching problems on various levels. Consider that as a human service provider you are committed to eradicating violence within society. You might choose to work with survivors of domestic violence, focusing on their personal empowerment. This approach would involve micro practice— practice with individuals. You might also decide to facilitate treatment groups for batterers, believing that the greatest likelihood of change can be accomplished by addressing the perpetrators of violence in a group setting where each group member can learn from others and hold each other accountable. This approach would involve mezzo practice—practice with groups. But if you decided to address the problem of violence by working with an entire community, locally, nationally, or perhaps even globally, by conducting a public awareness campaign to educate the population about the prevalence of violence, or by lobbying for the passage of antiviolence legislation, then you would be engaging in macro practice—practice with communities and organizations.

Macro practice is a multidisciplinary field shared by those in the human services, social sciences, political sciences, and urban planning disciplines. Macro practice involves addressing and confronting social issues on a community and societal level that can act as barriers to getting one's basic needs met by creating structural change through social action of some type. The most basic themes involved in macro practice include advocating for social and economic justice and human rights for all members of society to end human oppression and exploitation (Weil, 1996). There are several ways **social change** is accomplished through macro practice, including community development, community organizing, and policy practice. Thus, although direct practice is important, working with entire systems to promote positive structural change on all fronts is equally important.

Some human service professionals work solely in macro practice in administrative positions or policy practice, conducting no direct practice whatsoever. But a great many human service professionals involved in micro practice are also involved in macro practice at least to some extent. For instance, when I was the director of victim-witness assistance at a county state attorney's office, I provided generalist counseling to victims of violent crime, but I also served on community policy action committees and engaged in legislative action with community coalitions, making recommendations to the state legislature on behalf of victims' advocacy groups.

Human service professionals might ask themselves why they should be concerned about what is happening to people in an entire community, in a different part of the country, or in a completely different part of the world. The rationale for engaging in broad-based activities lie in human services profession's commitment to social justice and human rights achieved through social action and social change. This foundational commitment to social justice is so integral to the human services profession that the professional obligation to social action is reflected in the ethical principles of the discipline. For instance, the National Organization for Human Services (NOHS) (2015) ethical standards reference the human service professionals' responsibility to society, which includes remaining aware of social issues that impact communities, and initiating social action when necessary by advocating for social change.

As human service professionals we must be aware of the history of social injustices and human rights against certain populations so that we may better understand the context within which they currently struggle. These insights will also help us to gain an awareness of what groups are most likely to be targets of discrimination and oppression in the future. At all times we must be vigilant in avoiding the temptation to become influenced by the stigma surrounding many challenges experienced by historically marginalized and oppressed populations, such as ethnic minority populations that experience disparities within the criminal justice system or populations that are underserved in the areas of mental and physical health (Calkin, 2000).

In some respects, the human service profession has shifted away from its original call to community action, turning instead to a model of individualized care (Mizrahi, 2001; Rothman & Mizrahi, 2014). This is likely due to the increased popularity of direct (micro) practice within all the mental health professions in the 20th century. This doesn't mean that macro practice or social advocacy has ceased. Rather, as those in the human services fields have moved away from community work, other disciplines have moved in to fill the gap, such as urban and public planners and the political sciences. This shift in priorities has resulted in the human services profession often being out of the loop of community building and organizing efforts (Johnson, 2004).

Concerns have also been expressed regarding the neglect of macro and community practice in human services and social work educational programs, which has compounded the tendency for human service professionals to avoid macro practice in their careers as they feel ill equipped and unprepared (Polack, 2004). The movement away from macro practice is apparently an international trend as well. For instance, Weiss (2003) cited examples of how many human service professionals in Israel do not feel competent addressing social issues on a community or global level because the majority of their training focused on practice with individual clients. Weiss encourages those in the human services professions both in Israel and abroad to reengage in policy-related activities and social advocacy on a macro level. The reality is that structural issues contributing to poverty, racism, violence, labor abuses, and other forms of human exploitation must be addressed through advocacy efforts for social change on a macro level as well as a micro level to create much-needed changes within society.

At-Risk and Marginalized Populations

Before beginning any discussion on social advocacy efforts on a macro level it is important to identify populations that are often the target of marginalization, social injustice, oppression, and human rights violations. In essence, an at-risk population can include any group of individuals who are vulnerable to exploitation due to lifestyle, lack of political power, financial resources, and societal advocacy and support, and generally, lack of a powerful voice in society. Some of the current at-risk and oppressed populations include ethnic minorities, immigrants, and refugees (particularly those who do not speak English), indigenous people, older adults, women (particularly women of color), children in foster care, prisoners, the poor, the homeless, single parents, LGBTQ+ populations, members of religious minorities, and the physically and intellectually disabled. At-risk populations often share unique characteristics not shared by others within a particular culture, and it is often this uniqueness that can increase the risk of oppression, discrimination, injustice, and exploitation. At-risk populations are thus at greater risk of experiencing a variety of social problems compared to other populations within the mainstream of society (Brownridge, 2009).

An individual or population's risk of marginalization, oppression, and exploitation increases with the interconnectedness or **intersectionality** of multiple vulnerabilities. The more oppressive institutions individuals face—racism, sexism, xenophobia, homophobia—the more they are at risk for a range of social injustices, including increased risk of disadvantage, stigmatization, and oppression. The concept of intersectionality was originally applied to race and gender, although the concept is now applied to a variety of marginalizing categories, such as level of disability, sexuality and gender expression, social class and socioeconomic status, immigration status, nationality, and family status (Knudsen, 2005; Meyer, 2002; Samuels & Ross-Sheriff, 2008). An example of intersectionality of vulnerabilities would be an African American, older, transgendered woman who is economically disadvantaged, physically disabled, and struggling with homelessness. This profile reveals a woman who experiences multiple forms of vulnerability to injustice on a variety of levels, likely needing various types of advocacy (Martin, 2014). Other social forces that can increase the risk of discrimination, prejudice, oppression, and injustice include **white privilege**, **nativism**, and **xenophobia** (Martin, 2014).

A Just Society

Before human service professionals can effectively engage in work on a macro level, they must first become aware of what a just society looks like. At the root of any discussion of an ideal society is the assumption that all human beings have inalienable rights simply because they are human. History is replete with examples of egregious human rights violations, often waged in the belief that such actions are justified on some level. Slavery, a **caste system** that deems one group of people more worthy than another, a patriarchal system that subjugates females within society, the genocide or **ethnic cleansing** of a particular cultural group, and the sale and exploitation of women and children for sexual purposes, are all examples of the gross mistreatment of individuals, often because there is some defining characteristic that makes them different from groups possessing political and social power. Such differences are often used to justify mistreatment, where members of a more powerful group place themselves above members of less powerful groups.

Members of a just society recognize that one group should not have oppressive power over another because all human beings have basic rights that must be protected. Human service professionals work on a macro level, partnering with at-risk populations and communities to become the voice of the voiceless (Martin, 2014). There are many ways this activity occurs—community development, community organizing, and policy practice. Gaining at least a cursory understanding of the different types of macro practice and the associated activities can aid in understanding how human service professionals' work transitions from identifying social problems within society to finding ways of effectively addressing them.

Types of Macro Practice

Within the general field of macro practice, models and approaches have been developed to frame the various ways of approaching social concerns on a broad level. The Internet has in many ways changed the way that macro practice occurs. Whether engaging in macro-related activities solely online, or using the Internet as a vehicle for facilitating offline activities, the Internet, particularly social media, has dramatically increased the reach and power of social activists in ways not dreamed of in pre-Internet eras. Although there are many models and approaches to macro practice, most have at their core the basic goal of social transformation where a community on any level (local, national, or global) incorporates values that reflect the human dignity and worth of *all* its members.

Community Development

Community development dates back to the settlement house movement when Jane Addams and her colleagues worked with politicians, various community organizations, political activists, and community members to create a better community for all members. Addams was concerned about many civic issues and social ills, including immigrant rights, civil rights, child labor, compulsory education, and **women's suffrage**. By engaging residents, community leaders, local politicians, and other community organizations, Addams was able to develop a sense of community cohesion in urban Chicago, which resulted in collective social action and several laws being passed that benefited the members of her community, including those who resided in the settlement houses.

Community development in Addams's day is similar in many respects to civic and political activism today, where effective community building depends on the participation of community organizations and community members working together to address issues that are of concern to the entire community (Austin, 2005). The issues involved could include civic or political issues, such as addressing crime in the community; educational concerns, such as low state test scores and developing an after-school program to combat juvenile delinquency; bringing new businesses to the community to create jobs for community members; or rallying community leaders to develop more open spaces, such as parks, in densely populated neighborhoods.

Empowerment strategies are used in most macro practice approaches focusing on civic issues, such as social and economic development that involves creating liaisons between community organizations and community members. Partnering with those within the community who are most impacted by the identified problems is vitally important since an empowerment approach presumes that community members are experts at solving their own problems and just need guidance, resources, and political power. A community development approach can tackle problems in ways not possible through individual efforts. A particularly empowering aspect of community development is how the collaboration process can create a sense of collective self-sufficiency that often leads to civic pride for community members. In fact, effective community development is based on the conviction that any community is capable of mobilizing necessary resources to support families (Austin, 2005).

The various aspects of macro practice will vary depending on the area of concern and the at-risk population most affected. However, virtually all models of macro practice include a focus on community development, which can refer to the development of a geographic community, such as a neighborhood or city, or a community of individuals, such as women, immigrants, or children (Netting, Kettner, & McMurtry, 2016).

There are several necessary components of effective community development, including diversity among group members, a sense of shared values among members, positive and collaborative teamwork, good communication, equal participation of all team members, and a good network of connections outside the community (Gardener, 1994). Good community development also depends on the ability to secure enough funding to support group members' efforts and activities. Good networking skills are also essential as are good technology skills because so much of networking in contemporary society is accomplished through email and other technological means (Austin, 2005; Weil, 1996).

Community Organizing

Community development depends on community organizing efforts, which in turn depend on the efforts of community organizers. The first step in community organizing is to create a consensus on what the community needs, in particular what challenges the community is facing or areas of needed improvement. Once community members agree on the problems to be addressed, community organizers set about to recruit members to join in the effort to effect change. It is important to once again note that the term *community* does not necessarily refer to a geographic community, but might also refer to a community of people, such as women, survivors of domestic violence, prisoners, or foster care children.

Community organizers can be professional policy makers or licensed practitioners, or they can be individual people with a particular passion and calling for social action. A schoolteacher who gets a group of his students together to remove graffiti from public buildings is a community organizer. The single mother of three who organizes a voluntary after-school tutoring program for the kids in her neighborhood is a community organizer. The father of a child victim of sexual abuse who organizes a campaign to increase prison time for sexual offenders is a community organizer. The human service provider whose agency is hired to canvas a neighborhood in an antidrug educational campaign is a community organizer. There are many famous community organizers—Jane Addams, who organized community action around immigrant rights, Rev. Martin Luther King Jr., who organized community action around civil rights, and Cesar Chavez, who organized community action around farmworkers' rights.

Community organizing efforts usually begin with the *identification of a problem* that is of concern to many people in a community. Once a problem has been identified, community organizers must *conduct research* to define the issues so they can better understand how the problems developed and what, if any, forces exist that are keeping the problems in place. For instance, the community activist who is organizing efforts to increase the labor rights of undocumented immigrants may encounter opposition from factory owners who benefit by paying untaxed low wages to undocumented workers. Thoroughly researching

A stressed out Cesar Chavez (1927–1993) was a community organizer and co-founder of United Farm Workers (UFW) of America, the first farmworkers' union in the United States, working on behalf of exploited farmworkers, initially in California's agricultural valleys. La Paz, California, 1970s

CATHY MURPHY / HULTON ARCHIVE / GETTY IMAGES

this issue will enable community organizers to identify constituents in the community who will support their cause as well as those who may oppose it. Research will also enable community organizers to identify additional harm done by unfair labor practices not initially identified that might increase the strength of any collating forces.

Once the problem has been identified and research has been conducted, *a plan of action* must be determined based on the research conducted. Community organizers might decide to picket factories where they believe abuse of undocumented workers is occurring. They might decide to distribute press releases and have a press conference to gain media involvement, organize a work walkout, or conduct a letter-writing campaign to local political leaders. Effective community organizers also organize fundraising efforts to support their social activism. Fundraising can include a number of strategies including a direct request for donations, auctions, fundraising dinners, membership fees, or government grants.

Policy Practice

Policy practice is a narrower form of community practice in which the human service professional works within the political system to influence government policy and legislation on a local, state, federal, or even global level. The form that policy practice takes depends in large part on the issues at hand, but certain activities in policy practice are consistent despite the issues involved. This is a relatively new field within human services, with few researchers focusing on policy practice prior to the 1980s. Policy practice remains an often neglected area, both within human services and social work education and within human services practice settings. One reason for this may be that effective policy practice relies on a broad range of skills that reach far beyond the clinical realm (Rocha & Johnson, 1997).

Policy practice activities center on either reforming current social policy or initiating the development of new policies that address the needs of the underserved and marginalized members of society, with the primary goal of achieving social justice through social action and reform. Policy practice is based on the belief that many problems in society, such as poverty, are structural in nature and can be addressed through making structural changes within society, including the passage of fair and equitable legislation (Weiss, 2003).

Iatridis (1995) has defined several skills necessary for effectively integrating social policy practice. The first skill involves the human service professionals' ability to *understand the nature of social policy*, including what it is, how it develops, its influences and effect on society, as well as how social welfare policies are most often implemented. The second skill involves the ability to *view policy practice from a systems perspective*, where policy practice is seen as a part of a greater whole. In other words, human service professionals engaged in policy practice must be able to link issues confronted in direct service to structural problems. Another equally important skill involves the human service professionals' *commitment to improving social justice* within society by working toward a more equitable distribution of the community's resources. Those who engage in policy practice also research various social issues in an attempt to determine the short- and long-term effects of new policies and legislation.

Policy activists and analysts might focus their attention broadly on social injustices in general, or they may focus on particular issues, such as the quality of mental health delivery systems. Or their focus may be extremely narrow, such as the lack of access of quality mental health services for people of color living in urban communities. Human service professionals engaging in policy practice must be able to identify key trends and issues, as well as become familiar with legislation or pending legislation that will affect the areas of concern.

Let's assume you are involved in policy practice working for an agency concerned with the older adult population. The federal administration's policies regarding Social Security funding would be a matter of great concern to you. If you were involved with policy practice advocating for the rights of the children of undocumented immigrants, you'd be very concerned about possible legislation that would prohibit these children from attending public school. Regardless of the area of concern, those engaging in policy practice must be able to identify the "ripple effect" of new policies and legislation to identify their potential benefit or harm to the target population as well as the entire community.

Policy practice may be a singular activity or a part of community development and community organizing. Consider the group of human service professionals who are working with a coalition of agencies and concerned citizens on building a park in town where kids can play rather than loitering in the streets. Then consider that a few months after organizing efforts have begun, the coalition learns of an old law that permits the building of a park only in areas zoned for commercial use, and that the land donated to the coalition is zoned for residential use only. Members of the coalition would likely need to engage in policy practice to change the zoning laws, alongside community development efforts and community organizing. In other words, while there may be times where those engaging in macro practice will only be involved in one macro approach, most often numerous approaches are used in order to best address the issues so that macro goals can be achieved.

Cyberactivism

Community organizers and social justice activists are increasingly using the Internet, and particularly social media, to draw attention to social issues, as well as for civic engagement and political advocacy (Castells, 1997, 2001, 2007; Margolis & Resnick, 2000; Vissers, Hooghe, Mahé, & Stolle, 2008). People and organizations around the globe now use the Internet for creating awareness, increasing social mobilization, and effecting change on local, national, and global levels. For instance, a recent study by the Pew Research Center's Internet and American Life Project found that about 66 percent of social media users have used a social media site, such as Facebook or Twitter, for civil engagement and political purposes. Examples include liking, posting, and reposting content about civic, social, and political issues on their social media account; encouraging others to take action on an issue; joining a politically related group on a social media site; and following an elected official or political candidate on a social media site (Rainie, Smith, Schlozman, Brady, & Verba, 2012).

Online advocacy is referred to by many different names, but one of the more popular terms is **cyberactivism** (Morris & Langman, 2002). Macro-level practitioners use the Internet in a variety of ways to engage in cyberactivism. For instance, they can use social media to increase awareness about a particular issue, mobilize supporters, create alliances and encourage action, whether in the form of letter writing or attending protests. One of the many challenges traditional activists face is targeting groups most likely to be interested in their cause (Taylor & Van Dyke, 2003). The Internet and particularly social media have made this much easier. Since social media already "herds" like-minded people together in a variety of ways, cyberactivists can more easily develop a sense of solidarity among like-minded users, leading to greater engagement and action.

Many social media sites also allow users to engage in cyberactivism, both individually and collectively. For instance, Facebook allows individuals and organizations to create campaigns for a nominal fee. Users create the content of their campaign, which may include information, a petition, and/or a link to a website. Users can target their campaigns broadly (Facebook users in the United States), or they can target a particular demographic (women between the ages of 25 and 45, with elementary school-aged kids) using Facebook targeting algorithms. The campaign will then appear on the newsfeeds of Facebook users who meet the campaign's specified criteria. Users receive regular updates on their campaigns, including how many people clicked on the campaign post or took some other action, such as liking or commenting on the post.

Cyberactivism is more successful than traditional forms of activism because it's less expensive, faster, allows for far broader dissemination of information, and increases the ease of engagement. Consider how a petition was circulated in the pre-Internet era: organizations used professional printers to mass produce informational leaflets, which were then passed out via the U.S. postal service, door-to-door through in-person canvassing, and perhaps even placed on the windshields of cars in parking lots. Activists stood in shopping malls or busy streets for hours disseminating information in an attempt to increase concern and empathy. They asked for signatures on petitions, for volunteers to make phone calls or attend demonstrations, and if they were fortunate perhaps one person in 25 was effectively engaged. The process was slow, expensive, and cumbersome, and results were often minimal compared to other mobilizing efforts. Now consider civic and political campaigns facilitated through cyberactivism. People can click a link, type their name, and then click share.

The Internet has also enabled activists to dramatically increase empathy among the population, a challenge among all activists and community groups. People are not going to get involved in any civic or political campaign if they don't care about the issues, and they typically only care about issues that in some way they can relate to. It is the activists' job to get people to care by closing the gap between the observer and victim—a distance that typically allows the general public to remain emotionally distant and aloof. Carty and Onyett (2006) refer to this strategy as the creation of radical empathy, which increases the general public's empathy for the plight of others by immersing them into their life experiences. By closing the gap between "us and them," solidarity is enhanced. This is far more easily accomplished in an online environment where photo streams, videos, and personal testimonies of those impacted by a particular problem bring distant dynamics into the livingrooms of potential supporters.

Another strategy often used by cyberactivists is called **swarming**, the virtual organizing of multiple wired groups and individuals for advocacy purposes—signing a petition, making phone calls, emailing, or attending an offline demonstration—seemingly spontaneously. The activities of supporters are intended to appear disconnected, but with swarming, there is considerable "behind the scenes" organization that result in hundreds of thousands of emails, phone calls, or even simultaneous demonstrations across a large geographic area (Carty & Onyett, 2006).

Social media has enabled social movements and protests to grow in size far faster than in previous generations. Often, social and political movements have no identifiable leader or no traditional top-down organization, thus they are difficult to counteract through traditional means. Formerly disconnected groups from all over the country (and world) can now easily connect and coordinate through online social networks in a free-flowing and non-hierarchical fashion. Where in the past a political demonstration had to be organized over several months by a few key organizers who mailed paper flyers and made hard-wired telephone calls, social media permits information about protests to be disseminated instantly and broadly, allowing news of an issue or an event to **go viral** through shared status posts on Facebook, Twitter, and other popular social media sites.

Essentially, the Internet's ability for mass mobilization, and the creation of what researchers are calling **smart mobs**, allows community organizers and political activists to reach hundreds of thousands of people (in some cases, millions) in a matter of minutes, something not possible in the pre-Internet era. The power of the Internet is enabling formerly powerless people to quickly gain new social and political power (Rheingold, 2002). Cyberactivism can be used for both good and bad purposes. Consider the activities of community groups such as a group of concerned citizens creating awareness about child hunger or raising money for their local library. Very good! Now consider how the terrorist group the Islamic State of Iraq and Syria (ISIS) uses YouTube to recruit supporters and mobilize terrorism, or how advocates of pedophilia use Facebook to swap information on how to abuse children without detection. Very bad!

There are several online advocacy platforms used by many cyberactivists as a tool for engaging in macro-level activities online. Two of the most popular are MoveOn.org and Change.org, both of which boast millions of followers on their social media sites, and more than a 100 million users on their civic and political action websites.

MoveOn.org describes itself as a service for busy but concerned citizens who want to assert their collective power. Its motto is "Democracy in Action," and its mission is to elevate the voices and power of real people in the political process. Change.org describes itself as the world's largest online platform allowing everyday people to transform their worlds on a local, national, and global level. Its motto is "The World's Platform for Change," and its mission is to use technology to empower users to create the change they want to see.

MoveOn.org and Change.org leaders engage in online civic and political advocacy via their websites as well as via social media on behalf of issues important to the respective organizations. Each organization also serves as a platform for the general public engaging in their own cyberactivism. For instance, social media users can "like" the MoveOn.org or Change.org's Facebook community pages, and will then see the organizations' advocacy posts on their social media timelines and newsfeeds, which they can then share with their own social networking sites. Both organizations also allow cyberactivists to create online petitions on their websites, which can be disseminated via social media sites, such as Facebook and Twitter, as well as via email and text. Once an online petition is created and disseminated, social media users are encouraged to digitally sign the petition and then share it with their virtual communities via online social networking. Supporters are often asked to engage in some activity beyond signing the petition, such as contacting their Congressional representatives in support of or against various causes. Cyberactivists can also link their campaigns to **crowdfunding** sites such as GofundMe and Kickstarter for fundraising purposes.

Examples of successful MoveOn.org and Change.org campaigns abound—some focusing on local issues, such as providing some type of support for a community member or cause, and some campaigns focusing far more broadly, such as the cage-free egg movement that has influenced numerous stores and restaurants to commit to using only cage-free eggs. Community organizers and social justice activities have been flocking to online platforms such as MoveOn.org and Change.org in the last few years because such platforms not only allow for immediate and broad dissemination of information, but also because they facilitate agency cooperation, which increases reach and effectiveness. For instance, recently Greenpeace, the League of Conservation Voters, and Environment America teamed up in support of clean air protections. By using Change.org to facilitate

Watch this video on how MoveOn.org has been used for mobilization and action by cyberactivists. How might you use this or similar online platforms for a civic, social, or political issue of importance to you, or an agency for which you work?
ENHANCEDetext *video example 4.5*

www.youtube.com/
watch?v=oMHH7FL66fo

their campaign, they were able to collect 1.4 million digital signatures and 2.1 million comments in less than 10 weeks, successfully countering the very powerful anti-EPA lobbyists. Change.org asserts that the Clean Air Protection campaign resulted in the most signatures and largest number of comments ever submitted to a federal agency (Change .org, n.d.). MoveOn.org has also been used successfully by a number of cyberactivists, ranging from restoring funding to a popular music program at a local high school to stopping the passage of anti-gay legislation (MoveOn.org, n.d.).

ENHANCEDetext *self-check 4.5*

CONCLUSION

Human service professionals work with a wide range of clients presenting with an equally diverse range of psychosocial problems and challenges. Generalist skills and intervention strategies can be broadly applied in generalist practice, both during the assessment phase as well the intervention stage of practice. Understanding that people are not pathological by nature, but often are responding to real traumas, tragedies, and crises in a natural way, helps the human service professional look for a client's strengths rather than solely assessing a client's perceived deficits.

The unique nature of the human services profession encourages practitioners to view the individual as a part of a greater whole. Thus, a client's social world is assessed and evaluated in context, which enables human service professionals to help their clients better navigate their world. Essentially, the human service professional is committed to working with displaced populations on micro or macro levels, assessing not only their clients but the worlds in which they live, and then applying various culturally competent intervention techniques designed to encourage, empower, and integrate some of society's most marginalized members and communities, helping them to function on a more optimal level.

SUMMARY

- The ways in which the generalist practice model serves as a theoretical foundation for human service practice is described. The generalist practice model within the context of the role and function of human service practitioners working with a wide range of populations is explored, with a particular focus on historically disenfranchised populations experiencing complex system problems and challenges.
- The ways in which generalist practice competencies and skills are integral to building rapport with clients and better understanding them and their situations are described. Generalist practice competencies and skills, including the identification of basic helping characteristics such as the ability to empathize with clients and to set healthy boundaries with oneself and with clients are explored. These competencies and skills serve as the foundation of a human service professional's ability to effectively interview and assess clients and their situations.
- The ways in which effective interviewing skills are used during the assessment process are explained. The nature of effective interviewing skills most commonly

used during the assessment phase of a counseling relationship, including communication skills, such as active listening, observation skills, and interviewing skills are discussed.

- The ways in which intervention strategies are used in generalist practice are described. Generalist counseling skills are discussed within the context of working with a range of client populations in case management and generalist counseling roles. The importance of using culturally appropriate and culturally sensitive intervention strategies is also discussed with a particular focus on the importance of appropriate cultural training for human service professionals.
- Intervention strategies used on the macro level are explored. The nature of macro practice within the context of advocating for at-risk populations is discussed. Community practice, community organizing, and policy practice are explored within a human rights framework. Macro strategies using the Internet are explored, including the use of online advocacy platforms such MoveOn.org and Change.org.

Internet Resources

Conduct an Internet search for "Competencies" on the American Counseling Association website.

Conduct an Internet search for the "Generic Human Services Professional Competencies" on the National Organization for Human Services website.

Conduct an Internet search for the article "Revisiting Tarasoff" in the Psychology Today website.

Conduct an Internet search for the "Eight Concepts" on the Bowen Center website.

Conduct an Internet search for "Understanding Cultural Competency" on the HumanServicesEdu website.

Conduct an Internet search for MoveOn.org, and then click on Campaigns, and then click on "Featured Campaigns."

Conduct an Internet search for Change.org, and then click on "Victories every day," and review the recent Victory Highlights.

References

American Counseling Association. (2005). *ACA code of ethics*. Alexandria, VA: Author.

American Psychiatric Association. (2013). *Diagnostic and statistical manual of mental disorders* (5th ed.). Washington, DC: Author.

American Psychological Association. (2002). *Ethical principles of psychologists and code of conduct*. Washington, DC: Author.

Austin, S. (2005). Community-building principles: Implications for professional development. *Child Welfare, 84*(2), 105–122.

Barker, R. L. (2003). *The social work dictionary* (5th ed.). Washington, DC: NASW Press.

Bowen, M. (1978). *Family therapy in clinical practice*. New York, NY: Jason Aronson.

Brownridge, D. (2009). *Violence against women: Vulnerable Populations*. New York, NY: Routledge.

Carty, V., & Oynett, J. (2006). Protest, cyberactivism and new social movements: The reemergence of the peace movement post 9/11. *Social Movement Studies, 5*(3), 229–249.

Castells, M. (1997). *The power of identity*. Oxford: Blackwell.

Castells, M. (2001). *The Internet galaxy*. Oxford: Oxford University Press.

Castells, M. (2007). Communication, power and counter-power in the network society. *International Journal of Communication, 1*, 238–266.

Calkin, C. (2000, June). Welfare reform. *Peace and Social Justice: A Newsletter of the NASW Committee for Peace and Social Justice, 1*(1). Retrieved from http://www.naswdc.org/practice/peace/psj0101.pdf

Center for Credentialing & Education. (2011). Human Services-Board Certified Practitioner Exam Candidate Handbook. Retrieved from http://www.cce-global.org/Downloads/HS-BCPHandbook.pdf

Change.org. (n.d.). Victories. Retrieved from https://www.change.org/victories.

Child Welfare Information Gateway. (2016). *Mandatory reporters of child abuse and neglect.* Washington, DC: U.S. Department of Health and Human Services, Children's Bureau.

Cloud, H. C., & Townsend, J. (1992). *Boundaries.* Grand Rapids, MI: Zondervan.

Conner, K., & Grote, N. (2008, October). Enhancing the cultural relevance of empirically-supported mental health interventions. *Families in Society, 89*(4), 587–595. Retrieved from Academic Search Premier database.

Cunningham, P., Foster, S., & Henggeler, S. (2002, July). The elusive concept of cultural competence. *Children's Services: Social Policy, Research & Practice, 5*(3), 231–243. Retrieved September 14, 2009, from Academic Search Premier database.

Duffy, M., Gillig, S. E., Tureen, R. M., & Ybarra, M. A. (2002). A critical look at the DSM-IV-TR. *The Journal of Individual Psychology, 58*(4), 362–373.

Escalas, J. E., & Stern, B. B. (2003). Sympathy and empathy: Emotional responses to advertising dramas. *Journal of Consumer Research, 29,* 566–578.

Fortier, J. P., & Shaw-Taylor, Y. (2000). *Assuring cultural competence in healthcare: Recommendations for national standards and an outcomes-focused research agenda.* Resources for Cross-Cultural HealthCare and the Center for the Advancement of Health. Rockville, MD: U.S. Department of Health and Human Services, Office of Minority Health.

Fulero, S. M. (1988). Tarasoff: 10 years later. *Professional Psychology: Research and Practice, 19,* 184–190.

Gardener, J. W. (1994). *Building community for leadership training programs.* Washington, DC: Independent Sector.

Greenberg, L. S., Elliot, R., Watson, J. C., & Bohart, A. C. (2001). Empathy. *Psychotherapy: Theory, Research, Practice, Training, 38*(4), 380–384.

Iatridis, D. (1995). Policy practice. In R. L. Edwards (Ed.), *Encyclopedia of social work* (19th ed., pp. 1855–1866). Washington, DC: NASW Press.

Johnson, A. (2004). Social work is standing on the legacy of Jane Addams: But are we sitting on the sidelines? *Social Work, 49*(2), 319–322.

Kirst-Ashman, K., & Hull, G. (2014). *Brooks/Cole Empowerment Series: Understanding Generalist Practice.* Cengage Learning.

Knudsen, S. (2005). Intersectionality: A theoretical inspiration in the analysis of minority cultures and identities in textbooks. Presented at the Eighth International Conference on Learning and Educational Media "Caught in the Web or Lost in the Textbook?" *IUFM DE CAEN (France) 26–29 Octobre 2005.* Article accessed on March 25, 2008, at http://www.caen.iufm.fr/colloque_iartem/pdf/knudsen.pdf

Margolis, M., & Resnick, D. (2000). *Politics as usual: The cyberspace "revolution."* London: Sage.

Martin, M.E. (2014). *Advocacy for social justice: A global perspective.* Upper Saddle River, NJ: Pearson Publishing.

Meyer, B. (2002). Extraordinary stories: Disability, queerness, and feminism. *NORA 3,* 168–173.

Mizrahi, T. (2001). The status of community organization in 2001: Community practice context, complexities, contradictions, and contributions. *Research on Social Work Practice, 11,* 176–189.

Morris, D., & Langman, L. (2002). Networks of dissent: A typology of social movements in a global age. In M. Gurstein & S. Finquelievich (Eds.), *Proceedings of the 1st International Workshop on Community Informatics.* Montreal, Canada, October 8, 2002.

MoveOn.org. (n.d.). Success stories. Retrieved from http://petitions.moveon.org/victories.html.

National Organization for Human Services. (2015). *Ethical standards of human services professionals.* Washington, DC: Author. Retrieved from http://www.nationalhumanservices.org/ethical-standards-for-hs-professionals.

Netting, E., Kettner, P., & McMurtry, S. (2016). *Social work macro practice.* Boston, MA: Pearson Publishing.

Park, C. L., & Fenster, J. R. (2004). Stress-related growth: Predictors of occurrence and correlates with psychological adjustment. *Journal of Social and Clinical Psychology, 23*(2), 195–215.

Polack, R. (2004). Social justice and the global economy: New challenges for social work in the 21st century. *Social Work, 49*(2), 281–290.

Prest, L. A., & Protinsky, H. (1993). Family systems theory: A unifying framework for codependency. *American Journal of Family Therapy, 21*(4), 352–360.

Rainie, L., Smith, A., Schlozman, K., Brady, H., & Verba, S. (2012). Social media and political engagement. *Pew Research Center's Internet & American Life Project/Pew Research Center.* http://pewInternet.org/~/media/Files/Reports/2012/PIP_SocialMediaAndPoliticalEngagement_PDF.pdf

Reid, W. J. (1975). A test of a task-centered approach. *Social Work, 20*(1), 3–9.

Rheingold, H. (2002) *Smart mobs: The next social revolution.* New York, NY: Perseus Books Group.

Rocha, C., & Johnson, A. (1997). Teaching family policy through a policy framework. *Journal of Social Work Education, 33*(3), 433–444.

Rothman, J., & Mizrahi, T. (2014). Balancing micro and macro practice: A challenge for social work. *Social Work, 59*(1), 91–93.

Saleebey, D. (2005). The strengths perspective in social work practice. 4th ed. Boston, MA: Allyn & Bacon.

Samuels, G. M., & Ross–Sheriff, F. (2008). Identity, oppression, and power: Feminisms and intersectionality theory. *Affilia, 23*, 5–9.

Tarasoff v. Regents of the University of California, 118 Cal. Rptr. 129, 529 P.2d.533 (Cal. 1974).

Tarasoff v. Regents of the University of California, 113 Cal. Rptr. 14, 551 P.2d.334 (Cal. 1976).

Taylor, V., & Van Dyke, N. (2003). Get up, stand up: Tactical repertoires of social movements. In D. Snow, S. Soule & H. Kriesi (Eds.), *The Blackwell Companion to Social Movements Reader* (pp. 262–293). Oxford: Blackwell.

Vissers, S., Hooghe, M., Mahé, V., & Stolle, D. (2008). The potential of political mobilization: An experiment on Internet and face-to-face mobilization. *Conference Papers—American Political Science Association,* 1–43.

Weil, M. O. (1996). Community building: Building community practice. *Social Work, 41*(5), 481–499.

Weiss, I. (2003). Social work students and social change: On the link between views on poverty, social work goals and policy practice. *International Journal of Social Welfare, 12*, 132–141.

Whitaker, T., Weismiller, T., & Clark, E. (2006). Assuring the sufficiency of a frontline workforce: A national study of licensed social workers— Executive summary. Retrieved from the NASW website: http://workforce.socialworkers.org/studies/nasw_06_execsummary.pdf

5

Child Welfare Services

Overview and Purpose of the U.S. Child Welfare System

The field of child and family services generally involves the care and provision of children who cannot be appropriately cared for by their biological parents, as well as providing assistance for those who need support in the management and provision of their families. This practice setting is primarily concerned with abused and neglected children in foster care placement, but may also involve family preservation and adoption services. A human service professional working in a child and family services setting may be involved in the following activities:

- Child abuse investigations
- Child abuse assessments
- Case management and counseling of the child in placement, foster families, and biological parents
- Case management and counseling of families in crisis
- Case management and counseling of potential adoptive parents, adult adoptees, and birth parents

The clinical issues involved in this field are quite broad but involve issues related to abandonment and loss, **post-traumatic stress disorder** (PTSD), cultural sensitivity, child development, parenting issues, substance abuse, anger management, and the ability to work with a broad range of life stressors and maladaptive responses that might lead to breakdowns within the family.

In addition to this wide range of activities, there is also a wide range of practice settings where human service professionals might work, the largest being a state's **child protective services** (CPS) agency. Human service professionals also work for not-for-profit agencies, some of which are contracted by the state to provide mandated services to children in substitute care and some of which provide voluntary services to any family in crisis. Within these agencies a human service professional may be involved in a number of activities, including counseling, case management, **policy advocacy**, and writing grants for service funding. Many human service professionals working in the field of child welfare may do so on a volunteer basis, and although these individuals are not paid professionals, the work they do is so vital that their role in the welfare of children must be mentioned. For instance, **court-appointed special advocates** (CASA) advocate for children who are placed into state care, working to protect the best interest of the children by being their voice in all court proceedings.

THE HISTORY OF CHILD WELFARE IN THE UNITED STATES

The child welfare system in the United States has undergone significant changes in the last several hundred years due to numerous factors such as urbanization, industrialization, immigration, mass life-threatening illness, changes within the family system, changing social mores (including the reduction of shame associated with divorce, out-of-wedlock births, and single parenting by choice), and the eventual availability of government financial assistance for those in need. Thus, to truly understand the current child welfare system it is vital to understand its past.

In 2001, ABC's *Nightline* aired a documentary featuring the horrible plight of the street children of Romania (Belzberg, 2001). After the show, U.S. citizens flooded the network with telephone calls, expressing outrage at the images that flashed across their television screens for almost two hours. The documentary revealed children as young as six years old living on the streets, with no food to eat, and with only liquid glue to keep them warm at night. The reporter explained how political events in Romania created a situation where impoverished families could no longer care for their offspring, leading to the streets becoming flooded with children, in desperate search of money and food. These children, who often resorted to pickpocketing and other petty crimes, were considered by many mainstream Romanians to be the scourge of society, pests to be avoided.

The U.S. response was one of literal horror, not only at the conditions in which the children were forced to live but also at the apparent apathy of many Romanians, particularly those in government, including the Romanian police force. The documentary showed numerous incidences of police mistreatment, including one young boy whose leg was broken in a scuffle with a police officer. This seeming indifference shocked viewers, who expressed outrage at the heartlessness necessary to not only accept orphans living on the street, but actually perceive these orphans as social pariahs. These concerned and outraged Americans were apparently unaware that our own recent past included alarmingly similar conditions and attitudes toward orphans, with only 150 to 200 years separating the United States from Romania in this regard.

Child Labor in Colonial America: Indentured Servitude and Apprenticeships

There were many ways in which children were mistreated in early America, but in this section I will be exploring primarily two areas of mistreatment of children in Great Britain and **Colonial America**, which in many respects served as the foundation for child welfare laws in the United States. First, the use of children in the labor market, otherwise known as **child labor** will be explored, and second, the treatment of children who were, for whatever reason, without parents, including orphans and street children. By exploring primarily child labor and the treatment of orphans and street children, it should not be presumed that other forms of maltreatment did not occur in America's early history. The rationale for exploring these two areas of historic maltreatment is that they represent a significant departure in how children are treated today. Another rationale is that these areas of maltreatment highlight key areas within child welfare, with regard to early child welfare advocacy and the development of laws, policies, and programs intended to protect children.

During Colonial America, children were expected to work, often within their own households and farms alongside their families. The hope of parents was that their children would be able to afford to buy farms of their own when they grew to adulthood. But children from poor and immigrant families were often expected to work in adult-like capacities, with children under 12 working alongside their parents in factories or other industrial-like settings, and children 12 and older working in apprenticed positions outside of their homes, and away from their families.

During the many waves of early immigration, people seeking a better life in America often paid for their passage to the United States through a process called indentured service, which required that servants work off the cost of their travel by working for a master in some capacity once they arrived in America. If a family immigrated to the United States in this manner, their children, regardless of age, were required to work as well.

The economic system of **indentured servitude** was extremely exploitative. Ship owners would often recruit unsuspecting and desperate individuals from other countries, with stories of abundant life in America. Many individuals and families accepted the call, believing they could make a better life for themselves in Colonial America where opportunities for economic self-sufficiency were believed to be abundant. They were often told that the terms of their service would last for about three years, and then they would be free—free to buy land and to make a life for themselves that was not possible in many European countries (Alderman, 1975). In reality, the cost of their passage would be paid off in only one year, and the remaining years of service were considered free work. Masters often treated their bonded labor quite poorly. Servants received no cash wages, but were supposed to be provided with basic necessities, which depending on the nature and means of the master might range from sufficient sustenance to meager sustenance and substandard shelter. Thus, while indentured servants were not considered slaves *per se*, the treatment of them was quite similar (Martin, 2014).

Children were not allowed to enter into bonded labor contracts without the permission of their parents. However very poor and orphaned children, particularly in London, were often kidnapped and sold to ship captains, who then brought them to America and sold them as indentured servants, most often to masters who used them as house servants. Also, local governments that were responsible for the poor would **bind out** poor and orphaned children in early America as a form of poor relief (Katz, 1996). Most local laws favored masters since virtually all judges were masters themselves, and they stipulated that **child bonded servants** could be kept until 24 years of age. If they ran away, their treatment became even worse and their time in bonded servitude was often doubled (Kellow, 1984).

Indentured servitude eventually waned during the 17th century in favor of slavery, but the binding out of children who were poor and orphaned continued well into the 19th century. During the 300 years of the Atlantic slave trade over 15 million Africans were brought to the United States through the West Indies, or directly from Africa. Among these Africans were many children who were either forced or born into slavery along with their parents. In time masters realized that slaves who had once experienced freedom were far more difficult to control than those born into captivity; thus, a market developed for captive slave children because they tended to be more submissive servants.

Children under the age of about seven were more often sold with their mothers, but once the children reached the age of about 10, they were often sold off and separated from their families, particularly to fill this growing need for young African slave children born into captivity. Slavery was outlawed in 1865 with the passage of the Thirteenth Amendment to the U.S. Constitution, but the plight of African children did not improve significantly, and in fact, the legacy of slavery continues to impact African American children to this day. For instance, infant mortality of African slave children under the age of four was double that of white children during the time when slavery was legal due to disease and poor nutrition. Not only has this trend continued well into the 21st century, but it has gotten far worse with infant mortality rates among African American infants being about three times that of Caucasian infants (Mathews, MacDorman, & Thorna, 2015).

Another form of work that children engaged in during the early years of America was **apprenticeship**, which involved the training of children in some type of craft or artisan work such as making shoes or woodworking. Essentially apprenticeship involved an artisan taking on an apprentice in early adolescence and teaching him a trade. Some children went to live with the artisan who trained them and others did not (Schultz, 1985). Often apprentices left their families and lived with the artisan, serving as an unpaid assistant. In fact, parents often had to pay to have their children apprenticed because they knew this was likely the only way their children would learn a trade. While most apprenticeships did not involve overt exploitation, the practice did reflect the focus on working children, rather than on education and play. Apprenticeships eventually became less popular as industrialization began in the late 18th century, as machines were developed replacing the need for many craftsmen.

Child Labor during the Industrial Era: Children and Factories

By the mid-19th century, virtually all apprenticeships and indentured contracts had disappeared, and families were moving into the cities to work in factories (Bender, 1975). Children were the bulk of the workforce in many factories throughout the 19th century, with some children working six days a week, 14 hours a day. Child labor scholars

© UNIVERSAL HISTORY ARCHIVES / UIG / GETTY IMAGES

Child laborers in Cherryville Manufacturing Company, January 1, 1909.

estimate that hundreds of thousands of children—some as young as six—were employed in factories in the mid-19th century, with the bulk working in the textile industry, such as cotton mills. Excerpts of autobiographies written by individuals who worked in factories throughout their childhoods reference dismal conditions, with poor sanitation and air quality, repetitive work on machinery that left small hands bleeding, and very long days on their feet, which in many cases significantly shortened the life spans of these child workers.

Garment industry sweatshops began to spring up throughout New York and other large cities in the mid- to late-19th century. Although sweatshops eventually occurred in factory-like settings, their origin involved what was called "outwork," where workers sewed garments and other textiles in their homes. Women and children were primarily hired for these tasks since they could be paid a lower wage. Because they were paid by the piece, they often worked 14 or more hours per day, seven days a week. Children worked alongside their mothers, because their small fingers enabled them to engage in detail work, such as sewing on buttons—work that was challenging for adults.

The Fight for Child Labor Laws

Jane Addams and her friend Ellen Gates Starr founded the Hull-House of Chicago, the first U.S. **settlement house** that provided advocacy and what we now call **wraparound services** to marginalized populations working in sweatshop conditions in Chicago. Addams was appalled by the conditions of those living in poverty in urban communities, particularly the plight of recently arrived immigrants, who were forced to live in substandard tenement housing and work long hours in factories, often in very dangerous working conditions.

Hull-House offered several services for children and their widowed mothers, including after-school care for those children whose mothers worked long hours in factories. Providing comprehensive services to those in need and living among them in their own community were some of the ways in which Addams became aware of the plight of children forced to work in the factories. In her autobiography *Twenty Years at Hull-House*, Addams wrote of her first encounter with child labor, including how during their first Christmas party at Hull-House, when they knew nothing of child labor, they noticed several young girls who refused to eat the candy at the party. When asked why, the girls stated that because they worked in a candy factory, they could no longer stand the sight of candy. Addams noted how girls as young as seven would work at the candy factory from early in the morning until late at night. Because of unsafe conditions many of the children were injured, and a few of the child workers were even killed. Addams described the indifference on the part of factory owners and the lack of recourse of parents, who signed away all of their rights when they "allowed" their children to work (Addams, 1912).

Addams and her colleagues began an advocacy campaign against sweatshop conditions in Chicago factories early in the Hull-House's existence, advocating in particular for the women and children who were the most likely to work in these factories.

Their activism seemed to pay off quickly when the Illinois state legislature passed a law limiting the work day to just eight hours (from the previous 12 to 14-hour day). Their excitement was soon tempered though when the new law was quickly overturned by the Illinois Supreme Court as being unconstitutional.

Addams and the Hull-House networked quite extensively, joining efforts with trade unions and even the Democratic Party, which in 1892 adopted into its platform union recommendations prohibiting children under the age of 15 years old from working in factories. In her autobiography Addams discussed how the greatest opposition to child labor laws came from the business sector, which considered such legislation as radicalism. Business leaders, such as those who worked in the Chicago area candy factories and glass manufacturing companies, argued that their companies would not be able to survive without the labor of children (Addams, 1912; Martin, 2014).

Addams and her Hull-House colleagues advocated on a federal level as well, with their support for the *Sulzer Bill*, which when passed allowed for the creation of the Department of Labor. In 1904 the National Child Labor Committee was formed, and Addams served as chairman for one term. In 1912, Julia Lathrop, Addams's Hull-House colleague, was appointed chief of a new federal agency by President William Taft, focusing on child welfare, including child labor. As chief of the Children's Bureau, Lathrop was responsible for investigating and reporting all relevant issues pertaining to the welfare of children from all classes, and spent a considerable amount of time researching the dangers of child labor (Martin, 2014).

After several failed attempts federal legislation barring child labor was finally passed in 1938, and signed into law by President Franklin D. Roosevelt, three years after Addams' death. The Fair Labor Standards Act is a comprehensive bill regulating various aspects of labor in the United States, including child labor. The act outlawed what was deemed *oppressive child labor* and set minimum ages of employment and a maximum number of hours children were allowed to work. This act is still in existence today and has been amended several times to address such issues as equal pay (Equal Pay Act of 1963), age discrimination (Age Discrimination in Employment Act of 1967), and low wages (federal minimum wage increases).

The U.S. Orphan Problem

Throughout early America one of the most vulnerable groups of children were **orphans**, both in terms of how they were treated as well as how they were exploited in the labor force. During the 1700s and 1800s in particular, attitudes toward children were harsh, and many orphaned or uncared for children roamed the streets, particularly in growing urban areas such as New York and Chicago. Street children were often treated harshly and punitively. If children were on the streets because their parents were destitute, they were sent to almshouses to work alongside their homeless parents. Older orphaned children were sold into indentured servitude or forced into apprenticeships, which provided cheap labor during an era that saw many economic depressions and a shortage of available workers (Katz, 1996).

The plight of the orphan did not appear to tug at the heartstrings of the average American during that era, not only because of the vast number of abandoned and orphaned children, but also because during the 17th through the early-19th century, children were not perceived to be in need of special nurturing because childhood was not considered a distinct stage of development. The influence of Puritanical religious beliefs as well as the general **social mores** of the times led to the common belief that children needed to be treated with harsh discipline and compelled to work or they would fall victim to sinful behaviors such as laziness and vice (Trattner, 1998).

A significant shift in child welfare policy occurred in the mid-19th century (1861 to 1865), when the Civil War left thousands of children orphaned, making tragedy a visitor in some respect to virtually every family in America. Coinciding with an increased concern for the plight of orphaned and disadvantaged children was a dramatic transition in the way childhood was viewed. The development of psychology as an academic discipline and a profession in the early 1900s led to the emerging belief that children were essentially good by nature and needed to be treated with kindness, love, and nurturing to enhance their development and ultimate potential as adults (Trattner, 1998). As a result, settlement house workers, **Charity Organization Societies** (COS), and government officials were eager to address the problem of orphaned and abused children in the latter part of the 19th century. The most commonly suggested solution was the creation of institutions designed solely for the care of orphaned and needy children, which at the time seemed a quite compassionate alternative to living in almshouses or on the streets.

Although some orphanages existed in the 1700s, they did not become the primary method of caring for needy and orphaned children until the middle to late 1800s. By the 1890s there were more than 600 orphanages in existence in the United States (Trattner, 1998). Orphanages, or orphan asylums as they were often called, did not house solely children who lost both parents to death, but also became the solution for many of the economic and environmental conditions of the time. Even though mortality rates were down in both the United States and Europe during the Industrial Age, several factors existed that resulted in the increasing need for orphanages (Condran & Cheney, 1982).

Poor safety conditions in factories resulted in a relatively high prevalence of work-related injuries and death among the poorest members of society, leaving many children orphaned or half-orphaned. Additionally, a significant influx of poor immigrants in the late 1800s and early 1900s resulted in a vulnerable segment of society that often did not have an extended family on which to rely in cases of parental death or disability. Families who were for whatever reason unable to support their children could leave them in the temporary care of an orphanage for a small fee, but if they missed some monthly payments, the children would become wards of the state and the parents would lose all legal rights to them (Trattner, 1998). In addition, although infectious disease was nothing new to early America, several epidemics of infectious disease spread throughout urban cities between the mid-1800s and the early part of the 1900s, including smallpox, influenza, yellow fever, cholera, typhoid, and scarlet fever, leaving many children without parental care (Condran & Cheney, 1982).

Although the orphanage system was originally perceived as a significant improvement over placing children in almshouses or forcing them into indentured servitude, these institutions were not without their share of trouble, and in time, reports of harsh treatment and abuses became commonplace. Although some orphanages were government run, most were privately run with governmental funding, but had little if any oversight or accountability. Because the government paid on a per child basis, there was a financial incentive to run large operations, with some orphanages housing as many as 2,000 children under one roof. Obedience was highly valued in these institutions out of sheer necessity, whereas individuality, play, and creativity were discouraged through strict rules and harsh discipline.

The Orphan Train Movement

The next wave of child welfare reform involved the gradual shift from institutionalized care to substitute family care—the placing-out of children into private homes. This transition was prompted by a few different social trends, including increased complaints about institutionalized care, the development of compulsory public education (which meant that the education of an orphan was no longer linked with the provision of housing), and a growing problem of street children in big cities. In fact, have you ever wondered where the expression "farming kids out" came from? The origin of this term is rooted in the Orphan Train Movement, a program developed by The New York Children's Aid Society that sent kids living on the streets to farms out west.

Rev. Charles Loring Brace founded the **Orphan Train** program in the mid-19th century. Brace estimated that as many as 5,000 children were homeless and forced to roam the streets in search of money, food, and shelter. Brace was shocked at the cruel indifference of most New Yorkers, who called these children "Street Arabs" with "bad blood." He was also appalled at reports of children as young as five years old who were arrested for **vagrancy** (Bellingham, 1984; Brace, 1967).

Many factors contributed to the serious orphan problem in New York. Historians estimate that approximately 1,000 immigrants flooded New York on a daily basis in the mid-1800s (Von Hartz, 1978). Additionally, mass urbanization was occurring with poor rural families flocking to the cities looking for factory work. Industry safety standards were essentially nonexistent, and thus factory-related deaths were at an all-time high. An outbreak of typhoid fever also left many children orphaned or half-orphaned, their widowed mothers having no way to support them because there was no federal social welfare safety net. Harsh social conditions, coupled with the absence of any organized governmental subsidy, left many children to fend for themselves on the streets of New York, resorting to any means available for survival.

Brace feared that the temptations of street life would preclude any possibility that orphaned children would grow up to be God-fearing, responsible adults. He reasoned that children who had no parents, or whose parents could no longer care for them, would be far better off living in the clean open spaces of farming communities out west, where fresh air and the need for children and workers were plentiful. Because the rail lines were rapidly opening up the West, Brace developed an innovative program where children would be loaded onto trains and taken west to good Christian farming families who were open to caring for more children. Notices were sent in advance of train arrivals, and communities along the train line would come out and meet the train so that families who had expressed an interest in taking one or more children could examine the children and take them right then, if they desired.

Watch this video produced by Prairie Public Broadcasting on the history of the Orphan Trains. What are the benefits and drawbacks of this program?
ENHANCEDetext *video example 5.1*

www.youtube.com/watch?v=w3-kh5IPMm8

Many survivors of the orphan trains have described their experiences of being paraded across a stage like cattle, with interested foster parents checking their teeth and feeling their muscles before deciding which child they would take. Few parents would take more than one child, and thus siblings were most often split up, sometimes without even a passing comment made by the child care agents or the new parents (Patrick, Sheets, & Trickel, 1990). It was almost as if the breaking of lifelong family bonds was considered trivial compared to the gift these children were receiving by being rescued from their hopeless existence on the streets.

Most children on the orphan train were not legally adopted, but were placed with a family under an indentured contract, which served two purposes. First, this type of contract allowed the placement agency to take the children back if something went wrong with the placement. Second, children placed under an indentured contract could not inherit property; thus, farming families could take in boys to work on the farm or girls to assist with the housework, but didn't have to worry about them inheriting family assets (Trattner, 1998; Warren, 1995).

The orphan trains ran from 1853 to 1929, delivering approximately 150,000 children to new homes across the west, from the Midwestern states to Texas, and even as far west as California. Whether this social experiment was a glowing success or a miserable failure (or somewhere in between) depends on who one asks. Some children were placed in and eventually legally adopted by wonderful and loving parents, and they grew up to be happy and responsible adults. But others have shared stories of heartache and abuse, describing their new lives as no better than that of slaves, where they were taken in by families for no reason other than to provide hard labor for the cost of bed and board. Some orphan train survivors describe stories of having siblings torn from their sides as families chose one child (typically a younger child), leaving brothers and sisters on the train. And still others tell stories of failed placements, where farming families exercised their one-year right-of-return option, sending the children back to the orphanage or allowing the children to drift from farm to farm to earn their keep (Holt, 1992).

Eventually new child welfare practices caught up with new child development theories, leading to a shift in focus from one of work and virtue to one of valuing childhood play. By the early 20th century the practice of farming out children received increasing criticism, and the last trainload of children was delivered to its many destinations in 1929. Despite the controversy surrounding the Orphan Train Movement and similar outplacement programs across the country, even its harshest critics agree that it was a far better alternative than allowing children to fend for themselves on the streets of New York and other large urban cities. The Orphan Train Movement is also considered the forerunner of the current foster care system in the United States, representing a shift away from institutionalized care and toward a system where children are placed in private homes with substitute families.

ENHANCEDetext *self-check 5.1*

OVERVIEW OF THE CURRENT U.S. CHILD WELFARE SYSTEM

Children living in contemporary Western societies face very different challenges than children living 100 or so years ago. Child labor laws prohibit child exploitation in the workforce, and federal and state social welfare programs now exist that help to alleviate poverty and also help protect families from the impact of various catastrophes, such as natural disasters and health pandemics. Also, vulnerable groups of children are far better protected from disparity in treatment through the passage of such federal legislation as the Civil Rights Act of 1964 and the Americans with Disabilities Act. Yet, there remains significant disparity in treatment of children from certain ethnic groups, such as African Americans, Latinos, and Native Americans.

There also remain serious issues with how older children are treated within U.S. society. For instance, very few effective systems are in place to assist runaway and homeless youth. Thus, many adolescents who experience physical and sexual abuse in their homes choose to live on the streets rather than trust the "system" to provide for their safety and care. In addition, far too many children are charged as adults for crimes they commit as children, and most of these children are children of color—primarily African American boys. African American girls also experience disparity in treatment by organizations charged with the responsibility for their protection. For instance, there is a growing recognition that African American girls are far more likely to be victims of **domestic sex trafficking**; yet, if they are apprehended, rather than being treated as victims, they are far more likely to be charged with prostitution and sent back onto the streets (Martin, 2014).

With regard to child protection and the care of orphaned and abused children, care has slowly transitioned over the past 100 years from institutionalized care to primarily substitute family care or foster care. By 1980, virtually no children remained in institutionalized care in the United States, excluding group homes for adolescents, treatment centers, and homes for developmentally disabled children (Shughart & Chappell, 1999). Essentially, government public assistance programs in the 1960s reduced much of the necessity for the removal of children from their homes due to poverty. Thus, most removals currently are for issues related to maltreatment (Trattner, 1998).

The demographic makeup of children currently in the foster care system has changed considerably as well since the 1800s. Gone are the days where the majority of children placed into substitute care were orphaned due to industrial accidents, war, or illness. Instead, the majority of children currently in child protective custody have been removed from their homes due to serious maltreatment. Also, unlike earlier eras when orphanage placements were most often permanent, just over half of all children currently in foster care will be reunified with their biological parents (U.S. Department of Health and Human Services, 2016).

In 2014 (the most recent statistics available), there were approximately 415,129 children in the U.S. foster care system. This represents a 4 percent increase since 2012, reversing a several-year trend of decreases. In 2014, 264,746 new children entered care, joining 238,230 children who remained in care. There were more boys in care (52 percent) than girls (48 percent), 40 percent of children in foster care were over five years of age or younger, 23 percent were between the ages of six and ten years old, 22 percent were 11 to 15 years old, and 16 percent were 16 to 20 years old. With regard to race, the majority of children in foster care were Caucasian (42 percent), 24 percent were African American, and 22 percent were Hispanic. Among all children in foster care in 2014, 46 percent were in non-relative foster homes, 29 percent were in relative placement, 4 percent were in pre-adoptive placement, 6 percent were in group homes, and 8 percent were in institutional settings. Among those children who left foster care, about half were reunited with their parents, just over 20 percent were adopted, and almost 10 percent were either emancipated or placed with a guardian (respectively), and 7 percent moved in with relatives (U.S. Department of Health and Human Services, 2016).

The U.S. child welfare system exists to provide a safety net for children and families in crisis, with the primary objective of keeping families together or reuniting children with their biological parents if they have to be removed from the home (Sanchirico & Jablonka, 2000). Federal and state laws have established three basic goals for children in the child welfare system:

- To ensure *safety* from abuse and neglect
- To ensure *permanency* in a stable, loving home (preferably with the biological parents)
- To ensure *well-being* of children with regard to their physical health, mental health, and developmental and educational needs

So, how does a child end up in foster care? Made-for-television movies might have the public believing that child welfare workers have the power to remove children from homes with minimal evidence of abuse. Yet, in reality, several criteria must be met to place a child into protective custody, and a child cannot be removed from a family home without a judge's approval. The U.S. Constitution guarantees certain liberties to parents by giving them the right to parent their child in the manner they see fit. But such liberties have limits, and as such are balanced by the parents' duty to protect their child's safety and ensure their wellbeing. If parents cannot or will not protect their children from *significant* harm, the state has the legal obligation to intervene (Goldman & Salus, 2003).

The U.S. Congress has passed several pieces of legislation that support the state's obligation to protect children, including the *Child Abuse Prevention and Treatment Act* (CAPTA) of 1974, which was established to ensure that child maltreatment is reported to the appropriate authorities. This act (which was most recently amended in 2010) also provides minimum standards for definitions of the different types of child maltreatment. *The Adoption Assistance and Child Welfare Act of 1980* focuses on family preservation, with the goal of keeping families together by requiring that states develop supportive programs and procedures enabling maltreated children to remain in their own homes. This act also provides for the assistance of family reunification following out-of-home placements, as well as providing funding for adoption assistance, particularly for children with special needs.

Other legislation is aimed at (1) improving court efficiency so that child abuse cases will not languish in the court system for years, (2) providing assistance to foster care children approaching their 18th birthday, and (3) bolstering **family preservation programs** designed as early intervention measures to circumvent out-of-home placement (Goldman & Salus, 2003). In 1997 President Bill Clinton signed into law the *Adoption and Safe Families Act* (ASFA), which amended *The Adoption Assistance and Child Welfare Act of 1980*. The primary goal of the ASFA of 1997 was to amend problems in the foster care system presumably caused by the previous legislation, including placing family reunification as a priority over a child's health and wellbeing. Although this was not necessarily the intention of legislators when passing *The Adoption Assistance and Child Welfare Act of 1980*, many caseworkers interpreted this legislation as requiring that biological families remain intact regardless of circumstances, which resulted in children remaining in foster care for much of their childhoods. The ASFA of 1997 was passed as a way of addressing this ambiguity in the former legislation, making the best interest of the child a clear priority. Among the various amendments of the act are shortening the timeframe for a child's permanency hearing, financial incentives to states for increasing the number of adoptions of children in the foster care system, new requirements for states to petition for termination of parental rights, and the reauthorization of the Family Preservation and Support Program, which was renamed the Safe and Stable Families Program.

There have been both positive and negative consequences of the ASFA. Certainly no one wants abused and neglected children to languish in temporary placement, but expediting finding permanent homes should not be at the expense of biological parents' rights to have an appropriate amount of time to meet the state's criteria for regaining the custody of their children. Balancing the rights of the biological parents with the best interest of their child is challenging, particularly in light of the complexity involved in many foster care cases, but most human services professionals believe that striving for this balance must remain a priority.

In 2006, the *Safe and Timely Interstate Placement of Foster Children Act* (Pub. L. No. 109-239) was passed, which made it easier to place children in another state, if necessary. This legislation holds states accountable for the orderly, safe, and timely placement of children across state lines by requiring that home studies be completed in less than 60 days and that the children be accepted within 14 days of completion. The legislation also provides grants for interstate placement and requires caseworkers to make interstate visits when necessary.

Quite likely, the most significant federal legislation passed recently is the *Fostering Connections to Success and Increasing Adoptions Act of 2008* (Pub. L. No. 110-351), which former president Bush signed into law in October 2008. This law amends the Social Security Act by enhancing incentives, particularly in regard to kinship care, including providing the kinship guardian financial assistance as well as providing family connection grants designed to facilitate and support **kinship care**. This legislation also includes provisions related to education and health care, particularly for children in kinship care, many of whom were not eligible for special assistance programs unless they were in nonrelative care. And finally, in 2011, the *Child and Family Services Improvement and Innovation Act* was passed, reauthorizing Title IV-B of the Social Security Act (P.L. 112-34), and extending funding authorization for the Stephanie Tubbs Jones Child Welfare Services Program and the Promoting Safe and Stable Families Program through fiscal year 2016.

An earlier act that bears mention is the *Indian Child Welfare Act of 1978* (ICWA), which is a federal law that seeks to keep Native American children with Native American families. The ICWA was passed in response to a long history of forced child removal from Indian reservations, including forced removal of children into Indian boarding schools from about the 1880s through the early part of the 1900s, and then the subsequent removal of Native children by state child protection service agencies for maltreatment and placement into white homes. The intention of Congress was to protect the best interest of Native American children and promote the stability and security of Native tribes and families.

The ICWA serves as a policy framework for how to handle the placement of children who are eligible for membership in a federally recognized tribe, with the goal of promoting the role of tribal governments and preserving tribal families (on and off the reservation). The ICWA requires training for social workers about the law (including the historical injustices and reasons for this legislation) and its implementation, the development of tribal-based family programs, the development of intergovernmental agreements, funding for tribes to develop family supportive programs, and case consultation to tribal family members, agencies, human service practitioners, attorneys, and the court system. Essentially the ICWA requires that prior to a Native American child being placed with a non-Native family, the identified tribe must first be contacted with the goal of keeping the child within the tribal community. Although there has been some erosion of the ICWA with recent court decisions that critics claim violated the ICWA in contested adoption proceedings, the overall goals of the ICWA remain intact with the goal of promoting Native families and righting the wrongs of past injustices against the Native American population (NICWA, n.d.).

ENHANCEDetext *self-check 5.2*

CHILD ABUSE INVESTIGATIONS

There are several ways that a child abuse investigation may be initiated, but all have their origin in a concern that a child is being mistreated in some manner. **Mandated reporters** are required by law to file a report with their state's child abuse hotline immediately if they suspect that a child is being abused or neglected. Mandated reporters typically fall into several categories and include professionals who work with children as a part of their normal work duties, such as mental health professionals (social workers, counselors, and psychologists), teachers (and other school personnel), medical personnel (such as physicians and nurses), and law enforcement personnel.

Most states have strict laws that define the parameters of child abuse reporting, including delineating what constitutes a reportable concern, the timeframe in which a mandated reporter must report the suspected abuse, and the consequences of failing to report, including professional sanction such as probation or the temporary suspension of one's professional license. In fact, in most states, the failure to comply with mandated reporting requirements is a crime (a misdemeanor or even a felony for repeated failures). The most common reasons for not reporting a case of suspected child abuse include not being properly trained on the signs of potential abuse, not wanting to get a client in trouble, and failing to recognize that a mandated reporter is not an investigator, and thus does not need conclusive evidence of abuse prior to making a report.

The majority of calls made to the child abuse hotline are from mandated reporters, but this does not preclude private citizens from calling the child abuse hotline if they suspect a child is being abused or neglected by a parent or caregiver. Thus, it is not uncommon for neighbors, friends, or even relatives to report suspected child abuse. Those who are not mandated reporters are allowed to call anonymously.

Due to the intrusive nature of an abuse investigation, federal and state laws exist to protect the privacy of family life. Thus, child abuse hotline workers must adhere to strict guidelines regarding what reports can and cannot be accepted, and which reports rise to the level of warranting an investigation. If the report of alleged abuse meets the stated criteria, then the report will be accepted and investigated in a reasonable timeframe. In fact, federal funding of state CPS agencies is tied to compliance with federal mandates that all child abuse reports be screened immediately and investigated in a timely manner (CAPTA, 2010). Although federal law does not specify a particular timeframe for conducting an investigation, most states have compliance laws stipulating specific guidelines mandating that reports of abuse be investigated anywhere from immediately for cases involving imminent risk to 10 days for cases involving moderate to minimal risk to the child (Kopel, Charlton, & Well, 2003).

Once a child abuse report is accepted, the case is sent to the appropriate regional agency and assigned to an abuse investigator, who is a licensed social worker or other licensed human service professional. The actual investigation will vary depending on the specific circumstances of the allegations, but most investigations will involve interviewing the child, the non-offending parent(s), and the alleged perpetrator. Although the sequence of the interviews might change depending on the specific circumstances of the case, oftentimes investigators prefer to interview the child before the parents or caregivers to avoid the potential for the alleged abusive parent(s) influencing or intimidating the child.

Types of Child Maltreatment

Child maltreatment is a crime regardless of who the perpetrator is and should always be reported to legal authorities, but CPS becomes involved only when the abuse is perpetrated by someone in a caregiving role to the child. This includes a parent, a relative, a parent's boyfriend or girlfriend, a teacher, a childcare provider, or even babysitter. The federal government has developed a definition of what constitutes the minimum standard for child abuse and neglect, establishing four general categories of child maltreatment: neglect, physical abuse, sexual abuse, and emotional abuse. Each state and U.S. territory has the responsibility of defining child abuse and neglect according to state statute, in accordance with federal definitions. The following is the U.S. Health and Human Services' definition of each type of abuse and maltreatment. However, again it is important to remember that each state, although bound to this minimum standard, will likely have additional criteria and scenarios that qualify as abuse (National Clearinghouse on Child Abuse and Neglect, 2005).

Neglect of a child involves the failure to provide for a child's basic needs. Neglect may be

- Physical (e.g., failure to provide necessary food or shelter or lack of appropriate supervision)
- Medical (e.g., failure to provide necessary medical or mental health treatment)
- Educational (e.g., failure to educate a child or attend to the child's special education needs)
- Emotional (e.g., inattention to a child's emotional needs, failure to provide psychological care, or permitting the child to use alcohol or other drugs)

The existence of some of these indicators does not necessarily indicate child neglect, particularly because cultural values, standards of care in the community, and poverty may be contributing factors in caregiving challenges in meeting a child's physical, medical, and educational needs. Rather, the manifestation of certain problems within a family system, such as not sending a child to school, may be an indicator of an overwhelmed family's need for information and general assistance. Yet, if a family fails to utilize the information, assistance, and resources provided for them, and the child's health and/or safety is determined to be at risk, then a CPS intervention may be warranted.

A child cowers in a corner. The human services professional working in child welfare may be presented with children who experience child maltreatment in various forms.

© POLOLIA / FOTOLIA

Physical abuse of a child includes intentional or unintentional physical injury ranging from burning, minor bruises, severe fractures, or even death, as a result of punching, beating, kicking, biting, shaking, throwing, stabbing, choking, hitting with a hand, stick, strap, or other object. *Sexual abuse* includes activities by a parent or caretaker that include fondling a child's genitals, penetration, incest, rape, sodomy, indecent exposure, and exploitation through prostitution or the production of pornographic materials. Emotional abuse of a child involves a pattern of behavior that impairs a child's emotional development or sense of self-worth. This may include constant criticism, threats, or rejection, as well as withholding love, support, or guidance. Emotional abuse is often difficult to prove, and therefore most CPS agencies may not be able to intervene without evidence of significant harm to the child or an indication of another form of abuse (which almost always occurs alongside emotional abuse).

It's important to understand the nature of child abuse, particularly how it can be transmitted from one generation to the next (Bentovim, 2002, 2004; Ehrensaft, Cohen, & Brown, 2003; Newcomb, Locke, & Thomas, 2001; Pears & Capaldi, 2001), and although the majority of parents who have been abused in childhood do not go on to abuse their own children, those who commit child abuse have likely been abused in their own childhoods. Homes marked by violence, drug abuse, neglect, and sexual abuse contribute to the development of maladaptive patterns that can be passed down to the next generation. Although it might not make intuitive sense that someone who endured the pain of abuse would inflict this same abuse on their own child, the complex nature of child abuse oftentimes renders abuse patterns beyond the control of the abuser without some form of intervention. For instance, consider Case Study 5.1 about Rick and then ask yourself how this information would impact your work as a child abuse investigator or child welfare caseworker.

The case study about Rick illustrates some of the dynamics at play with the intergenerational transmission of abuse and why it is so important for caseworkers to understand what may occur in the mind of someone who has endured physical, emotional, and sexual abuse at the hands of parents and other caregivers. Individuals who have suffered significant childhood abuse often suffer from low frustration tolerance, displaced anger, inability to delay gratification, impulse control problems, problems with emotional regulation, difficulty attaching to others, and an unstable self-identity (Bentovim, 2002, 2004). Issues such as poor parental modeling, lack of understanding about normal child development, and an individual's level of residual anger and frustration tolerance affect a person's ability to positively parent their children. This does not mean that all parents who come from abusive homes are destined to repeat the mistakes of their parents; far from it in fact. Rather, what it does mean is that child abuse does not exist in a vacuum, and the more child welfare professionals understand the systemic nature of child abuse and maltreatment, the better they will be able to serve the families on their caseloads.

The Forensic Interview

In the past few decades, allegations of child abuse, particularly child sexual abuse, have skyrocketed. Reasons for this include increased public awareness, mandatory reporting requirements, a significant change in attitudes regarding what constitutes child abuse, as well as the belief that abuse is no longer a private family matter. Yet, as the pendulum swung, the 1970s witnessed a sort of frenzy in child sexual abuse reporting, fueled in part by a popular contention among mental health experts that children were incapable of making false allegations. This belief fostered overzealousness among some therapists, who used inappropriate interviewing techniques to encourage disclosures, many of which were false. Examples of the types of questions most likely to lead to false confessions include leading questions, such as: "Did he touch you on your privates?", forced choice questions, such as: "Did he touch you under your clothing or over your clothing?", option posing questions, such as: "I heard that your uncle has been bothering you", or suggestive questions, such as: "Many kids at your school have said that your teacher has touched them. Did he touch you too?"

The use of these types of leading questions used by well-meaning therapists was eventually met with harsh criticism, particularly among members of the legal

Case Study 5.1   Case Example of the Intergenerational Cycle of Child Abuse

Rick grew up in a home marked with domestic violence, which oftentimes extended to the children. Rick's mother was chronically depressed and often resorted to using alcohol to avoid dealing with her feelings. Rick recalls days and sometimes weeks where she refused to get out of bed, and he was responsible for caring for his younger siblings. His father also had an alcohol problem and would fly into nightly rages where he would physically abuse his mother. When Rick got older, he attempted to intervene and protect his mother, which only resulted in his father physically abusing him. In addition to physical abuse, Rick was also the victim of emotional abuse and neglect. Rick's father would often call him derogatory names and humiliate him by telling him that he would amount to nothing in life. It seemed as though Rick could do nothing right, and when he was about 12 years old he promised himself that he would never allow anyone to hurt or humiliate him again.

Rick married when he was 21 and was hopeful that his life of being victimized was over. He loved his wife very much and was determined to be the best husband and father he could possibly be. He vowed not to repeat the mistakes of his parents. But deep inside he was plagued with fears that he wasn't good enough for his wife and that she would eventually leave him. He became increasingly jealous and accused his wife of wanting to leave him. If she tried to convince him otherwise, he accused her of lying. When she became pregnant he was thrilled, but after the baby was born he became upset because his wife seemed to want to spend all her time with the baby, leaving him to fend for himself.

One day Rick's boss called him into his office and pointed out a mistake that Rick had made. All Rick could think of was the promise he had made to himself years ago to never allow anyone to hurt or ridicule him again. Even though his boss's comments would have seemed reasonable to most people, to Rick it was a recreation of the abuse he endured as a child. He lost control of his temper, slammed his fist into the wall, and quit his job. When he got home he told his wife and fully expected her to sympathize with him and support his decision to not tolerate such abuse, but instead she complained that his act was selfish, particularly in light of his responsibilities as a father. Rick completely lost his temper and in a blinding rage accused his wife of betraying him. In the blur that followed, Rick accused her of cheating on him, of caring about the baby more than him, and of even getting pregnant by another man. In the midst of his angry outburst he shoved his wife against the wall. All he could think of was how this woman who he thought was his savior was really his enemy, and at that moment he hated her for allowing him to lower his guard and trust her. All the pain of his childhood, with all the hurt and humiliation, came rushing back, and he began to choke her. When his baby interrupted his rage, he screamed at his son to shut up. When his baby's crying got louder, he picked him up and shook him violently.

community who represented those individuals falsely accused of sexually abusing children in their charge. By the 1990s considerable research existed that showed how asking children leading questions during abuse investigations significantly increased the likelihood of false and erroneous disclosures, particularly with preschool-aged children (Hewitt, 1999; Peterson & Biggs, 1997; Poole & Lindsay, 1998). In response to criticism and new research, CPS agencies across the country developed pilot programs that combined the resources of several investigative agencies, including CPS, police departments, and prosecutors' offices. This coordinated approach not only prevents the trauma of duplicative interviews by separate enforcement agencies, but also allows for the highly specialized training of investigators on **forensic interviewing techniques** that avoid any type of suggestive or leading questions.

Although there is a general understanding among investigators of what constitutes a forensic interview, there was still concern that many interviewers used questions that were somewhat leading in nature, including an interviewer's inadvertent reaction to a child's response that either encouraged or discouraged an honest disclosure. For instance, an investigator who strongly believes that a child has been abused may inadvertently respond with frustration if a child denies the abuse, which may influence a child who wants to please the investigator to give a false disclosure of abuse. Even an expression of sympathy on the part of the interviewer in response to disclosures of abuse can inadvertently encourage a child to embellish somewhat to receive more of the interviewer's compassion.

The National Institute of Child Health and Human Development (NICHD) developed a forensic interviewing protocol that teaches interviewers how to ask open-ended questions, using retrieval cues that rely on free recall. "Can you tell me everything you can remember?" is an example of an open-ended question. "Tell me more about the room you were in" is an example of a retrieval cue (Bourg, Broderick, & Flagor, 1999; Sternberg, Lamb, & Orbach, 2001). New research is being conducted all the time, examining a range of issues related to interviewing children when suspected abuse is involved, including exploring appropriate interview settings, how to build rapport with the child, how to pace the interview, the use of body maps, as well as best practice regarding how to interview special populations such as immigrant children (Fontes, 2010; Morgan, Dorgan, & Hayne, 2013).

Models for Decision-Making in Child Welfare Investigations

Child abuse investigators are responsible for assessing the safety of children who are at risk of maltreatment, deciding what types and levels of services may be immediately needed to keep children safe, and determining under what conditions children are placed in out-of-home care for their protection. (DePanfilis & Scannapieco, 1994). Many variables influence the outcome of an investigation, including the criteria a CPS agency uses to determine whether abuse is occurring and if so, whether it rises to the level of warranting an intervention.

The process of investigating an incident of potential child abuse and maltreatment is complex and wrought with the possibility for bias. For instance, how does an investigator evaluate parental cooperation versus resistance? What about forthrightness versus deception? Such decisions require good clinical skills, the ability to read people, to determine whether someone is being truthful or hiding something significant. In other words, the process of investigating a suspected case of child abuse is wrought with the potential of personal bias influencing the investigative process, which could lead to some cases of abuse being unfounded, as well as cases where the family is meeting the federal minimum parenting standard being founded.

Because of the potential for bias entering into the investigative process leading to unreliable and inconsistent evaluations, it is important for CPS agencies to adopt a risk assessment and decision-making model when assessing a case of suspected child abuse. According to the Child Welfare League of America (CWLA) there are several approaches to making risk assessments of child maltreatment in child protection. Most models rely on either actuarial (statistical) analyses or the consensus of experts in the field. Actuarial models of risk assessment assess families based on factors and characteristics that are statistically associated with the recurrence of maltreatment, whereas consensus-based models of risk assessment rely on the professional opinions of child maltreatment experts. Because the actuarial models of risk assessments are based on a statistical calculation, the validity of the inventories may be considered higher than the consensus-based model risk assessments. Yet, many within the child welfare fields express concern that actuarial models do not rely enough on clinical judgment. An example of an actuarial model for risk assessment and decision-making is the CRC Actuarial Models for Risk Assessment (Austin, D'Andrade, Lemon, Benton, Chow, & Reyes, 2005).

Consensus-based approaches include theoretically and empirically guided approaches that rank a series of factors that have empirical support for their association with child maltreatment (CWLA, 2005). Some examples of consensus-based models for risk assessment and decision-making include the Washington Risk Assessment Matrix (WRAM), the California Family Assessment and Factor Analysis (CFAFA or the "Fresno Model"), the Child Emergency Response Assessment Protocol (CERAP) (Austin, D'Andrade, Lemon, Benton, Chow, & Reyes, 2005), and the Child at Risk Field System (CARF). The CARF provides the following guidelines for abuse investigators making a determination about abuse:

Where children were determined to be maltreated and unsafe, the offending parents

1. were out of control,
2. were frequently violent,
3. showed no remorse,
4. may actually request placement,
5. did not respond to previous attempts to intervene, and/or
6. location was unknown.

And the caseworker believed that

1. the parents were a flight risk,
2. the child had special needs the parents could not meet,
3. the conditions in the home are life-threatening, and/or
4. the nonoffending parent could not protect the children.

Where children were determined to be maltreated and safe, the parents

1. possessed a sufficient amount of impulse control,
2. accepted responsibility for the situation in their home,
3. had appropriate understanding of the child, showed concern for the child and remorse for the maltreatment,
4. had a history of accessing help and services, and
5. exhibited knowledge of good parenting skills.

It is important to note that although definitions of child maltreatment are statutorily defined, there is a certain amount of latitude an investigator has in determining whether child maltreatment is occurring and whether the extent of the abuse warrants intervention. Primarily, it is through the use of an effective and well-tested decision-making model that an abuse investigator will have the greatest likelihood of making an appropriate determination in a child abuse and maltreatment investigation.

ENHANCEDetext *self-check 5.3*

WORKING WITH CHILDREN IN PLACEMENT AND THEIR FAMILIES

When an abuse investigator determines a child must be placed into protective custody, the child may be removed from the home and placed in one of many environments, including relative foster care, nonrelative foster care, or an emergency shelter pending more permanent placement. The case is then transferred to a family caseworker who evaluates all the relevant dynamics of the case (i.e., reason for placement, nature of abuse, attitude of the parents). The family caseworker also assesses the strengths and deficits of the biological parent(s) as well as the family structure. A permanency goal for the child is then determined and can include:

1. Reunification with the biological parents
2. Living with relatives (kinship care)
3. Guardianship with close friends
4. Short-term or long-term nonrelative foster care
5. Emancipation (with older adolescents)
6. Adoption with termination of parental rights

Although reunification with the biological parents remains the most common permanency plan, recent changes in many state and federal laws have shifted the focus from protecting the biological family unit to considering the best interest of the child. The reason for this shift can be traced to several high-profile cases in the mid-1990s where children were either seriously abused or killed after being reunified with their biological parents. In response, well-meaning child advocates launched campaigns in Washington, D.C., appealing to Congress to do something about the horrible plight of children who were returned to their biological families only to face further abuse and sometimes their deaths in a failed effort to save troubled families.

Although there was no documented increase of child maltreatment during this time period, newspaper and magazine articles highlighting tragic (albeit rare) cases of continued abuse or deaths when children were reunited with their biological parent(s) were passed around Congress. Articles such as "The Little Boy Who Didn't Have to Die" were utilized in an effort to make an emotional appeal to legislators to shift priorities from family reunification to parental termination and subsequent adoption (Spake, 1994). The result of this campaign was the passage of the ASFA of 1997, which marked a clear departure away from family preservation and toward adoption.

The **best interest of the child doctrine** may sound great on the surface. Who wouldn't want the best interest of the child to be the standard when considering the future of an abused child's future? The problem noted with this standard among child welfare experts is that the doctrine does not specify who makes the determination of what is actually in the best interest of the child. In other words, the best interest of the child according to whom? According to the foster parents? The courts? The caseworker? Congress? Society in general? It doesn't take much analysis to recognize how easily this standard could be abused. For instance, what if the caseworker determines that it is in the best interest of the child to be adopted by a family with two parents who are financially secure rather than be returned to the child's poor single mother who, regardless of how diligently she tries to regain custody, works late nights and has no supportive family? The potential to make permanency plans that discriminate against biological parents who are marginalized members of society—such as parents who are poor, single, an ethnic minority, undocumented immigrants, gay or lesbian, who work too many jobs, who are too young or too old (and the list goes on)—is significant.

Dorothy Roberts, author of *Shattered Bonds: The Color of Child Welfare* (2002), cautions that the AFSA of 1997 and the ensuing best interest of the child doctrine create many problems, including a conflict when caseworkers are required to pursue two permanency plans at the same time to comply with the new permanency plan timeframes—reunification with the biological family and adoption. What many caseworkers do to accomplish this task is to place foster children in *preadoptive* homes, while at the same time planning for reunification with the biological parent(s). This creates a situation where the biological parents' rights are often in conflict with the children's rights, and where foster care families, who are by definition charged with the responsibility of fostering a relationship between the children and their biological parent(s), are now competing with the biological parent(s) for the children.

Another possible conflict according to Roberts includes the act's adoption incentive program, where states are given financial incentives of $4,000 for each child placed for adoption (above a baseline), $4,000 for foster youth identified as special needs, and $8,000 for youths between the ages of 9 and 18. The potential for agency conflict of interest, and in some cases abuse, is evident as states scramble to replace lost revenue due to a poor economy. Roberts warns that this new legislation was not directed at effecting faster termination of parental rights in cases with severe abuse because these cases were already relatively "open-and-shut." Rather, it is the cases involving poverty-related maltreatment, most often in African American and Native American homes, that have been most affected by this new federal law. Roberts fears the new priorities have led to increases in social injustice in many CPS agencies, particularly against the poor, people of color, immigrants, and indigenous populations.

For this reason as well as many others, the caseworker must be careful in determining what criteria to use in making permanency determination recommendations. For instance, some experts have suggested using attachment ties as a guide in deciding a permanent placement plan, suggesting that a child should remain with the family they appear to have the greatest attachment to avoid further emotional ruptures (Gauthier, Fortin, & Jéliu, 2004). Yet, the potential for extending bias toward the foster parent is significant, particularly in light of the fact that the foster parents will have a greater advantage over the biological parents because of where the child resides. This is especially true if the biological parents are restricted from participating regularly in the child's life through regular visitation. U.S. history is filled with reports of abuses of this sort, where parents considered unworthy have experienced unfair treatment by child protective agencies (see discussion on Native Americans), and legislation that is based on the best child doctrine risks escorting in a new dawn of similar abuses.

The Biological Parent Case Plan

Once a child has been placed into foster care, the caseworker must prepare a detailed service plan, typically within 30 days, outlining goals the biological parents must meet before regaining custody of their child. The specific goals must be related to the identified parenting deficits, but can include goals such as counseling, **parenting classes**, treatment for substance abuse, **anger management**, securing employment, securing housing, and maintaining regular contact with their children. It is the responsibility of the caseworker to facilitate the biological parents' meeting of these goals. This might involve giving referrals to the parents or securing services for them, as well as monitoring their ongoing progress.

It is also important for caseworkers to be aware that biological parents who have had their children removed from the home may be enduring emotional trauma in response to this loss, which may result in them behaving in ways that could be uncharacteristic. The strain of having to be accountable to external forces that have control over their lives makes many biological parents vulnerable to feeling overwhelming shame, which may manifest in defensiveness that could be misinterpreted as indifference or a lack of remorse. An effective caseworker will understand this possible dynamic and will create an environment where biological parents will be able to overcome the barrier of defensiveness and shame and work on the issues identified in their service plan.

In fact, a part of any good case plan will involve a visitation schedule that supports and encourages the child's relationship with the biological parents and provides them with opportunities to apply new parenting techniques that they've learned in parenting classes and counseling (Sanchirico & Jablonka, 2000). An effective caseworker will give consistent feedback to the biological parents about their progress toward meeting service plan goals, will balance constructive feedback with encouragement, and will protect the parent–child relationship. The effective caseworker will do whatever possible to remove barriers to complying with service plans, such as finding alternate mental health providers when waiting lists would cause unreasonable delays or resolving conflicts between goals, such as not scheduling visitation during the parents' working hours when maintaining stable employment is a service plan goal.

The Impact of Foster Care on Children and Their Families

The clinical issues that a child welfare caseworker may experience when working with children in foster care will vary depending on variables such as the age of the child, the length of time in placement, the reasons for placement (and the nature of the abuse and maltreatment), and the **permanency plan** (i.e., adoption or **family reunification**). Younger children are typically easier to place and may display less oppositional behaviors than adolescents, who are often placed in residential group homes.

Children who have been sexually abused will often manifest emotional problems that require sophisticated handling on the part of the caseworkers, therapists, and foster parents. Sexually abused children may act out sexually with their foster parents as well as other children, which can create an uncomfortable situation, particularly for those who are unfamiliar with such acting out behaviors. In addition, most children who have been mistreated in some manner may behave appropriately during the honeymoon phase of placement, but then act out once they begin to feel more secure. This dynamic can lead to disrupted placements if the foster parents are unaware of the dynamics behind this shift in behavior, are poorly trained, or lack proper resources.

The reality is that most children who have been removed from their homes due to abuse and maltreatment will experience psychological and emotional problems on a short- or long-term basis and it should never be forgotten that while the abuse of a child is of course highly traumatizing, so is moving a child from his or her home. In fact, a national survey of approximately 4,000 children in foster care, ages 2 through 14, who had been removed from their homes due to maltreatment, showed that nearly half of the children had clinically significant psychological and/or behavioral problems. Alarmingly though, only about half of these children had received any counseling in the past year. The children who were the most likely to receive mental health services were younger children who had been victims of sexual abuse. African American children were the least likely to receive mental health services, as were children who remained living with their biological parents (Burns et al., 2004).

Siu and Hogan (1989) identified five clinical themes experienced by most children in foster care and made recommendations for how child welfare caseworkers should respond. These include issues related to:

- Separation;
- Loss, grief, and mourning;
- Identity issues;
- Continuity of family ties; and
- Crisis.

Watch this video on a child who is abused and reflect on the complexity of her situation and her feelings.
ENHANCEDetext *video example 5.2*

www.youtube.com/watch?v=lOeQUwdAjE0

Separation

Children involved in the child welfare system are contending with either issues related to separation from their biological family members or the threat of separation. Siu and Hogan (1989) recommended that caseworkers be familiar with the psychological dynamics involved in such separations as they relate to each developmental stage. It is important for caseworkers to acknowledge that these children are not just being separated from their biological parents, but are experiencing multiple separations, such as separation from their extended family, perhaps their siblings and their familiar surroundings, including their bedroom, house, neighborhood, and even their family pets. Caseworkers need to confront these separation issues head on with the children on their caseload, resisting the temptation to avoid them in response to their own separation anxiety.

Children often go through different stages when confronted with significant separation, beginning with the *pre-protest* stage, where children accept removal from their home with little protest. But this stage is ultimately followed by the *protest* stage, where children can respond with outright combative and oppositional behavior or with a subtler uncooperative attitude. The third stage is marked by *despair,* where the child often submits to the placement with a sense of hopelessness. The final stage involves *adjustment* to the placement, but also involves a sense of detachment to that which the child had previously been attached—namely, their biological families and environments (Rutter, 1978).

Caseworkers can respond to children dealing with separation issues by being honest with them (in an age-appropriate manner) regarding what is happening with their families, and by helping to prepare them for upcoming changes in order to reduce the anxiety associated with anticipating the unknown. Younger children are far more likely to be operating in the "here and now." Thus, it is important for the caseworker to reassure the child that the separation is only temporary (if the goal is family reunification) and that the feelings of sadness and discomfort experienced after being separated will not last forever.

Children who have been removed from their homes also need to be reassured that they are not the cause of the family disruption. It is quite common for foster care children to feel responsible for their parents "getting into trouble," and they may even be tempted to recant their disclosures of abuse in the hope that they can return home. Such children often reason that enduring the abuse is better than having their family torn apart and their parents being in trouble. In fact, some abusive parents tell their children that if they disclose the abuse the parents will go to jail and the children will be taken away. Thus, it is important that caseworkers anticipate the possibility of such prior conversations between children and parents and address this by reassuring the children that the current course of action will ultimately benefit and strengthen the entire family system.

Loss, Grief, and Mourning

It may be counterintuitive that children would experience a sense of **grief** in response to being removed from an abusive home. But this is often the case, and an inexperienced caseworker may erroneously believe that an abused child will experience only relief and gratitude when placed in a safe and loving foster home. On the contrary, many children who have been removed from their families experience grief in response to a range of losses, including the loss of their parent(s), their siblings, their home, their family pets, their bedrooms, their neighbors, friends, and oftentimes even their schools. Coming alongside children who have experienced a loss by permitting them to grieve openly and **mourn** their losses, regardless of the nature of the abuse, involves having a high tolerance for a wide range of emotions.

Lee and Whiting (2007) discuss the concept of ambiguous loss with regard to children in foster care. Ambiguous loss is defined as loss that is unclear, undefined, and in many instances, unresolvable. Ambiguous loss in foster care situations can involve losses that are confusing for the child, such as the loss of an abusive parent. Children who are removed from an abusive home and placed in a foster home with caring, nonabusive parents may feel conflicted about the loss of the biological parent and entry into the child welfare system. Feelings may include confusion, ambivalence, and guilt.

Earlier research studies have found that people who endure ambivalent loss tend to experience similar reactions and feelings, including:

- "Frozen" grief, including outrage and an inability to move on
- Confusion, distress, and ambivalence
- Uncertainty leading to immobilization
- Blocked coping processes
- Feelings of helplessness, depression, and anxiety, and relationship conflicts
- Denial of changes or losses, including a denial of the facts
- Anger at the lost person being excluded
- Confusion in boundaries and roles (e.g., who the parental figures are)
- Guilt, if hope has been given up
- Refusal to talk about the individuals and the situation (Boss, 2004 as cited in Lee & Whiting, 2007).

With these reactions and feelings in mind Lee and Whiting (2007) interviewed 182 foster children, ages 2 through 10. Children were asked about each of the reactions and feelings identified in Boss' study as typical responses to ambiguous loss. The study showed that virtually all of the children interviewed exhibited these typical feelings, particularly feelings associated with confusion, ambiguity, and outrage about their situation. Several children noted confusion about their future—not knowing when they would see their parent(s) again, or how long they would be in foster care. The children also expressed feelings of uncertainty, guilt, and immobility.

Lee and Whiting (2007) recommend using the model of ambiguous loss when working with children in foster care, cautioning against pathologizing children's feelings (and the consequential behaviors). In describing the application of this model of loss, Lee and Whiting urged child welfare professionals, including therapists, case managers, court personnel, and foster family members, not to see these feelings and their associated behaviors as pathological, but as coping strategies that were understandable considering their circumstances. Lee and Whiting discouraged child welfare professionals from encouraging children in protective care to suppress their feelings and behaviors just because it might be easier for the foster parents. In fact, they theorize that the behaviors that often cause a disruption in foster care placements are the very behaviors that need to be expected and understood since they are manifestations of fears of interdependency and self-fulfilling prophesies that they are unlovable. If child welfare professionals adopt a strengths-based approach they will no longer perceive grief-based behaviors as deficits, but rather as strengths.

Siu and Hogan (1989) also cite the importance of caseworkers understanding the nature of grieving and thereby assisting foster care children to grieve the loss of their families. It is vital for caseworkers to be familiar with the range of possible expressions of depression among grieving children, which often manifest as irritability and can easily be mistaken for oppositional behavior. It is also quite common for children to express heartfelt grief for parents who have abused them. Even children who have been sexually abused may express that they miss an abusive parent. Effective caseworkers can express understanding and empathy for children as they express their grief and mourn their losses, without necessarily minimizing the reasons why the children are in placement.

Identity Issues

Personal identity is a multifaceted concept referring primarily to one's **self-knowledge**, **self-appraisal**, and **self-assessment**. Developmental theorist Erik Erikson (1963, 1968, 1975) believed that identity formation involves the integration of numerous and sometimes conflicting childhood identities. Erikson believed that this convergence of identities took place during the adolescent stage of development, when the adolescent developed an internal continuity and consistency that integrated all different aspects of the self, allowing one's real identity to emerge. Our individual identities are based on several factors, some involving internal traits and some involving external traits.

As individuals mature, their basis for identity becomes more internally based. But children, particularly younger children, will typically base their identity more on external than internal attributes. For instance, if someone were to ask you to describe yourself, you might begin by saying that you are a college student (external). You might then share that you are a soccer player (external) and on student counsel (external). But, you might then describe yourself as an extrovert (internal), who is courageous (internal), loyal (internal), and kind (internal). The more internally based one's identity, the more resilient a person will be in times of crisis and transition.

Children tend to be far more external in their self-identity, and their self-appraisal can be quite fragile, varying dramatically if they're separated from their external structure. Siu and Hogan (1989) suggested that caseworkers become familiar with the process of identity development and how the removal of children from their family of origin can significantly affect their sense of personal identity. The nature of this impact will depend, of course, on the age of the children and their stage of development, but can also be affected by several other variables. Some of the factors involved in identity formation include one's gender, ethnic and cultural identity, extracurricular activities, talents, socioeconomic status, and relationships with others. Children are often

A child's identity is often external, such as playing baseball and having a pet

unaware of how they are affected by things such as their socioeconomic status, but it affects them nonetheless.

One's **positive identity** is dependent on an affirming reciprocal exchange between the various aspects of identity and one's environment. In other words, we tend to value what others value in us, or what our environment tells us is valuable. This type of reciprocal exchange can be conceptualized as a mirror reflecting back either positive or negative images of how one is perceived and valued by others. Individuals who are extremely talented musically may only perceive this talent as a positive part of their identity if their family and community perceive musical talent as valuable. Children who are exceptionally good at science and math but are raised in families that value athletic prowess may not perceive their intellectual abilities as a positive and valuable trait.

Children who are removed from their home because of maltreatment and placed in a new environment will almost always struggle with identity issues because, despite being in a more positive environment, they are, for instance, no longer the youngest sibling, no longer the owner of a small dog, no longer the funniest student in the class, and no longer the best bike rider in the neighborhood. Now they are foster children, different and set apart, perhaps living in a home much nicer than their own, leaving them feeling somewhat deficient and "less than"; they are, for instance, no longer funny because they know no one in class, or they are not the youngest kid because they are the only foster child in their new homes.

Because so much of children's identities reside outside of themselves and they are dependent on external validation and encouragement, child welfare caseworkers will be more effective if they know the various dynamics of identity development and understand how removing children from their homes, even highly abusive homes, can undermine a child's identity development. Post-placement acting out is often caused, at least in part, by identity disruption, and the caseworker can respond by providing comfort and encouragement to the child during this time of transition. Children who have only received praise for their ability to play basketball well are likely going to struggle with their identity if placed in a home that values academic performance or musical ability over sports. A child welfare caseworker can assist these children in recognizing that their worth is internal and should not be based solely on the approval and affirmation of others.

Continuity of Family Ties

Picture yourself in a boat moored to a dock on the shore of a large lake. Being anchored to the dock provides you with a connection to the mainland and a sense of security, without fearing that you'll become adrift at sea. But what if you need to get to the other side of the lake? You would have to pull up your anchor and drift across the water, and it wouldn't be until you reached the other side and safely anchored yourself against that shore that you would feel secure and stable again. Many significant life transitions are like this—adrift at sea, caught between two shores, where continuity and stability are temporarily lost (Martin, 2016). Children who have been removed from their biological homes will undoubtedly lose their sense of continuity with their biological families and will feel adrift at sea during the time period when they have not yet established new bonds with their foster family. This is a temporary phenomenon and will pass in time, thus continuity and stability can be reestablished once again.

Siu and Hogan (1989) strongly recommend that caseworkers consider the importance of **family continuity** and stability when considering where to place a child. Ready access to the biological family and even close friends should be a priority in placement decisions. Although this can become challenging, particularly in areas where there is a limited number of available foster families, consideration should still be given to a placement that will facilitate ongoing parental involvement and the possibility of continuing ties with family members and friends. For instance, at times siblings must be placed in separate foster homes, and consideration to continuity issues needs to be extended in this situation. Far too often siblings in foster families do not visit each other regularly because of the geographic constraints placed on foster families, who are often responsible for providing transportation.

Caseworkers may find themselves in double-bind situations, though, where they must make difficult choices regarding keeping siblings together by placing them in a foster home that is a significant distance away from a parent who does not have transportation, or placing the children in different foster homes that are closer to their biological parents, but preclude family visitation due to difficulties in coordinating visits among various foster families. Caseworkers must rely on their clinical skills in deciding the right course of action and should then recognize and acknowledge how this interruption of family continuity and stability will affect the children, particularly early in the placement.

Far too often the foster care system, with all its complications, is ill-equipped to effectively *foster* a relationship between children in placement and their biological families. This is because if children do not have ready access to their biological families, they will most likely search for continuity and connectedness with their foster families, which, although necessary and important, can pose a risk to the continuing bond with their biological parents. Research has clearly shown that children who visit their biological parents more frequently have a stronger bond with them and have fewer behavioral problems, are less apt to take psychiatric medication, such as antidepressant medication, and are less likely to be developmentally delayed. This underscores the importance of strengthening the attachment between foster children and their biological parents through regular and consistent visitation (McWey & Mullis, 2004). Restricting visitation for any reason other than the safety of the child will have a negative effect on this attachment and might even be subsequently used against the biological parents when the time comes to make reunification plans.

Crisis

Removing children from their biological homes and placing them into foster care constitutes a crisis. Siu and Hogan (1989) referred to this crisis as a critical transition which throws an already fragile family system into complete disequilibrium. In fact, most child welfare experts put foster care placement in the category of a catastrophic crisis. Crises are not always bad though, and a popular contention among mental health experts is that a crisis provides one of the best opportunities for personal growth and authentic change. However, ordinary coping skills are typically not going to be enough to help a child deal with the trauma associated with being placed in foster care. An effective and seasoned caseworker can help children develop more effective coping skills that can help them respond to the multiple crises of being removed from their home and placed with strangers.

Of primary concern to child welfare caseworkers is actively working to limit the level and nature of the crises involved in decision-making, including balancing the risk of keeping the child in the home with the risk of the multiple crises involved with removal. More recent research supports Sui and Hogan's recognition of the crisis nature of out-of-home placements. For instance, Doyle (2007) found that children assigned to caseworkers who had higher removal rates tended to have higher rates of juvenile delinquency and teen motherhood compared to children with similar types of abuse who remained in their homes with family preservation services. Doyle's research contributes to the policy debate on whether maltreated children are best served through family preservation or child protection.

Working with Foster Parents

Foster care can involve many different types of placement settings, including kinship care, a foster care emergency shelter, a child residential treatment center, a group home, or even an independent living program for older adolescents, but most frequently foster care involves placing a child with a licensed foster family (two-parent or single-parent family). Every state has certain guidelines and standards that prospective foster parents must meet (Barth, 2001). Licensure typically requires that families participate in up to 10 training sessions focusing on topics such as the developmental needs of at-risk children, issues related to child sexual abuse, appropriate disciplining techniques for at-risk children, ways that foster parents can support the relationship between the foster children and their biological parents, and ways to manage the stress of adding new members to their family. In addition, individuals who will be foster parenting children of a different ethnicity will undergo training focusing on transcultural parenting issues.

Foster parents provide an invaluable service by accepting abused and maltreated children into their homes and providing love, nurturing, and security, even though they know the children may be in their homes for only a short time. In addition to good training, foster parents benefit from caseworkers who are consistently supportive and available to them, particularly during high stress times when foster children are acting out. Foster placement will be far less likely to fail if the foster parents feel sufficiently well prepared and supported by their caseworker.

The success of a reunification plan depends largely on the cooperation of the foster parents. A foster parent who eagerly facilitates visitation and the sharing of vital information with the biological parents will help protect and maintain the continuity between the foster children and their biological parents. The caseworker plays a pivotal role in providing support and assistance to foster parents. A foster parent who feels unsupported by the caseworker will be far more likely to either purposely or inadvertently undermine the relationship between the foster child and the biological parents. Much of the time this action comes in the form of advocacy for the child, but unfortunately, this advocacy, as well meaning as it may be, has the potential of disrupting the necessary process of reunification. Thus, although it is certainly understandable that the process of emotional bonding with the foster child may make foster parents vulnerable to advocating for their perception of the best interest of their foster children, foster parents who take it upon themselves to protect their foster child by discouraging the relationship with the biological parents in any way are violating their designated roles, and their effectiveness as foster parents will likely be seriously compromised.

The Public Broadcasting Service (PBS) documentary entitled *Failure to Protect: The Taking of Logan Marr* documents the removal of five-year-old Logan and her baby sister, Baily, from their young biological mother, Christie Marr. The documentary reveals how Maine's child welfare system, the Department of Human Services (DHS), removed Logan from her mother's care on the presumption that the child might be abused at some *future* time based on some dynamics in the home. After years of jumping through hoops to get Logan back, Christie had another child, but ultimately lost both of her girls after marrying someone who the DHS did not believe was a suitable parent. Regardless of Christie's compliance with her parenting plan, the caseworker placed her girls with another DHS worker who was also a licensed foster parent. The foster mother wanted to adopt the Marr girls and actively hindered the relationship between the girls and their mother. As is typically the case, the foster mother was responsible for providing transportation for visitation, as well as for keeping Christie apprised of major events in the girls' lives. Thus, she had tremendous power to limit visitation if she so desired or to be begrudging with vital information about the girls.

Logan ultimately died in this foster mother's care, and her death led to an uproar over the treatment of Christie, the apparent "cozy" relationship between the foster mother and the DHS caseworker, as well as the caseworker's refusal to investigate Logan's earlier complaints that her foster mother had abused her. Fortunately cases such as these are quite rare, but they do exist, and they illustrate how vital it is for foster parents to be well trained and sufficiently supported by their caseworker. An effective caseworker will be able to sense when a foster parent is either burning out or overstepping appropriate boundaries and will respond with support and limit setting as necessary.

The Process of Reunification

Decisions about reunifying children in foster care placement with their biological parents are based on many factors, including the biological parents' success in meeting their service plan goals. Even if these goals are sufficiently met, the timing of reunification will depend on factors related to minimizing disruptions in the child's life, such as not switching schools during breaks if possible. If reunification is the plan from the beginning of placement, then the caseworker should be planning for this event from the initial stages of the case.

Problems arise when issues such as court postponements, additional service plan goals, changes in caseworker assignments, and other factors lead to delays in reunification. A judge may deem it perfectly reasonable to postpone a reunification hearing so that a child can complete the final four months of school without disruption. Such a decision can be devastating for the biological parents though, who have worked diligently to reach all service plan goals and go to court expecting to leave with their biological child, only to be told they must wait an additional four months to avoid their child changing schools in the middle of the school year. The potential for a biological parent to give up attempting to regain custody and to relapse into unhealthy behaviors out of discouragement and frustration is great, and caseworkers must be sensitive to the possibility of such frustrations leading to despair or relapse.

Therefore, even though reunification with biological parents is associated with several changes in the child's life, many of which may be negative in nature (Lau, Litrownik, Newton, & Landsverk, 2003), an effective caseworker will begin preparing the child for these transitions from the beginning of placement in foster care. Simply verbalizing what is going to happen, telling the child what to expect in the future, and giving children a voice in expressing their fears and frustrations, even if they do not have decision-making power, will go a long way in minimizing the negative effect of reunification, particularly for children who have been in placement for a significant amount of time.

Reunification is not just stressful for the child, it is stressful for the biological parents as well, and many biological parents are the most vulnerable to stress-related relapse in the weeks leading up to and following reunification. The combination of increased stress and the acting out of the child due to yet another transition can create a potentially volatile situation where negative behavior patterns resurface and unhealthy coping mechanisms are resumed. Any good reunification plan involves ongoing monitoring and provision of in-home services to prevent such problems during the reunification process. These services can be provided by the county child welfare office directly or by a contracted agency-based practice that specializes in providing services such as in-home case management and support. With good support services, many reunifications go quite smoothly, and in time the children and parents settle in to a regular routine where healthier communication patterns and positive parenting styles will eventually lead to a positive response from the children.

Family Preservation

Family preservation programs are comprised of a variety of short-term, intensive services designed to immediately reduce stress and teach important skills designed to reduce the need for out-of-home placement by intervening in a family crisis process before the dynamics deteriorate to the point of requiring the removal of the children. Services can include family counseling, parenting training, child development education, child behavior management, life-skills training, assistance with household budgeting, stress management, respite care for caregivers, and in some cases, cash assistance. Overall, family preservation programs are considered an effective way of avoiding out-of-home placement, with over 80 percent of families remaining intact four years after receiving services (CWLA, n.d.).

There are many types of family preservation programs, including different goals, program elements, services provided, and theoretical orientations. Most states will typically adopt a particular program and then implement it within the state's county CPS agencies. Most family preservation programs typically offer 24-hour referral and response, in-home services offered on a 24-hour, 7-day-a-week availability, small caseloads, and emergency services. An example of a family preservation programs is the Homebuilders® program from the Institute for Family Development, which provides a range of in-home services for identified at-risk families involved in the child welfare system, including crisis intervention, parenting training, life-skills education, and counseling. Currently, more than half of all states in the United States use the Homebuilders® program.

Project Connect is another family preservation program that provides a wide array of services to identified at-risk families in the child welfare system, with a particular focus on parental substance abuse. Project Connect also provides 18 weeks of in-home skills training to parents focusing on child behavior management, child health care skills, and home safety training. Another family preservation program, Functional Family Therapy (FFT), provides in-home services to identified at-risk parents with adolescents.

ENHANCEDetext *self-check 5.4*

ETHNIC MINORITY POPULATIONS AND MULTICULTURAL CONSIDERATIONS

Children of color, particularly African Americans, are overrepresented in every stage of the U.S. Child Welfare system (Boyd, 2014; Child Welfare League of America, 2002). Gaining a more comprehensive understanding of this **disproportionality** and the history between people of color and the U.S. child welfare system requires that human service professionals recognize the role of cultural competence in gaining greater insights into why some minority groups may not trust child welfare professionals to have their best interests in mind.

The child welfare professional may not be aware of the long-standing negative history between U.S. government child welfare agencies and a particular racial group, but members of that particular group are most likely aware of this history. It is vital that human service professionals develop cultural competencies regardless of whether they are actively working with ethnic minority populations. It is only through a comprehensive understanding of the history of child welfare policies and abuses of power that the U.S. child welfare system will achieve its goal of respecting the autonomy and dignity of all people regardless of race, gender, age, nationality, and sexual orientation.

Watch this video on racial disproportionality in the child welfare system and consider how you may respond to this issue if working with children.
ENHANCEDetext *video example 5.3*

www.youtube.com/watch?v=fb32deeM4UU

African American Children in the U.S. Child Welfare System

African American children constitute the most overrepresented population within the U.S. foster care system, representing 25.7 percent of children in foster care placement even though they consist of only 14 percent of the general U.S. population (Woods & Summers, 2014). While the current disproportionality represents a decrease from 2002 when African American children represented over 35 percent of the children in foster care placement, the continued overrepresentation of African American children in the U.S. foster care system reflects longstanding factors impacting the African American population, such as **social oppression**, chronic and intergenerational poverty, racial discrimination, **historic marginalization**, including **exclusion from the labor market**, and other forms of **economic injustice**. Other contributing factors relate to racial discrimination and **implicit bias** within the child welfare system itself (Harris & Benton, 2015), including the following:

1. *Racial bias in referring families for family preservation programs versus out-of-home placement.* Certain populations, including African American families, are not consistently targeted for family preservation programs. Reasons for this include caseworker bias based on the belief that the needs of the African American community may be too great to be appropriately handled by most family preservation programs (Denby & Curtis, 2003).

2. *Racial partiality in assessing parent–child attachment, leading to delays in returning children to their biological parents.* A 2003 study of approximately 250 black and white children in foster care placement found that racial partiality existed in assessing the parent–child attachment when the caseworker was of a different race than the biological parent. Although this result was reciprocal (i.e., black caseworkers showed partiality to black families and white caseworkers show

partiality to white families), the effect of this trend has particular relevance to the African American community because the majority of caseworkers are Caucasian, and African American children are disproportionately represented among children in foster care. The results of this study revealed that Caucasian caseworkers might have erred when they concluded that African American mothers were poorly attached to their children because of the caseworker's lack of understanding of cultural differences between Caucasian and African American customs (Surbeck, 2003).

3. *Caseworkers who are poorly trained in cultural competencies.* For a caseworker to accurately assess many of the factors necessary in determining whether out-of-home placement is warranted, such as the level of violence in the home, the ability of parents to protect their children, or the level of parental remorse, a caseworker must be aware of commonly held negative stereotypes of various racial groups. It is unacceptable for a member of the majority culture to claim not to hold any negative stereotypes, and it is only through the honest admission of overt and subtle negative biases toward other cultures that a caseworker can begin to work effectively with a variety of ethnic groups.

African American children are not just overrepresented in the foster case system, but they also remain in care for longer than other racial groups, including Caucasian, Latino, and Asian children, and receive disproportionately fewer services. In response to this crisis the Multiethnic Placement Act (MEPA) was enacted, which prohibits states or other placement entities from receiving federal funding if they delay or deny a child placement in either a foster care or an adoptive home based on the child or prospective parent's race, color, or national origin. The act also prohibits the denial of individuals as foster or adoptive parents on the basis of the foster parent's or the child's race, color, or national origin. And finally, the act requires that child welfare agencies activity recruit foster and adoptive parents with racial and ethnic backgrounds that reflect the demographics of the children in the foster care system.

Considerable controversy exists though regarding the placement of African American children in Caucasian homes. Many advocacy organizations do not support **transracial adoption**, whereas others claim that it is not in the best interest of children to experience placement delays simply because there are no foster families available that are the same race as the child. From a micro perspective, this latter argument makes sense. If an African American child is in desperate need of a long-term foster home, how much sense would it make to have a policy in place that prevents placement in a suitable home only because the foster family is Caucasian? After all, all children deserve loving homes, and the color of their skin should not keep them from being placed in one. Right?

Yet, from a macro perspective, a different viewpoint is revealed. Consider the equity of a majority culture systematically destroying an entire race, as the United States did to the African American population during the slavery and post–Civil War era or to the Native American population during colonial times and the era of early occupation of the United States. How do you think these racial groups would perceive this same majority culture then rushing in to "rescue" the children who were maltreated in large part because of this cultural genocide and the resultant social breakdown?

Advocates of placing children of color in homes of the same race cite such treatment in their arguments. Alternatives to transracial placement include the development of kinship care programs, where members of a child's extended family act as foster parents, often made possible through financial assistance. The National Association of Black Social Workers (NABSW) cites the longstanding tradition of informal kinship care within the African American community extending back to the Middle Ages and solidified during the slavery era, when many African Americans acted in the informal capacity of parents for children whose biological parents were sold and sent away. Such cultural traditions can serve as a precursor for federally funded programs that promote kinship care foster programs, which respect cultural identity and tradition (NABSW, 2003; Smith & Devore, 2004).

Recent studies support the concerns expressed by the NABSW and others about the difficulties faced by even the most wellmeaning white adoptive parents to appropriately and accurately teach their black adopted children lessons about race in a culturally appropriate manner. A recent study by Smith, Juarez, and Jacobson (2011) found that the majority of adoptive families of black adoptees were white, middle to upper-class families from primarily white communities, and despite their attempts to teach their children about matters of race and instill in them a sense of cultural pride, most of the black adoptees were often left to struggle with racial discrimination and racial enculturation on their own. The primary reason for this dynamic was that their white adoptive families more often than not experienced race quite differently than their black adopted children, viewing racial dynamics through a white **Eurocentric** lens (Smith, Juarez, & Jacobson, 2011).

In their study on the attempts of white parents to teach their black adopted children about race and racism in America, Smith, Juarez, and Jacobson (2011) caution that as a part of the dominant culture, white adoptive parents inadvertently pass on cultural misunderstandings and interpretations about whiteness in society, including notions of white privilege. Their study revealed that while a majority of white transracial adoptive parents cited the importance of their children developing a sense of pride in their cultural heritage, they framed "cultural pride" as an individual process, not a collective one. Since the majority of transracial families interviewed in the study lived in primarily white communities, their black children did not participate or engage in communities of color; thus, any development of cultural pride was done in collective isolation.

Most of the white parents in this study taught their children about African American culture, including the nature of race relations in America, through books, films, and cultural events such as attending black camps. For instance, several white adoptive parents shared that they taught their black adoptive children about overcoming racism through the telling of stories of famous black individuals who became successful despite racial barriers through personal fortitude and a lot of hard work. Yet Smith, Juarez, and Jacobson (2011) point out how this type of racial framing illustrates Western notions of individualism, rather than community efforts more reflective of African American culture and history. Nor did it teach black adoptees about racial inequality involved in societal structure that contributed to some groups not having to work as hard as **racialized others** to be economically and socially acceptable.

This study revealed just how committed the white adoptive parents who were interviewed were in their attempts to appropriately validate their black adoptive children's racial heritage and culture pride, but they did so in ways that were distinctly white. For instance, the white adoptive parents taught their black children to feel positively about racial differences but to subvert personal needs and feelings by confronting racial discrimination through an educational approach that avoids conflict at all costs.

Framing racial and cultural dynamics in such a white Eurocentric and individualist way contradicted sharply how most African American parents handle matters of race with their children. Although the white parents in this study clearly loved their adopted children and appeared very committed to addressing matters of race with regard to cultural pride and dealing with racial prejudice, by presuming that racism was the result of white ignorance that could be overcome only through education and hard work, the white parents were inadvertently drawing from historic white cultural narratives of racial inequality rather than black ones, which are far more likely to emphasize the purposeful agenda of racial oppression and inequality within American society, and the collective struggle of African Americans to fight against it.

Although Smith, Juarez, and Jacobson (2011) do not specifically advocate against transracial adoption, they do caution white parents to be very careful about the ways in which they choose to teach lessons about race to their adopted children, so to avoid even the inadvertent inculcation of white racist framing of the black experience in America. They suggest doing this through the reframing of race and racial issues through the experiences of the black community rather than through the lens of white America. It is difficult to say whether this is possible, but further research on ways in which race lessons can be taught to black adoptees will inform this growing area of research, particularly if informed by black adoptees themselves.

Latino Children in the U.S. Child Welfare System

Latino children—including native born children to native born or immigrant parents (64 percent) and foreign born (36 percent), primarily from Mexico, Cuba, the Dominican Republic, and Central and South America—have historically been slightly underrepresented in the child welfare system on a national level. But this trend has shifted in the past two decades, with Latino children now being slightly overrepresented in the child welfare population. For instance, in 2000 Latino children represented about 14 percent of the child welfare population while they represented just over 15 percent of the U.S. population, but by 2007 Latino children represented just over 20 percent of the child welfare population (Dettlaff & Earner, 2012; Dettlaff, Earner, & Phillips, 2009). On a state-by-state basis Latino children are significantly overrepresented in at least six states, particularly border states with a higher Latino population.

There is very little research on inter-group differences within the broader Latino population, but this should not be interpreted as there being complete homogeneity between the various country-of-origin sub-populations, or between native and foreign born children. The research that does exist reveals differences in the demographic characteristics and nature of maltreatment between native born and immigrant children. For instance, native children were more likely to be emotionally and physically abused, as well as have neglectful supervision, while immigrant children were more likely to be emotionally and sexually abused, as well as experience far higher rates of family stress. Additionally, immigrant children were far more likely to be living in a two-parent home with at least one grandparent also residing in the home (Dettlaff & Earner, 2014). A new demographic trend includes Latino immigrant children who come across the border alone. These unaccompanied migrant youth represent a rather small percentage of the total Latino child welfare population, but they are a group worth noting because their numbers are increasing, they tend to be highly traumatized with complex needs, and they have little to no in-country social support (Frydman, Dallam, & Bookey, 2014).

Risk factors for abuse in native Latino families involved in the child welfare system include alcohol abuse, drug abuse, poor parenting skills, domestic violence, excessive discipline, a history of child maltreatment, a recent arrest, low social support, high family stress, and difficulty meeting children's basic needs. Risk factors in immigrant families include alcohol abuse, poor parenting skills, domestic violence, excessive discipline, a history of child maltreatment, low social support, high family stress (often related to their immigration experience), and difficulty meeting children's basic needs. With regard to community risk factors, **native-born** families are far more likely to live in unsafe neighborhoods with high crime rates and with large numbers of unsupervised teens compared to immigrant families (Dettlaff & Earner, 2012).

Latinos in general have a number of cultural strengths that child welfare professionals can tap into when working with Latino families involved in the child welfare system. For instance, culturally, Latino families tend to have very close attachments to their children, have strong connections to their community, and have strong intergenerational ties and family-centered traditions. Additionally, although the stereotype of the Latino culture is that it is patriarchal in nature, the reality is that many subcultures within the larger Latino culture, such as Puerto Ricans, have a long history of feminism (CASCW, 2014).

Child welfare professionals using a strengths-based approach and who are appropriately trained can draw on these cultural values and traditions when working with Latino families, providing culturally congruent services. Another important factor relates to the history of trauma many Latino families and children experience, primarily as a part of their immigration experience. Thus, it's highly beneficial for child welfare workers working with Latino families to be trauma-informed so that they can both recognize and appropriately respond to acute and chronic trauma within their caseloads of migrant populations (Igelman, Conradi, & Ryan, 2007).

Indigenous Populations and the U.S. Child Welfare System

References to U.S. **indigenous populations** often conjure up images of a cohesive and homogeneous group of "American Indians" who share a single culture, yet there are 566 federally recognized tribes within the United States, each with their own language, culture, and traditions. There is considerable controversy surrounding the correct name to use to refer to indigenous populations that reflects their distinct nature without grouping all under one umbrella. For instance, while the term **Native American** is popular, particularly among journalists, politicians, and academics, typically Native Hawaiian and other Pacific Islanders (NHPIs) are not included, and although Alaskan Native tribal entities are federally recognized, often anecdotal considerations of Native American tribes and cultures do not include Alaskan Natives.

The British colonization of North America involved an organized and methodical campaign by European settlers and then later by the U.S. government to decimate mainland Native American populations and culture. This was done through invasion, trickery (such as trading land for alcohol), and ultimately the forced relocation of all Native Americans onto government-designated reservations, where the assimilation into the majority culture became a primary goal of the U.S. government (Brown, 2001). The few Native Americans who survived this genocide were broken physically, emotionally, and spiritually, and many suffered from alcoholism, rampant unemployment, and debilitating depression.

In the early part of the 19th century the U.S. government assumed full responsibility for educating Native American children. It is estimated that from the early 1800s through the early part of the 20th century, virtually all Native American children were

Native Americans in a mathematics class at Indian School, Carlisle, Pennsylvania

Watch this video on the sexual abuse of children on Native American reservations. How do you think Native autonomy can be balanced with appropriate intervention strategies that can keep children safe?

ENHANCEDetext *video example 5.4*

www.youtube.com/
watch?v=ctnGWQPW6Nc

forcibly removed from their homes on the reservations and placed in Indian boarding schools, where they were prohibited from speaking in their native tongues, practicing their cultural religion, or wearing their traditional dress. During school breaks many of these children were placed as servants in Caucasian homes rather than being allowed to return home for visits. The result of this forced assimilation amounted to cultural genocide where an entire generation of Native Americans was institutionalized, deprived of a relationship with their biological families, and robbed of their cultural heritage.

The ongoing campaign to assimilate Native Americans into Eurocentric white American culture became even more aggressive between 1950 and 1970, when social workers with governmental backing removed thousands of Native American children from their homes on the reservations for alleged maltreatment, placing them in adoptive Caucasian homes. In reality, many of the problems on the reservations were the product of years of governmental oppression resulting in extreme poverty and other commonly associated social ills. The U.S. government's response to this was to tear Native American families apart rather than intervene with mental health services and family preservation programs.

Between 1941 and 1978, approximately 70 percent of all Native American children were removed from their homes and placed either in orphanages or with adoptive Caucasian families (Marr, 2002). In truth, few of these children were removed from their homes due to maltreatment as it is currently defined. Rather, approximately 99 percent of these children were removed because social workers believed that the children were victims of social deprivation due to the extreme poverty common on most Indian reservations (U.S. Senate, 1974). The result of this government action has been nothing short of complete social devastation. Native Americans have one of the highest suicide rates in the nation, with Native American youth, particularly those who have spent time in U.S. boarding schools, having on average five to six times the rate of suicide compared to the non-Native American population. When these children graduated from high school, they were adults without a culture—no longer feeling comfortable on the reservation after years of being negatively indoctrinated against their cultural heritage, yet not being accepted by the white population either. The response of many of these individuals was to turn to alcohol in an attempt to drown out the pain and sense of alienation. The Indian Child Welfare Act of 1978 (Pub. L. No. 95-608) has for the most part stemmed the tide of mass removal of thousands of Native American children from their homes on the reservations. However, unfortunately many caseworkers still do not understand the reason why such a bill was passed in the first place, or why it is necessary, and mistakenly believe that this act hampers placing needy children in loving homes.

Overall Native American families experience disproportionately high rates of poverty, alcohol and substance abuse, and health problems. Native American children experience neglect and physical abuse at higher than average rates, and Native American children on reservations experience excessively high rates of sexual abuse and assault, with lower than average rates of criminal justice intervention. Child welfare professionals are faced with complex challenges, including broken family systems, tribal corruption, remote and isolated communities, chronic and intergenerational substance abuse, domestic violence, and poverty-related stressors. Culturally appropriate intervention strategies can address these complexities in a way that honors and reflects cultural traditions and values.

Native Hawaiians and Other Pacific Islanders

Native Hawaiians and Other Pacific Islanders (NHPIs) consist of a group of diverse people indigenous to the State of Hawaii and the U.S. territories of American Samoa and Guam, with Polynesian, Micronesian, and Melanesian backgrounds. There are approximately 1.2 million NHPIs living in the United States, constituting .05 percent of the U.S. population. While the majority of NHPIs reside in Hawaii, other states with high NHPI populations include California, Washington, and Florida. NHPIs are the fastest growing and most diverse racial groups in the United States.

NHPIs generally experience poorer health than other cultural groups in the United States, with higher than average rates of alcohol consumption, smoking, obesity, and diabetes. They also have the highest rates of cancer than any other U.S. cultural group and have the second highest rates of HIV infection, and have the second shortest survival rate (White House, n.d.). NHPIs also experience higher than average poverty rates and higher than average levels of family stress related to social conditions and histories of mistreatment and bias. They also experience disproportionate rates of poverty, barriers to educational opportunities, and quality health care (Communities, 2014).

All of these factors impact family systems and increase vulnerability to becoming involved in the child welfare system. While the overall numbers of NHPI children involved in the child welfare system is small, they are overrepresented in all aspects of the child welfare system, including the juvenile justice system, particularly in Hawaii (Fong, Dettlaff, James, & Rodriguez, 2014; OHA, 2010; Okamoto, 2011). Additionally, NHPIs experience disproportionate rates of incarceration, which also has implications for children and the child welfare system (OHA, 2010). These issues are actively being addressed with the human services and broader advocacy communities. However, the complex nature of the dynamics involved, the overt and covert racial bias and discrimination, along with the highly diverse nature of the NHPI population, creates a challenging situation for child welfare professionals that can only be addressed through extensive culturally-based training and a multi-pronged approach that pairs case management, counseling, and advocacy on a micro and macro level.

Alaska Natives

Alaska Natives consist of 13 federally recognized tribes of people indigenous to the State of Alaska. Although many Alaskan Natives are genetically similar to Native Americans in mainland United States and South America, their histories of migration, cultures, and treatment by Russian and European settlers and the U.S. government are somewhat different. Similar to other indigenous populations, Alaskan Natives have a long history dating back to the 1700s of oppression, marginalization, exploitation, and annihilation, including being treated as servants and slaves and losing their land to Russia and later American ruling powers. Also similar to mainland Native Americans, in an attempt to raise their status, Alaskan Natives were historically not allowed to practice their native traditions or speak their native languages.

Many Alaskan Natives fought against such treatment and attempts to rob them of their culture. While many of the remaining tribes remain strongly attached to their cultural traditions, the impact of centuries of mistreatment has resulted in a range of problems within their social structure and family systems, resulting in, among other dynamics, an overrepresentation in the child welfare system. In fact, children from Alaska are twice as likely to be placed in foster care than children from other states, with

Watch this video on the incidence of gender-based violence in Alaska. What are some intervention strategies you believe might work with this population? ENHANCEDetext *video example 5.5*

www.youtube.com/
watch?v=Lly7YffJJZE

Alaska Native children being seven times more likely to be in foster care than non-native children (Vadapalli, Hanna, & Passini, 2014). Native Alaskan children are physically and sexually abused at significantly higher rates than the rest of the population. Girls are particularly vulnerable to rape and other forms of violence and abuse, exacerbated by excessively high rates of alcohol abuse, long dark winters, and a culture of secrecy.

A unique challenge facing child welfare professionals in Alaska is the remote location of many of the tribes, which makes regular visits and the offer of support difficult. But research clearly shows that, historically, child welfare caseworkers showed a lack of the cultural integrity of Alaskan Natives by removing children from tribal lands despite members of the community being willing to care for them (Rieger & Kandel, 1999). More recent macro interventions focus on social justice issues and cultural rights of Alaskan Natives as autonomous people who continue to suffer the consequences of mistreatment by the majority white culture. As with other indigenous people, child welfare professionals working with these populations must be appropriately trained so they can provide culturally congruent services that allow native children to remain within their communities whenever possible.

ENHANCEDetext *self-check 5.5*

CONCLUSION

Human service professionals who work with families in crisis have the opportunity to effect change that positively affects not only the currently involved families, but all future generations within that family system as well. Child welfare caseworkers often experience high caseloads and can feel overwhelmed and burned out in the face of such immensely complicated dynamics commonly involved in child welfare cases.

An increased focus on family preservation programs and other early intervention programs offer the best opportunity for reducing out-of-home placements, but these programs must be offered to all potentially appropriate families without bias. This can occur through sufficient federal and state funding of child welfare programs and the effective recruitment and training of human service professionals willing to work with a variety of families, from various cultures dealing with a wide range of life challenges.

SUMMARY

- The ways in which children were treated historically in the United States, with a particular focus on children from marginalized populations, are examined. The treatment of children since Colonial times, including how poor, migrant, and children of color were abused and exploited within the labor market, as well as how orphaned and children without parental care were managed and cared for, are explored.
- The role and function of the human services professional in the current U.S. child welfare system are analyzed. The structure and purpose of the U.S. child welfare system, with a particular focus on the role and function of human services professionals working within each phase of the child welfare system process is explored.

- The various ways that child abuse investigations are initiated and managed are assessed. The child abuse investigation process within the U.S. child welfare system within the context of the various types of child maltreatment and abuse is explored.
- The role and function of child welfare professionals working with children in placement and their families are explored. The impact on children of being involved in the child welfare system is explored, with a particular focus on removal, as well as how human services professionals can effectively respond to children in placement.
- The relationship between historic mistreatment of ethnic minority populations and their current involvement in the U.S. child welfare system is analyzed. The disproportionality of children of color in the child welfare system is explored, including the role of racial bias in decision-making and the nature of historic mistreatment of many ethnic minority populations, including African American, Latino, Asian, Native American, Native Hawaiian and other Pacific Islanders, and Alaska Natives.

Internet Resources

Conduct an Internet search for "Concept and History of Permanency in U.S. Child Welfare" on the Child Welfare Information Gateway website.

Conduct an Internet search for "Child Abuse and Neglect" on the Child Welfare Information Gateway website.

Conduct an Internet search for "Position Statements" on transracial adoption and kinship care on the National Association of Black Social Workers website.

Conduct an Internet search for "Orphan Trains" on the Children's Aid Society website.

Conduct an Internet search for an Issue Brief entitled "Immigration and Child Welfare" on the Child Welfare Information Gateway website.

Conduct an Internet search for the "Indian Child Welfare Act" on the National Indian Child Welfare Association website.

References

Addams, J. (1912). Twenty Years at Hull House; with autobiographical notes. Kindle Edition.

Alderman, C.L. (1975). *Colonists for sale: The story of indentured servants in America*. New York, NY: Macmillan.

Austin, M. J., D'Andrade, A., Lemon, K., Benton, A., Chow, B., & Reyes, C. (2005). *Risk and safety assessment in child welfare: Instrument comparisons*. University of California, Berkeley, School of Social Welfare (BASSC), 2, 1–16. Retrieved from http://cssr.berkeley.edu/bassc/public/risk_summ.pdf

Barth, R. P. (2001). Policy implications of foster family characteristics. *Family Relations, 50*(1), 16–19.

Bellingham, B. (1984). *Little wanderers: A socio-historical study of the nineteenth century origins of child fostering and adoption reform, based on early records of the New York Children's Aid Society*. Unpublished doctoral dissertation, University of Pennsylvania. (Available from University Microfilm Incorporated (UMI), Ann Arbor, MI.)

Belzberg, E. (Director). (2001). *The forgotten children underground* [Docudrama]. Childhope International.

Bender, T. (1975). *Toward an urban vision: Ideas and institutions in nineteenth century America*. Baltimore, MD: The John Hopkins University Press, 1975.

Bentovim, A. (2002). Preventing sexually abused young people from becoming batterers, and treating the victimization experiences of young people who offend sexually. *Child Abuse & Neglect, 26*(6–7), 661–678.

Bentovim, A. (2004). Working with abusing families: General issues and a systemic perspective. *Journal of Family Psychotherapy, 15*(1–2), 119–135.

Bourg, W., Broderick, R., & Flagor, R. (1999). *A child interviewer's guidebook*. Thousand Oaks, CA: Sage Publications.

Boyd, R. (2014). African American disproportionality and disparity in child welfare: Toward a comprehensive conceptual framework. *Children and Youth Services Review, 37*, 15–27.

Brace, C. L. (1967). *The dangerous classes of New York and twenty years work among them.* Montclair, NJ: Patterson Smith.

Brown, D. (2001). *Bury my heart at wounded knee: An Indian history of the American west.* New York, NY: Henry Holt and Company.

Burns, B. J., Phillips, S. D., Wagner, H. R., Barth, R. P., Kolko, D.J., Campbell, Y., et al. (2004). Mental health need and access to mental health services by youths involved with child welfare: A national survey. *Journal of the American Academy of Child & Adolescent Psychiatry, 43*(8), 960–970.

CAPTA Reauthorization Act of 2010 (P.L. 111-320). Retrieved from http://www.govtrack.us/congress/bills/111/s3817/text

Child Welfare League of America. (n.d.). Family preservation services factsheet. Retrieved from http://66.227.70.18/programs/familypractice/fampresfactsheet.htm

Child Welfare League of America [CWLA]. (2002). Minorities as majority: Disproportionality in child welfare and juvenile justice. *Children's Voice.* Retrieved from http://www.cwla.org/articles/cv0211minorities.htm

Child Welfare League of America [CWLA]. (2005). *A comparison of approaches to risk assessment in child protection and brief summary of issues identified from research on assessment in related fields.* Retrieved from http://www.childwelfare.gov/responding/iia/safety_risk/

Center for the Advanced Studies in Child Welfare [CASCW]. (2014). Latino cultural guide building capacity to strengthen the well-being of immigrant families and their children: A prevention strategy. Retrieved from http://cascw.umn.edu/wp-content/uploads/2014/02/CulturalGuide-Latino.pdf

Communities, E. P. I. (2014). Native Hawaiians and Pacific Islanders in the United States: A community of contrasts. Los Angeles, CA: Empowering Pacific Islander Communities. Retrieved from http://empoweredpi.org/wp-content/uploads/2014/06/A_Community_of_Contrasts_NHPI_US_2014-1.pdf

Condran, G. A., & Cheney, R. A. (1982). Mortality trends in Philadelphia: Age and cause-specific death rates 1870–1930. *Demography, 19*(1), 97–123.

Denby, R. W., & Curtis, C. M. (2003). Why special populations are not the target of family preservation services: A case for program reform. *Journal of Sociology & Social Welfare, 30*(2), 149–173.

DePanfilis, D., & Scannapieco, M. (1994). Assessing the safety of children at risk of maltreatment: Decision-making models. *Child Welfare, 73*(3), 229–246.

Dettlaff, A. J., & Earner, I. (2012). Children of immigrants in the child welfare system: Characteristics, risk, and maltreatment. Families in Society: The Journal of Contemporary Social Services, 93, 295–303.

Dettlaff, A. J., Earner, I., & Phillips, S. D. (2009). Latino children of immigrants in the child welfare system: Prevalence, characteristics, and risk. *Children and Youth Services Review, 31*(7), 775–783.

Doyle Jr., J. J. (2007). Child protection and child outcomes: Measuring the effects of foster care. *The American Economic Review, 97*(5), 1583–1610.

Ehrensaft, M. K., Cohen, P., & Brown, J. (2003). Intergenerational transmission of partner violence: A 20-year prospective study. *Journal of Consulting & Clinical Psychology, 71*(4), 741–753.

Erikson, E. H. (1963). *Childhood and society* (2nd ed.). New York, NY: W. W. Norton & Co.

Erikson, E. H. (1968). *Identity: Youth and crisis.* London: Faber & Faber.

Erikson, E. H. (1975). *Life history and the historical moment.* New York, NY: Norton.

Fong, R., Dettlaff, A., James, J., & Rodriguez, C. (Eds.). (2014). *Addressing racial disproportionality and disparities in human services: Multisystemic approaches.* Columbia University Press.

Fontes, L. A. (2010). Interviewing immigrant children for suspected child maltreatment. *Journal of Psychiatry & Law, 38*(3), 283–305.

Frydman, L., Dallam, E., & Bookey, B. (2014). A treacherous journey: Child migrants navigating the US immigration system. Center for Gender & Refugee Studies. University of California Hastings College of the Law. Retrieved from http://www.uchastings.edu/centers/cgrsdocs/treacherous_journey_cgrs_kind_report.pdf

Gauthier, Y., Fortin, G., & Jéliu, G. (2004). Clinical application of attachment theory in permanency planning for children in foster care: The importance of continuity of care. *Infant Mental Health Journal, 25*(4), 379–396.

Goldman, J., & Salus, M. (2003). *A coordinated response to child abuse and neglect: The foundation for practice.* Washington, DC: U.S. Department of Health and Human Services, National Center on Child Abuse and Neglect.

Hewitt, S. K. (1999). *Assessing allegations of sexual abuse in preschool children: Understanding small voices.* Thousand Oaks, CA: Sage Publications.

Holt, M. (1992). *The Orphan Trains: Placing out in America.* Lincoln, NE: University of Nebraska Press.

Igelman, R., Conradi, L., & Ryan, B. (2007). Creating a trauma-informed child welfare system [Electronic version]. *Focal Point, 21*(1), 23–26.

Katz, M. B. (1996). *In the shadow of the poorhouse: A social history of welfare in America*. New York, NY: Basic Books.

Kellow, M. (1984). Indentured Servitude in Eighteenth-Century Maryland. *Histoire sociale/Social History, 17*(34).

Kopel, S., Charlton, T., & Well, S. J. (2003). Investigation laws and practices in child protective services. *Child Welfare, 82*(6), 661–684.

Lau, A. S., Litrownik, A. J., Newton, R. R., & Landsverk, J. (2003). Going home: The complex effects of reunification on internalizing problems among children in foster care. *Journal of Abnormal Child Psychology, 31*(4), 345–358.

Lee, R. E., & Whiting, J. B. (2007). Foster children's expressions of ambiguous loss. *American Journal of Family Therapy, 35*, 417–428.

Marr, C. (2002). Assimilation through education: Indian boarding schools in the Pacific Northwest. Seattle, WA: University of Washington Libraries Digital Collections Retrieved from http://content.lib.washington.edu/aipnw/marr/marr.html

Martin, M. (2016). Why our grown-up need for stability isn't always good. Huffington Post. Retrieved from http://www.huffingtonpost.com/michelle-martin/grown-up-need-for-stability_b_8918014.html?.

Martin, M. (2014). Advocacy for social justice: Local and global implications. Upper Saddle River, NJ: Pearson Publishing.

Mathews, T.J., MacDorman, M.F., Thorna, M.E. (2015). Infant mortality statistics from the 2013 period linked birth/infant death data set. National vital statistics report, 64, 9. Hyattsville, MD. National Center for Health Statistics.

McWey, L., & Mullis, A. K. (2004). Improving the lives of children in foster care: The impact of supervised visitation. *Family Relations: Interdisciplinary Journal of Applied Family Studies, 53*(3), 293–300.

Morgan, K., Dorgan, K., & Hayne, H. (2013). Body maps do not facilitate older children's report of touch. *Scandinavian Journal of Psychology, 54*(1), 51–55.

National Association of Black Social Workers. (2003). *Kinship care.* Retrieved from http://www.nabsw.org/mserver/KimshipCare.aspx?menuContext=760

National Clearinghouse on Child Abuse and Neglect. (2005). *Definition of child abuse and neglect state statutes.* Series 2005. U.S. Department of Health and Human Services, Administration for Children & Families. Retrieved from http://www.childwelfare.gov/systemwide/laws_policies/statutes/define.cfm

National Indian Child Welfare Association (NICWA). (n.d.). Indian Child Welfare Act of 1978. Retrieved from http://www.nicwa.org/Indian_Child_Welfare_Act/

Newcomb, M., Locke, D., & Thomas, F. (2001). Intergenerational cycle of maltreatment: A popular concept obscured by methodological limitations. *Child Abuse & Neglect, 25*(9), 1219–1240.

Office of Hawaiian Affairs [OHA]. (2010). The Disparate Treatment of Native Hawaiians in the Criminal Justice System. Retrieved from http://www.justicepolicy.org/uploads/justicepolicy/documents/10-09_exs_disparatetreatmentofnativehawaiians_rd-ac.pdf

Okamoto, S. K. (2011). Current and future directions in social work research with Native Hawaiians and other Pacific Islanders. *Journal of Ethnic & Cultural Diversity in Social Work, 20*(2), 93–97.

Patrick, M., Sheets, E., & Trickel, E. (1990). *We are a part of history: The Orphan Trains.* Virginia Beach, VA: The Donning Co.

Pears, K. C., & Capaldi, D. M. (2001). Intergenerational transmission of abuse: A two-generational prospective study of an at-risk sample. *Child Abuse & Neglect, 25*(11), 1439–1461.

Peterson, C., & Biggs, M. (1997). Interviewing children about trauma: Problems with "specific" questions. *Journal of Traumatic Stress, 10*(2), 279–290.

Poole, D. A., & Lindsay, D. S. (1998). Assessing the accuracy of young children's reports: Lessons from the investigation of child sexual abuse. *Applied & Preventive Psychology, 7*(1), 1–26.

Rieger, L., & Kandel, R. (1999). Child welfare and Alaska Native tribal governance: A pilot project in Kake, Alaska—Report of findings.

Roberts, D. (2002). *Shattered bonds: The color of child welfare.* New York, NY: Basic Civitas Books.

Rutter, B. (1978). *The parents' guide to foster family care.* New York, NY: Child Family League of America.

Sanchirico, A., & Jablonka, K. (2000). Keeping foster children connected to their biological parents: The impact of foster parent training and support. *Child and Adolescent Social Work Journal, 17*(3), 185–203.

Schultz, C.B. (1985). Children and childhood in eighteenth century. In Joseph M. Hawes and N. Ray Hiner (Eds.), *American childhood: A research guide and historical handbook* (Vol. 70, pp. 79–80). Westport, CT: Greenwood Press.

Shughart, W. F., & Chappell, W. F. (1999). Fostering the demand for adoptions: An empirical analysis of the impact of orphanages and foster care on adoptions in the U.S. In R. D. McKenzie (Ed.), *Rethinking orphanages for the 21st century* (pp. 151–171). Thousand Oaks, CA: Sage Publishers.

Siu, S., & Hogan, P. T. (1989). Common clinical themes in child welfare. *Social Work, 34*(4), 229–345.

Smith, C. J., & Devore, W. (2004). African American children in the child welfare and kinship system: From exclusion to over inclusion. *Children & Youth Services Review*, 26(5), 427–446.

Smith, D. T., Juarez, B. G., & Jacobson, C. K. (2011). White on Black: Can White parents teach Black adoptive children how to understand and cope with racism? *Journal of Black Studies*, 42(8), 1195–1230.

Spake, A. (1994, November). The little boy who didn't have to die. *McCall's*, p. 142.

Sternberg, K. J., Lamb, M. E., & Orbach, Y. (2001). Use of a structured investigative protocol enhances young children's responses to free-recall prompts in the course of forensic interviews. *Journal of Applied Psychology*, 86(5), 997–1005.

Surbeck, B. C. (2003). An investigation of racial partiality in child welfare assessments of attachment. *American Journal of Orthopsychiatry*, 73(1), 13–23.

The White House. (n.d.). White house initiative on Asian Americans & Pacific Islanders (WHIAAPI) fact sheet: What you should know about Native Hawaiians and Pacific Islanders (NHPI's). Retrieved from https://www2.ed.gov/about/inits/list/asian-americans-initiative/what-you-should-know.pdf

Trattner, W. (1998). *From poor law to welfare state* (6th ed.). New York, NY: Free Press.

U.S. Department of Health & Human Services, Administration for Children and Families, Administration on Children, Youth and Families, Children's Bureau. (2016). Child maltreatment 2014. Retrieved from http://www.acf.hhs.gov/programs/cb/research-data-technology/statistics-research/child-maltreatment

Vadapalli, D., Hanna, V., & Passini, J. (2014). Trends in age, gender, and ethnicity among children in foster care in Alaska. Retrieved from http://www.iser.uaa.alaska.edu/Publications/2014_12-TrendsInAgeGenderAndEthnicityAmongFosterChildrenInAlaska.pdf

Von Hartz, J. (1978). *New York street kids*. New York, NY: Dover.

Warren, A. (1995). *Orphan Train rider: One boy's true story*. Boston, MA: Houghton Mifflin Co.

Woods, S., & Summers, A. (2014). Technical assistance bulletin: Disproportionality rates for children of color in foster care (Fiscal Year 2012). National Council of Juvenile and Family Court Judges: Reno, NV.

6

Adolescent Services

© PIKSELSTOCK / SHUTTERSTOCK

"One second she's curled up in my lap asking me to stroke her hair as she cries about a fight she had with one of her girlfriends, and the next second she's screaming at me, telling me she doesn't need a mother, and that her father and I are ruining her life. She is so dramatic, and her moods shift from moment to moment. She's driving us crazy, and I'm wondering where my sweet little girl went." So complains one of my clients about her 15-year-old daughter. The stage of adolescence is as confusing for adults as it is for adolescents. This stage of development serves as the bridge from childhood to adulthood, and crossing this bridge often involves several circuitous routes that sometimes appear to parents as though no progress toward maturity is being made.

Adolescence is an interesting stage of development for many reasons. The concept of this stage is rather new as there was little acknowledgment or understanding of adolescence as a separate stage of development until the latter part of the 19th century. But even now, when adolescence is accepted as a distinct stage of development, there are significant differences in how the stage of adolescence is perceived among various cultures, both within the United

LEARNING OBJECTIVES

- Evaluate adolescent behavior from a developmental perspective
- Compare and contrast psychosocial challenges and psychological disorders diagnosed in adolescence
- Explore the role and function of human service professionals within practice settings serving the adolescent population
- Evaluate the role of culture in both adolescent behavior and intervention strategies

CHAPTER OUTLINE

States and internationally. In addition, many societal changes have occurred in the last 150 years that have had a dramatic impact on adolescents themselves, creating new dynamics and issues reflected in developmental theories.

ADOLESCENT BEHAVIOR AS VIEWED THROUGH A DEVELOPMENTAL LENS

Considering adolescence as a distinct stage of development is a relatively new phenomenon. G. Stanley Hall conducted the first-ever study of adolescence and published a book about it in 1904, in which he described adolescents as possessing a "lack of emotional steadiness, violent impulses, unreasonable conduct, lack of enthusiasm and sympathy"— behaviors not terribly different than contemporary descriptions (as cited in Demos & Demos, 1969, p. 635).

Of course the stage of adolescence has likely always existed, even prior to its acknowledgement among developmental theorists. However, there have been significant societal changes in the past few hundred years that have influenced how we perceive not only the stages of childhood and adolescence but also the course of development itself. Lifestyles were quite different 200 years ago when the United States was a new country. The U.S. economy was different, livelihoods were different, and families were different. Chief among these various changes is the expectations society has of adolescents—youth between the ages of about 13 and 19 years. Consider that not too long ago, adolescent boys as young as 13 (and sometimes even younger) were expected to work in support of their families, and in past generations a mandatory draft meant that most boys went off to war by the time they turned 18. Just one generation ago it was commonplace for teens to graduate from high school, get married, and start their adult lives before their 20th birthdays. That certainly is not the case now for most adolescents, many of whom are either away in college or living at home attending a local college or working toward establishing their independence.

One of the major driving societal forces that has changed our expectations of adolescents is the economic structure of U.S. society. There is no question that the mass urbanization of the past 200 years has had an impact on individual and family life, including the lives of adolescents. Today, adolescents have far fewer vocational responsibilities and far more responsibility in the academic realm as educational requirements have increased over the years. This shift has not only extended childhood several years but also created a dynamic where teens today spend far more time surrounded by their peers than their family members (Larsen, 2003; National Center for Education Statistics, 1999; Raywid, 1996). Changes in the U.S. economic structure contributed to changes in other realms as well, including family structure and the educational system, each of which has had an impact on the lives of adolescents.

Many theories of development propose that individuals progress through predictable stages of growth, with earlier stages of development serving as foundations for successive stages. One way to better understand the behavior of children and adolescents is to study their developmental patterns within the context of the cognitive, emotional, psychosocial, moral, and even spiritual domains. Having a competent grasp of normative development can be a guide for human service professionals who work with adolescents and must evaluate and assess their behavior before determining the appropriate level of intervention or whether intervention is warranted at all.

Most developmental theorists agree that adolescence is a time of searching for one's identity and developing a sense of autonomy. Trying on different "selves" is a common mental and behavioral activity of adolescents who are in the process of developing an internally anchored sense of who they are rather than defining themselves by what others think or expect of them (including their parents) (Erikson, 1968; Kerpelman & Pittman, 2001). Many normative and healthy adolescents can be quite dramatic and ego-centric in their behavior, and although this might give many parents cause for concern, most adolescents grow out of this stage to become giving and compassionate adults.

There are many developmental theories that describe normative and nonnormative development in adolescents. Erik Erikson's theory of psychosocial development posits that children and adolescents proceed through linear stages where they navigate a psychosocial crisis that leads to either deficits in psychosocial skills or the successful navigation of the crisis. This then serves as a foundation for more advanced challenges related to their psychosocial maturity (Erikson, 1968). Jean Piaget developed a theory of cognitive development where he described the process of intellectual development of children and adolescents, where **abstract reasoning ability** is increasingly developed and relied upon in intellectual functioning (Piaget, 1950).

Watch this video on Jean Piaget's experiment on concrete and abstract reasoning ability. What role does abstract reasoning ability play in adolescent decision-making?
ENHANCEDetext *video example 6.1*

The human services discipline has in recent years shifted away from reliance on **meta-theories**—broad, overarching, and universally applied theories of development and human behavior, such as those posited by Erikson and Piaget. Instead the human services discipline has moved toward evaluating children and adolescents through the lens of key developmental theories to better understand their behavior. No theory can be applied prescriptively to all people, in all eras, from all cultures, since the course of development is influenced by many factors on an individual and on a broader societal level. Thus, it is important to consider the course of developmental growth and maturity of children and adolescents within various contexts. Considering the course of development within physical, cognitive, moral, and psychosocial domains, within various contexts, is consistent with ecological systems theory. In this regard, individuals are evaluated within the context of their environment, ranging from **microsystems**, such as family and friends, to **macrosystems**, such as societal influences.

With regard to *historical context,* it is important to consider the normative aspects of adolescent development. What is expected of an adolescent and what is considered adaptive and healthy behavior depend on what is occurring in the world during the time in which the adolescent lives. A world war with a mandatory draft forces adolescents to grow up quickly, just as the Great Depression shortened childhoods across the country as adolescents were expected to help support their families. Yet, in contemporary society, childhoods are often considered lengthened by a good economy, which reduces the need for adolescent employment and increases educational requirements for professional employment. Adolescents who did not work during the Great Depression would likely have been considered irresponsible for not being willing to assist in the support of their families, but adolescents who do not work in contemporary society are likely presumed to be responsible if they are focused on their academic studies in preparation for college.

It is also important to consider developmental dynamics within a *cultural context.* What is considered normative and emotionally healthy within one culture may be considered maladaptive in another, and what is considered respectful and honorable behavior in one culture may be a sign of an emotional disorder or **maladaptive behavior** in another. For instance, in many cultures, remaining in the family home until marriage is considered the norm. It is common in collectivist cultures, such as Asian, Hispanic/Latino, and even some European cultures, for unmarried adult children as old as 30 years to live at home with their parents. In many of these cultures it would be considered a sign of disrespect for a single adult, particularly a female, to move from the family home to gain independence prior to getting married.

The United States is, for the most part, an individualistic society that values independence and autonomy; thus, many people may perceive that the unmarried 30-year-old male living with his parents has an unhealthy emotional attachment, even **enmeshment**. Considering the cultural background of adolescents on our caseloads, such as their ethnic background, nationality, and religion, can explain a lot, including influences on their development. Examples of these considerations might be how their cultural background informs perspectives about expectations of males and females, whether independence and autonomy are perceived as something positive or negative, and even how individual expression is handled, including which expressions are stigmatized and which are not.

Finally, it is important to consider development within a *regional context*. Although urbanization over the last 200 years within the United States has resulted in the majority of people living in urban centers or suburban communities, rural life still exists in the United States, and some research suggests that there are significant differences between adolescent life in rural communities and adolescent life in urban communities. Although there is not a wide body of research comparing urban and rural adolescents, a study conducted in 2001 found that rural adolescents differed from urban adolescents in that they felt less pressure to become involved in gang activities, were confronted with less violence both on and off campus, and felt less academic pressure from both their school and their parents (Gandara, Gutierrez, & O'Hara, 2001). And yet, other research shows that rural adolescents may not have as much access to mental health services compared to nonrural adolescents (Cummings, Wen, & Ross, 2013), and adolescents who identify as a sexual minority may experience greater stigmatization compared to nonrural adolescents because of conservative attitudes in rural communities (Cohn & Hastings, 2010; Yarbrough, 2004).

Keeping historical context in mind helps human services professionals remember that expectations of the current generation of adolescents are different than adolescents of one or more generations ago. Keeping cultural and regional contexts in mind will assist the human service practitioner in not mischaracterizing certain behaviors because their origin is either misunderstood or not valued by the majority culture. It may also help provide context for other behaviors, such as when the adolescent is reluctant to disclose family information because of cultural or religious influences that value privacy, or the adolescent avoids direct eye contact not because they are being evasive or dishonest, but because their culture interprets direct eye contact with authority figures a sign of disrespect.

ENHANCEDetext *self-check 6.1*

COMMON PSYCHOSOCIAL CHALLENGES AND PSYCHOLOGICAL DISORDERS DIAGNOSED IN ADOLESCENCE

The common stereotype of adolescents being generally rebellious and out of control is both true and untrue. Many adolescents are quite responsible and do not have mental health problems. But adolescence is a time of stress; a time of trying on different "selves"; and of exploring undiscovered issues, attitudes, and behaviors. Most developmental theorists consider this time in one's life to be transitional, and typically all transitional times can be stormy. There are many dynamics unique to this transitional stage that renders adolescence unique among the various developmental stages of life, which in turn have an impact on service delivery and intervention strategies.

Piaget's theory of cognitive development is still the dominant theory of intellectual development. Among Piaget's many findings is his discovery that children, adolescents, and adults each think differently. Most notably, Piaget discovered that younger children think concretely, meaning that they lack the ability to understand many adult concepts, such as metaphors and analogies, as well as other abstract concepts. If a group of adults were asked what it meant to "let the chips fall where they may," they will most likely explain that this is an idiom meaning to let things happen naturally. But if a group of children were asked what this statement meant, they would most likely reply that one should not pick up chips that have fallen on the ground.

Piaget (1950) believed that as children approached adolescence, they began to develop the ability for logical reasoning involved in abstract thought. Abstract thought or reasoning enables us to have empathy by putting ourselves in someone else's shoes. It allows us to think metaphorically, to understand sarcasm, to deduce, to analyze, to synthesize, and to rationalize. Abstract reasoning allows us to understand, and thus internalize, moral standards—to not just know that something is wrong, but to understand *why* it is wrong. If children at the age of five are asked why it is wrong to hit another child on the playground, they might state that it is wrong because they will get in trouble. But most adults would be able to explain that this act is wrong because it violates another person's personal rights, that violence does not resolve conflict, and that they would not want to be hit, even if someone were angry with them. This type of reasoning requires empathy, the ability to see situations from multiple perspectives, the ability to learn from past experiences, and the ability to connect the immediacy of hitting someone to the generalized concept of violence, and then to the possible consequences, both internal and external—all of which require abstract reasoning ability.

It is through the development of abstract reasoning ability that adolescents discover that their parents might not always be right, that lying can be rationalized, that breaking the rules can sometimes be fun, and that authority can be questioned. When a child asks, "Why?" the question usually relates to why the sky is blue or why they can't eat candy for dinner. But when adolescents ask, "Why?" it often relates to asking why sexting is discouraged among minors, why certain drugs are illegal and others are not, why war exists, and even existential questions such as whether God is real or why they were put on this earth. Abstract reasoning is a useful and powerful intellectual tool but can at times be rather destructive in the hands of an emotionally unstable and angry adolescent. Existential questions about the meaning of life can quickly spiral into questioning why one should exist at all, and questions about the concept of authority can quickly evolve into abandoning the concept of obeying authority altogether.

Disruptive, Impulse-Control, and Conduct Disorders

Casually defined, adolescent **acting out behavior** can include any behavior that is marked by opposition to standard rules, either within the family or within society in general. Determining what specifically constitutes acting out behavior, though, can be a bit more challenging and often depends on current social mores, as well as one's own personal value system. Behaviors that involve outright destruction and the breaking of laws are easily characterized as rebellious. But whether the more subtle challenging of rules is considered acting out is certainly in the eye of the beholder, where one person's rebellion is another person's sign of autonomy and individuation. For instance, most would agree that behaviors such as taking illegal drugs, habitual lying, and engaging in chronic truancy are rebellious behaviors, but what about the occasional drinking of alcohol or the intermittent breaking of a curfew? Many mental health experts and even some parents might normalize this behavior as being typical of the majority of adolescents who are striving for increased independence and testing limits along the way. In general, though, any behavior in adolescents should be considered potentially maladaptive if it interferes with normal functioning and causes problems in the adolescent's everyday life. For instance, adolescents who skip one day of school in an entire year would not be considered "rebellious," but adolescents who are truant several times per week, thereby affecting their ability to pass their classes, would likely be characterized as acting out through rebellious behavior.

When acting out moves beyond normative rebellion then an adolescent may meet the criteria for conduct disorder (CD) and oppositional defiant disorder (ODD), which are disorders diagnosed during adolescence to describe problems in emotional and behavioral self-control. CD, the more serious of these two disorders, involves a consistent pattern of behaviors in which social norms and rules are habitually broken and the rights of others are consistently violated without regard for the other person's feelings. To avoid a child being diagnosed with CD in response to uncharacteristic or minor acting out, children cannot receive this diagnosis unless they meet at least three of the four criteria in the preceding 12-month period. The criteria relate to the expression of aggression toward people or animals, the destruction of property, deceitfulness, and serious violation of rules (APA, 2013).

Again, what most often determines the difference between the adolescents who are harmlessly spreading their wings and adolescents with CD is the *frequency, persistence,* and *seriousness* of the maladaptive behaviors. A 12-year-old who "runs away" to the next-door neighbor's house or a 16-year-old who breaks curfew by 30 minutes on just a few occasions would certainly not be diagnosed with CD. But a 12-year-old who runs away for weeks at a time or a 16-year-old who comes home whenever he pleases certainly might.

ODD is another psychological disorder commonly diagnosed during adolescence and is characterized by a milder set of behavioral problems, including negative, hostile, and defiant behavior such as losing one's temper, arguing with adults, and consistently refusing to obey rules. Other criteria include blaming others for personal mistakes, being easily annoyed, frequent feelings of anger and resentment, spite, and vindictiveness. Intermittent explosive disorder (IED) is characterized by sporadic and unprovoked episodes of explosive anger during late childhood and adolescence. The anger can be either physical or verbal (the latter was added in the *DSM-5*). In order to meet the criteria for IED, the angry outbursts must be impulsive in nature, relatively frequent, and cause considerable distress and impairment. This criteria helps clinicians distinguish IED from more normative and intermittent temper tantrums (particularly in children and younger adolescents).

Because human service professionals always evaluate the mental health of individuals within the context of their environment, it is vital to examine any potential environmental causes or influences of an adolescent's maladaptive behavior so that errors are not made in the assessment process and so that a more holistic picture of the adolescent's personal dynamics and situation can be drawn. For instance, socioeconomic status, gender, parenting styles, environment, genetic influences, cognitive deficits, and temperament have all been associated with juvenile delinquency (Lahey, Moffitt, & Caspi, 2003). It is important to note that although such research indicates some type of a relationship between behavioral disorders and these various influences, they do not specify whether any of these variables cause conduct disorders in adolescents. Thus, it would be incorrect to assume that adolescents from lower socioeconomic backgrounds will automatically engage in juvenile delinquency. It may be that families that are chaotic, perhaps even abusive, are likely to be from a lower socioeconomic level because such behaviors are often not amenable to the skill sets required to be a high wage earner, or perhaps there is a third variable that contributes to both dynamics (economic challenges and juvenile delinquency), such as substance abuse, violence or structural variables, racism, and oppression.

I have worked with adolescents for years—first in a residential setting, then in a school setting, and later in a private practice. In my experiences I found that adolescents typically act out for a reason. Evaluating the entire picture is extremely important, as many children and adolescents who meet the criteria for CD, ODD, and IED are expressing signs of earlier abuse, neglect, and general chaos in the home environment (Frick, 2004). In general, if children and adolescents cannot talk out their feelings, they will be more likely to act them out, often in a negative manner. Thus, if adolescents have neither the opportunity nor the maturity to connect their feelings with their behaviors, they will be at greater risk of expressing negative feelings in destructive ways.

Depression and Anxiety in Adolescence

Everyone experiences depression from time to time, but when feelings of sadness become so pronounced and long-standing that these emotions become barriers to normal functioning, the adolescent may be suffering from clinical depression, also referred to as major depressive disorder. The *DSM-5* lists several criteria for major depressive disorder, including abnormally depressed mood; loss of interest and pleasure; inappropriate guilt; disturbances in sleep, appetite, energy level, memory, and concentration; and, in serious cases, frequent thoughts of suicide. In children and adolescents sadness and melancholy can often appear as irritability, which can lead to confusion in diagnosing the appropriate disorder because an irritable teenager can look far more oppositional than a sad or melancholy one. Depression can be caused by many things, including life events (such as the death of a loved one or a trauma), biological factors, and various emotional struggles that cause enduring symptoms and significant impairment in the adolescent's life and level of functioning.

The **comorbidity** of depression and anxiety is quite high, with approximately 80 percent of those with depression also suffering from anxiety of some type (Cummings, Caporino, & Kendall, 2014; Gorwood, 2004). Although anxiety has a completely different set of diagnostic criteria, if one examines the possible origin of mood disorders, then it makes sense that the emotional issues that can make someone feel depressed are likely to cause anxiety as well. There are many treatments for depression and anxiety, ranging from counseling to drug therapy. However, working with adolescents is a special challenge because adolescents can be impulsive, dramatic, and self-centered as a normative part of development, but a depressed adolescent who is impulsive, dramatic, and self-centered can create a dangerous situation because of an increased risk of suicide.

Girl cuts arm with knife blade

Nonsuicidal Self-Injury Disorder

Another way that some adolescents deal with their problems is by turning their emotions inward. For instance, adolescents experiencing depression and anxiety may manifest many self-destructive behaviors, the most serious being suicide. But there are many other self-destructive behaviors that emotionally disturbed adolescents may engage in that, although certainly not as serious as suicide, still warrant serious clinical intervention. One of these types of behaviors is called nonsuicidal self-injury (NSSI) and involves the deliberate attempt to hurt oneself without suicidal intent (Nock & Prinstein, 2005). NSSI (also referred to as deliberate self-harm) can involve scratching, cutting, and burning oneself, typically on the arms and legs, but can also include head banging. NSSI is thought to occur when someone shifts emotional pain to physical pain because it is perceived to be more easily managed (Hicks & Hinck, 2009).

NSSI used to be considered a component of borderline personality disorder (BPD). However, the *DSM-5* includes it as a separate disorder, but in the section containing disorders in need of further studies. This is a positive step since many clinicians recognized that NSSI occurred in populations that did not also experience BPD. Once further research studies have been conducted on the nature of NSSI then diagnostic criteria can be further defined and presumably NSSI can be included as a distinct diagnostic category.

NSSI typically, begins in early adolescence between the ages of 12 and 14, peaking in middle adolescence, and declining in adulthood. Just under 7 percent of the general adolescent population engages in NSSI, compared to 40 percent of the psychiatric inpatient adolescent population (Hamza & Willoughby, 2013). Additionally, approximately 40 percent of college students have admitted to engaging in some type of self-injury (Whitlock, Purington, & Gershkovich, 2009). The majority of adolescents who engage in NSSI do so quite frequently and in time may become desensitized to the pain (Turner, Chapman, & Layden, 2012). There are many negative consequences of NSSI, including physical consequences such as infection and scarring. Social consequences can include scrutiny and rejection by peers, family members, and even health care workers. In fact, some health care workers stigmatize adolescents who self-harm, believing they are manipulative and attention seeking (Cohen, 2014; Law, Rostill-Brookes, & Goodman, 2009).

The precise reasons why adolescents engage in NSSI behaviors is unknown, but NSSI has been associated with various emotional and psychological problems, including depression and anxiety, eating disorders, chronic feelings of hopelessness and despair, sexual abuse, physical abuse, severe emotional abuse, perfectionism, and a pervasive sense of loneliness (Nock & Prinstein, 2005). The National Institute of Mental Health (NIMH) estimates that approximately 50 to 60 percent of adolescents who cut themselves were sexually abused as children (Crowe & Bunclark, 2000). Many adolescents who engage in NSSI cite many reasons for physically harming themselves, including the belief that the cutting or burning allows them to feel something in the midst of emotional numbness. NSSI is difficult to treat because it can become a habit, and those who engage in this type of behavior have difficulty controlling the urge to self-abuse, particularly because the body develops a tolerance to the pain and can become addicted to the endorphins that are released when tissue is damaged (Cohen, 2014; The Cornell Research Program on Self-Injury and Recovery, 2013).

A human service professional will likely encounter adolescent clients who engage in NSSI in a variety of practice settings, including adolescent residential facilities, group homes, foster homes, schools, and any other settings where adolescents are served. It is important that clinicians always be on the lookout for common warning signs of self-injury, even if the adolescent or the parents deny the behavior. Adolescents who self-mutilate for attention will often flaunt their "work" by showing off what frequently amounts to superficial cuts on the forearm or thighs. But serious self-mutilators will often hide their wounds; thus, a human service professional would be wise to note suspicious behaviors, such as consistently wearing long sleeves and pants, even on warm days. More obvious signs of **self-injury** may include parallel scars on the forearm or thighs, burn marks in these same places or even on the fingertips, or any unexplained or suspicious wound, particularly wounds that tend not to heal (due to chronic reinjury).

The most successful treatment programs include a combination of individual, group, and family therapy with the goal of increasing the adolescent's personal insight and awareness of the dynamics underlying the compulsion to self-injure. Issues such as **impulse control** and **emotional regulation** are paramount in any successful treatment plan, as is assisting the adolescent client in learning how to understand and effectively manage intense or uncomfortable emotions in a direct manner. This approach will allow self-abusive adolescents to own their emotions, rather than deny or suppress them.

Watch this video on the case of Sarah, who is engaging in deliberate self-harm, and reflect on how you might respond to Sarah if she were your client.

ENHANCEDetext *video example 6.2*

Suicide and Suicidal Ideation

Suicide involves the intentional ending of one's life, whereas suicidal ideation involves the process of thinking about and considering suicide, which may or may not lead to the actual killing of oneself. Of particular interest to social scientists and mental health practitioners is discovering how to most effectively prevent suicide attempts. Adolescents are at particularly high risk of suicide and **suicidal ideation** for several reasons, including their propensity for impulsivity, the turbulence common in adolescence, as well as their frequent feelings of omnipotence in the sense that they often do not believe bad things can actually happen to them.

Suicides are increasing among the general population, and as of 2013 suicide was the second leading cause of death among adolescents and young adults, with about 5,400 suicide attempts by kids in grades 7th to 12th grade (Kann, Kinchen, et al., 2014). Adolescent suicidal behavior can include suicidal gestures, suicide attempts, serious suicide attempts, and suicide completions. Each of these behaviors can result in a completed suicide, even if that is not the intention of the adolescent, but it is important to distinguish between each of these types of suicidal behavior for the purposes of intervention, as well as developing an understanding of what goes on in the mind of an adolescent who engages in any type of suicidal behavior.

A **suicidal gesture** typically involves behavior on the part of an adolescent that is unlikely to result in a completed suicide, but is more often a cry for help or attention. Even if practitioners do not believe that their adolescent clients actually wish to kill themselves, these gestures should not be taken lightly because it is possible that adolescents will kill themselves even if death wasn't the intended outcome. Certainly the most serious of all suicidal behaviors involve actions that are intended to end one's life.

As with the adult population, it is not necessarily the adolescents who scream their suicidal intentions from the rooftop whom clinicians need to be the most concerned about, but the sad, hopeless, and depressed adolescents who quietly slink away, without drawing any attention, determined to kill themselves, in a manner that precludes intervention. Fortunately, not all serious suicide attempts are successful. Some adolescents experience a last-minute change of heart and call a family member or friend, reach out to a suicide hotline, or call 9-1-1.

The types of adolescents who attempt suicide tend to be different than those who complete suicide. For instance, research indicates that about 85 percent of "attempters" are female (Andrus et al., 1991), whereas about 80 percent of "completers" are male (Arias, Anderson, Kung, Murphy, & Kochanek, 2003). Reasons for this might be related to the social acceptance of males completing suicide rather than making an attempt (Moskos, Achilles, & Gray, 2004). Other reasons may relate to the ways in which males and females attempt suicide, such as the male tendency to use lethal methods, such as guns, and the tendency for women to use less lethal methods, such as drugs (Vörös, Osváth, & Fekete, 2004).

Recognizing whether an adolescent is at real risk of attempting suicide or is experiencing suicidal ideation is an important clinical skill that develops with education and experience. One of the most intimidating issues facing any human service professional is knowing how to predict suicidal behavior. How do we know for sure that a client is going to commit suicide? The answer to that question is that we don't. But there are indicators and precursors that practitioners can look for in helping to render the best possible clinical judgments, such as recognizing the **psychosocial risk factors** often associated with increased suicide risk. Rutter and Behrendt (2004) conducted a study of 100 at-risk adolescents, focusing on psychosocial risk factors. Their research revealed that those adolescents who were plagued by feelings of hopelessness, had little to no social support, had feelings of hostility, and had a negative self-concept were at the greatest risk for attempting suicide.

Other risk factors for suicide include having a friend commit suicide, and for males, having a gun available was a significant risk factor and for females, low self-esteem. Research also showed that deep involvement in school activities markedly decreased the potential for suicidal behavior (Bearman & Moody, 2004). Treatment will then emanate directly from any deficits found in these areas of functioning and will include the development of emotional insight and better coping skills to deal with all challenges as they arise. Spirito and his colleagues found that the most powerful predictors of continued suicidal behavior was the existence of depression and family dysfunction. Therefore, any treatment plan designed to address suicidal behavior must seriously address what is most likely the interplay between maladaptive family relations and the adolescent's feelings of depression (Hazell & Lewin, 1999; Spirito, Valeri, Boergers, & Donaldson, 2003).

Although it's true that human service professionals should have a "safety first" approach to treatment, there are valid concerns for not calling 9-1-1 each time an adolescent client sounds hopeless or is immersed in despair, including not wanting to destroy the counseling relationship by overreacting. When adolescent clients share that they sometimes wonder what it might feel like to die, and an anxious practitioner responds by having the adolescent involuntarily committed, trust can certainly be destroyed. But in light of the alarming increase in adolescent suicides since the mid-1990s, particularly within the adolescent male population, safety is of paramount importance. Thus, some sort of balance must be struck between honoring the privacy and safety of the counseling relationship and making sure that the adolescent remains safe.

If an adolescent is assessed to be a suicide risk, a safety plan is developed with the parents or primary caregivers, because the desire to commit suicide can only come to fruition if there is opportunity. Thus, it is important for the adolescent's environment to be as free of risk as possible. For instance, a good home-safety plan will include the removal of all pharmaceutical drugs, guns, kitchen knives, and loose razor blades. A depressed and socially isolated adolescent who is not actively suicidal but who thinks about dying from time to time may not need to be hospitalized, but should be monitored so that any escalation in depressive symptoms can be addressed immediately. At any time that an adolescent client acknowledges a suicidal intent, or discloses having a suicide plan, the human service professional may decide hospitalization is warranted, and in that case, the family will be directed to either call 9-1-1 or take their teen to their local emergency room.

The best intervention strategy for teen suicide is to prevent it altogether. Current suicide prevention programs include school-based suicide prevention education programs, crisis centers including teen suicide hotlines, screening programs aimed at identifying high-risk adolescents within the community, peer support programs that target suicide risk factors, and public awareness campaigns, including pleas to remove guns from homes with at-risk adolescents. Suggestions for future programs include recommendations that the juvenile justice system coordinate efforts with the school-based programs and other youth outreach agencies, because over 60 percent of adolescents who committed suicide also had a history of involvement with the justice system (Moskos, Achilles, & Gray, 2004).

Human service professionals must be prepared to deal with the growing trend of suicidal behaviors in the adolescent population, particularly Caucasian males. Through education, prevention, and intervention strategies, including a multidisciplinary approach that addresses many of the risk factors for suicide, far more needs to be done to confront what many consider an epidemic. While many new prevention and intervention programs are promising, more research needs to be done on their effectiveness in reducing suicide among the adolescent population (Katz, Bolton, et al., 2013).

Feeding and Eating Disorders in the Adolescent Population

Another set of disorders common to adolescents is eating disorders, including anorexia nervosa and bulimia nervosa. Although individuals of all ages suffer from eating disorders, the primary onset of eating disorders occurs during adolescence (Ray, 2004). Females tend to suffer from eating disorders far more often than males, comprising approximately 85 to 90 percent of all documented cases of eating disorders, though the incidence of eating disorders in males is increasing, particularly among male athletes (Walcott, Pratt, & Patel, 2003). Additionally, men who have eating disorders tend to overeat, whereas women tend to under-eat (Striegel-Moore, Rosselli, Perrin, DeBar, Wilson, May, & Kraemer, 2009).

In general, it is estimated that approximately one-third of all adolescents have a diagnosable eating disorder. Around 90 percent of college students (primarily females) report having attempted to control their weight regularly and over 50 percent of female adolescents reported using unhealthy methods for controlling their weight, such as severe restriction, vomiting, and the use of laxatives. Only about 10 percent of adolescents who suffer from an eating disorder receive treatment, which is alarming since eating disorders are among the most deadly of all mental disorders (Arcelus, Mitchell, Wales, & Nielsen, 2011; Crow, Peterson, et al., 2009).

Anorexia nervosa involves the intentional starving of oneself and the refusal to maintain expected body weight. The *DSM-5* criteria for anorexia includes a body weight of less than 85 percent of normal body weight, an intense fear of gaining weight, and distortion of how one's body is perceived (American Psychiatric Association, 2013). Among the various theories of the causes of anorexia, the most popular tend to focus on maladaptive family patterns where the adolescent's anorexia is presumed to help protect unhealthy family dynamics. These maladaptive patterns can include conflict avoidance, rigidity, and family enmeshment (Lock & le Grange, 2005). It is for this reason that family counseling is the most common recommended treatment for adolescents suffering from anorexia, in addition to in-patient treatment for adolescents who are at risk of serious health complications (Fairburn, 2005).

Bulimia nervosa involves a pattern of binge eating, indicating a lack of control, followed by purging in the form of self-induced vomiting, use of laxatives, or excessive exercise in an attempt to rid oneself of the abundance of food (American Psychiatric Association, 2013). Bulimia is far more prevalent than anorexia in the adolescent population (van Hoeken, Seidell, & Hoek, 2003). Common risk factors of adolescents suffering from bulimia include perfectionism, body dissatisfaction, and low self-esteem (Vohs et al., 2001). Adolescents who engage in binge eating behavior often experience significant shame once the binging phase is over. These feelings of shame are often dealt with by purging to rid the body of the excess food. This binging–purging cycle often becomes a compulsion, robbing the adolescent of the ability to stop the behavior.

Treatment for bulimia often includes **insight therapy**, family therapy, and cognitive behavioral therapy (CBT), which focuses on the negative self-statements the adolescent thinks in response to life events, as well as negative self-appraisals (Gowers & Bryant-Waugh, 2004). Depression and anxiety are often associated with both anorexia and bulimia; thus, a course of antidepressant or antianxiety medication is often considered appropriate.

Watch this video on Jessica, who struggles with anorexia nervosa and bulimia nervosa. Consider how you might respond to Jessica if she were your client.
ENHANCEDetext *video example 6.3*

Other Clinical Issues Affecting the Adolescent Population

There are several other psychological and emotional issues impacting the adolescent population, such as substance abuse, bullying, unplanned pregnancy, homelessness, and engagement with the juvenile justice system due to criminal activity such as gang involvement, but these issues and their associated dynamics will be explored in other chapters, such as the chapters on schools, homelessness, and violence.

ENHANCEDetext *self-check 6.2*

PRACTICE SETTINGS SPECIFIC TO ADOLESCENT TREATMENT

There are many practice settings where adolescents receive clinical services, as well as many ways in which these services are provided. Some adolescents may receive individual counseling from therapists who are in private practice. These counseling services can be provided by anyone who has a license to provide independent counseling services such as psychiatrists, psychologists, marriage and family therapists, licensed clinical professional counselors, and licensed clinical social workers. Counseling typically occurs in the counselor's office as often as the practitioner and parents deem necessary, but once or twice a week is the most common schedule.

Counseling also occurs in many other settings, such as in schools by school social workers, counselors, and psychologists; human service agencies that specialize in adolescent issues; outreach organizations such as after-school programs; religious organizations such as Jewish Community Centers; organizations that provide **therapeutic foster care**; and the juvenile justice system. Residential treatment centers are practice settings where human service professionals are most likely to work with the adolescent population. Such settings are often utilized for adolescents who are severely behaviorally disordered and at high risk of self-harm and destructive behaviors. Although institutionalized care has steadily decreased for most segments of the population, institutionalized care for the adolescent population skyrocketed in the 1980s (Wells, 1991), but has steadily decreased ever since (Child Trends Data Bank, 2015). These institutions can be locked or open, private or governmental, short or long term, therapeutic or more punitive in nature, but all provide some level of mental health services in relatively large, dormitory-like settings, where the adolescent residents sleep and attend school. Although care tends to focus more on chronic mental health care needs than urgent ones, some studies report that between 70 and 80 percent of adolescents in locked facilities suffer from mental illnesses that go untreated (Shufelt & Cocozza, 2006).

Residential treatment programs vary widely in type and nature. Some residential programs offer services that make them sound more like a boarding school than a treatment facility, boasting equine programs, river rafting, and therapeutic skiing programs, whereas others are far more sterile and punitive in nature, offering few extracurricular activities. One reason for this difference may be related to the range of populations served. For instance, behavior on the part of an adolescent that results in court intervention and detention in the juvenile justice system would not necessarily be conducive to a therapeutic ski trip to Colorado.

Placement times can also vary, with some adolescents placed in a residential facility for a few months with others requiring several years of treatment, again depending on the severity of the target problems. One popular short-term residential program is Outward Bound, a wilderness therapy program that uses physical challenges to help adolescents deal more effectively with their emotional challenges. Wilderness therapy camp programs are offered in various locations throughout the United States and have programs ranging in length of days and endurance levels.

Group homes (also called therapeutic foster homes) offer less-structured residential care, with various community services accessed by adolescents who attend the local public high school. **Treatment modalities** used in residential treatment programs and group homes often include a combination of behavior modification where desirable behaviors are rewarded and undesirable behaviors are punished, individual therapy, group therapy, and family therapy.

Male counselor (l) walking with arm around male camper outside Camp E-Hun-Tee wilderness-therapy camp

The most structured and most serious of all residential treatment programs include correctional institutions for adolescents, most commonly referred to as juvenile halls or juvenile detention centers. These facilities are reserved for adolescents who have been convicted of breaking some law, and although there is far more of an emphasis on rehabilitation than in an adult correctional facility, there is a far greater emphasis on corrections and punishment than in a therapeutic residential treatment center.

A creative version of the juvenile correctional institution that has received mixed reviews is the correctional boot camp, which offers rehabilitation as well as restraint in the form of a military-like, highly structured environment. The philosophy behind boot camps is that adolescents or young adults who have poor impulse control, low self-esteem, and high rates of acting out behaviors can benefit from a highly structured environment that pushes them to their limit (both physically and emotionally). The high emphasis on structure and self-discipline, coupled with the push to achieve, is believed to have a positive impact on both self-esteem and self-respect, which is hoped to generalize into more respectful behavior within society. Many parents and participants commonly claim dramatic changes in the behavior of participants after a boot camp experience, but research appears to indicate that boot camps do not necessarily reduce recidivism rates in young offenders, and thus they have reduced in popularity in the last decade or so (Mitchell, 2014).

Another type of treatment facility for adolescents experiencing mental health problems is the in-patient psychiatric hospital. These programs tend to be acute (short term) and focus on stabilizing the adolescent's high-risk behaviors, such as suicidal behavior, self-abuse, substance abuse, and eating disorders. Some in-patient programs specialize in one or more of these disorders while some are more general in nature, offering short-term acute services to any adolescent who cannot be maintained safely within their home environment. Many of the same type of therapies are available in an in-patient setting as in a residential treatment center, with the exception of drug therapies, which are more prevalent in a psychiatric hospital. In-patient hospitals also rely heavily on discharge planning, a task that typically falls to a hospital social worker or other human service professional who works with the family and community resources to ensure that the adolescent will transition back to home and school with enough outpatient support to minimize the need for rehospitalization.

ENHANCEDetext *self-check 6.3*

CULTURAL CONSIDERATIONS

Race and **ethnicity** have a significant effect on adolescent development, including the types of problems adolescents of various racial and ethnic backgrounds experience as well as the various responses to those problems, both within the family and within the community. Human services professionals must be aware of the way in which race and ethnicity affect adolescent development and behavior, any negative stereotypes that might affect the types of diagnoses adolescents receive, and the types of treatment.

A 2001 study found that African American adolescents were more commonly diagnosed with conduct disorders, whereas Caucasian adolescents more often received a diagnosis of depression (DelBello, Lopez-Larson, & Soutullo, 2001). Is this because more African American adolescents actually have conduct disorders? Or is this because the negative stereotype that African American males are typically more violent influenced the practitioner rendering the diagnosis? DelBello et al. (2001) doubted that the difference in diagnosing adolescents of color reflected any real variation in disorders among different races and suggested it is more likely attributable to variables such as misdiagnosing based on cultural differences and misperceptions.

Other research indicates that Latino adolescents, specifically Mexican Americans, are at higher risk for delinquency, depression, and suicide than Caucasians (Roberts, 2000). African American youth tend to show the greatest need for mental health services yet were the most underserved among all racial and ethnic groups, and although most African American adolescents with mental illnesses had a long history of diagnosable mental health problems, often their first exposure to treatment was within the juvenile justice system. One reason for this might be that there is a negative stigma associated with mental health disorders and counseling in certain ethnic minority groups.

Another equally significant reason for disparity in diagnosing and treatment is likely the lack of affordable mental health services in ethnically diverse neighborhoods. For instance, a 2011 study revealed that African American, Latino, and Asian adolescents with major depression were significantly less likely to receive mental health treatment, including prescription medication, than non-Hispanic white adolescents, regardless of income levels and health insurance (Cummings & Druss, 2011). Another study found that despite having greater need, African American and Asian American/Pacific Islander youths were half as likely as non-Hispanic white youths to receive any mental health services (Garland, Lau, et al., 2014). It is also interesting to note that Latino adolescents were rated as the most underserved of all racial groups, despite the fact that they had significant needs, and Caucasians were reported to have the highest rate of mental health utilization, although they have less serious mental health diagnoses compared to other racially diverse groups (Rawal, Romansky, & Jenuwine, 2004).

Watch this video on the mental health delivery services for Latinos living in California. What is the impact of the challenges noted in the film on Latino youth?
ENHANCEDetext *video example 6.4*

www.youtube.com/watch?v=78EwXz1qahY

Certainly not all differences in adolescent diagnoses and treatment patterns can be attributed to cultural misperceptions, misdiagnoses, and underutilization of services. Social conditions, such as poverty, high crime neighborhoods, and unemployment likely contribute to a significant proportion of mental health problems in ethnic minority youth as well. Rawal et al. (2004) noted that African American adolescents were far more likely to be raised in single-parent households, be placed in foster care, and experience significantly higher rates of familial abuse and neglect, all of which can be expected to have a negative impact on their mental health. Latino adolescents also exhibited higher incidences of acting out and antisocial behaviors, such as juvenile delinquency, compared to Caucasians; yet, they also had greater familial support, with their caregivers exhibiting greater understanding and involvement in their mental health issues, which might act as an intervention negating the necessity of more serious intervention.

Regardless of the reasons for the differences in mental health issues among adolescents of different ethnic groups, it is imperative that human service professionals be trained to deliver culturally competent counseling in a variety of contexts. Education that addresses all these issues, including the nature of institutionalized racism, both within the community and within the juvenile justice system; culturally based stigmas associated with mental health issues; social conditions affecting adolescents of all races; and the relevant histories of various racially ethic minority groups within the United States will assist the human service professional render a bias-free mental health evaluation and provide the most appropriate treatment for the adolescent client.

ENHANCEDetext *self-check 6.4*

CONCLUSION

Adolescence is a developmental stage that marks the transition from childhood to adulthood, and as such may be filled with stormy and tumultuous times. Most adolescents (and their families) brave these storms quite well, while others struggle with a range of social, emotional, and psychological challenges. As our society becomes more technologically based, it appears to become more complex as well. Educational requirements have increased over the last 50 years or so, family systems have changed, and vocations are becoming less streamlined and guaranteed.

History reveals that adolescence has always been a difficult stage to navigate, long before it was even recognized as an official stage of development. The greatest hope one can offer parents and educators alike is that adolescents who often seem destined for a lifetime of narcissistic obsession and rebellion most often evolve into loving, caring, and responsible adults. Human service professionals can help families ensure that this is the path for as many adolescents as possible through effective program development and supportive services on all levels.

SUMMARY

- Adolescent behavior from a developmental perspective is evaluated. The stage of adolescence as a distinct stage of development is discussed, with a particular focus on the value of evaluating common dynamics, such as identity issues and psycho-social challenges, through the lens of developmental theory.
- Psychosocial challenges and psychological disorders diagnosed in adolescence are compared and contrasted. Psychosocial challenges and psychological disorders common within the adolescent population, including depression and anxiety, suicide, nonsuicidal self-injury, and eating disorders, are explored.
- The role and function of human service professionals within practice settings serving the adolescent population are explored. A range of practice settings serving the adolescent population are examined including residential treatment centers, group homes, school-based programs, correctional boot camp, and therapeutic day programs, with a particular focus on the role and functions of human services professionals.
- The role of culture in both adolescent behavior and intervention strategies is evaluated. The role of culture in forming adolescent identity and influencing behavior within the context of culturally competent helping approaches and intervention strategies is discussed. Racial inequality, disparity in access to effective treatment, and provider attitudes toward stigmatized populations are also explored.

Internet Resources

Conduct an Internet search for adolescent health topics on the U.S. Department of Health and Human Services website on the Office Adolescent Health website.

Conduct an Internet search for "Runaway and Homeless Youth" in the section "Family and Youth Services Bureau" on the U.S. Department of Health and Human Services website.

Conduct an Internet search for "Eating Disorders" on the National Eating Disorders Association website.

Conduct an Internet search for "Self-harm" under "Health Topics" on the National Institute of Mental Health website.

Conduct an Internet search for "Adolescent Health and Youth of Color Practice Update" on the National Association of Social Workers website.

References

American Psychiatric Association. (2013). *Diagnostic and statistical manual of mental disorders* (5th ed.). Washington, DC: Author.

Andrus, J. K., Fleming, D. W., Heumann, M. A., Wassell, J. T., Hopkins, D. D. Y., & Gordan, S. (1991). Surveillance of attempted suicide among adolescents in Oregon, 1988. *American Journal of Public Health, 81,* 1067–1069.

Arcelus, J., Mitchell, A., Wales, J., & Nielsen, S. (2011). Is there an elevated mortality rate in anorexia nervosa and other eating disorders? A meta-analysis of 36 studies. *Archives of General Psychiatry, 68,* 724–731.

Arias, E., Anderson, R. N., Kung, H. C., Murphy, S., & Kochanek, K. D. (2003). Deaths: Final data for 2001. *National Vital Statistics Reports, 52*(3). Hyattsville, MD: National Center for Health Statistics.

Bearman, P. S., & Moody, J. (2004). Suicide and friends among American adolescents. *American Journal of Public Health, 94*(1), 89–95.

Child Trends Data Bank. (2015). Juvenile detention: Indicators on children and youth. Retrieved from http://www.childtrends.org/?indicators=juvenile-detention

Clarke, L., & Whittaker, M. (1998). Self-mutilation: Culture, contexts and nursing responses. *Journal of Clinical Nursing, 7,* 129–137.

Cohen, L. (2014). Stepping out of the shadows: Non-suicidal self-injury as its own diagnostic category. *Columbia Social Work Review, 5,* 1–20.

Cohn, T. J., & Hastings, S. L. (2010). Resilience among rural lesbian youth. *Journal of Lesbian Studies, 14*(1), 71–79.

Cornell Research Program on Self-Injury and Recovery. (2013). Is self-injury addictive? Retrieved from http://www.selfinjury.bctr.cornell.edu/about-self-injury.html#tab8

Crow, S. J., Peterson, C. B., Swanson, S. A., Raymond, N. C., Specker, S., Eckert, E. D., & Mitchell, J. E. (2009). Increased mortality in bulimia nervosa and other eating disorders. *American Journal of Psychiatry, 166,* 1342–1346.

Crowe, M., & Bunclark, J. (2000). Repeated self-injury and its management. *International Review of Psychiatry, 12*(1), 48–53.

Cummings, C. M., Caporino, N. E., & Kendall, P. C. (2014). Comorbidity of anxiety and depression in children and adolescents: 20 years after. *Psychological Bulletin, 140*(3), 816.

Cummings, J. R., & Druss, B. G. (2011). Racial/ethnic differences in mental health service use among adolescents with major depression. *Journal of the American Academy of Child & Adolescent Psychiatry, 50*(2), 160–170.

Cummings, J. R., Wen, H., & Druss, B. G. (2013). Improving access to mental health services for youth in the United States. *JAMA, 309*(6), 553–554.

DelBello, M., Lopez-Larson, M. P., & Soutullo, C. A. (2001). Effects of race on psychiatric diagnosis of hospitalized adolescents: A retrospective chart review. *Journal of Child and Adolescent Psychopharmacology, 11*(1), 95–103.

Demos, J., & Demos, V. (1969). Adolescence in a historical perspective. *Journal of Marriage and the Family, 31*(4), 632–638.

Erikson, E. H. (1968). *Identity: Youth and crisis.* New York, NY: Norton.

Fairburn, C. G. (2005). Evidence-based treatment of anorexia nervosa. *International Journal of Eating Disorders, 37*(Suppl.), S26–S30.

Favazza, A. R. (1996). *Bodies under siege: Self-mutilation and body modification in culture and psychiatry* (2nd ed.). Baltimore, MD: Johns Hopkins University Press.

Frick, P. (2004). Developmental pathways to conduct disorder: Implications for serving youth who show severe aggressive and antisocial behavior. *Psychology in the Schools, 41*(8), 823–834.

Gandara, P., Gutierrez, D., & O'Hara, S. (2001). Planning for the future in rural and urban high schools. *Journal of Education for Students Placed at Risk, 6*(1–2), 73–93. (ERIC Document Reproduction Service No. UD522844)

Garland, A. F., Lau, A. S., Yeh, M., McCabe, K. M., Hough, R. L., & Landsverk, J. A. (2005). Racial and ethnic differences in utilization of mental health services among high-risk youths. *American Journal of Psychiatry, 162*(7), 1336–1343.

Gorwood, P. (2004). Generalized anxiety disorder and major depressive disorder comorbidity: An example of genetic pleiotrophy? *European Psychiatry*, 19(1), 27–33.

Gowers, S., & Bryant-Waugh, R. (2004). Management of child and adolescent eating disorders: The current evidence base and future directions. *Journal of Child Psychology & Psychiatry*, 45(1), 63–83.

Hamza, C. A., & Willoughby, T. (2013). Nonsuicidal self-injury and suicidal behavior: A latent class analysis among young adults. *PLoS One*, 8(3), 1–8.

Hazell, P., & Lewin, T. (1999). Friends of adolescent suicide attempters and completers. *Journal of American Academy of Child & Adolescent Psychiatry*, 32(11), 76–81.

Hicks, K., & Hinck, S. M. (2009). Best-practice intervention for care of clients who self-mutilate. *Journal of the American Academy of Nurse Practitioners*, 21(8), 430–436.

Kann, L., Kinchen, S., Shanklin, S. L., Flint, K. H., Kawkins, J., Harris, W. A., & Whittle, L. (2014). Youth risk behavior surveillance—United States, 2013. *MMWR Surveillance Summaries*, 63(Suppl 4), 1–168.

Katz, C., Bolton, S. L., Katz, L. Y., Isaak, C., Tilston-Jones, T., & Sareen, J. (2013). A systematic review of school-based suicide prevention programs. *Depression and Anxiety*, 30(10), 1030–1045.

Kerpelman, J. L., & Pittman, J. F. (2001). The instability of possible selves: Identity processes within late adolescents' close peer relationships. *Journal of Adolescence*, 24(4), 491–512.

Lahey, B. B., Moffitt, T. E., & Caspi, A. (Eds.). (2003). *Causes of conduct disorder and juvenile delinquency.* New York, NY: Guilford Press.

Larsen, M. (2003). *Violence in U.S. public schools: A summary of findings.* New York, NY: ERIC Digest. (ERIC Document Reproduction Service No. ED482921)

Law, G. U., Rostill-Brookes, H., & Goodman, D. (2009). Public stigma in health and non-healthcare students: Attributions, emotions and willingness to help with adolescent self-harm. *International Journal of Nursing Studies*, 46(1), 108–119.

Lock, J., & le Grange, D. (2005). Family-based treatment of eating disorders. *International Journal of Eating Disorders*, 37(Suppl.), S64–S67.

Miniño A. M. (2010). Mortality among teenagers aged 12–19 years: United States, 1999–2006. NCHS data brief, no. 37. Hyattsville, MD: National Center for Health Statistics.

Mitchell, O. (2014). History of Boot Camps. In *Encyclopedia of Criminology and Criminal Justice* (pp. 2099–2106). Springer New York.

Moskos, M. A., Achilles, J., & Gray, D. (2004). Adolescent suicide myths in the U.S. *Journal of Crisis Intervention & Suicide Prevention*, 25(4), 176–182.

National Center for Education Statistics. (1999). *Digest of education statistics.* Washington, DC: National Research Council Panel on High Risk Youth, National Academy of Sciences.

Nock, M. K., & Prinstein, M. J. (2005). Contextual features and behavioral functions of self-mutilation among adolescents. *Journal of Abnormal Psychology*, 114(1), 140–146.

Piaget, J. (1950). *The psychology of intelligence.* London: Routledge & Kegan Paul.

Rawal, P., Romansky, J., & Jenuwine, M. (2004). Racial differences in the mental health needs and service utilization of youth in the juvenile justice system. *Journal of Behavioral Health Services & Research*, 31(3), 242–254.

Ray, S. L. (2004). Eating disorders in adolescent males. *Professional School Counseling*, 8(1), 98–102.

Raywid, M. (1996). *Downsizing schools in big cities.* New York, NY: ERIC Clearinghouse on Urban Education. (ERIC Document Reproduction Service No. ED393958)

Roberts, R. E. (2000). Depression and suicidal behaviors among adolescents: The role of ethnicity. In I. Cuéllar & F. A. Paniagua (Eds.), *Handbook of multicultural mental health* (pp. 360–389). San Diego, CA: Academic Press.

Rutter, P. A., & Behrendt, A. E. (2004). Adolescent suicide risk: Four psychosocial factors. *Adolescence*, 39(154), 295–302.

Shufelt, J. L., & Cocozza, J. L. (2006). Youth with mental health disorders in the juvenile justice system: Results from a multi-state prevalence study. National Center for Mental Health and Juvenile Justice. Retrieved from http://www.unicef.org/tdad/usmentalhealthprevalence06(3).pdf. See more at: http://www.childtrends.org/?indicators=juvenile-detention#_edn9

Spirito, A., Valeri, S., Boergers, J., & Donaldson, D. (2003). Predictors of continued suicidal behavior in adolescents following a suicide attempt. *Journal of Clinical Child and Adolescent Psychology*, 32(2), 284–289.

Striegel-Moore, R. H., Rosselli, F., Perrin, N., DeBar, L., Wilson, G., May, A., & Kraemer, H. C. (2009). Gender difference in the prevalence of eating disorder symptoms. *International Journal of Eating Disorders*, 42(5), 471–474.

Turner, B. J., Chapman, A, L., & Layden, B. K. (2012). Intrapersonal and interpersonal functions of nonsuicidal self-injury: Associations with emotional and social functioning. *Suicide and Life-Threatening Behavior*, 42(1), 36.

van Hoeken, D., Seidell, J., & Hoek, H. (2003). Epidemiology. In J. Treasure, U. Schmidt, & E. van Furth (Eds.), *Handbook of eating disorders* (2nd ed., pp. 11–34). Chichester, UK: Wiley.

Vohs, K. D., Voelz, Z. R., Pettit, J. W., Bardone, A. M., Katz, J., Abramson, L. Y., et al. (2001). Perfectionism, body dissatisfaction, and self-esteem: An interactive model of bulimic symptom development. *Journal of Social & Clinical Psychology, 20,* 476–497.

Vörös, V., Fekete, S., Hewitt, A., & Osváth, P. (2005). Suicidal behavior in adolescents—psychopathology and addictive comorbidity. *Neuropsychopharmacol Hung, 7*(2), 66–71. Hungarian. PMID: 16167457 [PubMed—indexed for MEDLINE]

Vörös, V., Osváth, P., & Fekete, S. (2004). Gender differences in suicidal behavior. *Neuropsychopharmacol Hung, 6,* 65–71.

Walcott, D. D., Pratt, H. D., & Patel, D. R. (2003). Adolescents and eating disorders: Gender, racial, ethnic, sociocultural, and socioeconomic issues. *Journal of Adolescent Research, 18,* 223–243.

Wells, K. (1991). Long-term residential treatment for children: Introduction. *American Journal of Orthopsychiatry, 61,* 324–326.

Whitlock, J. L., Purington, A., & Gershkovich, M. (2009). Influence of the media on self injurious behavior. In M. Nock (Ed.), *Understanding non-suicidal self-injury: Current science and practice* (pp. 139–156). American Psychological Association Press.

Yarbrough, D. G. (2004). Gay adolescents in rural areas: Experiences and coping strategies. *Journal of Human Behavior in the Social Environment, 8*(2–3), 129–144.

7

Gerontology: Human Services with Older Adults

© MONKEY BUSINESS IMAGES / SHUTTERSTOCK

Carrie looked at the sea of faces before her. They looked empty—almost as if they had no souls. The only sounds in the camp were the incessant, never ceasing buzzing of hungry flies. Even the children were quiet. Carrie reasoned that the calm was due to hunger—people were often subdued when they hadn't eaten well in days, but she knew this calm was related to something far removed from hunger. Just three days ago many people in this camp were victims of a resurgence of fighting among rebel groups and government forces in the Democratic Republic of the Congo, a country in Central Africa with a long history of conflict rooted in the 1994 Rwanda genocide against the Tutsi. The camp in the southern part of Rwanda was receiving about 500 refugees per day, most of whom needed medical care. Carrie reflected on how she got here and how much different her life turned out than she expected.

When Carrie became a widow at the age of 71, she thought her life was over. She hadn't worked in years and had spent the last several years traveling for pleasure with her husband. However, when a long-time friend approached her with an idea of how her vast experience as an emergency room nurse could help others, she became intrigued. Apparently there was great need for medical personnel, particularly nurses, in refugee countries like Kenya, Thailand, Rwanda, and Serbia. When she met men and women like her—older adults, many long retired, working in medically related positions in various refugee camps around the world with families and children—she finally realized that this was something she could do.

Of course, Carrie's adult children thought she'd lost her mind. They even questioned whether her decision to travel alone to a faraway country and create a new life in a tented camp was a sign of early Alzheimer's disease! But they eventually grew to understand her decision—her desire to feel relevant and productive again, her need to have something of value to look forward to, and, finally, her need to have one last adventure in her life. Carrie's contemplative thoughts were interrupted with the announcement of the most recent influx of refugees from the latest cycle of fighting. She ventured out of the makeshift hospital to meet the new arrivals and to provide medical and wellbeing checkups.

Sean was shocked as he walked down La Salle Avenue, in the heart of the business district in Chicago. He was used to seeing homeless people, either standing or sitting along the side of the road with signs asking for money, but he had never before seen an older couple begging for money. What was unique about this couple was that they looked as though they could be his parents. He began to walk by them, avoiding their stare as he usually did when people begged for money, but this time was different, and he could not resist approaching this couple. "Hi, my name is Sean, and I'd love to give you some money." The couple looked at him sheepishly, and he noticed the shame in their eyes. "Thank you," the woman said quietly, diverting her glance downward. Sean handed them a $10 bill and started to walk away, but curiosity got the better of him. He turned around and asked them if he could talk to them about their situation. The husband and wife looked at each other, and Sean did not know if it was with suspicion or simple caution, but they eventually agreed once Sean offered to buy them lunch.

Over their meals of hot soup and sandwiches, Rosemary and Donald shared about their all-American lives. They raised two children in a suburb of Chicago, owned a home, and even had a family dog. They were like anyone else in the neighborhood or their church, until Donald was laid off two years before his scheduled retirement when the company he had worked for 40 years downsized. Donald was unable to find a job due to his age, and eventually they had to let their health insurance lapse because they could no longer financially handle the extremely high monthly premiums.

Unfortunately, Rosemary became ill the following month with a bout of influenza that ultimately developed into pneumonia. The hospital bill for her two-week stay was almost $10,000. With no retirement and only Social Security benefits to count on, and with their two adult children serving overseas in the military, Donald and Rosemary began a downhill financial descent that didn't stop until they depleted their life savings and ultimately lost their house. Thus, although most couples like Donald and Rosemary spend their golden years playing golf in Florida, Donald and Rosemary spend their days sitting outside the train station begging for money.

These two vignettes highlight the vast range of experiences Americans living in the United States can have in the last decades of their lives—what is normally called *old age*. And although there are some similarities between the older adults of today and the older adults of 100 years ago, there are also significant differences brought on by many of the societal changes referenced in earlier chapters, particularly in relation to social welfare policy explored in Chapter 2, including ongoing urbanization, changes in the family structure, and the dawning of the technological era. However, there have also been transitions in culture and society that have affected the older adult community in a unique way. These include issues such as increasing longevity, the global community and economy, other economic shifts, the advent of long-distance travel enabling family members to move farther and farther away from one another, the health care "crisis," significant demographic shifts, as well as the increasing complexity of society in general. Each of these issues and their impact on the older adult population affects the human services field as it attempts to meet the complex needs of this growing population.

THE GRAYING OF AMERICA

Watch the video produced by the Alliance for Aging Research. What role can human services professionals play in meeting the needs of a growing older adult population?
ENHANCEDetext *video example 7.1*

www.youtube.com/
watch?v=7rGpJDyiUXs

AARP representatives from each of the 50 states attended a rally in the Senate Park to urge Congress to pass legislation providing senior citizens with a prescription drug benefit through Medicare

The opening vignettes illustrate the range of experiences of those considered "old" in the United States. Today's older adults experience a broader range of lifestyles than ever before, but they also experience a broad range of challenges. There are several dynamics that have led to increased opportunities and lifestyle choices for older adults, including an increase in the human lifespan, changes in the perception of old age in general, changes in the economy, and finally changes in the nature and definition of the American family in the United States, including an increase in divorce and two-parent working families.

The term **graying of America** refers to the increase in the older adult population in the United States (as well as in most parts of the world). The current population increase coupled with a projected increase in the U.S. older adult population between now and 2050 is directly related to the aging of a cohort of individuals referred to as the **baby boomers**. The baby boomers are popularly defined as those having been born between 1946 and 1964. The name refers to the *boom* of births after World War II, which caused an unusual population spike in the United States.

Approximately 76 million individuals (roughly 29 percent of the U.S. population) fall into the baby boomer cohort; thus it is obvious why this cohort has been the focus of interest to social scientists, the media, politicians, and others. For one thing, despite the somewhat broad range of ages within this cohort, similarities between members are numerous, including their socioeconomic status, which tends to be higher than earlier cohorts, consumer habits, and political concerns. As the boomers age, there has been much discussion and some concern regarding the consequences of this large cohort heading into their retirement years, including their increased lobbying power. The graying of America, then, refers to the projected increase in the older adult population because of the aging boomers.

The aging of the baby boomers is not the only variable leading to the increase in the older adult population. Other factors include the 50 percent increase in the human life expectancy in the United States during the 20th century. In 1900 the average human lifespan in the United States was about 47 years, but by 1999 life expectancy had increased to about 77 years, which is where it stands today.

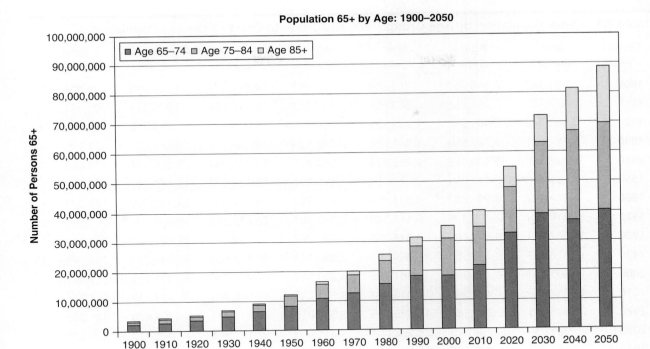

Figure 7.1

Increase in U.S. Population by Age,1900 to 2050, Showing Increase in Population Age 65+

Compiled by the U.S. Administration on Aging using data from Table 5. Population by Age and Sex for the United States: 1900 to 2000, Part A. Number, Hobbs, Frank and Nicole Stoops, U.S. Census Bureau, Census 2000 Special Reports, Series CENSR-4, Demographic Trends in the 20th Century.

Population experts expect life expectancy for most demographic groups to increase at least another 15 years by the year 2100 (Arias, 2004). This life expectancy increase is due to improved medical technology, medical discoveries such as antibiotics and immunizations for various life-threatening diseases, and generally safer lifestyles.

Currently there are approximately 46 million people over the age of 65 living in the United States (see Figure 7.1 and Table 7.1), but that number is projected to double by the year 2050, growing to more than 88 million (U.S. Bureau of the Census, 2014). Additionally, the U.S. Census Bureau projects that the population of those 85 and older is expected to grow from 5.8 million in 2010 to just over 20 million by the year 2050 (U.S. Bureau of the Census, 2014). When one considers that from 1900 to 2050 the over-65 population in the United States will have grown from about 3 million to about 88.5 million, it is not difficult to understand why the field of gerontology has received so much attention in recent years!

So far this all sounds pretty good—we're living longer, and in the next 10 or 20 years a third of the population will be classified as older adults, which will no doubt increase attention paid to social and political issues important to those in their later years of life. However, the landscape for older adults in the United States is not without concern; quite the opposite, in fact. Some older adults will enjoy their longer lifespan, but for many, their additional years on this earth may be spent in a long-term care facility with chronic health problems far too complex to make remaining in their home a possibility. Increases in rates of dementia, depression, and alcohol abuse are valid concerns for older adults and their family members, as they face a multitude of challenges in a rapidly changing world that has not quite kept up pace with the growing needs of the older adult population.

Table 7.1   Older Population by Age Group: 1900 to 2050 with Chart of the 65+ Population

Census Year	Age 60–64	Age 65–74	Age 75–84	Age 85+	Age 60 and older	Age 65 and older	Total, all ages
1900	1,791,363	2,186,767	771,369	122,362	4,871,861	3,080,498	75,994,575
1910	2,267,150	2,793,231	989,056	167,237	6,216,674	3,949,524	91,972,266
1920	2,982,548	3,463,511	1,259,339	210,365	7,915,763	4,933,215	105,710,620
1930	3,751,221	4,720,609	1,641,066	272,130	10,385,026	6,633,805	122,775,046
1940	4,728,340	6,376,189	2,278,373	364,752	13,747,654	9,019,314	131,669,275
1950	6,059,475	8,414,885	3,277,751	576,901	18,329,012	12,269,537	150,697,361
1960	7,142,452	10,996,842	4,633,486	929,252	23,702,032	16,559,580	179,323,175
1970	8,616,784	12,435,456	6,119,145	1,510,901	28,682,286	20,065,502	203,211,926
1980	10,087,621	15,580,605	7,728,755	2,240,067	35,637,048	25,549,427	226,545,805
1990	10,616,167	18,106,558	10,055,108	3,080,165	41,857,998	31,241,831	248,709,873
2000	10,805,447	18,390,986	12,361,180	4,239,587	45,797,200	34,991,753	281,421,906
2010	16,757,689	21,462,599	13,014,814	5,751,299	56,986,401	40,228,712	310,232,863
2020	21,008,851	32,312,186	15,895,265	6,597,019	75,813,321	54,804,470	341,386,665
2030	20,079,650	38,784,325	24,562,604	8,744,986	92,171,565	72,091,915	373,503,674
2040	20,512,884	36,895,223	30,145,467	14,197,701	101,751,275	81,238,391	405,655,295
2050	23,490,423	40,112,637	29,393,295	19,041,041	112,037,396	88,546,973	439,010,253

Source: From "Administration on Aging (AoA). Projected Future Growth of the Older Population". Published by Administration for Community Living © 2000.

The **Great Recession of 2007** caused, among other things, forced retirement and unanticipated layoffs of many older adults within the workforce. In addition, changes in the U.S. and global economic landscape resulted in many individuals approaching retirement in economically vulnerable positions as companies shifted away from offering lifelong and secure pensions and toward self-funded and less secure retirement strategies. Sharp increases in the cost of medical care, increased housing costs, and other complexities of life are also putting some older adults at risk of financial insecurity. Thus, a growing older population is having a significant impact on the economic, housing, medical, mental health, and even transportation needs of the older adult population, their families, and communities in which they reside.

Additionally, changes in the U.S. family structure, such as the significant increase in divorce rates, have put some older adults, particularly women, in economically fragile positions. Other older adults are in the position of having to provide day care for their grandchildren and, in some cases, even parenting their grandchildren. Thus, although some older adults will be able to take advantage of the many medical advances, healthier lifestyles, and increased opportunities for enjoying life, many others may not.

This chapter will explore the wide range of issues and challenges many in the older adult population experience in the United States, as well as explore some issues projected to be relevant in the future. The role of the human service professional will be explored as well, with a special focus on how the field of gerontology has changed in recent years, expanding the role of the human service professional in various practice settings.

ENHANCEDetext *self-check 7.1*

UNDERSTANDING OLDER ADULTS FROM A DEVELOPMENTAL PERSPECTIVE

Adults do not go through systematic and uniform developmental stages in the same way that children do; thus, many developmental theories typically stop at early adulthood or lump all adult development into one category stretching from post-adolescence and beyond. One reason for this approach is that if development is conceptualized as involving the combined impact of physical, cognitive, and emotional development, then development must involve progression, such as children who push themselves from a crawl to a walk in their quest to explore their social worlds. Yet, once one has reached physical and cognitive maturity, this interplay between physical ability and emotional desire (where one dynamic serves as the incentive for the other) subsides, and the motivation to pursue a particular life course becomes based more on personal choice and internal motivation, making adult maturity anything but systematic or universal.

Most of us have heard about the infamous **midlife crisis** marking the entry into middle age, or **empty nesting**, the life transition some women experience in response to their adult children leaving home. Regardless of the validity of the universality of such life events, it does seem reasonable to assume that individuals within a particular society will respond and adapt in similar ways to both internal and external demands and expectations placed on them by cultural mores and norms. For example, cultural expectations in the United States, such as marriage, parenting, employment, and home ownership, certainly have an impact on those in early and middle adulthood, just as retirement, increased physical problems, and widowhood will have an impact on those in later adulthood. Yet, because the options and choices available to adults are so broad, any developmental theory must be considered in more general and descriptive terms compared to the narrower and more prescriptive terms often used to evaluate and consider child developmental theories.

Erik Erikson (1959, 1966), a psychodynamic theorist who studied under Sigmund Freud (the father of psychoanalysis), developed a theory of psychosocial development, beginning with birth and ending with death. According to Erikson, each stage of development presented a unique challenge or crisis brought on by the combining forces of both physiological changes and psychosocial needs. Successfully resolving each developmental crisis resulted in being better prepared for the next stage of development. The eighth stage of Erikson's model is *integrity versus despair* and spans from the age of 65 to death. Although Erikson's theory is no longer considered universal in the sense that we cannot assume that all individuals progress through these stages in a uniform manner, his theory is useful as a lens to better understand the psychosocial experiences of the older adult population.

Erikson believed that adults over the age of 65 reflected on their lives, taking stock of their choices and the value of their various achievements. If this reflection results in a sense of contentment with their choices and life experiences, older adults will be more likely to accept death with a sense of integrity. But if they do not like the choices they made, the relationships they developed, and the wisdom they gained throughout their lives, they risk facing death with a sense of despair.

Because the successful navigation of each stage is dependent on the successful navigation of the preceding stages, Erikson believed that individuals who did not develop a sense of basic trust in others or in the world (Stage 1) struggled with developing a sense of personal autonomy (Stage 2), had difficulty developing any personal initiative (Stage 3) or a sense of accomplishment (Stage 4), faced challenges in adolescence when attempting to discover a personal identity (Stage 5). This made it difficult to develop truly intimate relationships with others (Stage 6), leaving them incapable of offering true guidance and generativity to the younger generations (Stage 7), which meant they would be less likely to reflect back on their lives with a sense of contentment and satisfaction, and would likely face impending death with a deep sense of despair.

A ninth stage was added posthumously by Erikson's wife, Joan Erikson. That ninth stage was based on discussions she and her husband had prior to his death in recognition of the lengthening lifespan, as well as his notes from interviews (Erikson & Erikson, 1998). The ninth stage, *very old age* (despair and disgust versus integrity) pertains to those in their 80s and 90s, who are dealing with the reality of death in a way not experienced in previous generations. Joan Erikson cites the increasing isolation of the *old-old adult* as they deal with loss in numerous realms. She cites cultural implications common in many Western countries, noting that older adults are often marginalized and dismissed and no longer perceived as sources of life wisdom, but instead as burdens (Erikson & Erikson, 1998). This is an extremely challenging time, according to Joan Erikson, where the old-old adult must in some respects rework or confront earlier stages, with the negative outcome at times becoming more dominant. She argues that many cultural determinants are destructive forces, negating the "grand-generative" contributions adults in their 80s and 90s (and older) can make.

Similar to Joan Erikson's conceptualization of grand-generativity is Tornstam's theory of **gerotranscendence**, which posits that the *old-old* transcend above their everyday realities toward a more cosmic connection with the universe. Tornstam (1994) describes the changes individuals experience from middle to older adulthood on emotional, cognitive, and physical levels as gerotranscendence (Tornstam, 1994). This theory explores how an individual moves from a strong connection to the material world to transcending above material aspects of the world into a more existential approach to living. Tornstam describes how individuals progressing from midlife onward transition from an externalizing perspective, where they are focusing outward toward the world, to a more internally focused approach in life.

According to Tornstam (2003) there are three dimensions of transcendence. The first is the cosmic dimension, in which individuals change their notions of time and space, such as reorienting themselves to how they view life and death, ultimately accepting death with a sense of peace. The second dimension relates to "the self" where individuals increasingly move away from self-centeredness, transcending above a focus on the physical and move toward more altruism. The third dimension involves social and individual relationships, where relationships are viewed in a new light with new meaning, including developing new insights into the differences between "the self" (who they really are) and the roles they play in life (mother/father, son/daughter, friend, etc.), and the ability to rise above black-and-white thinking and embrace the gray in life (Degges-White, 2005).

There are key issues involved in the process of personal transcendence across the three

Watch the video produced by Davidson Films, Inc., featuring a conversation with Joan Erikson on old age. How is the lengthening lifespan impacting the developmental stage of old age?

ENHANCEDetext *video example 7.2*

www.youtube.com/watch?v=00DUXNQLAjQ

Meditation is one way that older adults can transcend above their daily realities and focus intrinsically on themselves

© BST2012/FOTOLIA

dimensions (cosmic, self, and relationships with others). For instance, Degges-White cites the importance of counselors becoming personally comfortable with the concept of death within, so they can help their aging clients accept the inevitability of death without overwhelming fear and anxiety. With regard to transcendence in the "self" domain, Degges-White describes how counselors can help their older clients conduct a "life review" where they seek to better understand and accept their life choices, thus finding a level of peace and self-acceptance about their choices and experiences, particularly the challenging and painful ones. The ultimate goal of counseling older adults using a gerotranscendence model is to assist older adults move toward increased self- and other-acceptance and wisdom in various dimensions and domains in life—in a sense, giving them permission to draw intrinsically inward as they let go of the more transitory dimensions of life and move toward a more existential existence.

Daniel Levinson (1978, 1996) is probably one of the most well-known adult developmental theorists, having developed a lifespan theory extending from birth through death. Levinson wrote two books explaining his theory, *The Seasons of a Man's Life* (1978) and *The Seasons of a Woman's Life* (1996), where he focused on middle adulthood. What is rather revolutionary about his theory is his argument that adults do continue to grow and develop on an age-related timetable. Levinson noticed that adults in the latter half of their lives are more reflective, and as they approach a point in their lives where they have more time behind them than ahead of them, this reflection intensifies. Levinson also believes that individuals progress through periods of stability followed by shorter stages of transition (and instability). The themes in his theory most relevant to human service professionals include the notion of life reflection—the taking stock of one's life choices and accomplishments, the need to be able to give back to society, which encompasses an acknowledgment that at some point the goal in life is not solely to focus on one's own driving needs, but to give back to others and to one's community through the sharing of gained wisdom and mentoring.

Finally, Levinson's belief that as people age they need to become more intrinsically focused rather than externally based is equally relevant. Consider the man who in his 30s gains self-esteem and a sense of identity through working 80 hours per week and running marathons. How will this same man define himself when he is 70 years old and no longer has the physical stamina or agility to perform these activities? Levinson believes that a developmental task for aging adults is to become more internally anchored, more intrinsic in their self-identify, lest they develop a sense of despair and depression later in life when they are no longer able to live up to their previous youthful expectations.

ENHANCEDetext *self-check 7.2*

SUCCESSFUL AND ACTIVE AGING

Successful aging refers to the process of adding years to one's life and getting the most out of life in later years (Havighurst, 1961). Researchers have examined individuals who age better than others to determine what differences might account for their success. Some of the variables at play in healthy longevity include maintaining a moderately high physical and social activity level, including keeping active with hobbies, social events, and regular exercise (Warr, Butcher, & Robertson, 2004). Research shows that when older adults participated in some type of social activity, such as paid or unpaid work, religious activities, and political involvement, mortality and cognitive impairment were reduced. Yet disparity in opportunities for meaningful social activities left some older adults more vulnerable to physical and cognitive decline (Hsu, 2007).

The World Health Organization (WHO) describes a similar concept called **active aging**, which involves enhancing the quality of one's life by taking advantage of opportunities for better health and security (WHO, 2002). Similar to the concept of successful aging, active aging focuses on potential, well-being, and active participation in all life has to offer within a range of life domains, including social, economic, cultural, spiritual, and civic aspects of life. In other words, those who are actively aging are engaged in life—not solely physically and vocationally, but in many other ways as well. The goal of programs and policies focusing on enhancing active aging is to extend the lifespan, as well as maximize one's quality of life.

The natural aging process, though, seems to discourage high activity levels in many domains of life, particularly for certain populations. Employment provides many people with one of the greatest opportunities for social interaction, and when individuals retire, opportunities for social interaction decline. Physical limitations can also discourage active engagement, such as poor night vision that can keep an older adult from being able to hop in the car and visit family. Thus, many older adults naturally begin withdrawing from the world, both physically and socially, in response to diminished capability and opportunity. With such disengagement comes an increase in physical and psychosocial problems, such as depression and even alcohol abuse to combat loneliness.

A recent study seems to indicate that good psychological health is one of the most important factors in ensuring good quality of life in later years (Bowling & Iliffe, 2011). For instance, the ability of older adults to rely on their psychological resources, such as good **self-efficacy** and **resilience**, were more strongly linked to successful and active aging than were biological and social factors. This does not mean that good physical health and an active social life aren't important, but as Tornstam (2005) and Degges-White (2005) suggest, older adults who can mentally and emotionally transcend the physical and social limitations inherent in the aging process seem to have a better quality of life compared to older adults who lack these psychological resources.

Many older adults must not only face increased health problems and physical limitations but also deal with multiple losses as they begin to lose friends, siblings, and even their spouses to death. Many older adults may also need to move from their long-time home into residential care or the home of a family member, and the loss of independence can have a devastating effect on their ability to optimize opportunities for active engagement. Those with better coping mechanisms, psychological resilience, and optimism will be able to manage these multiple losses in a healthier manner, even perhaps finding some existential meaning in facing these losses with a sense of wisdom and acceptance, despite the deep pain and sense of powerlessness many older adults may feel. Those who have a lifetime of poor coping mechanisms, who are not particularly resilient and who tend toward pessimism will likely fare much worse.

In anticipation of the increase in the older adult population as well as an increase in the complex nature of the challenges facing many older adults, the **Older Americans Act** (OAA) was signed into federal law in 1965. This act led to the creation of the **Administration on Aging**, which among other things fund grants at the state level for various community and human service programs and provide money for age-related research and the development of human service agencies called **Area Agencies on Aging** (AAA) operating on the local level.

Watch the video produced by Tedx Talks on tips to keep your brain young. How can you incorporate these tips with older adult clients?

ENHANCEDetext *video example 7.3*

www.youtube.com/watch?v=2tcEgqTWbxQ

The Administration on Aging also acts as a clearinghouse, disseminating information about a number of issues affecting the older adult population in the United States, including dementia, elder abuse, nutrition, age-based discrimination and ageism, housing needs including long-term care, depression, anxiety, suicide prevention, and grandparents parenting. Those in the human services field are often included in the group of professionals most likely to come into contact with the older adult population, either through direct service or through providing counseling services to a family member of an older adult. Therefore, they must be familiar with the psychosocial issues facing many older adults so that they can assist this population in maintaining an optimal functioning level.

ENHANCEDetext *self-check 7.3*

COMMON PSYCHOSOCIAL CHALLENGES IN OLDER ADULTHOOD

There are many challenges facing the older adult population in the United States, many of which have a direct impact on the aging process. Some examples include age-related discrimination (ageism), economic disadvantage impacting housing stability (and quality of housing), challenges associated with retirement, depression, dementia, and elder abuse. Of particular concern to human service professionals and others working in the field of gerontology are the populations that are disproportionally impacted by these challenges, such as some ethnic minority populations, women, and veterans, particularly those experiencing a lifetime of economic disadvantage.

Ageism

Ask some typical young Americans what they think it's like to be a man in his seventies, and they may well tell you that an average 75-year-old man is in poor health, drifts off to sleep at a moment's notice, talks of nothing but the distant past, and unproductively sits in a rocking chair, rocking back and forth all day long. They might even throw in a comment or two about his general grouchy disposition. Ask if older adults still have the desire for sexual intimacy, and you might get a good hearty laugh in response. However, this description of older adults is a myth based on deeply entrenched negative stereotypes of older adults and can serve as a foundation of a form of prejudice and discrimination of older adults called **ageism**.

The term *ageism* was first coined by Robert Butler (1969), chairman of a congressional committee on aging in 1968. He described ageism in a similar vein as racism and sexism, where older adults are negatively stereotyped on a systematic basis and are then discriminated against on that basis. Butler theorized that at the root of this negative stereotyping was perhaps a fear of growing old. Ageism typically involves any attitude or behavior that negatively categorizes older adults based either on partial truth (often taken out of context) or on outright myths of the aging process. Such myths often describe old age as inherently involving poor health, senility, depression, irritability, a sexless life, a lack of vitality, an inability to learn new things, and a loss of productivity (Thornton, 2002).

Gerontologists caution that the promotion of such negative stereotypes of old age not only trivializes older adults but also risks displacing the older adult population as communities undervalue them based on the perception that older adults are a drain on society. A further risk of ageism is that older adults may internalize negative stereotypes held by the majority population, creating a self-fulfilling prophecy of sorts, in much the same way that some marginalized ethnic minority groups internalize historic negative perceptions held by the majority population (Snyder, 2001; Thornton, 2002).

Old age hasn't always been viewed negatively in the United States. In fact, earlier in the 20th century, societal attitudes reflected a relatively positive view of older adults and the aging experience. Older adults were respected for their wisdom and valued for their experience; thus they were not perceived as a drain on society. Yet, sometime around the mid-1900s, as life expectancy began to grow in response to safer lifestyles and medical advances, professionals such as physicians, psychologists, and gerontologists began discussing older adults in terms of their burden rather than their contributions (Hirshbein, 2001).

Many social psychologists and gerontologists cite the media as contributing to the creation of negative stereotypes of older adults and the aging process, noting the consistent negative portrayal of older adults in television shows and commercials as dimwitted individuals who live in the past. And yet, the results of a study conducted in 2004 did not support these concerns. The study's authors reviewed television commercials from the 1950s through the 1990s and found that media depictions of older adults have been generally positive during this time period and actually improved in the latter two decades (Miller, Leyell, & Mazacheck, 2004). This study is not only good news, but also highlights the power of the media and how it can be used to confront existing negative stereotypes as older adults are cast in active and vibrant roles.

NBC's hidden camera show *Off Their Rockers*, starring Betty White, is an excellent example of a television show that confronts negative stereotypes of older adulthood. The premise of the show is similar to other popular shows about pranks being played on unsuspecting people in front of a hidden camera. The twist with this show is that the pranks involve scenarios designed to not just confront stereotypes, but to shatter them with humor. Each episode begins with a "warning" screen informing viewers that the show involves senior citizens who play pranks on real unsuspecting young people. The theme song is "We're Not Going to Take It." Betty White then welcomes viewers, describing the show as one where seniors prefer to age disgracefully.

Most pranks involve stark contradictions, each beginning with an expected stereotype of an older adult, and concluding with something that is unexpected—a nun cruising down the street in an electric wheelchair (expected), swearing at people to get out of her way (unexpected); an older woman asking a younger woman on the street for help with her smartphone (expected), and then asking her to help decipher sexts from her senior citizen boyfriend (unexpected); an old blind man with a red-tipped cane asking a younger man for assistance walking across a path (expected), and then getting into his convertible and driving off at a fast speed (unexpected); and finally, Betty White in several skits talking about the importance of remaining active in later years (expected), and then walking away with a shirtless younger man (unexpected). What has been so effective about this show is that it uses humor to confront negative stereotypes about older adults (and confront them it does!).

It's very important that human service professionals explore their own misconceptions and negative stereotypes of older adults and the aging process, such as assuming that older adults are incapable of learning something new, gaining new insights, resolving old conflicts, and growing emotionally. Since research shows that internalized negative stereotypes about aging can increase feelings of loneliness and dependency, practitioners are wise to address any misconceptions they personally have prior to working with the older adult population (Coudin & Alexopoulos, 2010). Practices such as talking down to older adult clients and not directly addressing difficult issues based on a belief that the older client lacks the capacity to understand will undoubtedly affect the level of investment the client makes in the counseling relationship. This type of behavior on the part of the practitioner can also encourage a **self-fulfilling prophecy** within older adult clients, where they begin to act the part of the incompetent, unproductive, and cognitively dull individual. Making positive assumptions about older adult clients will increase the possibility of bringing out the most authentic and dynamic aspects of older adult clients.

Housing

Medical technology may be allowing people to live longer, but longer doesn't always equate with healthier. Although the majority of older adults remain in their homes throughout their lives, some older adults may find themselves needing to move out of their homes when they reach a certain level of physical and/or cognitive decline. They might move into the home of a family member or they might move into a retirement community, where they can still enjoy their independence while also enjoying many facility-offered services to meet their needs, such as shuttle services, handicapped-accessible facilities, and childfree living.

Older adults needing more consistent care with their **activities of daily living** (ADL) sometimes enter assisted-living facilities. These facilities offer apartment-like living in a more structured environment and often include a range of services. Most assisted-living facilities offer help with eating, bathing, dressing, housekeeping, and medication, and some even have fully functioning medical centers. Many assisted-living apartments have alarm systems in every unit and offer a restaurant-style cafeteria, a club for social activities, a hairdresser, medical staff, home health care, and a relatively full array of human services, such as case management, support groups, and individual counseling. The services are far more intensive than in a retirement community, as residents in assisted-living facilities are there because they cannot manage their ADL without assistance.

Private residential communities for the older adult population are typically quite costly though, with the price increasing substantially in relation to the services provided. As a consequence, many older adults find themselves in situations where they cannot afford the exorbitant cost of many private communities. Government-subsidized senior housing, such as Section 202 Supportive Housing for the Elderly program, Section 8 Housing for the general population (choice vouchers and project-based), and Section 515 for rural communities, can make housing costs more affordable for low income older adult populations by providing a subsidy directly to older adults in the form of tax credits, loans, or rental vouchers or to housing communities, which then pass on this discount to residents. There are several problems with government subsidy programs, though, including a lack of available units and the inappropriateness of many units for older adults due to location and condition.

The goal of many assisted-living facilities is to keep residents active and engaged

© JAMIE HOOPER/SHUTTERSTOCK

A 2003 longitudinal study that followed 1,200 older adults in their transition from independent living to age-restricted housing found that older adults who transitioned to more expensive communities fared the best with regard to physical health and overall life satisfaction, while those who transitioned to government-subsidized housing programs fared the worst. Although the study investigators acknowledged that levels of life satisfaction might be related to a cumulative effect of a lifetime of poverty, they concluded that, overall, the quality of housing had a direct relationship to life satisfaction (Krout, 2003).

Homelessness and the Older Adult Population

One of the opening vignettes of this chapter highlighted the issue of homelessness in the older adult community. Although older adults are at a lower risk for homelessness than other age groups, homelessness in the older adult population is a growing concern because the percentage is expected to grow as the baby boomer generation ages (Gonyea, Mills-Dick, & Bachman, 2010). Additionally, for years the problem of homelessness among the older population has been for the most part ignored by policy makers and legislators, rendering this population somewhat invisible (Gonyea, Mills-Dick, & Bachman, 2010).

The common causes of homelessness in the older adult population include many of the same underlying factors as in the general population, such as a lack of affordable housing, a lack of employment opportunities (Burke, Johnson, Bourgault, Borgia, & O'Toole, 2013), mental illness (Creech, Johnson, Borgia, Bourgault, Redihan, & O'Toole, 2015), and a breakdown in the family, including violence (Fisher, Ewing, Garrett, Harrison, Lwin, & Wheeler, 2013). But the older adult population in general has additional risk factors, such as not being able to sufficiently recover from a job loss, as well as experiencing a chronic illness that interferes with work responsibilities or destroys them financially (Kutza & Keigher, 1991). Homeless older adults are a particularly vulnerable subgroup because of age-related physical vulnerabilities, which may be exacerbated by poor nutrition and difficult living conditions. They are also at a much higher risk of becoming a victim of crime while living on the streets (Hecht & Coyle, 2001).

Understanding the demographics of the older adult homeless population is an important factor in designing appropriate programs for older adults. One study found that homelessness among adults increased from 11.2 percent to 32.3 percent between 1990 and 2000 (Hahn, Kushel, Bangsbert, Riley, & Moss, 2006). Older adult homelessness is expected to continue to increase as well. In 2010 in the United States there were approximately 58,772 unsheltered adults over the age of 62 years of age, and according to the National Alliance to End Homelessness this number is expected to double by 2050 (Sermons & Henry, 2010). This projection is a cause of great concern, particularly in light of the limited availability of subsidized affordable housing units. For instance, the Section 202 program has only 300,000 available units across the country, with only modest increases in federal funding (the FY 2016 budget included only a 3 percent increase in funding over the prior year) (Sermons & Henry, 2010).

Gaining more insights into the differences between younger homeless and older homeless populations becomes important when considering programs designed to assist the older adult homeless population. And yet, while some research has been conducted that indicates several differences, including older adult populations having significantly lower incidences of substance abuse and domestic violence, more research is needed to better understand the patterns of older adult homelessness, including frequency and duration of homeless episodes, the nature of their needs, and their patterns of service utilization. Any human services programs designed to assist the older adult subgroups with housing issues need to focus on issues related specifically to the older adult population, such as insufficient income, health concerns, low-income housing needs, and supportive services designed for an older adult population.

Retirement

The concept of retirement is so common to the 21st century that it rarely needs explanation. The most common conceptualization of retirement involves an employee permanently surrendering his or her position at approximately 65 years of age, and drawing on a pension or retirement account that has likely been accruing for decades. Of course, there are numerous variations on this theme—some people never fully retire, choosing instead to dabble in part-time work, and some people work in fields that have mandatory retirement ages, such as the airline industry, which requires all pilots retire at the age of 65. For others, retirement is simply not an option due to financial constraints. The traditional notion of retirement is an experience that only those with higher incomes can afford, thus it would be inappropriate to assume that everyone in the workforce has accrued a pension sizeable enough to permit them to live on for years. But despite the range of retirement experiences, certain generalizations can be made about the retirement experience for the majority of those living in the United States during the 21st century.

Robert Atchley (1976) was one of the first researchers who attempted to describe the retirement experience for men and women. He identified five distinct yet overlapping stages that most retirees progress through when they formally retire:

1. The honeymoon phase: Retirees embrace retirement and all their newfound freedom in an optimistic but often unrealistic manner.

2. Disenchantment: Retirees become disillusioned with what they thought retirement was going to be like and get discouraged with what often feels like too much time on their hands.

3. Reorientation: Retirees develop a more realistic view of retirement with regard to both increased opportunities and increased constraints.

4. Stability: Retirees adjust to retirement.

5. Termination: Retirees eventually lose independence due to physical and cognitive decline.

There has been some controversy about whether retirees actually progress through such distinct stages or whether there is just too much of a range of experiences among retirees in the United States to categorize experiences in a **linear stage theory**. A study by Reitzes and Mutran (2004) appears to support Atchley's stage theory, finding that retirees experience a temporary lift right after retiring (for about six months), but then develop an increasingly negative attitude after about the 12-month mark, with some retirees starting to experience increased optimism after about two years. The study also found that an individual's level of self-esteem preretirement seemed to have an effect on their overall mental health after retirement, with those who had higher levels of self-esteem faring better.

A more recent study on postretirement dynamics seems to support some of Atchley, and Reitzes and Mutran's findings, while refuting others. The study, which was funded by the National Institute on Aging, found that men and women who continued to work for a period of time after retirement, on a part-time or temporary basis (called **bridge employment**), had much better physical and psychological quality of life during their later years. This would seem to indicate that sudden and complete retirement without any transition period may have negative consequences for an older adult's physical and mental health. Interestingly, the positive effects gained from bridge employment existed regardless of the retiree's preretirement mental and physical health status (Zhan, Wang, Liu, & Shultz, 2009).

Because nearly 50 percent of the U.S. population is now over the age of 50, the implications of retirement preparation and adjustment to retirement for the human services field cannot be ignored. Human service professionals will likely come into contact with retired or retiring adults in many different settings. Thus, it is important to realize that impending retirement can become an issue for someone even in middle adulthood.

Finally, race and gender have a significant effect on retirement experiences. Research has shown that women and many ethnic minority groups often have different attitudes and experiences surrounding retirement issues due to disparity in income and education levels (McNamara & Williamson, 2004). Thus, the human service professional must understand that most factors affecting a client's retirement experience are going to be influenced by the client's gender and racial status.

Grandparents Parenting

The practice of grandparents raising grandchildren is not new, but it has increased dramatically over the past several years, signaling many challenges in U.S. society that have emerged since the 1970s. In response to an increase in grandparents becoming primary caregivers to their grandchildren, beginning in 2000 the U.S. Census includes questions regarding grandparents residing with grandchildren, including whether they had primary responsibility for them and what length of time they had acted in a parental role (i.e., revealing whether the situation is temporary or permanent).

About 10 percent of all children in the United States live with a grandparent. The number of children residing in grandparent-maintained households (where grandparents have primary caregiving responsibilities) has doubled in the last several decades increasing from 3 percent in 1970 to 6 percent in 2012. Additionally, about 60 percent of these households involved a single grandparent, totaling 2.7 million households. Grandparent caregivers also tend to be younger, belong to ethnic minorities, be poor with low education levels, and suffer from depression. Additionally, grandparent caregivers in the Southeast and in urban areas have the highest levels of poverty and the lowest levels of education (Simmons & Dye, 2003; Whitely & Kelley, 2007). Even though older African American grandmothers are disproportionately represented in custodial grandparent arrangements, a recent research study indicates that older grandparents may experience less emotional strain related to their primary parenting role than do younger grandparents, likely related to their increased ability to manage stressful life situations (Conway, Jones, & Speakes-Lewis, 2011).

Ethnic minority children are far more likely to be raised by a grandparent than Caucasian children, with African American children in the Southeastern states having a significantly higher rate of living with custodial grandparents than children in other regions in the United States. African American grandparents are far likelier to experience poverty (despite being in the workforce). They are also far likelier to be underinsured and experience greater physical and emotional stressors (Whitely & Kelley, 2007). There are several reasons why grandparents become surrogate parents, but the chief reasons include the following:

1. The high divorce rate, leaving many women facing potential poverty, resulting in them returning home to live with parents

2. The sharp rise in teen pregnancies, resulting in the mother residing with her parents for economic (and oftentimes emotional) reasons

3. The increase in relative foster care in response to a sharp increase in child welfare intervention due to child abuse

4. The increase in parents serving time in prison, primarily for drug and drug-related offenses punishable by high prison sentences due to the U.S. government's War on Drugs

5. The sharp increase in drug use, particularly among women of color whose use of crack cocaine has literally exploded over the past 10 years

6. The AIDS crisis that has devastated many communities, leaving children orphaned and in need of permanent homes. These cases become even more complicated when the children have contracted HIV and have significant medical needs.

The issues facing grandparents raising grandchildren are complex involving emotional as well as financial, legal, and physical challenges. Many grandparent caregivers are forced to live in limbo, not knowing how long they will remain responsible for their grandchildren, particularly when the biological parents are either in jail or suffering from drug addiction that prevents them from resuming their primary parenting role. The choice to act as a surrogate parent is in many instances made in a time of crisis. Thus, older adults who may have been planning their retirement for years often find themselves in a position to either take on this parenting role in the face of the situation that rendered the biological parents unable to continue parenting or to allow their grandchildren to enter the foster care system. Parenting younger children has its unique challenges, but often comes with some level of social support, at least within the primary school system, but this is often not the case with older children, particularly adolescents.

Parenting adolescents often presents significant challenges for grandparents, particularly when the grandparent caregivers are advanced in years. Parenting adolescents can be an exhausting endeavor for the young or middle-aged parent, but imagine the demands placed on someone who is an older adult, who has limited physical capacity and even more limited financial means. Adolescents who have endured significant loss through death or abandonment, have been raised in abusive homes, or have been raised by parents who abuse drugs or are serving time in prison may act out emotionally and even physically, putting even greater stress on an already fragile family system.

Human service professionals may enter a grandparent-led family system in numerous ways—they could be the school social worker or counselor working with the children, they might be the child welfare caseworker assigned to assist the grandparent who is serving as a kinship foster care parent, or they might work for a human services agency offering outreach services to grandparent caregivers. The generalist skills human service professionals must have are relatively expansive due to the nature of the work they will likely be doing within the family system. These include knowledge of adolescent development, cultural competence, knowledge of a range of psychosocial issues ranging from effective parenting styles to knowledge of grief and loss processes, and excellent case management skills.

Depression in Older Adulthood

Another significant concern affecting the older adult population is the increased incidence of clinical depression and depressive symptoms. In fact, the National Institute of Mental Health (NIMH) estimates that approximately two million individuals over the age of 65 suffer from some form of depression and as many as five million more suffer from some form of depressive symptoms that do not meet all the criteria for clinical depression. Although prevalence rates can vary rather widely within the population, due in part to how depression is defined, these statistics indicate that at any given time anywhere from 5 to 30 percent of the older adult population may suffer from some form of depression, compared to a 1 percent prevalence rate in the general population (Birrer & Vemuri, 2004; Center for Behavioral Health Statistics and Quality, 2015).

Depression rates in nursing homes are even higher, with some studies finding up to 50 percent of the residents meeting the criteria for clinical depression. Older adults are also disproportionately at risk for suicide. For instance, although individuals aged 85 years and older make up about only 1.4 percent of the U.S. population, they account for 19.3 percent of all completed suicides in 2014 (CDC, 2015). White widowed males over the age of 85 are at the highest risk of suicide among all age and racial groups (Birrer & Vemuri, 2004; Kraaij & de Wilde, 2001; McIntosh, 2004; NIMH, 2007).

Depression is not a natural part of growing older and can be avoided in many cases with increased attention and early intervention. Due to misdiagnoses and misunderstandings about the nature of depression and depressive symptoms and how they manifest in the older adult population, many older adults remain undiagnosed and untreated. For instance, depression is frequently mistaken for early signs of dementia or some other form of cognitive impairment (Birrer & Vemuri, 2004). Human service professionals can play a significant role in early identification and prevention efforts by being observant of the signs of depression in their older adult clients. Watching for the many risk factors for depression is also important, such as anxiety, chronic medical conditions, unmarried status, a history of alcohol abuse, stressful life events (such as the recent death of a spouse or a recent move), and minimal social support (Birrer & Vemuri, 2004; Lynch, Compton, Mendelson, Robins, & Krishnan, 2000; Waite, Bebbington, Skelton-Robinson, & Orrell, 2004).

Dementia

Dementia is a progressive degenerative illness experienced during old age that impairs brain function and cognitive ability. Dementia is an umbrella term encompassing numerous disorders, but the two most common forms of dementia are **Alzheimer's disease** and **multi-infarct dementia** (small strokes in the brain). Dementia involves the comprehensive shutting down of all bodily systems. In general, the symptoms include progressive memory loss, increased difficulty concentrating, a steady decrease in problem-solving skills and judgment capability, confusion, hallucinations and delusions, altered sensations or perceptions, impaired recognition of everyday objects and familiar people, altered sleep patterns, motor system impairment, inability to maintain ADL (such as dressing oneself), agitation, anxiety, and depression. Ultimately, the dementia sufferer enters a complete vegetative state prior to death.

According to the NIMH, multi-infarct dementia accounts for nearly 20 percent of all dementias, affecting about 4 in 10,000 people. Even more individuals suffer from some form of mild cognitive impairment but do not yet meet the criteria for full-blown dementia (Palmer, Winblad, & Fratiglioni, 2003). Alzheimer's disease affects approximately 4.5 million Americans or about 5 percent of the population between the ages of 65 and 74 years, and the incident rate increases to 50 percent for those over 85 years of age. Diagnosis is based on symptoms and it is only through an autopsy that a definitive diagnosis is made. In the latter part of the 20th century, the United States has experienced a dramatic increase in the incidence of dementia primarily due to the increased human lifespan. It is theorized that dementia did not have an opportunity to develop prior to the 1900s, when the average lifespan was about 47 years. There is no known cure for dementia, and thus treatment is focused on delaying and relieving symptoms.

Human service professionals may work directly with clients diagnosed with dementia or with the caregiver (typically a spouse or adult child) if they work in a practice setting that serves the older adult population. However, dealing with dementia as a clinical issue can occur in any practice setting because any client may have a relative suffering from dementia and may therefore need counseling and perhaps even case management. Consider the practitioner who assists clients in managing an ailing parent. The practitioner may need to help the client with questions about whether the parent is suffering from cognitive impairment, with grieving the slow loss of the parent they love, and with support in making difficult decisions such as determining when their parent can no longer live alone. Or, consider the school social worker who is counseling a student whose grandfather has recently been diagnosed with Alzheimer's disease. The pressure on the entire family system will affect the student in numerous ways—academically, emotionally, perhaps even physically—and may even magnify any existing issues with which the student is currently struggling.

Elder Abuse

The National Center on Elder Abuse (NCEA) defines elder abuse as any "knowing, intentional, or negligent act by a caregiver or any other person that causes harm or a serious risk of harm to a vulnerable adult." The specific definition of elder abuse varies from state to state, but in general elder abuse can include physical, emotional, or sexual abuse; neglect and abandonment; or financial exploitation. Older adults are at an increased risk of abuse due to factors such as their physical frailty, dependence, social isolation, and any existence of cognitive impairment.

Elder abuse was not legally defined until 1987, when it was directly addressed in an amendment of the Older Americans Act. While it's difficult to determine with any level of accuracy how many older adults are being abused and/or neglected, reports of elder abuse have increased significantly over the last several years. For instance, in 1986 there were 117,000 reports of elder abuse nationwide, and by 1996 the number had more than doubled, reaching 293,000 reported cases (Tatara, 1997). By the year 2000 the number of elder abuse reports had risen to an alarming 47,281. Other estimates place the rate of abuse and neglect among the older adult population at about 10 percent (Acierno et al., 2010).

One reason for the rise in abuse reports is that the newest figures include not only abuse in domestic settings, but also abuse in institutional settings. Despite the more comprehensive data collection methods, there is no escaping the fact that elder abuse is increasing within the United States (Teaster, 2000). Elder abuse is expected to continue to rise in the coming years due to the increased lifespan and the resultant increase in chronic illnesses, changing family patterns, and the complexity involved with contemporary caregiving.

Watch the video produced by Dan Rather Reports *on a case of elder financial abuse. What role can human service professionals play in working with older adults who either have been exploited financially or are at risk of financial exploitation?*

ENHANCEDetext *video example 7.4*

www.youtube.com/
watch?v=N0cXyl3xdjQ

Sixty percent of all reported abuse victims are women, 65 percent of all abuse victims are white, more than 60 percent of abuse incidences occurred in domestic settings, and about 8 percent of abuse incidences occurred in institutionalized settings. Family members were the most commonly cited perpetrators, including both spouses and adult children (Teaster, 2000). A recent study found that elder abuse and neglect were associated with being single (separated or divorced), poverty, being in poor health, and having a disability The study also found that Hispanics were less likely to be abused and/or neglected (Burnes et al., 2015).

In March 2010, the Elder Justice Act of 2009 (EJA) was passed and signed into law by President Obama as part of the Patient Protection and Affordable Care Act (ACA). The act sets forth numerous provisions for addressing the abuse, neglect, and exploitation of older adults, with both preventative and responsive measures. For instance, the legislation provides grants for a number of training programs focusing on prevention of abuse and exploitation of older adults; provides measures for expanding long-term care services, including a long-term care ombudsman program; establishes mandatory reporting requirements for abuse against older adults occurring in long-term care facilities; and includes provisions for creating national advisory councils (National Health Forum Policy, 2010).

Every state is required to have an **adult protective services (APS) agency**. There is significant variation among states with regard to how abuse is to be reported and investigated. Some states have separate agencies handling elder abuse, and some combine the protection of older adults with the protection of disabled adults of all ages. Despite increases in reporting requirements, elder abuse is still considered to be grossly underreported not only due to the range of reporting requirements, but also due to the hidden nature of elder abuse. It is for this reason that it's essential that those working in the human services field be aware of the elder abuse reporting laws and requirements in their state in addition to the early signs of abuse and neglect, including financial abuse.

Caregiver burnout is one of the primary risk factors of elder abuse. The most common scenario involves a loving family member who becomes intensely frustrated by the seemingly impossible task of caring for a spouse or parent with a chronic illness such as dementia. Providing continuous care of someone with Alzheimer's disease, for example, can be frustrating, provoking an abusive response from someone with no history of abusive behavior. One of the most effective intervention strategies can be a caregiver support group. These groups are typically facilitated by a social worker or other human services provider and focus on providing caregivers, many of whom are older adults themselves, a safe place to express their frustrations, sadness, and other feelings related to caring for their dependent older adult loved one.

ENHANCEDetext *self-check 7.4*

PRACTICE SETTINGS SERVING OLDER ADULTS

Working with older adults is gaining in popularity within the human services field, driven in part by an increased focus on gerontology in human services educational programs. For human service professionals wishing to provide direct services to the older adult population, a wide array of choices in practice settings awaits them. AAAs, discussed earlier in this chapter, often serve as human service agencies offering direct service to the older adult community on a local level. Generally these agencies offer a multitude of services for older adults, such as nutrition programs, services for homebound older adults, low-income minority older adults, and other programs focusing on the needs of older adults within the local community. Many AAAs also act as a referral source for other services in the area. For instance, the Mid-Florida AAAs offer programs for those suffering from Alzheimer's disease (including **caregiver respite**), a toll-free elder hotline that links older adults in the area with resources, an emergency home energy assistance program, paralegal services, home care for older adults, Medicaid waivers, and practitioners who work with older adults in helping them make informed decisions.

Most AAAs offer both in-house services, many of which are facilitated by human service professionals, and off-site programs. Human service professionals working at an AAA-funded center might facilitate caregiver respite programs, or they might provide case management for an agency that provides employment services for clients over 60 years old. Even at centers where services are primarily medical in nature, human service professionals often provide counseling and case management as a support service.

Other practice settings include adult day cares, geriatric assessment units, nursing home facilities, veterans' services, elder abuse programs, adult protective services, bereavement services, senior centers, and hospices. A human service professional working in one of these practice settings may engage in direct services, consultations, and educational services focused on assisting older clients maintain or improve their quality of life, independence, and level of self-determination. Tasks are typically performed using a multidisciplinary team approach and can include conducting psychosocial assessments, providing case management, developing treatment plans, providing referrals for appropriate services, and providing counseling to older adult clients and their families. Services are also provided to family caregivers offering support and respite care.

Watch the video produced by the Veterans Health Administration on dementia care. What activities could human service professionals engage in with a veterans dementia population in a unit such as this?
ENHANCEDetext *video example 7.5*

www.youtube.com/
watch?v=3rMa0Ap_cfA

Multicultural Considerations

As the frail older adult population has increased in numbers, the government has shifted its priorities to long-term health care needs, with a particular focus on at-risk populations such as women, ethnic minorities, nursing home residents, and older adults living in rural communities who are socially isolated. It's difficult to define who among the adult population is at particular risk of a range of psychosocial problems because in many senses all older adults are at-risk in that they are vulnerable to social, economic, physical, and psychological harm or exploitation simply by virtue of their advanced age and corresponding dependency needs. But many gerontologists classify various subpopulations as more vulnerable than others for various reasons. For instance, successful aging has been linked to good economic status, good health care, relatively low stress levels, and high levels of social connections. A 2004 study also showed a link between good health and financial stability, finding that Caucasians tend to have greater economic wealth and better health than African American and Latino populations (Lum, 2004). A more recent study found that predictors of successful aging are rooted in early childhood, with those who had positive childhood experiences, including a higher socioeconomic status, having a greater likelihood of aging more successfully (Brandt, Deindl, & Hank, 2012).

Women are often considered a special population because as a group they are more prone to depression and typically have a worse response to antidepressant medication (Kessler, 2003). Women also experience greater financial vulnerability, particularly if

Older male veterans are at high risk of a range of psychosocial problems, including poverty, homelessness, and physical and mental health problems

divorced or widowed, and are often in lower-wage jobs, undereducated, and underinsured. Widowhood is a common occurrence for women because they live an average of seven years longer than men, and although the majority of women in the United States marry, 75 percent of women are unmarried by the age of 65. Widowhood puts women at increased risk for lower morale and other mental health problems, even though these symptoms abate with time and intervention (Bennett, 1997). Other research indicates that in some settings, women tend to fare better, at least in assisted living facilities (Kozar-Westman, Troutman-Jordan, & Nies, 2013). This may be due to the tendency for women to engage in social activities in such settings at a higher level compared to men.

Another at-risk population is older veterans, and while most older veterans rate themselves as aging successfully (Pietrzak, Tsai, Kirwin, & Southwick, 2014), other studies show that in war cohort, exposure to trauma, pre- and post-service socio-economic status, and health status impact successful aging in this population. For instance, veterans who experienced combat had a history of financial insecurity and mental health problems, including depression and post-trauma stress disorder (PTSD) experienced more challenges in their advanced years (Daniels, Boehnlein, & McCallion, 2015). In fact, it appears as though exposure to combat-related trauma in early adulthood may decrease veterans' ability to effectively manage stressors later in life. Sachs-Ericsson et al. (2016) found that veterans who had been exposed to combat-related trauma earlier in life actually developed PTSD symptoms in older adulthood, becoming more reactive to stressors in older adulthood than non-veterans.

Research has also shown that racism can affect quality of life in later years for certain populations. A study conducted in 2002 found that racism, and particularly **institutionalized racism** (such as government-sanctioned racism through discrimination in housing, education, employment, and health care), had a detrimental effect on older African Americans, particularly men, who experienced greater stress throughout lives and lower life satisfaction during older adulthood (Utsey, Payne, Jackson, & Jones, 2002). In fact, institutionalized racism has been linked to feelings of invisibility, stress, depression, and ultimately despair as affected individuals experience a sense of futility in combating a lifetime of discrimination and disparity in treatment related to white privilege (Franklin, Boyd-Franklin, & Kelly, 2006).

Identifying special populations within the older adult population will allow the human service professional to explore issues that can potentially place older adult clients at increased risk of a lower quality of life during old age. A human service professional who is well versed in common risk factors for older adults in the United States, as well as for the increased risk factors facing special populations, will be far more effective in protecting and advocating for their older adult clients.

ENHANCEDetext *self-check 7.5*

CONCLUSION

The older adult population is increasing at a dramatic rate in the United States (as well as globally), rendering this one of the fastest growing target populations of human services agencies. As the baby boomer cohort continues to age and as life continues to become increasingly complex, many within the older adult population will rely on human service professionals to meet many of their psychosocial needs. Many human services educational programs are adding the field of older adult care, or social gerontology, as an area of specialization in response to the growing need for practitioners committed to working with this population.

Future considerations include continued efforts to identify at-risk populations, as well as addressing ongoing concerns such as the shortage of available affordable housing, the availability of long-term care and health care services directed at the older adult population, and the increased role of parenting responsibilities placed on the older adult population. Human service professionals can make a positive impact on the lives of older adults and their family members by addressing both ongoing and anticipated needs of this population.

SUMMARY

- The impact of changing demographics associated with the current and projected growth of the older adult population is examined. Changing population demographics involving the dramatic growth of the older adult population, also referred to as the graying of America, is explored. Dynamics include the impact of the extended lifespan on older adults, their family systems, and society in general.
- The stage of older adulthood within a developmental context is explored. Older adulthood from a developmental perspective is discussed, including discussion of Erikson's theory of psychosocial development, Tornstam's theory of gerotranscendense, and Daniel Levinson's work on middle age.
- Key aspects of successful and active aging are identified. The concepts of successful aging and active aging are discussed within the context of what factors are related to aging well, such as remaining physically active and engaged on a social level.
- Major challenges facing many older adults are examined. Challenges facing many older adults are discussed, including ageism, housing and homelessness, retirement, grandparents parenting, depression, dementia, and elder abuse. Populations that are at increased risk of experiencing these challenges are also explored as are underlying factors, such as economic disadvantage and ethnic minority status.
- The roles and functions of human service professionals working with the older adult population in a range of practice settings are explored. Practice settings serving the older adult population are explored within the context of the roles and functions of human service professionals. Practice settings such as AAAs, adult day cares, geriatric assessment units, nursing home facilities, veterans' services, elder abuse programs, adult protective services, bereavement services, senior centers, and hospices are also explored as are multicultural considerations.

Internet Resources

Conduct an Internet search for Aging Services on the National Association of Area Agencies on Aging.

Conduct an Internet search for the article "Not Your Father's Retirement" on the AARP website.

Conduct an Internet search for the article "Ageism in the U.S. Workplace: A Persistent Problem Unlikely to Go Away" on the Reuters' website.

Conduct an Internet search for "Information for Senior Citizens" on the U.S. Department of Housing and Urban Development website.

Conduct an Internet search for the "Fact Sheet: Age and Socioeconomic Status" on the American Psychological Association website.

Conduct an Internet search for the article "Ethnic Disparities Persist in Depression Diagnosis and Treatment among Older Americans" on the National Institute of Mental Health website.

References

Acierno, R., Hernandez, M. A., Amstadter, A. B., Resnick, H. S., Steve, K., Muzzy, W., & Kilpatrick, D. G. (2010). Prevalence and correlates of emotional, physical, sexual, and financial abuse and potential neglect in the United States: The National Elder Mistreatment Study. *American Journal of Public Health,100*(2), 292–297.

Arias, B. (2004). United States life tables, 2002. *National Vital Statistics Reports, 53*(6). Hyattsville, MD: National Center for Health Statistics.

Atchley, R. C. (1976). *The sociology of retirement.* New York, NY: John Wiley.

Bennett, K. M. (1997). Widowhood in elderly women: The medium- and long-term effects on mental and physical health. *Mortality, 2,* 137–148.

Birrer, R. B., & Vemuri, S. P. (2004). Depression in later life: A diagnostic and therapeutic challenge. *American Family Physician, 69*(10), 2375–2382.

Bowling, A., & Iliffe, S. (2011). Psychological approach to successful ageing predicts future quality of life in older adults. *Health and Quality of Life Outcomes, 9*(1), 13–22.

Brandt, M., Deindl, C., & Hank, K. (2012). Tracing the origins of successful aging: the role of childhood conditions and social inequality in explaining later life health. *Social Science and Medicine, 74*(9), 1418–1425.

Burke, C., Johnson, E. E., Bourgault, C., Borgia, M., & O'Toole, T. P. (2013). Losing work: Regional unemployment and its effect on homeless demographic characteristics, needs, and health care. *Journal of Health Care for the Poor and Underserved, 24*(3), 1391–1402.

Burnes, D., Pillemer, K., Caccamise, P. L., Mason, A., Henderson, C. R., Berman, J., & Salamone, A. (2015). Prevalence of and risk factors for elder abuse and neglect in the community: A population-based study. *Journal of the American Geriatrics Society, 63*(9), 1906–1912.

Butler, R. N. (1969). Ageism: Another form of bigotry. *Gerontologist, 9,* 243–246.

Center for Behavioral Health Statistics and Quality. (2015). *Behavioral health trends in the United States: Results from the 2014 National Survey on Drug Use and Health* (HHS Publication No. SMA 15-4927, NSDUH Series H-50). Retrieved from http://www.samhsa.gov/data/

Centers for Disease Control and Prevention [CDC]. (2015). *Data & Statistics Fatal Injury Report for 2014.* Retrieved September 25, 2016, from http://www.cdc.gov/injury/wisqars/fatal.html.

Conway, F., Jones, S., & Speakes-Lewis, A. (2011). Emotional strain in caregiving among African American grandmothers raising their grandchildren. *Journal of Women and Aging, 23*(2), 113–128.

Coudin, G., & Alexopoulos, T. (2010). "Help me! I'm old!" How negative aging stereotypes create dependency among older adults. *Aging and Mental Health, 14*(5), 516–523.

Creech, S. K., Johnson, E., Borgia, M., Bourgault, C., Redihan, S., & O'Toole, T. P. (2015). Identifying mental and physical health correlates of homelessness among first-time and chronically homeless veterans. *Journal of Community Psychology, 43*(5), 619–627.

Daniels, L. R., Boehnlein, J., & McCallion, P. (2015). Aging, depression, and wisdom: A pilot study of life-review intervention and PTSD treatment with two groups of Vietnam veterans. *Journal of Gerontological Social Work, 58*(4), 420–436.

Degges-White, S. (2005). Understanding gerotranscendence in older adults: A new perspective for counselors. *Adultspan: Theory Research and Practice, 4*(1), 36–48.

Erikson, E. H. (1959). Identity and the life cycle. *Psychological Issues, 1,* 1–171.

Erikson, E. H. (1966). Eight ages of man. *International Journal of Psychiatry, 2,* 281–300.

Erikson, E. H., & Erikson, J. M. (1998). *The life cycle completed (extended version).* WW Norton & Company.

Fisher, R., Ewing, J., Garrett, A., Harrison, E. K., Lwin, K. K., & Wheeler, D. W. (2013). The nature and prevalence of chronic pain in homeless persons: an observational study. *F1000Research, 2.*

Franklin, A., Boyd-Franklin, N., & Kelly, S. (2006, June). Racism and invisibility: Race-related stress, emotional abuse and psychological trauma for people of color. *Journal of Emotional Abuse, 6*(2/3), 9–30. Retrieved September 14, 2009, from doi:10.1300/J135v06n02-02

Gonyea, J. G., Mills-Dick, K., & Bachman, S. S. (2010). The complexities of elder homelessness, a shifting political landscape and emerging community responses. *Journal of Gerontological Social Work, 53*(7), 575–590.

Hahn, J., Kushel, M., Bangsbert, D., Riley, E., & Moss, A. (2006). The aging of the homeless population: Fourteen-year trends in San Francisco. *The Journal of General Internal Medicine, 21*(7), 775–778.

Havighurst, R. J. (1961). Successful aging. *Gerontologist, 1*(1), 8–13.

Hecht, L., & Coyle, B. (2001). Elderly homeless: A comparison of older and younger adult emergency shelter seekers in Bakersfield, California. *American Behavioral Scientist, 45*(1), 66–79.

Hirshbein, L. D. (2001). Popular views of old age in America, 1900–1950. *Journal of American Geriatrics Society, 49*, 1555–1560.

Hsu, H. (2007, November). Does social participation by the elderly reduce mortality and cognitive impairment? *Aging and Mental Health, 11*(6), 699–707. Retrieved from doi:10.1080/13607860701366335

Kessler, R. C. (2003). Epidemiology of women and depression. *Journal of Affective Disorders, 74*(1), 5–13.

Kozar-Westman, M., Troutman-Jordan, M., & Nies, M. A. (2013). Successful aging among assisted living community older adults. *Journal of Nursing Scholarship, 45*(3), 238–246.

Kraaij, V., & de Wilde, J. (2001). Negative life events and depressive symptoms in the elderly life: A life span perspective. *Aging and Mental Health, 5*(1), 84–91.

Krout, J. A. (2003). *Residential choices and experiences of older adults: Pathways for life quality.* New York, NY: Spring Publishing Company.

Kutza, E. A., & Keigher, S. M. (1991). The elderly "new homeless": An emergency population at risk. *Social Work, 36*(4), 283–293.

Levinson, D. (1978). *The seasons of a man's life.* New York, NY: Knopf.

Levinson, D. (1996). *The seasons of a woman's life.* New York, NY: Knopf.

Lum, Y. (2004). Health-wealth association among older Americans: Racial and ethnic differences. *Social Work Research, 28*(2), 106–116.

Lynch, T. R., Compton, J. S., Mendelson, T., Robins, C. J., & Krishnan, K. R. R. (2000). Anxious depression among the elderly: Clinical and phenomenological correlates. *Aging and Mental Health, 4*(3), 268–274.

McIntosh, J. L. (2004). *U.S.A. suicide: 2004 official final data.* Retrieved from http://www.ct.gov/dmhas/lib/dmhas/prevention/cyspi/AAS2004data.pdf

McNamara, T. K., & Williamson, J. B. (2004). Race, gender, and the retirement decisions of people ages 60 to 80: Prospects for age integration in employment. *International Journal of Aging and Human Development, 59*(3), 255–286.

Miller, D., Leyell, T., & Mazacheck, J. (2004). Stereotypes of the elderly in U.S. television commercials from the 1950s to the 1990s. *International Journal of Aging and Human Development, 58*(4), 315–340.

National Health Forum Policy. (2010, November). *The Elder Abuse Act: Addressing elder abuse, neglect and exploitation.* Retrieved from http://www.nhpf.org/library/the-basics/Basics_ElderJustice_11-30-10.pdf

National Highway Safety and Traffic Administration [NHSTA]. (2009). *Traffic safety facts 2009 data: Older population.* Retrieved from http://www-nrd.nhtsa.dot.gov/Pubs/811391.pdf

National Institute of Mental Health. (2007). *Older adults: Depression and suicide facts* (NIH Publication No. QF 11-7697). Bethesda, MD: National Institutes of Health.

Palmer, K., Winblad, B., & Fratiglioni, L. (2003). Detection of Alzheimer's disease and dementia in the preclinical phase: Population based cohort study. *BMJ: British Medical Journal, 326*(7383).

Pietrzak, R. H., Tsai, J., Kirwin, P. D., & Southwick, S. M. (2014). Successful aging among older veterans in the United States. *The American Journal of Geriatric Psychiatry, 22*(6), 551–563.

Reitzes, D. C., & Mutran, E. J. (2004). The transition to retirement: Stages and factors that influence retirement adjustment. *International Journal of Aging and Human Development, 59*(1), 63–84.

Sachs-Ericsson, N., Joiner, T. E., Cougle, J. R., Stanley, I. H., & Sheffler, J. L. (2016). Combat exposure in early adulthood interacts with recent stressors to predict PTSD in aging male veterans. *The Gerontologist, 56*, 83–91.

Sermons, M. W., & Henry, M. (2010, April 1). Demographic of homelessness series: The rising elder population. Homelessness Research Institute. National Alliance to End Homelessness. Retrieved from http://www.endhomelessness.org/page/-/files/2698_file_Aging_Report.pdf

Simmons, T., & Dye, J. L. (2003, October). *Grandparents living with grandchildren: 2000.* Washington, DC: U.S. Bureau of the Census.

Snyder, M. (2001). *Self and society.* Malden, MA: Blackwell Publishers.

Tatara, T. (1997). *Summaries of the statistical data on elder abuse in domestic settings.* Washington, DC: National Center on Elder Abuse.

Teaster, P. B. (2000). *A response to the abuse of vulnerable adults: A 2000 survey of state adult protective services.* Washington, DC: National Center on Elder Abuse.

Thornton, J. E. (2002). Myths of aging or ageist stereotypes. *Educational Gerontology, 28,* 301–312.

Tornstam, L. (1994). Gerotranscendence—A theoretical and empirical exploration. In L. E. Thomas & S. A. Eisenhandler (Eds.), *Aging and the religious dimension.* Westport, CT: Greenwood Publishing Group.

Tornstam, L. (2003). *Gerotranscendence from young old age to old age.* Retrieved from www.soc.uu.se/Download .aspx?id=SpeY85XbP%2Bg%3DShare

Tornstam, L. (2005). *Gerotranscendence: A developmental theory of positive aging.* New York, NY: Springer Publishing.

U.S. Bureau of the Census, Population Estimates Program (PEP). (2014). Updated annually. http://www.census .gov/popest/.

Utsey, S. O., Payne, Y. A., Jackson, E. S., & Jones, A. M. (2002). Race-related stress, quality of life indicators, and life satisfaction among elderly African Americans. *Cultural Diversity and Ethnic Minority Psychology, 48*(3), 224–233.

Waite, A., Bebbington, P., Skelton-Robinson, M., & Orrell, M. (2004). Life events, depression and social support in dementia. *British Journal of Clinical Psychology, 43,* 313–324.

Warr, P., Butcher, V., & Robertson, I. (2004). Activity and psychological well-being in older people. *Aging and Mental Health, 8*(2), 172–183.

Weiss, I. (2005). Interest in working with the elderly: A cross-national study of graduating social work students. *Journal of Social Work Education, 41*(3), 379. Retrieved September 14, 2009, from MasterFILE Premier database.

Whitley, D. M., & Kelley, S. J. (2007, January). Grandparents raising grandchildren: A call to action. (Prepared for the Administration for Children and Families, Region IV.) Retrieved from http://www.acf.hhs.gov /opa/doc/grandparents.pdf

World Health Organization. (2002). Active ageing: A policy framework. Retrieved from http://apps.who .int/iris/bitstream/10665/67215/1/WHO_NMH _NPH_02.8.pdf

Zhan, Y., Wang, M., Liu, S., & Shultz, K. S. (2009). Bridge employment and retirees' health: A longitudinal investigation. *Journal of Occupational Health Psychology, 14,* 374–389.

8

Mental Health Services

© TINXI / SHUTTERSTOCK

The mental health field is quite multifaceted, in large part due to the highly complex nature of mental illness and mental health disorders. *Mental illness* is a term that, in its broadest sense, refers to a wide range of mental and emotional disorders, such as depression and anxiety disorders, and, in its narrowest sense, to those individuals who suffer from severe and chronic mental illness requiring at least intermittent custodial care. Because of the broadness of the terms *mental illness* and *mental disorders*, it can be challenging to reach a consensus on just how many people suffer from mental illness at any one time within the United States. However, using the *Diagnostic and Statistical Manual of Mental Disorders*, 5th edition (*DSM-5*), the primary tool for diagnosing mental disorders in the United States, can help.

In 2014 about 43.6 million Americans over the age of 18 experienced some type of mental illness. This included 7.9 million of whom experienced a co-occurring mental and substance use disorder, and 9.8 million of whom experienced a **serious mental illness**, defined as any mental, behavioral, or emotional disorder that significantly interferes with their life activities, such as their relationships, employment, parenting, or personal life management skills (Center for Behavioral Health Statistics and Quality, 2015). That's close to 20 percent of the entire adult U.S. adult population that is struggling with some diagnosable mental disorder. If substance use disorders are included as independent disorders (not co-occurring), the number jumps to almost 64 million adult or 26.5 percent of the U.S. population.

THE HISTORY OF MENTAL ILLNESS: PERCEPTIONS AND TREATMENT

Early in human history mental illness, called madness, lunacy, insanity, or feeble-mindedness, was commonly believed to be caused by demon possession. Archeologists have found skulls dating back to at least 5000 BCE with small holes drilled in them, presumably to allow the indwelling demons to escape. This practice, called trepanning, was practiced through the Middle Ages. Demonic possession, including witchcraft, was still thought to be the cause of most mental illnesses throughout the Middle Ages. A common "cure" involved tying up those suspected of being witches or demon-possessed with a rope and lowering them into freezing cold water. If they floated, they were believed to be witches and were then killed. If they sunk, they were not considered witches, and the cold water was believed to be a cure for whatever ailed them (Porter, 2002).

During Colonial times mental illness was considered a private family matter to be handled at the local level by family and perhaps the church. But as populations in the cities grew, those suffering from some form of mental illness increasingly became a problem for the entire community. Almshouses, typically used as poorhouses or work-houses, were often used to house the mentally ill. By the mid-1700s many towns in **Colonial America** were following the trend in Europe of building separate almshouses and even specialized hospitals for the insane (Torrey & Miller, 2002). Yet, reports of mistreatment were common. In fact, the trend of abuse noted in the **Middle Ages** continued throughout the 18th and 19th centuries, where members of society who were considered insane or feeble-minded (including those whose behavior was not in line with the general expectations of social norms) were subjected to public beatings, incarceration, and sometimes were even killed, particularly if their behavior was perceived as threatening (Torrey & Miller, 2002).

By the early 18th century, mental health reform had begun with the **moral treatment movement**, led in part by Dr. Philippe Pinel, a French physician, who rejected the prevailing belief that insanity was caused by demonic possession. Pinel became interested in mental illness when a friend developed symptoms, which Pinel referred to as a "nervous mania" that eventually evolved into a full mania. Pinel was ultimately forced to admit his friend into an asylum where his treatment was mismanaged. Pinel's friend left the asylum to return home with his parents, where his condition continued to deteriorate, leading to his untimely death when he wandered into the forest and was found dead several weeks later. This experience prompted Pinel to seek employment in 1792 at La Bicêtre hospital, which had an asylum for the incurably insane. Pinel served as chief physician at La Bicêtre for five years (Goldstein, 2002).

The conditions Pinel found at the hospital shocked him—patients chained to walls, some for decades, regular beatings, and some patients being put on public display for money. Although Dr. Pinel receives most of the credit for stopping this inhumane treatment at the hospital by unchaining thousands of patients, it was actually Jean-Baptiste

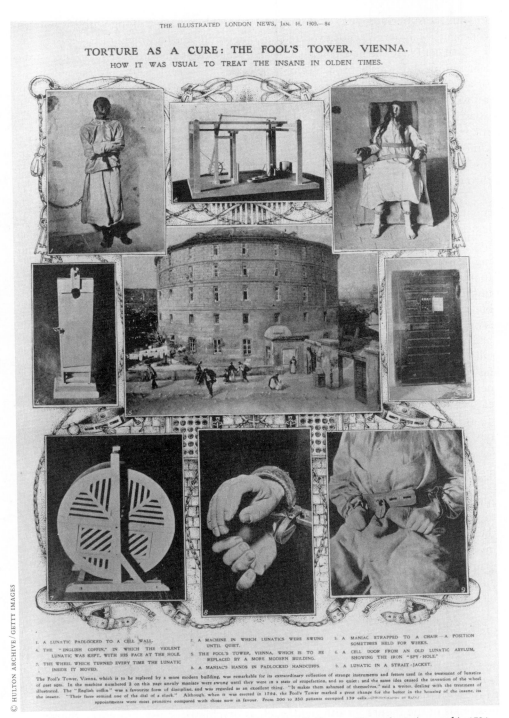

Circa 1850: How the insane were treated in days gone by at the Fool's Tower at Vienna (center), erected in 1794. Torture was looked upon as a cure. Original Publication: Illustrated London News—Torture As a Cure: The Fool's Tower, Vienna—to published 1909

Pussin, the superintendent of the mental ward who in 1784, along with his wife and colleague, Marguerite, who advocated for a more humane treatment of patients.

In 1793 Pinel, the new chief physician of the hospital, visited Pussin in the ward to learn more about his approach to patient care. In 1797 Pinel officially banned the use of all chains and shackles as well as other forms of abuse at the hospital. Pinel and Pussin worked together again at another hospital where Pinel was chief and Pussin was his assistant. Together they instituted what is now referred to as moral treatment of the mentally ill, described in detail in Pinel's book *Treatise on Insanity*, published in 1800. Unfortunately, Pinel and Pussin's work did not end the abuse of the mentally ill, and in time, the cruel treatment of those considered insane and incurable became prolific throughout both Europe in the United States.

Dorothea Dix was a leader in advocating for more compassionate treatment of the mentally ill in insane asylums in the United States. Her plea to the Massachusetts state legislature in 1843 poignantly described the deplorable conditions those with mental illness were forced to endure, including being held in cages by chains, often naked, enduring beatings with rods, and whipped to ensure obedience. Dix pleaded for the legislators to intercede on behalf of society's most vulnerable members. Dix's efforts resulted in an improvement in the conditions in both hospitals and asylums (Torrey & Miller, 2002), but these improvements were rather short-lived.

By the beginning of the 20th century most of the almshouses and insane asylums had closed, and state mental institutions became the primary facilities housing the mentally ill. While institutionalized care was considered revolutionary, compassionate, and far better than almshouses and asylums, rampant abuses involving cruel treatment, neglect, and physical and emotional abuse were increasingly reported throughout the early and middle 1900s. In fact, Dix's description of mid-century insane asylums could easily have described early the 20th century state system, which ultimately led to what is now referred to as deinstitutionalization.

The Deinstitutionalization of the Mentally Ill

Although horrible abuses in state and private mental hospitals were well documented through the mid-1900s, institutionalized care remained the primary method of treating the seriously mentally ill for another 50 years. The U.S. government's first legislative involvement in the care of the mentally ill occurred in 1946, when President Harry Truman signed the National Mental Health Act into law. The signing of this act allowed for the creation of National Institute of Mental Health (NIMH) in 1949, one of the first of four institutes under the National Institutes of Health.

In 1955 the Mental Health Study Act was passed, which directed the convening of the Joint Commission on Mental Health and Illness under the auspices of the NIMH. The Joint Commission was charged with the responsibility of analyzing and assessing the needs of the country's mentally ill, as well as making recommendations for a more effective and comprehensive national approach to the treatment of those with mental disorders and disabilities. The committee was comprised of professionals in the mental health field, such as psychiatrists, psychologists, therapists, educators, and representatives from various professional agencies, including the American Academy of Neurology, the American Academy of Pediatrics, the American Psychological Association, the National Association of Social Workers (NASW), and the National Association for Mental Health.

Generally, in addition to making recommendations for increasing funding for both research and training of professionals, the committee recommended transitioning from an institutionalized treatment model to an outpatient community mental health model, where patients were treated in the **least restricted environment** within the community. This report led to the creation of the Community Mental Health Centers (CMHC) Act of 1963, which was passed under the Kennedy administration. The CMHC enabled the funding of a new national mental health care system focusing on prevention and community-based care rather than on institutionalized custodial care (Feldman, 2003). The passage of the CMHC Act set the **deinstitutionalization movement** into motion, prompted by dissatisfaction with public mental hospitals, as well as the development of psychotropic medications and a new focus on the brain–behavior connection (Mowbray & Holter, 2002).

Several decades after President Kennedy described the CMHC program as a bold new approach to dealing with mental illness, many in the mental health field cited frustration and discouragement with what was perceived as numerous failures of the deinstitutionalization process and the new national system. A part of the challenge of implementing a community-based program was related to over-optimism about new treatments and an underestimation of the complexity of mental illness.

Early proponents of deinstitutionalization had hoped that through early detection, increased research, psychotropic medication, and better intervention strategies, mental illness could be greatly reduced and perhaps even eliminated. Yet, mental illness remained pervasive regardless of significant efforts to curb its devastating impact on individuals, families, and society. The most serious criticisms of the deinstitutionalization movement are leveled at the federal government, which many claim fell short of funding commitments, resulting in far fewer community mental health centers being opened across the United States.

Among those centers that did open, most were poorly staffed and generally unprepared to deal with the rapid transition from institutionalized to community care. With insufficient funding and an inability of government services to keep pace with need, the burden of care for the country's mentally ill shifted from the public mental hospital system to nursing homes, the prison system, and even the streets (Dear & Wolch, 2014; Kim, 2016; Raphael & Stoll, 2013). Patients seeking treatment with community mental health centers appear to have been a previously undertreated population that were experiencing life challenges, such as substance abuse and child welfare issues, not chronic and severe mental illness (Grob, 2010).

ENHANCEDetext *self-check 8.1*

SERIOUS MENTAL ILLNESSES AND MENTAL DISORDERS

Human service professionals may encounter mental illness directly when clients seek therapy for previously diagnosed disorders or they may encounter mental illness indirectly when clients seek services from a human services agency for reasons unrelated to their own mental health and then symptoms of mental illness begin to surface in the midst of the counseling relationship. Whether clients present with prior diagnoses or have no previously identified mental health issues, mental health providers must be able to recognize the common signs and symptoms of mental illness in their clients.

The *DSM-5* categorizes mental disorders based on common symptomology, and certain criteria must be met to diagnose someone with a mental, emotional, or behavioral disorder. There is some controversy surrounding the possibility that the *DSM-5* contributes to pathologizing people rather than focusing on their strengths, but it is to date the most effective evidence-based tool available for assessing individuals in a systematic and organized manner (APA, 2013).

The *DSM-5* is organized into three sections—Section 1 includes introductory information, Section II includes diagnostic criteria and diagnostic codes, and Section III includes information on emerging measures and models (e.g., alternative models, conditions for further study). One of the most significant changes from the *DSM-IV* is that the *DSM-5* no longer uses a multiaxial system to categorize mental disorders. Disorders formerly diagnosed on Axis I (clinical disorders), Axis II (personality disorders and intellectual disabilities), and Axis III (general medical conditions) are now all included in Section II. Axis IV, which clinicians used to note psychosocial and contextual functioning that affected the client's functioning, has now been omitted (although counselors are encouraged to holistically note psychosocial and environmental in their primary diagnosis). Axis V, formerly the Global Assessment of Functioning (GAF)—a hypothetical continuum of mental health and functioning ranging from 0 to 100—was discontinued due a perception that a singular score of functioning was unreliable and not particularly useful.

A complaint of many in the human services field is the mental health community's general tendency to approach mental illness from a pathological perspective. This inclination to see human behavior in polarized terms of good and bad, acceptable and unacceptable, desirable and undesirable has contributed to the promotion of the stigmatization of mental illness. Viewing mental illness solely through the lens of biology can also contribute to the tendency to pathologize the mentally ill where individuals are seen as "sick" and "broken." Although the discovery that many forms of mental illness have biological roots can relieve the mentally ill and their family of unnecessary guilt, it also suggests limited potential on the part of the mentally ill, increasing both social stigma and social rejection (Sullivan, 1992).

An alternative approach is to use a strengths perspective, or **strengths-based approach**, also referred to as the strengths-based approach, which is a model for helping clients commonly used in the human services field and an alternate to a pathological approach. This theoretical perspective encourages the practitioner to recognize and promote a client's strengths rather than focusing on deficits. A strengths perspective also presumes clients' ability to contribute to addressing their own problems through the development of self-sufficiency and self-determination. Although there are several contributors to strengths-perspective models in the human services field, Saleebey (1996) developed several principles for practitioners to follow that can help clients experience a sense of empowerment in their lives. Saleebey encourages practitioners to recognize that all clients:

1. have resources available to them, both within themselves and their communities;

2. are members of the community and as such are entitled to respect and dignity;

3. are resilient by nature and have the potential to grow and heal in the face of crisis and adversity;

4. need to be in relationships with others in order to self-actualize; and

5. have the right to their own perception of their problems, even if this perception isn't held by the practitioner.

Sullivan (1992) was one of the first theorists to apply the strengths perspective to the area of chronic mental illness where clients suffering from mental illness are encouraged to recognize and develop their own personal strengths and abilities. Sullivan compared this approach to one often used when working with the physically challenged, where focusing on physical disabilities is replaced with focusing on the development of physical *abilities*. Sullivan claimed that by redefining the problem (rather than continuing to search for new solutions), by fully integrating the mentally ill into society, and by focusing on strengths and abilities rather than solely on deficits, an environment can then be created that is more consistent with the early goals of mental health reformers who sought to remove barriers to treatment and promote respectful, compassionate, and comprehensive care of the mentally ill. Operating from a strengths perspective is important regardless of what the clinical issues are or what intervention strategies are used.

Every society has members who struggle with some form of mental illness—those people whose behavior is considered outside what is considered normal and appropriate. Each society has also developed ways in which to handle or manage such individuals so that healthy societal functioning is not disrupted. But because the criteria for what is considered normative behavior changes from era to era, as well as from culture to culture, it is important to keep cultural mores and generational issues in mind when characterizing someone's behavior as maladaptive or unhealthy.

The following section includes some of the more serious mental illnesses that human service professionals may encounter when working with clients who have been (or could be) diagnosed with a mental, behavioral, or emotional disorder that significantly interferes with multiple life domains, warranting extensive case management and counseling services. Clients experiencing a serious mental illness may come into contact with a human service professional in a range of agencies, such as an outpatient community mental health center, an inpatient psychiatric facility, the court system (mental health court or a probation department), a prison, or a homeless shelter. It is important, then, that generalist human service professionals be familiar with some of the more common disorders so their clients' cases can be managed as effectively possible.

Watch the video about Georgina and her description of what it feels like to have schizophrenia. How could you as a human service professional work with Georgina as a part of a broader treatment plan? ENHANCEDetext *video example 8.1*

Psychotic Disorders

Psychotic disorders are among the most serious of all mental illnesses because they impact an individual's sense of reality, often resulting in the marked impairment in most, if not all, life domains. Common symptoms of a psychotic disorder include hallucinations, delusions, and generally bizarre and eccentric behavior. The most common psychotic disorder is **schizophrenia**, an umbrella term for a number of brain disorders with similar symptoms, manifesting most often in late teens and early adulthood. Schizophrenia affects how people think, perceive, feel, and act. While there is no known cause of schizophrenia, researchers believe there are genetic components involved and likely numerous causes.

According to the *DSM-5*, symptoms of schizophrenia are divided into four domains: **positive symptoms**, including psychotic symptoms such as hallucinations; **negative symptoms**, including an absence of appropriate emotion and/or loss of speech; **cognitive symptoms**, including neurocognitive deficits such as issues with memory, attention, and social skills; and **mood symptoms**, including alterations in mood manifesting in either excessive happiness or sadness (APA, 2013).

According to the *DSM-5*, an individual may be diagnosed with schizophrenia if they experience two of the following five symptoms for at least one month.

1. **Delusions**: Strongly held false beliefs or misperceptions that are not consistent with the person's culture, many of which could not possibly be true. Examples include believing that the government is monitoring one's activities through the television set or that one has special powers such as speaking to others through mental telepathy.

2. **Hallucinations**: Sensations that are experienced as real, but are not, such as hearing voices, seeing things that are not there, smelling smells that do not exist, or feeling sensations when nothing is present.

3. **Disorganized speech**: Speech often reflects thinking that makes no sense, with frequent trailing off into incoherent talk often referred to as **word salad**.

4. Disorganized or **catatonic behavior**: Inability to dress oneself, poor self-care, or catatonic behavior such as holding a rigid pose for hours.

5. Negative symptoms: **Affective flattening**, alogia (a complete lack of any speech), and extreme apathy or disinterest.

Schizophrenia used to be diagnosed based on subtype (paranoid, disorganized, catatonic, undifferentiated, and residual types), but because patients often experience overlapping symptoms, the APA omitted subtypes in its most recent edition of the *DSM* (APA, 2013).

There is no cure for schizophrenia, and thus treatment consists primarily of custodial care and medication to minimize symptoms, particularly destructive ones. Antipsychotic medication has been available since the mid-1950s, but negative side effects of these medications, such as sexual impotence, tardive dyskinesia (involuntary jerking spasms of the muscles), and tranquilizing effects, often result in many patients refusing to take their medication consistently. New **atypical antipsychotic drugs**, such as Vraylar (approved by the FDA in September 2015), Seroquel, and Risperdal, have shown promise in reducing symptoms of schizophrenia such as hallucinations and delusion without nearly the number of side effects.

Bipolar Disorder

Bipolar disorder is a disorder of the brain that causes dramatic shifts in mood, called mood episodes, where affected individuals swing from periods of mania to periods of depression. Manic episodes can include inflated self-esteem, insomnia, rapid speech, a rush of ideas, impulsive or dangerous behavior in response to elation and overexcitement, as well as irritability, particularly in response to someone attempting to stop their activities. People with bipolar disorder often feel isolated and misunderstood. During a manic episode, an individual may believe they have special powers or a unique contribution to make to the world that do not match the reality of their situations. They may go days without sleep, appear extremely restless, talk rapidly, act in a grandiose manner, behave impulsively, and experience a mental rush in response to rapidly firing ideas and extreme creativity. They may go on unrestrained spending sprees, have unprotected sex with strangers, or engage in other high-risk behaviors.

Depressive episodes are more frequent than manic episodes and involve deep depression or complete despondency. During a depressive episode, individuals with bipolar disorder may experience profound guilt and feelings of worthlessness, they may have difficulty thinking and making decisions, they often have no appetite, they may want to do nothing but sleep, and they may think about or plan their suicide. If an individual experiences both manic and depressive symptoms, they are experiencing what is called a mixed episode. When bipolar disorder first manifests, patients often experience what is called rapid cycling—a more extreme form of bipolar involving four or more mood episodes within a 12-month period (APA, 2013).

While the exact cause of bipolar disorder is unknown, earlier studies show a genetic link and recent stem cell research found that people with bipolar disorder had significant differences in their brains compared to those without bipolar disorder. Specifically, researchers found that people diagnosed with bipolar disorder experienced genetic vulnerabilities in their early brain development, including differences in how calcium signals were sent and received (Chen et al., 2014). The most common treatment of bipolar disorder involves a combination of drug therapy, including mood stabilizers, lithium (a salt), and psychotropic medications, along with case management and counseling.

Denver, CO, May 03: Timothy Heckler pulls himself out of bed at his apartment in the Capitol Hill neighborhood of Denver, CO, May 03, 2014. He says he hasn't been sleeping well recently and wakes up in the middle of the night, "my mind starts getting into thoughts. My loneliness is amplified by anger. I try to maintain good thoughts. And then there's the conspiracy theories." Timothy says he has suicidal thoughts at times "Do I want to do it? No, I can't quit until the miracles happen." He jokes that there are too many people in the world "So I'm pro-suicide. I'd take one for the team but I feel I have something to offer." Timothy has been diagnosed with bipolar disorder, which he believes has been amplified by a traumatic brain injury

Depressive Disorders

People who suffer from depressive disorders often feel sad, anxious, empty, hopeless, irritable, guilty, worthless, helpless, and lethargic. While there are several types of depressive disorders, one of the most common is major depressive disorder. Everyone feels depressed sometimes. We experience heartbreak when our partner breaks up with us or a dear friend or family member dies, and we are likely going to have difficulty sleeping, eating, and concentrating as a result. We may even experience a stomachache or headache and other somatic symptoms. But major depressive disorder is far more than a temporary down mood in response to a difficult time in life.

According to the *DSM-5*, in order for a diagnosis of major depressive disorder to be given, an individual must experience two episodes of five or more of the following symptoms for at least a two-week period:

1. Depressed mood most of the day
2. Lack of interest or pleasure in all or almost all activities
3. Significant unintentional weight loss or weight gain
4. Insomnia or sleeping too much
5. Agitation or cognitive slowness that is noticed by others
6. Fatigue or loss of energy
7. Feelings of worthlessness or excessive or toxic guilt
8. Difficulty concentrating or making decisions
9. Recurrent thoughts of suicide

Additionally, the symptoms must cause significant impairment in the individual's import-ant areas of life, such as work, their social life, and interpersonal relationships (APA, 2013).

Depression is quickly becoming one of the most significant disorders of our time, with an estimated 350 million people experiencing major depression throughout the world (World Health Organization, 2015). In fact, depression is projected to be a leading cause of disability by 2020 (Michaud, Murray, & Bloom, 2001). The impact of depression is broad and deep, particularly for women, who experience depression in greater num-bers than men. Depression doesn't just rob people of joy and happiness; it also has a neg-ative impact on society in the form of lost productivity and the residual impact on family members who are caring for a loved one suffering from chronic depression.

Depression is not a new disorder even though it seems to be increasing in prevalence. References to depression date back to the beginning of recorded time. Hippocrates wrote about melancholy in the 4th century, believing such sadness was caused by an imbalance in the body's "humors" or liquids (blood, bile, phlegm, and black bile). Depression is considered productive if it motivates people to change themselves and their circumstances, when complacency might otherwise keep someone in an unhealthy situa-tion. But debilitating depression is rarely productive and can leave people feeling ashamed, particularly in a productive-oriented society such as the United States. Such shame and guilt only serve to add an increased burden to the depressed person though, exacerbating depressive symptoms, which can lead to a downward emotional spiral.

There are several theories regarding the cause of major depression, and most experts agree there are likely numerous causes of depression, involving a combination of psychological and biological systems. One popular theory of depression is drawn from cognitive-behavioral theory—a somewhat hybrid model incorporating aspects of Aaron Beck's cognitive theory of depression and behaviorism theory. Cognitive-behavioral the-ory hypothesizes that depression is often the result of negative and irrational thinking. Thoughts such as "I'm a horrible person," "Nothing good will ever happen to me," or "I will always fail," if thought consistently enough, can ultimately lead to feelings of sadness, despair, and hopelessness (Beck, 1964, 2006).

Another popular theory, particularly with human service professionals and social workers, draws from social-contextual theory. In this theory negative life events within one's social world, such as racial discrimination, gender bias, and poverty, are believed to contribute to depression, particularly if the depressed individual does not have adequate coping skills to deal with these negative experiences in a productive manner (Swindle, Cronkite, & Moos, 1989).

In the last several decades a biological model of depression has emerged positing genetic vulnerabilities and neurohormonal irregularities, such as problems with neu-rotransmitter functioning. Most human service professionals tend to embrace a **biopsy-chosocial model** of depression that recognizes the biological basis of many depressions, as well as other influences, such as those in the psychological and social realms. Because depression often co-occurs with other disorders, such as anxiety, eating disorders, and substance abuse disorders, it is essential that all human service professionals involved in direct service be able to screen for depression, even if a client is not seeking services for this purpose.

Human service professionals utilize many tools and interventions when working with clients struggling with depression. Some of these intervention strategies include insight counseling, where clients develop self-awareness skills intended to help them cope more effectively with their mental health–related challenges. A popular and effective intervention strategy often used to treat depression is cognitive behavioral therapy (CBT) based on Beck's (1964) theory of depression. CBT is an intervention strategy used with a range of client populations, including those struggling with depression and anxiety disorders. CBT is a hybrid theory drawing from **cognitive theory** and **behaviorism**.

Essentially, CBT is based on the premise that people will function more effectively if they change their negative and maladaptive thinking and behavioral patterns. Examples of negative thinking include self-statements such as "Nobody will ever love me" or "I can't do anything right." CBT theorists believe that such statements not only influence our beliefs, but also our behaviors. People create meaning around their experiences, and the meaning they create is based on their belief system, which is built up over years of conditioning. CBT challenges client's negative beliefs about themselves, others, and the world in an attempt to undo previous negative conditioning and replace limiting negativity with more hopeful and optimistic beliefs and behaviors (Beck, 2006).

CBT was originally developed as an intervention with depression, but it has since been used with a range of disorders, including anxiety, eating disorders, and OCD (Fava, Rafanelli, Grandi, Conti, & Belluardo, 1998; McKay et al., 2015; Norton & Price, 2007). In addition to individual counseling, group counseling can be effective in assisting clients gain strength and support from others in similar situations—some a few steps ahead of them and some a few steps behind. Psychotropic medications are often used in collaboration with individual and group counseling, and they offer many clients hope of controlling the often debilitating symptoms common to many serious mental illnesses.

Boulder, CO, July 12, 2007— University of Colorado doctoral candidate Brendan Depue looks over functional magnetic resonance images (FMRI) of the brain that highlight areas (in red) that control our cognitive behaviors and in his studies have been shown to actively help suppress emotional memory. The study may help clinicians develop new therapies for those unable to suppress emotionally distressing memories associated with disorders like post-traumatic stress disorder, phobias, depression, anxiety, and obsessive-compulsive disorder, he said. He studies these scans in a lab in Boulder. Depue is a neuroscience and cognitive psychology doctoral candidate at Professor Marie T. Banich's cognitive neuroscience lab at the University of Colorado at Boulder

Anxiety Disorders

Other disorders that are frequently experienced by clients seeking treatment in human service agencies include anxiety disorders, such as generalized anxiety disorder (GAD), which involves excessively worrying (that cannot be easily controlled) about a number of different things more days than not for at least six months. Symptoms of GAD include restlessness, being easily fatigued, difficulty concentrating, irritability, muscle tension, and disturbances in sleep, although a client only needs to experience three of these symptoms in order to be diagnosed with GAD, and the symptoms cannot be associated with a substance, medication condition, or post-traumatic stress disorder.

Obsessive compulsive disorder (OCD) is also quite common and includes compulsive behaviors, such as intrusive thoughts and impulses that the individual realizes are coming from inside, not being imposed from the outside (to distinguish OCD from psychotic disorders). In addition, OCD includes as compulsions, or ritual behaviors, such as repetitive handwashing, used to manage the obsessive thoughts. For example, an individual who has intrusive thoughts about family members dying might flip his blinds seven times every hour based on the irrational belief that this activity will keep his family safe (while knowing that the behavior is irrational). Another OCD-type

© GLENN ASAKAWA / DENVER POST / GETTY IMAGES

disorder includes body dysmorphic disorder, a body image disorder where people are preoccupied with imagined or exaggerated flaws in their appearance.

Because human service professionals work in practice settings that serve high-crisis clients, they often come into contact with individuals who have experienced a significant amount of trauma. Some of these clients will then likely be experiencing trauma-and-stressor-related disorders, such as post-traumatic stress disorder (PTSD); PTSD is a particular clinical focus when working with survivors of domestic violence and veterans. PTSD involves a history of exposure to a traumatic event, referred to as the stressor, which results in symptoms that fall into four clusters:

- *Intrusive recollections* involving, for instance, mental images or intrusive thoughts about the original traumatic event repeatedly playing through the person's mind;
- *Avoidance behaviors* that serve as strategies to avoid psychological triggers related to the trauma, such as avoiding people, places, or things that remind the person of the original traumatic event;
- *Negative cognitions*, such as blaming oneself for the traumatic event or believing that the world is a bad place;
- *Moods*, such as ongoing depression and rage; alternations in arousal or reactivity, such as generalized anxiety; or hypervigilance, such as a heightened startle reflex (APA, 2013).

Personality Disorders

People with personality disorders view themselves and others in a way that significantly and negatively impacts their lives and ability to function across in many areas of their lives. Personality disorders used to be diagnosed on Axis II of the *DSM-IV*, but the *DSM-5* now includes personality disorders and clinical disorders in the same section based on the contention that distinguishing between clinical disorders and personality disorders is arbitrary (APA, 2013).

Students and newer clinicians often express confusion about how to tell the difference between clinical disorders and personality disorders because some of the symptomology is overlapping, but more seasoned counselors can pretty easily make a distinction. In fact, when I was in graduate school I had a professor who told us that the easiest way a clinician could tell the difference between someone with a clinical disorder and a personality disorder is that clients with clinical disorders express fears that there is something terribly wrong with them, whereas clients with personality disorders express outrage that there is something wrong with everyone else. Of course my professor was exaggerating to make a point, and while there is certainly no validity to such universal catchall phrases, anyone who has known someone with a diagnosable personality disorder would understand my professor's point.

Generally speaking, a key difference between clinical disorders and personality disorders is that those with clinical disorders for the most part have insight and awareness into the maladaptive nature of their feelings and behaviors, whereas those with personality disorders often do not. For instance, clients with OCD for the most part know their intrusive thinking and obsessive need to engage in rituals is irrational and they will often come into counseling expressing fears that they are "crazy," while clients with obsessive compulsive personality disorder believe their way is the right way, and they may come into counseling complaining that the entire world is out of step except them (IOCDF, 2014).

Individuals with personality disorders often experience rigid and inflexible patterns of feelings and behavior, including unhealthy and maladaptive patterns of perceiving things, difficulty controlling or regulating emotions, and difficulty controlling emotional impulses. People with personality disorders will often perceive things differently than others, including misperceiving another's behavior and intentions. Up to 30 percent of all individuals seeking mental health care services have at least one diagnosable personality disorder (Dingfelder, 2004), but treatment options remain limited due to defensive posturing, rigidity, and limited insight common with many personality disorders.

Before you begin diagnosing your family and friends (or your exes!), it's important to know that just because someone has personality traits that are irritating or somewhat eccentric, it does not mean they have a personality disorder. One of my best friends can be defensive if someone is criticizing her children. She often misperceives innocent comments as slights or criticism of her parenting. But does this mean she has a personality disorder? Not necessarily. But what if her defensiveness was so intense that she started arguments constantly with friends and family members? What if she could not enjoy going out socially because all she could think about was protecting her children? What if she perceived insults everywhere and could not get along with anyone, including her children's teachers? This behavior might then push her in the direction of a personality disorder—a collection of maladaptive and rigid personality traits that are exhibited across different life domains and that interfere with one's ability to function effectively in life, including interfering with one's ability to enjoy reasonably healthy relationships with others.

For instance, it might be perfectly normal for a woman to feel emotionally attacked whenever she gets into an argument with her husband if he has an aggressive way of expressing his needs and frustrations. But it is not necessarily healthy or normative for a woman to feel emotionally attacked whenever she receives constructive feedback that she perceives as criticism from her husband, friends, family, coworkers, supervisor, teachers, and children. It also might be perfectly healthy for a man to consistently focus on himself in certain situations where perhaps he feels somewhat insecure, such as in large social environments. But it might not be considered normative and healthy if this person excessively focuses on himself in virtually all areas of his life—at home, at work, with family, in social situations large and small, often at the expense of others.

The relative health or adaptive nature of one's personality traits is judged on a continuum, like so many other mental and emotional conditions. If someone is a bit on the rigid side with certain issues, it wouldn't necessarily be appropriate to diagnose this person with a personality disorder. Yet, if someone gets far enough out on the continuum with regard to rigidity, for example, so that it interferes with an ability to function at work, with family, or in social situations, then this person might have what is considered a disordered personality. According to the *DSM-5*, the key difference between someone who has a normally structured personality and one who has a personality disorder is that the structure of a disordered personality must cause distress and impairment of functioning in several important areas of functioning (APA, 2013).

The *DSM-5* categorizes the 10 personality disorders into three groups, or clusters, based on similar features and symptoms. Although all personalities share some factors in common, such as the tendency to misperceive social cues and others' intentions, rigidity, pervasive problems in interpersonal relationships, and emotional regulation, each cluster of personality disorders varies with regard to both symptoms and cause. Table 8.1 reflects each cluster type and the associated personality disorders.

Table 8.1   Personality Disorders Organized by Clusters

Cluster	Cluster Description	Personality Disorders	Personality Disorder Characterization
A	Odd and eccentric	Paranoid	A pattern of suspicion and mistrust of others that is irrational and not based in reality
		Schizoid	A lack of interest and detachment from social relationships, feelings of apathy toward others, and a restricted range of emotions
		Schizotypal	A pattern of extreme discomfort in social interaction with distorted thinking and perceptions
B	Dramatic, emotional, or erratic	Antisocial	A pervasive pattern of disregard for others with a violation of others' rights, a lack of empathy, bloated self-image, manipulative and impulsive behavior
		Borderline	A pervasive pattern of instability in relationships, self-image, identity, and behavior. Emotions often lead to self-harm, intense anger in response to perceived abandonment, and impulsivity
		Histrionic	A pervasive pattern of attention-seeking behaviors and excessive emotionality
		Narcissistic	A pervasive pattern of grandiosity, a constant need for admiration, and a general lack of empathy toward others
C	Anxious and fearful	Avoidant	Pervasive feelings of social inhibition and feelings of inadequacy, extreme sensitivity to negative evaluation
		Dependent	A pervasive psychological need to be cared for by others, highly dependent on the approval of others, inability to make choices on their own
		Obsessive compulsive	A pervasive and rigid conformity to rules, perfectionism, an excessive need for control

Counseling individuals with personality disorders is often frustrating for practitioners because progress is slow, and clients are often resistant to change due to the inherent nature of personality disorders. Yet, many new counseling techniques are being developed, some with a fair amount of success. One reason for the slower progress is because authentic change requires that clients with personality disorders change the entire way they perceive the world and themselves within it. They must also learn how to "sit with their emotions" and control their impulses rather than act on them, which can be particularly challenging when the personality disorder involves impulsivity and high emotionality like those in Cluster B. Antidepressant and antianxiety medications are often used in combination with individual and group counseling, where even clients who struggle with insight can focus on skillbuilding, such as anger management, delaying gratification, and increasing social skills.

ENHANCEDetext *self-check 8.2*

COMMON MENTAL HEALTH
PRACTICE SETTINGS

Human service professionals working with the mentally ill population do so in a variety of practice settings, including outpatient mental health clinics, community mental health centers, not-for-profit agencies, outreach programs, job training agencies, housing assistance programs, prisoner assistance programs, government agencies such as departments of mental health and human services, and probation programs. Generalist human service practitioners might be case managers responsible for conducting needs assessments and coordinating the mental health care of clients, they might be providing counseling services on an individual and/or group basis, or they may provide more concrete services such as job training. In truth, a human service practitioner will likely encounter clients with serious mental illnesses in just about any practice setting, but in this section I will focus on those settings where the seriously and chronically mentally ill are the target population.

Community mental health centers provide direct services to the seriously and chronically mentally ill population. These centers are typically licensed by the state and designated to serve a certain catchment area within the community. Services offered often include outpatient services for adults and children, 24-hour crisis intervention, case management services, community support, psychiatric services, alcohol and drug treatment, psychological evaluations, and various educational workshops. They might also offer partial hospitalization and day treatment programs. Although most community mental health centers operate on a sliding scale, because most centers are funded through federal grants they typically will not turn clients away who have no ability to pay, thus they are highly reliant on public funding.

The seriously mentally ill are often served by full-service not-for-profit human services agencies, which typically offer an array of services aimed at various target populations, including the seriously mentally ill. Human services agencies can range broadly in terms of the level of services they provide, and what client populations they target, but generally most agencies provide general counseling and case management services, group counseling, family intervention services, as well as a range of special programs specific to the agency's mission, such as vocational programs, housing assistance, parenting training, child care, crisis intervention, and substance abuse counseling.

A human service practitioner might work in a number of capacities within a human services agency, depending in large part on what types of programs the agency offers. For instance, a human service practitioner might offer general case management services coordinating all the care the client is receiving, acting as the point person for the psychologist, psychiatrist, and any other service providers involved in a client's case. They might provide direct counseling services or run support groups focusing on a number of psychosocial and daily life issues. If the agency provides outreach services, the human service practitioner might be out in the community providing emergency crisis intervention services for the local police department or other emergency personnel. The list of program services that a human services agency may offer is almost endless, particularly because a part of the role of the human services agency is to identify needs within a community and address those needs whenever possible.

Watch this video of a news report on a partial hospitalization program for women experiencing postpartum depression. Why is this program so innovative?

ENHANCEDetext *video example 8.2*

www.youtube.com/
watch?v=ZhYQFd1FBBk

An alternative to inpatient hospitalization is partial hospitalization or day treatment programs. These programs, often operated within a hospital setting, are intensive and offer services for individuals who are having difficulty coping in their daily lives but are not at a point where inpatient hospitalization is a necessity. Clients typically attend the program five days a week, for approximately seven hours a day, and work with a multidisciplinary team of professionals, including a psychiatrist, psychologist, and social worker. Family involvement is highly encouraged. Certain partial hospitalization programs focus on specific issues, such as eating disorders, self-abuse, or substance abuse, whereas others focus on a wider range of clinical issues, such as severe depression, anger management, and past abuse issues. The nature of the program will also vary depending on whether the target population consists of adults, adolescents, or children. These structured programs can either serve as an alternative intervention to inpatient hospitalization or they can be utilized when a patient is transitioned out of inpatient hospitalization back into the community.

Although the deinstitutionalization movement has resulted in a dramatic reduction in long-term hospitalization of the severely mentally ill, some individuals who are acutely disturbed or suicidal are hospitalized on a short-term basis for diagnostic assessment and stabilization in inpatient or acute psychiatric hospitals. Psychiatric units are typically locked for the safety of the patients, who are often actively psychotic and may be a danger to themselves or others. Again, services are focused on assessment and stabilization with a particular emphasis on discharge planning. Human service practitioners often provide case management and discharge planning in inpatient settings. Licensed mental health care providers engage in more intensive counseling services such as facilitating individual and group counseling, as well as behavioral management if the program is focused on children and adolescents.

Mental Illness and the Homeless Population

One unanticipated consequence of deinstitutionalization was the shifting of literally thousands of mentally ill patients from institutions to the streets due to a shortage of housing for the severely mentally ill (Torry et al., 2015). In fact, a 2005 study found that nearly one in six mentally ill individuals are homeless (Folsom, Hawthorne, & Lindamer, 2005). And since it is so difficult to track intermittent homelessness—where a mentally ill person cycles in and out of homelessness—the actual number is likely far higher.

Many of these individuals would have previously been institutionalized, but with the closing of the majority of public mental hospitals and the transitioning of most psychiatric units to a focus on short-term stays, the severely mentally ill who do not have a network of supportive and able family members are often left with no place to live except on the streets. Even individuals who do have supportive families may live on the streets due to the nature of psychosis, which clouds judgment and impairs the ability to think without distortion, leading some individuals to disappear for years at a time.

The link between homelessness and mental illness is not solely related to deinstitutionalization. Certainly warehousing the mentally ill kept them off the streets, but the nature of this association is far more complex and likely reciprocal in nature. Severe mental illness leaves many incapable of providing for their basic needs, and the stressful nature of living on the streets—not knowing where one will sleep at night, dealing with exposure to violence and inclement weather, not knowing where ones next meal will come from— would put the healthiest of individuals at risk for developing some mental illness.

Government sources estimate that approximately 26 percent of the homeless population is severely mentally ill (HUD, 2009; U.S. Conference of Mayors, 2011), and if mental illness is broadened to include clinical depression and substance abuse disorders (often used to self-medicate), that percentage jumps to 35 to 50 percent (North, Eyrich, Pollio, & Spitznagel, 2004; Shern et al., 2000). The mentally ill homeless population is a diverse group, but African American single men and veterans are most likely to be homeless and suffering from mental illness (Folsom et al., 2005; Koerber, 2005; Shern et al., 2000).

Although deinstitutionalization is credited for being the primary cause of increases of the mentally ill homeless population, the increase escalated in the 1980s due to a shortage in affordable housing and a lack of funding of housing assistance programs targeting at-risk middle-aged men and veterans. One of the biggest challenges in getting individuals with ness off the streets is engaging them in treatment. One of the rights the mentally ill achieved in post-deinstitutionalization legislation was the right to refuse treatment. A deeper look into this issue reveals that it may not be as simple as individuals in need not wanting help, but may be far more related to the difficulty and complexity of accessing needed services (Shern et al., 2000).

Barriers to accessing services often include difficulties in applying for government assistance such as Medicaid and Medicare to pay for both treatment and medication. Another barrier involves the actual service delivery model most popular in counseling and mental health centers, where the client comes to the psychologist, not the other way around. History clearly reveals that this model simply does not work with most seriously mentally ill individuals, particularly those living on the streets. Such individuals are often confused, disoriented, and frequently distrusting of others, particularly if they are suffering from some sort of psychotic disorder. To expect a person who is homeless and suffering from some mental illness to remember a weekly appointment and somehow figure out how to navigate transportation to a doctor's office in a business center or other urban location is likely unrealistic.

Another barrier to seeking treatment involves the many stipulations and requirements common in standard treatment models used by many community mental health centers. Most standard mental health programs have strict participation requirements, particularly related to behavioral issues such as maintaining sobriety to remain in a housing assistance program or requiring clients to participate in weekly counseling support groups in order to receive other services. In fact, most standard programs are directive with seriously mentally ill clients, often determining treatment goals and interventions for the client, rather than empowering clients to assist in determining their own treatment goals and interventions (Shern et al., 2000).

The problem of homelessness among the mentally ill population will not be resolved until sufficient long-term housing assistance can be provided. Housing assistance programs typically have long waiting lists and often allow only women with children accelerated access to the program. Because African American men and veterans are overrepresented in the mentally ill homeless population, more programs need to be developed that target these populations. Such programs must also be designed to address issues related to alcohol and substance abuse problems as well because many within the mentally ill homeless population have co-occurring substance abuse problems.

Watch the PBS video on homelessness and the mentally ill in Los Angeles. Why is the Housing First program successful with co-occurring mental illness and substance abuse?
ENHANCEDetext *video example 8.3*

www.youtube.com/
watch?v=mGQoEBKEsxY

Military Personnel and Veterans

A relatively recent phenomenon within the armed services involves a dramatic spike in mental health disorders, including suicide, among military personnel—both within service members who have been deployed to combat zones as well as those deployed within the United States. Suicides among military personnel (active duty and post-enlistment) have skyrocketed in recent years, particularly between 2007 and 2009 (during the Iraqi and Afghanistan conflicts). In fact, despite efforts to confront this epidemic, in 2012 the number of military suicides outpaced the number of soldiers killed in combat (Briggs, 2013). The mental health community is scrambling to figure out why and also to find viable and enduring solutions to this mental health crisis. These wars have been protracted and extremely violent, involving unprecedented re-deployments and longer-than-average deployment times. Soldiers are returning home with a range of mental, physical health, and psychosocial challenges, including traumatic brain injuries, stress-related disorders such as PTSD and "combat stress," intimate partner violence, substance abuse, trauma resulting from sexual abuse and assault, and readjustment issues. Soldiers often return to face a lack of support, including insufficient (and stigmatized) mental health services, financial difficulties, and challenges finding employment. Consider the following case study detailing true events:

> On March 11, 2012 Staff Sgt. Robert Bales, a U.S. Army Staff Sergeant, who was serving his fourth combat deployment since enlisting in the Army in November 2001 shortly after the 9/11 terrorist attacks, opened fire on 17 innocent Afghani civilians, primarily women and children. The Kandahar Province massacres were committed in the middle of the night, solely by Sgt. Bales, following a night of drinking with his buddies. The married father of two from Washington described in court how he brutally attacked victims in two villages by gunning them down, and then stacking some like firewood and setting them on fire. This incident is certainly disturbing (to say the least), but what is almost equally disturbing is what Sgt. Bales' defense attorney described as a normal family man turned homicidal maniac due to the horrific stress endured on the battlefield—four combat deployments in high violence combat zones; two injuries, one including traumatic brain injury (TBI); exposure to high levels of violence and trauma, including numerous roadside bombings and carrying dead bodies, some burned beyond recognition, off the battlefield—coupled with excessive drinking to relieve stress and taking valium and steroids allegedly supplied by his superiors. Fellow soldiers described Sgt. Bales as "competent and positive." His wife described him as a wonderful husband and father. But when he returned from each of his tours, he described how his depression and anger worsened, how his drinking and misuse of sleeping pills increased, and how ineffective counseling caused him to withdraw from family and friends even more. In court Sgt. Bales stated that while he could not explain the murders, he believed he just snapped because he could no longer manage his mounting anger and stress resulting from the trauma he had endured from multiple deployments. Brown, his defense attorney, described Sgt. Bales as "crazed and broken" the night of the attack—"He's broken, and we broken him." (Johnson, 2013).

Mental health issues, such as PTSD, depression, explosive disorders, and substance abuse have long been associated with military service and are increasingly prevalent among the veteran population. There has been increased attention on the mental health of military personnel recently due to several high profile cases involving homicide, suicide, and domestic violence. Research on the impact of trauma on military personnel and their families focuses on answering important questions about the causes, nature, and extent of mental illness. For instance, was Sgt. Bales' murderous rampage a result of longstanding homicidal tendencies rooted in childhood or adolescence? Or was it brought on solely by the stress of multiple deployments and untreated PTSD and a TBI? What were the warning signs, if any, that Bales' struggles were beyond his ability to cope? What structures did the Army have in place to deal with Bales' deteriorating mental health status?

In response to the recent spike in mental health disorders and suicides among service members, the Army, in cooperation with the National Institutes of Mental Health, has initiated the largest research study of military service members and veterans ever commissioned. The study is called the Army Study to Assess Risk and Resilience in Servicemembers (STARRS). STARRS consists of a series of studies categorized into five study types including:

- The Historical Administrative Data Study—The examination of administrative and health records of 1.6 million active duty soldiers between 2004 and 2009 in search of evidence of psychological risk (e.g., a past history of depression) and protective factors (e.g., evidence of psychological resilience).
- The New Soldier Study—The assessment of the health, personalities, and prior experiences of new soldiers.
- The All Army Study—The assessment of soldiers' psychological and physical health during combat and non-combat periods.
- The Soldier Health Outcomes Study—Two studies that compare service personnel who have experienced suicidal behavior with those who have not.
- Special Studies—Examines the effects of deployment to a combat zone with the goal of identifying risk factors for suicide and factors relating to psychological resiliency among service members who have faced combat.

Many military personnel and veterans are provided with service dogs to help with anxiety, depression, and the symptoms of PTSD

According to three STARRS studies published in March of 2014, suicide rates more than doubled for soldiers who served in Iraq and Afghanistan between 2004 and 2009, but almost even more alarming was that suicide rates nearly tripled for soldiers who were not deployed, but remained in the United States (Schoenbaum et al., 2014). Additionally, most subjects who were diagnosed with post-deployment mental disorders (e.g., PTSD, anxiety, depression, attention-deficit-hyperactivity disorder [ADHD], anger management, substance abuse), as well as those who experienced suicide ideation and suicide attempts, had a history of pre-enlistment mental disorders, most often rooted in childhood and adolescence (Nock et al., 2015; Ursano et al., 2014). These findings are vitally important because not only do they highlight the nature of the problems experienced by many current and former service members (active duty, deployed, and veterans), but also provide insights into ways that the mental health community can better support recruits, soldiers, and veterans through better mental health screening and the development of prevention and treatment programs.

Human service practitioners have long been members of multidisciplinary teams serving on military bases as both officers and civilian employees, dating back to at least World War I. Currently, a range of human service practitioners contribute to the development and facilitation of effective treatment programs to address contemporary issues facing soldiers and their family members. Human service practitioners work within all branches of the armed services throughout the world, Department of Defense (DoD), and the U.S. Department of Veteran's Affairs hospitals (the VA). They serve on emergency response teams that are deployed in times of crisis, such as a violent incident occurring on a military base or during a natural disaster, providing humanitarian and disaster relief.

The Criminalization of the Mentally Ill

Another unintended by-product of deinstitutionalization is the inadvertent shifting of chronically mentally ill patients from public mental hospitals to jails and prisons. In fact, many mental health advocates have argued that prisons are now the primary institutions within the United States warehousing severely mentally ill individuals. About 60 percent of state and federal prisoners have a diagnosable and often untreated mental illness and about 15 percent have a diagnosable severe mental illness (e.g., schizophrenia, bipolar disorder) (Fields & Phillips, 2013; Palermo, Smith, & Liska, 1991; Raphael & Stoll, 2013; Torrey, 1995).

There are more mentally ill men than mentally ill women in jails and prison. However, mentally ill women are overrepresented in the prison population, with approximately 31 percent of women in state prisons suffering from some form of serious mental illness compared to about 14 percent for men (Torrey, Kennard, Eslinger, Lamb, & Pavle, 2010). Most mentally ill prisoners are poor and were either undiagnosed prior to their incarceration or were untreated in the months prior to entering the prison system. Mentally ill inmates were twice as likely to have a history of physical abuse and four times as likely to have been the victim of sexual abuse. In fact, almost 65 percent of mentally ill female inmates reported having been physically and/or sexually abused prior to going to prison (Ditton, 1999).

But what does this really mean? Could it simply mean that mentally ill individuals break the law more than mentally healthy individuals? Couldn't it be argued that one must certainly be mentally ill to commit serious crimes in the first place? After all, what sane person sexually abuses children, or robs a bank, or drinks alcohol and drives? Depending on how mental illness is defined, it could be argued that those who commit heinous crimes are by definition mentally ill, and that their mental illness does not and should not negate the appropriateness of sending them to prison for their crimes. But even in situations where offenders clearly should be incarcerated, a retrospective look at their mental health histories might reveal a history of poor service utilization, including multiple barriers to effective treatment.

While prisons have always held mentally ill prisoners, the number of incarcerated mentally ill has increased, in large part because of a decrease in treatment options available for the mentally ill population within the general population. The reasons for this decrease include a reduction in funding of community mental health centers, barriers to access for lower income and ethnic minority populations, and increasing difficulty in securing involuntary hospitalization of the severely mentally ill. The majority of the mentally ill who are incarcerated have been convicted of nonviolent petty crimes related to their mental illness. In fact far too often mentally ill prisoners, particularly those in the general prison population, are consistent targets of victimization, particularly sex-related crimes, many of which go unreported (Marley & Buila, 2001).

The incarceration of the mentally ill is not a simple problem, and thus it has no simple answers. Mental health and prison advocates cite barriers to accessing mental health services, problems with early intervention, and the high cost of mental health care as direct causes of seriously mentally ill individuals ending up in the penal system rather than in psychiatric facilities. The **Affordable Care Act** (ACA), with the inclusion of **mental health parity**, is a promising step forward, but challenges related to service availability, cost, and patient compliance remain significant.

Once again the controversial issue of an individual's right to refuse treatment is relevant in this matter as well, evidenced by the many family members of the mentally ill who consistently complain that the courts have refused to order involuntary treatment, only to have their mentally ill family member commit a violent crime some time later. What is so unfortunate in these incidences is that the majority of mentally ill defendants are amenable to treatment, but many were not receiving any treatment at the time of their incarceration (Marley & Buila, 2001).

Many steps are currently being taken by those in the criminal justice system and mental health and human services fields to address the issue of the incarceration of the mentally ill and the many factors that contribute to this complex cycle of reincarceration. The development of the **Mental Health Courts Program** is an example of a significant step in the right direction. The Mental Health Courts Program is administered under the Bureau of Justice Assistance (BJA), a component of the U.S. Department of Justice, in cooperation with the Substance Abuse and Mental Health Services Administration (SAMHSA). The goal of the BJA is to offer alternatives to incarceration for adult, non-violent offenders. Mental Health Courts Program goals include the following:

- Increased public safety for communities—by reducing criminal activity and lowering the high recidivism rates for people with mental illnesses who become involved in the criminal justice system.
- Increased treatment engagement by participants—by brokering comprehensive services and supports, rewarding adherence to treatment plans, and sanctioning nonadherence.
- Improved quality of life for participants—by ensuring that program participants are connected to needed community-based treatments, housing, and other services that encourage recovery.
- More effective use of resources for sponsoring jurisdictions—by reducing repeated contacts between people with mental illnesses and the criminal justice system and by providing treatment in the community when appropriate, where it is more effective and less costly than in correctional institutions.

The goal of the BJA program is to have a mental health court in every jurisdiction. In 2007 there were only 175 nationwide, and by 2015 that number had doubled to over 350. Research indicates that mental health courts are successfully diverting the mentally ill from jails to mental health programs offering much needed services. One study exploring the effectiveness of one of the first mental health courts (located in Broward County, Florida) found that participants spent 75 percent less time in jail, received needed mental health services on a more frequent basis, and were no more likely to commit a new crime, compared to mentally ill defendants who proceeded through the traditional courts and corrections system (Christy, Poythress, Boothroyd, Petrila, & Mehra, 2005).

ENHANCEDetext *self-check 8.3*

MULTICULTURAL CONSIDERATIONS

Early studies have shown that ethnic minority populations are often poorly served in mental health centers because of a lack of culturally competent and bilingual counselors, as well as a lack of available services offered in ethnic minority communities (Alegría et al., 2015; Marcela Horvitz-Lennon, 2015; Sue, 1977). Other studies have shown that while Latino, Asian, and Pacific Islander populations were underrepresented in community mental health center settings, those within the African American and Native American populations were overrepresented (Diala, Muntaner, Walrath, Nickerson, LaVeist, & Leaf, 2001; Hernandez et al., 2015; Sue & McKinney, 1975). This pattern may be partly due to cultural acceptance or rejection of psychotherapy within different cultural groups, and it may also be related to the relative complexity of issues facing the populations served, particularly Native Americans, who traditionally have high rates of substance abuse and depression and often reside in remote areas. Regardless of inter-ethnic minority utilization comparisons, the research clearly shows that lower income ethnic minority populations are poorly served in almost all respects, including a lack of the availability of individual counseling, case management, and front-line psychotropic medications (Hernandez et al., 2015).

Cultural competence on the part of the human service practitioners is an important factor in combating these disparities. Racial bias on the part of the mental health provider can influence many factors associated with mental health care and counseling. For instance, a relatively recent study found that African Americans were far more likely to be diagnosed with disruptive behavioral disorders in mental health counseling when compared to Caucasians, who were far more likely to be diagnosed with less serious clinical disorders, such as adjustment disorder (Feisthamel & Schwartz, 2009). Racially disproportionate clinical diagnostic assessment may be due to personal racial biases on the part of human service professionals, but may also be due to counselors not taking into consideration the disproportionate challenges facing many ethnic minorities, such as increased levels of poverty, racial oppression, and higher rates of unemployment, compared to Caucasians (Feisthamel & Schwartz, 2009).

Other types of bias can enter the counseling relationship as well. Consider the bias that many in the United States (particularly European-Americans) have about time. The U.S. culture tends to highly value time and promptness. When someone is timely, they are often considered to be respectful, responsible, considerate of others, and organized. Conversely, those who are consistently late are often presumed to be disrespectful, irresponsible, inconsiderate of others, disorganized, and perhaps even lazy. Yet, not all cultures value or perceive time in the same manner and a stereotyped bias is that individuals from cultures that do not perceive time in a similar manner as the majority culture are in some way deficient.

Human service professionals who have been enculturated in U.S. values might not even realize they hold this stereotype and might unconsciously attribute negative traits to clients who consistently show up late to their appointments. Thus, although it might be worth exploring whether a pattern of lateness is related to lacking motivation or resistance, a human services professional should consider whether racial bias is resulting from negative assumptions about a client's character based solely on the fact that the client is from a culture that does not value time in the same manner as U.S. culture. Hence, although rarely is someone eager to admit holding negative stereotypes and biases about

Watch the video produced by the University of New Mexico on suicide prevention in the Native American population. Which issues does this film highlight regarding cultural competency, particularly when working with smaller ethnic minority populations?

ENHANCEDetext *video example 8.4*

www.youtube.com/watch?v=ZRpJaap-En0

certain races, cultures, or lifestyles, it is imperative, particularly when working with the seriously mentally ill population that these negative stereotypes are explored, challenged, and discarded. Otherwise they will remain powerful forces in how human service professionals subtly or overtly evaluate and assess client actions, motivations, strengths, and deficits, including assessing accountability and causation for their life circumstances.

ENHANCEDetext *self-check 8.4*

CONCLUSION

The field of mental health is a dynamic practice area for the human service professional for many reasons. Human service professionals have the ability to truly make an impact while working with some of society's most vulnerable members. Because mental illness is such a broad term, encompassing such a wide array of psychological, emotional, and behavioral issues, the human service professional works as a true generalist whether in a direct service capacity or whether providing advocacy within the community. The United States has experienced dramatic shifts in its mental health delivery system during the past 60 years and will no doubt continue to experience future changes, some intended and some unintended. Human services professionals are on the front lines of many intended changes, lobbying for increased funding, changes in legislation, and new programs to meet the complex needs of the seriously mentally ill population.

SUMMARY

- The ways in which people with mental illness have historically been perceived and treated are examined. The history of mental health treatment dating back to 18th century France and through deinstitutionalization in the United States in the 1960s is discussed. The ways in which advocacy efforts impacted the treatment of the seriously mentally ill are examined.
- Serious mental illnesses and common mental disorders within the context of diagnostic approaches used in the human services field are explored. A range of mental disorders experienced by client populations commonly encountered by human service professionals is discussed, including psychotic disorders, depressive disorders, anxiety disorders, and personality disorders. *DSM-5* criteria are explored and compared to using a strengths perspective in evaluating clients.
- The roles and functions of human services professionals within common mental health practice settings serving mainstream and special populations are described. Practice settings serving client populations experiencing serious mental illnesses within the context of the roles and functions of human services professionals are examined. An exploration of special populations, including the homeless mentally ill and mentally ill prisoners, is also included.
- The relationship between racial bias and disparity in treatment among ethnic minority populations is critically examined. Multicultural considerations with a particular focus on people of color are examined, including the nature of barriers to and disparities in treatment for ethnic minority populations. The importance of cultural competence is stressed.

Internet Resources

Conduct an Internet search for American Experience a Brilliant Madness Timeline of Treatment of Mental Illness on the PBS website.

Conduct an Internet search for information about the *DSM-5* development on the American Psychiatric Association website.

Conduct an Internet search for Health Topics on the National Institute of Mental Health website.

Conduct an Internet search for the article "Deinstitutionalization: A Psychiatric 'Titanic'" on the PBS Frontline website.

Conduct an Internet search for the "Key Features of the Affordable Care Act by Year" on the U.S. Health and Human Services website.

Conduct an Internet search for the Army STARRS studies by navigating to the Army Starrs website.

Conduct an Internet search for the "Mental Health Courts Program" on the BJA website.

Conduct an Internet search for Diverse Communities on the National Alliance for the Mentally Ill website.

References

Alegría, M., Chatterji, P., Wells, K., Cao, Z., Chen, C. N., Takeuchi, D., & Meng, X. L. (2015). Disparity in depression treatment among racial and ethnic minority populations in the United States. *Psychiatric Services*.

American Psychiatric Association. (2013). *Diagnostic and statistical manual of mental disorders* (5th ed.). Washington, DC: Author.

Bandelow, B., Krause, J., Wedekind, D., Broocks, A., Hajak, G., & Rüther, E. (2005). Early traumatic life events, parental attitudes, family history, and birth risk factors in patients with borderline personality disorder and healthy controls. *Psychiatry Research, 134*(2), 169–179.

Beck, A. T. (1964). Thinking and depression: 2. Theory and therapy. *Archives of General Psychiatric, 10*, 561–571.

Beck, J. S. (2006). Cognitive-behavioral therapy. *Primary Psychiatry,13*(4), 31–34.

Center for Behavioral Health Statistics and Quality. (2015). Behavioral health trends in the United States: Results from the 2014 National Survey on Drug Use and Health (HHS Publication No. SMA 15-4927, NSDUH Series H-50). Retrieved from http://www.samhsa.gov/data/

Chen, H. M., DeLong, C. J., Bame, M., Rajapakse, I., Herron, T. J., McInnis, M. G., & O'shea, K. S. (2014). Transcripts involved in calcium signaling and telencephalic neuronal fate are altered in induced pluripotent stem cells from bipolar disorder patients. *Translational Psychiatry, 4*(3), e375.

Christy, A., Poythress, N. G., Boothroyd, R. A., Petrila, J., & Mehra, S. (2005). Evaluating the efficiency and community safety goals of the Broward county mental health court. *Behavioral Sciences and the Law, 23*, 227–243.

Dear, M. J., & Wolch, J. R. (2014). *Landscapes of despair: From deinstitutionalization to homelessness*. Princeton University Press.

Diala, C. C., Muntaner, C., Walrath, C., Nickerson, K., LaVeist, T., & Leaf, P. (2001). Racial/ethnic differences in attitudes toward seeking professional mental health services. *American Journal of Public Health, 91*(5), 805–807.

Dingfelder, S. (2004). Treatment for the untreatable. *Monitor in Psychology, 35*(11), 48–49.

Ditton, P. M. (1999). *Mental health and treatment of inmates and probationers* (Special report NCJ 174463). Washington, DC: U.S. Department of Justice, Office of Justice Programs, Bureau of Justice Statistics.

Fava, G. A., Rafanelli, C., Grandi, S., Conti, S., & Belluardo, P. (1998). Prevention of recurrent depression with cognitive behavioral therapy: Preliminary findings. *Archives of General Psychiatry, 55*(9), 816–820.

Feisthamel, K. P., & Schwartz, R. C. (2009). Differences in mental health counselors' diagnoses based on client race: An investigation of adjustment, childhood, and substance-related disorders. *Journal of Mental Health Counseling, 31*(1), 47–59.

Feldman, S. (2003). Reflections on the 40th anniversary of the U.S. Community Mental Health Centers Act. *Australian and New Zealand Journal of Psychiatry, 3*, 662–667.

Fields, G., & Phillips, E. E. (2013). The new asylums: Jails swell with mentally ill. *Wall Street Journal, 25*.

Folsom, D. P., Hawthorne, W., & Lindamer, L. (2005). Prevalence and risk factors for homelessness and utilization of mental health services among 10,340 patients with serious mental illness in a large public mental health system. *American Journal of Psychiatry, 162*(2), 370–376.

Goldstein, J. E. (2002). *Console and classify: The French psychiatric profession in the nineteenth century*. University of Chicago Press.

Hernandez, M., Nesman, T., Mowery, D., Acevedo-Polakovich, I. D., & Callejas, L. M. (2015). Cultural competence: A literature review and conceptual model for mental health services. *Psychiatric Services*.

Housing and Urban Development, U.S. Department of (HUD). (2009). The 2008 Annual Homeless.

International OCD Foundation [IOCDF]. (2014). What is obsessive compulsive personality disorder factsheet. Retrieved from https://iocdf.org/wp-content /uploads/2014/10/OCPD-Fact-Sheet.pdf

Kim, D. Y. (2016). Psychiatric deinstitutionalization and prison population growth: A critical literature review and its implications. *Criminal Justice Policy Review, 27*(1), 3–21.

Koerber, G. (2005). *Veterans: One-third of all homeless people*. National Alliance on Mental Illness, Issue Spotlight. Retrieved from http://www.nami.org/Template .cfm?Section=Issue_Spotlights&template= /ContentManagement/ContentDisplay. cfm&ContentID=26958

Marcela Horvitz-Lennon, M. D., Frank, R. G., Thompson, W., Seo Hyon Baik, M. S., Alegría, M., Rosenheck, R. A., & Normand, S. L. T. (2015). Investigation of racial and ethnic disparities in service utilization among homeless adults with severe mental illnesses. *Psychiatric Services*.

Marley, J. A., & Buila, S. (2001). Crimes against people with mental illness: Types, perpetrators, and influencing factors. *Social Work, 46*(2), 115–124.

McKay, D., Sookman, D., Neziroglu, F., Wilhelm, S., Stein, D. J., Kyrios, M., Matthews, K., & Veale, D. (2015). Efficacy of cognitive-behavioral therapy for obsessive–compulsive disorder. *Psychiatry Research, 225*(3), 236–246.

Michaud, C. M., Murray, C. J., & Bloom, B. R. (2001). Burden of disease—implications for future research. *Journal of the American Medical Association, 285*(5), 535–539.

Mowbray, C. T., & Holter, M. C. (2002). Mental health & mental illness: Out of the closet? *Social Service Review, 76*(1), 135–179.

Nock, M. K., Ursano, R. J., Heeringa, S. G., Stein, M. B., Jain, S., Raman, R., . . . & Gilman, S. E. (2015). Mental disorders, comorbidity, and pre-enlistment suicidal behavior among new soldiers in the US Army: results from the Army Study to Assess Risk and Resilience in Service members (Army STARRS). *Suicide and life-threatening behavior,45*(5), 588–599.

North, C. S., Eyrich, K. M., Pollio, D. E., & Spitznagel, E. L. (2004). Are rates of psychiatric disorders in the homeless population changing? *American Journal of Public Health, 94*(1), 103–108.

Norton, P. J., & Price, E. C. (2007). A meta-analytic review of adult cognitive-behavioral treatment outcome across the anxiety disorders. *The Journal of Nervous and Mental Disease,195*(6), 521–531.

Palermo, G. B., Smith, M. B., & Liska, F. J. (1991). Jails versus mental hospitals: A social dilemma. *International Journal of Offender Therapy and Comparative Criminology, 35*(2), 97–106.

Porter, R. (2002). *Madness: A brief history*. New York, NY: Oxford University Press.

Powell, J. (2003). Letter to the editor. *Issues in Mental Health Nursing, 24*(5), 463.

Raphael, S., & Stoll, M. A. (2013). Assessing the contribution of the deinstitutionalization of the mentally ill to growth in the US incarceration rate. *The Journal of Legal Studies, 42*(1), 187–222.

Saleebey, D. (1996). The strengths perspective in social work practice: Extensions and cautions. *Social Work, 41*(3), 296–305.

Sentencing Project. (2010). Racial disparity. Retrieved from http://www.sentencingproject.org/template/page .cfm?id=122.

Shern, D. L., Tsemberis, S., Anthony, W., Lovell, A. M., Richmond, L., Felton, C. J., et al. (2000). Serving street-dwelling individuals with psychiatric disabilities: Outcome of a psychiatric rehabilitation clinical trial. *American Journal of Public Health, 90*(12), 1873–1878.

Schoenbaum, M., Kessler, R. C., Gilman, S. E., Colpe, L. J., Heeringa, S. G., Stein, M. B., ... & Cox, K. L. (2014). Predictors of suicide and accident death in the Army Study to Assess Risk and Resilience in Service members (Army STARRS): results from the Army Study to Assess Risk and Resilience in Service members (Army STARRS). *JAMA psychiatry,71*(5), 493–503.

Sue, S. (1977). Community mental health services to minority groups: Some optimism, some pessimism. *American Psychologist, 32*, 616–624.

Sue, S., & McKinney, H. (1975). Asian Americans in the community mental health system. *American Journal, 45*, 111–118.

Sullivan, W. P. (1992). Reclaiming the community: The strengths perspective and deinstitutionalization. *Social Work, 37*(3), 204–209.

Swindle, R. W., Cronkite, R. C., & Moos, R. H. (1989). Life stressors, social resources, coping, and the 4-year course of unipolar depression. *Journal of Abnormal Psychology*, *98*(4), 468–477.

Torrey, E. F. (1995). *Surviving schizophrenia*, 3rd ed. New York, NY: Harper-Perennial.

Torrey, E. F., Entsminger, K., Geller, J., Stanley, J., & Jaffe, D. J. (2015). The shortage of public hospital beds for mentally ill persons. *Montana,303*(20.9), 6–9.

Torrey, E. F., Kennard, A, D., Eslinger, D., Lamb, R., and Pavle, J. (2010). More mentally ill persons are in jails and prisons than hospitals: A survey of the states. Report for the Nation al Sheriff's Association and the Treatment Advocacy Center.

Torrey, E. F., & Miller, J. (2002). *The invisible plague: The rise of mental illness from 1750 to present.* New Brunswick, NJ: Rutgers University Press.

U.S. Conference of Mayors. (2011). *Hunger and homelessness survey: A status report on hunger and homelessness in America's cities.* Washington, DC: Author.

World Health Organization. (2015, October). Depression: Fact Sheet No 369. Retrieved from http://www.who.int/mediacentre/factsheets/fs369/en/

9

Housing and Homelessness

© EMA WOO / SHUTTERSTOCK

I met Sarah when she was homeless and looking for permanent housing and attempting to put the pieces of her life together. Sarah was raised in an unstable and abusive home environment where she had been told repeatedly throughout her childhood that she was worthless and that no one would ever love her. Her every move was criticized and served as proof that she was no good. She had the natural need and desire to be loved and accepted, and by the time she was 17 this need peaked to a point that she could not resist the affections of an older man who promised her the world. Although she initially resisted his attempts to become sexual with her, he eventually convinced her by telling her that the only way he would know she loved him was if they had sex, and that if she refused he would leave her. Sarah's immense insecurities and her deep need to be cared for made her vulnerable to his manipulative threats, so she relented and agreed to become sexual with him, believing that she had finally found someone who truly loved and accepted her. Yet when she became pregnant, he became abusive and used many of the same abusive statements she had confided that her father had used to manipulate and control her. She believed that her father must have been right all along, because how else could she explain yet another man seeing such ugliness in her? Ultimately he abandoned her and her unborn child, and when her father learned of her pregnancy he kicked her out of the house and refused to allow her to return.

For the next four years Sarah was intermittently homeless, finding temporary stability through various transitional housing programs that helped her secure employment and an apartment. However, any crisis put her on the streets again, such as the time her son got the chicken pox, resulting in her needing to stay home with him for two weeks. Sarah was fired even though she had medical verification of her son's illness. This led to yet another financial downward spiral and another episode of homelessness. By the time her son was five he was acting out, considerably adding to her sense of frustration and burden. So when she met a new man who showered her with attention and compliments, all she could think of was that she had finally met the man of her dreams. He said all the right things, offered to let her and her son move in with him, and offered to manage every part of her life. He even told her that she would not have to work and could stay home with her son, so she gladly quit her job and embraced being a stay-at-home mom at last—something she had wanted to do for years.

Sarah wanted desperately to believe this was real and accepted this man's seemingly generous offers because she believed that to do otherwise would mean robbing her son of his only opportunity for a real home and family. When her new boyfriend told her that she was the first woman he ever wanted to have a baby with, she was so flattered she agreed immediately to get pregnant. She believed with all her heart that she finally had it all, and that all the years of suffering were behind her.

Sarah became pregnant quickly and dreamed of her new life with her new boyfriend. Although she would have preferred they got married, he claimed to not be ready yet. Because she did not want to create waves in the relationship, she did not push the subject. She talked endlessly to her son about their good fortune in finding this man who was going to take care of them forever. When her new boyfriend hit her for the first time, she convinced herself that it was a one-time incident caused by the stress of having a new family. When she noticed that he drank too much alcohol and seemed impatient with her son, she convinced herself that he needed time to adjust to having an instant family. Then one day he did not come home from work, and when a few days had gone by and he still did not return with her car, she came to the agency where I worked asking for financial assistance because she had no money to pay for the rent due in a few days.

Unfortunately, we learned that this man had a pattern of treating women in this way. This was not the first time he had encouraged a single mom to depend on him only to flee when the good feelings ended. Equally unfortunate was that she had absolutely no recourse against him, even for taking her car, because to make insurance matters easier, she had agreed to put his name on the title—a decision that seemed foolish in hindsight, but at the time it seemed the least that she could do in light of what he was offering her. Now she had no money, no job, no car, a devastated and angry child, and a baby on the way. She would also be homeless again within the month.

Adding to her burden was the intense sense of humiliation she felt when she realized that she had once again been taken advantage of. She firmly believed that she deserved this treatment and argued that there must be something terribly defective about her because these things kept happening to her. She was devastated that she was so completely abandoned in the wake of breathing her first sigh of relief in years. She was extremely depressed, which increased her risk for either inadvertently abusing her child or neglecting him in some way, particularly when he expressed anger at her for driving his new daddy away. And, her additional loss of self-esteem left her in no shape to solve problems by gaining employment, finding low-cost housing, and searching out assistance programs, most of which would require her to disclose her reasons for becoming homeless. She simply did not have it in her to repeatedly tell her story of blind trust and exploitation. Although we suggested she go to the hospital for a suicide evaluation due to her severe depression, she refused because she feared that hospitalization would mean placing her son in temporary foster care.

The last time I spoke with Sarah she had lost her home and was "couch surfing"—doubling-up with friends for a few weeks at a time while she tried to save enough money to afford to stay in a motel. She admitted that on a few nights, when they had no place to go, she and her children slept in her car. She had no solid plan for permanent housing, was slipping further and further into a depression, and had no idea where to turn. Assistance seemed out of reach and all she could think about was taking care of her children by waking up each morning and focusing on nothing other than knowing where they would sleep that night. Sarah's case may sound complicated, but it is all too familiar to those human service professionals working with the homeless population.

THE CURRENT STATE OF HOMELESSNESS IN THE UNITED STATES

Homelessness is a very complex social problem, as reflected in the opening case study, often encompassing issues related to physical and mental health, domestic violence, child welfare, and chronic financial insecurity. The rate of homelessness began to increase between 1970 and 1980 due to a decrease in **affordable housing** and an increase in poverty. The 2007 recession has exacerbated this trend of financial vulnerability, as indicated by about two-thirds of cities in the United States reporting increases in requests for food and emergency shelter in 2014. Among those cities reporting an increase in emergency service requests, 56 percent were families, 38 percent were employed, and just over 20 percent were older adults (U.S. Conference of Mayors, 2014). Not all of those requesting emergency food assistance were homeless, but the two are certainly related. City officials identified the lack of affordable housing as one of the primary causes of homelessness among families with children, but unemployment, poverty, and low-paying jobs were referenced as well. For single individuals, housing and unemployment, poverty, untreated mental illness, and untreated substance abuse were all correlated to homelessness (U.S. Conference of Mayors, 2014).

Homeless Counts and Demographics

There is currently no universally agreed-upon definition of homelessness, which creates challenges for service providers, particularly those seeking government funding. The federal definition of homelessness includes only those individuals or families who do not have a fixed, regular, or adequate nighttime residence, and who spend the night in a shelter or in an area not intended as a regular sleeping accommodation for humans, such as a car, abandoned building, a train station, or an airport. In other words, federal definitions include only those people who are sheltered or unsheltered, and do not include the **hidden homeless**, such as those in jail for factors related to their homelessness, such as loitering; those in mental hospitals and rehabilitation facilities; individuals and families

Watch the video on the hidden homeless in rural America. Which aspects of living in a rural community increase the risk of homelessness for certain populations, and why are they considered "hidden"?

ENHANCEDetext *video example 9.1*

www.youtube.com/
watch?v=FSI3kFY8TuE

living in **single room occupancy** (SRO) units; and those living in substandard living conditions. Advocates for the homeless have long criticized the federal definition for being far too narrow, thus failing to capture the entire scope of the homeless problem.

The federal government counts homelessness in two ways—**point-in-time counts**, which provide an estimated number of people who are sheltered or unsheltered on any given night in the last week of January of a particular year (thus, a "snapshot"), and estimates of the total number of people who experience homelessness (sheltered and unsheltered) within a year. Clearly the second estimate is going to be far higher, but it may be less accurate since some homeless individuals may be counted more than once. The federal government began requiring that local community agencies (called **Continuum of Care (CoC) programs**) provide annual point-in-time counts to Congress in 2005. The estimates are then released in an annual report by HUD, called the **Annual Homeless Assessment Report (AHAR)**, and provided to Congress. The report is also published on the **U.S. Housing and Urban Development (HUD)** Exchange website.

In response to criticism that the federal definition of homelessness was too narrow, it was broadened somewhat when the McKinney-Vento Act was reauthorized and amended as the **Homeless Emergency Assistance and Rapid Transition to Housing (HEARTH) Act** in 2009. The definition now includes those who are in imminent danger of losing their housing, whether it is a home they own, rent, live in without paying rent, or share with others. Also included in the definition of homelessness are those who have been evicted from their homes and have no home to move into because they lack the resources to obtain permanent housing. Much of the impetus for the expanded definition of homelessness was the 2007 recession that resulted in over seven million home foreclosures, affecting not only homeowners, but renters as well. The HEARTH Act also expanded the definition of homelessness to include unaccompanied youth and families with chronic housing instability due to health problems, such as physical disabilities and illnesses, mental health conditions, substance abuse, and domestic violence and child abuse (42 U.S.C. § 11302, et seq., 2009).

Advocates for the homeless still complain that the federal definition of homelessness is too narrow because point-in-time counts still only include sheltered and unsheltered persons. This impacts service provision eligibility and funding, since the federal government significantly underestimates the homeless population. For instance, federal point-in-time counts estimated that on any given night in 2015 there were 564,708 homeless people, 69 percent of who were sheltered and 31 percent who were unsheltered (Henry et al., 2015; National Alliance to End Homelessness, 2015a). When definitions are broadened to include the hidden homeless, estimates of homelessness jump to between 2.5 and 3.5 million people (National Law Center on Homelessness and Poverty, 2006). When people who are temporarily **doubling-up** with family and friends for economic reasons are included, estimates jump an additional 7.4 million!

According to federally mandated point-in-time counts, in 2015 64 percent of the homeless population consisted of individuals, 36 percent were families, 25 percent were children under

Doubling-up for economic reasons has increased significantly in the last 10 years

Table 9.1   Homeless Rates by Year (Individuals and Families)

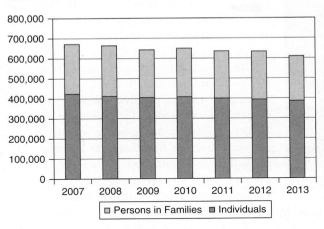

Table 9.2   Number of People Doubling-Up with Family and Friends by Year

As sheltered and unsheltered homeless counts have declined, people doubling-up with family and friends for economic reasons as increased

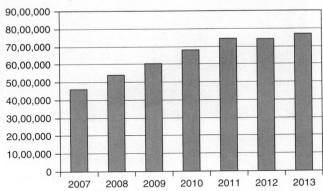

the age of 18, about 10 percent were veterans, and about 7 percent were unaccompanied youth between the ages of 18 and 24. Additionally, about 17 percent of the homeless population are considered **chronically homeless** (Henry et al., 2015). Overall, homelessness appears to be declining, having decreased about 10 percent in the last decade. More good news is that homelessness among veterans has decreased about 35 percent between 2009 and 2015. Families experienced a decline of about 20 percent in homelessness as well, and chronic homelessness declined about 21 percent (Doran, 2015). (See Table 9.1 for homeless rates between 2007 and 2013).

These are very positive trends and are likely happening in response to ambitious government programs targeting homelessness among these subgroups. However, alongside these reductions have been some disturbing trends, including a significant increase in the number of people doubling-up due to economic reasons (about 7.7 million in 2015) (see Table 9.2), an increase in the number of people who spend more than 50 percent of their income on housing (about 6.4 million in 2015), and an increase in the number of shelters that turned away families with children due to lack of space (about 73 percent in 2014) (National Alliance to End Homelessness, 2015b; U.S. Conference of Mayors, 2014). Thus, it is too early to determine whether the overall decline in homelessness is a sign of a successful government strategy or is more representative of a shift in demographics, where some of those living in shelters and on the streets are now a part of the hidden homeless (Table 9.2).

ENHANCEDetext *self-check 9.1*

PERCEPTIONS OF THE POOR

Homelessness, particularly among certain subpopulations, tends to be highly stigmatized, which can lead to a lack of sympathy toward the homeless, particularly those living on the streets. This can in turn negatively affect funding for homeless services as

© PHOTOGRAPHEE.EU / SHUTTERSTOCK

The stereotypical homeless person is an unkempt alcoholic man

well as general service provision, when homelessness is either perceived as too complex of a problem to effectively manage or the homeless population is perceived as causing their own problems through "poor choices," such as substance abuse.

In general, most people's attitudes toward the poor and the homeless are negative, and the stigma that is typically associated with poverty in general seems to increase when the poor become homeless. Some of the reasons for the stigmatization of homelessness are related to the public nature of homelessness. Many people who are homeless are forced to live out in the open, such as on the streets or alleyways, in parks or automobiles, where good hygiene is impossible and begging for money and food is often the only means of survival (Phelan, Link, Moore, & Stueve, 1997). The common association of mental illness and substance abuse with homelessness also contributes to the negative stigma of homelessness.

The negative attitude about those who are poor and homeless is reflected in several studies and national public opinion surveys. Generally, it appears as though most people blame the poor for their bad lot in life. For instance, a seminal national survey conducted in 1975 found that the majority of those in the United States attributed chronic poverty to personal failures, such as having a poor work ethic, poor money management skills, a lack of any special talent that might translate into a positive contribution to society, and low personal moral values. Those questioned ranked social causes, such as economic disadvantage, racism, poor schools, and the lack of sufficient employment, the lowest of all possible causes (Feagin, 1975).

More recent surveys conducted in the mid-1990s revealed an increase in the tendency to blame the poor for their poverty (Weaver, Shapiro, & Jacobs, 1995), even though a considerable body of research points to social and structural dynamics as the primary causes of poverty, such as a bad economy and a lack of opportunity (Shelton et al., 2015). A 2007 study comparing attitudes toward homelessness among respondents in five countries—the United States, the United Kingdom, Belgium, Germany, and Italy—found that respondents in the United States and the United Kingdom, the only two English-speaking countries, reported higher rates of lifetime homelessness and fewer social programs, yet had lower levels of compassion for the homeless population (Toro et al., 2007).

Watch the CBS video clip on the history of class warfare in America. What is the role of class conflict in economic inequality? And what is the relationship between class conflict and perceptions of the poor?
ENHANCEDetext *video example 9.2*

www.youtube.com/
watch?v=bGS2G79IxTc

Compassion for poverty-related homelessness tends to be greater during difficult economic times and lower during economic booms, and general compassion for families tends to be greater as well, particularly if the family members do not match the negative stereotype of homeless people living on the streets. Recent studies reflecting attitudes about poverty during the most recent economic crisis revealed increased compassion, but they also showed an increase in **class conflict** (also called class warfare), where lower income individuals expressed resentment toward the wealthy. A 2012 study conducted by the Pew Research Center found that negative perceptions of each class—the poor of the rich and the rich of the poor—commonly referred to as class conflict, had significantly increased in recent years.

Attitudes toward the wealthy, something not explored in earlier attitudinal surveys about income levels, reveal that about 46 percent of people surveyed believed that most wealthy people earned their wealth through inheritance and social connections, whereas 43 percent of people surveyed believed that wealthy people became rich through hard work, ambition, and education (Taylor, Parker, Morin, & Motel, 2012). Based on these studies it appears as though there remains at the least a fair amount of confusion about the causes of poverty and wealth, whether poverty and homelessness are caused by behavioral factors or social conditions, and whether wealth is a result of privilege and inheritance or hard work.

Despite intermittent increases in compassion toward the poor and homeless, the general public does not appear to understand the underlying causes of poverty and homelessness, which may make it easier for them to jump to incorrect conclusions based on negative stereotypes. Negative perceptions of homeless people do not seem to be consistent across the board though, as some subgroups are more stigmatized than others, including single men, ethnic minorities, alcoholics, and undocumented immigrants. One concept that may help explain why certain groups are more stigmatized than others is the fundamental attribution error (FAE), a tendency for people to attribute causality of events and circumstances incorrectly due to bias. In normal circumstances when people attempt to explain why they failed, or someone they know well or can relate to failed, they will have a tendency to blame situational factors outside of the person's control. But if they are attempting to explain why a complete stranger failed, particularly someone they cannot relate to, they will have a tendency to blame personal factors (personality traits or choices), such as personal moral failing, and disregard situational ones. In the latter case, they are likely committed FAE, where under certain circumstances they overemphasize personal factors in attributing causality.

Assuming that FAE is at play when people are trying to figure out why someone is homeless, the average person would have a tendency to assume that those they don't know and/or cannot relate to are homeless due to their own personal shortcomings, such as an inability to manage money well, a history of poor choices (e.g., promiscuity), a poor work ethic, and substance abuse. Yet, if they or someone they knew well became homeless, they would most likely attribute the homelessness to situational factors, such as being unfairly laid off from work or abruptly leaving an abusive relationship.

Human service professionals must understand the stigmas associated with homelessness as well as why they occur so they can acknowledge and challenge them. Recognizing how ingrained negative stereotypes and stigmas can be within U.S. society is also important so that human service providers can avoid the possibility of internalizing negative biases, which can influence perceptions of their clients experiencing homelessness. Human service professionals who internalize macro negative stereotypes about certain populations risk being influenced by these stigmas in their practice, which can contribute to homeless clients' existing sense of invisibility and lost sense of self.

ENHANCEDetext *self-check 9.2*

POPULATIONS AT-RISK FOR BECOMING HOMELESS

There are many risk factors associated with homelessness. For instance, the most recent U.S. Conference of Mayors report found that about 28 percent of homeless adults were severely mentally ill, 22 percent were physically disabled, 15 percent were victims of domestic violence, 13 percent were veterans, and 3 percent were HIV-positive, reflecting the very complex nature of homelessness (U.S. Conference of Mayors Report, 2014). Additionally individuals who have adverse childhood experiences, such as child maltreatment, a parent with mental illness or substance abuse, and witnessing violence, are at far higher risk of homelessness (Montgomery, 2013; Montgomery et al., 2013; Shelton et al., 2015). Domestic violence and chronic economic insecurity also increase the risk of homelessness, particularly among single mothers and their children (Staggs et al., 2007). And finally, single middle-aged men, many of whom are veterans, are also at increased risk of homelessness for a variety of reasons that include post-war social isolation and untreated mental health issues such as post-traumatic stress disorder (PTSD), depression, and substance abuse (Creech et al., 2015; Rosenbeck & Fontana, 1994).

The Rise in Homeless Single Parent Families

For years, families have been one of the fastest growing subgroups among the homeless population. Although family homelessness has declined in recent years, single mothers and their children remain a highly vulnerable group. The increase of homeless single mothers began several decades ago due to a lack of affordable housing, an increase in divorce, and a decrease in the stigmatization of single parenting. The consequences associated with these dynamics, particularly the latter two, resulted in many single mothers not being able to support their children financially for a variety of reasons, including the decline in material support available through the social welfare system, a difficult economy, and a family court system that is based on the male breadwinner model and has not kept pace with changing social or economic dynamics.

Women of color are overrepresented in the single parent homeless population, with African American women comprising the majority of female head-of-household homeless families (43 percent), followed by Caucasian (38 percent), Hispanic (15 percent), and Native American (3 percent). Despite this disparity among ethnic groups, the overwhelming majority of homeless single mothers are native-born U.S. citizens, not immigrants. Even states that border Mexico have a relatively low percentage of homeless immigrants. Families of color are at greatest risk of becoming homeless, although single-parent homelessness among Caucasians is significant as well.

Most homeless single mothers have never been married, and although more than half are high school graduates, most have never established a solid work history for many reasons. Many single mothers cite either never having had stability in their housing situations (some dating back to their childhoods) or having experienced unstable housing for several years prior to becoming homeless. Most have experienced homelessness chronically on a cyclical basis, securing housing for a short time only to experience a financial crisis, such as a job loss, which resulted in a domino effect of negative life events and ultimately another episode of homelessness.

Causes and Correlates of Single Mother Homelessness

About three-quarters of all single mothers work, but most are in low-wage jobs, such as those in the service industry, which often pay minimum wage, have unstable hours (or are seasonal), and do not provide benefits. The median annual income of a working single mother is about $26,000 per year, compared to $84,000 per year for a married couple (U.S. Census Bureau, 2014). What this means is that on average among single mothers in the United States, about 90 percent live in poverty, of whom 50 percent meet the criteria for extreme poverty. Among single mothers who work full time in minimum wage jobs, 80 percent paid more than 30 percent of their income toward the cost of housing in 2014 and nearly one-third paid over 50 percent, a trend being driven by stagnated wages and increasing rents (Joint Center for Housing Studies of Harvard University, 2015).

The high cost of child care remains one of the most significant barriers to meaningful employment among the single parent population. In most states, the cost of full-time center-based child care ranges from $10,000 to $13,000 per year per child, which is between one-third and one-half of the average single mother's annual take-home pay (Bugbee, 2015). Additionally, most service sector jobs, in which the bulk of low-income single mothers are employed, offer employment with nontraditional hours, such as evenings and weekends, which makes it even more difficult and cost-prohibitive to secure appropriate and accessible child care services. Additionally, child care subsidies are very difficult to obtain and most states have either long waiting lists or have frozen their subsidy programs (Schulman & Blank, 2013).

Unfortunately, safety nets in the form of public assistance programs have significantly shrunk since the passage of federal welfare reform legislation in 1996. Welfare reform effectively ended the Aid to Families with Dependent Children (AFDC) program and initiated the **Temporary Assistance for Needy Families (TANF)** program, which provides assistance at about one-third of the federal poverty level (Nickelson, 2004). A driving force behind the change in approaches to poverty alleviation was the belief that poverty was more effectively addressed through increased personal accountability, a focus on employment (and less reliance on government), and a policy strategy that decreased out-of-wedlock births and increased incentives for single mothers to marry.

Essentially, the change in policy priorities and approaches shifted the rhetoric from a focus on macro-level poverty dynamics to characterizing single-parent homelessness as one of poor women of color having sex outside of marriage and getting pregnant. Such a characterization negates the complexity of the problem and also contributes to a perception that single-parent poverty and homelessness is not a social problem but a personal one that needs to be managed through increased stigmatization and punishment.

Research on single-parent homelessness reveals a quite different picture of the one painted by proponents of welfare reform—one of incredible complexity where the "problem" of single-parent homelessness is deeply rooted in numerous other social issues related to race, gender, violence, and mental illness. For instance, over 90 percent of homeless single mothers report unstable childhoods filled with physical and sexual abuse (Nunez & Fox, 1999; Shelton et al., 2015). About 85 percent of homeless single mothers surveyed experienced domestic violence as adults, with most reporting that they became homeless after leaving a relationship. Other issues include high rates of mental health problems, including co-occurring substance abuse disorders at about four times that of the non-homeless population (Shelton et al., 2015). These types of social problems are exacerbated by longstanding societal disparities, such as the overrepresentation of children of color in the child welfare system (Bradley-King, Perry, & Donohue, 2013) and increased barriers to mental health treatment experienced by many ethnic minority populations (Alegría et al., 2015).

Single Parent Families and Shelter Living

The increase in single-mother homelessness has resulted in the need for significant changes in social welfare policy regarding how homelessness is managed on local, state, and federal levels. When the homeless population was more homogeneous, consisting

In many emergency shelters teenage boys are required to stay on the men's side of the shelter rather than remain with their mothers and sisters

primarily of single men living in SROs or on **skid row**, the community response was less complex, focusing on low-cost housing and substance abuse counseling. But the current homeless demographic presents more challenging problems requiring a more multifaceted approach. For instance, emergency shelters are not equipped to serve families, which poses a considerable number of challenges for single mothers and their children, which in turn can exacerbate existing problems.

Single parents and their children often proceed through a series of unstable housing situations, such as doubling-up with family and friends prior to living in a shelter, living in a motel, and entering (and exiting) romantic relationships quickly. When a single-parent family does become homeless, the parent often attempts to avoid traditional shelter setting, but that is not always possible. There are a lot of studies showing just how unhealthy traditional shelter living is for families, particularly children, but probably one of the most compelling studies involved interviewing single mothers who were living in shelters with their children (Lindsey, 1998). In this study single homeless mothers discussed the vast number of outdated rules, such as not allowing their sons to sleep in the same area as them (some boys as young as eight years old, were required to sleep alone on the men's side of the shelter). If the mothers refused, for fear of their sons' safety, the only choice they had available to them was to allow their sons to enter the county foster care system.

Several single mothers in the study also shared how shelters applied the same rules to families as they did to singles, forcing single mothers and their children to leave the shelter between 7:00 A.M. and 5:00 or 6:00 P.M., even if they had infants or preschool-aged children. This policy was enforced regardless of weather conditions or the lack of safety of the community where the shelter was located. Many single mothers also complained that there was no way to look for a job when they had to stay out of the shelter with their kids for most of the day. Other complaints included staff who seemed insensitive to their children's needs, for instance enforcing rules barring children from running around and playing, creating a difficult situation for parents who were required to keep their children quiet at all times though the children lacked distractions such as television or toys. If the mothers didn't or couldn't comply, they risked being asked to leave the shelter.

By far the most difficult aspect of shelter living according to the single mothers surveyed involved staff who would override their parenting decisions. For example, staff might correct a mother in front of her child and other shelter residents for how she was disciplining her child. Such actions on the part of shelter staff made the mothers feel as though their authority was diminished in the eyes of their children. Other shelter rules that made parenting difficult included not being able to have food at any time other than during designated meal times, including not allowing mothers to give snacks to their young children.

Lindsey (1998) concluded that most rules and policies in traditional shelters were not created with families in mind and had a potently devastating effect on the parent–child relationship. Most mothers she interviewed felt as though they were no longer the head of household with the power to make parenting decisions in the best interest of their children—even basic decisions such as when to bathe and feed their children were taken away from them, leaving many of them feeling just as powerless as they felt when living with an abusive partner. Lindsey also noted that the disintegration of the mother–child relationship was often not a temporary disruption, but rather one that continued on long after the family left the shelter, degrading and disempowering parents who were already feeling shamed and powerless by their homeless status.

It is important to also discuss the strengths that many homeless single mothers exhibit, particularly because human service professionals will need to work with the single-parent client to identify and build on existing strengths. A 1994 study found that single mothers living in shelters had a surprising level of determination, a sense of personal pride, and an ability to confront their problems directly. Many of the single mothers interviewed exhibited a strong commitment to the welfare of their children (such as choosing homelessness over remaining in an abusive relationship) and had strong moral values that acted as a guide in decision-making. Many homeless single mothers also had deep religious convictions that provided them with a sense of purpose and meaning. Many overcame what seemed to be insurmountable odds to keep their children with them rather than have them placed in foster care, despite harsh living conditions (Montgomery, 1994).

A more recent study evaluating the resiliency of single mothers in general (not solely homeless families) found that single mothers were very resilient, despite all of the challenges they faced. Most shared that they disagreed with the negative stereotypes of single mothers as inadequate and immoral, and believed they had personally grown through the challenges they faced in raising their children alone. Many also shared that they found the experience of single parenting transformative and confidence-building (Levine, 2009). Human service professionals can tap into these strengths when working with single parents in order to help them gain self-sufficiency in the face of multiple challenges.

Homeless Children and School Attendance

Children are the fastest growing segment of the homeless population. According to the Department of Education (which uses the broader definition of homelessness) there are over 1.2 million students under the age of 18 who identified as homeless in the 2012–2013 school year, which is an 87 percent increase since 2007. Most of these children are living with at least one parent and were doubling-up with family and friends, but the report also found that over 76,000 were living on the streets or in a shelter alone (National Center for Homeless Education, 2014).

The staggering increase in homeless students creates challenges for social service agencies and schools. Homeless children are at increased risk of a range of social problems and challenges, including physical illnesses, such as asthma; mental disorders, such as depression and anxiety; behavioral problems; learning problems; and low self-esteem (Davey, 2004; Masten, Fiat, Labella, & Strack, 2015; Needle, 2014). Developing effective programs designed to address the wide array of risk factors associated with homelessness, as well as keeping homeless children in school and succeeding academically, is essential; otherwise they will be at increased risk of homelessness in their adulthood, in addition to experiencing a host of other social problems, including chronic poverty.

Enrolling in school and maintaining a consistent pattern of attendance is a significant challenge for homeless children due to the transient nature of homelessness, as well as other problems that result from homelessness. For instance, about 42 percent

Watch the 60 minutes video excerpt on homeless children. How can human service providers in schools meet the needs of children such as those featured in the video?
ENHANCEDetext *video example 9.3*

www.youtube.com/watch?v=L2hzRPLVSm4

of homeless children transfer schools at least once and 51 percent transfer twice or more (National Coalition for the Homeless, 2007). Some of the many barriers to school enrollment and attendance for homeless children include chronic illness, falling too far behind in their academics, and emergency shelter residency limits that result in multiple moves, often out of the child's home school district (National Coalition for the Homeless, 2007).

Even though the McKinney-Vento act (reauthorized as the HEARTH Act) requires that schools allow homeless children to remain at their home school if they move out of the district, regardless of residency requirements, it is often just not feasible due to difficulties in transportation and other complications. In addition to family mobility, other barriers to school enrollment and attendance include delays in the transfer of school records, poor health and hygiene, a lack of clothing, and an inability to obtain required school supplies (National Coalition for the Homeless, 2007).

I recall when I was working as a school social worker in Los Angeles having several school-aged homeless children on my caseload. The children would get settled and acclimated to their classroom and start the long process of building a trusting relationship with their teachers and me, and then suddenly, one day, they would disappear. I would typically learn at some point that the family was forced to move to a different shelter, and even if remaining at the school of origin was a legal possibility, it was not a realistic one because there was no guarantee that the next shelter would be anywhere close to our school. Even if our school could offer transportation, the commute was often several hours each way, which was simply not sustainable.

Homeless Individuals

The largest portion of the homeless population consists of homeless individuals—primarily middle-aged men who are often of color and are sometimes veterans—living alone in shelter or on the streets. Reasons for homelessness vary. Some are similar to the causes noted in single-parent families—childhood histories of abuse, growing up in the foster care system, having little or no family or social support, being undereducated and stuck in minimum wage jobs, physical illness and disabilities, and mental illness and co-occurring substance abuse disorders. Social causes of homelessness among middle-aged and older African American men include institutionalized racism and oppression, lack of opportunity, and a lack of appropriate mental health services.

Many homeless veterans suffer from PTSD after having served in the military during wartime, as well as have physical disabilities, such as traumatic brain injury. Changes in the economic infrastructure resulting in fewer well-paying jobs as well as difficulty transitioning from military life to civilian life are only some of the underlying dynamics associated with veteran homelessness. Veterans services address many of these issues in programs designed to meet the complex needs of the veteran population. However, most programs, especially those offered through the Veterans Administration (VA), have long waiting lists and generally poor track records in meeting the needs of veterans, particularly homeless ones. Several recent efforts have been made to increase service provision for veteran populations, including increased funding for provider training. Veteran homelessness has declined in recent years, but this population remains highly vulnerable to housing insecurity as well as a host of other social problems, such as depression and risk of suicide (Briggs, 2013; Shoenbaum et al., 2014).

Runaway and Homeless Youth

No one is certain just how many adolescents and youth are homeless and living on the streets, but some estimates put that number as high as two million in the United States alone. This is a unique population among the entire homeless population because the reasons, risk factors, and intervention needs of runaway and homeless youth are often markedly different than the general homeless population. Adolescents are far more likely to be living on the streets than in a shelter. They are also far more likely to participate in dangerous behaviors such as drug abuse (including needle sharing), panhandling, theft, and survival sex (sex for food, money, and shelter). These risky behaviors put homeless adolescents at risk for HIV, hepatitis B, hepatitis C, and sexually transmitted diseases (Beech, Meyers, & Beech, 2002). Runaway and homeless youth are also at high risk for physical and sexual violence, both by other teens and by adults.

Most homeless adolescents are living on the streets because they have run away from an abusive home, have been kicked out of their homes by parents who no longer wish to take care of them (**throw-away youth**), or have aged out of the foster care system. The majority of runaway and homeless youth interviewed in various research studies reported a history of both physical and sexual abuse, which served as a primer for being similarly victimized on the streets (Whitbeck, Hoyt, & Ackley, 1997). Another study of over 600 runaway youth found that sexual abuse was the chief reason adolescents chose to live on the streets rather than remaining in their homes (Yoder, Whitbeck, & Hoyt, 2001). The fact that many of these teens will continue to experience sexual exploitation while living on the streets, whether through outright attacks or through survival sex, is certainly a tragedy, and one that can be addressed by those in the human services field.

Most urban runaway and homeless youth operated as a somewhat cohesive group on the streets, protecting each other and helping one another survive. More seasoned youth often took newer homeless teens under their wings, teaching them survival tactics and welcoming them into the fold. Newer homeless youth expressed relief about having someone mentor them about surviving street life. Runaway and homeless youth have also shared stories of the horrors of living on the streets, including being exploited by older youth and adults who forced them into dealing drugs and prostitution (Auerswalk & Eyre, 2002).

Many runway and homeless youth have also reported having a strong belief in God, who they believed watches out for them and keeps them safe. In a 2000 study, one teen stated that when he was not really in need, he would often get no offer of food and little money while panhandling. Yet when he was really in need, having gone without food for a few days, whatever he needed would just come to him. He attributed this pattern to God knowing what he needed and providing for him when he needed it the most (Auerswalk & Eyre, 2002). In fact, in another study, researchers found that over half of all runaway and homeless youth interviewed cited faith in God as the primary motivation for survival (Lindsey, Kurtz, Jarvis, Williams, & Nackerud, 2000).

Yet even with this surprisingly high percentage of faith-seeking homeless teens, an estimated 40 percent of homeless youth attempt suicide (Auerswalk & Eyre, 2002). They are also at high risk for PTSD, anxiety disorders, depression, substance abuse, and delinquency (Thrane, Chen, Johnson, & Whitbeck, 2008). Many runway and homeless youth report losing all contact with people in their former lives, even siblings, extended family, and those who had been supportive of them in the past. Most runaway and homeless youth talked about feeling extremely lonely and distrustful of others, but in desperate need of love and affection. Because the majority of runaway and homeless youth ran away from abusive homes, it's likely that many were suffering from some form of emotional disturbance even prior to entering street life (Kidd, 2003).

Unfortunately, because of their histories of abuse, many runaway and homeless youth are highly suspicious of all adults, including outreach workers with human services agencies serving the homeless youth population. The prevailing belief was that human services organizations would force the teens to return to an abusive home environment or that they'd be turned over to the police. Youth who accepted assistance from these agencies were often considered sellouts and foolish by other youth living on the streets. Knowing these attitudes can aid human services agencies in developing outreach programs and other services designed to overcome these negative perceptions. Research studies have also found that homeless adolescents are acutely aware of their outsider status, and many of them manage by embracing being an outsider, for example they may get multiple piercings which sets them apart from their fellow youths. By incorporating their outsider status into their identity, they take control of something that could potentially make them feel even more vulnerable (Auerswalk & Eyre, 2002). Successful intervention programs need to address the issue of the teens feeling like they don't belong.

Targeting the many strengths exhibited by runaway and homeless youth can be a starting point for human service professionals working with this often resistant population. But this is challenging when many intervention systems view homeless youth as deviant: first because they are "runaways" and second because many of the behaviors engaged in by this population while living on the streets are against the law. Consider the adolescent who is kicked out of his family home because he stands up to physical abuse he's been enduring for years. Then consider that there are no appropriate and available shelters available for him, so he is forced to live on the streets. In order to survive, he panhandles, pickpockets, and every once in a while, in order to obtain money for food, he engages in survival sex with grown men. His only contact with mainstream society is when he's arrested for loitering. After being placed in juvenile detention, imagine that a psychologist or social worker evaluates the teen, and noting the long list of acting out and rebellious behaviors as well as the adolescent's uncooperative attitude, diagnoses the teen with conduct disorder or oppositional defiance disorder. This can be a humiliating and shaming experience for an adolescent who is acting out in response to being victimized in his family of origin. To then enter into the juvenile justice system that continues to pathologize his behavior and responds in punitive measures rather than supportive ones only adds to his feelings of victimization.

Human service professionals working with runaway and homeless youth must provide consistent encouragement, compassionate care, and understanding that promote both self-esteem and self-efficacy (a sense of competence). This can be accomplished while focusing on basic needs such as providing food, shelter, and good health care, while using a strengths-based approach to build a positive alliance as a basis for intervention. Yet again the barrier that human services agencies must overcome is significant because so many runaway and homeless youth have been rejected and abandoned by their families, and then are further exploited and abused by adults on the streets, causing them to remain very distrustful.

ENHANCEDetext *self-check 9.3*

COMMON PRACTICE SETTINGS SERVING HOMELESS POPULATIONS

There are many agencies that offer services for the homeless and those experiencing housing insecurity. Agencies that provide direct services to the homeless population are likely the recipient of grants provided in response to the McKinney-Vento Act. Under the McKinney-Vento Act (prior to reauthorization), government funding for homeless programs was facilitated through a number of competitive grant programs within the federal Homeless Assistance program. These included the Shelter Plus Care Program, the Supportive Housing Program, and the Section 8 Moderate Rehabilitation Single Room Occupancy Program. Under the HEARTH Act grants were consolidated into a single program called the Emergency Solutions Grants program, which funds community-based programs through the Continuum of Care (CoC) program. The CoC program provides competitive grants for not-for-profit agencies as well as State and local governments. Programs focus on **rapid rehousing** to minimize the trauma of homelessness, as well of funding permanent housing programs, transitional housing programs, supportive services, and programs that focus on homelessness prevention.

Permanent housing programs, also called supportive housing, include any housing program that doesn't have a limit on the amount of time a client can stay. Permanent supportive housing provides services to individuals with disabilities, and rapid rehousing involves services that assist homeless individuals and families with obtaining permanent housing as quickly as possible. Other examples of permanent housing that are not necessarily funded through the CoC program include subsidized housing programs facilitated through HUD. An early type of government-subsidized housing consisted of clusters or communities of apartments, often in high rises. **Housing projects**, as such communities were often called, did not effectively resolve homelessness, in large part due the inadvertent creation of segregated communities of poverty and crime.

Gang activity, drug dealing, and other crimes often associated with low-income urban communities were common in what became known as "the projects." Once government policy makers realized that congregated housing projects were causing more harm than good, an organized effort was made to close the projects down, particularly in large cities such as Chicago and Philadelphia, and transition residents to new low-rise housing units scattered throughout the community.

A more current form of permanent low-cost housing includes HUD's voucher program, which is based on the scattered model: **Section 8 housing** for the general population (although women with children have priority) and **Section 811 housing** for individuals with disabilities (including mental illness). Section 8 and 811 programs involve recipients finding their own rental that accepts a government voucher for rental payment. Theoretically the voucher can be used with any approved rental property, but either through bias or because of a competitive rental market, many landlords in more expensive communities will not accept Section 8 or 811 rental vouchers. Thus, even though one intention of the voucher program was to avoid segregation, the result in some communities is still much the same because the landlords most likely to accept Section 8 or 811 vouchers are owners of large apartment complexes in low-income, higher crime areas. Unfortunately, the need for low-cost housing has not kept pace with availability.

Emergency and **transitional housing programs** offer temporary housing on an emergency or longer basis, with comprehensive programs sometimes offering housing

Watch the video about homelessness among the veteran populations. How are the programs referenced in the film addressing veteran homelessness?

ENHANCEDetext *video example 9.4*

www.youtube.com/
watch?v=P6g3LxofaZ0

Standing Rock Reservation, North/South Dakota, USA, January 2009: Mary Kelly and Jill Lawrence, her daughter, both victims of domestic violence, now work for Bridges Against Domestic Violence, a shelter bordering the reservation in the city of Mobridge. Jill, a mother of three, feels it is safer for her three sons to be raised outside the reservation

for up to 24 months. Housing is usually only one part of the program package, and residents are often required to participate in a wide range of adjunct social services such as job training, budgeting classes, adult literacy, substance abuse treatment, and parenting training. Other support services may include child care, job placement, medical care, and counseling. Most transitional housing programs focus on a specific target population, such as survivors of domestic violence, single-mother families, single men struggling with a substance abuse disorder, runaway and homeless youth, or the older adult population.

Emergency shelters and daytime drop-in centers offer crisis services for individuals who have no other housing options available. While emergency shelters are definitely needed, particularly when dealing with a population that might experience a crisis resulting in sudden homelessness, many emergency shelters are criticized for their often unsafe and inflexible environments where residents must leave after only a short stay. Transitional housing programs that offer housing for a year or two tend to be more successful, particularly if they provide a wide range of intensive services aimed at addressing the root causes of chronic poverty and homelessness. Transitional housing programs are also challenging to facilitate due to the complexity of the issues being addressed and the cost associated with administering programs offering comprehensive services. Other permanent housing programs focus on subpopulations, such as veterans. There has been a push in recent years to address veterens' homelessness. In addition, many new programs have been developed to provide comprehensive services, as well as permanent housing in the form of rental apartments that are subsidized through government grants and grassroots organizations.

Domestic violence shelters offer transitional housing to women and children who are fleeing violent partners. Domestic violence shelters operate on a 24-hour emergency basis, providing safe houses whose locations remain confidential. Many domestic violence shelters have various homes and apartments spread throughout the community, each shared by a few women and children. Shelter stays range from one month to several months, and residents and their children participate in a broad range of services, including age appropriate support groups. Human service professionals provide counseling, case management, and advocacy services, including assisting clients in obtaining orders of protection through the court system and advocating for them during any criminal or civil court hearings. Support groups focus on empowerment issues, including educating the women on the nature of intimate partner violence, parenting from a perspective of strength, developing self-sufficiency skills, and understanding healthy relationship boundaries. Services may also include job training skills and job networking, locating child care services, referral for substance abuse treatment (if necessary), and assistance in locating permanent housing. In general, human service professionals provide as many services as are needed by the client.

Supportive services provided in any practice setting that focus on homeless populations can include anything from outreach to sheltered and unsheltered homeless persons and families,

© STEPHAN GLADIEU / GETTY IMAGES

to linking clients with housing or other necessary services. Programs may include mental health counseling and case management for homeless individuals, budgeting assistance, and substance abuse counseling—really any services that focuses on an associated risk factor or correlate to homelessness. The one thing that all homeless programs have in common though is a focus on housing. Homeless prevention programs can include any community-based services that focus on stabilization in order to prevent homelessness.

ENHANCEDetext *self-check 9.4*

CONCLUSION

Homelessness is a complex social problem with multifaceted causes and risk factors, including domestic violence, substance abuse, mental illness, and physical disabilities. Social causes include institutionalized racism and oppression and structural causes related to a changing U.S. economy. Structural issues include increasing income inequality, salaries that have not kept pace with cost of living, escalating housing prices, which when combined create an abundance of low-income renters competing for fewer affordable housing units. The development of affordable housing, although a good idea in theory, is challenging due to the high cost of land and appropriate housing in safer areas. Regardless of how rental subsidies are structured, focusing on affordable subsidized housing as the primary resolution to the homeless problem negates the complex nature of homelessness (Wright, 2000).

It appears that programs offering a wide array of social services focusing on the personal root causes of homelessness, as well as addressing structural causes, will have the greatest likelihood of successfully addressing the homeless problem with long-term solutions in mind. Human services agencies are on the front lines of developing such programs designed to promote self-sufficiency and personal security.

SUMMARY

- Past and current demographic trends within the homeless population are identified, with a particular focus on how the definitions of homelessness impact funding and service provision. Homelessness demographics are explored, with an examination of overrepresented populations.
- The ways in which negative perceptions of the poor and homeless impact funding and service provision are examined. Stigmatization of homelessness is examined, with a focus on the origin of negative stereotypes of poverty and homelessness, particularly of certain subgroups, and the impact stigmatization has had on funding and service provision.
- The nature of homelessness within a range of subpopulations at risk of housing insecurity is explored. The nature of homelessness within a range of subpopulations that are at risk of housing insecurity, including single mothers and children, individuals, and run-away and homeless youth, is explored.
- The nature of service provision at agencies serving homeless populations is identified, including various types of housing programs serving at-risk populations.

Internet Resources

Conduct an Internet search for the U.S. Conference of Mayors and locate the most recent Hunger and Homelessness Survey.

Conduct an Internet search for the National Alliance to End Homelessness and explore the section on a Snapshot of Homelessness under About Homelessness.

Conduct an Internet search for HUD Exchange and search for AHAR reports and Continuum of Care (CoC) programs.

Conduct an Internet search for the National Coalition for the Homeless, and search for Homelessness in America.

References

Alegría, M., Chatterji, P., Wells, K., Cao, Z., Chen, C. N., Takeuchi, D., & Meng, X. L. (2015). Disparity in depression treatment among racial and ethnic minority populations in the United States. *Psychiatric Services*.

Auerswalk, C. L., & Eyre, S. L. (2002). Youth homelessness in San Francisco: A life cycle approach. *Social Science and Medicine, 54*, 1497–1512.

Beech, M., Meyers, L., & Beech, D. J. (2002). Hepatitis B and C infections among homeless adolescents. *Family Community Health, 25*(2), 28–36.

Bradley-King, C., Perry, M. A., & Donohue, C. (2013). Race, racial disparity, and culture in child welfare. In *Contemporary issues in child welfare practice* (pp. 159–181). Springer New York.

Briggs, B. (2013). One every 18 hours: Military suicide rate still high despite hard fight to stem deaths. NBC News. Retrieved from http://usnews.nbcnews.com/_news/2013/05/23/18447439-one-every-18-hours-military-suicide-rate-still-high-despite-hard-fight-to-stem-deaths?lite

Bugbee, K. (2015). The cost of child care: 2015 Care.com report. Care.com . Retrieved from https://www.care.com/a/the-cost-of-child-care-2015-carecom-report-20150727162954

Creech, S. K., Johnson, E., Borgia, M., Bourgault, C., Redihan, S., & O'Toole, T. P. (2015). Identifying mental and physical health correlates of homelessness among first-time and chronically homeless veterans. *Journal of Community Psychology, 43*(5), 619–627.

Davey, T. L. (2004). A multiple-family group intervention for homeless families: The weekend retreat. *Health and Social Work, 29*(4), 326–329.

Feagin, J. R. (1975). *Subordinating the poor.* Englewood Cliffs, NJ: Prentice Hall.

Henry, M., Shivji, A., de Sousa, T., Cohen, R., Khadduri, J., & Culhane, D. P. (2015). The 2015 annual homelessness assessment report (AHAR) to Congress, Part 1: Point-in-time estimates of homelessness.

Joint Center for Housing Studies of Harvard University. *The State of the Nation's Housing.* (2015). Cambridge, MA: Joint Center for Housing Studies of Harvard University. Retrieved from http://www.jchs.harvard.edu/sites/jchs.harvard.edu/files/jchs-sonhr-2015-full.pdf

Kidd, S. A. (2003). Street youth: Coping and interventions. *Child and Adolescent Social Work Journal, 20*(4), 235–261.

Levine, K. A. (2009). Against all odds: resilience in single mothers of children with disabilities. *Social Work Health Care, 48*(4) 402–419.

Lindsey, E. W. (1998). The impact of homelessness on family relationships. *Family Relations, 47*(3), 243–252.

Lindsey, E. W., Kurtz, D. P., Jarvis, S., Williams, N. R., & Nackerud, L. (2000). How runaway and homeless youth navigate troubled waters: Personal strengths and resources. *Child and Adolescent Social Work Journal, 17*(2), 115–140.

Masten, A. S., Fiat, A. E., Labella, M. H., & Strack, R. A. (2015). Educating homeless and highly mobile students: Implications of research on risk and resilience. *School Psychology Review, 44*(3), 315.

Montgomery, C. (1994). Swimming upstream: The strength of women who survive homelessness. *Advances in Nursing, 16*(3), 34–45.

Montgomery, A. E. (2013, November). Relationship between adverse childhood experiences and adult homelessness: A secondary analysis of behavioral risk factor surveillance system data. In *141st APHA Annual Meeting and Exposition (November 2–November 6, 2013)*. APHA.

Montgomery, A. E., Cutuli, J. J., Evans-Chase, M., Treglia, D., & Culhane, D. P. (2013). Relationship among adverse childhood experiences, history of active military service, and adult outcomes: Homelessness, mental health, and physical health. *American Journal of Public Health, 103*(S2), S262–S268.

National Alliance to End Homelessness. (2015a). The state of homelessness in America 2015. Retrieved from

http://www.endhomelessness.org/page/-/files
/State_of_Homelessness_2015_FINAL_online.pdf

National Alliance to End Homelessness. (2015b). The state of homelessness in America 2015, blog. Retrieved from http://www.endhomelessness.org/blog/entry /just-released-the-state-of-homelessness-in-america-2015#.Vt2_gmQrLow

National Center for Homeless Education. (2014). Education for homeless children and youths: Consolidated state performance report data 2. http://center.serve.org/nche/downloads/data-comp-1011-1213.pdf

National Coalition for the Homeless. (2007). Education for homeless children and youth. Retrieved from http:// www.nationalhomeless.org/publications/facts /education.pdf

National Law Center on Homelessness and Poverty. (2006). Some facts on homelessness, housing and violence against women. Retrieved from http://www. nlchp.org/content/pubs/Some%20Facts%20on%20 Homeless%20and%20DV.pdf

Needle, C. M. (2014). *Another piece of baggage: A literature review and data analysis on the needs of young homeless children in emergency shelter programs* (Doctoral dissertation, University of Pittsburgh).

Nickelson, I. (2004). *The district should use its upcoming TANF bonus to increase cash assistance and remove barriers to work*. Washington, DC: DC Fiscal Policy Institute. Retrieved from http://dcfpi.org/?p=69

Nunez, R., & Fox, C. (1999). A snapshot of family homelessness across America. *Political Science Quarterly, 114*(2), 289–307.

Phelan, J., Link, B. J., Moore, R. E., & Stueve, A. (1997). The stigma of homelessness: The impact of the label "homeless" on attitudes toward poor persons. *Social Psychology Quarterly, 60*(4), 323–337.

Rosenbeck, R., & Fontana, A. (1994). A model of homelessness among male veterans of the Vietnam War generation. *American Journal of Psychiatry, 151*, 421–421.

Schoenbaum, M., Kessler, R. C., Gilman, S. E., Colpe, L. J., Heeringa, S. G., Stein, M. B., & Cox, K. L. (2014). Predictors of suicide and accident death in the army study to assess risk and resilience in servicemembers (Army STARRS): Results from the army study to assess risk and resilience in servicemembers (Army STARRS). *JAMA Psychiatry*.

Schulman, K., & Blank, H. (2013). *Pivot point: State child care assistance policies 2013*. Washington, DC: National Women's Law Center.

Shelton, K. H., Taylor, P. J., Bonner, A., & van den Bree, M. (2015). Risk factors for homelessness: evidence from a population-based study. *Psychiatric Services*.

Staggs, S. L., Long, S. M., Mason, G. E., Krishnan, S., & Riger, S. (2007). Intimate partner violence, social support, and employment in the post-welfare reform era. *Journal of Interpersonal Violence, 22*(3), 345–367.

Taylor, P., Parker, K., Morin, R., & Motel, S. (2012). Rising share of Americans see conflict between rich and poor. Pew Research Center. Social and Demographic Trends. Retrieved from http://www.pewsocialtrends .org/files/2012/01/Rich-vs-Poor.pdf

Thrane, L., Chen, X., Johnson, K., and Whitbeck, L. (2008). Predictors of post-runaway contact with police among homeless adolescents. *Youth Violence and Juvenile Justice, 6*(3), 227–239.

Toro, P. A., Tompsett, C. J., Lombardo, S., Philippot, P., Nachtergael, H., Galand, B., Schlienz, N., Stammel, N., Yabar, Y., Blume, M., MacKay, L., and Harvey, K. (2007). Homelessness in Europe and the United States: A comparison of prevalence and public opinion. *Journal of Social Issues, 63*(3), 505–542.

U.S. Census Bureau. (2014). America's families and living arrangements: 2014 family groups [Table FG10]. Retrieved from Table FG10. Family Groups: 2014.

U.S. Conference of Mayors. (2014, December). *Hunger and homelessness survey*. Retrieved from http:// usmayors.org/pressreleases/uploads/2014/1211-report-hh.pdf

Weaver, R. K., Shapiro, R. Y., & Jacobs, L. (1995). Trends: welfare. *Public Opinion Quarterly, 59*(4), 606–627.

Whitbeck, L. B., Hoyt, D. R., & Ackley, K. A. (1997). Abusive family backgrounds and later victimization among runaway and homeless adolescents. *Journal of Research on Adolescents, 7*(4), 375–392.

Wright, T. (2000). Resisting homelessness: Global, national and local solutions. *Contemporary Sociology, 29*(1), 27–43.

Yoder, K. A., Whitbeck, L. B., & Hoyt, D. R. (2001). Event history analysis of antecedents to running away from home and being on the street. *American Behavioral Scientist, 45*(1), 51–65.

Medical, Health Care, and Hospice

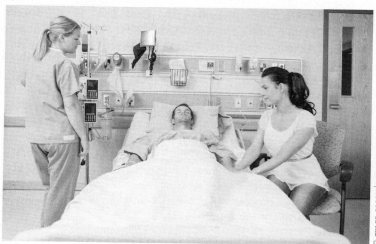

© TYLER OLSON/SHUTTERSTOCK

At 9 A.M. Glenn is called to the labor and delivery department of a large hospital where he tries to talk with a teenage girl who just had a baby. The young girl holds her new infant as Glenn initiates a conversation with her. He explains that he is visiting her because it is hospital policy for a human service professional to visit with all adolescents who have just had babies. He asks the young mother a few basic questions, such as whether she has a place to live once she and her infant leave the hospital, whether her parents knew about her pregnancy, whether the father of the baby is involved, and whether she has a plan for raising her child. The young mother admits that her parents knew nothing of her pregnancy, as she managed to hide it by wearing large clothing and spending a lot of time in her room. She admits she is frightened that if she shares the news with them, they will force her to leave their home. And she admits that the father is no longer in her life and that she has no ability, nor any real desire, to raise a child.

Glenn understands that this mother's ambivalence about raising her child is far more related to her age than her character. After some further discussion, Glenn asks her if she'd be interested in talking with a counselor who can assist her in sorting through all of the options available to her. After learning that her parents were generally supportive and loving people, he offers to call them for her so that they can help her decide how to best manage this unplanned pregnancy. The young mother appears relieved and admits that she considered just leaving the hospital without her baby because she was so desperately frightened and didn't know what else to do. When Glenn returns to his office, he makes the call to the parents; after a 20-minute emotional phone call, he makes plans to meet them in 30 minutes in their daughter's hospital room. After meeting with the entire family, he supplies them with several names of counseling agencies that can assist the young mom in either parenting or placing her infant for adoption.

While walking out of the hospital room Glenn is paged to the emergency room. When he arrives, he finds the entire unit in chaos. Three cars collided and many people were injured. After talking to the emergency room nurses and physicians, Glenn learns that one of the cars had several children in it, many of whom were seriously injured. Glenn gets to work right away collecting identifying information, making sure that each child's parent is accounted for, and obtaining numbers of parents who need to be notified of the accident and their child's condition. After obtaining all necessary information, Glenn makes himself available to the parents who had children in surgery—parents who were not in the accident, whom he recently called to the hospital—and the children who are not seriously injured but had parents who were. He offers to contact friends and family for support. After contacting spouses and two family pastors, Glenn sat with one family who had two seriously injured children and provided crisis counseling so that they could be calm enough to understand all that was going on with their children. Glenn also offers to be the conduit between the waiting families and the medical team, so for over an hour he goes back and forth between the medical personnel working on the injured and delivering any new information to the family members. Two hours later, all parties were out of crisis and had support systems by their sides, and Glenn was cleared to return to his office.

Next, Glenn began working on several discharge planning cases for various patients who were scheduled to be released from the hospital within the next two days. One was an older patient who was not healthy enough to return home, and it was Glenn's responsibility to assist the family in finding either appropriate alternate housing or in-house services that would enable the patient to remain in his home. Another case involved a survivor of a serious car accident who needed continued therapy, but could no longer remain in the hospital. Glenn's job was to locate a rehabilitation center close to family that would be covered under his insurance plan.

As Glenn's day was coming to a close, he was paged again to the emergency room, where he learned there was a potential victim of sexual assault. Glenn asked the victim if she was comfortable talking to him, but she stated that she was not—she preferred a female counselor. Glenn then called the local county rape crisis center and asked for a volunteer to come to the hospital immediately to counsel and support a sexual assault victim.

On his way out of the emergency room he was asked to consult on a potential child abuse case. Glenn interviewed the parents of a six-year-old boy who suffered a spiral fracture of the arm. Glenn became concerned when he interviewed each parent separately and their stories differed significantly. Because of this and the child's inability to describe in detail how he injured his arm, Glenn felt the case warranted a call to child protective services (CPS). He explained to the parents that he would be making an abuse allegation report and that the child would not be released until a CPS caseworker came to the hospital and interviewed everyone in the family.

Prior to Glenn leaving for the day, he was asked to visit with a patient and her adult son who just learned of her terminal diagnosis. Glenn provided both with some crisis counseling and made a referral to a local hospice agency. He offered to meet with them again tomorrow and to meet with them and the hospice team if they wished. Glenn's last case for the day was to provide counseling to a 60-year-old man who recently underwent a liver transplant and was about to be released from the hospital. Research indicates that transplant patients often experience depression after being released from the hospital. Therefore, Glenn's focus was to help this patient adjust to the realities of being a transplant patient, as well as preparing him for experiencing some depression in the coming weeks. He made sure this patient left armed with names of counselors who had experience working with transplant patients.

HUMAN SERVICES IN MEDICAL AND OTHER HEALTH CARE SETTINGS

Glenn's day depicted in the opening case study reflects a typical day of a human service professional working in a medical or health care setting—essentially a day with very little predictability. In other words, there is no such things as a "typical day" in the life of a human services professional working in a medical or health care setting! In fact, someone interested in a career in the human services field and looking for structure and predictability would probably not fare well in a health care setting, whereas human service providers who embrace change and unpredictability will likely thrive in a typical health care setting.

Human service providers have traditionally worked in hospital settings in a variety of capacities. Yet as the health care field branched out to other arenas, including community-based health care centers, primary care full-service clinics, and specialized health centers serving particular populations (such as HIV-positive patients, women, cancer patients, children, etc.), human service providers can now be found in a variety of health care-related practice settings.

Health care is one field in which most professionals working in human services are required to be licensed human service providers in some capacity—licensed social workers, therapists, or psychologists. There is some variation from state to state, but health care settings in particular are highly regulated fields and as such mental health providers working in these environments are typically required to have both advanced degrees and state licenses. For instance, most human service providers working in a hospital setting are required to have an MSW and be registered as a **licensed clinical social worker (LCSW)** with the state. Psychologists working in health care settings must typically have a PsyD or PhD and also be licensed by the appropriate professional and state agency.

Human service providers working in medical settings are true generalists. They must be flexible and able to deal with a variety of issues, in a setting that is often wrought with crisis and trauma. But despite their broad generalist functions, the scope of human service functions in medical and health care settings, such as hospitals, can be quite specific. These functions and responsibilities may include:

- conducting psychosocial assessments on patients as needed
- providing information and referrals for patients
- preadmission planning

- discharge planning
- psychosocial counseling
- financial counseling
- health education
- post-discharge follow-up
- consultation with colleagues
- outpatient continuity of care
- patient and family conferences regarding health status, care, and future planning
- case management for patients
- facilitation of and referral to self-help and emotional support groups for patients and families
- patient and family advocacy
- trauma response
- assistance in exploring bioethical issues
- outcome evaluations on best practice committees.

In addition to performing these various functions, some of the issues addressed by human service providers working in medical and health care settings include addressing patient problems related to **activities of daily living** (ADL), assisting patients and their family members in dealing with illness adjustment, assessing possible physical and sexual abuse (including child abuse and domestic violence), and assessing patients with potential mental health problems.

Crisis and Trauma Counseling

A large part of a human service professional's role in a medical or health care setting is comprised of providing crisis and trauma counseling to patients who are experiencing a medical crisis, as well as their family members. In fact, when a hospital has notified a family of a patient's injury or illness, it is often someone from the human services or social work department who meets the family at the emergency room doors.

A good model for how to approach an individual or family in crisis is one based on a theory developed by Abraham Maslow. Maslow (1954) created a model focusing on needs motivation that helps us to better understand how people are motivated to get their needs met, and how we, as mental health providers, can help them meet their needs. As the illustration shows, Maslow believed that people are motivated to get their most basic physiological needs met first (i.e., the need for food and oxygen) before they meet higher level needs, such as their need for safety (i.e., the security we find in the stability of our relationships with family and friends), or their need to develop self-esteem (i.e., to gain respect from others and have confidence in who they are). According to Maslow, most people would find it difficult to focus on developing a more positive self-esteem when they are hungry and homeless. In other words, thoughts about how to gain more self-confidence would quickly take a back seat as worries about mere survival took hold.

Maslow's hierarchy of needs reflects how a person will be compelled to meet lower level needs before higher level needs

SELF-ACTUALIZA-TION
morality, creativity, spontaneity, acceptance, experience purpose, meaning and inner potential

SELF-ESTEEM
confidence, achievement, respect of others, the need to be a unique individual

LOVE AND BELONGING
friendship, family, intimacy, sense of connection

SAFETY AND SECURITY
health, employment, property, family and social abilty

PHYSIOLOGICAL NEEDS
breathing, food, water, shelter, clothing, sleep

© ELENARTS/ SHUTTERSTOCK

Hospital social workers and other mental health providers working in a medical setting understand that when individuals are facing a significant crisis they often feel compelled to get their most basic needs met before anything else. In situations where family members or close friends have been called to a hospital in response to a loved one having been in a serious accident or suffering from a life-threatening illness, their first priority is often to obtain information about the medical status of the patient. Therefore, it is very important for the human service professional to provide as much information as possible without escalating in panic or anxiety along with the family. In fact, it is vital that professionalism be maintained in the midst of the crisis so the human service professional can serve as a calming influence that the family can rely on as they attempt to navigate the crisis and regain emotional stability.

Each family handles a crisis differently and an effective human service professional will recognize the family's particular coping style quickly. Some families will focus on seemingly mundane details, such as inquiring about meals or clothing, while others will focus more directly on crisis-related issues. Some families may ask the same questions repeatedly, or ask questions that have no answers, such as repeatedly asking whether the patient will survive the surgery, even though there might be no way to answer such a question at that time.

Regardless of people's individual coping styles, the human service professional must be able to read between the lines, recognizing that a family confronted with the shocking news of a loved one having a life-threatening condition often leaves them feeling disoriented and powerless, and many of the questions or actions of family members are likely attempts to regain some sense of control over the situation. By understanding this dynamic, the human service professional can take concrete steps to assist the family in gaining as much control as possible in a chaotic situation with numerous unknowns. For instance, the human service professional can act as the conduit between the medical staff and the family, can assist the family in developing an immediate plan of action, such as finding child care for younger children or having someone go to the patient's house to care for pets, and can help notify friends and employers on behalf of the patient. By addressing clients' more basic needs, the human service professional meets clients where they are.

Human service professionals' role may be limited to the immediate crisis. Though they also may only meet with patients and family members for a few hours, they may also continue working with the family as the situation progresses, perhaps for days or even weeks, depending on the nature of the health care crisis. In the latter instance, providers may assist the patient and family in adjusting to any limitations posed by the patient's condition or injury, as well as assist the family and patient in securing necessary resources as a part of discharge planning when the patient is well enough to leave the hospital. The human service professional may even follow up with the patient and family after discharge to check on their progress, and ensure that they've been able to successfully connect with services within their community.

For many patients and their family members, the trauma associated with a serious illness or injury will continue for years. In fact, in the last few decades considerable research has shown that trauma can have a profound effect on an individual's life, at times evolving into **post-traumatic stress disorder** (**PTSD**). Those who meet the criteria for having features of PTSD exhibit physical and emotional symptoms that are pervasive and interfere with daily functioning. When individuals experience a significant trauma, their brains react accordingly, going into a "survival mode," which often doesn't go away when their lives return to normal. People with PTSD continue to react in many respects as if they are still in danger. They may have an exaggerated startle reflex, they often replay various aspects of the trauma again and again in their minds, and they may experience heightened anxiety and a fear response to new experiences, particularly those experiences that remind a person of the original trauma (called triggers).

Human service providers can respond with trauma-informed counseling, a healing approach to trauma that was developed in recognition of the powerful and profound impact trauma has on people physically, psychologically, emotionally, and even spiritually. According to SAMHSA's National Center for Trauma Informed Care (NCTIC), a trauma-informed approach acknowledges the significant impact of trauma on people's lives and integrates the knowledge of the nature of trauma and its comprehensive impact on individuals, family systems, and society into policies, procedures, and practices, with the dual goal of helping people heal and avoiding retraumatization (SAMHSA, 2015). The six key principles of a trauma-informed approach focus on creating an environment that emphasizes the importance of (1) *safety*, developing relationships with clients based on (2) *trustworthiness and transparency*, the importance of (3) *peer support*, (4) *collaboration and mutuality* between client and counselor, providing clients with a sense of (5) *empowerment, voice, and choice*, and respecting and honoring (6) *cultural, historical, and gender issues*.

Using a trauma-informed approach in a hospital setting requires that human service providers become aware of the nature of trauma, including how it impacts people across the lifespan, how it affects the human brain, and common ways that individuals who have and are experiencing trauma may react at various stages of the trauma experience. An example of a trauma-informed approach to policies in a hospital setting would be to have more flexible visitation policies, including providing family members with the option of spending the night. A trauma-informed policy may also require an expansion of the definition of "family" to include close friends and partners with no legal status, but who are integral parts of a patient's life. A trauma-informed approach to case management involves recognizing the importance of ensuring patients and their family members are provided trauma-focused resources within their community.

Single Visits and Rapid Assessment

Because lengths of stays in hospitals are decreasing, the reality for most human service providers is that they will have very brief access to the majority of their patients in a hospital setting. In fact, it may be that a human service professional working in a hospital setting will see patients only one or two times. Because of the abbreviated nature of client work in medically related settings, there is a growing body of literature on single session encounters with clients, addressing how human service providers can develop a set of skills that allow for rapidly assessing the patient and his or her situation, as well as how to assist clients most effectively in a short period of time.

Gibbons and Plath (2009) explored the area of rapid assessment by interviewing several patients and asking what they found helpful in these single sessions, including what skills and qualities were helpful and which were not. They isolated seven basic skillsets that medical social workers needed in order to engage successfully with patients during a single session. These included the ability to

1. quickly put the patient at ease
2. establish a rapport and a sense of trust quickly

Watch the video on the importance of a trauma-informed approach. How might you use this approach when working with a family who just learned their teenaged son was involved in a serious accident involving a drunk driver, and he may have sustained potentially life-threatening injuries, including a possible traumatic brain injury? **ENHANCEDetext** *video example 10.1*

www.youtube.com/watch?v=jFdn9479U3s

3. exhibit a sense of competence
4. engage in active listening and exhibit empathy
5. be nonjudgmental
6. provide needed information quickly, and
7. organize support services.

Since many hospitals hire human service providers with certificates and bachelor's degrees to conduct discharge planning, case management, and patient advocacy, as well as other functions related to patient care, the skill set discussed by Gibbons and Plath can be applied to a broader range of roles within the human services profession.

ENHANCEDetext *self-check 10.1*

WORKING WITH THE HIV/AIDS SPECTRUM

Human service providers working in a medical setting, particularly in public health, commonly work with various health-related crises and epidemics, such as **HIV/AIDS**. Human service providers, such as social workers, psychologists, counselors, and behavioral health care providers, work not only with those diagnosed with HIV/AIDS, but also with their families members; thus, there is a wide spectrum of psychosocial issues involved. Examples of commonly associated psychosocial issues include: grief and loss, learning to manage the stigma associated with an **HIV-positive status**, adjustment issues related to learning to live with a chronic disease that requires a daily medical regime, and co-occurring mental illnesses such as substance abuse issues and disorders.

HIV and AIDS were first discussed in the medical literature in 1981 (Gottlieb et al., 1981). Medical treatment during these early years typically occurred in a crisis setting with patients presenting in the emergency room with advanced or end-stage AIDS infections, such as **Pneumocystis carinii pneumonia (PCP)** or **Kaposi's sarcoma**, both opportunistic infections common in end-stage AIDS patients. In August 1981, 108 AIDS cases were reported in the United States by the Centers for Disease Control and Prevention (CDC), and by 1988 the CDC estimated that approximately 1.5 million people were living with the HIV infection. The dramatic increase in the HIV infection rate indicates just how quickly HIV/AIDS spread throughout the United States (CDC, 1988).

The World Health Organization (WHO) (2013) estimates that 78 million people in the world have been infected with the HIV virus and 39 million people have died from AIDS worldwide since 1981, with 1.5 million people dying worldwide in 2013. When HIV/AIDS first emerged in the United States, there were no medical treatments available to address the actual disease process, thus treatment was focused on symptomatic relief only. By the 1990s significant medical advances were gained, in large part through grassroots efforts that led to significant fund-raising efforts for medical research. Currently, HIV/AIDS is considered a chronic rather than terminal disease for those individuals fortunate enough to have access to expensive antiviral therapy. Despite medical advances, however, the treatment of HIV/AIDS remains a serious public health concern, particularly for those individuals who have no access to advanced medical treatment or who do not respond positively to the most aggressive antiviral therapy (ART), commonly referred to as the **AIDS cocktail**.

During the early years of the AIDS crisis, the role of human service providers focused almost exclusively on the crisis of receiving a terminal diagnosis and included conducting emergency discharge planning, death preparation, arranging for acute care, and initiating hospice services. By the 1990s education efforts led to earlier diagnoses and better medical treatment for those who could afford it and clinical intervention focused more on the psychosocial issues involved with having a chronic, debilitating, and sometimes terminal disease that was highly stigmatized. These psychosocial issues typically included a fear of discrimination, concerns about receiving quality medical care, job accommodations and finding other income sources when they could no longer work, and housing accommodations when a client's physical health began to decline (Kaplan, Tomaszewski, & Gorin, 2004). More current treatment protocols for working with HIV/AIDS-affected clients include evaluating a spectrum of biopsychosocial issues impacting the entire family system.

The most recent statistics available from the Centers for Disease Control and Prevention (CDC) (2014) indicate that at the end of 2013, about 933,941 people in the United States were living with a diagnosed case of HIV/AIDS. The CDC estimates that there are approximately 50,000 people newly diagnosed with HIV each year in the United States. According to the CDC, the populations at greatest risk of infection are **men who have sex with men** (**MSM**), as well as people of color. For instance, African American men and women have an HIV incidence rate that is almost eight times greater than Caucasians.

Despite aggressive public awareness campaigns in both the general public and the professional community designed to increase general awareness and remove stigma, many individuals with the HIV/AIDS virus endure numerous barriers to getting their basic needs met—some of which are related to the stigma associated with HIV/AIDS, some related to institutionalized racial discrimination, and some related to a combination of both (Kaplan et al., 2004).

An example of disparity in treatment is the lack of quality medical care available on most Native American reservations. Native American advocates argue that the reason for this deficit relates to racial disparity and historic mistreatment and oppression. When reservations were first confronted with rapidly increasing rates of HIV/AIDS, the U.S. government did very little to address the issue, and Native American elders complained that the medical neglect experienced on most reservations was yet another form of racial discrimination and **marginalization** (Weaver, 1999). Human service providers working within the medical field must be aware of the various ways that racial **prejudice** and **discrimination** play out within ethnic minority and other displaced communities, whether such prejudice and discrimination is direct and overt or institutionalized (such as the allocation of federal funding). This awareness can then translate into advocacy and outreach as well as increased sensitivity as practitioners challenge their own perception of the HIV/AIDS crisis, including their attitudes about those populations that are currently most affected by this disease.

A woman marches in the Twin Cities Gay Pride Parade to raise awareness of the impact HIV stigma has on people living with HIV and AIDS, on June 30, 2013

© MIKER/SHUTTERSTOCK

Three-Pronged Approach to Working with the HIV/AIDS Population

When confronting the HIV/AIDS crisis, human service providers engage in a three-pronged approach to psychosocial care, including prevention and educational awareness (such as the practice of safe sex), client advocacy, and case management/counseling. Human service providers are actively involved in both practice and policy aspects of the HIV/AIDS pandemic. This includes: focusing on meeting the psychosocial needs of those diagnosed with HIV/AIDS; being on the front lines of prevention efforts, and community and patient educational and awareness campaigns, advocating for increased funding of intervention and treatment programs; and participating in lobbying efforts and advocating for the passage of laws designed to protect the privacy and legal rights of HIV-positive populations.

Other tasks involve helping HIV-positive clients obtain necessary medical services, including advocating for the necessary funding for treatment and providing counseling for HIV-positive clients and their families and caregivers. The nature of the counseling will change depending on the progression of the virus and the personal dynamics associated with each client. Newly diagnosed clients will likely need counseling focusing on acceptance of a potentially terminal disease, whereas other clients will need counseling focusing more on living with a chronic illness, accepting a life of potential disability, accepting a life that includes multiple medications taken on a daily basis, and learning to live with the consequences of a stigmatized disease.

Depending on the demographic nature of the patient, the human service professional may also help secure child care, help the patient apply for financial assistance, obtain home health care, maintain or obtain employment, housing, and medical care, including care for other health-related issues, such as substance abuse, and finally, help the patient and family contend with the various stressors involved with having a stigmatized illness (Galambos, 2004).

HIV/AIDS and the Latino Population

According to the CDC (2016), the HIV infection poses a serious risk to the Latino population. While Latinos represent about 17 percent of the general population, they constituted about 21 percent of all new HIV diagnoses in 2010, an incidence rate three times that of Caucasians (relative to their representation in the population). Latino men are most affected by HIV/AIDS with close to 90 percent of new HIV infections being diagnosed in the Latino male population, primarily Latino MSM. Among the U.S. Latino population, those living in the southern United States, where the population has grown by over 200 percent since 1990, are particularly vulnerable to HIV infection for a variety of reasons. A report focusing on a two-year fact-finding and cooperation program facilitated by the *Latino Commission on AIDS* explored the extent and nature of the HIV/AIDS problem within the Latino population living in the Deep South, which includes Alabama, Georgia, Louisiana, Mississippi, North Carolina, South Carolina, and Tennessee (Frasca, 2008).

The Latino Commission on AIDS program, also referred to as the *Deep South Project,* found evidence that Latinos are being infected with HIV at disproportionate and rising rates in the South, and yet are often excluded from the health care system, as well as HIV/AIDS-related services (such as prevention and educational programs), due to their immigration status, fear related to an increase in anti-immigrant hostility, and the stigmatization of the disease within the Latino community. Many members of the Latino community also lack access to HIV/AIDS-related services due to geographic isolation. In general, there are insufficient HIV/AIDS-related programs in the Deep South focusing on the Latino population and an insufficient number of bilingual service providers. The report found that due to a lack of awareness of the nature of the disease and lack of access to quality health care, many within the Latino population are diagnosed in the later stages of the disease, which limits the success rate of the antiviral therapy (ART) protocol (Frasca, 2008).

Many Latino relationships tend to reflect more traditional gender roles consistent with machismo culture, which increases the risk of contraction and transmission of the HIV/AIDS virus. For instance, within the machismo culture, men commonly engage in high-risk sexual behaviors in order to prove their manhood, such as having multiple sex partners, despite being married, and not wearing a condom. Latina women often cite an awareness that their male partner's sexual behavior places them at greater risk for contracting the HIV virus, but they do not believe they have enough power in the relationship to make demands for safe-sex practices, such as fidelity and wearing a condom (Acevedo, 2008).

Human service providers working within the Latino population must develop a level of cultural competence, becoming aware of the many culturally related risk factors at play. They must also be aware of how racial prejudice, social exclusion based upon immigration status (or perceived status), and various stigmas impact the Latinos' access to educational and prevention services as well as access to quality and timely health care (Acevedo, 2008).

The Deep South project report makes several recommendations, including public health departments conducting needs assessments of the Latino population, increasing outreach efforts in high Latino communities, increasing the number of bilingual service providers, increasing the cultural competency of service providers working with the Latino population, and increasing HIV/AIDS research on Latino populations so that the literature more accurately reflects their needs (Frasca, 2008).

Engaging Resistant At-Risk Clients

When human service providers and allied health workers engage with populations that are at higher risk for HIV infection and the AIDS virus and have lower levels of health care engagement, such as the Latino MSM population, cultural competence and sensitivity are vitally important, as is creativity in accessing this difficult to reach population. The intersectionality of characteristics that increase a population's level of vulnerability is considerable among the ethnic minority populations who are in same-sex relationships or are bisexual, and are HIV-positive. When evaluating clients within the context of stigmatizing characteristics and issues, it is understandable why HIV-positive Latino MSM can be a challenging population to engage in counseling and active health care management.

The CDC (2012) reports that more than half of all people diagnosed with HIV are not actively engaged in their own health care, which is of great concern since research clearly shows a strong relationship between personal health care engagement and positive health outcomes. Within the context of HIV-infected patients, research shows that individuals who are not actively engaged in their medical care are more likely to be diagnosed later in the disease progression and begin taking antiviral drugs late or not at all

Watch this video about the work of the Latino Commission on AIDS. In what ways is this organization addressing the social factors contributing to Latinos being at higher risk for HIV infection in the Deep South?
ENHANCEDetext *video example 10.2*

www.youtube.com/watch?v=UQFW1V5mckc&spfreload=10

(Mugavero, Amico, Horn, & Thompson, 2013). This makes sense of course—if patients aren't proactive about their health care, including accessing medical care on a regular basis and accessing accurate information about HIV/AIDS (transmission, treatment, etc.), they will be less likely to advocate for themselves in receiving the best possible medical care. This is particularly important information for human service providers working with ethnically diverse HIV-positive clients who are known to have lower levels of health care engagement.

The Internet and smartphones are an excellent outreach and educational tool for all HIV-positive clients, but particularly for more resistant clients. In fact, recent research on Internet usage for health purposes and the effectiveness of online engagement with the HIV-positive population reveals just how powerful this medium is in breaking through a number of barriers. For instance, there is a positive connection between using the Internet for health-related purposes (e.g., engaging with medical personnel via email, using a smartphone calendar for appointment reminders, asking health-related questions on social media and blogs, watching educational health-related online videos, reading health-related articles posted on social media and blogs) and better psychosocial and health outcomes (Mbuagbaw et al., 2013).

But research also shows that HIV-positive African Americans and Latinos, particularly those with lower education levels and lower incomes, tend not to use the Internet nearly as often as Caucasians or those with higher education levels and higher incomes (Saberi & Johnson, 2015). Thus, one way of promoting better psychosocial and health-related outcomes among ethnically diverse HIV-positive clients is to encourage their use of social media and mobile messaging devices for health care purposes. Human services professionals can make suggestions that their HIV-positive clients email their doctors or use online calendars and smartphone reminders for appointments, and they can provide them with valid and relevant online sources for information about HIV/AIDS, such as social media sites, informational websites, online articles, and blogs. HIV-positive clients who are hesitant to reach out to the medical community because they are embarrassed or afraid may be far more likely to take initial steps in the direction of more active health care engagement if they can do so from the privacy of their own homes.

ENHANCEDetext *self-check 10.2*

THE U.S. HEALTH CARE CRISIS: A LEGISLATIVE RESPONSE

In 2007, Michael Moore, American film director, writer, and social advocate, released his documentary called *Sicko*, highlighting a range of problems with the U.S. health care system. Throughout the film, Moore featured everyday Americans who faced insurmountable challenges in attempting to receive quality health care. In some cases, patients did not have sufficient health care insurance either because it was unaffordable or because they were unable to receive health care insurance due to a range of insurance industry policies designed to avoid providing coverage—policies that Moore alleged were designed to benefit the for-profit insurance industry, not the consumer. The crux of Moore's film was that the United States was the only industrialized country where an individual could potentially face financial ruin and in some cases death because of increasingly unaffordable health care and unsavory practices by a for-profit insurance industry that, according to Moore, was more concerned about its financial bottom line than the health care of its consumers.

After a contentious partisan battle over the role of government in ensuring that all Americans have access to quality and affordable health care, the Patient Protection and Affordable Care Act (ACA) was signed into law by President Obama on March 23, 2010. Proponents of the ACA (also referred to as "Obamacare" and the PPACA) framed the health care crisis in the United States as a human rights issue, often relying on arguments that all individuals deserve affordable health care, and that to deny people quality medical care because of they couldn't afford it is a violation of their human rights. Advocates of the ACA cited the recent trend of employer-provided health care benefits to employees being drastically reduced, either by increasing employee contributions or by restricting benefits to only a small pool of employees. This trend was making it impossible for many lower and middle class individuals to afford health care insurance despite being employed full-time.

Linking compulsory health care insurance coverage to employment dates back to the early 1900s, when Congress passed legislation limiting wage increases, and employers responded by offering employees "fringe benefits" to increase the rank of quality workers (Scofea, 1994). Employment-provided insurance benefits were also thought to guarantee a full-time work force, since people would be required to work in order to receive much-needed benefits. Yet many of the employer incentives to provide employee health care benefits (such as government tax breaks) have not kept pace with the cost of health care; thus many employers have found it necessary to reduce their benefit packages. In other words, a system that worked for decades—employers offering employees health care benefits to secure a strong full-time workforce—no longer appears to be feasible because of changes in the U.S. health care and economic structure.

The concept of a single-payer government-sponsored health care program is not new. In fact, President Truman attempted to introduce such a program for all Americans and had considerable public support, but any reference to a universal health care program was vehemently opposed by the American Medical Association (Corning, 1969). In response to strong opposition to a government-sponsored single payer system, no such program was implemented in the United States (despite several attempts), until, that is, when the ACA was voted into law in 2010. The ACA isn't a true universal health care program, but rather it is a complex network of legislative policies and requirements that place limitations on third-party payers (e.g., private insurance companies) and employers with regard to the nature of the benefits they provide and how such benefits are to be facilitated. Implementation of the ACA was incremental, with various components of the legislation being rolled out between 2010 and 2014.

The goal of the ACA is to reform health care insurance in the United States by expanding coverage, making health care more affordable, and increasing consumer protections. The ACA includes an emphasis on prevention and wellness and taking steps to limit rising health care costs. The following list includes key provisions of the legislation:

- Employers must provide health insurance for their employees (citizens and legal residents), or pay penalties, with exceptions for small employers.
- Tax credits are provided for certain small businesses that reimburse certain costs of health insurance for their employees (began in 2010).

Watch the video on the Affordable Care Act and Alaska Natives. Imagine that you are a human service provider in Alaska. What barriers exist for Native Americans signing up for insurance through the Health Insurance Exchange (marketplace), and what would you do to encourage a higher level of engagement? **ENHANCEDetext** *video example 10.3*

www.youtube.com/
watch?v=Lja5TinFFug

- Citizens and legal residents were required to sign up for health insurance by April 1, 2014, with some exceptions such as financial hardship or religious belief.
- Policies must provide what is called "Essential Health Benefits," at varying rates of coverage, starting at the bronze level (covers 60 percent of health care costs) or the platinum level (covers 90 percent of health care cost) (Note: the minimum benefit level is referred to as "Essential Health Benefits").
- The creation of state-based insurance exchanges to help individuals and small businesses purchase insurance. Federal subsidies are provided for individuals and families to 2 percent of income for those with incomes at 133 percent of federal poverty guidelines and 9.5 percent of income for those who earn between 300 percent and 400 percent of the poverty guidelines.
- Medicaid was expanded to cover people with incomes below 138 percent of federal poverty guidelines.
- Creation of temporary high-risk pools for those who cannot purchase insurance on the private market due to preexisting health conditions (began in 2010).
- Young adults covered under parents' policies until age 26 (began in 2010).
- National, voluntary long-term care insurance program for "community living assistance services and supports" (CLASS) established (established in 2012).
- The enactment of a range of consumer protections to enable people to retain their insurance coverage (began in 2010), such as allowing no lifetime monetary caps or exclusions for preexisting conditions, prohibiting insurance plans from rescinding coverage (unless fraud is involved) if consumers become ill, or limiting insurance premium increases due to illness and/or gender, etc.

Experts estimate that ACA has extended health insurance coverage to at least 32 million people (Gorin, 2010). Human services professionals have played a key role in the debate about health care by being advocates for individual's rights to quality and affordable health care. Human service providers also serve an important role in providing assistance to clients as they navigate their way through what can be a confusing process of obtaining health insurance through the government **Health Insurance Marketplace** and can also help clients better understand the nature of their benefits.

The government Health Insurance Marketplace is an easy to navigate website that enables consumers to select a health insurance plan that complies with the ACA

The ACA is not without its critics though, from both sides of the political fence. Some common criticisms include the government's ability to compel millions of uninsured (or underinsured) individuals to purchase health care insurance or else face financial penalties. Some critics are also concerned about the high cost of implementing the ACA, particularly in the first several years. There are also concerns about the impact the ACA will have on small businesses, as well as on the medical community, particularly in terms of whether physicians will accept policies generated through the marketplace, or whether insurance providers will pull out of certain markets (there is already some indication that this latter trend is occurring in some states).

A significant concern relates to the fact that consumers must reapply for insurance on an annual basis, providing insurers with an opportunity to raise rates. Under the law, insurance providers must disclose if they will be raising their rates more than 10 percent. They did just that on June 1, 2015 when several health care insurance companies filed a notice that they intended to increase their rates for 2016 on an average of 5 to 40 percent. As an example, Blue Cross Blue Shield increased the cost of health plans offered through the government Health Insurance Marketplace an average of 13.5 percent in 2015 and an additional 25.7 percent in 2016 (Tajlili, 2015). Despite consistent gains in profits each year, the company cited an increase in costs as justification for the almost 40 percent rate hikes in the last two years, and yet many of the losses involved moving funds into reserves for anticipated losses (Wang, 2014).

While it is too early to evaluate the long-term impact of the ACA on consumers as well as the economy, there are economic indicators that third-party insurance companies participating in the government Health Insurance Marketplace are doing quite well financially, dispelling early warnings that the ACA meant certain financial disaster for insurance companies, as well as the economy in general (Winkler, 2015). However, that doesn't appear to be stopping insurance providers from increasing their rates. Although government reports have shown that the ACA has improved access and affordability of quality health care, improved collaboration between private and public sectors, and created new initiatives to focus on prevention and wellness, and consumer awareness, the election of Donald Trump has thrown the future of the ACA into question. Trump and the Republican majority in Congress have expressed the intention to repeal the ACA and replace it with an alternative health care program—not yet defined—that they feel will better serve the American people. The coming months and years will be sure to feature heated debates regarding the future of American healthcare.

ENHANCEDetext *self-check 10.3*

THE HOSPICE MOVEMENT

Hospice care is a service provided to the terminally ill that focuses on comprehensive care addressing their physical, emotional, social, and spiritual needs. Although hospices have existed since about the 4th century, the biblical and Roman concepts of hospice involved providing refuge for the poor, sick, travelers, and soldiers returning from war. Hospice as a refuge or service for the terminally ill was not developed until the mid-1960s.

The modern hospice movement emerged from the general dissatisfaction with how dying individuals were being treated by the established medical community. Western medicine is curative by design with a focus on restoring individuals back to a state of healthy functioning. This model left the majority of the traditional medical community at a loss as to how to treat those who were beyond the hope of recovery. Dying patients often felt neglected and isolated in depersonalized hospital settings where they were typically subjected to needless and futile medical interventions. The hospice movement challenged the treatment provided by the traditional medical community that often failed to address pain management effectively and often neglected the psychosocial and spiritual needs of the dying patient.

Dame Cicely Saunders, the founder of the modern hospice movement, recognized this lapse of appropriate care for the dying and set about to make significant changes that would affect how the world viewed the dying process. Originally trained as a nurse, Saunders eventually earned her degree in medicine and quickly challenged what she saw as the medical community's failure to address the comprehensive needs of terminally ill patients. Saunders was passionate about the care of the terminally ill and in 1958 wrote her first paper, entitled "Dying of Cancer," addressing the need to approach dying as a natural stage of life. Through her work with the terminally ill, Saunders recognized that dying patients required a far different approach to treatment than the traditional one that tended to see death as a personal and medical failure.

In Saunders's personal letters, she describes in detail her discussions with terminally ill patients in the hospice where she worked, as well as her dedication to the prospects of developing a system of care committed to a dying process without pain while enabling terminally diagnosed patients to maintain their sense of dignity throughout the dying process (Clark, 2002). Saunders founded St. Christopher's Hospice of London in 1967. Her model of care used a multifaceted approach, where dying patients were treated with compassion so that their final days were spent in peace rather than undergoing invasive and futile medical treatments and where they were free to attend to the business of dying, such as saying good-bye to their loved ones.

The Connecticut Hospice, Inc., was the first hospice opened in the United States in 1974 in New Haven, Connecticut, funded by the National Cancer Institute (NCI). The hospice was created for many of the same reasons noted by Saunders—the belief that good end-of-life care was severely lacking within the U.S. hospital system and the belief that the dying process was a meaningful one worthy of honor and respect (Stein, 2004). When the HIV/AIDS crisis first began in the 1980s, and prior to the development of antiviral treatment, hospices took on a significant role in the end-of-life care of those dying of the AIDS virus. Although there are some freestanding hospices, hospice is not a "place," but rather it is a concept of care and can be provided anywhere a patient resides (Paradis & Cummings, 1986).

The hospice movement has grown immensely in a relatively short period of time, and what began as a grassroots effort of trained volunteers supported by philanthropic agencies, such as the United Way, has become a highly regulated and profitable industry staffed by a team of professional service providers. Although the core goals and philosophy of hospice remain the same, the professionalization and governmental regulation of this field has influenced its service delivery model. For instance, although hospice care was originally developed as an alternative to hospital care, many hospices in the United States are now in some way affiliated with a hospital or other health care organization, most are accredited, and almost all are Medicare certified (Paradis & Cummings, 1986).

The Hospice Philosophy

The hospice philosophy employed today is similar to the one envisioned by Saunders. Dying is seen not as a failure, but as a natural part of life in which every human being has the right to die with dignity. Hospice care involves a team approach to the care and support of the terminally ill and their family members. A core value of the hospice philosophy is that each person has the right to die without pain and that the dying process should be a meaningful experience. Because Western culture often perceives accepting death as synonymous with giving up, individuals battling illness are often inadvertently encouraged to fight for their survival to the "bitter end"; thus, the hospice philosophy is counterintuitive to Western cultural wisdom.

Hospice treatment involves **palliative care** rather than curative care. The hospice movement is highly supportive of patients remaining in their homes, but when that is not possible, hospice service is provided in hospitals, nursing homes, and long-term care facilities and can be an adjunct to other medical services provided. The only stipulation of most hospice agencies is that the patient has stopped pursuing **curative treatment** and that the patient received a terminal diagnosis of six months or less.

The hospice team is interdisciplinary by design, and although there is considerable overlap in many of the roles of the various service providers, the hospice human service professional serves a unique purpose on the team, emanating from the distinct values underlying the human services discipline (MacDonald, 1991). The hospice team typically consists of a hospice physician who makes periodic visits and monitors each case through weekly reports from other team members; a nurse who visits patients wherever they reside at least three times per week; and a human service professional, most often a social worker, who provides case management services and counseling to the patient and family. The social work professional might help the patient say goodbye to friends and family, help resolve any past conflict, and assist with end-of-life issues, including preparation of legal documents such as wills and advance directives (which will be explored in the next section). The hospice team might also include a chaplain who provides spiritual support; a home health aid who provides daily care such as personal hygiene; a trained volunteer who provides companionship, including reading to patients or taking them for strolls in a wheelchair; and a bereavement counselor, a human service provider (licensed, paraprofessional, or volunteer) who provides counseling and support to surviving family members after the death of the patient. One might question whether the interdisciplinary team model works when so many varied professions are involved, but research indicates that the hospice interdisciplinary team model is effective as long as there is good communication, trust, and mutual respect among team members as well as administrative support (Oliver & Peck, 2006).

The Hospice Team and the Role of the Hospice Human Service Provider

The hospice team is interdisciplinary by design, and although there is considerable overlap in many of the roles of the various service providers, the human service provider serves a unique purpose on the team, emanating from the distinct values underlying the human services discipline (MacDonald, 1991).

The hospice social worker provides numerous services to hospice patients and their families, including providing advocacy for patients, particularly in regard to obtaining services and financial assistance; crisis intervention when emergencies arise; case management and coordination of services for the comprehensive care of patients and their family members; case consultation services among hospice and other health care staff; assisting

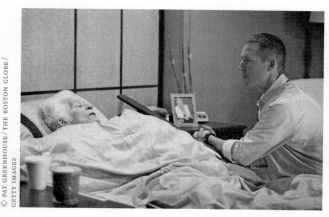

A hospice social worker visits a terminally ill patient, providing counseling and case management

the patient and family in planning for the patient's eventual death; and bereavement counseling to assist patients in accepting their terminal illness and in saying goodbye to loved ones, as well as counseling surviving family members after the patient's death. Bereavement counselors provide counseling and support to surviving family members after the death of the patient, including regular outreach, providing telephone support, making home visits, facilitating support groups and educational workshops, and even sending condolence cards on the anniversary of the death.

Prior to engaging in any intervention strategy with hospice patients, human service providers working in the capacity of counselor and case manager will complete a thorough psychosocial assessment to evaluate the strengths and deficits of the patient and family members. How are the client and family accepting the reality of the terminal illness? What are the family's emotional, social, and financial resources? Is there a history of mental illness in the family and/or the client? Can the family realistically provide for the current and future needs of the patient? Family members who are still reeling from the news or their loved one's terminal diagnosis are often unrealistic in their expectations of the rigors involved with caring for a terminally ill person and may need help to recognize their limitations and need for outside assistance.

Conducting a thorough psychosocial assessment is the first step in making these clinical determinations and ascertaining what services are needed. Although there are basic criteria of a psychosocial assessment, the information sought and the focus of the assessment change depending on the issues at hand. Thus, a psychosocial assessment of a hospice patient living at home will focus more on the patient's current living conditions, including whether they are appropriate in relation to the patient's declining health, as well as focusing on end-of-life issues. Other dynamics explored may include the state of the patient's current relationships, and whether there are any unresolved issues that need to be resolved before the patient's death. Once a thorough psychosocial assessment has been conducted, the human service professional will determine the nature and level of intervention necessary to meet the needs of the patient and family members. In fact, the psychosocial assessment in many respects acts as a blueprint for the human service provider, determining the course of case management and counseling intervention strategies for the patient and involved family members.

One of the most common roles for human service providers working in hospice includes providing case management and bereavement counseling services to patients and their family members that address the issues noted in the psychosocial assessment. For instance, issues related to how the patient and family are dealing with the terminal illness, the patient's loss of control because of increasing debilitation, and the impending death are all explored and counseling is provided as necessary. Because each family is different, the counseling will vary pretty significantly from patient to patient. For instance, if the patient is a five-year-old child dying of cancer, the counselor will need to assess the needs of the parents and siblings involved. Yet, if the patient is 85 years old with an ailing spouse and adult children in their 60s, the clinical issues will be different, and although it would be incorrect to automatically assume that the level of grief is lessened simply because this death is expected in the natural course of life, the needs of the different parties involved are obviously going to vary significantly. Thus, the actual nature of the illness or condition, the age of the patient, and the specific demographics and characteristics of the family members, including their cultural and religious background, all combine to determine the nature of the counseling.

I recall working with one client who was dying of amyotrophic lateral sclerosis (ALS), also known as Lou Gehrig's disease. She was suffering from almost complete paralysis and was unable to communicate once hospice was hired, thus I worked primarily with her husband. This couple was in their early 80s and had been married for over 50 years. The surviving spouse was heartbroken at the prospect of losing his wife who was also his best friend. Our counseling relationship lasted for months and consisted primarily of him talking about his wife, their relationship, and how agonizing it was for him to watch his once capable, articulate wife, who was a leader both in the community and within their family, become slowly imprisoned and paralyzed by ALS.

My role was not to reframe this tragedy in some more positive light, as might be appropriate in another type of counseling in another practice setting. Rather, my role was to remain comfortable when in the presence of his emotional expressions of grief and sadness, which in some sense gave him permission to have these necessary feelings. I did my best to provide comfort and a forum for his sadness, but I never gave him the impression that his feelings were in any way wrong, or that he should work harder to see the positive side of the situation. Rather I accompanied him on his grief journey as best I could, making sure he knew I was emotionally available and comfortable with his emotions.

Well-meaning but misguided counselors are often uncomfortable when confronted with a client's intense emotions of sadness and anger and in an attempt to alleviate their client's pain and their own discomfort, try to make the client feel better by pointing out the positive side of a crisis or encouraging the client to avoid dwelling on feelings of sadness and anger. This approach often leaves grieving clients feeling as though their emotions are somehow unacceptable, or at the least burdensome, which in turn results in them potentially withdrawing and struggling in isolation. Hence, one of the greatest challenges facing hospice workers lies in their ability to increase their comfort level with painful and unpleasant emotions. Many people who are grieving can intuitively sense the comfort levels of those around them, and many hospice clients report that hospice counselors are the only people with whom they feel safe and comfortable sharing their deepest and most painful feelings of loss, grief, sadness, and anger. We don't need to offer magic words to make it better to be effective counselors, we just need to be present, open, and accepting.

There are several common issues that human service providers may encounter when working with terminally ill patients and their family members. Ways in which patients and family members manage the impending death on an emotional and practical level often determine the nature of the intervention strategies used in the counseling process. For instance, do the patient and family accept the diagnosis and grieve openly and collectively? Or do they perceive such acceptance as a sign of lost hope and giving up? Are they prepared to deal with the more practical aspects of dying, such as getting the affairs of the patient in order? What coping mechanisms do they use to help them through difficult life experiences?

Most likely human service providers will encounter a broad range of attitudes, approaches, and coping strategies used by their clients, with some families presenting a unified approach and others presenting a complex system of contradictory perspectives and approaches to

Watch the video on the role of the hospice social worker. How have your feelings and beliefs about hospice changed after watching this film?
ENHANCEDetext *video example 10.4*

www.youtube.com/
watch?v=00jXVr7v3Qs

death—many of which are rooted in intergenerational, cultural, and/or religious traditions. An effective human service provider helps terminally ill patients and their families navigate this difficult path, using a range of client-centered and culturally sensitive strategies.

Accepting the Reality of the Death

Hospice patients and their family members often struggle with the realities associated with a terminal diagnosis. As mentioned earlier, embracing death often feels all too much like letting go of life, and North American culture encourages embracing life, and even fighting for it. Many people are fearful that if they accept the reality of the terminal diagnosis, they are essentially letting go of their loved one, which they fear not only sends the wrong message, but also feels like they're giving up. This culturally-based attitude has helped create a sort of taboo surrounding death where many people don't want to think about their own deaths, let alone the impending death of a loved one.

In some families, if accepting the reality of the terminal diagnosis is synonymous with losing hope, then resisting the acceptance of a terminal diagnosis can feel like fighting for life, and a human service provider might be seen as someone who is trying to rob the patient and family of their hope. Thus many times families make the decision to either reject social services when first signing up for hospice care or prohibit the human service provider (the social worker or bereavement counselor) from talking about the terminal diagnosis in front of the patient. Yet, because many of the issues addressed by hospice workers are anticipatory, meaning that they are designed to also deal with problems that may confront surviving family members at some point in the future, it is important that the human service provider address the family's denial and assist them in understanding that to accept the impending death of their loved one is not synonymous with hastening the death or with losing hope. Rather, it is more about seeing death as a natural part of life, as a transition.

Counseling can be particularly challenging when the patient is asking for information and the family does not want the information about the terminal diagnosis to be shared. In this situation, the human service provider must be sensitive to the family's feelings, but clear that the patient is the identified client, and what is in the best interest of the patient will also eventually be in the best interest of the family, even if they do not initially recognize this. A human service provider will assist the family with the task of accepting the terminal illness, facing this approaching loss, and addressing each emotional complication that arises with as much sensitivity and compassion as possible.

Human service providers working in hospice must be comfortable confronting the realities of death within themselves before they will be comfortable dealing with this often-taboo or at least uncomfortable subject with patients and families. Knowing how to respond effectively and compassionately when a family accepts social services, but prohibits any discussion of the terminal illness, requires clinical skills based not only on good training and education, but also on the human service provider's self-awareness and own comfort level in dealing with these difficult issues.

Planning for the Death

Human service providers working in hospice settings also assist the patient and family with the practical aspects of planning for increased disability and eventual death. Such practical planning may include something as specific as assisting the patient and family prepare **advance directives** or as broad as helping the patient and family sort through their feelings of sadness and even anger in response to the impending death. Generally, advance directives include the spelling out of one's end-of-life wishes. Legal documents such as **do-not-resuscitate (DNR)** orders, **living wills**, and a **medical power of attorney** are designed to clearly define a patient's wishes regarding the nature of their medical care if and when they reach a point where they are no longer able to make decisions for themselves. Preparing advance directives is an emotional process though. Imagine sitting with a patient who recently learned he is terminally ill and will likely die in less than six months and discussing whether or not the patient and his family want extraordinary measures taken to save his life when a point is reached in his disease process where he is unresponsive and stops breathing. The clients may respond with shock and confusion—why are you asking us these questions when we already know he's going to die? The process may seem unnecessary, but it is not, because these are legal documents required by medical settings providing care in end-of-life situations.

Making a decision that essentially will mean allowing a family member to die without intervention, either through the removal of a feeding tube or not using cardiopulmonary resuscitation (CPR) to revive their loved one, often generates feelings of immense guilt at the prospect of abandoning their family member and allowing him to die. Such emotional turmoil has the potential to create significant conflict and rifts within a family system that may already be buckling under the emotional strain of their impending loss. A human service provider's role then is not simply to assist the patient and family with the practical matters involved with preparing advance directives, but to help the family navigate this emotionally rocky path as well.

Another role of the human service provider is to assist the patient with the preparation of funeral arrangements. The thought of planning one's own funeral might seem rather morbid to some, but it can actually be rather therapeutic for someone who is facing a terminal illness or other life-limiting condition. Consider experiencing a life event that stripped you of all control—you can no longer plan for your future because you have only six months to live, you can no longer bound out of the door for a morning jog or even run errands whenever the mood strikes. A terminal illness robs people of their hopes for the future, but it also robs them of their control in their present, and patients—even aging patients—often struggle with the reality of their increasing dependence on others. Planning their funeral, such as selecting scriptures, music to be played, whether it will be a celebration of life or a more traditional and formal funeral, a graveside service, or a memorial service, gives patients a sense of control in the midst of their increasing powerlessness.

The hospice human service provider can utilize what might initially appear to be a practical matter (making funeral arrangements) to facilitate discussions with clients and elicit feelings about their increasing debilitation, confinement, and dependence. I recall working with a hospice patient who at the age of 93 shared heartfelt grief at the thought that he could no longer take his dog for a walk or run to catch up with a friend. In his confinement to a bed, he recalled how he had taken his physical freedom for granted and felt powerless and hopeless in response to the realization that his body could no longer cooperate with what his mind wanted it to do. Planning his funeral was the one thing he felt he still had control over in the midst of the powerlessness he felt in every other aspect of his life.

The Spiritual Component of Dying

Hospice care has its roots in the caring of the dying by religious orders, because religious leaders recognized the spiritual component of facing one's mortality and eventual death. Even though religious issues and spiritual concerns may technically fall under the purview of the hospice chaplain, every professional on the hospice team will likely be asked by a patient or family member to pray with them, and human service providers, including bereavement counselors, are more effective if they are comfortable in doing so, even if they do not happen to share the same faith as the patient. Facing one's mortality can be a frightening experience for many, and relying on or reconnecting to the faith of one's youth is a common experience for those dying of a terminal illness.

Counseling commonly takes on a spiritual tone as hospice patients attempt to make sense out of their terminal diagnosis. Patients might experience anger, confusion, and a loss of hope, and may seek answers from God yet pose these questions to the human service provider. Although no one expects someone in human services to be an expert in theology, it is important that the human service provider feel comfortable enough to help the patient sort through these questions, and even if questions cannot be answered, the human service provider can then direct a pastor or other religious leader to the patient to provide answers and comfort.

Death and Dying: Effective Bereavement Counseling

Several research surveys have noted that about 60 percent of human services and social work programs at both a bachelor's and a master's level offered courses related to death and dying, these courses were primarily offered as electives, and only about 25 percent of students actually took them. Related studies found that over 60 percent of new human service providers felt as though their educational program did not adequately prepare them for counseling clients dealing with end-of-life issues (Kramer, Hovland-Scafe, & Pacourek, 2003). This is unfortunate because many human service providers work directly or indirectly with death and dying issues, including issues related to grief and loss. In light of this, it is essential that those in the human services field obtain the necessary education and training so they feel competent in providing services to clients dealing with death and dying.

Several theoretical models are available for dealing with grief and loss related to death and dying. Traditional grief models, including Elisabeth Kübler-Ross's (1969) model of grief, depict grieving as a process involving overlapping stages, where a mourner meets a loss initially with a sense of denial and disbelief, then moves on to the anger stage, where the mourner feels a sense of injustice and rage in response to the loss. The object of the anger varies depending on the circumstances surrounding the loss and the values of the mourner, but might include being angry with God, the loved one who died, at themselves for not doing more, or at the world in general. The next stage is marked by the mourner bargaining to avoid the loss. Individuals whose loss is due to a death may bargain with God—perhaps promising a sinless life if their loved one can be returned to them, or they wish they were the ones to die, rather than their loved one. The stage of *depression* is marked by sadness where mourners experience deep melancholy, hopelessness, and despair. The final stage of grieving involves the mourner's acceptance of the loss, which allows the mourner to move on in life. Although Kübler-Ross's stage theory has dominated the field of grief and loss for many years, there has been a recent turn away from perceiving the mourning process as one where mourners progress through distinct emotional stages, culminating in acceptance.

A more contemporary approach focuses on task theories, which suggest that mourners are confronted with tasks or needs to address as they navigate their grief journey. Alan Wolfelt (1996), a **thanatologist**, developed a task-based practice theory for grief and loss that involves seven reconciliation needs that both adults and children need to address to find healing. It is interesting to note that Wolfelt does not discuss healing in terms of acceptance, which he believes puts too much pressure on the bereaved, particularly those mourning a significant loss, such as the death of a child.

Wolfelt's seven reconciliation needs include (1) acknowledging the reality of the death, (2) embracing the pain of the loss, (3) remembering the person who died through memories, (4) developing a new self-identity in the absence of the loved one, (5) searching for some meaning in the loss, (6) receiving ongoing support from others, and (7) reconciling the grief, which is different than acceptance. Bereavement counseling can be facilitated by human service providers from various disciplines, including a human service generalist with a bachelor's or master's degree, a licensed therapist or social worker, or even hospice volunteers. In fact, it is often a volunteer bereavement counselor who follows up with family members after the death of the patient to explore how the surviving family members are faring, as well as to determine the need for ongoing bereavement counseling.

Human service providers who conduct bereavement counseling may do so on an individual basis, but may also facilitate support groups focusing on a particular loss. Support groups for children surviving the loss of a parent or groups for widows or widowers are examples of grief-specific support groups. Most hospices offer free bereavement counseling for up to one year after the death of the patient as a part of the full continuum of care. Bereavement counseling is an important component of hospice care, particularly because knowing their loved ones will be cared for after their death can provide a sense of comfort for dying hospice patients.

Multicultural Considerations

Individuals from many ethnic minority and migrant groups tend to underutilize hospice care. The reasons for this underrepresentation are related to numerous factors, including a general lack of awareness of hospice care; Medicare regulations, which create barriers for immigrants, low-income populations, and certain minority groups from accessing hospice; a lack of diversity within the hospice staff leading to a general mistrust and discomfort with hospice services; and a lack of knowledge of hospice care among many physicians who serve ethnic minority populations.

Many ethnic groups perceive the acceptance of death negatively, values that are inconsistent with hospice values. For instance, one study that examined barriers to hospice service for African Americans found that many African Americans held religious beliefs that conflicted with the hospice philosophy. Subjects stated that they did not feel it was appropriate to talk about, plan for, or accept their impending death. In addition, a majority of the subjects interviewed stated they felt more comfortable turning to those within their own community, particularly their church, for support during times of crisis, rather than turning to strangers within the health care system (Reese, Ahern, Nair, O'Faire, & Warren, 1999).

It's important not to push hospice services on any cultural group if they are culturally and morally opposed to the hospice philosophy. However, if the reason why hospice care is rejected lay more in the lack of knowledge about the services provided, then it is appropriate for hospice workers to advocate for increased access to underutilizing populations. Thus, rather than accepting differences in philosophy on their surface, hospice agencies can adapt their services to meet the needs of the African American community and other ethnically diverse groups (Greiner, Perera, & Ahluwalia, 2003; Reese et al., 1999).

Little research has been conducted on usage patterns or barriers to service for Asian Americans, Latino Americans, or Native Americans, but similar issues are likely to emerge within these communities as well. By remaining flexible in their policies and practices, hospice agencies can meet the needs of a range of culturally diverse groups, particularly those that either directly or inadvertently discriminate against ethnic minority groups, such as strict admittance requirements. Although there may be multiple barriers facing some populations in receiving hospice care services—some financial and some cultural—one of the foundational values of the hospice philosophy is that hospice care will be available to every dying individual.

Certainly hospice administrators are responsible for developing admittance policies that do not directly or inadvertently discriminate against low-income patients while protecting the financial status of the hospice. But human service providers who are professionally committed to advocating for economically disadvantaged and underserved populations are in the unique position of securing financial assistance in the form of private and government assistance.

Another ethical dilemma facing hospice staff involves the issue of **euthanasia** and physician-assisted suicide. Dr. Jack Kevorkian made national headlines in the 1990s for assisting numerous terminally ill patients in the ending of their lives and was then sent to prison for his actions. Currently, euthanasia remains illegal in most states, but **physician aid-in-dying (PAD)** is legal in California, Oregon, Washington, Vermont, and some parts of New Mexico. The difference between euthanasia and PAD is that in the former, a physician administers the lethal dose of medication, whereas with PAD, the patient does. Requests for PAD or physician-assisted suicide presents a particularly challenging ethical dilemma for conservative faith-based hospice agencies that believe that issues related to death and dying fall under the sole dominion of God (Burdette, Hill, & Moulton, 2005).

Those who believe that PAD should be legalized typically cite an argument based on the inalienable human right to choose death when pain and suffering robs a person of a meaningful life. Although a counterargument could be based on the meaningful nature of suffering, a better argument might be based on the hospice philosophy that dying persons have a right to die without physical, emotional, and spiritual pain—the heart of palliative care. In fact, several studies examining similarities among terminally ill patients expressing a desire to hasten their deaths found that the chief reasons cited included (1) depression and a sense of hopelessness, (2) poor symptom management, (3) poor social support, (4) fear of becoming a burden on family members, and (5) a poor physician–patient relationship (Kelly et al., 2002; Leman, 2005). If these issues could be addressed effectively, would these same patients still seek physician-assisted suicide? That is a difficult question to answer and likely would vary from person to person.

Although the hospice philosophy advocates for neither hastening nor postponing death, hospice agencies have more in common with supporters of physician-assisted suicide than one might initially think. In fact, the leading reasons among terminally ill patients for requesting a quicker end to their lives include the very issues hospice care is designed to manage. Hospice workers can respond to this ethical dilemma by advocating for the meaningful nature of the dying process from spiritual, psychological, and social perspectives, made possible when patients are helped to confront feelings of sadness and hopelessness, when symptoms are well managed, when social support is bolstered, when families are assisted with the care of the patient, and when the hospice physician maintains a close relationship with patients based on a palliative care model. In fact, one human service professional working in hospice explained that if a choice is made to cut the dying process short, then many opportunities for growth and even last-minute revelations may be lost, as it is often the last weeks, days, hours, or even minutes of a person's life that many lifelong problems are resolved. Hospice advocates cite the value of every life experience and remind us how these types of end-of-life realizations and resolutions also benefit surviving family members and friends (Mesler & Miller, 2000).

ENHANCEDetext *self-check 10.4*

CONCLUSION

Hospital social workers and other human service providers provide crisis counseling, case management, discharge planning, and a range of other generalist services focused on the care of clients receiving services in relation to a medical issue. Some examples include providing counseling and case management services to patients and their family members experiencing a medical emergency and providing psychosocial support to those struggling with HIV/AIDS. Hospital social workers and other human service providers commonly work on interdisciplinary teams and possess an array of skills that equip them to manage a wide range of issues within a client population seeking medical services. The passage of the ACA health care delivery, management, and reimbursement models have changed the health care model dramatically in the United States, impacting both patients receiving medical care and those who care for them.

Hospice care grew out of a general discontent with Western curative treatment models, which often involves subjecting the terminally ill to unnecessary, futile, and often painful treatment, as well as a loss of dignity in their final months of life. The hospice philosophy is based on a palliative model, which involves a patient and family-centered approach that allows patients to die with dignity with the least amount of pain possible. Although hospice care has been around for over four decades, many patients and their families are resistant to accepting hospice services because they believe that doing so is tantamount to accepting defeat and losing hope. Human service providers play a key role in helping families perceive hospice care in a different light, where embracing the dying process recognized as an important and meaningful part of living.

SUMMARY

- The role and functions of human service providers in medical and other health care settings are explored.
- The ways human service providers can engage HIV-positive populations are identified.
- The nature of the ACA and how it has changed the U.S. health care system is examined.
- The role and function of the human service professional working with patients in a hospice care setting is explored.

Internet Resources

Conduct an Internet search for the National Association of Social Workers (NASW) website and search for the "NASW Standards for Social Work Practice in Health Care Settings."

Conduct an Internet search for the U.S. Department of Health and Human Services website, click on Programs and Services, and then click on Public Health and Safety.

Conduct an Internet search for the Substance Abuse and Mental Health Services Association (SAMHSA) website, and search for "Trauma-Informed Approach and Trauma-Specific Interventions."

Conduct an Internet search for the Latino Commission on AIDS website, click on the Programs tab in the top menu, and then click on "Latinos in the Deep South Program."

Conduct an Internet search for the Hospice Foundation of America website, click on the Grief tab in the top menu, and then on Helpful Grief Articles.

Conduct an Internet search for the National Hospice and Palliative Care Society, click on Resources, and then on Hospice Care, and then on "Hospice Video Series."

References

Acevedo, V. (2008). Cultural competence in a group intervention designed for Latinos living with HIV/AIDS. *Health and Social Work*, 33(2), 111–120.

Burdette, A. M., Hill, T. D., & Moulton, D. E. (2005). Religion and attitudes toward physician-assisted suicide and terminal palliative care. *Journal for the Scientific Study of Religion*, 44(1), 79–93.

Centers for Disease Control and Prevention [CDC]. (1988). Quarterly report to the domestic policy council on the prevalence and rate of spread of HIV and AIDS—United States. *Morbidity and Mortality Weekly Report*, 37(36), 551–554.

Centers for Disease Control and Prevention [CDC]. (2012). HIV in the United States: The stages of care. Atlanta: CDC.

Centers for Disease Control and Prevention [CDC]. (2015). HIV Surveillance Report: Diagnosis of HIV infection in the United States and dependent areas, 2014 (No. 26). Retrieved from http://www.cdc.gov/hiv/library/reports/surveillance/.

Centers for Disease Control and Prevention [CDC]. (2016, August). HIV among Latinos: CDC Fact Sheet. Atlanta: CDC. Retrieved from https://www.cdc.gov/nchhstp/newsroom/docs/factsheets/cdc-hiv-latinos-508.pdf.

Clark, D. (2002). *Cicely Saunders: founder of the hospice movement: selected letters 1959–1999*. Clarendon Press.

Corning, P. A. (1969). *The evolution of Medicare: From idea to law* (No. 29). US Social Security Administration, Office of Research and Statistics;[for sale by the Supt. of Docs., US Govt. Print. Off.

Frasca, T. (2008). Shaping the new response: HIV/AIDS and Latinos in the Deep South. Latino Commission on AIDS. Retrieved from http://img.thebody.com/press/2008/DeepSouthReportWeb.pdf

Galambos, C. M. (2004). The changing face of AIDS. *Health and Social Work*, 29(2), 83–85.

Gibbons, J., & Plath, D. (2009). Single contacts with hospital social workers: The clients' experiences. *Social Work in Health Care*, 48(8), 721–735.

Gorin, S. H. (2010). The Patient Protection and Affordable Care Act, cost control, and the battle for health care reform. *Health & Social Work*, 35(3), 163–166.

Gottlieb, M. S., Schroff, R., Schanker, H. M., Weisman, J. D., Fan, P. T., Wolf, R. A., et al. (1981). *Pneumocystis carnii* pneumonia and mucosal candidiasis in previously homosexual men: Evidence of a new acquired cellular immunodeficiency. *New England Journal of Medicine*, 305(24), 1425–1431.

Greiner, K. A., Perera, S., & Ahluwalia, J. S. (2003). Hospice usage by minorities in the last year of life: Results from the National Mortality Follow Back Survey. *Journal of the American Geriatrics Society*, 51, 970–978.

Kaplan, L. E., Tomaszewski, E. S., & Gorin, S. (2004). Current trends and the future of HIV/AIDS services: A social work perspectives. *Health & Social Work*, 29(2), 153–159.

Kelly, B., Burnett, P., Pelusi, D., Badger, S., Varghese, F., & Robertson, M. (2002). Terminally ill cancer patients' wish to hasten death. *Palliative Medicine*, 16, 335–339.

Kramer, B. J., Hovland-Scafe, C., & Pacourek, L. (2003). Analysis of end-of-life content in social work textbooks. *Journal of Social Work Education*, 39(2), 299–320.

Kübler-Ross, E. (1969). *Living with death and dying*. New York, NY: Macmillan Publishing Co.

Leman, R. (2005). *Seventh annual report on Oregon's death with dignity act*. State of Oregon, Department of Human Services, Office of Disease Prevention and

Epidemiology. Retrieved from http://oregon.gov/DHS/ph/pas/docs/year7.pdf

MacDonald, D. (1991). Hospice social work: A search for identity. *Health and Social Work, 16*(4), 274–280.

Maslow, A. (1954). *Motivation and personality.* New York, NY: Harper.

Mbuagbaw, L., Van Der Kop, M. L., Lester, R. T., Thirumurthy, H., Pop-Eleches, C., Smieja, M., & Thabane, L. (2013). Mobile phone text messages for improving adherence to antiretroviral therapy (ART): a protocol for an individual patient data meta-analysis of randomised trials. *BMJ open, 3*(5), e002954.

Mugavero, M. J., Amico, K. R., Horn, T., & Thompson, M. A. (2013). The state of engagement in HIV care in the United States: from cascade to continuum to control. *Clinical Infectious Diseases, 57*(8), 1164–1171.

Mesler, M. A., & Miller, P. J. (2000). Hospice and assisted suicide: The structure and process of an inherent dilemma. *Death Studies, 24,* 135–155.

National Association of Human service providers. (1990). *Clinical indicators for social work and psychosocial services in the acute care medical hospital.* Washington, DC: Author.

Oliver, D., & Peck, M. (2006, September). Inside the interdisciplinary team experiences of hospice human service providers. *Journal of Social Work in End-of-Life and Palliative Care, 2*(3), 7–21.

Paradis, L., & Cummings, S. (1986). The evolution of hospice in America toward organizational homogeneity. *Journal of Health and Social Behavior, 27*(4), 370–386.

Reese, D. J., Ahern, R. E., Nair, S., O'Faire, J. D., & Warren, C. (1999). Hospice access and use by African Americans: Addressing cultural and institutional barriers through participatory action research. *Social Work, 44*(6), 449–559.

Saberi, P., & Johnson, M. O. (2015). Correlation of Internet use for health care engagement purposes and HIV clinical outcomes among HIV-positive individuals using online social media. *Journal of Health Communication, 20*(9), 1026–1032.

Scofea, L. A. (1994). The development and growth of employer-provided health insurance. *Monthly Labor Review, 117*(3), 3–10.

Substance Abuse and Mental Health Services Administration [SAMHSA]. (2015). About NCTIC. National Center for Trauma-Informed Care & Alternatives to Seclusion and Restraint. Retrieved from http://www.samhsa.gov/nctic.

Stein, G. (2004). Improving our care at life's end: Making a difference. *Health and Social Work, 29*(1), 77–79.

Tajlili, B. (2015). Yes, you'll probably pay more for your health insurance in 2016, and here's why. Health Care: Health Care Reform. Blue Cross Blue Sheild. Retrieved March 9, 2016, from http://blog.bcbsnc.com/2015/06/yes-youll-probably-pay-more-for-your-health-insurance-in-2016-and-heres-why/

Wang, A. (2014, March 5). Blue Cross parent expecting losses in 2014 due to Obamacare. Crain's Chicago Business. Retrieved from http://www.chicagobusiness.com/article/20140305/NEWS03/140309917/blue-cross-parent-expecting-losses-in-2014-due-to-obamacare

Weaver, H. N. (1999). Through indigenous eyes: Native Americans and the HIV epidemic. *Health and Social Work, 24*(1), 27–34.

Winkler, M. (2015). Ask investors whether Obamacare is working. Bloomberg View. Retrieved from http://www.bloombergview.com/articles/2015-10-16/obamacare-gives-a-boost-to-u-s-health-care-stocks

Wolfelt, A. (1996). *Healing the bereaved child: Grief gardening, growth through grief, and other touchstones for caregivers.* Fort Collins, CO: Companion Press.

World Health Organization. (2013). Global health observatory data: HIV/AIDS. Retrieved from http://www.who.int/gho/hiv/en/

Human Services in Public Schools

© MONKEY BUSINESS IMAGES / SHUTTERSTOCK

Mario is a junior at a public high school in a large urban school in a state bordering Mexico. He does not have a behavior problem and does relatively well in his academic studies, but he has come to the attention of school social workers due to excessive absences. His teachers also report that he seems particularly "stressed out" lately, and is not himself. There is concern that he may be withdrawing emotionally and socially due to an increase in anti-immigrant sentiment exhibited among some students and school personnel. A psychosocial evaluation reveals that Mario is the oldest of four children. Mario's parents are undocumented immigrants from Mexico, who have been living in the United States for approximately 15 years, having been recruited to work in the United States by a large agricultural company.

Mario's parents do not speak English, and Mario disclosed that he often misses school so that he can translate for his parents or intercede on behalf of his parents who are often scared to seek out services themselves in light of anti-immigration legislation recently passed in the state. Mario also disclosed that he has in fact been the target of anti-immigrant sentiment in the form of derogatory statements and scapegoating. For instance, on several occasions while walking down the halls in school he has heard random students shout out to him asking for proof of his legal status. He has also experienced negative statements directed toward all Latina/o immigrants, including a few teachers and some office assistants who have made statements appearing to scapegoat this population for everything from escalating violence in the drug war to scapegoating Latinos for high regional unemployment rates. The school social worker, Kate, responds to Mario and his parents reassuringly and explains that Mario can receive supportive services—both from government social services and from programs within the school. At this point in the session, Mario admits that he just learned that he does not in fact have legal status. Mario grew up believing that he was born in the United States, but after a recent meeting with a state social service agency, he was informed that his Social Security number was not valid. His parents then told him that he was six months old when they emigrated from Mexico and they used false papers provided to them by men from the agricultural company that recruited them. Mario became extremely distraught when sharing this secret, expressing discouragement and fear that he would not be able to attend college and receive financial aid, despite having lived in the United States almost his entire life and working so hard to do well in school, or worse, that he could be legally deported to a country he has never visited and where he knows no one.

Before Kate can competently provide guidance, services, and referrals to Mario and his family, she must be aware of several areas of law that impact the migrant population—both those who are documented and undocumented. These overlapping areas include federal and state immigration laws (much of which changed significantly post-9/11), changes in public assistance policies in response to 1996 welfare reform (that barred the majority of residents, documented and undocumented, from receiving any public assistance), differences in legislation and policies on various levels (federal, state, county, and school), as well as having an awareness of pending legislation that may have an impact on Mario and his family, such as the Dream Act, federal legislation that would make it possible for students like Mario to attend college under certain circumstances. Gaining this level of awareness of macro issues affecting the Hispanic students at Kate's school is a vital part of providing culturally-competent social work services. One way to learn more about current issues affecting undocumented students is to attend workshops and conferences focusing on this issue, as well as seeking out resources identifying key issues and dynamics published by advocacy organizations or other authoritative organizations. For instance, the National School Boards Association and the National Education Association jointly published an online report in 2009 in cooperation with several professional organizations, including School Social Work Association of America, entitled "Legal Issues for School Districts Related to the Education of Undocumented Immigrants" (Borkowski & Sorensen, 2009). This publication would be a great place for Kate to start learning about a public school's obligations and responsibilities regarding the education of undocumented students.

Human service professionals are an integral part of the public school system providing academic support, psychosocial counseling, and career guidance to millions of students every year, as well as programmatic leadership and support within the public school system. Generally, three types of professionals provide these services to students on public school campuses: school social workers, school counselors, and school psychologists. Together, these support professionals comprise what is often called the **student services team**—a multidisciplinary team where each support professional works within their respective specialties meeting students' psychosocial and academic needs, increasing student success in a range of important domains.

School social workers, school counselors, and school psychologists each provide psychosocial services, but they use somewhat different approaches to counseling and student support provision, having different standards of practice, and even different service and treatment goals. Social workers tend to focus more on the psychosocial aspects of students' lives, providing counseling and case management that focus on traditional social work concerns such as the students' overall mental health, diversity and cultural competence, and social problems within the community that can impact students' lives in a way that creates barriers to learning (e.g., violence, homelessness, poverty). School counselors have a similar focus as school social workers, but tend to focus more on academic counseling and career guidance, while also focusing on emotional or psychological issues that pertain to student achievement. School psychologists focus more on testing, particularly in response to numerous federal and state mandates that require the academic testing of students to place them in the proper educational setting, but school psychologists may also provide counseling for students who are experiencing emotional difficulties affecting their academic achievement.

In general, the goals of each member of a student services team focuses on (1) supporting academic achievement, (2) fostering emotional and mental health, (3) encouraging prosocial behavior, (4) supporting diverse learners and students from diverse backgrounds, (5) creating safe school environments, and (6) building strong connections between school, home, and community. Thus while there is some overlap in the duties and functions of school social workers, school counselors, and school psychologists, each professional serving on a student services team accomplishes these goals in ways that reflect the evidence-based and data-driven practices and foundational values unique to their respective professional disciplines.

SCHOOL SOCIAL WORK

School social workers serve as important liaisons between students and their families, the school system, and the community. Most states require that school social workers have an MSW with a specialization in school social work, accrue 1200 hours in an internship, which includes 720 hours in a public school setting, and pass a state content-area test. School social workers serve the vital role of providing students with psychosocial support in a range of contexts—in the classroom, at home, in the community–addressing dynamic challenges that present barriers to academic success.

The Historical Roots of Social Work in Schools

Social workers have served an important role in supporting a wide range of at-risk and marginalized students and their families for over 100 years, ensuring that students were attending school regularly, that children's adjustment needs were met, and that children with disabilities received the services they needed (Allen-Meares, 2006; McCullagh, 1993). Early school social workers were called visiting teachers and were a part of the **Visiting Teacher Movement**, beginning in 1906 and ending in 1940.

Visiting teachers were primarily social workers from **settlement houses**—community-based organizations that provided services primarily to low-income immigrant populations in large urban areas. Thus most of the children who were the original focus of early school social work services were the children of immigrants, many from non-English-speaking countries. The communities where settlement houses were located were frequently overcrowded, both within the neighborhoods as well as within the classroom, where some schools had as many as 50 students per classroom (McCullagh, 1993, 1998).

The role of visiting teachers expanded quickly though to focus not only on immigrant children but also on maladjusted children (including those with conduct problems), and children with intellectual disabilities (often referred to as **feeble-minded** or unintelligent in the early education literature). Among the many goals of visiting teachers was to save the unadjusted child—those children who were not faring well amidst all of the dramatic social and economic changes occurring during that era that were impacting children and their families, and thus the educational system as a whole.

In addition to mass immigration, another social force driving the need for increased psychosocial support in the public school system was the passage of **compulsory education laws** from the mid-1800s through about 1920. Mandatory attendance laws meant that thousands of children who had previously been omitted from the educational system—poor children, orphans, immigrant children, and children who were cognitively disabled—were now compelled to attend school or face sanctions, which in some states involved the termination of parental rights. **Mass urbanization** was another socioeconomic force involving scores of people moving away from their farms and into the cities for factory jobs. With them came children, many of whom struggled in their adjustment to city life, particularly when it involved living in cramped quarters with parents who worked long hours. The maladjustment of these children created challenges within the school systems in large cities, such as New York, Philadelphia, and Chicago, in the form of conduct problems and truancy.

By the 1920s the number of visiting teachers placed in schools had increased significantly, with boards of education and teachers in low-income, high-need, urban neighborhoods looking to visiting teachers for advice and assistance with several psychosocial issues related to their students. In fact, many larger school districts were lobbying to have school social workers become paid members of the school district and board of education, rather than being contracted volunteers of the settlement houses supported by philanthropic organizations (McCullagh, 1993, 1998; Terry, 1925).

One of the first professional organizations representing visiting teachers was the National Committee of Visiting Teachers and Home and School Visitors, established in 1919. In 1929 the name of the organization was changed to the American Association of Visiting Teachers, and in 1942 the name was changed again to the American Association of School Social Workers, and just a few years later, the name was changed again to the National Association of School Social Workers (NASSW) to reflect the growing professionalization of school social workers as a distinct field.

In 1955 the American Association of Social Workers (AASW), American Association of Medical Social Workers (AAMSW), American Association of Psychiatric Social Workers (AAPSW), American Association of Group Workers (AAGW), Association for the Study of Community Organization (ASCO), Social Work Research Group (SWRG), and the National Association of School Social Workers (NASSW)—merged to form the NASW. The NASSW still exists but it is now under the auspices of the NASW.

The role of the school social worker continued to grow and expand through the 1960s and 1970s, fueled in part by the social turbulence that marked these decades, as well as the passage of the Individuals with Disabilities Education Act [IDEA] (Pub. L. No. 94–142), which required that public schools provide "free and appropriate" public education to all school-aged children between 3 and 21 years of age, regardless of their disability. The passage of IDEA meant that schools were now legally required to serve a far broader student population, many with complex needs. Social workers contributed to compliance efforts, along with other members of the student services team. Today, school social work remains a growing field that offers excellent practice opportunities for those wanting to work with school-aged children. Issues such as international academic competition, concerns about increasing violence in schools, and continued reliance on social work services for the regular as well as special education students have continued to propel school social work forward into the 21st century.

Duties and Functions of School Social Workers

The traditional model of school social work involves the social worker providing school-based social work services as an employee of the school district and as a part of a multidisciplinary team. Although some districts utilize school-based social workers employed by outside agencies (primarily as a cost-saving measure), most school districts in the United States still use the traditional school social work model. School social workers' roles and functions are typically generalist in nature, but have become increasingly specialized as challenges experienced by students have become more complex (Lewis, 1998).

School social workers perform a variety of duties, serve numerous functions, and operate within several different roles depending on the demographics of the school population, the age of children served, and the capacity in which the social worker is functioning. In general, school social workers assist children in managing psychosocial issues that are creating a barrier to learning and academic achievement. These could include physical barriers to learning in the form of a physical disability, cognitive barriers such as intellectual or learning disabilities, and behavioral barriers such as students who are depressed, anxious, or acting out. School social workers also work to develop, enhance, and maintain a close working relationship between student families and the school, advocating for students and their family members in a variety of situations.

According to the NASW (2008), school social workers should be competent in providing individual, group, and family counseling; they should be well versed in theories of human behavior and development; and should have knowledge of and be sensitive to the demographic makeup of the school population in which they work, including students' socioeconomic status (SES), gender, race, sexual orientation, and any community stressors that might affect a student's ability to perform (such as a high crime rate or community gang infiltration). School social workers must also have competencies in the areas of psychosocial assessment, be familiar with local referring agencies, and be committed to the values and ethics of the social work profession, including those relating to social justice, equity, and diversity.

School social workers may work with the general school population or may work solely within the special education department, with physically, cognitively, or behaviorally disordered students. Direct practice often includes individual and group counseling, as well as family counseling if necessary. In many school settings, social work services are designated as a required part of a student's **Individualized Education Plan (IEP)**, which serves as a sort of contract between the school and family for students identified with special education needs. But school social workers are often called upon to work with the general population of students, as needed.

The intervention tools a school social worker uses depends on the age of the students and the issues they are experiencing, but often the school social workers will facilitate support groups focusing on issues such as anger management, the development of better social skills, the management of grief and loss, divorce recovery, and perhaps even a newcomer club for new students who are struggling making friends. There are ample resources in the marketplace to help school social workers facilitate such groups, such as anger management and social skills curriculum, and therapy games such as the **Ungame**.

Case management is also provided by school social workers and can include the organization and coordination of numerous services received by a student. For instance, a student's case might involve an outside therapist who is providing psychological counseling, a psychiatrist who supervises psychotropic medication such as antidepressants, a truancy officer, the police department, a child welfare agency, the family, all the student's teachers, and the school principal. Thus, depending on the issues the student is experiencing, the social worker will likely be involved in the coordination of services and the appropriate dissemination of information to a number of involved parties (assuming confidentiality has been waived).

Crisis intervention is also an important function of a school social worker. Crises may include a natural disaster, such as a tornado or earthquake; a student suicide; or on-campus violence, such as student-on-student assaults. School social workers, in coordination with other members of the student services team, provide crisis counseling to the entire student population, families, and school staff as needed. Crisis

Watch the video on adolescent cliques. Cliques can help adolescents develop their identity, but sometimes cliques are used to isolate and ostracize certain students, which can be very damaging and hurtful. How should school social workers respond to situations in which cliques are causing harm to other students?
ENHANCEDetext *video example 11.1*

The ruins of an elementary school in Joplin, Missouri after a powerful tornado that cut a path seven mile long and half mile wide on May 22, 2011

© DUSTIE/SHUTTERSTOCK

counseling includes helping students face the initial shock of a tragedy and also includes ongoing counseling as a part of a safety and prevention plan. For instance, the suicide of a student often elicits emotional distress among a student population and can lead to the increased risk of other students committing suicide. A school social worker will be involved in creating awareness (through classroom presentations or staff meetings), maintaining a visible presence on campus, and conducting outreach services to vulnerable students.

School social workers also work as a part of a multidisciplinary team when a natural disaster occurs within a school community, such as a tornado, hurricane, flood, wildfire, or earthquake. Natural disasters create a series of traumas, beginning with the acute reaction to a life-threatening experience, followed by subsequent traumas related to loss and secondary loss. For instance, once students recover from the shock of living through a tornado, they will experience additional traumas, perhaps related to losing their home, losing friends or family, and witnessing others' traumas (vicarious trauma). School social workers provide crisis counseling in response to natural disasters, but also provide important follow-up services once the initial crisis has calmed and students (and their families) are continuing to deal with the crisis.

Ethical Dilemmas Facing School Social Workers

Like many in other social work settings, school social workers face many ethical dilemmas on a daily basis that require knowledge of NASW ethical standards, as well as an awareness of common ethical dilemmas experienced in a school setting. Some ethical dilemmas are pretty straightforward, such as maintaining confidentiality of student counseling and related records and reporting child abuse in accordance with mandatory child abuse reporting laws. But there are other areas of ethical concern that are not so clearcut, requiring school social workers to rely on a systematic method for managing difficult situations.

For instance, consider the Caucasian school social worker who, without awareness seems to automatically show bias toward Caucasian students and against students of color because he relates better to students he better understands. At what point does a personal affinity become bias toward one subpopulation and against another? Or consider the Latina school social worker who is passionate about advocating for Latina students because of what she endured in school with racially biased teachers. Her motivation to advocate for Latina students is good, but if she doesn't thoroughly evaluate the circumstances surrounding situations involving similar dynamics, she might be biased toward Latina students and against students and staff from other ethnic groups.

School social workers deal with very complex situations on a daily basis, and must make decisions about how to best handle these situations based on their professional training as well as their own personal experiences. Having personal experiences that allow us to empathize with certain situations that clients are experiencing is absolutely fine. In fact, it is often those very experiences that draw people to the social work career to begin with. But it is important for school social workers (and social workers in general) to be aware of how an emotional desire to help can easily evolve into ethical breaches, as passionate advocacy blinds wellmeaning social workers to important ethical boundaries. School social workers are bound by the NASW Code of Ethics and can benefit from additional training in ethical management from a variety of sources. School social workers can also seek additional guidance from the specialty practice section of the NASW website that focuses on school social work, where, for example, articles on issues related to confidentiality and boundary setting are posted.

ENHANCEDetext *self-check 11.1*

SCHOOL COUNSELING

School counselors serve a vital role in maximizing student success (Lapan, Gysbers, & Kayson, 2007; Dahir & Stone, 2006). They are licensed professionals with a minimum of a master's degree in school counseling, typically offered within the education department at universities offering this degree. School social workers provide leadership, advocacy, and collaboration, with the goal of promoting equity in access to the best educational experience possible for all students. School counselors work on student services teams to promote safe and effective learning environments for all students by delivering culturally relevant services as a part of a comprehensive school counseling program (Lee, 2005).

The Historical Roots of School Counseling

School counseling also has a history dating back to the late 1880s and early 1900s, with roots in the vocational guidance counseling movement (Schmidt & Ciechalski, 2001). In fact, early school counselors focused primarily on matching male high school graduates in an appropriate vocational or job placement. In the 1920s, theories of intelligence and cognitive development became popular, influencing the work of school guidance counselors who, with the advent of intelligence and aptitude testing, now had new tools with which to do their jobs.

The 1930s saw advancements in the areas of personality development and motivation, which directly influenced the field of school counseling, enabling counselors to further assist students in identifying areas of aptitude, as well as developing motivational techniques to increase academic performance and all-around personality development. Social trends and political movements were chief among various influences that led to a gradual shift from a primary focus on guidance and the vocational needs of students to a more comprehensive focus where school counselors proactively meet various developmental and psychosocial needs of students (Schmidt & Ciechalski, 2001). As with school social work, the passage of IDEA—which required, among other things, that children with special needs receive all support services necessary for their academic success—led to school counselors becoming involved in special education departments. Government committee reports, such as *A Nation at Risk* (1983), and additional federal legislation, such as the **No Child Left Behind Act** of 2001 (now referred to as the *Elementary and Secondary Education Act* [ESEA]) have meant an increase in funding for many schools, some of which was directed to school counseling programs.

Duties and Functions of School Counselors

School counselors perform vitally important services in public schools, providing a range of direct and indirect services to students, parents, the school, and the community. The American School Counselor Association (ASCA) has developed a national framework for school counseling programs with the goal of promoting student achievement by addressing students' personal, social, educational, and career needs. The framework ensures the development of skills, knowledge, and attitudes necessary for students to achieve success in school, and their lives in general, so they can become well-adjusted and successful adults (ASCA, 2012).

A national model for school counseling programs was developed by the ASCA to ensure that school counseling across the nation had a unified vision based on four themes: (1) leadership, (2) advocacy, (3) collaboration, and (4) systemic change. The model has four components, including:

1. *Foundation:* Includes the foundation upon which the program is built. Program foundations include components such as a vision and mission statement that articulates the program's focus; a plan for goal setting for student achievement; the development of student competencies that focus on academic, career, and personal development; and professional competencies for school counselors based on the ASCA Ethical Standards for School Counselors.

2. *Delivery:* Includes all activities necessary to deliver the school counseling program, including guidance curriculum, which is integrated into the broader K-12 curriculum; individual student planning; services that respond to students' needs, such as individual counseling focusing on psychosocial issues and academic needs; and systems support that facilitates the administration of the school counseling program.

3. *Management:* Includes the development and ongoing management of organizational processes involved in the school counseling program, including ways in which school counselors manage the delivery of services, including the overall facilitation of the program to ensure that program goals are met.

4. *Accountability:* Includes information on the collection and evaluation of data to illustrate how the program is meeting the needs of students and its organizational and program goals (ASCA, 2012).

School counseling programs generally focus on three basic areas: academic counseling, career development, and personal–social development (Dahir, 2001). What form this counseling takes depends in large part on whether the school counselor is working at an elementary school, middle school, or high school. Other issues influencing the nature of the counseling include the size of the student population, whether the school is in an urban or rural area, the nature of the surrounding community, and the demographic makeup of the school. For instance, a school counselor who works at a high-crime, overcrowded high school in inner-city Chicago will perform different duties and functions than a school counselor working in a high-income suburban elementary school. Despite the variation in duties and functions, all school counseling activities are drawn from the ASCA school counselor competencies (ASCA, 2012).

School counselors work as an important part of the multidisciplinary student services team, collaborating with school social workers, school psychologists, teachers, and school administrators on student matters related to student academic performance and behavior. In general, school counselors provide individual student guidance, such as helping students develop good study skills, develop effective coping strategies, and foster good peer relationships through the development of prosocial skills, such as exhibiting empathy, showing kindness to others, and managing anger appropriately. School counselors also develop and facilitate programs on substance abuse awareness and multicultural

Watch the video on collaborating with a school counselor. Can you think of other ways the school counselor could help with this case of a resistant student?

ENHANCEDetext *video example 11.2*

A school counselor runs a group on diversity and multicultural awareness

awareness, including perhaps running a diversity support group. They assist students with goal setting, academic planning, and planning for college. They facilitate crisis intervention with individual students, the student body, families, and the school as a whole as a part of the student services team.

School counselors also collaborate with parents, teachers, and school administrators and provide community referrals as necessary. They may also facilitate programs focusing on making the transition to the next level of schooling or to a working environment. School counselors identify and then work with at-risk students, managing behavioral and mental health issues such as substance abuse, suicide threats, classroom disruptions, student–teacher conflicts, and other issues as they arise. Finally, they are leaders in educational reform and the ability to effectively communicate with and collaborate with other educational professionals (ASCA, 2012; Lee, 2005).

Common Ethical Dilemmas Facing School Counselors

As with many other human service-related disciplines, school counselors face ethical dilemmas on a daily basis that require them to not only be aware of the ethical standards of the school counseling profession, but also the common dynamics they may face that could result in unintentionally transitioning from genuine caring about students to the violation of ethical boundaries. Some of these challenges are pretty straightforward, such as maintaining confidentiality of student counseling and related records or reporting child abuse in accordance with mandatory child abuse laws. But there are other areas of ethical concern that are not so clear cut.

Several articles posted on the ASCA website focus on common ethical dilemmas encountered by school counselors with the goal of assisting school counselors to recognize the ethical and unethical nature of various approaches to student problems and situations. For instance, one article entitled *Boundary Crossing: The Slippery Slope* features a vignette of a student from a particularly chaotic and neglectful home who develops a strong attachment to the school counselor, popping into her office spontaneously whenever he needs some additional support. The student then invites the school counselor to a wrestling match a considerable distance from the school on a Saturday evening. The school counselor attends the match, and then drives the student home, stopping for dinner on the way home as a gesture of congratulations for a job well done. Readers are asked whether any aspect of this scenario violated ethical boundaries and why. Most respondents were somewhat mixed on whether the fluidity of the office visits and traveling a long distance to attend a student's school-related event were ethical, but all respondents perceived the school counselor driving the student home from the match and stopping for dinner as clearly representing an ethical boundary violation, or at least a potential one (Stone, 2011).

Stone (2011) explains each type of boundary violation and the associated risks, including the violation of boundaries regarding *roles* (confusing the role of school counselor with a caregiver), the violation of boundaries regarding *time* (allowing the student to so frequently make impromptu office visits, an arrangement that cannot be maintained for all students), and the violation of boundaries regarding *place* (attending an event outside of school hours and such a long distance away, driving the student home, and stopping for dinner). Such boundary violations, while coming from a place of good intentions on the part of the school counselor, can lead to confusion on the part of the student who may develop unrealistic expectations of the school counselor. The behavior of the school counselor may also reflect bias toward one particular student, when many students have similar backgrounds and needs.

Stone believes that many ethical boundary violations among school social workers, even more significant ones, most often come from good intentions on the part of the school counselor, and not from bad character or an overt attempt to behave unethically. Ethical breaches often begin with a desire on the part of the school counselor to be helpful and supportive, but at some point either because of **counter-transference** or some other dynamic, ethical boundary lines are crossed, and originally gray situations become much clearer (particularly in retrospect).

ENHANCEDetext *self-check 11.2*

SCHOOL PSYCHOLOGISTS

School psychologists provide services that focus on the academic, social, and emotional success of students with the goal of creating healthy and safe learning environments. They also focus on developing strong connections between the school and students' home. While the goals of school psychologists are similar in nature to school social workers and school counselors, their duties and functions are quite different in that school psychologists focus on student learning, which also includes supporting teachers in their efforts to teach all learning styles. School psychologists have either a master's degree in educational psychology or a doctoral degree. They complete a 1,200-hour internship in a school setting and complete a licensing exam, which enables them to obtain a special credential designating them as a school psychologist.

Duties and Functions of School Psychologists

School psychologists work directly with students, teachers, administrators, families, and other members of the student services team with the goal of helping students achieve their optimal level of academic performance. Some of their specific duties include conducting psychological and academic testing, developing programs that increase student motivation and engagement, and creating individualized education programs that include instructional programs and interventions tailored to a student's specific needs. School psychologists also monitor student progress through observation, testing, and evaluation.

School psychologists focus on the promotion of positive mental health, which includes assessing students' emotional and behavioral needs and providing direct service to students to foster better life skills, including communication skills, social skills, coping skills, and problem-solving skills. School psychologists develop these skills through individual and group counseling, as well as through coordination with other members of the multidisciplinary student services team and through collaborative efforts with community agencies.

Similar to the mission of the school social work and school counseling professions, school psychologists are committed to supporting diverse learners. Diversity can include a student's ethnic minority status, immigration status, gender identity, sexual orientation, ability level, or learning style. Some of the ways school psychologists perform this function are conducting testing to assess diverse learning needs and providing culturally appropriate services to students with diverse backgrounds. They may also modify curricula and instruction methods as needed and as appropriate. School psychologists communicate regularly with students' parents and guardians, fostering the connection between home and school.

School psychologists also work with other members of the student services team to create and foster a positive and safe learning environment. Their activities in this regard may include developing programs focused on the development and support of prosocial skills, such as character building and ethical behavior. They also develop and facilitate programs addressing online and offline bullying, conflict resolution, violence prevention, and crisis intervention. They do this through the development and facilitation of prevention programs, positive discipline programs that address negative behaviors, and restorative justice programs that help foster an environment of healing and positive growth.

Common Ethical Dilemmas Facing School Psychologists

The National Association of School Psychologists (NASP) Principles for Professional Ethics (2010) are based on four broad themes: (1) respecting the dignity and rights of all persons, (2) professional competence and responsibility, (3) honesty and integrity in professional relationships, and (4) responsibility to schools, families, communities, the profession, and society. Similar to the other student services team professions, school psychologists often face ethical dilemmas when they are attempting to help students. Ethical dilemmas can also occur when ethical principles conflict, such as when a school psychologist attempts to balance a student's right to privacy with the parents' rights to know what's going on with their child (Iyer & Baxter-MacGregor, 2010). Other ethical dilemmas relate to complying with federal legislation, such as IDEA (2006) and the No Child Left Behind Act (2002), in a way that respects the rights of students with disabilities, while at the same time not compromising the learning of mainstream students or a safe school environment.

Achieving this balance can be challenging when students with significant disabilities have psychiatric or behavioral disorders that can disrupt learning environments or pose a danger to other students (Koppelman, 2004). For instance, students with serious behavioral problems may require restraint and seclusion, practices that are highly controversial among education and child development experts who question their effectiveness (Ryan & Peterson, 2004; Scheuermann, Peterson, Ryan, & Billingsley, 2015). Experts also cite the history of abuse and trauma to children when such tactics are used inappropriately (Frueh et al., 2005). There are times though when students behave in ways that require restraint to ensure their safety or the safety of others. School psychologists are often responsible for developing programs that assess the appropriateness of **restraint** and **seclusion**, including under what circumstances they are used and how restrain is to be carried out.

But what if parents refuse to agree to the program of restraint or seclusion, even if their child's behavior warrants it? In a situation such as this, a school psychologist faces an ethical dilemma because NASP Ethical Standard I.1.5 stipulates that school psychologists respect the wishes of parents who object to school psychology services. But consider the example posed by Yankouski, Masserelli, and Lee (2012) of a significantly disabled child with a history of self-injurious behavior, including banging her head against a wall so hard she has caused damage to her head and potentially to her vision. Her parents refuse to allow her to be restrained under any circumstance because they believe that restraining their child in the past did not help her or discourage her self-injurious behavior. Thus the ethical dilemma—the school psychologist cannot keep the child safe and respect the parents' wishes at the same time.

In cases where ethical and legal standards conflict, the use of an ethical and legal decision-making model that provides school psychologists with evidence-based options for dealing with difficult situations is recommended. Using an ethical and legal decision-making model in the case of the head-banging child whose parents object to her being restrained would likely recommend that the school psychologist contact the parents when the child is banging her head and require they pick her up immediately. In the event that the student has already injured herself, then the appropriate course of action would be to contact emergency services (Yankouski, Masserelli, & Lee, 2012).

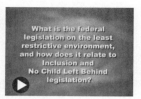

Watch the video on the least restrictive environment (LRE). What ethical challenges might a school psychologist face when working with teachers to create LRE options for students with disabilities?
ENHANCEDetext *video example 11.3*

ENHANCEDetext *self-check 11.3*

MENTAL HEALTH AND OTHER PSYCHOSOCIAL CONCERNS

In 2014 approximately 2.8 million children between the ages of 12 and 17 experienced at least one episode of major depression, with female youth experiencing almost double the rate of depression than male youth (Center for Behavioral Health Statistics and Quality, 2015). Additionally, close to three-quarters of youth surveyed, with major depression, reported that their depression caused significant problems in functioning, in one or more areas of their lives, including in school (Center for Behavioral Health Statistics and Quality, 2015). Symptoms of depression in children and adolescents are similar to those of adults, except that oftentimes children exhibit symptoms of irritability rather than melancholy (Abrams, Theberge, & Karan, 2005).

Abrams, Theberge, and Karan (2005) recommend that school mental health providers in school settings use an **ecological model** as a lens for evaluating students struggling with major depression. For instance, in assessing and evaluating a potentially depressed student, the human services provider would evaluate the relationship the student has with peers, family members, even teachers, and then consider whether the student is experiencing conflict with one or both parents, and whether the student recently experienced fights with peers or teachers. Other considerations include understanding the nature of the relationship between the student and the broader community, including whether the student has been involved with the legal system or with a truancy officer.

In general, school-based human service providers not only evaluate anything that might be a contributing factor to the student's current mental health status, but also evaluate strengths and support within the student's world (Abrams et al., 2005). Does the student belong to a faith community that offers or has the potential of offering support? Does the student have any extended family members who might come forward and offer support to the student during a difficult time? Students experiencing depression because a military parent has been deployed, for instance, might have an untapped support system, such as a support group for children facilitated by the U.S. Armed Services. By using an ecological model, members of the student services team can assist the student in expanding his or her existing support system, thus helping to not only address existing depression, but also potentially stemming the tide of future psychosocial problems that might evolve if core issues are left unaddressed.

The value of the ecological model is that it is complementary with the overall model of human services, which relies on a **person-in-environment approach** to nearly all psychosocial issues. The ecological model also enables human service providers to provide more effective case management once contributing factors and support systems are identified. This model also encourages inter-professional collaboration on a variety of levels.

Parental involvement is a key factor in the treatment of students experiencing major depression, and members of the student services team should evaluate any barriers that might prevent parents from being involved in the school-based counseling of their child. Barriers might be cultural in nature, such as a less-than-welcoming environment for non-English-speaking parents, or environments where parents do not feel well treated by school personnel (Vanderbleek, 2004). Barriers can also be more concrete, such as a parents' lack of transportation or a work schedule that makes meeting with school personnel during prescribed times impossible. Flexibility on the part of schools, particularly school services teams, is important, and may include a willingness to conduct home visits—after school hours, if necessary.

Substance Abuse in the Schools

Substance abuse, both on and off campus, continues to be a growing problem across the United States, primarily in high schools, but also in some middle schools. School services teams must be able to identify the signs of substance abuse as well as be prepared to intervene when substance abuse is suspected. Although many graduate programs in the mental health–related fields are addressing this issue by including more courses on substance abuse, the majority of programs still only offer substance abuse courses as electives, leaving many within the human services fields feeling unprepared to deal with substance abuse, particularly with regard to complicated family systems (Lambie & Rokutani, 2002).

The reality is that 74 percent of high school seniors in suburban high schools have reported using alcohol sometime in the past and 40 percent of high school seniors in suburban high schools have reported using illegal drugs in the past (Greene & Forster, 2004).

Watch the video on adolescent substance abuse. Based on the video, what prevention program do you believe would be most successful in a high school setting?
ENHANCEDetext *video example 11.4*

Although rates of substance abuse have been declining in recent years, substance abuse remains one of the most significant issues confronting school personnel. In terms of current use, about 140 million adolescents admitted to drinking alcohol in the past month (about 50 percent of the adolescent population) and about 2.3 million adolescents admitted to using illegal drugs (about 9.4 percent of the entire U.S. adolescent population), representing a slight decrease from prior years (Center for Behavioral Health Statistics and Quality, 2015).

Human service providers need to be able to identify adolescent substance abuse and respond with an effective intervention strategy, which includes school engagement, as well as the involvement of outside referral sources that will engage the entire family system. The model most often used to describe the nature of adolescent substance abuse is similar to an adult model but often does not take into consideration factors related to adolescent development. Adolescents tend to be developmentally egocentric in the sense that they often act in more self-focused ways than adults. They also tend to display behaviors that are impulsive, not always considering the consequences of their use of alcohol and drug use and abuse. This seeming sense of omnipotence, coupled with normative developmental egocentrism, often complicates the application of traditional models of substance abuse to the adolescent population.

Lambie and Rokutani (2002) suggest using a systems perspective in evaluating substance abuse in the adolescent population. Rather than viewing substance abuse in the adolescent as an individual problem, a systems perspective views the substance abuse as a sign of something going on within the family system. The substance-abusing adolescent may also serve as a symptom of deeper problems within the family system that are purposely hidden from view, such as when a child is scapegoated for family problems, such as domestic violence or general marital problems. The family that works hard to appear normal and healthy may be compelled to deal with underlying dysfunction when one or more of the children begin acting out in ways that require outside attention and intervention—in this case abusing drugs and alcohol.

Another issue to consider when using a systems perspective is whether the adolescent's substance abuse is mirroring a parent's substance abuse. A parent's abuse of alcohol or drugs has been shown to influence an adolescent's decision to begin drinking early (Lambie & Sias, 2005; Piercy, Volk, Trepper, Sprenkle, & Lewis, 1991). Families that have serious systemic problems such as parental substance abuse and other forms of maladaptive behavior are often closed-family systems and may lack the ability or capacity to handle the increased stressors associated with children entering the adolescent years. Adolescents demanding changes to longstanding rules, pushing for more privileges, developing a far wider circle of peers, and questioning family rules, including unspoken rules to keep family dysfunction a secret, can often leave a family that is wary of outsiders with few effective coping skills to adapt to these changes. In addition, problems that have their roots in early childhood often manifest during adolescence.

A human service provider working with substance-abusing adolescents must first be able to identify the common signs of abuse, including erratic behavior, mood swings, red eyes, and slurred speech. They must then be able to provide support to the student and the family, acting as a liaison between student, family, school, and community-based treatment programs. On a broader level, student services teams can help institute prevention programs in the school, such as the Drug Abuse Resistance Education (DARE) program that involves police and other community agencies coming into the schools and

Students becoming emotional at an Every 15 Minutes program at a high school in Los Angeles, California

creatively (through plays, dance, and songs), and in an age-appropriate manner, educate students about the dangers of drug abuse and provide students with avoidance strategies and avenues for assistance, if needed. Another program that has been very successful at the high school level is the *Every 15 Minutes* program, where four times an hour a student is taken from a classroom, made to look dead (with makeup), and then returned "dead" by the police. A letter is then read by the student's parents, often framed as an obituary, and a mock funeral often follows during a school assembly designed to make the consequences of teen drinking and driving very real to the students. The *Every 15 Minutes* program is a collaborative effort that involves school, home, community, and student engagement.

Teenage Pregnancy

Teenage pregnancy has been on the decline since an all-time high in 1991. In fact, teen pregnancies in girls between the ages of 15 and 19 decreased 9 percent in 2014 from 2013 (Hamilton et al., 2015). While no one really knows the exact reason for the decrease, there is some speculation that adolescent girls are not as sexually active as in earlier years, and when they are, they are more likely to use birth control. And yet, teen pregnancy remains a serious issue in high school because over 60 percent of high school seniors report that they are sexually active (Greene & Forster, 2004).

There is considerable disparity in teen pregnancy and birth rates among certain ethnic groups, warranting increased attention and intervention (Hamilton et al., 2015). For instance, although birth rates among socioeconomically disadvantaged African American, Latino, Native American, Alaska Native, and Hawaiian and Pacific Islanders youth decreased between 7 and 12 percent between 2013 and 2014, according to the CDC,

Latino and African American teen births still represented almost 60 percent of all births among 15 and 19 year olds in 2013 (Hamilton et al., 2015).

Various research studies have identified many factors that might influence pregnancy. Beyond sexual activity in the adolescent population, other factors include early alcohol use (Stueve & O'Donnell, 2005) and poverty (Young, Turner, Denny, & Young, 2004). Research on prevention points to religiosity (Rostosky, Regnerus, & Wright, 2003), peer influence, appropriate parental supervision, good and direct parental communication, higher socioeconomic status, race and ethnicity (Corcoran, Franklin, & Bennett, 2000), and involvement in sports that is correlated with remaining abstinent in high school or at least becoming sexually active later in adolescence.

Sex and pregnancy prevention programs have been included in school curriculums for several decades with mixed reviews. Sex prevention programs in the 1970s and 1980s focused primarily on sexual health and birth control, but in the 1990s *abstinence-only* programs became popular. Proponents of abstinence-only sex education cite research showing a decrease in adolescent sexual activity after participating in an **abstinence-only program** evidence that they are successful (Toups & Holmes, 2002). Yet others have questioned whether these programs are as successful as some of these studies indicate, citing poor study designs and a wide range of abstinence programs with some defining abstinence as postponing sex until early adulthood and some more religiously based programs sending the message that premarital sex should always be avoided. Without a clear definition of "abstinence," critics claim that it's impossible to determine the success of these programs (Kirby, 2002). A large federally funded study published in 2007 may have provided the definitive word on this issue, when the results clearly showed that youth who had completed abstinence-only programs were no more likely to delay becoming sexually active, have fewer sexual partners, or abstain from sex altogether (Trenholm et al., 2007).

Reasons for the lack of success of abstinence-only programs may be related to the lack of immediate consequences for adolescents who engage in sexual activity. One of the most popular and evidence-based programs currently used in high schools across the nation is the *Baby Think It Over* (BTIO) program, which provides immediate feedback to teens making child raising a reality. The BTIO program uses a computerized doll programmed to cry and fuss intermittently throughout the day and night to educate teenagers on the realities of having a baby. Whether this program is successful at deterring teen pregnancy is also uncertain, with some studies showing a positive effect (Somers & Fahlman, 2001; Somers, Johnson, & Sawilowsky, 2002) and other studies showing no impact (Barnett, 2006).

Identifying the reasons why populations of adolescents engage in unsafe sex practices may provide more information on why some prevention programs work and others don't. For instance, developing culturally sensitive empowerment support groups has shown some success in increasing awareness among a demographic of adolescent girls that often report feeling powerless in making decisions about their sexuality (citation). All-girl empowerment groups can provide at-risk girls a safe place to talk about their feelings about sex and support each other in their right to say no to sex (or no to sexual activity without using a condom). They can also provide girls with educational information and tools for boundary setting that reflects their actual desires, increasing an overall sense of personal empowerment, which is likely to result in a reduction of unplanned pregnancies.

This approach involves a shift from sex and pregnancy prevention to personal empowerment and healthy sexual choices. One of the first states to transition from a risk-focused paradigm to a youth development model that perceives sexual activity as a normal part of adolescent development is Oregon. A youth development model engages adolescents as partners in the issue, focusing on sexual health and positive choices, destigmatizing sexual activity and instead focusing on personal empowerment (Nystrom, Duke, & Victor, 2013).

ENHANCEDetext *self-check 11.4*

DIVERSITY IN THE PUBLIC SCHOOL SYSTEM

In virtually every school, some students fit into the mainstream and others do not. It is often the students who do not fit in who are most likely to be vulnerable to scapegoating, bullying, violence, and other psychosocial problems. Students who do not feel safe in school, who are subject to bullying, and who are made to feel like outcasts because of their gender, race, sexual orientation, religion, body type, family constellation, or any other factor that seems to set them apart from the mainstream are at increased risk for academic failure or at least academic difficulty. Although the responsibility for keeping students safe rests with all adults associated with the student—teachers, all school personnel, and even parents—school social workers, school counselors, and school psychologists are in a unique position to identify potential problems related to diversity and difference and intervene by advocating for diverse students.

Working with Racial and Ethnic Minority Populations

Racial and ethnic diversity can be a wonderful asset to any school environment, leading to a richness in experiences for students and teachers alike. But in some school environments, racial prejudice and discrimination can lead to violence and conflict among many within the student population. Students who comprise a part of a racial minority either within the school or within broader society are at risk for academic failure for many reasons including social, economic, and political conditions such as poverty, racial intolerance, and higher rates of violence often associated with the urban school environment discussed earlier in this chapter. For example, a school environment that is hostile to racial and ethnic minorities contributes to the creation of an unsafe school environment where students feel uneasy, unsafe, and unprotected.

School social workers, school counselors, and school psychologists can assist teachers and school administrators in recognizing and addressing racial and ethnic discrimination and prejudice on campus. They can also assist in the development of cultural diversity training focusing on racial and ethnic sensitivity and respect for diversity. Equally important is the cultural competence of the student services team professionals themselves. It is vital that school-based human service providers undergo additional diversity training, focusing on the nature of counseling from a multicultural perspective (Holcomb-McCoy, 2004).

This type of training is particularly important since research shows that traditional counseling theories and interventions are often biased against racial and ethnic minorities, particularly African Americans. For instance, many traditional Euro-American theories tend to pathologize racial minorities rather than recognizing the social oppression that contributes to violence, gang activity, and juvenile delinquency (Fusick & Charkow,

2004). Any theory (or theorist) that disregards the power of long-standing racism and the affect that intergenerational oppression has on a population would be hard pressed to explain why these groups experience significantly higher rates of poverty and violence than other groups that haven't experienced intergenerational racism and oppression. Are the former merely more innately violent? Are they just lazy? Less moral as a whole? Of course the answer is no, which means that credence must be given to the possibility that behavior deemed maladaptive is not solely a result of individual psychopathology, but must be the result of social causes and clinical interpretation as well.

Many of the psychosocial assessment tools used in the public school system (and within the mental health field in general) are also biased against racial and ethnic minorities, having been developed for the assessment and evaluation of the majority culture based upon Caucasian middle-class values (Fusick & Charkow, 2004). Cultural competency training can aid school-based human service providers in assessing the appropriateness of using standard assessment tools and adapting them when possible for racial and ethnic minority populations. This practice will contribute to alleviating the broad-based problem of over-identifying racial and ethnic minority students for social work services due to behavioral problems.

Bias-Based Bullying and Cyberbullying

Bullying within the public school system is gaining increasing attention among the general U.S. population, as well as among school administrators and policymakers on a local and national level. The increased attention is at least in part due to what appears to be a vast increase in bullying incidents, including **bias-based bullying**—bullying based on a federally protected characteristic, such as race/ethnicity, religion, nationality, gender identity/expression, gender, sexual orientation, or disability—and **cyberbullying**—bullying and harassment using an electronic medium, such as texting, instant messaging, or social media.

A recent study found that over a quarter of all U.S. students reported being victims of bullying while at school (over seven million students), and about six percent of U.S. students reported being a victim of cyberbullying on or off campus (just over 1.5 million students) (DeVoe & Murphy, 2011). Whether bullying incidents are actually increasing, or whether reporting rates have increased, remains unclear, but this is an important issue that directly affects the human services profession, particularly those working in schools because about 75 percent of students surveyed have reported they do not know how to report bullying incidents (Asian American Legal Defense and Education Fund, 2009).

Bullying can include name-calling and insults, being the object of rumors, threats of harm, physical assaults (shoving, hitting, tripping, spitting), being purposely excluded from activities, and property destruction. Cyberbullying can include posting hurtful, harassing, and threatening information on the Internet, as well as unwanted contact via email, text, online gaming sites, or other online community such as Facebook. Cyberbullying can also include the purposeful exclusion from an online community, such as a Facebook group (DeVoe & Murphy, 2011).

Bullying of males and females tends to be relatively equal, with slightly more girls than boys being victims of school-based bullying (DeVoe & Murphy, 2011). Students who are perceived as different are at the greatest risk of bullying, particularly those from racial and ethnic minority groups, students of lower socioeconomic status, and students who are perceived to deviate from expected gender norms (whether or not they actually identify as gay or lesbian) (DeVoe & Murphy, 2011; Kosciw, Greytak, Diaz, & Bartkiewicz, 2010), and students who are overweight (Biggs, Simpson, & Gaus, 2009).

Bullying in schools, particularly bias-based bullying, is an important issue for many reasons, but chief among them include evidence that victims being bullied experience both short- and long-term consequences, including poor school performance, depression, and increased health problems (Rigby, 2003). And while research is not conclusive in this area, there is growing evidence that extreme bullying may cause retaliation with devastating consequences. For instance, the U.S. government's bullying website notes that in 12 out of 15 student-initiated campus shootings in the 1990s, the shooters disclosed histories of being bullied, some severely. Research also suggests that many incidents of bullying go unreported to parents and school, which hinders a school's ability to determine the scope of bullying within a school system as well as effectively addressing the problem (Petrosino, Guckenburg, DeVoe, & Hanson, 2010). When bullying is bias-based, the damage to the victim can be even more significant, such as the victim committing suicide, since the target of bullying relates to the victim's identity—race, gender, gender identity, or sexual orientation—something that cannot be changed and something that may make the child or adolescent already feel different and socially isolated.

Although to date there is no federal legislation mandating how schools must respond to bullying, there is considerable encouragement from the White House as well the Department of Education for schools to adopt proactive measures to address bullying on campus, off campus, and online. For instance, in March of 2011 former President Obama and the First Lady reached out to students, parents, educators, and education advocates across the country as well as other concerned parties at the *White House Conference on Bullying Prevention*, acknowledging the very serious nature of school bullying, and announcing several programs designed to assist schools, nonprofit organizations, and other advocates in putting a stop to bullying, both on campus as well as in cyberspace. The StopBullying website was launched as a part of this conference, providing information from numerous government agencies on the nature of bullying, including bullying prevention and intervention strategies.

School-based human service providers are aptly placed to be leaders in the fight against bullying, but far too often they lack the training and resources to effectively address bullying on a macro and micro level. For instance, in a recent study on cyberbullying about half of social workers surveyed reported they felt ambivalent about their role in addressing cyberbullying, despite the majority reporting their recognition of the seriousness of this form of bullying (Slovak & Singer, 2011). Other research indicates that a part of the challenge in effectively addressing school bullying, including cyberbullying, involves a lack of clear school policies and a general lack of training in managing all aspects of the school bullying problem (Mason, 2008).

Biggs, Simpson, and Gaus (2009) recommend that school-based human service providers develop a strategy to address school bullying that involves a multidisciplinary team approach, using a strengths-based perspective. The team approach allows each professional distinction to provide support for the others on the team, as well as serving as inter-disciplinary consultants sharing resources from a variety of professional perspectives. Most anti-bullying prevention programs are based on a combination of education, awareness, and outreach, such as the Pink Shirt Day anti-bullying campaign, Project Change, use of anti-bullying posters as educational tools, and hosting an anti-bullying workshop with speakers.

Watch the video about Rebecca Preston's experience of being cyberbullied after she came out at the age of 13. What do you believe student support team members can and should do to ensure that cyberbullying does not occur among their student population, even if the cyberbullying occurs outside of school time?

ENHANCEDetext *video example 11.5*

www.youtube.com/
watch?v=bPw9GQi4fMQ

Lesbian, Gay, Bisexual, Transgendered, and Questioning Youth

Students who are in the sexual minority—such as lesbian, gay, bisexual, transgendered youth, those students who are questioning their sexuality in some way, and other sexual minorities (LGBTQ+)—are often the victims of bias-based bullying, including verbal and physical violence. Many of these children spend a considerable amount of time feeling different and isolated, often believing that no one will understand their feelings and accept them unconditionally. Such individuals have an alarmingly high rate of suicide attempts, with over 30 percent admitting to having attempted suicide at some point in their lives. Approximately 75 percent of LGBTQ+ students admit to having been verbally abused at school and over 15 percent have been physically abused (Pope, 2003).

Most of the youth in Pope's study reported that the violence they experienced was a direct result of their sexual orientation, with boys being abused more often than girls. Pope discussed this type of abuse in terms of the pressure on most high school students to conform to the norms of their peer group. When faced with the overwhelming demands to be just like everyone else, students who stand out because they look or act differently can quickly become outcasts. In 2009, the advocacy organization Gay, Lesbian and Straight Educational Network (GLSEN) conducted a national survey of LGBTQ+ students about their experiences with the following issues:

- hearing biased and homophobic remarks in school;
- feeling unsafe in school because of personal characteristics, such as sexual orientation, gender expression, or race/ethnicity;
- missing classes or days of school because of safety reasons; and
- experiences of harassment and assault in school.

The results of the study found that a significant majority of LGBTQ+ students experience verbal and physical harassment on a daily basis in school, with little to any intervention or advocacy on the part of school personnel. For instance, between 75 percent and 90 percent of LGBTQ+ students surveyed heard homophobic terms used in a derogatory manner, such as "gay," "dyke," and "faggot," in school, and most respondents reported feeling distress in response. Almost 85 percent reported that they had been verbally harassed at school due to their sexual orientation, and almost as many reported that they'd been verbally harassed because of their gender expression (not being feminine or masculine enough). About 40 percent of respondents reported that they had been victims of physical harassment at school because of their sexual orientation and about 20 percent were physically assaulted. Over 50 percent of respondents were victims of cyberbullying and harassment through text messaging, emails, and social media. In most of these cases, there was little to no response on the part of school personnel, leaving the majority of these students feeling very unsafe in their respective school environments.

The report details the most frequent consequences of these various types of bullying related to a student's sexual orientation and gender expression, including higher-than-average school absenteeism, lower educational achievement, and a negative impact on their psychological well-being (higher rates of depression, anxiety, and lower levels of self-esteem). GLSEN recommends that schools offer **gay-straight alliance clubs (GSAs)**, inclusive curriculum (course curriculum that includes positive representations of LGBTQ+ people and events, currently and historically), supportive educators (training educators in LGBTQ+ awareness and advocacy), and the incorporation of strict bullying and harassment legislation and policies. Schools that had incorporated these remedies show marked reductions in LGBTQ+ bias-based bullying (Kosciw, Greytak, Diaz, & Bartkiewicz, 2010).

It is vital that school-based human service providers address the harassment that so many gay and lesbian students experience on a daily basis in the public school system and help to develop programs to combat poor treatment of students in the sexual minority. The first step in this effort is to establish a *zero-tolerance policy*, where teachers, school administrators, and student services team professionals make it clear to the student population through policy and action that harassment will not be tolerated in any respect. Developing a plan for making school safe for all vulnerable students begins with the education of school personnel.

School social workers, school counselors, and school psychologists are the ideal candidates to educate both school staff and students on the importance of accepting diversity. Such a program must begin with the school staff, particularly the teachers, who are most likely to be present when the abuse of LBGTQ+ students occurs. The focus of such programs center on a belief that regardless of personal opinion respect for human dignity and everyone's basic right to self-determination cannot be compromised.

A particularly effective program facilitated by schools across the nation is called the Making Schools Safe project (Otto, Middleton, & Freker, 2002). This program was developed by the American Civil Liberties Union (ACLU) and was designed to combat antigay harassment on school campuses. The ACLU recommends that all teachers and administrators use this curriculum, which focuses on the importance of creating a safe learning environment for all children by challenging the status quo that exists on many school campuses, ranging from overt bullying to more subtle forms of harassment, such as the generalized use of the word "gay" and other terms deemed derogatory and offensive to the LGBTQ+ population.

Terrorism and "Islamophobia"

In the wake of the September 11, 2001, terrorist attacks in New York and Washington, D.C. the media was filled with reports of potential future attacks, many of which have since come to fruition. Many school districts scrambled to develop programs to address students' feelings about the attacks and their concerns about future attacks, particularly for students close to the origin of the attacks (Calderoni, Alderman, Silver, & Bauman, 2006). Programs were also developed to prevent bias-based bullying and scapegoating of Muslim students (Zempi, 2014).

The events of September 11, 2001, were difficult for adults, but were particularly hard on children, many of whom lacked the ability to effectively communicate their feelings. A 2004 study found that about 65 percent of students experienced moderate to high levels of distress in the weeks following the attacks (Auger, Seymour, Roberts, & Waiter, 2004). The most frequently reported symptoms included fear, worry, anxiety, sadness, anger, and aggression. Students who were personally affected by terrorist attacks or who were already suffering from some mental health issues, such as depression, were the most at risk for developing symptoms consistent with PTSD. Auger et al. (2004) also noted that although many schools took appropriate action in responding to students' needs, 12 percent took no responsive action. In addition, the majority of the schools surveyed took no action to assist school personnel in dealing with their own feelings about increases in terrorism. In fact, over one-third of school counselors stated that they did not feel prepared to respond to a serious trauma, suggesting that ongoing training of all school personnel is essential.

There have been many long-term consequences to terrorist attacks but one particularly troubling reaction is a marked increase in what is called **Islamophobia**—the irrational fear and hatred of Muslims (or those perceived to be Muslims) (Conway, 1997). A 2011 policy brief published by the Institute for Social Policy and Understanding states that bullying of Muslim children in school environments is on the rise since the September 11, 2001, terrorist attacks (Britto, 2011). While the increase in bias-based bullying is on the rise in general, this brief identifies that the chief reason why Muslim children are being bullied is due to a pervasive misperceptions about the Muslim community and negative stereotypes about Muslims in general. Britto cites the influence of the media on the attitudes of non-Muslim youth, which frequently depict all Muslims as potential terrorists and ideological extremists.

Some examples of Islamophobia include making constant references to Muslim children as being terrorists, and making jokes about Muslim children and their families making bombs (Abdelkader, 2011). Such bias-based bullying should not be tolerated and school-based human service providers, in coordination with teachers, school administrators, parents, and other students, can counteract Islamophobia through the implementation of educational programs designed to increase awareness of the diversity within mainstream Muslims, both in the United States and abroad.

The Plight of Urban Schools

The plight of urban schools has received considerable attention in the past several years due to a range of socioeconomic problems. In response to these concerns, the Education Trust, a not-for-profit agency committed to working for high academic

© DAVID MCNEW / GETTY IMAGES

Many urban schools have a police presence on campus to monitor student activity, including dress codes

achievement among all children, has made numerous recommendations regarding school mental health programs, including developing systematic programs designed to address many of the issues currently confronting urban schools, such as gang activity, poverty, homelessness, child abuse, violence on and off campus, increasing rates of clinical depression, unplanned pregnancy, and low academic performance (Baggerly & Borkowski, 2004; Holcomb-McCoy, 2005; Lee, 2005). In addition, urban schools face what is referred to as an achievement gap when compared to suburban youth. Urban youth are far more likely to drop out of high school and are less likely to meet the minimum standard on national standardized tests. Urban schools have far greater difficulty retaining quality teachers, must contend with political issues often not confronting suburban schools, and are often located in high-crime areas of concentrated poverty (Olson & Jerald, 1998).

Other issues facing urban schools and, thus, school social workers, school counselors, and school psychologists working in these settings include dealing with high student absenteeism and unstable family systems, including a high percentage of students living in foster care and high student transience, where students transfer in and out of school frequently (Green, Conley, & Barnett, 2005; Lee, 2005). Increased funding for prevention programs and an increase in mental health services can be effective measures in combating many socioeconomic challenges experienced by urban youth. By creating community partnerships and establishing strong ties within the communities of concern, including partnering with area human service agencies, law enforcement, and even local government agencies, schools can be active partners in finding long-term solutions to chronic problems within many urban communities.

ENHANCEDetext *self-check 11.5*

CONCLUSION

The need for mental health services and psychosocial support in public school settings has never been greater (Johnson, Oliff, & Williams, 2011). Teachers are increasingly reporting that children with behavioral problems fare worse in their academic performance and overall school adjustment (Baker, Kamphaus, Home, & Winsor, 2006). For instance, poverty is known to increase psychosocial problems in children (Smith, Stagman, Blank, Ong, & McDow, 2011), and child poverty has increased markedly in recent years, particularly between 2000 and 2013 (Fanjul, 2014; Wight, Chau, & Aratani, 2011). Other psychosocial issues that can present barriers to academic achievement include mental health problems, community and neighborhood crime, bias-based bullying, and a whole host of other dynamics plaguing our school systems.

It is with the complexity of student psychosocial challenges in mind that there has been an increased focus on ways in which school social workers, school counselors, and school psychologists can move beyond mere cooperation toward real collaboration (Kim, 2012). Collaboration within a public school context is defined as a process where professionals within each discipline (school social work, school counselor, and school psychology) provide reciprocal information, informing mutual understanding of the client(s) while acknowledging the expertise and roles played by each respective profession (Axelsson & Axelsson, 2009).

There is the increased need for interprofessional collaboration not only due to shrinking budgets (requiring the pooling of resources) but also because of a national movement toward school-based mental health programs that are dependent on professionals from each helping profession to work together more effectively (Kim, 2012). An example is the Expanded School Mental Health (ESMH), a three-tiered framework incorporating prevention, early intervention, and treatment. The ESMH framework expands on existing core mental health services provided in the public school system, and emphasizes shared responsibility among all school service professionals, as well as community mental health providers. Recognizing the vital role that each student services team member plays in the public school system in addressing children's mental and psychosocial well-being is important because working together to remove barriers to learning offers students their best opportunity for academic success.

SUMMARY

- The nature of school social work in the public school system, including the duties, roles, and functions of a school social worker, is explored. The history of the visiting teacher movement and the roots of social work in the settlement house movement are explored within the context of how the profession evolved into the career today. Ethical dilemmas facing many school social workers are also explored.
- The nature of school counseling in the public school system, including the duties, roles, and functions of a school counselor, is explored. The history of the school counseling profession's roots in academic guidance and its evolution to a broader focus to include psychosocial counseling and support is discussed. Ethical dilemmas facing many school counselors are also explored.
- The nature of school psychology in the public school system, including the duties, roles, and functions of a school psychologist, is explored. The duties of school psychologists in the public school system and their role on the student services team, including their expanding role beyond academic testing, are discussed.
- Responses of school-based human service providers to mental health challenges, such as depression and substance abuse, are examined. The way in which mental health concerns create barriers to student academic achievement is explored, with a focus on how student services teams collaborate to support students with mental health care concerns and other psychosocial challenges, such as depression, substance abuse, and teen pregnancy.
- The ways in which school-based human service providers become culturally competent in working with and advocating on behalf of diverse student populations are explored. Issues related to diversity in the public school system, with a focus on how school social workers, school counselors, and school psychologists collaborate to create safe and bias-free learning environments, are examined. Cultural competence within the context of working with ethnic minority populations is explored, as well as how school-based human service providers respond to a range of challenges in public school settings, such as bias-based bullying, cyberbullying, disparate treatment of LGBTQ+ students, and challenges in urban school settings.

Internet Resources

Conduct an Internet search for the American School Counselor Association, navigate to School Counselors and Members, and then Legal and Ethical, and click on Ethical Standards for School Counselors.

Conduct an Internet search for the National Association of School Psychologists, navigate to About School Psychology, and click on Who Are School Psychologists?

Conduct an Internet search for the School Social Work Association of America, navigate to the About Us tab, then click on About School Social Work (SSW), and then click on the National School Social Work Practice Model.

Conduct an Internet search for the National Association of School Social Workers and search for School Social Work.

References

Abdelkader, E. (2011, October 24). Islamophobic bullying in our schools. Huffington Post: Religion.

Abrams, K., Theberge, S. K., & Karan, O. C. (2005). Children and adolescents who are depressed: An ecological approach. *Professional School Counseling*, 8(3), 284–292.

American School Counselor Association [ASCA]. (2012). *The ASCA national model: A framework for school counseling programs, Third Edition*. Alexandria, VA: Author.

Asian American Legal Defense and Education Fund. (2009). Bias-based harassment in New York City public schools: A report card on the Department of Education's implementation of chancellor's regulation A-832. Retrieved from http://www.aaldef.org/Bias-based-Harassment-in-NYC-Public-Schools.pdf

Auger, R. W. (2005). School-based interventions for students with depressive disorders. *Professional School Counseling*, 8(4), 344–352.

Auger, R. W., Seymour, J. W., Roberts, W. B., & Waiter, B. (2004). Responding to terror: The impact of September 11 on K-12 schools and schools' responses. *Professional School Counseling*, 7(4), 222–230.

Axelsson, S. B., & Axelsson, R. (2009). From territoriality to altruism in interprofessional collaboration and leadership. *Journal of Interprofessional Care*, 23(4), 320–330. doi:10.1080/13561820902921811

Baggerly, J., & Borkowski, T. (2004). Applying the ASCA national model to elementary school students who are homeless: A case study. *Professional School Counseling*, 8(2), 116–124.

Baker, J. A., Kamphaus, R. W., Horne, A. M., & Winsor, A. P. (2006). Evidence for population-based perspectives on children's behavioral adjustment and needs for service delivery in schools. *School Psychology Review*, 35(1), 31.

Barnett, J. E. (2006). Evaluating "baby think it over" infant simulators: A comparison group study. *Adolescence*, 41(161), 103.

Biggs, M. J. G., Simpson, C. G., & Gaus, M. D. (2009). A case of bullying: Bringing together the disciplines. *Children and Schools*, 31(1), 39.

Borkowski, J. W., & Sorensen, L. E. (2009). *Legal issues for school districts related to the education of undocumented students*. Alexandria, VA: National School Boards Association. Retrieved from http://www.nsba.org/SchoolLaw/COSA/Search/AllCOSAdocuments/Undocumented-Children.pdf

Britto, R. (2011). Global battleground or school playground: the bullying of America's Muslim children, Policy Brief #49. Washington, D.C.: Institute for Social Policy and Understanding. Retrieved from http://ispu.org/pdfs/ISPU_Policy%20Brief_Britto_WEB.pdf

Calderoni, M. E., Alderman, E. M., Silver, E. J., & Bauman, L. J. (2006). The mental health impact of 9/11 on inner-city high school students 20 miles north of Ground Zero. *Journal of Adolescent Health*, 39(1), 57–65.

Center for Behavioral Health Statistics and Quality. (2015). *Behavioral health trends in the United States: Results from the 2014 National Survey on Drug Use and Health* (HHS Publication No. SMA 15-4927, NSDUH Series H-50). Retrieved from http://www.samhsa.gov/data/

Conway, G. (1997). *Islamophobia: A challenge for us all*. London: Runnymede Trust.

Corcoran, J., Franklin, C., & Bennett, P. (2000). Ecological factors associated with adolescent pregnancy and parenting. *Social Work Research*, 24(1), 29–39.

Dahir, C. A. (2001). The national standards for school counseling programs: Development and implementation. *Professional School Counseling*, 4(5), 320–327.

Dahir, C. A., & Stone, C. B. (2006). Preparing the next generation: Implementing new paradigms for school counseling preservice and practice. *Vistas: Compelling Perspectives on Counseling, 43–47.*

DeVoe, J., & Murphy, C. (2011). Student reports of bullying and cyber-bullying: Results from the 2009 school crime supplement to the National Crime Victimization Survey. Web Tables. NCES 2011-336. *National Center for Education Statistics.*

Fanjul, G. (2014). *Children of the recession: the impact of the economic crisis on child well-being in rich countries,* UNICEF (No. inreca733). Retrieved from https://www.unicef-irc.org/publications/pdf/rc12-eng-web.pdf.

Frueh, B. C., Knapp, R. G., Cusack, K. J., Grubaugh, A. L., Sauvageot, J. A., Cousins, V. C., & Hiers, T. G. (2005). Special section on seclusion and restraint: Patients' reports of traumatic or harmful experiences within the psychiatric setting. *Psychiatric Services.*

Fusick, L., & Charkow, B. (2004). Counseling at-risk Afro-American youth: An examination of contemporary issues and effective school-based strategies. *Professional School Counseling, 8*(2), 102–116.

Garvey, M. (2005, September). Preggo high school: Kids are readin', writin' & reproducin'. *New York Post,* p. 19.

Green, A. G., Conley, J. A., & Barnett, K. (2005). Urban school counseling: Implications for practice and training. *Professional School Counseling, 8*(3), 189–195.

Greene, J. P., & Forster, G. (2004). *Sex, drugs, and delinquency in urban and suburban public schools* (Education Working Paper 4). New York, NY: Center for Civic Innovation, Manhattan Institute. (ERIC Document Reproduction Service No. ED483335)

Hamilton, B. E., Martin, J. A., Osterman, M. J. K., et al. (2015). Births: Final data for 2014. *National Vital Statistics Reports, 64*(12). Hyattsville, MD: National Center for Health Statistics.

Holcomb-McCoy, C. C. (2004). Assessing the multicultural competence of school counselors: A checklist. *Professional School Counseling, 7*(3), 178–186.

Holcomb-McCoy, C. C. (2005). Investigating school counselors' perceived multicultural competence. *Professional School Counseling, 8*(5), 414–423.

Individuals with Disabilities Education Improvement Act of 2004, Pub. L. 108-446. 118 Stat. 2647. (2006).

Iyer, N. N., & Baxter-MacGregor, J. (2010). Ethical dilemmas for the school counselor: Balancing student confidentiality and parents' right to know.

Johnson, N., Oliff, P., & Williams, E. (2011). An update on state budget cuts. *Center on Budget and Policy Priorities. Updated February, 9.*

Kim, A. J. (2012). *Interdisciplinary collaboration in school social work: building relationships for ecological change.* Doctoral dissertation.

Kirby, D. (2002). Effective approaches to reducing adolescent unprotected sex, pregnancy and childbearing. *Journal of Sex Research, 39*(1), 51–57.

Koppelman, J. (2004). Children with mental health disorders: Making sense of their needs and the systems that help them. *National Health Policy Forum Issue Brief, 799,* 1–24.

Kosciw, J. G., Greytak, E. A., Diaz, E. M., & Bartkiewicz, M. J. (2010). *The 2009 National School Climate Survey: The experiences of lesbian, gay, bisexual, and transgender youth in our nation's schools.* New York, NY: GLSEN.

Lambie, G. W., & Rokutani, L. J. (2002). A systems approach to substance abuse identification and intervention for school counselors. *Professional School Counseling, 5*(5), 353–359.

Lambie, G. W., & Sias, S. (2005). Children of alcoholics: Implications for professional school counseling. *Professional School Counseling, 8*(3), 266–273.

Lambie, G. W., & Williamson, L. L. (2004). The challenge to change from guidance counseling to professional school counseling: A historical proposition. *Professional School Counseling, 8*(2), 124–131.

Lapan, R. T., Gysbers, N. C., & Kayson, K. (2007). *How implementing comprehensive guidance programs improves academic achievement for all Missouri students.* Jefferson City, MO: Missouri Department of Elementary and Secondary Education, Division of Career Education.

Lee, C. C. (2005). Urban school counseling: Context, characteristics, and competencies. *Professional School Counseling, 8*(3), 184–188.

Lewis, M. R. (1998). The many faces of school social work practice: Results from a research partnership. *Social Work in Education, 20*(3), 177–190.

Mason, K. L. (2008). Cyberbullying: A preliminary assessment for school personnel. *Psychology in the Schools, 45*(4), 323–348.

McCullagh, J. G. (1993). The roots of school social work in New York City. *Iowa Journal of School Social Work, 6,* 49–74.

McCullagh, J. G. (1998). Early school social work leaders: Women forgotten by the profession. *Social Work in Education, 20*(1), 55–64.

National Association of School Psychologists. (2010). Principles for professional ethics. Retrieved from https://www.nasponline.org/assets/Documents/Standards%20and%20Certification/Standards/1_%20Ethical%20Principles.pdf

National Association of Social Workers. (2008). *NASW standards for school social work services*. Washington, DC: Author.

No Child Left Behind Act of 2001, Pub. L. 107–110., 115 Stat. 1425 (2002).

Nystrom, R. J., Duke, J. E., & Victor, B. (2013). Shifting the paradigm in Oregon from teen pregnancy prevention to youth sexual health. *Public Health Reports,* 89–95.

Olson, L., & Jerald, C. D. (1998). *Quality counts '98: The urban picture.* Retrieved from http://rc-archive.edweek.org/sreports/qc98/challenges/tables/ta-n.htm

Otto, N., Middleton, J., & Freker, J. (2002). *Making schools safe: An anti-harassment program from the Lesbian & Gay Rights project of the American Civil Liberties Union.* New York, NY: Lesbian & Gay Rights Project, American Civil Liberties Union. (ERIC Document Reproduction Service No. ED475274).

Petrosino, A., Guckenburg, S., DeVoe, J., & Hanson, T. (2010). What characteristics of bullying, bullying victims, and schools are associated with increased reporting of bullying to school officials? Issues & Answers. REL 2010-No. 092. *Regional Educational Laboratory Northeast & Islands.*

Piercy, F. P., Volk, R. J., Trepper, T., Sprenkle, D. H., & Lewis, R. (1991). The relationship of family factors to patterns of adolescent substance abuse. *Family Dynamics of Addiction Quarterly, 1*(1), 41–54.

Pope, M. (2003). *Sexual minority youth in the schools: Issues and desirable counselor responses.* Information Analysis. (ERIC Document Reproduction Service No. ED480481).

Rigby, K. (2003). Consequences of bullying in schools. *The Canadian Journal of Psychiatry, 48*(9), 583–590.

Rostosky, S. S., Regnerus, M. D., & Wright, M. L. C. (2003). Coital debut: The role of religiosity and sex attitudes in the add health survey. *Journal of Sex Research, 40*(4), 358–367.

Rumberger, R. W., Larson, K. A., Ream, R. K., & Palardy, G. J. (1999). *The educational consequences of mobility for California students and schools.* Berkeley, CA: Policy Analysis for California Education. (ERIC Document Reproduction Service No. ED441040).

Ryan, J., & Peterson, R. (2004). Physical restraint in school. *Behavioral Disorders, 29*(2), 154–168.

Scheuermann, B., Peterson, R., Ryan, J. B., & Billingsley, G. (2015). Professional practice and ethical issues related to physical restraint and seclusion in schools. *Journal of Disability Policy Studies,* 1044207315604366.

Schmidt, J. J., & Ciechalski, J. C. (2001). School counseling standards: A summary and comparison with other student services' standards. *Professional School Counseling, 4*(5), 328–333.

Slovak, K., & Singer, J. B. (2011). School social workers' perceptions of cyberbullying. *Children and Schools, 33*(1), 5–16.

Smith, S., Stagman, S. M., Blank, S., Ong, C., & McDow, K. (2011). Building strong systems of support for young children's mental health: Key strategies for states and a planning tool.

Somers, C. L., & Fahlman, M. M. (2001). Effectiveness of the "baby think it over" teen pregnancy prevention program. *Journal of School Health, 71*(5), 188–195.

Somers, C. L., Johnson, S. A., & Sawilowsky, S. S. (2002). A measure for evaluating the effectiveness of teen pregnancy prevention programs. *Psychology in the Schools, 39*(3), 337–342.

Stone, C. (2011, July). Boundary crossing: The slippery slope. ACSA School Counselor. Retrieved January 27, 2012, from http://www.ascaschoolcounselor.org/article_content.asp?edition=91&section=140&article=1221

Stueve, A., & O'Donnell, L. N. (2005). Early alcohol initiation and subsequent sexual and alcohol risk behaviors among urban youths. *American Journal of Public Health, 95*(5), 887–893.

Terry, P. (1925). Review: The visiting teacher movement, with special reference to administrative relationships by Julius John Oppenheimer. *The Elementary School Journal, 26*(4), 313–315.

Toups, M. L., & Holmes, W. R. (2002). Effectiveness of abstinence-based sex education curricula: A review. *Counseling and Values, 46*(3), 237–240.

Trenholm, C., Devaney, B., Fortson, K., Quay, K., Wheeler, J., & Clark, M. (2007). *Impacts of Four Title V, Section 510 Abstinence Education Programs. Final Report.* Mathematica Policy Research, Inc.

Vanderbleek, L. M. (2004). Engaging families in school-based mental health treatment. *Journal of Mental Health Counseling, 26*(3), 211–224.

Wight, V., Chau, M. M., & Aratani, Y. (2011). Who are America's poor children? The official story. National Center for Children in Poverty. Retrieved from http://www.nccp.org/publications/pub_1001.html

Yankouski, B., Masserelli, T., & Lee, S. (2012, December). Ethical issues regarding the use of restraint and seclusion in schools (Practice Forum). Washington, DC: Division of School Psychology, American Psychological Association. Retrieved from http://www.apadivisions.org/division-16/publications/newsletters/school-psychologist/2012/12/restraint-in-schools.aspx

Young, T., Turner, J., Denny, G., & Young, M. (2004). Examining external and internal poverty as antecedents of teen pregnancy. *American Journal of Behavior, 28*(4), 361–373.

Zempi, I. (2014). Responding to the needs of victims of Islamophobia. *Responding to Hate Crime: The Case for Connecting Policy and Research,* 113.

12

Religion, Spirituality, and Faith-Based Agencies

© MARK SKALNY / SHUTTERSTOCK

Helping the poor and those in need is integral to many faith traditions. In fact, religious institutions have a long history of caring for the poor and disadvantaged, providing counsel to those in pain, and responding in times of crisis. Who is helped and how the help is provided has been highly influenced by religious teachings, particularly teachings within the **Judeo-Christian** traditions, and then reinforced by church authorities. A policy of charity is not limited to Judeo-Christian faiths though; in fact, most religions and faith traditions include charity as a requirement of faith, not only in the form of financial assistance but also through compassionate service and kindness.

THE ROLE OF RELIGION AND SPIRITUALITY IN HUMAN SERVICES

Spirituality is a part of everyday life for many people. In fact, research studies have shown that between 80 and 90 percent of people identify themselves as being either religious or spiritual, stating that their faith is an important aspect of their daily lives (Gallup & Lindsey, 1999; Grossman, 2002). Faith provides people comfort during difficult times, binds people together, and provides communities with a framework for coming together and depending on one another during good times and bad. And yet despite the core role that religion and spirituality play in the lives of so many people, the human service profession as a whole has been rather reluctant to incorporate faith and spirituality into practice. Perhaps this reticence is out of a fear that practitioners will be too directive, thus robbing clients of their right to self-determination, or perhaps there is simply a lack of knowledge about how practitioners can integrate spirituality in practice well, particularly if they are not religious or practice a religion that differs from their client.

Integrating Christianity into human services practice has been of particular concern to human service professionals since Christianity is the dominant faith tradition in the United States. Yet, in light of the fact that such a high percentage of people cite faith as integral to their identity and a primary source of support during difficult times, many within the human service profession have acknowledged that exploring this area has merit.

Integrating faith and spirituality into practice is a broad topic and often means something different to different people. For instance, there are many faith-based agencies in the United States, but not all faith-based agencies provide services that are religious and/or spiritual in nature. Similarly, not all mental health counselors who provide spiritual or faith-based counseling work with faith-based agencies. In fact, in many instances, it would be difficult to determine any substantive difference between the services provided by a secular agency and those provided by a faith-based agency. And yet some faith-based agencies do operate from a distinctly religious value system, and some providers integrate faith in their practice in a range of ways.

Religion or religiousness is not the same as **spirituality** though. Religiousness is often defined as a social or cultural experience grounded in a religious tradition, whereas spirituality is often defined as the experience of having an independent relationship with a deity, involving a search for the sacred—a process that involves seeking out that which is considered holy or the divine (Miller & Thoresen, 2003; Pargament & Mahoney, 2009). Of course, people can be religious *and* spiritual (searching for the divine within the context of a particular religious tradition), religious without being particularly spiritual (a cultural or secular involvement in a religious faith), or spiritual without being grounded in a particular religious tradition (searching for the divine within the context of various spiritual practices), such as **New Age spirituality** or **Eastern religious philosophies**. When clients use these terms, it's important for human service providers to explore what religiousness and spirituality mean to them, so that everyone is speaking the same language.

Several research studies in the last two decades have focused on the mind–body–soul connection in an attempt to understand the reciprocal relationship of each, with a specific focus on how spirituality affects an individual's overall physical and mental well-being (Idler & Kasl, 1992; Koenig et al., 1998; Koenig, Larson, & Weaver, 1998; McLaughlin, 2004; Powell, Shahabi, & Thoresen, 2003). What has been found in most of these studies is that personal spirituality has been linked to a decrease in depression, an increase in greater social support, an increase in cognitive functioning (Koenig, George, & Titus, 2004), an improvement in the ability to cope with crises (McLaughlin, 2004), and a better ability to cope with substance abuse problems (Fallot & Heckman, 2005). So it would seem that having a relationship with a faith community and believing in something bigger than ourselves is good for our physical health, our mental health, and our psychosocial well-being.

It is quite likely that as human service providers we will serve our clients more effectively if we can accompany them on *their* faith journey, at least to some extent. Several research studies suggest that counselors should acknowledge and address the religious and spiritual dimensions of mental and emotional disorders within the counseling relationship, particularly if clients identify themselves as being spiritually grounded, at least to some extent (Fallot, 2001; Kliewer, 2004; Miller, Korinek, & Ivey, 2004). And yet, as much as incorporating spirituality into the counseling relationship may be helpful for many clients, there is also the potential for harm, particularly when the religion of a provider is pushed onto a client in a directive manner.

The question pertinent to all human service providers then is to how to remain client-centered while incorporating spirituality into practice. This process will undoubtedly involve engaging in some conceptual or paradigm shifts, from a Western model to a more holistic one. Traditionally, the mental health and medical communities in Western societies have had a tendency to divide human beings into biological, intellectual, social, emotional, and spiritual domains, with minimal recognition of how each of these dimensions interacts with the other. But in recent years there has been a growing interest, both within professional circles and within the general public, in moving away from such a compartmentalized view of the human experience, and toward regarding humans more holistically, where one is considered as a whole with each part or dimension of the person being inextricably interwoven with the others.

Essentially, a holistic approach to psychosocial health involves the process of acknowledging, addressing, and evaluating the mind, the body, and the spirit (or soul) when considering issues affecting one's psychosocial functioning. In other words, rather than attempting to determine whether depression is a biological disorder with psychological manifestations or a psychological disorder with biological implications, depression would be considered a condition having a reciprocal impact on the whole person: mind, body, and soul.

Cultural Competency and Religious Literacy

Religious values and ethics are core components of many religious faiths, and it is important to have a basic working understanding of the values of various religions in the event that a human service provider works with clients who practice a different faith. Possessing inter-faith competency and religious literacy will enhance the human service provider's ability to provide faith-based or spiritual counseling by enabling them to move beyond their own belief system. It's also important to move beyond the common negative stereotypes of other religions and denominations and see the value of religious diversity. Incorporating spirituality into a counseling relationship requires counseling skills reflecting cultural competence, as well as religious literacy, because many religious traditions are rooted in cultural tradition.

A human service provider who does not possess cultural competence risks inflicting harm onto the client, even if the harm is unintentional. For instance, the human service provider may feel unprepared to address the client's spiritual needs, and in response, may simply ignore the client's references to spiritual matters, which may result in the client feeling ashamed or trivialized. Prior to the recent surge of interest in **holistic health**, practitioners in the West were often dismissive of Eastern philosophies, which have acknowledged the mind–body–soul connection for centuries (Tseng, 2004), rendering many in the human services profession ill-equipped to provide effective services to Asian clients (for instance) from Buddhist or Hindu traditions (Hodge, 2004).

A more overt form of lacking cultural competence is when human service providers are inappropriately directive in pushing their religious beliefs onto their clients. This can be particularly egregious if the human service provider is a member of the dominant culture and practices the dominant religion and is providing human services to members of a minority religious group. Cultural competence in religion and spirituality requires that human service providers practice religious humility, sensitivity, and receptivity, integrating spirituality into their practice in a way that is client-driven and client-centered (Hall, Dixon, & Mauzey, 2004).

ENHANCEDetext *self-check 12.1*

THE NATURE OF FAITH-BASED HUMAN SERVICE DELIVERY

Human service providers can incorporate matters of spirituality in virtually any practice setting in response to their clients' disclosure that faith is an integral part of their lives or something they wish to explore. In addition, there are thousands of faith-based agencies that operate locally and globally, providing valuable services to a range of populations in need. Human service providers who work with these agencies may or may not practice the same faith as the agency, and the populations served may or may not practice the same religion. Some faith-based agencies incorporate spirituality into practice and some do not. This all leads to the logical question then of what, if anything, makes a faith-based organization different—in nature and service delivery—than a secular agency.

It's easy to identify a faith-based agency when it's a synagogue, church, or mosque filled with religious symbols and a mission statement that identifies serving God as a primary function and purpose of the organization. But what about agencies that are **parachurch organizations** that do not function as churches but more as a human services agencies? Or human services agencies that have their roots in a particular religious tradition but don't integrate religion or faith into practice? Would those agencies be considered "faith based"? These are more challenging questions than they might appear when the courts are not particularly clear on what makes a human service organization religious or faith-based in nature (Ebaugh, Pipes, Chafetz, & Daniels, 2003).

The difficulty lies in the fact that many secular agencies provide almost identical services as faith-based agencies and there is often no distinguishable difference between the two. Policy makers, social scientists, and historians have defined faith-based organizations in various ways in the past, with most criteria relating to an organization's dependency on religious entities or denominations for financial support, whether the **mission statement** identifies agency goals that reflect core values that are religious in nature, and whether the employees of the organization are religious and adhere to a **statement of faith** (Ebaugh et al., 2003).

However *faith based* is defined, it is important to remember that a faith-based agency does not necessarily mean Christian, as might be presumed in many Western countries, such as the United States. In fact, a number of religiously oriented agencies provide faith-based human services grounded in faiths other than Christianity. Thus, although it is true that the majority of faith-based agencies in the United States are Christian in nature, many are not. Faith-based agencies may be Jewish, Christian, Muslim, Buddhist, Hindu, or **interfaith**, each serving communities either broadly or electing to serve only individuals of that particular faith.

Faith-based human services can be facilitated as a ministry of a house of worship, such as a synagogue or church counseling center or food bank, or they can be facilitated as a program within a religious organization that functions as a distinct agency, such as the Salvation Army. Some faith-based agencies have the goal of converting clients to that particular faith (evangelism), believing that conversion is the first step toward wholeness, or they might deliver human services in a manner consistent with the agency's mission—justice, compassion, and kindness, for instance—without integrating religion into practice. It's important for human service providers to be aware of the church or agency's mission because it will have a significant impact on how human services are delivered.

Federal Funding of Faith-Based Agencies

Historically, it has been difficult, if not impossible, for a faith-based agency to receive government funding. The Fourth Amendment of the U.S. Constitution, which guarantees freedom of worship, has been interpreted by the courts to mean there must be a separation between government and religion. Thus, unless the agency operated as a secular organization and did not incorporate faith into practice, for the most part it could not receive government funding. The government remains sensitive to those members of society who do not share the same faith as the majority culture and, as such, attempts to protect these individuals with policies and legislation that ensure equity in access and services for those who do not practice a particular faith, or are members of a religious minority.

In 2001, then president George W. Bush signed the Faith-Based Community Initiatives Act, also known as Charitable Choice, or Care Services Act (CSA), which made it easier for faith-based agencies to receive federal funding as long as religious worship, religious instruction, or **proselytizing** was not a part of service provision (at least within the aspect of the agency or program seeking federal funding). Many saw this as a positive step toward reengaging religious organizations in the care of those in need, though yet others expressed concern that the CSA would remove the federal government as the primary entity responsible for human service provision.

While acknowledging the important role of faith-based agencies in human service provision, critics recalled the history of some faith-based organizations enforcing arbitrary conditions on service delivery based on religious or moral grounds. These practices directly or indirectly discriminated against certain groups, such as gays and lesbians, single parents, the poor, or individuals who embraced different values than the majority population, such as indigenous populations (National Association of Social Workers [NASW], 2002).

Some might question whether there is anything inherently wrong in making services contingent on the performance of some behavior. Do compliance-based services rob clients of self-determination and risk, forcing culturally based moral values on those who do not share these same social mores? Take, for example, single women in the 1940s and 1950s who had children out of wedlock. It was not uncommon for these women to have services denied to them unless they agreed to place their babies for adoption—a practice based on the culturally rooted moral belief that premarital sex was wrong and that it would be immoral for a single mother to raise an out-of-wedlock child (Edwards & Williams, 2000). Or what about the common practice of denying services to homeless individuals who are actively engaging in alcohol and drug abuse? Do those without homes and dependent on others for sustenance have the right to consume alcohol, even if it is not in their best interest? The goal of this chapter is not to determine which side of this debate has a stronger argument. Certainly each side has merit, and a meaningful debate must continue. What is important though, is understanding the complexities involved in qualifying services based on behavior, particularly when behavioral standards are religiously based.

Most critics of the CSA are not necessarily against faith-based agencies providing services to those in need. Rather, they argue that faith-based agencies should not become the primary human service providers in the United States. For instance, the NASW advocates for the government remaining responsible for providing comprehensive human services programs to the public, which ensures that everyone has equal and available access to services, that utilization remains voluntary, that human service delivery systems remain accountable to the public and professional community, and that human service providers have appropriate levels of education and are professionally licensed in their field (NASW, 2002).

In February 5, 2009, President Obama signed Executive Order 13199, establishing the White House Office of Faith-Based and Neighborhood Partnerships. After signing the order, President Obama pledged not to favor one faith tradition or denomination over another, changing how decisions on funding practices were made from his predecessor. Among the key priorities of the Office of Faith-Based and Neighborhood Partnerships is a commitment to foster interfaith dialogue with community leaders and scholars (White House, 2009). The shift in priorities alleviated many of the fears of the NASW and other human service organizations, which recognize the long-term contributions of faith-based agencies but advocate for distribution of agency funding to a wide range of religious agencies, with an equally wide range of views and objectives.

The Benefits of Faith-Based Services

The majority of Americans identify religion and spirituality as an important part of their lives and also identify themselves as being members of a particular faith community. Many members of faith communities rely on their congregations when going through a difficult time. Faith communities provide individuals with a valuable support system during times of crises, providing both guidance and emotional support. One goal of human services is to connect people to a broad support system, and a faith community can provide this for its active members.

Religious coping has been found to provide more benefits over other coping methods, such as general social support, including mental health counseling (Pargament, Tarakeshwar, Ellison, & Wulff, 2001). For instance, one study questioned individuals within a church congregation who had recently experienced a crisis. The subjects were asked to rank various resources they found helpful during the crisis, such as family, friends, religious beliefs, praying, reading scripture, and professional services, including counseling, legal services, and psychological services. The researchers were surprised to learn that most people ranked professional services last as far as helpfulness and ranked religious beliefs and praying the highest (Stone, Cross, Purvis, & Young, 2003).

Another study conducted after the September 11 terrorist attacks on the World Trade Center and the Pentagon revealed that of 560 adults questioned in a national telephone survey, 90 percent sought out positive religion, often in the context of a faith community, as a way of coping with this tragedy. Examples of positive religion include seeing God as a source of strength and support and perceiving God and a faith community as supportive rather than a source of judgment (Meisenhelder & Marcum, 2004). These studies confirm what many therapists would likely say: that in times of crisis, people tend to draw strength and support from their faith communities, which provide them with a sense of comfort and familiarity while giving them a sense of being a part of a larger whole and reminding them they are not alone.

ENHANCEDetext *self-check 12.2*

THE RANGE OF FAITH-BASED HUMAN SERVICE AGENCIES

In this section I will explore examples of faith-based human service agencies operating from **Abrahamic religions** (Jewish, Christian, and Islamic), as they are the major providers of human services, both on a local and global level. I will also explore the role of the human service provider working in these faith-based agencies, noting any significant differences between their role and those played by human service providers in secular agencies. Most of the agencies featured in this section operate separately from any church or religious entity but are either supported by a particular religious tradition or operate as an extension or branch of a particular religious tradition or denomination. I will also explore ways in which human service providers can incorporate spirituality in practice using spiritually-based intervention strategies drawn from Eastern philosophies and religions, since oftentimes clients are seeking a spiritual connection outside of a traditional mainstream religious framework.

Jewish Human Service Agencies

> If one of your countrymen becomes poor and is unable to support himself among you, help him as you would an alien or a temporary resident, so he can continue to live among you. (Leviticus 25:35)

Judaism is an Abrahamic religion that is based on the belief that the Jews are the chosen people of God. Judaism is considered an ancient religion with a history of profound blessings and persecution. The Hebrew Bible, called the *Tanakh* (what Christians call the Old Testament), contains three books, the first of which is called the **Torah**. The Torah contains oral tradition and written law providing Jews with guidance on how to live and treat others.

Tzedakah is the Hebrew word for giving to the disadvantaged. The literal translation of Tzedakah means fairness or justice, as in doing what is fair and just for the poor. Tzedakah is not really like charity in that charity is voluntary and based on altruism, while Tzedakah is obligatory. While Jewish law, the **Halakhah**, doesn't necessarily prohibit charitable giving, it does recognize that charity alone isn't sufficient in caring for the poor; thus Tzedakah is an obligation, somewhat like a public tax, imposed on Jewish followers. Poverty is not considered virtuous in the Jewish religion, as it is in some Christian denominations, and in fact, it is considered pointless and something to be avoided through hard work and good financial stewardship (Eisenberg, 2010). While Jews are required to provide for the poor through mandatory giving, because poverty is not considered a natural state, the most ideal type of giving is providing someone with employment (Lifshitz, 2008).

Jewish human service agencies operate under an umbrella agency that provides coordination and macro services, such as financial support, educational services, and policy support, including political lobbying for social justice causes. For instance, the Jewish Federations of North America (JFNA) serves as an umbrella organization for a network of over 100 Jewish federations and Jewish community centers across North America. The JFNA also provides international funding and coordination for rescue and resettlement of Jews living in high-conflict or unsafe areas worldwide, including regions where anti-Semitism is prolific.

A component of the JFNA is the Human Services and Social Policy Pillar (HSSP), which is responsible for political lobbying action on local and national levels in an attempt to influence policymakers. Whether it's lobbying for increased funding for geriatric services, homeless resources, or refugee programs, the HSSP, or *the pillar* as it is commonly called, relies on human service professionals and volunteers to coordinate services of human services agencies inside and outside the Jewish community.

The Association of Jewish Family and Children's Agencies (AJFCA) serves as an information clearinghouse and support for Jewish Family Services (JFS) agencies located across the country. The AJFCA provides funding, advocates for social justice causes on a policy level, and provides information on education and training opportunities for JFS agencies. Local JFS agencies offer a number of different services including individual and family counseling, marital counseling, substance abuse counseling, AIDS counseling and educational awareness programs, anger management courses, employment services, parenting workshops, domestic violence services, children's camps, teen programs, and geriatric programs including Kosher Meals on Wheels and hospice. No one is denied services due to an inability to pay, and payment for services is typically on a sliding scale.

Many JFS agencies also have refugee resettlement programs, which assist Jewish and non-Jewish migrants who have fled persecution and need legal and resettlement assistance in the United States. Services typically include providing short-term housing on arrival, emergency financial support, case management, medical care, assistance with school enrollment, job placement, and language courses. JFC agencies have excellent reputations in assisting refugees gain financial independence, particularly in light of the often tragic circumstances many refugees have faced prior to coming to the United States.

A counselor for Jewish Family Services helps students deal with emotions through therapy that is often aimed at improving students' self-esteem

Refugee resettlement services may be coordinated with the United Nations and U.S. Department of State, or at times are facilitated without government funding and assistance.

Services focused exclusively on the Jewish community include Holocaust survivor services to Jews who lived under Nazi rule between 1933 and 1945 or were affected by the Holocaust in some manner. In addition to providing counseling services related to post-traumatic stress disorder (PTSD), in-home services related to geriatric care are also provided for Jewish older adults. Other Jewish-related services include counseling and case management services for Jewish armed services personnel, Jewish chaplaincy services, family services, and outreach focusing on assisting families reconnect with their Jewish roots by learning how to incorporate Jewish traditions and values into their family systems. Premarital and marriage services are also offered to Jewish and interfaith couples, focusing on marriage and parenting within the Jewish faith.

The primary difference between the manner in which human service providers deliver services at a JFS agency versus a secular agency is the focus on connecting Jewish clients to the broader Jewish community, both domestically and worldwide, as well as the incorporation of Jewish values throughout the various programs. Counselors and case managers are also primarily Jewish and well connected to the Jewish community, including being familiar with local synagogues and other Jewish services within the local community.

Case Example of a Client at a Jewish Faith-Based Agency

Raisa, a 77-year-old Jewish widow, began counseling at a local Jewish community center about one year ago for depression. Her initial psychosocial assessment revealed a long history of mild depression with mild anxiety that escalated in recent years to a point where intervention was necessary. Raisa shared that her normal sadness increased dramatically when she lost her husband four years ago and did not abate even when she found herself feeling more at peace with her husband's death. Raisa and her husband were married for 45 years, both having migrated from Europe shortly after World War II. They were unable to have children of their own and thus adopted one child, a daughter, who resides in a different state about three hours away by car. Raisa's daughter is married and has one child, also through adoption.

Sarah, her counselor, presumed that Raisa may have been a Holocaust survivor, and that some of the earlier trauma and grief issues were likely at play in her current depressive state, but Sarah chose not to address this possibility in counseling, choosing to wait until Raisa was ready to share her experience. Despite weekly counseling sessions and several courses of antidepressant medication, Raisa's depression and anxiety continued to worsen. During one session approximately nine months into their counseling relationship, Raisa was discussing the difficult early years of her marriage when she and her husband first moved to the United States. Raisa became extremely emotional as she shared that they were both orphans because of the war and thus had no family to help or guide them, either in their migration experience or in their marriage.

Sarah recognized the grief Raisa was reexperiencing, and also noted that once Raisa became obviously distressed, she became very uncomfortable, apologizing for her "outburst," and then quickly changing the subject. Sarah did not push Raisa, understanding that Raisa's decision to share her distant but obviously still-powerful memories was just that—Raisa's decision. As the months progressed Raisa began to pensively share more stories of her early marriage, which seemed to be marked by considerable loss and struggle.

Watch the video on the services provided by Jewish Family Services of Detroit. What are some differences that you note between JFS human service agencies and secular agencies?
ENHANCEDetext *video example 12.1*

www.youtube.com/watch?v=z43-B_ri6qA

She was 18 when the war ended. She met her husband, Reuben, one year later, although they had met once or twice several years earlier. They became inseparable almost immediately, likely out of loneliness, Raisa suspected, rather than any type of love at first sight. Although in retrospect Raisa shared, she wasn't sure there was a difference—both were emotions encompassing a significant amount of passion and intensity. Raisa and Reuben spent two years searching for family members immediately after the war with the hope of relocating from their home in Amsterdam. Her husband located an aunt and uncle in the United States and Raisa learned that her brother had escaped to Israel at the beginning of the war. They never located any other surviving family members.

After some thought and consideration, they decided to move to the United States in the hope of connecting with her husband's relatives. When they first arrived in New York, they experienced a long-overdue measure of relief, but this was to be short lived when Reuben's aunt and uncle announced plans to move to California. Deciding not to follow, Raisa and Reuben were left to survive on their own in a big city that offered as much risk as opportunity.

Although Raisa spent most of her time focusing on the physical and financial hardships of her early life, she appeared to avoid any discussion of her feelings. In fact, Sarah noted that whenever Raisa risked becoming emotionally upset, such as when Sarah asked any question that required Raisa to reflect on her childhood (even positive aspects of her youth), Raisa became emotionally and physically rigid, as if she were talking herself out of the "nonsense" of her feelings to regain composure.

Sarah became increasingly concerned about Raisa's psychological stability, particularly in light of her very recent increase in anxiousness. In fact, there were two recent occasions where Raisa was so anxious she did not feel comfortable leaving her home to attend her counseling session. In light of Raisa's worsening condition and a fear that Raisa might be at risk of suicide, Sarah made the decision to have a session with Raisa where she would more assertively address Raisa's Holocaust experience, believing that to be the root of her unresolved grief and the source of complicated mourning related to many of the losses she experienced after the war. Sarah went to Raisa's house for this session so that Raisa could remain in the safety of her surroundings if the session became too difficult. Sarah also implemented a safety plan for Raisa, including collecting a list of emergency numbers and the number of a local geriatric outreach center that Raisa had been involved with intermittently for several years.

Sarah began her session with Raisa by gently expressing her concern about her emotional well-being, as well as sharing her belief that Raisa may be suffering long-term effects from being a Holocaust survivor. Sarah shared her belief that unless Raisa addressed her past grief and losses, her depression and anxiety might not abate and may, in fact, continue to worsen. Raisa was immediately uncomfortable, but Sarah reassured her that although she wanted to push Raisa a bit, she'd made sure she could remain with Raisa for the entire afternoon, thus Raisa could take her time. Although Sarah had spent considerable time in counseling sessions with Raisa conducting "psychoeducation"—teaching Raisa about the normal stages of grief and the common psychological responses to trauma—Sarah reiterated this information now in the hope that Raisa would begin to accept that her feelings were normal.

During this session Raisa shared that her early childhood was one of constant happiness. Her father was a professor at a local university in Amsterdam. Although they were not very religious, they attended synagogue weekly and observed the Sabbath. Without realizing it at the time, Raisa's family was quite immersed in the Jewish culture, which in her family meant close ties to extended family and friends within the community who had a shared culture, customs, and life perspective. Raisa recalled the emergence of a different feeling in her neighborhood when she was about 11 years old. She is not sure if this marked the slow invasion of the Nazi party into her small town, but she did recall that it was about this time that her parents could no longer protect her brother and her from the fact that their lives were about to change forever.

Raisa shared that her family started closing the front door and drawing the shades more frequently and that various neighbors suddenly began to disappear. She recalls the day, at the age of 13, when almost everyone in her neighborhood was forced to wear yellow stars on their sleeves, and she marked this as the day she realized that some of her favorite neighbors were apparently not Jewish, because they did not have to wear the yellow star.

Raisa shared with great emotion the night she and her brother, two years older than she, were awakened in the middle of the night by their parents and told to dress quietly in the dark. They were going on a long trip but had to remain quiet. She shared that she did not recall thinking much about what was happening. Perhaps she was too scared, or maybe she had experienced so much change and shock in the past year, she simply accepted this as one more confusing event in a long line of bewildering experiences.

Months earlier Raisa's father had told her that it was important for her to obey him without asking questions because not obeying him might have serious consequences. She recalled crying when he said this to her because he was so firm, an emotion she rarely saw in her father. He responded by telling her that tears were useless now—they would not help, and that she needed to be strong. She obeyed him now as she folded one change of clothing into a small dark knapsack, confused and afraid, but resolved not to cry.

The next thing Raisa remembers is that she and her family were crouching down outside in the dark and running along the hedge line. She recalled that there was no moon, and the night was so dark she was certain she would lose her brother, who was directly in front of her. She kept running, though, trusting that someone would come back for her eventually if she lost her way. They arrived at a stranger's house, and her father knocked on a back door that appeared to lead to a basement. A young woman opened the door and hurried Raisa and her brother through the door.

Raisa had only a quick moment to look back and see her mother and father, who to her horror were not following behind them. Instead, her father and mother were crying, peering into the dark basement with a look of sadness on their faces. Raisa recalled her mother telling her earlier that she loved her very much, yet Raisa could not recall having said it in return. This was something that would haunt Raisa for years. Did she tell her mother that she loved her? She would never be sure that she had. That was the last time that Raisa and her brother saw their parents. Raisa learned after the war that their parents were forced to leave their home shortly after arranging to smuggle their children out of Amsterdam and after a short stay in what became known as a Jewish ghetto, they were sent to a concentration camp. Although she was never able to obtain exact information, Raisa learned that both of her parents had been executed, likely sometime in early 1943.

Raisa and her brother remained in the dark basement with little food or water for about three days before being driven, during the middle of the night, to another home. Raisa recalled crying sometimes but her brother, like her father, told her to stop and to be strong, and she complied. This time period was particularly difficult for both Raisa and her brother, who were tempted to escape and return home to their parents. She is not sure whether it was fear or wisdom that kept them from this course, but she realizes now that had they returned home, their fate would have been the same as their parents'.

The next trauma for Raisa occurred when she learned that she would be separated from her brother. Although her parents had arranged for them to remain together, increased risk led her rescuers to conclude that two children suddenly showing up in a home was far riskier than one; thus in the middle of one night several weeks into their frightening journey, Raisa's brother was hurried into one car, and she into another. This, too, would remain a source of considerable pain for Raisa, as she realized that once again she was denied a proper good-bye. Her last memory of her brother was his surprised face looking out the car window as he realized that she was being escorted into a different car.

Raisa fled to Italy, where she lived in a converted attic, and although enjoying some measure of freedom, she had to remain relatively hidden until the war was over. Her foster parents were nice, but stern. They were not Jewish, thus Raisa was compelled to live a lifestyle very different from the one she had enjoyed in Amsterdam. She dressed differently, attended church rather than synagogue, and ate food very different from what she was used to.

It did not occur to Raisa until she was much older that there wasn't any possibility of seeing her family again. Her attitude during the balance of her childhood was one of "waiting it out" until the war was over and she could go home and resume life as she had known it before the war. But of course that was a dream that would never come true. When the war ended, her host family wished her good fortune, and at 17 years of age Raisa was completely on her own.

Although God had never played much of a role in her life before, Raisa now found herself praying to the God of her childhood that her family was safe and waiting for her at home. She got a job in town so she could earn enough money to return to Amsterdam, and that is where she met Reuben. It was Reuben who told her there was nothing to return to—that his family, and likely hers, were dead, and the only choice Jews had was to go somewhere safe, outside of Europe, perhaps Israel or America. Raisa had been sheltered by her host family and had heard nothing of the concentration camps and the unchecked slaughter of millions of Jews. She had difficulty describing the way she felt once she learned that her entire family was likely dead. She described it as both surreal and numbing. She had no idea where her brother had been taken, and she had fantasized for years about finding him walking down an Italian street or shopping center in town. He was all she could think of now. She had to find him.

She and Reuben made the singular goal of finding whatever family they had left. At some point in their planning, they became a couple and decided to marry. Raisa learned through a charitable organization that her brother was living in Israel. She shared with Sarah earlier that their decision to immigrate to New York to join Reuben's family was a practical one. She shared now that Reuben was afraid that if they immigrated to Israel, they might find themselves in the same situation as in Amsterdam—in the center of a war—and he could not risk becoming involved in another war ever again. Raisa let go of her hope to return to her brother when Reuben decided it would be wiser for them to move to the United States.

Raisa did reconnect with her brother eventually, but they never enjoyed the closeness of their childhood. When she and Reuben visited her brother in Israel many years later, it felt to Raisa as if she were visiting a complete stranger. Her brother had become quite religious, embracing the faith of their youth—a choice antithetical to Raisa's, who chose to distance herself from her Jewish roots. Raisa shared all these stories with emotion, but no tears; she was still being "strong."

Although Sarah decided to hold off on approaching the subject of Raisa and Reuben's infertility she made a mental note that she would visit this issue in a later session. Sarah knew this too would likely be a very difficult subject for Raisa and a source of great pain—both from a generational perspective (issues related to infertility were typically not discussed in earlier generations) and from a loss perspective. Sarah assumed that Raisa and Reuben looked forward to having their own children not simply as a way of starting a family as so many couples do, but as a way of *replacing* the family that had been taken from them both. Sarah would learn later that Raisa's first child was a stillbirth, that the loss was almost too much for Raisa to bear, and that this was likely when Raisa's melancholy transitioned into a clinical depression. Even when Raisa and Reuben experienced the joy of adopting their daughter, Raisa shared that a sense of sadness remained hidden within her.

After this intense and very long session, Sarah developed a treatment plan for Raisa—one that involved both trauma and grief counseling. Sarah suspected that in addition to depression and anxiety Raisa also suffered from PTSD, thus she incorporated aspects of **trauma-informed therapy** designed to help her deal more effectively with being a survivor of trauma and loss. Sarah suspected that Raisa was in many ways still operating with a survivor mentality, which compelled her to obey her father's distant admonition to resist crying and remain strong. Raisa's tendency to equate crying with weakness could be addressed through cognitive behavioral therapy, where Raisa would be encouraged to recognize that such rules about emotion may have been necessary in wartime, but were no longer necessary and were actually damaging. The challenge for Raisa would likely lie in a fear that to change her perspective on crying might indicate a betrayal of her father and his wishes.

One of Sarah's ultimate treatment goals for Raisa was to help her develop a more realistic and timely definition of authentic strength that did not dishonor her father's guidance. Another treatment goal involved helping Raisa learn to grieve all her past losses and finally to rebuild the community she lost so many years ago. Although Raisa had a daughter, she had avoided ever getting too involved in the Jewish community, perhaps out of a fear that she might lose again what she had lost as a child—a close-knit community of neighbors who shared a culture and a faith and who operated in many respects as an extended family. Although Sarah suspected that Raisa might have some objections to getting involved in the local Jewish community, Sarah planned to explore the possibility of reconnecting with the faith and culture of her childhood.

A significant portion of Raisa's healing came from a pilgrimage of sorts that Sarah helped her plan involving returning to Amsterdam with her daughter and her brother. During this long overdue visit Raisa and her brother tearfully revisited their childhood home, as well as other places of nostalgia, and although things had changed significantly since their youth, Raisa and her brother found great healing in their trip "home." The final leg of their trip involved creating a memorial for Raisa and her brother's parents and all her lost family and friends. Raisa's last session with Sarah prior to her trip involved writing a poem they would leave at the site where the Chelmno concentration camp once stood. The trip helped Raisa create meaning around the death of her parents, and it also helped her to reconnect emotionally with her brother and involve her daughter in a part of her life she had previously kept hidden.

In succeeding years Raisa's debilitating depression lifted, and her anxiety receded. She learned how to genuinely grieve her past losses and learned to recognize how her early trauma and loss impacted virtually every area of her life. She did ultimately become involved in her community, and in the years preceding her death, she even resumed attending synagogue. Sarah's relationship with Raisa involved more than counseling. It involved incorporating aspects of faith and culture into sessions, case management that involved connecting Raisa to a community from which she had been generally estranged. It also involved Sarah drawing on her own Jewish faith, which enabled her to understand much of what Raisa experienced both in her past and in her current life.

Christian Human Services

> For I was hungry and you gave me something to eat, I was thirsty and you gave me something to drink, I was a stranger and you invited me in, I needed clothes and you clothed me, I was sick and you looked after me, I was in prison, and you came to visit me . . . I tell you the truth, whatever you did for one of the least of these brothers of mine, you did for me. (Matthew 25:35–36, 40)

Christianity is an Abrahamic religion that evolved when a sect of Jews professed their belief that Jesus was the promised Messiah and savior of the world. Christians believe that Jesus is the Son of God and died for their sins. They consider this sacrificial act "the good news" and they consider themselves the adopted children of God. Christians follow both the Old and New Testaments, which contain admonitions to care for the poor, particularly widows, orphans, and the sick. Christians are instructed to provide materially for those in need, as well as tending to their emotional and spiritual needs.

A considerable number of faith-based agencies in the United States are Christian in nature, operating from a wide range of denominations and faith traditions. The Catholic Church and traditional Protestant denominations have a long history of providing for the financial, emotional, spiritual, and social needs of those in need. An earlier Protestant movement called the **social gospel** represented a renewal of commitment to address the social causes of many problems experienced by people in need, particularly poverty and oppression.

Many **conservative Christians**, such as evangelicals, fundamentalists, and Pentecostals, have moved away from the social gospel, focusing instead on individual sin as the cause of many problems in society. Evangelism is seen as the initial priority in helping others, based on the belief that repenting of one's sins and becoming a new creation in Christ, will in most situations alleviate suffering. Ethical dilemmas can arise when Christian agencies and providers practice evangelism as a component of human service provision since professional standards in the human services fields, whether human services, social work, counseling, psychology, or psychiatry, prohibit proselytizing to clients, particularly when clients are not driving this process. Critics of evangelical practitioners who evangelize clients as a part of the counseling and case management process suggest that evangelism is more appropriately conducted in the vein of pastoral counseling or ministry efforts, not human services (Belcher, Fandetti, & Cole, 2004).

The black church, particularly in the rural South, has a long history of providing valuable and important services to the African American community—a typically underserved population (Blank, Mahmood, Fox, & Guterbock, 2002). Many historically black churches provide for the social and mental health care needs of individuals within the churches and communities. Research shows that many African Americans prefer to seek support, guidance, and counsel from their pastors, rather than seeking assistance from formal human service agencies, which underscores the importance of the black church and the services they provide. African American churches tend to offer far more human services than predominantly White churches, which may be a reflection of many African Americans' general sense of distrust of the mainstream mental health community, as well as their historic (and current) exclusion from formal services within their communities (Blank et al., 2002; Thomas, Quinn, Billingsley, & Caldwell, 1994).

As part of the 2013 Feeding Our Neighbors: An Interfaith Response campaign, Cardinal Timothy Dolan and other members of Catholic Charities of the Archdiocese of New York and the United Jewish Appeal (UJA) Federation helped to distribute Thanksgiving meals to over 400 residents

Catholic Charities USA is a network of human service agencies linked to the Roman Catholic Church that has a long tradition of caring for those in need, regardless of religious affiliation or ability to pay. Currently, there are about 1,600 local Catholic Charities agencies across the United States offering a wide variety of human services designed to serve those in need within the particular community served. According to the Catholic Charities website, services provided at most of its local agencies focus on advocacy and direct services related to reducing poverty, supporting families, and empowering communities. They do this by facilitating programs that focus on child welfare and adoption, housing, counseling, after-school youth programs and youth athletic programs, child care, domestic and international adoptions, domestic violence victim advocacy, employment and job training, health care education, senior services, and homeless services, including providing holiday meals to those in need (Catholic Charities USA, 2010). The majority of funding for Catholic Charities comes from federal and state sources, with only a small percentage coming from the Catholic Church. Catholic Charities has not had significant problems obtaining federal funding because providing services directly linked to religious ministry is not typically an aspect of services the agencies provide. Human service professionals are not required to be Catholic to work at Catholic Charities, and services are not dependent on a client's faith, although service delivery is facilitated in a manner consistent with Catholic teachings.

An example of a Protestant human service agency is Prison Fellowship Ministry (PFM), founded by Chuck Colson, former President Richard Nixon's aide. In 1973 Colson became a Christian, and in 1974 he pleaded guilty to obstruction of justice charges in association with the **Watergate scandal**. Colson served seven months of a three-year sentence and on his release founded PFM in 1976, based on his own religious conversion and his belief that no one was beyond hope. His ministry is now one of the largest prison ministries in the world, serving thousands of prisoners, ex-prisoners, their families, and victims. PFM is also involved in criminal justice reform through a PFM affiliate, Justice Fellowship, which focuses on numerous social justice issues including prison safety and eliminating prison rape.

Such social advocacy is particularly important for groups of individuals who do not evoke sympathy in the average person, and prisoners certainly fall into this category. Yet, it is essential for people to realize that prisoners are not a uniform group of "evildoers" and "sociopaths" who deserve whatever hardship the prison system can dish out. Most

Watch the video on Prison Fellowship Ministries. What are the benefits and drawbacks of this faith-based agency? Do you believe it should qualify for federal funding? Why or why not?

ENHANCEDetext *video example 12.2*

www.youtube.com/watch?v=_
cYBH4I63Vs

prisoners have had childhoods marked by poverty and abuse, many serve longer sentences because they could not afford adequate legal counsel, and some are innocent, or at least not guilty of the crimes for which they are charged and sentenced. PFM is committed to stopping the intergenerational cycle of crime and poverty by offering prisoners hope for a second chance through the Christian faith.

PFM volunteers facilitate Bible studies and topical seminars, mentor at-risk youth, counsel prisoners and crime victims, serve in youth camps, organize Angel Tree programs, visit prisoners regularly, counsel ex-prisoners and crime victims, and write letters to prisoners in the pen pal program. PFM does not receive federal funding because its volunteers focus extensively on the evangelism of prisoners and their family members.

Case Example of a Client at a Christian Faith-Based Agency

Castle Christian Counseling Center (CCCC) is a not-for-profit, ecumenical counseling center contracted by the county to provide mandated counseling services, including anger management and alcohol counseling for individuals who have been charged with an alcohol offense. Julie was required to attend anger management as a part of her probation for a domestic battery charge. Julie's initial psychosocial assessment recommended that she participate in both group and individual counseling. The group counseling consisted of a 26-week program focusing on anger management and personal accountability.

Julie's individual counseling was designed to help her deal with the underlying reasons for intense anger and inappropriate behavior, such as verbal and physical abuse. Julie was 24 years old when she was charged with domestic battery against her husband of three years. When Julie began counseling she was both emotionally needy and defensive. Her counselor, Dana, suspected that beneath Julie's defensiveness lay a tremendous amount of shame, so she chose not to confront Julie until much later in their counseling relationship.

During the first several months of counseling Julie expressed considerable anger and frustration with her husband, who she perceived as being quite passive. In response to his seeming inability to make decisions or take the lead in any aspect of their life, Julie expressed extreme disappointment and at times rage. It became clear to Dana that Julie's husband was in many respects being set up for failure by Julie. For instance, Julie often expressed to her husband that she wished he would be more proactive in their social life, but if he did forge ahead and make plans without checking with her first, she would become irate that he chose an activity he should have known she would not like. Yet if he checked with her first before making plans, she would become angry that he did not have the confidence to make plans without her input, and she would accuse him of ruining the surprise for her.

The incident that resulted in the charge of domestic battery involved a fight that escalated over their finances. Julie had decided to quit her job and try to get pregnant, even though her husband had expressed concerns that he did not make enough money to be the sole provider. He ultimately supported her decision, and Julie quit her job, but after a few months, when money got tight, and they ultimately did not have enough money to pay bills, Julie lost her temper. During her tirade she accused her husband of not caring about their finances and of sabotaging their plans to start a family. Julie became physically abusive toward her husband when he attempted to stand up to her by telling her that he had not in fact wanted her to quit her job because he feared their current situation would come to fruition. Julie became hysterical, accusing her husband of hating her and of just looking for an excuse to leave her.

Dana recognized Julie's tendency to alter the facts to support whatever theory she was attempting to prove at the moment. She also recognized Julie's all-or-nothing thinking—people either loved her or hated her, were for her or against her. According to secular psychology Julie may have met the criteria for borderline personality disorder, but Dana recognized her behavior as indicative of a contemporary form of idol worship. Julie was expecting her husband to be God, yet there was only one God who could meet all of Julie's needs. Dana knew that over the next several months she would be Julie's representative of God—showing her unconditional love as well as truth. She made a commitment to Julie that she would always be honest with her, and there would be nothing that Julie could do that would lead Dana to end their relationship. She trusted that Julie could handle the truth if it were delivered in love, not shame.

It was only a few days later that Julie seemed to test Dana's commitment. Julie called Dana and left a frantic message, stating that she was very upset and needed to talk immediately. When Dana had not returned her call within the hour, Julie called again and but this time was enraged. She accused Dana of being like everyone else—making promises but then abandoning her when she was most in need. Before returning Julie's call, Dana prayed for wisdom and insight. She immediately had an image of truth as light, and for Julie, any truth at all was like a flashlight blaring into her eyes, causing Julie to have to bat the light away to avoid the pain. Dana knew immediately from then on that she would have to be gentle not only in the amount of truth she shared with Julie but also in the way she shared her wisdom.

In the face of Julie's intense and abrasive defensiveness, Dana resisted the natural tendency to force truth on her. Instead she indulged Julie a little, suspecting that Julie's initial feeling when she made a mistake was intense shame, but before she could respond to this emotion she reacted by flipping her shame outward into anger against anyone who represented the source of shame—anyone who made her feel guilty in some way, who exacted accountability, and even who reacted emotionally to one of her rages. Dana's intuition told her that if she could relieve some of Julie's shame—take her off the hook in some manner–this might give Julie the emotional space to explore her feelings of intense shame and guilt. When Dana did call, she suspected that Julie would already be feeling immense shame and guilt, regretting her episode of anger.

Dana also suspected that Julie would not be able to emotionally manage these feelings, thus would have a need to rationalize her behavior by escalating Dana's "sin" to match her own reaction. Dana knew that if she admonished Julie for her tantrum, this would set this process in motion, so she did something different; she took Julie off the hook and rather than admonishing her, she praised her for her ability to communicate her feelings! Julie was so taken off guard that it actually enabled her to experience feeling a small amount of productive guilt. After Dana had finished complimenting Julie on her willingness to communicate, Julie admitted that she should have handled her feelings differently, that she should have been more patient, and that in some respects she believed she was expecting to be let down by Dana, thus she didn't even give her a chance to meet her needs. Success! By taking this counterintuitive approach and lifting the burden of shame, Julie was able to actually recognize her internal process without rationalizing her feelings away.

During the course of their counseling Dana addressed Julie's negative feelings about God. Julie shared that she felt very insignificant whenever she thought of God. She then shared new elements of her childhood. She had already disclosed a childhood fraught with abuse and emotional humiliation at the hands of both her father and her mother, but during this particular session, Julie shared that whenever she made a mistake as a child, her father would tell her she was going to hell, that she was a disappointment to God, and that she could not hide from God—he could see her wherever she was and he knew what she was doing and that what she was doing the majority of the time was bad. Julie's father would often physically abuse her, sometimes using a Bible to beat her on the head.

When Dana asked Julie to draw a picture of her relationship with God, Julie drew a picture where she was quite small, crouched down and running, and God, a large presence on the page, was looking down on her with a stern scowl on his face. Dana asked Julie if she ever turned to God when going through a difficult time. Julie looked shocked, expressing her belief that if she were in trouble, God would be the last source she would consider turning toward for support. In fact, Julie shared that she believed that the only time God paid any attention to her was when she had messed up. She imagined God saying, "There you go again—I knew you would blow it eventually!"

Dana told Julie that she would like to spend some time sharing a different type of God with her, not a punishing God, but a loving God who acted as a father to his children—guiding his children when they were walking down the wrong path, like any good father, and applauding when they did well. Dana shared about her own feelings toward her young son. She found herself chuckling even when he got himself into a bit of trouble, like the time he wrote his name in purple crayon all over his closet door, only to deny his culpability when Dana came upon his artwork. Dana was not harsh, nor punishing, but she did want to teach her son that defacing property was not the best choice. She did this in love, extending grace and forgiveness because she understood that at this age her son did not know any better. She also smirked as she admired her son's artwork, knowing that drawing on the wall with crayon was a perfectly normal thing to do. Julie could not fathom a God who was anything but condemning but she was very interested in learning about the concepts of grace and forgiveness.

Once Dana was confident that Julie trusted her, she began to respond to each of Julie's rage episodes by first empathizing with Julie's emotions—her disappointment, her fear, her anger—followed by gently sharing truth. When Julie asked if Dana thought she was wrong to have such high expectations of her husband, Dana said yes, but that did not mean Julie should have no expectations. Rather, Dana explained that once Julie developed a more solid emotional base within herself, including having a more solid relationship with God, her expectations of her husband would likely be more realistic.

Julie's counseling also consisted of a significant amount of grief counseling, mourning her lost childhood, gaining insight and understanding of the abuse she had endured, and learning her emotional triggers and ways to avoid them. Dana taught Julie to contain her emotions, so that she wouldn't have to react the moment she experienced an intense emotion, such as the intense fear that she was going to be abandoned, which would often turn toward anger. Dana used guided imagery directing Julie to imagine Jesus holding her firmly, but lovingly. Imagery exercises of this type also helped Julie make God more real in her life. Julie began to believe that God had good intentions for her, not evil ones, that He wanted the best for her, not the worst. He would not hide from her, and she did not have to hide from him. Julie continued counseling even after she met her mandated requirement.

In her second year of counseling Dana shifted focus from Julie's childhood to her current relationships, including the relationship with her husband. Julie's intense fear of abandonment often led her to be so self-focused that she was blinded to the damage she caused other people. As her fear of abandonment subsided and her shame diminished, Dana was able to coach Julie into looking through the eyes of her husband. This process would have been impossible a year ago because the shame would have paralyzed her, but with her increasing internal strength, Julie was able to accept her behavior and the pain it caused. Once she saw herself as deserving of forgiveness, she could address her own abusive behavior.

Within the second year of therapy, Julie's anger receded significantly, and she was able to talk through her feelings rather than act them out. She remained in counseling intermittently for years to maintain her program of faith building, emotional containment, and extending forgiveness to self and others.

Islamic Human Services

> And those in whose wealth is a recognized right; for the needy who asks and those who are deprived. (Qur'an 70:24–25)

Islam is another Abrahamic religion that is based on both the Jewish holy books, as well as the Christian Bible. The word *Islam* means submission, and followers of Islam submit themselves to **Allah**. The **Muslim** holy book is called the **Qur'an** and is considered by Muslims to be the recited words of God revealed to the Prophet Muhammad in the seventh century. Islam believes the Qur'an to be God's final revelation to humankind.

Islam is a religion that is often misunderstood and mischaracterized, both by the general public and by the media. This mischaracterization is due in part to the differences between more liberal Western values and the more conservative values held by many in the Islamic community. The terrorist acts of September 11, 2001, and subsequent acts of terrorism have increased cultural misunderstandings and promoted sentiments of **xenophobia** and **Islamophobia**. A negative stereotype of Islam is that the entire Muslim culture endorses violence, extremist dogma, and female oppression. In truth, every culture and every religious faction has its peaceful members and its violent ones, but the extremists do not define the entire population.

There are over one billion followers of Islam worldwide, which makes it the second-largest religion in the world. The majority of Muslims live in Southeast Asia, Northern Africa, and the Middle East. There are two primary sects within Islam due to an early dispute over who should have been Muhammad's successor. The Sunnis tend to be more religiously and politically liberal (for instance, they believe that Islamic leaders should always be elected). Approximately 90 percent of all Muslims are Sunnis. Shiites, on the other hand, tend to be more orthodox in their religious beliefs and political philosophies, having developed a more strictly academic application of the Qur'an. Shiites believe that all successors to Muhammad (imams) are infallible and sinless. They appoint their clergy and hold them in high regard.

The majority of Muslims who live in the United States are Sunnis, 75 percent of whom are foreign born. The Muslim community tends to be both college educated and middle class, and Muslims in general tend not tend to rely on government-sponsored human services to meet their basic needs. Much of the focus of Islamic charity is directed toward Muslims in other parts of the world who are suffering, either because of war or some other form of oppression. Local Muslim human services tend to focus on marriage and family services.

Because Muslims come from many different countries there is considerable diversity within the Islamic community, particularly in the United States. Yet despite the variability of cultural beliefs and practices, Islam shares five basic pillars of faith:

- *Shahada:* Faith in one God
- *Salat:* Ritual prayer five times a day while facing Mecca
- *Zakat:* Charitable giving to the poor with the understanding that all wealth belongs to God
- *Sawm:* Fasting from sunrise to sunset during the month of Ramadan
- *Hajj:* Pilgrimage to Mecca

According to the Qur'an (9:60), there are eight categories of people who qualify to receive zakat. These include the poor, the needy, those who collect zakat, those who are being converted, captives, debtors, and travelers. The three foundational values within the Islamic community include community, family, and the sovereignty of God. Family is often defined as the joining of two extended families, thus what might be considered **enmeshment** in North American society is often seen as a sign of respect, as extended families are drawn close and remain an active part of the immediate family's life. Men and women typically adopt traditional roles in families that are close adherents to the Islam faith, with men working outside of the home and women caring for the home and children. This trend is changing though, even in more traditional families, just as it is in other cultures within U.S. society. Modesty is seen as an important value necessary for keeping order within society, and women often wear clothing (*hijab*) that covers the greater part of their body (Hodge, 2005).

Areas of obvious conflict between Islamic values and liberal North American values include Western culture's values of individualism, self-expression, and self-determination, compared to Islamic culture values of community, self-control, and consensus (Hodge, 2005). Thus, whether working with an Islamic human services agency, coordinating services with one, or directly serving the Islamic community, Hodge cautions human services workers not to view Islamic values through the eyes of Western culture. For example, it is common for Westerners to view the Islamic tenet of modesty as primitive and oppressive to women, which for some Westerners may seem synonymous to endorsing domestic violence. Yet the Qur'an states that husbands and wives must express respect and compassion toward one another, and domestic violence is not endorsed. To truly understand the values of modesty and traditional roles embraced within the Islamic culture, one must take the time to understand what these values mean to the men and women who embrace them because as with many other social dynamics, people interpret Islamic gender roles in many different ways. Hence, although human service providers might not share Islamic belief systems, working in association with Islamic human service agencies can provide them with an opportunity to gain greater cultural competence.

There has been a recent surge of interest in developing human services programs within mosques and Islamic centers across the United States in response to growing concerns about social issues and demonstrated needs within the Muslim community, particularly related to marriage, family, and Islamophobia. The discipline of human services is relatively new to the Islamic community, but charity is not new and has been practiced within Islamic and broader Arab communities for generations. Islamic human service providers may include social workers, counselors, and psychologists, but an **imam** can also provide human services. Islamic human service agencies provide services to those within Muslim and non-Muslim communities, and are increasingly relied on to serve as a liaison for Western aid agencies in Muslim communities experiencing a crisis (De Cordier, 2009).

Islamic charities have suffered since the September 11 terrorist attacks, though, because many Muslims in the United States are afraid that monies they donate in good faith to an Islamic charity may be frozen by the U.S. government and not directed to humanitarian causes as planned. Muslims are also giving less because they are afraid they might be held in suspicion if a charity they donate money to is later investigated for diverting funds to terrorist causes. Mosques and Islamic centers across the nation are reaching out to legislators in a campaign called Charity Without Fear, asking them to establish a list of Islamic charities in good standing, so that devout Muslims can give to charity without fear of being accused of supporting terrorist organizations (Council of Islamic Organizations, 2005). To date, the federal government has not responded to the request for a "clean" list of Muslim charitable organizations.

There are several Islamic human service agencies operating within the United States, and although not as prolific as Jewish or Christian organizations, Islamic agencies are increasing in numbers, and offer important services to the Muslim community. The Islamic Social Services Association (ISSA) acts as an umbrella organization for all Muslim human service agencies in the United States and Canada. The ISSA provides training and educational services, acting as a network linking and equipping Muslim communities. The Inner-City Muslim Action Network (IMAN) focuses on meeting the needs of those in the inner city in Chicago by operating food pantries, health clinics, and prayer services. IMAN, which is located in a storefront on Chicago's South Side, offers a free computer lab with free Internet service, General Educational Development (GED) courses, and computer training classes. IMAN is also involved in community activism such as lobbying against the granting of liquor licenses in high-crime areas, community development, and coordination of outreach events with other community agencies both Muslim and non-Muslim.

There is concern within the Islamic faith community that Muslim marriages are being negatively affected by the casual nature of divorce in the United States. Thus several Muslim human service agencies focus on providing marriage and family services with the goal of strengthening Muslim families. Muslim Family Services (MFS), a division of the Islamic Circle of North America (ICNA), is a national agency with offices located throughout the United States. They provide marriage and family services for families and couples, teaching them how to have a marriage according to Islamic principles. MFS provides education, such as workshops for married couples and training for Imams; premarital, marriage, and parenting counseling; emergency services; foster care; and advocacy in court and with departments of social services. Islamic values are stressed, including the belief that marriage is the foundation of society and the pillar on which family is built. Human service providers working for MFS understand that Muslim couples living in the United States are often caught between two cultures, and many are influenced by the more liberal Western values. This has led to increased divorce rates and also many parenting challenges as adolescents in particular challenge traditional Islamic values such as modesty and more liberal male–female relationships.

Another Muslim human services agency that focuses primarily on women is Niswa (which means "woman in community" in Arabic), located in Southern California. The goal of Niswa is to strengthen Muslim families by providing services to South Asian, Afghan, and Middle Eastern immigrant women. Niswa provides counseling, case

Watch the video on Muslim Family Services. List three ways that you could coordinate services with a Muslim Family Services agency.
ENHANCEDetext *video example 12.3*

www.youtube.com/
watch?v=VYYLpQjyvCo

Dr. Shamin Ibrahim puts together a baby crib at a shelter for South Asian and Middle Eastern women. Dr. Ibrahim is a Muslim woman who started Niswa House, a Muslim women's association for abused women from South Asian and Middle Eastern countries

management, crisis intervention, preventative health education, referrals, and domestic violence services, including a domestic violence shelter, called Niswa House. Niswa was founded in 1990 by Dr. Shamim Ibrahim, a psychologist and counselor, who recognized the need for culturally and linguistically competent services for incoming migrant and refugee Muslim women in need of advocacy. Niswa's primary focus is on women's advocacy and domestic violence, but has expanded considerably in the past several decades to keep pace with clients' needs.

In addition to Muslim human services, there are several human service agencies that provide services to the Arabic community, but outside of a religious context. For instance, Arab American Family Services (AAFS) provides services focused on domestic violence prevention and intervention, older adult and disabled services, cultural diversity training, immigration services, community health and education, youth programs, and mental health services. AAFS also provides advocacy services focused on dispelling negative stereotypes about the Arab culture, serving as a bridge between Arab-Americans and the mainstream American culture.

The U.S. Muslim community will continue to be confronted with issues related to acculturation and the eroding of traditional values, and problems within Muslim families will likely continue, particularly in light of rising incidences of Islamophobia. Human service agencies can assist Muslim families in feeling less isolated, can provide much-needed education and support, and can provide a sense of connectedness among Muslims who are feeling unsupported within their communities.

Case Example of a Client at a Muslim Faith-Based Agency

Maya is a 42-year-old Muslim woman who was referred to an Islamic women's center for advocacy and counseling. She has been married to Asad, a 44-year-old physician, for 18 years. Maya is the stay-at-home mother of their three children, aged 10, 12, and 14. Both Maya and Asad are originally from Egypt, having immigrated to the United States shortly after getting married. Maya reports that she and her husband have always been devout Muslims, being very involved in their local mosque. They have had what she considers a traditional Muslim marriage, where her husband is the leader of the home and provides for the family financially, and Maya takes care of the home and the children.

For the majority of their marriage Maya believed that their marriage has been a good one. She believed that her husband was always very respectful of her and relied on her wisdom and input in making decisions impacting the family, particularly with regard to the children. Because Maya was an accountant prior to getting married, Asad has relied on her to help with financial matters related to his medical practice. Maya reported that about five years ago Asad began to "bring his work home with him," which led to an increase in his general irritability and frustration. In the last two years Maya noted that he began to become more controlling of her whereabouts, getting angry with her if he could not reach her at a moment's notice. She did not reach out then because she believed Asad when he said that it was his right to control her in this manner. Although

Maya's father did not behave this way, she began to believe that perhaps she needed to endure Asad's behavior in order to be a good Muslim wife.

Maya shared that in the past few months Asad's aggression had escalated to the point of screaming at her, both at home and in public, backing her into corners. His drinking has escalated as well. The incident that prompted Maya to finally reach out for help occurred after she refused to sleep with Asad because he was extremely intoxicated and verbally abusing her. Asad became irate and began beating her, citing his rights according to the Qur'an (4:34–35).

Maya initially went to the imam at her mosque, who supported her completely and also explained that her husband's use of the Qur'an was a misinterpretation. He explained that Islam did not in any way condone abuse. He provided her with a considerable amount of information regarding the "cycle of violence" and services in the community for victims of domestic violence, including support groups for both adults and children. Maya contacted the Muslim women's center that day and saw a counselor later in the week.

During Maya's first counseling center she expressed relief that her community was so supportive of her, but she expressed sadness as well because the information and resources she received seemed so fatalistic and hopeless. Her counselor explained that her husband was acting in a manner inconsistent with the will of Allah and if he was truly committed to following Islam and being a good Muslim husband and father, then perhaps he would be open to receiving counseling as well. Domestic violence, the counselor explained, not only destroyed everyone in the family but also affected the entire community, thus the Muslim community was as concerned about Asad as it was about Maya.

During counseling Maya began to understand the underlying dynamics of her husband's behavior and gained wisdom regarding the difference between a husband who led his family with respect, as described by Muhammad, and the controlling and abusive behavior exhibited by her husband. As Maya gained confidence in herself and her decisions, she felt strongly that Allah was leading her to be strong for the sake of her family. Strength, according to her counselor, meant that she could not tolerate abuse. Asad met with the Imam for several weeks and then reluctantly agreed to attend a one-year anger management program that was led by an imam at the community Islamic center, and Maya agreed not to make any decisions about divorce until after Asad had finished his program. Both the imam and the counselor agreed that family counseling should not occur until after Asad had received enough counseling to recognize the root of the family and marital problems lay mostly within himself and his abusive behavior.

As Maya continued counseling, she began to realize the intergenerational cycle of abuse that existed in her husband's family and how important it was, particularly for the sake of her children, that she become strong enough to break the cycle. The most difficult aspect of this process for Maya was maintaining good boundaries with Asad and realizing that he had the choice not to change, which would force her hand in a sense, compelling her to leave the marriage to avoid repeating the patterns of abuse.

The Mindfulness Movement

Spiritual counseling need not always be facilitated within a traditional religious framework. It can also involve general spirituality, where the social worker provides resources and counseling focusing on a belief that all people are interconnected on some level and are guided by a divine presence. Many clients who wish to seek a deeper connection with a **higher power** but are not comfortable doing so within a particular theological frame-work can greatly benefit from exposure to general spirituality. Thus, although in this section the focus is more on mainstream traditions, it is important for social workers to be aware of a wide range of spiritual resources, which include traditions rooted in what would be considered Eastern or New Age philosophies, including some yoga traditions and the mindfulness movement.

New Age traditions approach the person from a **holistic** perspective, focusing on making connections between the person and the divine, and often rely on using all of the senses, as well as meditation practices, with the goal of helping individuals gain increased awareness and connectedness. The **mindfulness movement** (also called **contemplative practice**) rooted in the Buddhist tradition helps individuals develop a sense of awareness and presence in one's daily life.

Mindfulness traditions focus on cultivating an accepting awareness and enhanced attention to present moment experiences, and a belief that with this experience, a sense of interconnectedness to everything else emerges on its own. Practicing living each moment with this awareness promotes resilience in relating to life's obstacles as well as promoting healing, love, and compassion. Those practicing mindfulness believe that if one seeks wisdom and balance in life and a connection with that which is bigger than oneself, then conditions such as depression, anxiety, substance abuse, and unresolved grief can be overcome, and ultimately replaced with living mindfully with greater compassion, appreciation, and joy.

Watch the video on contemplative practice and end-of-life care. What do you believe are the advantages of this approach compared to traditional (Western) approaches to terminal illness?

ENHANCEDetext *video example 12.4*

www.youtube.com/watch?v=11sraBGqGG4

The Feldenkrais Method raises awareness of natural postures of the body to better live in harmony with oneself. Photo taken at Mac Mahon studio in Paris

Case Study in the Mindfulness Movement

Shira Vardi, a Chicago area social worker, recently began her own mindfulness organization called *Encounters in Motion*. Vardi uses her social work skills and training in a unique way that incorporates all aspects of the mind and body, with a particular focus on movement. *Encounters in Motion* is not psychotherapy in that problems aren't approached from the framework of mental illness and its healing or management. Rather, Vardi views the source of much of our suffering as a society rooted in disconnection: from ourselves (mind/body/spirit) and from those around us (see the research on vulnerability by Brené Brown and on happiness through connection by Barbara Fredrickson). Vardi therefore shares tools and facilitates experiences—for individuals, groups, and organizations—that support connection in the moment. Using Feldenkrais® Method practitioner training, she uses gentle touch to guide individual client movement and attention toward their physical structural support in relation to gravity. This enables clients to move through life with greater support, lightness, and ease. Using meditation and internal family systems training with individuals and groups, she helps clients relate to their thoughts and feelings with leadership and good will.

This process enables a client's whole self to work in harmony, rather than the internal chatter/infighting that often uses up so much of our energy. Using West African dance and

expressive movement, she helps clients sense, feel, and move their bodies and their spirits to music, from a place of connection, pleasure, and ease.

ENHANCEDetext *self-check 12.3*

CONCLUSION

Far too many of the world's conflicts center on religion, and religious dogma has far too often been at the heart of marginalization and the justification of oppression of members of the "out-group" population. Yet religion can also be a source of peace, faith, optimism, and hope. Despite the misuse and misapplication of religion by some, religion, particularly personal spirituality, is often key to the self-actualization of many. Thus human service providers must be comfortable integrating spirituality into practice, if this is in the best interest of the client. Further, faith-based agencies from a range of religious traditions have had a long history of providing assistance to underserved and at-risk populations and are often working in partnership with secular and government agencies providing valuable services to clients throughout the country and world.

As the field of human services evolves and matures, the scope with which this discipline is viewed will be broadened and the value of services provided by those not within the mainstream mental health community will be increasingly recognized. Whether these services are delivered informally through church-sponsored programs or through highly organized faith-based human service agencies, recognizing that human service delivery can occur through a variety of systems acknowledges the reality that different people seek help in different ways.

SUMMARY

- The ways in which human service providers can integrate religion and spirituality into practice are explored. The importance of human service providers to develop competency in integrating faith and spirituality in practice in a manner that is client-centered is discussed.
- The ways in which faith-based human service agencies operate are examined. The nature of faith-based institutions including comparisons with secular agencies is also examined. The history of government funding of faith-based agencies is explored within the context of federal legislation that determines parameters for which faith-based agencies qualify for federal funding. The benefits of faith-based services are also explored, such as the development of positive religious coping strategies.
- Service delivery approaches of faith-based agencies from a range of faith traditions are explored. The philosophies and human service delivery systems from a range of faith traditions, including Jewish, Christian, and Islamic human service agencies, are discussed. The mindfulness movement, an Eastern faith tradition, is also explored.

Internet Resources

Conduct an Internet search for the American Psychological Association, and then search for an article entitled "Religion and spirituality in the treatment room" by Karen Kersting.

Conduct an Internet search for the National Association of Social Workers, and then search for an article entitled "Eye on Ethics: Wrestling With Faith in Social Work Education" by Frederic G. Reamer, Ph.D.

Conduct an Internet search for the White House Office of Faith-Based and Neighborhood Partnerships, and then click on *About Us*.

Conduct an Internet search for Jewish Federations of North America, and then click on *How Federations Help*.

Conduct an Internet search for the Association of Jewish Family and Children's Agencies, and then click on *About Us*, and then *Member Agencies*.

Conduct an Internet search for Catholic Charities USA, and then click on *What We Do* in the middle menu bar.

Conduct an Internet search for Prison Fellowship and then click on *What We Do*, and then *Our Approach*.

Conduct an Internet search for Niswa, and then click on *Services*.

Conduct an Internet search for The Center for Contemplative Mind in Society, and then click on Contemplative Practices, and then *Practices in Daily Life*.

Conduct an Internet search for Shira Vardi's Encounters in Motion, and then click on *Tools*.

References

Belcher, J. R., Fandetti, D., & Cole, D. (2004). Is Christian religious conservatism compatible with the liberal social welfare state? *Social Work, 49*(2), 269–276.

Blank, M. B., Mahmood, M., Fox, J. C., & Guterbock, T. (2002). Alternative mental health services: The role of the Black church in the South. *American Journal of Public Health, 92*(10), 1668–1672.

Catholic Charities USA. (2010). Catholic Charities at a glance. Available online at: http://www.catholiccharitiesusa.org/document.doc?id=2853

Council of Islamic Organizations. (2005). *Charity without fear*. Retrieved from http://www.ciogc.org/Go.aspx?link=7654625

De Cordier, B. (2009). Faith-based aid, globalisation and the humanitarian frontline: An analysis of Western-based Muslim aid organisations. *Disasters, 33*(4), 608–628.

Ebaugh, H. R., Pipes, P. F., Chafetz, J. S., & Daniels, M. (2003). Where's the religion? Distinguishing faith-based from secular social service agencies. *Journal for the Scientific Study of Religion, 42*(3), 411–426.

Edwards, C. E., & Williams, C. L. (2000). Adopting change: Birth mothers in maternity homes today. *Gender and Society, 14*(1), 160–183.

Eisenberg, R. L. (2010). *What the Rabbis said: 250 topics from the Talmud*. ABC-CLIO.

Fallot, R. D. (2001). Spirituality and religion in psychiatric rehabilitation and recovery from mental illness. *International Review of Psychiatry, 13*, 110–116.

Fallot, R. D., & Heckman, J. D. (2005). Religious/spiritual coping among women trauma survivors with mental health and substance use disorders. *Journal of Behavioral Health Services and Research, 32*(2), 215–226.

Gallup, G., & Lindsey, D. M. (1999). *Surveying the religious landscape: Trends in U.S. beliefs*. Harrisburg, PA: Morehouse.

Grossman, C. L. (2002, March 7). Charting the unchurched in America. *USA Today*, p. D1.

Hall, C. R., Dixon, W. A., & Mauzey, E. D. (2004). Spirituality and religion: Implications for counseling. *Journal of Counseling & Development, 82*, 504–507.

Hodge, D. R. (2004). Working with Hindu clients in a spiritually sensitive manner. *Social Work, 29*(1), 27–38.

Hodge, D. R. (2005). Social work in the house of Islam: Orienting practitioners to the beliefs and values of Muslims in the U.S. *Social Work, 50*(2), 162–173.

Idler, E. L., & Kasl, S. (1992). Religion, disability, depression and the timing of death. *American Journal of Sociology, 97*, 1052–1079.

Kliewer, S. (2004). Allowing spirituality into the healing process. *Journal of Family Practice, 53*(8), 616–624.

Koenig, H. G., George, L. K., Hays, J. C., Larson, D. B., Cohen, H. J., & Blazer, D. G. (1998). The relationships between religious activities and blood pressure in older adults. *International Journal of Psychiatry Medicine, 28*, 189–213.

Koenig, H. G., George, L. K., & Titus, P. (2004). Religion, spirituality, and health in medically ill hospitalized elderly patients. *Journal of American Geriatrics Society, 52*(4), 554–562.

Koenig, H. G., Larson, D. B., & Weaver, A. J. (1998). Research on religion and serious mental illness. *New Directions in Mental Health Surveys, 80*, 81–95.

Lifshitz, J. (2008). Welfare, property and the divine image in Jewish law and thought. In Jonathan B. Imber

(Ed.), _Markets, morals and religion_ (pp. 117–129). New Brunswick, NJ: Transaction Publishers.

McLaughlin, D. (2004). Incorporating individual spiritual beliefs in treatment of in-patient mental health consumers. _Perspectives in Psychiatric Care, 40_(3), 114–119.

Meisenhelder, J. B., & Marcum, J. P. (2004). Responses of clergy to 9/11: Post-traumatic stress, coping and religious stress. _Journal for the Scientific Study of Religion, 43_(4), 547–554.

Miller, M. M., Korinek, A., & Ivey, D. C. (2004). Spirituality in MFT training: Development of the spiritual issues in supervision scale. _Contemporary Family Therapy, 26_(1), 71–81.

Miller, W. R., & Thoresen, C. E. (2003). Spirituality, religion, and health: An emerging research field. _American Psychologist, 58_, 24–35.

National Association of Social Workers. (2002, January). _NASW priorities on faith-based human services initiatives._ Retrieved from http://www.naswdc.org/advocacy/positions/faith.asp

Pargament, K. I., & Mahoney, A. (2009). Spirituality: The search for the sacred. In C. R. Snyder & S. J. Lopez (Eds.), _Oxford handbook of positive psychology_ (2nd ed., pp. 611–620). New York: Oxford University Press.

Pargament, K. I., Tarakeshwar, N., Ellison, C. G., & Wulff, K. M. (2001). The relationships between religious coping and well-being in a national sample of Presbyterian clergy, elders, and members. _Journal for the Scientific Study of Religion, 40_(3), 497–513.

Powell, L., Shahabi, L., & Thoresen, C. E. (2003). Religion and spirituality: Linkage to physical health. _American Psychologist, 58_, 36–52.

Stone, H. W., Cross, D. R., Purvis, K. B., & Young, M. J. (2003). A study of the benefit of social and religious support on church members during times of crisis. _Pastoral Psychology, 51_(4), 327–340.

Thomas, S. B., Quinn, S. C., Billingsley, A., & Caldwell, C. (1994). The characteristics of Northern Black churches with community health outreach program. _American Journal of Public Health, 84_(4), 575–579.

Tseng, W. S. (2004). Culture and psychotherapy: Asian perspectives. _Journal of Mental Health, 13_(2), 151–161.

White House, Office of the Press Secretary. (2009, February 5). _Obama announces White House Office of faith-based and neighborhood partnerships_ [Press Release]. Retrieved from http://www.whitehouse.gov/the_press_office/ObamaAnnouncesWhiteHouseOfficeofFaith-basedandNeighborhoodPartnerships/

13

Violence, Victim Advocacy, and Corrections

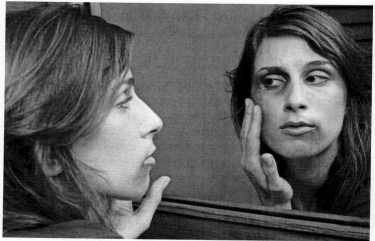

© DAXIAO PRODUCTIONS/SHUTTERSTOCK

Rick grew up in a home marked by domestic violence, which oftentimes extended to the children. Rick's mother was chronically depressed and often resorted to using alcohol to avoid dealing with her feelings. Rick recalls days and sometimes weeks where his mother refused to get out of bed, and he was responsible for caring for his younger siblings. His father also had an alcohol problem and would fly into nightly rages where he would physically abuse Rick's mother. When Rick got older, he attempted to intervene and protect his mother, which only resulted in his father physically abusing him.

In addition to physical abuse, Rick was also the victim of emotional abuse and neglect. Rick's father would often call him derogatory names and humiliate him by telling him that he would amount to nothing in life and that he was worthless. It seemed as though Rick could do nothing right, and when he was about 12 years old, he promised himself that he would never allow anyone to hurt or humiliate him again.

Rick married when he was 21 and was hopeful that his life of being victimized was over. He loved his wife Sarah very much and was determined to be the best husband and father he could possibly be. He vowed not to repeat the mistakes of his parents, but deep inside he was plagued with fears that he wasn't good enough for his wife and that she would eventually leave him.

He became increasingly jealous and accused his wife constantly of plotting behind his back to leave him, likely with another man. If Rick's wife tried to convince him otherwise, he accused her of lying. When she became pregnant he was thrilled, but after the baby was born he became upset because his wife seemed to want to spend all her time with the baby, leaving him to fend for himself.

One day Rick's boss called him into his office and pointed out a mistake that Rick made. All Rick could think of was the promise he had made to himself years ago to never allow anyone to hurt or ridicule him again. Even though his boss's comments would have seemed reasonable to most people, to Rick they were a recreation of the abuse he endured as a child. He lost control of his temper, slammed his fist into the wall, and quit his job.

When he got home he told Sarah and fully expected her to sympathize with him and support his decision to not tolerate such abuse, but instead she complained that his act was selfish, particularly in light of his responsibilities as a father. Rick completely lost his temper and in a blinding rage accused Sarah of betraying him. In the blur that followed, Rick accused her of cheating on him, of caring about the baby more than him, and even of getting pregnant by another man.

In the midst of his angry outburst he shoved Sarah against the wall and knocked her down, and then began kicking her in the stomach and head. All he could think of was how this woman, who he thought was his "savior," was really his enemy, and at that moment he hated her for allowing him to lower his guard and trust her. All the pain of his childhood, with all the hurt and humiliation, came rushing back, and he began to choke her. When his baby interrupted his rage, he screamed at his son to shut up. When his baby's crying got louder, he picked him up and shook him violently.

Rick was arrested on charges of felony domestic violence, unlawful restraint, and child endangerment. After Sarah was released from the hospital she listened to her voicemail and heard several frantic and pleading voicemail messages from Rick crying and profusely apologizing and expressing intense fear about being in jail. The next call was from a social worker at the Victim-Witness Assistance with the local prosecutor's office asking her to return the call so that she could provide her with information about the court case, her order of protection, and resources for counseling.

Sarah then received a call from the local domestic violence shelter. The social worker asked her several questions about her safety and whether she needed shelter. She also offered Sarah court advocacy and resources to help with her baby's medical care. Sarah was hesitant to say too much. Mostly she was overwhelmed and felt flood of emotions – fear, sadness, confusion, and guilt.

She felt sorry for Rick. She knew he was a good person and she couldn't stand the thought of him being in jail, alone and scared. The sound of Rick's voice on the voicemail rang in her ears and she began going over what happened in her mind again and again, questioning her original version of the events that night. Did Rick mean to knock her down? Did he really shake the baby? Why wasn't she more sympathetic? She really had been neglecting him lately . . . was she a bad wife?

During Sarah's first meeting with the prosecutor and court advocate about Rick's case she became immediately uncomfortable about the prospect of testifying against her husband. In fact, she couldn't imagine it! She felt sorry for Rick—he'd had a horrible childhood and she felt like she was the only one he could confide in and that made her feel good. She believed in her heart that good people forgave easily, especially their husbands.

Since Rick was released on bond, and even though he was not allowed to contact her, she had been receiving almost nightly calls from him, begging for her forgiveness. This Rick was the Rick she fell in love with—the soft Rick, the vulnerable Rick, the sweet Rick, and the kind Rick. She reasoned that as awful as this incident had been, maybe it was the wake-up call their family needed to get back on track.

When the prosecutor informed Sarah that she did not have the power to drop the charges or the order of protection, she became very upset. She neither wanted nor asked for their involvement. She was certain that she could handle this matter on her own, as a family, and she wanted no part of the free advocacy from Victim-Witness or from the local shelter. She found their perception of her as a "battered wife" embarrassing and humiliating.

Despite her numerous attempts to play down what happened, even blaming herself for what happened, denying that it was "that bad," and explaining that Rick has never kicked her and was actually trying to soothe the baby, not shake him, the prosecutor refused to budge, and in fact warned Sarah that if she allowed Rick back into the house, she too could be facing charges of child maltreatment for putting her baby at risk. Sarah left the courthouse upset and confused, feeling misunderstood, scared, embarrassed, and completely alone. She knew none of her friends and family would understand because no one understood Rick like she did and they didn't like him. In fact, the only person she believed she could rely on was the one person who was forbidden to see her—her husband Rick.

The field of forensic human services is a multidisciplinary practice area focusing broadly on the intersects between human services, the legal, judicial, and corrections systems. Human service providers who work in practice settings dealing with domestic violence, sexual assault, gang activity, and criminal justice agencies such as police departments, probation, state, and county prosecutors, as well as within correctional facilities such as jails and prisons are considered forensic human service providers. The role and function of human service providers working in the area of forensics may vary significantly depending on the legal issues involved, but most forensic human service providers require specialized training in areas such as deviant behavior, crime victimization, crisis counseling, trauma responses, and intervention strategies, as well as developing a thorough understanding of the legal and criminal justice system.

Violence seems to have always been a part of the human existence. A question that is often debated among philosophers and social scientists is whether violence is a *necessary* part of human existence. Is war necessary? Certainly war has always existed, but is our existence dependent on competition for resources won through violent means? At what point does the act of war become the act of genocide? How can ordinary people live side by side peaceably for years and suddenly commit heinous acts, such as was the case during the Holocaust or the more recent genocide in Rwanda? Perhaps having the ability to respond in intense anger that manifests in violence is necessary when one is defending oneself, but isn't it the unjust use of violence that makes this defensive response necessary in the first place?

Determining the answers to these questions lies at the heart of violence research within the social science disciplines, such as sociology, social psychology, anthropology, and criminology, as well as those who work in the applied fields of human services, social work, clinical psychology, and criminal justice. In this chapter various types of violence will be explored, such as domestic violence or intimate partner violence (IPV), rape and sexual assault, hate crimes against lesbian, gay, bisexual, transgender, questioning/queer (LGBTQ+) populations and **gender nonconforming populations**, and general crime victimization. Ways in which violence impacts victims, including how victims become survivors, will also be explored, as well as how society and those within the human services fields intervene to reduce violence.

INTIMATE PARTNER VIOLENCE

IPV involves physical violence, sexual violence, stalking, and psychological aggression toward an intimate partner (Breiding et al., 2015). IVP can occur between current or former spouses, cohabitating partners, boyfriends, and girlfriends, dates, and sexual partners. Intimate partners can be either heterosexual or same-sex. *Physical violence* can include hitting, punching, slapping, pinching, shoving, and throwing objects at or near the victim, or threatening to do so, or using one's body weight and strength to restrain someone, such as backing someone into a corner and not allowing them to leave. *Sexual violence* can include forced penetration of the abuser or someone else; psychological pressure or coercion to engage in unwanted sexual activity; unwanted sexual contact, such as being touching or being forced to touch someone else; and non-contact unwanted sexual activity, such as being forced to watch pornography, or being filmed while engaging in some sexual activity. *Stalking* involves a pattern of repeated unwanted contact or harassment that causes fear, such as phone calls or texts, driving by one's house, monitoring one online (**cyberstalking**), leaving notes on cars, and showing up where the victim is present. *Psychological aggression* involves the use of verbal or non-verbal communication to cause another person harm, and to exert control over that person, such as name-calling, harassment, taunting, put-downs, and ridiculing, using coercion, monitoring one's whereabouts, and using threats and intimidation to tear another person down and control him or her (Breiding et al., 2015).

IPV is a significant public health problem with consequences that extend far beyond the individual families involved in the violence. IPV affects the entire community in lost revenue, lost creativity, mental health problems, and uncompensated medical care. IPV is perpetrated against both men and women, but women are far more often the targets of violence in relationships. According to the most recent statistics available, over 10 million women and men experience physical violence in an intimate relationship per year in the United States (Breiding et al., 2015), resulting in over 1.3 million injuries and 2,350 deaths (Black et al., 2011).

One in five women (29 million) and one in seven men (16 million) report having experienced severe violence during their lifetimes (Breiding et al., 2015). While men are victims of IPV, women are far more likely targets of violence in intimate relationships, particularly of more severe forms of physical violence, such as intimate partner sexual assault and murder (Black et al., 2011; Johnson, 2008). In addition, compared to men, women who have experienced IPV also experience higher rates of psychological trauma and mental illness, including depression, PTSD, anxiety, worry, nightmares, memory problems, and suicidal ideation (Karakurt, Smith, & Whiting, 2014). Women also have significantly higher rates of physical health problems as a consequence of IPV, such as chronic pain, gynecological problems, HIV/AIDS, other sexually transmitted diseases,

Children are often silent witnesses to IVP and can be deeply impacted by the violence for their entire lives

gastrointestinal problems, unwanted pregnancy, miscarriage, and premature births. Because of social structures that support **patriarchy**, women are far likelier to be economically dependent on their abuser and may be culturally and / or socially expected to remain in the relationship and endure the abuse.

Children living in home with IPV are victims as well, even if the violence is not aimed directly toward them. For instance, children who witness **interparental violence** are at increased risk of experiencing a range of problems including being emotionally, physically, and sexually abused, developing emotional and behavioral problems that often extend well into adulthood, and experiencing a range of adversities in their lives, such as having violent relationships, vocational problems, and housing insecurity (Holt, Buckley, & Whelan, 2008).

Research also indicates that boys and girls who witness IPV, particularly against their mother, often respond differently, with boys externalizing their feelings by acting like "warriors" and girls internalizing their feelings by acting like "worriers" (Blair et al., 2015). Additionally, boys who witness interparent violence, where their fathers abuse their mothers, are socialized to become violent and more likely to perpetrate violence against women as adults, whereas girls in such situations are socialized to be submissive and compliant, thus are more likely to enter into a domestic violence relationship (Roberts et al., 2010).

The Cycle of Violence

Lenore Walker (1979) was the first to coin the phrase **cycle of violence** to describe the pattern of interpersonal violence in intimate relationships. Most abusive relationships begin in a *honeymoon-like state*, with the abusers often telling their new partners that they are the only people in the world they can trust—the only ones who understand them. New partners are usually swept off their feet with compliments and many promises for a wonderful future. Once the abusers feel comfortable in the relationship, a dual process occurs. The abusers begin to feel vulnerable by recognizing their partner's power to hurt them deeply, and as familiarity in the relationship increases, the abusers often increase their sense of entitlement to have all their needs met.

Abusers, plagued with fears that they will be abandoned, taken advantage of, and humiliated (as many were in their childhoods) exhibit jealousy and possessiveness, and accusations begin. Emotional immaturity often prevents abusers from being able to separate their internal feelings from possible causes (i.e., are their feelings of jealousy caused by their own insecurities or caused by their partner's unfaithfulness?); thus a common assumption among batterers is that if they feel bad that their partners must be doing something to cause their pain. In response to these threatening feelings of vulnerability and entitlement, and poised to be hurt once again, innocent partners often become the focus of the batterer's mistrust, fear, and ultimate rage. Abusers often misinterpret the intentions of their partners, mentally ticking off injustice after injustice. These types of negative misperceptions and misassumptions are prevalent and are rarely checked against fact.

Most partners of batterers will sense the increasing tension brought about by the abusers' underlying anger that is bubbling to the surface. Batterers might ask more questions, make sarcastic comments, ask why two cups are out rather than one, or question why the phone wasn't answered more quickly when they called. They will typically have a short fuse, becoming easily frustrated often without provocation. In response, most victims do their best to *walk on eggshells* to avoid an explosion. But no amount of running interference or offered reassurances will help because the process is an internal one, occurring within the mind of the abuser. In fact, most abusers have an actual need to be proven correct in their fear of being hurt and humiliated again because to a batterer, being too trusting is often synonymous with being an unsuspecting fool.

Eventually the *explosion* occurs despite all peacemaking efforts. Abusive rages can take on several forms including frightening bouts of screaming and yelling; intimidation; and physical abuse such as hitting, kicking, scratching, grabbing, slapping, and shoving. Attacks might also include throwing objects at or near the victim, punching walls, and making threats to harm either the person or the personal property of the victim. Once batterers have experienced a violent rage, they are often temporarily relieved of their internal feelings of rage and in many respects take on the persona of a remorseful child seeking reassurance and approval. Batterers often *honeymoon* their partners and other family members who were victims of the abuse, promising never to repeat the abusive behavior. There is commonly a manipulative aspect to the batterer's professions of regret and apologies, with the extent of authentic remorse being somewhat questionable. One reason for this is that the batterer's apologies are often riddled with a series of "buts": "I'm sorry I hit you, *but* you know how I hate to be awakened early in the morning." "I'm sorry I shoved you, *but* you know I don't like you talking to other men." "I'm sorry I slapped you, *but* you know how stressed I get when work is so busy."

Rarely is the batterer's focus authentically placed on the pain and trauma caused to the partner or other family members. Rather, the honeymoon phase involves more of a panicked pleading, begging the victim not to leave, to forgive and forget, to move on quickly by minimizing the extent of the abuse. Statements intended to reframe the abuse, such as "I can't believe you think I shoved you! I clearly remember me reaching out to you and you jerking away and tripping," are common. This can be an immensely confusing time for victims, who usually know instinctively that the batterer needs help, though any attempt to point out a pattern of abuse or to hold the batterer accountable (particularly after the batterer gets comfortable once again and stops apologizing) will hasten the tension-building phase, something victims desperately want to avoid. Attempts to demand authentic change in the abuser often result in the batterer accusing the victim of holding a grudge, being unforgiving, and being punishing. Comments such as, "How dare you rub my face in this when I've already apologized! What do you want me to do? I've already said I'm sorry 100 times. Let's move on!" are common.

With the hope that the honeymoon phase might just last forever, victims of IPV often comply with the dangerous demands of the batterer to relinquish their own sense of reality and accept the reality of the batterer instead—that the abuse was not that bad, that it was a one-time event, and that it will never happen again. Living in the here-and-now allows both the batterer and the victim to avoid seeing the broader pattern of abuse, which in some respects allows them both to avoid their fear of facing the truth and seriousness of the situation. But no matter how many promises the abusive partner makes or how desperately the victim wants to believe the abuse will never occur again, without intervention the cycle is destined to repeat itself.

Many women find leaving an abusive relationship very difficult, particularly because the cycle of violence means that a honeymoon is right around the corner. But there are other forces at play as well. For instance, many women remain in an abusive relationship citing their love and commitment to their abusive partner, despite the abuse (Smith & Randall, 2007). Such women often have a romanticized view of love as a powerful force that can conquer all, a belief system influenced by American culture, particularly the media (Power, Koch, Kralik, & Jackson, 2006). Many women in abusive relationships also cited a fear of being alone (and lonely) as a reason for staying, as well as a strong fear of abandonment (McWilliams, 1999).

While some dynamics place certain women at higher risk for domestic violence, for the most part women who are in an abusive relationship or have a history of abusive relationships come from all walks of life. And although there are many theories of shared personality factors, most are not supported by research. Walker (1979) theorized that many battered women shared a common orientation of **learned helplessness**— the tendency to see oneself as powerless in controlling life events. As such, Walker predicted that battered women would have an external locus of control (the tendency to place control of their lives and choices outside of their domain of responsibility), be more passive in relationships, and have poorer problem-solving skills, compared to women who had not experienced IPV. Research has supported aspects of Walker's theory, but not others. Battered women do tend to have significantly poorer problem-solving skills, and they were also more passive in their relationships, but research did not support Walker's theory that battered women had a more external locus of control (Launius & Lindquist, 1988).

Research has found connections between decisions to remain in an abusive relationship and how battered women attribute causality of the abuse. Women who attributed their partner's abuse to personality factors, such as an inability to manage anger, a refusal to take responsibility for his behavior, or a lack of empathy, were more likely to leave the abusive relationship (Pape & Arias, 2000; Truman-Schram, Cann, Calhoun, & Vanwallendael, 2000), whereas women who attributed their partners' abusive behavior to forces outside his control, such as work stressors or a bad childhood, were more likely to remain in the relationship (Gordon, Burton, & Porter, 2004). Research has also found that women who remain in abusive relationships long-term (six or more years) experienced far higher rates of self-blame and unreasonable guilt, often citing guilt associated with self-advocacy (such as calling the police) and a belief that they had betrayed their partners (Karakurt, Smith, & Whiting, 2014).

Domestic Violence Practice Settings

One of the most common practice settings where human service providers will encounter survivors of IPV is a **women's shelter**, also sometimes called a battered women's shelter, as well as a **transitional shelter** (long-term housing focused on gaining permanent self-sufficiency). Such shelters typically offer numerous services, including the following:

- A 24-hour hotline for immediate access to information and services
- Immediate safety shelters for domestic violence victims and their children
- Individual counseling for all victims
- Survivor support groups
- Court advocacy
- Children's programs

- Teen programs
- Information referral
- Medical advocates who provide on-site support at hospitals
- Immigrant programs (depending on the ethnic makeup of the community)

Most shelters involve communal living, where residents share their living space with other survivors. Residents are often required to participate in group counseling sessions with other residents as well as assist with the general functioning and maintenance of the shelter. Human service providers are often assigned to each shelter living space and facilitate in-house programs to maintain smooth functioning within the home, as well as among the residents. Human service providers will also be likely to engage in individual counseling, case management, and court advocacy. The focus of counseling will likely vary depending upon the needs of the residents, but most often focus on educational awareness, life skills, self-sufficiency, and learning about healthy relationships, including healthy parenting, and how to be safe.

It is particularly important for human service providers to be familiar with the Internet and social media, since perpetrators can now easily track a survivor's whereabouts online, and may even use social media to harass and intimidate the victim (cyberstalking and **digital abuse**). The growing awareness of ways that perpetrators can track the online activity of victims is reflected in domestic violence awareness websites having "quick escape" buttons that pop up when the page loads. Technology can also help in the fight against IPV through online awareness campaigns, such as the *No More* campaign, which includes actors providing public service announcements using YouTube videos. Facebook is also being used to provide an online space for virtual support groups, such as the open Facebook group *Domestic Violence Support Group*.

Intervention Strategies with Survivors of IPV

Working with IPV survivors requires specialized training above generalist human services education that focuses on the unique dynamics commonly at play in abusive relationships. Most human services agencies serving the IPV survivor population require that providers and volunteers complete a 40-plus hour domestic violence training and certification program that focuses on topics such as

- The history of domestic violence
- The complexity of domestic violence
- The impact of violence on victims
- The effect of domestic violence on children
- Cultural competency
- Advocacy strategies for victims
- Legal issues, such as orders of protection and domestic violence court

Because IPV involves an abuse of psychological, sexual, economic, and physical power in order to coerce and oppress a partner, most counseling intervention strategies are based on **empowerment theory**, which focuses on increasing the personal relationship and social power of victims (Goodman & Epstein, 2008). Empowerment theory is based on feminist values of social justice, self-determination (personal choice, finding one's voice), and resiliency (overcoming abuse and oppression) (Cattaneo, Colton, & Brodsky, 2014). Using empowerment theory as the foundation of an intervention strategy relies on a strengths-based approach and focuses on helping clients increase their personal empowerment within the context of their intimate relationship.

There are several theoretical models that can be used when working with survivors of IPV that provide structure and guidance to the clinician and client. A relatively new model is the empowerment process model, developed by Cattaneo and Goodman (2015). The model focuses on clients establishing empowerment goals and taking action to achieve these goals. The actions are based on a client's evolving **self-efficacy** (belief in one's abilities), skills (concrete capabilities), knowledge (information the client must learn to achieve empowerment goals), and access to community resources (formal and informal). In this respect, the empowerment process model utilizes a psychosocial approach to self-empowerment, guiding the process of self-evolution, while connecting clients to supportive resources within their communities. The model also encompasses a process of reflection, where clients reflect on their progress and make adjustments to their goals, if necessary.

Cattaneo and Goodman stress the importance of their model as encompassing both *process* and *outcome*. Far too often clients in violent relationships are assessed (and assess themselves) based on whether they leave their abusive relationship and become self-sufficient (psychologically, socially, and economically), and yet the process of achieving interim empowerment goals incrementally are highly valuable in and of themselves. Many clients, for instance, gain a personal sense of empowerment by gaining financial literacy, long before they leave an abusive relationship.

Human service providers using the empowerment process model can work with clients in abusive relationships in every step of their empowerment journey. The various "steps" in the empowerment process are interrelated in the sense that each promotes the others. For instance, providing guidance to a client in goal-setting provides opportunities to assist clients in increasing their self-efficacy as they assess their strengths and resources. The process of gaining knowledge, such as learning about their legal rights in a divorce process, naturally leads to skill development as clients explore taking concrete steps to protect their rights, such as contacting an attorney and filing an order of protection. The reflection process can increase clients' self-efficacy as they reflect on their progress and all that they've accomplished. Again, it is important to note that "accomplishments" do not necessarily mean leaving an abusive relationship, as there are numerous areas of accomplishment leading up to that point that providers can acknowledge, thus increasing a client's sense of personal empowerment.

What is so powerful about the empowerment process model is that the authors take into account the context within which a victim of domestic violence lives, and how it is their context that creates meaning in their everyday decisions to seek safety for themselves and their children. This context is different for every client and can vary dramatically from survivor to survivor. Rather than imposing options for survivors based on a clinician's or agency's timeline or goals, Goodman et al. (2016) suggest using a *survivor-defined approach* that takes into consideration the unique situation of clients and the complexity of their lives.

Using a survivor-defined approach considers clients within the context of their environments, encouraging providers to consider factors such as the client's cultural background, including their immigration status, their family situations, their financial status, their level of support outside the relationship, and so on. It's the unique complexity of survivors' lives that influences their individual goals and the path to achieve their goals (Goodman et al., 2009). Two clients can have the same goal of leaving an abusive relationship, but depending on contextual factors in their lives their decision-making may be quite different.

Consider the college-educated client who is in an abusive relationship with a husband of three years, has no children, has remained in the workforce, has a large support network, and has independent financial resources. Now consider the client who has been married for 15 years to an abusive partner, has three children under the age of 10, has been out of the workforce for over 10 years, did not graduate from high school, has few marketable skills, who is a Mexican immigrant with residency status dependent on her marital status, has very little family in the United States, comes from a family with intergenerational abuse, and has a history of substance abuse. Both women have the goal of leaving their abusive partners, but their paths will be quite different.

It's often tempting for clinicians, particularly those working in domestic violence agencies (such as transitional shelters) to push clients along, imposing timelines and enforcing goals (this is particularly common in transitional shelters). However, such a directive approach risks the clinician becoming just another external force exerting control in the client's life, which can have a devastating effect on the client's self-esteem and can also discourage continued engagement in the counseling process. Using a survivor-defined approach with the empowerment process model not only acknowledges (and in many respects honors) the unique circumstances of each client's life but also allows clients to take control of their lives, empowering them to take an active role in planning their future and their decision-making, which increases their sense of autonomy, self-esteem, and self-efficacy.

Violence Against Women Act

In 1994 the federal government passed the Violence Against Women Act of 1994. The Violence Against Women Act (VAWA) established policies and mandates for how states were to handle cases of domestic violence, sexual assault, and dating violence (including stalking). The act's policies and mandates included encouraging mandatory arrests, encouraging interstate enforcement of domestic violence laws, and maintaining state databases on incidences of domestic violence, as well as establishing a national domestic violence database. This act also provides for numerous grants for educational purposes (e.g., the education of police officers and judges), a domestic violence hotline, battered women's shelters, and improvements in the safety of public areas such as public transportation and parks.

VAWA was reauthorized in 2000, again in 2005 as the Violent Crime Control and Law Enforcement Act, and again, after a fierce bipartisan battle, in 2013, focusing on the expanded coverage of the legislation. Prior to the 2013 reauthorization, VAWA did not protect all women who were victims of domestic violence, sexual assault, and dating violence and stalking. The reauthorization, signed into law March 7, 2013 by then President Obama, extended protection to Native women, immigrants (including undocumented immigrants), and same-sex couples (the source of the bipartisan controversy).

The Violence Against Women Act spurred several states to pass similar legislation, which continues to change the nature of domestic violence prosecutions. With regard to current policies on the prosecution of domestic violence, it is important to note that unlike a civil case, where a plaintiff brings an action and thus has the right to subsequently drop the case, in criminal cases the plaintiff is the state and the victims are witnesses. But in the past, prosecutors have allowed victims to drop a case (typically at the urgings of the batterer). Domestic violence legislation has for the most part put a stop to this practice. Instead, domestic violence is typically treated as any other crime where the victim is

Intervention strategies can also be on a macro level with domestic violence awareness campaigns and public service announcements (PSA). The 2016 Super Bowl game featured several domestic violence PSAs, including this one called "No More: Listen" about a real 911 call from a victim of domestic violence. No More is an organization that raises public awareness about domestic violence. Why do you believe this PSA has been so successful? ENHANCEDetext *video example 13.1*

www.youtube.com /watch?v=5Z_zWIVRIWk

called as a witness and must appear at the trial to testify on behalf of the state. This can create emotional tension for victims, who may initially want court involvement immediately after experiencing violence, but then want to resist any intervention when the honeymoon phase begins and renewed hope for authentic change seems possible. Since the passage of the Violence Against Women Act, incidents of domestic violence have been cut by more than half, and the national hotline handles about 22,000 calls per month.

Intervention Strategies with Batterers

Strategies for reducing recidivism rates among batterers have varied through the years, with some approaches involving punishment via the criminal justice system and other strategies focusing on court-mandated psychological intervention. In the past the criminal justice system sought traditional forms of justice for those convicted of domestic violence in the form of incarceration. However, this approach was often unsuccessful because some judges were reluctant to break apart families, and some victims of domestic violence were reluctant to testify against their partners or spouses, particularly if it meant the possibility of incarceration. In response, many states developed specialized domestic violence courts with the goal of incorporating mental health and **psychoeducational approaches**, such as empowerment theory anger management training, in lieu of jail. If defendants successfully completed a batterer intervention program (and any other intervention requirements) their sentences were vacated, but if they did not, or they engaged in repeated violence, their sentences were reinstated.

Many batterer intervention programs are based upon the Duluth Model—a psychoeducational program drawn from feminist theory, which posits that domestic violence is caused by patriarchal ideology that promotes the concept that men have the right to control their female partners. Many batterer intervention programs are also based upon group treatment using cognitive behavioral therapy (CBT) and anger management training, although anger management training alone is insufficient because it does not address the underlying values of patriarchy and control (anger is not the root of the problem, but rather a tool used by the batterer). Newer programs use a multifaceted treatment design, based on the premise that battering is a complex problem encompassing a deeply rooted belief system of power and control, thus a combination of psychoeducation, CBT, and anger management in a group setting is more likely to be successful.

Programs range in duration from six weeks to one year and are often mandated by the court as a part of sentencing. Batterers are taught to respect personal boundaries, the difference between feelings and actions, and the concept of personal rights and egalitarian relationships. Dynamics of **social learning theory**, including modeling, are also explored so participants can discover how their violent behavior is likely patterned after a parent or some other influential person in their lives. Participants also learn how to identify their personal triggers and learn strategies for managing their anger, including how to control impulses and how to use "I" statements to avoid getting caught up in making accusations.

Most batterer treatment programs have similar goals, including *increasing awareness of violent behavior* and *encouraging the batterer to take responsibility for violent behavior*. Common program philosophies include the following beliefs:

- Violence is an intentional act
- Domestic violence uses physical force and intimidation as coercive methods to obtain and maintain control in the relationship
- Using violence is a learned behavior and as such can be unlearned

Many participants make authentic changes not only because of the curriculum but also because of the built-in accountability that a group setting provides. Ironically, it is the other group members who often challenge those participants who refuse to engage or who consistently blame the victim for their own abusive behavior. Unfortunately, at least an equal number of participants do not authentically change while in a program. Some batterers fail to complete the program, and others are reluctant to change because they actually love the adrenaline rush and power they get from feeling intense anger (Pandya & Gingerich, 2002).

Whether batterer intervention programs actually work is a question that remains unanswered for the most part. A 2003 study commissioned by the U.S. Department of Justice (DOJ) found little support for the success of batterer intervention programs with regard to recidivism rates, or attitudes toward domestic violence. The only significant difference found was in the re-offense rates of men who completed programs 26 weeks or longer. Yet, while these men had significantly lower recidivism rates, their attitudes about domestic violence did not appear to change much. For instance, men in the experimental group (the batterer intervention program) viewed their partners only slightly less responsible for the battering incident than men in the control group.

The study's authors cited numerous limitations of the study, which may have been responsible for the results, including a high drop-out rate among participants and questionable validity of the attitudinal surveys. Based upon these limitations, the authors recommended that batterer intervention programs be allowed to continue to evolve (since they are a relatively new tool in the fight against domestic violence), but in a manner that was responsive to the increased knowledge that is being gained about the nature of IPV, including common risk factors for becoming a batterer. A follow-up study on the Duluth Model in 2014 found that about one-third of participants eventually reoffended, and those who completed at least 24 weeks of treatment experienced the most positive outcomes among all participants, defined as decreases in physical and verbal aggression (Herman, Rotunda, Williamson, & Vodanovich, 2014).

Recent research on the effectiveness of batterer intervention programs has focused on participants' readiness to change—a batterer's personal motivation to effect a meaningful change in their attitudes and behaviors about violence and control in intimate relationships. Motivation to change was assessed through **motivational interviewing (MI)** assessments, as well as through the manner in which a participant entered a program (court-ordered vs. self-referral). The studies found that participants who were ready to change had far higher success rates after completing a batterer intervention program than those who had little motivation to change (Bowen & Gilchrist, 2010; Zalmanowitz, 2012). While these results may not seem surprising, they can be helpful for practitioners and other professionals working in the area of domestic violence in terms of assessing high-risk perpetrators, making sentencing decisions (based on assessments of who is most amenable to treatment), as well as exploring ways of increasing clients' motivations and readiness to change.

ENHANCEDetext *self-check 13.1*

RAPE AND SEXUAL ASSAULT

Another form of violence against a person is the act of rape or sexual assault. Sexual assault involves forcing some form of sexual act on another person without his or her consent. Determining the rate of sexual assault in the United States is difficult due to dramatic variations in the way sexual assault is defined. Although both men and women can be raped, women are victims of rape far more often than men. Approximately one in five women in the United States have been raped sometime during their lifetime, and more than half of them were raped by intimate partners (Black et al., 2011).

For the first time since 1927, the legal definition of forcible rape has been changed. According to the Uniform Crime Reports (UCR), the former definition was: "the carnal knowledge of a female, forcibly and against her will." That definition, unchanged since 1927, was outdated and narrow. It only included forcible male penile penetration of a female vagina. The new definition is: "[t]he penetration, no matter how slight, of the vagina or anus with any body part or object, or oral penetration by a sex organ of another person, without the consent of the victim." This is an important victory for advocates since this expanded definition now includes rape of both genders, rape with an object, and sexual acts with anyone who cannot give consent due to mental or physical disability.

According to the National Crime Victimization Survey (NCVS) there were 150,420 victims of rape or sexual assault (attack or attempted attack, including unwanted sexual contact) in 2014 (compared to 173,610 in 2013 and 118,700 in 2012), of which only about one-third were reported to police (Truman & Langton, 2015). About 75 percent of all women who were raped were assaulted by perpetrators they knew and about 25 percent were assaulted by strangers. African American women are raped at a higher rate (relative to the population) than White or Hispanic women. And indigenous populations (Native Americans, Alaskan Natives, Hawaiian Natives, and Pacific Islanders) are two-and-one-half times more likely to experience violent sexual assault in their lifetimes.

The Controversy Surrounding Rape

There is considerable controversy surrounding rape statistics though, including the methodology used to collect data, how questions are phrased, and even how rape and sexual assault are defined. Consider, for example, that according to the Centers for Disease Control (CDC) National Intimate Partner and Sexual Violence Survey, about two million adult women were raped in 2011. Compare this statistic to the U.S. Department of Justice NCVS, which estimated that there were 238,000 rapes and sexual assaults reported in 2011 (note that this does not mean that 238,000 individual women were raped, but that there were this many incidences of rapes and sexual assaults reported) (U.S. Department of Justice, 2011). Why is there such a difference in estimates? Critics cite gender bias, such as questions designed to elicit an affirmative response from women but a negative response from men (Young, 2014).

Consider that the CDC definition for rape or sexual assault against women is quite broad, whereas for men, it is quite narrow. For instance, the CDC survey includes incapacitated sexual acts—defined as sexual activity when the respondent was too intoxicated to consent—for women only. Incapacitated sexual acts constituted two-thirds of all reported rapes on the CDC survey, and yet did not include instructions to rule out instances of voluntary sex while intoxicated. Further, the CDC defined rape of men as forcible sexual activity by another man, but did not include instances where men were too incapacitated to consent to sexual activity with women, or instances where men were forced to penetrate a woman, or receive or give oral sex to a woman (rather these were included as "other sexual violence").

In other words, if a man reports being forced to have sexual intercourse with a woman, the CDC classifies that not as rape, but as "sexual coercion" or "other sexual violence," but if a woman reports being forced to have sexual intercourse with a man, or having sex while intoxicated (voluntarily or involuntarily), that is considered rape. Are the differences in definitions fair? Do they factually represent qualitative differences in sexual experiences where men have more power in society than women? Or do they reflect gender-based stereotypes where men always want sex (regardless of who it is with), and women are not responsible for the choices they make, even the foolish ones? Does presuming women are always victims and cannot be perpetrators of violence accurately capture the culture of rape and patriarchy in our society, or does it rob women of their free choice and agency? Some critics of the CDC approach believe that the latter is true, and that such an attitude trivializes the problem of female-perpetrated assaults on men (Young, 2014). Treating sexual assault in a gender-neutral manner may sound good on the surface, but the question must be asked whether this approach trivializes the long-standing problem of violence against women in our society. If this is the case, then perhaps relying on gender-contextualized definitions of rape and sexual assault is the most effective way of reflecting longstanding and deeply rooted gender power disparities in society. What do you believe?

The problem of sexual assault on college campuses, particularly **incapacitated sex**, has gained considerable attention, as well as generated controversy, in the past few years, in large part due to several high profile on-campus rape allegations. The attention was warranted because of the alarming rate of sexual assaults on campuses across the country, particularly incapacitated sex, and the perceived general indifference on the part of many college administrators.

Several researchers have reported that one in five women are raped while in college, but the variation of sexual assaults and misconduct across universities has put that estimate in question. The Association of American Universities (AAU) conducted a survey of 27 public and private universities across the United States and found that the rate of sexual assault ranged significantly across universities depending on the type of sexual violence or misconduct. The survey found that overall, about 23 percent of undergraduate female college students reported having been sexually assaulted by physical force, coercion, or while incapacitated since starting college. The rate of sexual assault ranged by year in college, with freshmen reporting the highest rate and seniors reporting the lowest (11.7 percent). Some universities reported rates as high as 30 percent, exceeded only by sexual assaults of transgender, **genderqueer**, and other nonconforming or questioning students (TGON). Additionally, the survey found that the distribution of female undergraduate students who reported having been subjected to sexual harassment ranged from an alarming 49 to 74 percent (Cantor & Fischer, 2015).

Unfortunately, there have been a few high-profile cases involving false allegations, such as the Rolling Stone story of "Jackie," the college student from University of Virginia who alleged being gang raped by a group of fraternity members (Coronel, Coll, & Kravitz,

Gallaudet University students, faculty, and staff use their phones as a light source as the power temporarily went out during a rally and protest against sexual violence on April 7, 2015 in Washington, DC. The university is promoting the "It's On Us" campaign, a White House-led initiative that asks men and women across America to make a personal commitment to be a part of the solution to combat campus sexual assaults

© RICKY CARIOTI/THE WASHINGTON POST/ GETTY IMAGES

Some male college students have complained about many universities' policy of expelling the accused before a criminal investigation, stating that it is unfair and biased because such policies rob them of due process. After watching the video on the lawsuit filed by two male college students against the University of Texas, write down three arguments in support of the male students' claims and three arguments in support of the university. What did you learn from this exercise?

ENHANCEDetext *video example 13.2*

www.youtube.com/watch?v=
mDDThO586LY&nohtml5=False

2015a). Jackie's story did not stand up to scrutiny and Rolling Stone magazine ultimately recanted the story, leading to a flurry of accusations and counter-accusations regarding definitions, allegations, and narratives (Coronel, Coll, & Kravitz, 2015b). Despite controversies regarding how rape is defined, how statistics are calculated, the role of gender bias against women and men, and the nature of campus policies and their effectiveness, the problem of rape and sexual assault in the United States, and particularly on college campuses, is very serious and in need of continued attention.

Recognizing the role patriarchy has played in creating a culture that stigmatizes female victims and makes excuses for male offenders does not negate the existence or seriousness of female-on-male rape. Sexual assault is a complex social problem that involves an abuse of power, most often targeting members of the population that lack power within society. Thus, while all forms of sexual assault warrant a serious response, rape and sexual assault targeting populations that have historically lacked power in society is at the core of sexual assault advocacy for women.

Why Men Rape

An important factor in prevention is understanding why men rape women, which includes being able to distinguish fact from myths. One of the more common myths of why rape occurs includes blaming the victim by asserting that the victim wanted it, liked it, or in some way deserved the sexual assault because she provoked the assailant (by dressing or acting provocatively, etc.). Myths about rapists include assertions that men just cannot control their sexual desires and thus are not responsible for sexually assaulting women (Burt, 1991). The damage done by the proliferation of these rape myths is plentiful because they blame the victim while exonerating the perpetrator, which undermines societal prohibition against sexual violence.

In fact, a 1998 study at University of Mannheim in Germany (Bohner et al., 1998) found that such myths actually encourage sexual assault by giving rapists a way of rationalizing their antisocial behavior. In other words, although Western social customs may claim to abhor rape, popular rape myths provide rapists a way around such social mores by encouraging the belief that victims in some way *asked for it* and that men simply *cannot control themselves,* and thus they really haven't done anything wrong, or at least nothing that many other men haven't done as well.

The Psychological Impact of Sexual Assault

The physical and psychological impact of sexual assault is serious and long-lasting and may include PTSD, depression, increased anxiety, fear of risk-taking, development of trust issues, increased physical problems including exposure to sexually transmitted diseases such as HIV/AIDS, chronic pelvic pain, gastrointestinal disorders, and unwanted pregnancy (CDC, 2005). In 1975 Lynda Holmstrom and Ann Burgess coined the term **rape trauma syndrome** (RTS), a collection of emotions similar to PTSD, commonly experienced in response to being a survivor of a forced violent sexual assault.

RTS includes an initial phase where the survivor experiences both psychological and physical symptoms such as feeling extreme fear, persistent crying, and sleep disturbances, as well as other reactions to the actual assault such as the common fear of being killed during the assault. Survivors in subsequent phases avoid social interaction, experience a loss of self-esteem, feel inappropriate guilt, and in some cases, develop clinical depression. Many survivors minimize their feelings and reactions to the assault and avoid seeking treatment because they do not want to be stigmatized, which can contribute to RTS. In fact, one of the primary reasons most rape crisis advocates refer to clients as *survivors* rather than as *victims* is to reduce this stigma by focusing on the strength it takes to survive sexual violence.

Male-on-Male Sexual Assault

Men are also victims of sexual assault, in the form of child sexual abuse, same-sex date rape, male-on-male stranger rape, prison rape, and female-on-male rape. Research on male-on-male sexual assault is sparse with the exception of some early efforts to identify the nature and dynamics of male rape. The reason for the lack of studies in this area may be related to the belief that male rape is rare, at least outside prison walls. In fact, historically, the legal definition of rape does not even account for the possibility of men being victims. Due to the stigma associated with being a victim of male-on-male sexual assault, most incidences of rape go unreported, and thus it is impossible to accurately assess incidence rates. Even rapes that occur in prisons often go unreported, not only because of the fear of retaliation, but also because of the shame men feel in response to being victimized in this manner.

Treating men who have been sexually assaulted is similar in some respects to serving the female survivor population except that the shame men feel, although equal in intensity, tends to be more focused on their gender identity as males. Heterosexual men who were victims of male-on-male rape reported questioning their sexual identity and orientation because they were unable to fight off their attackers. Men also have a greater tendency to turn toward alcohol and drugs in response to the rape. Men also experience sexual dysfunction and problems getting close to people, particularly in intimate relationships. In addition, as is the case with female victims, some male victims become sexually promiscuous after a sexual assault or abuse (Mezey & King, 1989).

More studies need to be conducted on both female-on-male rape and male-on-male rape, particularly on the differing dynamics of sexual assault in ethnic minority populations. What research there is on ethnic minority populations seems to indicate that victims of sexual assault who are Caucasian and have higher levels of academic education tend to seek mental health counseling more often than victims of color or those with less education (Ullman & Brecklin, 2002; Vearnals & Campbell, 2001). This certainly has practical implications for human service providers who through assessment or advocacy have the opportunity to reach out to survivors of sexual assault and abuse.

Rape Crisis Centers

Human service providers working in any practice setting will likely encounter a victim of sexual assault at some point in their careers. This might involve a recent victim seeking support services on the heels of an assault, but it is far more likely that rape victims will present for counseling at some point long after an assault, perhaps even years later, and might not even connect the problems they are currently experiencing with a past sexual assault.

Human service providers who work directly with victims of sexual assault usually do so at a rape crisis center or sexual assault advocacy organization. Many states require that each county have at least one rape crisis center that offers a wide range of services including a 24-hour hotline, around-the-clock on-site advocacy during medical examinations and investigative interviews, and crisis counseling, as well as long-term individual and group counseling.

Many human service providers who work with sexual assault victims receive from 40 to 50 hours of specialized training focusing on the history of the rape crisis movement, the nature of crisis counseling, the dynamics of RTS, rape myths, and the dangers of gender oppression. Training also includes information on normal child and adult developmental stages and how these stages are affected by sexual violence and trauma.

ENHANCEDetext *self-check 13.2*

HATE CRIMES AGAINST LGBTQ+ POPULATIONS

Historically, individuals (primarily men) who were considered to be "homosexual" were considered sinful and immoral, committing "unnatural acts," called either sodomy or buggery. Men who were suspected of engaging in "homosexual behavior" were often subjected to inhumane and unscientific examinations of their anuses in an attempt to determine if sexual intercourse with another man had occurred (this type of examination is still occurring in some parts of the world). In fact, not only were same-sex relationships criminalized in the United States, they were considered a mental disorder by the American Psychiatric Association (APA) until 1973.

Many of the hateful acts committed against members of **LGBTQ+ populations** can be better understood if viewed through the lens of **homophobia**—the irrational dread of, hostility toward, and prejudice against members of the LGBTQ+ populations. Although the term "homophobia" is now perceived as somewhat limiting in the sense that it does not capture the totality of oppression and discrimination that the LGBTQ+ community has experienced, considered in a broader context, it can be useful in better understanding anti-gay attitudes rooted in stigma and sexual prejudice (Herek, 2009).

Despite increased acceptance of LGBTQ+ populations, hate crimes are on the rise in the United States. In fact, according to the Federal Bureau of Investigation (FBI), hate crimes against those perceived to be gay or lesbian, or those with nonconforming gender expression, increased to over 20 percent of all documented hate crimes in the United States in 2011. This increase makes sexual orientation the second most common target of hate crimes in the United States, more common than religion, ethnicity/national origin, and disabilities (race remains the largest target of hate crimes in the United States).

In addition to an increase in the number of hate crimes in the United States, according to research the level of violence of crimes targeting sexual orientation and gender-nonconformance is considerably higher when compared to hate crimes targeting other types of differences (Dunbar, 2006). For instance, the majority of hate crimes committed against members of the LGBTQ+ populations, or those perceived to be LGBTQ+, are against the person, not property, and include physical assault, harassment, and intimidation. Also, most hate crime murders committed in the United States are committed against members of the LGBTQ+ and gender non-conforming populations.

Members of the LGBTQ+ population are acutely aware of the risks they face, and even if they haven't personally been targeted, the high number of hate crimes targeting this population can lead to a sort of vicarious trauma. This dynamic is reflected in a recent Gallup poll, which found that over 50 percent of LGBTQ+ populations reported being concerned about becoming victims of a hate crime, and of these, about one quarter report being extremely concerned. This percentage becomes even more meaningful when compared to that of the general population, where only about six percent of people reported being concerned about becoming a victim of a hate crime, and over half of the general population reported no concerns at all about hate violence (Marzullo, Libman, Crimes, Lesbian, & Ruddell-Tabisola, 2009).

On October 6, 1998 at around 8:00 P.M., a 21-year-old gay Wyoming college student Matthew Shepard was kidnapped by two men, driven to a remote area, tied to a fence, beaten ruthlessly, and left for dead. The perpetrators, both 21-year-old locals, saw Shepard in a bar and pretended to be gay in order to gain Shepard's trust. They targeted him because he was gay and their attack and ultimate murder of him was an intentional act.

The two men could not be charged with a hate crime because at the time, sexual orientation, gender, and gender identity were not protected classes in existing hate crimes legislation. In response to this heinous crime and the work of social justice advocates, in October 2009 then President Obama signed into law the Matthew Shepard & James Byrd, Jr. Hate Crimes Prevention Act (P.L. 111- 84).

The Hate Crimes Prevention Act makes it a federal crime to assault individuals because of their sexual orientation, gender, or gender identity. The passage of this somewhat contested legislation has been lauded by civil rights organizations as a significant step forward in the fight for equality and protection of the LGBTQ+ populations. However, far more must be done, particularly since hate crimes against LGBT people tend to be grossly underreported, particularly crimes that are highly violent (Human Rights Campaign, 2013).

The vulnerability of LGBTQ+ populations to marginalization, injustice, and violence due to their sexual orientation and gender identity expression is magnified considerably with increasing levels of vulnerability. The interaction between multiple aspects of identity, such as gender, race, class, and sexual orientation, and their impact on social inequality is often referred to as the intersectionality of vulnerability (McCall, 2005). In the context of sexual orientation, the theory of intersectionality posits that societal oppression in the form of various types of social injustice, such as racism, sexism, **ableism**, **ageism**, and homophobia, do not act independent of one another, and in fact interact creating increasingly magnified forms of social oppression depending upon the number of vulnerabilities an individual possesses.

While all women experience some form of gender bias, an economically disadvantaged African American woman will experience more social oppression than a middle-class Caucasian woman, because of the two identity categories of vulnerability (racial minority and poverty). However, add sexual orientation, a complex identity category, and the intersection of race, gender, sexual orientation, and perhaps gender identity expression and gender nonconformance will significantly increase this individual's vulnerability to social oppression, injustice, and bias-based violence (Meyer,

After watching the film about Matthew Shepard's murder, produced by the Matthew Shepard Foundation, describe what you believe is at the root of anti-gay hate crimes.
ENHANCEDetext *video example 13.3*
www.youtube.com/watch?v=TOsgy7CYnMI&nohtml5=False

NYC, October 19, 1998: Candlelight vigil for slain gay Wyoming student Matthew Shepard

© EVAN AGOSTINI / HULTON ARCHIVE / GETTY IMAGES

2012). In fact, a recent report revealed that transgendered women of color were disproportionately targeted in hate crimes (Chestnut, Dixon, & Jindasurat, 2013).

Human service providers working with a diverse population may not be aware of the sexual orientation or gender identity of their clients, but can more effectively advocate for them if they remain open to disclosures and remain aware of the vulnerability of LGBTQ+ populations to marginalization, **micro-aggressions**, and violence. Clients may or may not disclose whether orientation and gender identity initially arise due to fear of stigmatization, thus developing cultural competence in working with these populations is vitally important, as a provider's awareness and sensitivity will increase the likelihood that clients will feel more at ease disclosing any negative experiences.

Hate crimes targeting populations perceived as different in some way remain a serious problem, despite attempts to stop them through awareness campaigns and legislation. LGBTQ+ populations remain targets of hate crimes, which can have a lasting impact on those who are victimized, as well as their family and friends. Even if a member of the LGBTQ+ community is not personally a victim of bias-based violence, research shows that many within this population are afraid they will be; thus the experience of **vicarious trauma** is common. Creating an accepting environment and incorporating trauma-informed therapies into the counseling of LGBTQ+ and gender non-conforming populations can have a positive effect on clients who have experienced hate crimes and other types of violence.

ENHANCEDetext *self-check 13.3*

VICTIMS OF VIOLENT CRIME

In 2014 there were approximately 7.4 million violent and serious violent crimes committed in the United States (compared to just over 8 million in 2013). Although violent crime has declined in recent years, according to the National Crime Victimization Survey, serious violent crime has increased slightly between 2013 and 2014, particularly serious violence involving a weapon and stranger violence (Truman & Langton, 2015). Human service providers work with victims of violent crime in a variety of capacities and settings, providing advocacy and counseling, as well as engaging in advocacy on a micro and macro level.

Historically, victims of crime had virtually no rights in criminal proceedings because the U.S. criminal justice system is based on the presumption of innocence. Because defendants charged with a criminal offenses are innocent until proven guilty, legally there can be no victims until after a verdict is rendered. If there are no victims prior to a defendant being convicted, then there are no rights to enforce. In addition, in criminal proceedings the case is considered an action committed against the state, and thus other than being a witness, historically, victims of crime have had no special status. This logic, which is consistent with the U.S. criminal justice system, is completely backward for most victims and victim advocates.

The victims' rights movement gained momentum in the 1980s when victims of crime came together along with advocates in the human services fields to secure both a voice within the criminal justice community and some basic rights in the criminal justice system. The victims' movement is based not on the desire to lessen the rights of criminal defendants, but rather on the desire to increase the rights of victims. Rights include being notified of court hearings, appearing at all legal proceedings, making a statement at sentencing, and being kept apprised of the incarceration status of the perpetrator. Most crime victims and victim advocates state that a primary goal of the victims' movement is to ensure that crime victims have a voice within the community, specifically within the criminal justice system (Mika, Achilles, Halbert, Amstutz, & Zehr, 2004). How that voice gets heard is certainly up for debate. Whether through direct face-to-face meetings with criminal justice officials or through the active involvement in victim-sensitive training of police personnel, prosecutors, and judges, victims advocacy groups continue to work toward a system that sees victims as a central aspect of the criminal justice process (Quinn, 1998).

In response to the victims' movement and subsequent federal legislation (42 U.S.C. § 10606[b]), all states now have a Victim's Bill of Rights ensuring certain basic rights to victims as well as protection for victims of violent crime. Although there is some variation from state to state, most states ensure that victims of violent crime be afforded the following rights:

- The right to be treated with dignity and fairness and with respect for the victim's dignity and privacy
- The right to be reasonably protected from the accused offender
- The right to be notified of court proceedings
- The right to be present at all public court proceedings related to the offense, unless the court determines that testimony by the victim would be materially affected if the victim heard other testimony at trial
- The right to confer with the attorney for the government in the case
- The right to restitution
- The right to information about the conviction, sentencing, imprisonment, and release of the offender (Victim's Rights Act of 1998)

Victim–Witness Assistance Programs

In response to federal legislation and Victim's Bill of Rights, state prosecution units within prosecutors' offices (state's attorney, district attorney, and attorney general offices) developed specialized units called Victim–Witness Assistance, designed to enforce victims' rights and provide support for victims through the criminal justice process. Human service providers working within these departments offer the following services:

- Crisis intervention counseling
- Referrals to coordinating human services agencies, such as rape crisis centers, battered women's shelters, and crime victim support groups
- Referrals to advocacy organizations such as Mothers Against Drunk Driving (MADD), who have a presence in court to ensure enforcement of victims' rights
- Advocacy and accompaniment in court proceedings
- Special services or units for victims of domestic violence, child victims, older adults, and victims with disabilities
- Case status updates including notification of all public court proceedings
- Foreign language translation
- Assistance with obtaining compensation, such as reimbursement for counseling and medical costs
- Assistance in preparation and writing of victim impact statements to be read by the victim at the sentencing hearing

Victim–witness advocates may have a master's degree in any of the applied social science disciplines (social work, psychology, general human services), but often work at the bachelor's level with some specialized training in the dynamics involved in violent crime victimization. Advocates must also be familiar with the inner workings of the criminal justice system because victims of violent crime often feel revictimized when they must endure the often confusing labyrinth of the prosecution system.

The average person may not be familiar with the differing duties of a local police department and a state prosecuting office, nor with how a criminal case proceeds toward prosecution. Those individuals who have become victims of a crime must be quick studies so they can be prepared for what is going to happen next. Victim–witness advocates can help crime victims understand the process of a criminal trial and the importance and value of each step within the prosecution process.

If a case goes to trial the victim–witness advocate will work closely with the victims to help prepare them for testifying. The clinical issues involved depend on the nature of the crime and victimization. For instance, if the defendant is the victim's spouse who is charged with domestic battery, the clinical issues will likely involve fear of retaliation and guilt in response to testifying against a spouse, particularly if there is a possibility that the defendant might have to serve time in jail or prison. If the defendant was charged with sexual assault, the victim will likely experience feelings of shame, embarrassment, and fear. A victim of home invasion might experience intense fear of retaliation once the defendant becomes aware of the victim's cooperation and testimony. In each instance the victim–witness advocate will work with community human services agencies and advocates to provide support and assistance to the victim in preparation for trial.

Once a defendant is found guilty, either through trial or a **plea arrangement**, a sentencing hearing is scheduled. In a sentencing hearing both sides have an opportunity to advocate for a sentence they believe is appropriate. It is the responsibility of the victim–witness advocate to assist victims in writing their victim impact statements, which are often read in open court before the judge, jury, and defendant. Although the statements are written in the words of the victims, they have a dual purpose—giving victims a voice in court and assisting the prosecutor in obtaining the desired sentence. Thus, it is important that victims receive guidance in writing their statements. This also serves as another opportunity for victims to express and work through their pain, and thus it is often an effective clinical tool.

Surviving Victims of Homicide

Some of the most emotionally intense and difficult cases for victim–witness advocates are homicide cases, particularly when the primary victim is a child. The victim–witness advocate must develop a high threshold for dealing with another's emotional pain because the pain of losing a loved one through violence is often unlike any other loss. Revictimization through the criminal justice process is almost a certainty as surviving victims of homicide are forced to balance their desire to represent their loved one in court by being present at all hearings with the trauma inherently involved in having to hear about the gruesome details of the crime, including how their loved one suffered.

Research strongly suggests the importance of providing supportive counseling services and advocacy in the weeks immediately following a homicide. Surviving victims of **intrafamilial homicides**, where one family member kills another, are particularly prone to psychologically complex reactions involving both internal and external stressors. Most

Watch the video of Lizzi Marriott's mother, Melissa, delivering her victim impact statement at the sentencing hearing for her 19-year-old daughter's rapist and murderer, Seth Mazzaglia. What skills do you believe human service providers must develop in order to effectively assist survivors of violent crime to prepare a victim impact statement?

ENHANCEDetext *video example 13.4*

www.youtube.com/watch?v=qt0fF_sA8n0

experts suggest the use of crisis counseling immediately following the crime, focusing on the concrete needs of the surviving victims. This approach is important in light of research, which suggests that surviving victims of homicide are most likely to utilize advocacy services during the initial crisis phase (Horne, 2003).

The needs of surviving victims of homicide are complex, particularly in the weeks and months after the murder. Surviving victims of homicide must cooperate with various law enforcement agencies and attend court proceedings at the same time they are planning a funeral and contending with the effects and belongings of the murdered victim. This can be quite overwhelming during a time when they are dealing with the paralyzing shock of losing a loved one in a sudden and violent manner.

Regardless of the nature of the crime committed, victims of violent crime all have basic needs that can be addressed by the human service providers working with them in treatment (Courtois, 2004). Common treatment goals include:

1. Building formal and informal social support systems
2. Reinforcing ways to regain a sense of safety
3. Teaching victims how to manage their emotions, such as anger, sadness, and fear
4. Achieving physical and psychological stability
5. Building skills that will help victims regain a sense of personal power and control over their lives
6. Educating the client on the nature of the crime victimization so they know what to expect
7. Reconditioning victims to minimize negative triggering of the traumatic incident
8. Helping victims through the mourning process
9. Seeking resolution and closure which leads to personal growth and allows the victim to regain the confidence and strength to trust people once again

By focusing on these core issues, as well as addressing the factors and needs specific to each type of crime victimization, the human service provider will be instrumental in fostering healing and growth in victims of crime so they can begin the process of seeing themselves no longer as victims but as survivors.

ENHANCEDetext *self-check 13.4*

WORKING WITH PERPETRATORS OF CRIME

The human services profession has a long history of association with the criminal justice system, most notably working in jails, prisons, government probation departments, police departments, and agencies offering services to recently released offenders. Human service providers working within the criminal justice system may be employed as prison or correctional psychologists who conduct psychological evaluations on recently charged defendants or who provide assessment or counseling to offenders within the prison system.

Human service providers working with perpetrators of crime may be licensed social workers who provide counseling and facilitate support groups focusing on various forms of violence designed to reduce recidivism. They may be probation officers charged with the responsibility of coordinating treatment and supervising the offender's compliance with the conditions of probation (e.g., entering a drug treatment program, obtaining counseling, attending an anger management program, or completing community service), or they may be bachelor's level correctional treatment specialists or case managers who provide general counseling to the prison population, assisting them in preparing for release and reentry into society. They may also be aides or volunteers working with youth gang members in an after-school diversion program.

Human service providers may also work on a community level advocating for prison reform such as the development of mental health courts, substance abuse treatment programs in prisons, or increased mental health services for mentally ill prisoners. Thus, although this field of service is broad, the clinical issues are specialized, requiring training focusing on the common issues facing offenders both within prison and on release.

Gang Activity

Gangs consist of groups of individuals who actively participate in criminal activities on an organized or coordinated basis. Gang activity has become an increasingly severe problem in recent years, not only with regard to the number of gangs in operation within the United States (estimated to be somewhere between 700,000 and 800,000 nationwide), but also with regard to the type of violent activities in which many gang members participate. Gang activity remains primarily a big-city phenomenon, with some of the larger cities having more than 30 gangs operating at one time (National Youth Gang Center, 2005). Smaller towns and rural communities also experience gang problems, but these tend to be relatively sporadic with gangs that are loosely organized.

Gang members commit crimes such as theft, drug trafficking, assault, and intimidation. When gang members engage in turf wars where one gang is in conflict with another, gang fights often ensue, involving both serious assaults and homicides. In some urban communities, such as Chicago and Baltimore, drive-by shootings are a way of life, and parents respond by keeping their young children off the streets and away from windows. And even that doesn't keep some children safe, evidenced by the alarming number of children who are shot inadvertently by bullets that crash through living room windows.

Most gang members are between the ages of 13 and 25, but some studies found gangs that have members as young as 10. Most gang members come from backgrounds of poverty and racial oppression, live in high-crime urban communities, and live in neighborhoods with high gang activity (Vigil, 2003). Although there has been a recent increase in female gang activity (Chesney-Lind, 1999), most gangs are still primarily comprised of males.

Every year the FBI releases a report on gang activity in the United States called the National Gang Report (NGR), which provides an assessment of gang activity across the country. The report is based on surveys of law enforcement agencies throughout the United States. The report categorizes gang activity into four categories: (1) street gang activity (neighborhood gangs and national gangs), (2) prison gang activity, (3) **outlaw motorcycle gang (OMG)** activity, and (4) cross-border gang activity (gang activity between the U.S./Mexico border). This year's report shows an increase in the size of all gangs in the past two years, as well as increases in gang-related crime (National Gang Report, 2015).

Neighborhood gangs pose a threat to residents, industry, and law enforcement. Prison gangs pose a threat to prison efficiency and the safety of both staff and other prisoners, as well as to the community in general since there remains a strong connection between prison gangs and street gangs. Gangs in general are increasing their criminal activities as well as the seriousness of the crimes they are committing. For instance, gangs consistently engage in drug trafficking crimes (e.g., manufacturing, trafficking, distribution), intimidation (e.g., threats, assaults, murder), and financial crimes (e.g., identity theft, credit card theft, money laundering). More recently street gangs have been increasingly involved in sex trafficking (international and domestic) and prostitution and have formed alliances with other gangs across the country and international sex trafficking rings to increase sex trafficking across the country. Activity between U.S. gangs and gangs and cartels in Mexico, referred to as Mexican Transnational Criminal Organizations (MTCO), has also increased significantly in the last two years, with prison gangs often facilitating the connection between the two. Threats against law enforcement, while remaining stable in numbers, have increased in boldness and level of violence (National Gang Report, 2015).

According to the FBI, gangs have two primary goals: to make money and increase their power. They accomplish both goals through criminal activity, the former through trafficking and robbery, and the latter through intimidation and violence. The NGR (2015) also reports that street gangs and OMGs have increased their power and reach by seeking employment in law enforcement agencies, the military, and other government institutions, as well as coordinating with other criminal organizations, such as international sex trafficking rings and MTCOs.

Another interesting trend is the dramatic increase in gangs using social media for recruiting new members, communication between gang members and other gangs, the targeting of rivals, the facilitation of criminal activity, and circumventing law enforcement. Social media has also been used to make threats to law enforcement. The most popular social media sites used by gang members are Facebook, YouTube, Instagram, and Twitter. Additionally, prison gangs use smuggled cell phones to communicate with street gangs and new recruits via social media sites such as Facebook. In 2014 alone, the California Department of Corrections confiscated close to 15,000 cell phones from prisoners, many of which were smuggled in by corrupt prison staff in exchange for cash and sex (National Gang Report, 2015). In response to the dramatic rise of gangs using social media, law enforcement agencies are now actively monitoring social media as a part of their surveillance of gang activity.

Risk Factors of Gang Involvement

There are several theories regarding why people (primarily men) join gangs. Most sociological and anthropological theories focus on the sense of solidarity and feelings of belonging that gangs can provide members, particularly disenfranchised youth. Identifying risk factors is important so that effective intervention strategies can be developed and implemented.

A comprehensive study facilitated by the DOJ evaluated the gang membership and backgrounds of over 800 gang members from 1985 to 2001 in an attempt to identify some of the reasons why adolescents join gangs. This study, referred to as the Seattle Social Development Project, confirmed that the majority of gang members are men (90 percent) and that gang members came from diverse ethnic backgrounds including Caucasian (European American), Asian, Latino, Native American, and African American, with African Americans having the highest rates of gang membership. Interestingly, the study found that the majority of gang members joined for only a short time, with 70 percent of youths belonging to a gang for less than a year (Hawkins et al., 2003).

The study identified multiple risk factors for gang membership, including living in high-crime neighborhoods, coming from a single-parent household, poverty, parents who approved of violence, poor academic performance, learning disabilities, little or no commitment to school, early drug and alcohol abuse, and associating with friends who commit delinquent acts. The study's authors recommended early prevention efforts that target youth with multiple risk factors. Programs need to focus on all aspects of the adolescent's life, including family dynamics, school involvement, peer group, and behavioral issues such as drug and alcohol abuse as well as any antisocial and delinquent behaviors.

What this study seems to underscore is that for youth with multiple risk factors gang membership may be less an option and more a way of life. Adolescents who are fortunate enough to have cohesive families, where high-functioning parents work hard to maintain structure, provide accountability, and keep teens engaged in positive activities, can often avoid the temptation to join a gang. This is particularly true for black youth living in large urban areas (Walker-Barnes & Mason, 2001).

Adolescents without the benefit of such positive influences, including those who have neglectful and uninvolved parents, often face a reciprocal pull into gang life where they are targeted by existing gang members who recognize the existence of these risk factors. Many adolescents are drawn to gang life because of the benefits gangs appear to provide such as a sense of belonging, a life of excitement, and the feeling of empowerment. The NGR referenced aggressive attempts on the part of many gangs to recruit adolescents as young as 11. One example of recruitment tactics using social media include gang members posting rap music on YouTube in an attempt to engage interested youth and convince them to join their gang. Another example included a gang member who contacted a middle school student using an online chat platform and not only told him to join the gang but also demanded that he provide names of other middle school students.

Intervention Strategies with Gang Members

Human service providers who work with youth gang populations may do so on school campuses, in agencies that target at-risk youth, in faith-based outreach agencies, at police departments, or within the juvenile justice system. Most outreach programs target adolescents who live in large urban communities where gang activity is prolific and violent behavior a fact of life, especially those who come from single-parent homes, have poor academic histories, and have shown early signs of delinquent behaviors. Human service providers also target social conditions on a macro level, such as poverty, racism, and the lack of opportunities in urban communities, because these factors contribute to the development of gang activity.

Many human service programs that target at-risk adolescents operate after-school programs or evening community programs that give adolescents a place to go to socialize other than the streets. This is particularly important for youth who are in search of a sense of cohesion,

The L.A. Bridges Program is an early gang prevention program that targets middle schoolers with the goal of keeping them from joining gangs. The middle schoolers enjoy a recognition ceremony for their participation and completion of the program

© LAWRENCE K. HO / LOS ANGELES TIMES / GETTY IMAGES

security, and social belongingness, elements that might be missing from their home life. In light of the research indicating that most gang members have relatively loose, short-term affiliations with gangs, these types of programs have the potential of being success-ful in steering even active gang members away from gang life. Finally, human service programs committed to reducing the gang problem must be willing to engage in active and aggressive outreach efforts, maintain a highly visible presence in the community, coordinate services with other gang intervention programs, and be willing to engage at-risk adolescents and their family on multiple levels.

The War on Drugs

Many people might be surprised to learn that violent crime in the United States has steadily declined since the early 1990s. Homicides, rapes, assaults, robberies, firearms-related crimes, and even violent juvenile crimes have all plummeted in recent years; yet the population in prisons and jails across the country has skyrocketed. In fact, the United States has the high-est prison population of any country in the world (Walmsley, 2003). So what is to account for this seeming contradiction? Why, when virtually all forms of violent crime are on a downhill slide for many years, is the nation's prison system experiencing such a dramatic increase in population? Many social scientists agree that the primary reason for prison over-crowding relates to the U.S. war on drugs. In fact, approximately 55 percent of all federal prisoners are incarcerated for drug-related offenses (Harrison & Beck, 2003) and 80 percent of the increase in prisoners in the federal prison system between 1985 and 1995 is related to increased convictions of drug-related offenses (Bureau of Justice Statistics, 2004).

The U.S. war on drugs might seem like good policy on the surface. Certainly no one would argue that the using and selling of illicit drugs is good for the American public. But many argue that the federal government's aggressive policies related to the prose-cution and punishment of drug offenders unfairly targets poor, young ethnic minorities, many of whom are serving extremely long prison sentences due to minimum federal sentencing guidelines (sometimes 20 years to life), despite not committing any violent crime (Human Rights Watch, 2000a).

Human service providers should be concerned about any governmental policy that either directly or indirectly targets a certain segment of the population. The war on drugs appears to do just this, evidenced by the significant overrepresentation of ethnic minorities, particularly African American men, within the federal and state prison sys-tem (Human Rights Watch, 2000b). Human service providers working within the U.S. criminal justice system must be aware of potentially unfair political policies to develop a truly objective perspective of social conditions leading to the overrepresentation of minorities in correctional facilities. In addition, they must understand the reasoning behind sentencing guidelines for various criminal offenses, identifying social influences that tend to hold one behavior in a particular era as socially acceptable, only to criminal-ize it several decades later. For instance, determining what drugs are socially acceptable and which ones are not is influenced by constantly shifting social mores.

During the **Prohibition era** the use and sale of alcohol was considered criminal, yet today it is considered socially acceptable within legally prescribed limits. Marijuana was once considered a gateway drug, and its use and sale was punishable by jail or prison sentences. In the last few years though there has been a movement to legalize marijuana, and currently 23 states have new laws that legalize the use and sale of marijuana in vary-ing capacities (e.g., medical, recreational, etc.). Thus, there is a temporal aspect to the

Watch the ABC News video on women behind bars. What are your thoughts on the situations of the women featured in this news feature? What prevention strategies do you believe might be effective in addressing the issues explored in the film?

ENHANCEDetext *video example 13.5*

www.youtube.com/
watch?v=kRuTgdGEDj4

Amanda Lyles, a prisoner in an Indiana Women's prison, holds her baby girl while in her prison cell as a part of a prison family preservation program. In the last two years the program has expanded to include the Wee Ones Nursery, which allows eligible offenders who deliver while incarcerated at IWP to reside with their infant at the facility for up to 18 months or the mother's earliest possible release date, whichever is sooner

criminalization of certain behaviors, and it is important that human service providers recognize this dynamic.

Mental Health Programs in Correctional Facilities

The issues confronting human service providers working within the criminal justice system, particularly within a correctional facility, will vary depending on the demographics of the population and type of crime committed by the defendant. A key goal of the criminal justice system is to reduce recidivism. Therefore, "success" in terms of treatment is often focused on whether a prisoner, once released, reoffends and returns to prison. Behavioral programs within prisons can focus on many clinical issues, some related to criminal behavior and some related to other issues the inmates might be experiencing. Programs related to criminal behavior typically focus on issues such as drug abuse, sexual violence, domestic violence, anger management, and the development of social skills (for prisoners with antisocial tendencies). Programs designed to address psychosocial issues not directly related to criminal behavior typically focus on grief and separation issues, sexual abuse victimization (particularly for female inmates because a large proportion of the female inmate population has been the victim of sexual violence at some point in their lives), self-esteem, and issues related to the impact of being incarcerated.

Female inmates are often incarcerated for non-violent offenses related to drug addictions, and while African American women are overrepresented in the female prison population, the number of Caucasian women who are incarcerated for drug offenses, often pharmaceutical drugs, is increasing at an alarming rate. Advocates are concerned about the long prison sentences many women are receiving for nonviolent offenses, as well as the high rate of prisoners who struggle with mental illness and have histories of domestic violence and sexual abuse.

Women who are pregnant or parenting when in prison often have to rely on the county foster care system for the care of their children during their incarceration (Siefert & Pimlott, 2001). Human service providers working in a female correctional facility will likely encounter women who are grieving over the loss of their children or are anticipating their loss once they give birth. One of the roles of human service providers is to work with outside agencies that can arrange to transport children to see their incarcerated mothers to maintain the mother–child bond. Parenting issues are often explored with the goal of maintaining close family ties and reducing the incidence of prenatal damage and infant mortality related to drug use during pregnancy.

Some prisons have grant-funded programs that provide intensive prenatal care, nutrition counseling, substance abuse treatment, and individual and group counseling. One such program is called Women and Infants at Risk (WIAR), which helps mothers break intergenerational cycles of abuse, giving infants the best start in life possible. This

is particularly important in light of how the "cards" are already stacked against infants who are born behind prison walls (Siefert & Pimlott, 2001).

Another significant issue often confronting both inmates and human service providers involves the high rate of infectious diseases that exists within the prison population, made worse by the ongoing problem of sexual assaults. Diseases such as hepatitis B and hepatitis C are prevalent in some prisons, and HIV/AIDS remains a serious concern among prisoners and correctional staff alike. A 2002 report by the National Commission on Correctional Health Care (NCCHC) indicated that the incidence of AIDS in the U.S. prison population is five times that of the general population, and the primary method of transmission is sexual assault (Robertson, 2003).

The fear of being raped is the number one fear among men serving time in prison. Although no one is certain of the exact number of male-on-male sexual assaults within the prison system, it is estimated that between 7 and 12 percent of the male prison population have been victims of sexual assault while incarcerated, although the actual number is presumed to be far higher (Human Rights Watch, 2001), with many prisoners suffering multiple rapes throughout their incarceration.

A common complaint among mental health providers in correctional settings is the underfunding and understaffing of mental health programs often experienced in many jails and prisons across the country. Developing effective and comprehensive mental health services within correctional facilities is an important aspect of efforts to reduce recidivism rates among the prison population. However, the U.S. criminal justice system is punitive in nature and not based on a rehabilitation model, thus mental health programs are often not a priority within the criminal justice system, evidenced by a consistent lack of funding, understaffing, and limited outreach.

Yet even in prisons that have sufficient mental health services, barriers still exist that often prevent prisoners from accessing these services. A 2004 study surveying prisoner attitudes about mental health services identified several perceived barriers to service, including being uncertain how or when to access counseling, a belief that mental health services are for "crazy" people, the lack of confidentiality involved in the counseling relationship with a fear that the information shared would later be used against them, a fear that other prisoners would believe they were a snitch, a belief that people should deal with their own problems, a preference for talking with friends and family rather than a professional counselor, and having had a past bad experience with counseling (Morgan, Rozycki, & Wilson, 2004).

Human service providers need to be aware of these common perceptions held by prisoners so that strategies can be designed to overcome both real and perceptual barriers to seeking mental health counseling. Although many of these negative perceptions held are common among the general population as well, many are related to being in custodial care where prisoners' personal rights are extremely limited by necessity.

ENHANCEDetext *self-check 13.5*

CONCLUSION

Working within the criminal justice system offers rich opportunities for human service providers at all education levels. The opportunity to interact with several other advocacy organizations and to coordinate services with agencies offering complementary services provides the human service professional with a broad range of professional experiences. Human service providers facilitate counseling and case management and advocate on behalf of victims and offenders, thus making a difference in the lives of the members of society most in need.

Victims of violent crime such as domestic violence, sexual assault, hate crimes, and other violent crimes need advocacy and counseling to turn tragedy into triumph and powerlessness into empowerment. Human service providers are on the front lines of bringing issues formerly kept in the dark out into the open, removing stigmas, and creating change that is meaningful and long-lasting.

Criminal activity and subsequent incarceration leaves long-lasting scars on the families of offenders, often plunging them into a cycle of poverty and social isolation. This process significantly increases the likelihood of creating an intergenerational pattern of incarceration. Thus, some of the most important work that forensic human service providers do involves working with the family members of prisoners, particularly children who not only feel abandoned by their incarcerated parents but often are forced to enter the foster care system if no family members are available to care for them.

Rehabilitation offers the most hope of lowering recidivism rates among the prison population, yet a correctional philosophy that incorporates rehabilitation is controversial because in the eyes of many in the general public, counseling and other mental health programs feel too much like a luxury, not deserved by those who have committed crimes. However, not only are prisoners a heterogeneous group (i.e., many prisoners have been incarcerated for relatively minor offenses), but those who have committed the most serious offenses are in many cases those who need mental health services the most. Unfortunately, mental health programs are often the first to be cut from state and federal budgets because on the whole the prisoner population does not garner much sympathy within the general public. For this reason it is imperative that human service providers advocate for the basic rights and needs of prisoners, as they do with all vulnerable populations.

SUMMARY

- The role of the human service provider in working with survivors of intimate partner violence is critically analyzed. The nature of intimate partner violence, including the cycle of violence, motivations to commit violent acts on intimate partners, and the impact on survivors and their children, is discussed. The role of the human service provider working with survivors of IPV is explored, including an exploration of common practice settings and intervention strategies based on empowerment theory.
- The complex nature of rape and sexual assault is examined. Rape and sexual assault are explored within the context of patriarchy and other cultural factors that increase the vulnerability of women. Disparity in victimization among women of color, rape on college campuses, rape myths, and rape trauma syndrome is also explored within the context of the role and function of human service providers working with the survivor population.
- The ways in which LGBTQ+ and gender nonconforming populations respond to hate crimes are explored. The history and nature of hate crimes against LGBTQ+ and gender nonconforming populations are examined, with a particular focus on the intersectionality of vulnerability that render some populations at increased risk of violence. Hate crimes legislation as well as effective intervention strategies used by human service providers are explored.

- The role of the human service provider in working with perpetrators of violent crime is explored. The ways in which human service providers work with victims of violent crime, such as surviving victims of homicide, are examined. General crime victimization within the context of the role of human service providers working with victims of crime, such as survivors of homicide, is explored. The Victim's Bill of Rights is also explored in a broader discussion of the role of victims in the criminal justice process.

Internet Resources

Conduct an Internet search for the National Coalition to End Domestic Violence website, and navigate to Learn and then Statistics.

Conduct an Internet search for National Center for Victims of Crime website, and navigate to Library and then Training.

Conduct an Internet search for National Organization for Victim Assistance website, and then navigate to Victims of Crime, and then Victims of Crime Overview.

Conduct an Internet search for the Rape, Abuse and Incest National Network (RAINN) website, and then navigate to Get Info.

Conduct an Internet search for the Prisoner Policy Initiative website, and then navigate to Publications and then to the report entitled "Mass Incarceration: The Whole Pie 2016."

Conduct an Internet search for the GLAAD website, and then navigate to the NCAVP report: "2012 Hate Violence Disproportionately Targets Transgender Women of Color."

Conduct an Internet search for the FBI website, and then navigate to Stats & Services, and then click on Crime Statistics/UCR, then search for the 2015 National Gang Report, under Other Reports.

Conduct an Internet search for the Duluth Model website, and then click on What is the Duluth Model? Why it Works tab.

Conduct an Internet search for the National Women's Law Center website, and search for the report entitled "Mothers Behind Bars."

References

Black, M. C., Basile, K. C., Breiding, M. J., Smith, S. G., Walters, M. L., Merrick, M. T., Chen, J., & Stevens, M. R. (2011). *The national intimate partner and sexual violence survey (NISVS): 2010 summary report*. Atlanta, GA: National Center for Injury Prevention and Control, Centers for Disease Control and Prevention.

Blair, F., McFarlane, J., Nava, A., Gilroy, H., & Maddoux, J. (2015). Child witness to domestic abuse: baseline data analysis for a seven-year prospective study. *Pediatric Nursing, 41*(1), 23.

Bohner, G., Reinhard, M., Rutz, S., Sturm, S., Kerschbaum, B., & Effler, B. (1998). Rape myths as neutralizing cognitions: Evidence for a causal impact of anti-victim attitudes on men's self-reported likelihood of raping. *European Journal Social Psychology, 28*, 257–268.

Bowen, E., & Gilchrist, E. (2004). Do court-and self-referred domestic violence offenders share the same characteristics? A preliminary comparison of motivation to change, locus of control and anger. *Legal and Criminological Psychology, 9*(2), 279–294.

Breiding, M. J., Basile, K. C., Smith, S. G., Black, M. C., & Mahendra, R. R. (2015). *Intimate partner violence surveillance: Uniform definitions and recommended data elements*, Version 2.0. Atlanta, GA: National Center for Injury Prevention and Control, Centers for Disease Control and Prevention.

Bureau of Justice Statistics. (2004). *Crime in the United States, annual, uniform crime reports*. Washington, DC: U.S. Department of Justice, Office of Justice Programs. Retrieved from http://www.ojp.usdoj.gov/bjs/glance/tables/drugtab.htm

Burt, M. R. (1991). *Rape myths and acquaintance rape*. In A. Parrot & L. Bechhofer (Eds.), *Acquaintance rape: The hidden crime* (pp. 26–40). New York, NY: Wiley.

Cantor, D., & Fisher, W. B. (2015). Report on the AAU campus climate survey on sexual assault and sexual misconduct assault and sexual misconduct. Retrieved from http://sexualassaulttaskforce.harvard.edu/files/taskforce/files/final_report_harvard_9.21.15.pdf

Cattaneo, L. B., Calton, J. M., & Brodsky, A. E. (2014). Status quo versus status quake: Putting the power back in empowerment. *Journal of Community Psychology, 42*(4), 433–446.

Cattaneo, L. B., & Goodman, L. A. (2015). What is empowerment anyway? A model for domestic violence practice, research, and evaluation. *Psychology of Violence, 5*(1), 84.

Centers for Disease Control and Prevention. (2005). *Sexual violence: Fact sheet*. Atlanta, GA: National Center for Injury Prevention and Control. Retrieved from http://www.cdc.gov/ncipc/factsheets/svfacts.htm

Chesney-Lind, M. (1999). Challenging girls' invisibility in juvenile court. *Annals of the American Academy of Political and Social Science, 564*, 185–202.

Chestnut, S., Dixon, E., & Jindasurat, C. (2013). Lesbian, gay, bisexual, transgender, queer, and HIV-affected hate violence in 2012. New York, NY: A report from the National Coalition of Anti-Violence Programs (NCAVP).

Coronel, S., Coll, S., & Kravitz, D. (2015a). Rolling Stone and UVA: The Columbia University Graduate School of Journalism Report. *Rolling Stone, 5*.

Coronel, S., Coll, S. & Kravitz, D. (2015b). Rolling Stone's Investigation: A failure that was avoidable. Colombia Journalism Review. Retrieved from http://www.cjr.org/investigation/rolling_stone_investigation.php

Courtois, C. (2004). Complex trauma, complex reactions: Assessment and treatment. *Psychotherapy: Theory, Research, Practice, Training, 41*(4), 412–445.

Dunbar, E. (2006). Race, gender, and sexual orientation in hate crime victimization: Identity politics or identity risk? *Violence and Victims, 21*(3), 323–337.

Goodman, L. A., Glenn, C., Bohlig, A., Banyard, V., & Borges, A. M. (2009). Feminist relational advocacy: Processes and outcomes from the perspective of low-income women with depression. *The Counseling Psychologist, 37*, 848–876.

Goodman, L. A., Thomas, K., Cattaneo, L. B., Heimel, D., Woulfe, J., & Chong, S. K. (2016). Survivor-defined practice in domestic violence work measure development and preliminary evidence of link to empowerment. *Journal of Interpersonal Violence, 31*(1), 163–185.

Gordon, K. C., Burton, S., & Porter, L. (2004). Predicting the intentions of women in domestic violence shelters to return to partners: Does forgiveness play a role? *Journal of Family Psychology, 18*(2), 331–338.

Harrison, P. M., & Beck, A. J. (2003). *U.S. Department of Justice, Bureau of Justice Statistics, Prisoners in 2002*. Washington, DC: U.S. Department of Justice.

Hawkins, J. D., Smith, B. H., Hill, K. G., Kosterman, R., Catalano, R. F., & Abbott, R. D. (2003). Understanding and preventing crime and violence: Findings from the Seattle Social Development Project. In T. P. Thornberry & M. D. Krohn (Eds.), *Taking stock of delinquency: An overview of findings from contemporary longitudinal studies* (pp. 255–312). New York, NY: Plenum.

Herman, K., Rotunda, R., Williamson, G., & Vodanovich, S. (2014). Outcomes from a Duluth model batterer intervention program at completion and long term follow-up. *Journal of Offender Rehabilitation, 53*(1), 1–18.

Herek, G. M. (2009). Sexual stigma and sexual prejudice in the United States: A conceptual framework. In D. A. Hope (Ed.), *Contemporary perspectives on lesbian, gay & bisexual identities: The 54th Nebraska Symposium on Motivation* (pp. 65–111). New York, NY: Springer.

Holmstrom, L. L., & Burgess, A. W. (1975). Assessing trauma in the rape victim. *American Journal of Nursing, 75*(8), 1288–1291.

Holt, S., Buckley, H., & Whelan, S. (2008). The impact of exposure to domestic violence on children and young people: A review of the literature. *Child Abuse & Neglect, 32*(8), 797–810.

Horne, C. (2003). Families of homicide victims: Service utilization patterns of extra- and intrafamilial homicide survivors. *Journal of Family Violence, 18*(2), 75–81.

Human Rights Campaign. (2013). LGBT cultural competence. Retrieved from http://www.hrc.org/resources/entry/lgbt-cultural-competence.

Human Rights Watch. (2000a). *Key recommendations from punishment and prejudice: Racial disparities in the war on drugs*. Retrieved from http://www.hrw.org/campaigns/drugs/war/key-reco.htm

Human Rights Watch. (2000b). *Punishment and prejudice: Racial disparities in the war on drugs, 12*(2). Retrieved from http://hrw.org/reports/2000/usa/index.htm#TopOfPage

Human Rights Watch. (2001). *No escape: Male rape in U.S. prisons*. Retrieved from http://www.hrw.org/reports/2001/prison/report.html

Karakurt, G., Smith, D., & Whiting, J. (2014). Impact of intimate partner violence on women's mental health. *Journal of Family Violence, 29*(7), 693–702.

Launius, M. H., & Lindquist, C. U. (1988). Learned help-lessness, external locus of control, and passivity in battered women. *Journal of Interpersonal Violence, 3*(3), 307–318.

Marzullo, A., Libman, A. J., Crimes, H., Lesbian, V. A., & Ruddell-Tabisola, J. G. (2009). Research Overview: hate crimes and violence against lesbian, gay, bisexual and transgender people.

McCall, L. (2005). The complexity of intersectionality. *Journal of Women in Culture and Society, 30*(3), 1771–1800.

McWilliams, N. (1999). *Psychoanalytic case formulation.* New York, NY: Guilford.

Meyer, D. (2012). An intersectional analysis of lesbian, gay, bisexual, and transgender (LGBT) people's evaluations of anti-queer violence. *Gender & Society, 26*(6), 849–873.

Mezey, G., & King, M. (1989). The effects of sexual assault on men: A survey of 22 victims. *Psychological Medicine, 19*, 205–209.

Mika, H., Achilles, M., Halbert, E., Amstutz, L., & Zehr, H. (2004). Listening to victims—a critique of restorative justice policy and practice in the United States. *Federal Probation, 68*(1), 32–39.

Morgan, R. D., Rozycki, A. T., & Wilson, S. (2004). Inmate perceptions of mental health services. *Professional Psychology: Research and Practice, 35*, 389–396.

National Youth Gang Center. (2005). *Highlights of the 2002–2003 national youth gang surveys.* Washington, DC: U.S. Department of Justice, Office of Justice Programs, Office of Juvenile Justice and Delinquency Prevention.

Pandya, V., & Gingerich, W. J. (2002). Group therapy intervention for male batterers: A microethnographic study. *Health and Social Work, 27*(1), 47–55.

Pape, K. T., & Arias, I. (2000). The role of attributions in battered women's intentions to permanently end their violent relationships. *Cognitive Therapy and Research, 24*, 201–214.

Power, C., Koch, T., Kralik, D., & Jackson, D. (2006). Love-struck: Women, romantic love and intimate partner violence. *Contemporary Nurse: A Journal for the Australian Nursing Profession, 21*(2), 174–185.

Quinn, T. (1998). *An interview with former visiting fellow of NIJ, Thomas Quinn.* Washington, DC: The National Institute of Justice Journal, Office of Justice Programs, U.S. Department of Justice.

Roberts, A., Gilman, S., Fitzmaurice, Decker, M., & Koenen, K. (2010). Witness of intimate partner violence in childhood and perpetration of intimate partner violence in adulthood. *Epidemiology, 21*(6), 809–816.

Robertson, J. E. (2003). Rape among incarcerated men: Sex, coercion and STDs. *AIDS Patient Care and STDs, 17*(8), 423–430.

Siefert, K., & Pimlott, S. (2001). Involving pregnancy outcome during imprisonment: A model residential care program. *Social Work, 42*(2), 125–134.

Smith, M. E., & Randall, E. J. (2007). Batterer Intervention Program: The victim's hope in ending the abuse and maintaining the relationship. *Issues in Mental Health Nursing, 28*, 1045–1063.

Truman-Schram, D. M., Cann, A., Calhoun, L., & Vanwallendael, L. (2000). Leaving an abusive dating relationship: An investment model comparison of women who stay versus women who leave. *Journal of Social and Clinical Psychology, 19*, 161–183.

U.S. Department of Justice. (2011). *National crime victimization survey.* Washington, DC: Office of Justice Programs, Bureau of Justice Statistics. Retrieved from http://bjs.ojp.usdoj.gov/content/pub/pdf/cv10.pdf

Vearnals, S., & Campbell, T. (2001). Male victims of male sexual assault: A review of psychological consequences and treatment. *Sexual and Relationship Therapy, 16*(3), 279–286.

Victim's Rights Act of 1998, 42 U.S.C. § 10606(b) (West 1993).

Vigil, J. M. (2003). Urban violence and street gangs. *Annual Review Anthropology, 32*, 225–242.

Walker-Barnes, C. J., & Mason, C. A. (2001). Ethnic differences in the effect of parenting upon gang involvement and gang delinquency: A longitudinal, HLM perspective. *Child Development, 72*, 1814–1831.

Walmsley, R. (2003). *World prison population list* (5th ed.). London: Home Office Research, Development and Statistics Directorate.

Young, C. (2014). The CDC's rape numbers are misleading. *Time Magazine.* Retrieved from http://time.com/3393442/cdc-rape-numbers/

Zalmanowitz, S. J., Babins-Wagner, R., Rodger, S., Corbett, B. A., & Leschied, A. (2012). The association of readiness to change and motivational interviewing with treatment outcomes in males involved in domestic violence group therapy. *Journal of Interpersonal Violence.*

Rural Human Services

© MARIO TAMA / GETTY IMAGES

Carrie Lynn lives in the small rural town of Boonville in Eastern Kentucky—a part of central Appalachia. She has been struggling with alcoholism for most of her life and was recently referred for services with her community's itinerant counselor, Sandra, a licensed counselor who comes to town once or twice a month. Carrie Lynn has been drinking alcohol steadily since the eighth grade, quitting only during her pregnancies. Without any formal intervention, she resumed drinking once her babies stopped breastfeeding. Carrie Lynn's drink of choice is a homemade alcohol that her family and friends have been brewing for years because until recently her county had been dry, and though was legal to drink alcohol, one needed to drive a long distance to buy it. She wasn't certain of the alcohol content of this homemade brew, but she was certain it was high. In addition, she added the alcohol to just about everything she drank, even her morning coffee. As a widowed mother of four young children, the pressure of trying to keep a roof over the heads of herself and her children was almost unbearable, and drinking helped her to manage the everyday grind. Despite her alcoholism Carrie Lynn is a good mom, or at least she tries to be. She hung in after she and her husband lost the small farm that had been in her family for more than 100 years. She hung in after she lost one of her babies to "crib death." She hung in when she lost her two siblings to cirrhosis of the liver. She hung in when her husband lost his job in the coal mines, and when he died last year of lung cancer. She even hung in when she lost her part-time job at the local lumber mill, when it shut down a few months ago. Carrie Lynn now survives on government aid and the little bit of money she earns from babysitting some neighborhood kids. Booneville, Kentucky, like many small towns in Appalachia (a large swath of land encompassing portions of 13 states, stretching from northern Mississippi to southern New York), was a community mired in deep poverty. Located in Owsley County, in the Eastern Coalfield region of Kentucky, Booneville is the county seat. Once a thriving boomtown for common folks working in the coalmines and lumber mills, today the town is home to about 81 people according to the last U.S. census. Owsley County has the highest rate of child poverty in the country, and is considered the poorest county in the nation. The per capita income in Owsley County is just over $10,000 per year, and more than half of all families living in the county fell below the federal poverty line. Government benefits account for about 53 percent of personal income, and there is no indication that things will be turning around any time soon. Carrie Lynn is only 45, but she looks much older. A life of stress, loss, chronic back pain, obesity, and alcoholism has taken its toll on her body and her sense of wellbeing. While she's somewhat open to receiving counseling services, she's concerned about the stigma. Everyone knows everyone in the small town of Booneville, and Carrie Lynn knows that if her car is seen in the counselor's office parking lot, then people will start to talk. Sandra, the counselor, agreed to meet Carrie at the local park to avoid suspicion, and it was during their first meeting that Carrie Lynn expressed concern that her neighbors may no longer trust her with their kids if they think she's "crazy." The counselor is sympathetic and understands Carrie Lynn's concerns. Gossip is a big issue in small towns, which lack the anonymity of urban and suburban communities. Sandra works for a human services agency in central Kentucky and spends several days a week driving to different rural communities to provide macro and micro services, including substance abuse counseling, wellbeing checks for older adults, and counseling for people dealing with domestic violence and child welfare issues. She is considered an outsider to those living in the communities she serves, and because she is responsible for such a large geographic area, she can only visit each community once or twice per month—certainly not enough time to develop meaningful relationships and most important, trust. These challenges have required that she be creative in her approach to service delivery, meeting clients in places of their choosing, not keeping an eye on the clock, and accepting token gifts in exchange for payment, so that her clients, most of who pride themselves on their self-sufficiency, don't feel as though they're a burden on her.

A practice area that has recently gained nationwide attention is rural human services—the provision of human services, on a micro and macro level, in rural communities (Martinez-Brawley, 2000). The reasons for the recent attention are many, but essentially, despite the historic glamorization of small town life (think "Mayberry" of The Andy Griffith Show fame), rural communities have been struggling for decades—economically, with social isolation, and a number of other social ills. But before exploring the challenges facing many of America's small towns and rural communities, it's important to first clarify what we are talking about when we use the term rural.

THE STATE OF RURAL COMMUNITIES

Rural communities can be defined in several different ways—geographically, where people live in small isolated towns or farming and ranching communities; demographically, where population density is sparse; or functionally, where a community is characterized by its economy, rural identity, and social and community characteristics (Daley, 2015; Housing Assistance Council [HAC], 2011, 2012). While rural communities are often located in geographically remote areas, there are also **rural enclaves** located within larger cities. Rural enclaves can form when suburban communities encroach on formerly rural areas, or when people from rural towns move to the city for work, and therefore create a rural island in the midst of an urban area (Daley, 2015; Foulkes & Newbold, 2008). Rural enclaves are sometimes called rural ghettos if they are residentially bounded areas with high poverty, social isolation, and high unemployment. When rural ghettos are comprised primarily of ethnic minority or immigrant populations, then the community is often racially stigmatized in addition to being stigmatized for poverty and social disorganization (Burton, Lichter, Baker, & Eason, 2013).

According to government sources, approximately 46 million people live in rural communities, equaling about 15 percent of the U.S. population (Kusmin, 2016). Many rural communities were once thriving "boom towns," offering solid incomes and a safe and clean lifestyle for working class families. With the decline of family farming, the lumber industry, and the manufacturing industry (called **deindustrialization**), many rural communities have fallen on very hard times, resulting in the process of **rural depopulation**.

Some of the challenges many of America's small towns face include low educational attainment, high infant mortality rates, poor quality health care, social isolation, poor housing options, high unemployment rates, and limited formal services (Daley, 2015). People living in rural communities are more likely to smoke tobacco, abuse alcohol and other drugs without treatment options, as well as suffer from a range of chronic lifestyle-related health problems (such as diabetes, high blood pressure, and heart disease). Yet they are less likely to receive regular health care because of lack of access to quality medical services, lack of money, and poor (or no) health insurance (Office of Rural Health Policy, 2011).

The lack of available formal services means that people living in rural communities must travel longer distances for a medical and mental health care. This challenge is compounded by the fact that many people living in remote regions are struggling with poverty and do not have reliable transportation, if they have any transportation at all. Although rates of mental disorders and illnesses are not considerably different in rural communities compared to urban areas, there are far fewer treatment options available in small towns. In addition, with transportation challenges, as well as high stigmatization of mental health and substance abuse issues, many people in rural communities do not receive the help they need (Conway, BigFoot, & Sandler, 2011; Office of Rural Health Policy, 2011).

Geographical isolation tends to increase unhealthy behavior such as alcohol and drug abuse, sedentary lifestyles, and unhealthy eating, as people resort to informal ways of experiencing relief and comfort, which exacerbates existing issues (Lichter & Johnson, 2007). In fact, rural communities have experienced significantly higher rates of drug and alcohol abuse compared to urban communities for the past several decades

Watch the video on Kansas's legislation plan to counter rural depopulation. Do you think this program will work?

ENHANCEDetext *video example 14.1*

www.youtube.com/watch?v=d7Gj1wDfKFM

(Van Gundy, 2006). These challenges are intensified in areas with a lot of land mass and high population dispersion, such as Alaska, Montana, New Mexico, and North Dakota. The economic, cultural, and social isolation many rural people experience also fosters a sense of independence and local interconnectedness that can be both a strength as it relates to resiliency, but also a deficit when assistance from outsiders is shunned (Daley, 2015).

A dentist walks past waiting patients during the 16th annual Remote Area Medical (RAM) clinic at the Wise County Fairgrounds in Wise, Virginia. U.S. RAM, a nonprofit that delivers free medical care to people living in rural areas, treated a record setting 1,600 patients on its first day

Other challenges facing rural communities include higher rates of adolescent smoking, alcohol use, and bullying, and low adolescent educational attainment, with high rates of teens dropping out of high school. And while many small towns experience far lower rates of violence than in urban communities, in some rural communities violence is more tolerated by the community and law enforcement, including adolescent violence and acting out. Adolescents often engage in higher risk behaviors in rural communities, often out of boredom (Moreland, Raup-Krieger, Hecht, & Miller-Day, 2013). Some examples include excessive drinking of alcohol and partying, as well as engaging in high-risk pranks. Further, some researchers have noted that violence against women, while not necessarily more prevalent in rural communities, does tend to be more highly tolerated by local law enforcement and the community in general due to more patriarchal beliefs (DeKeseredy & Schwartz, 2008; Rennison, DeKeseredy, & Dragiewicz, 2013).

ENHANCEDetext *self-check 14.1*

RURAL POVERTY

There are approximately 430 counties in the United States that experience persistent poverty, and most of these counties are almost entirely rural. Many people who live in rural communities experience deep poverty—chronic and persistent poverty that shows no signs of abating. The income threshold for deep poverty for a family of four is a mere $11,157 (DeNavas-Walt, Proctor, & Smith, 2013), and while the cost of living in rural communities is often lower than urban regions, the difference does not account for the fact that it is impossible to effectively raise a family well on just over $10,000 per year. Imagine what it must be like to live in the United States, a country known for opportunity, social and economic mobility, and great excess, and yet you were born in poverty with little chance of escape. Can you imagine the sense of despair you might feel? Those who live in chronically poor rural communities, such as those in the **Appalachian Region**, understand that they live in a different America, one with few opportunities for advancement.

There are more than 21 million people living in counties marked by persistent poverty. Nearly 60 percent of the population in these communities are racial and ethnic minorities, with median household incomes of $31,581, more than 40 percent less than the national median. About 20 percent of all those experiencing poverty in the United States live in rural communities, but they are largely invisible, making their challenges difficult to address. Rural poverty in large part stems from a changing economic climate that has in many respects left rural communities behind. Deindustrialization, including the collapse of the auto manufacturing industry, the 1980s farming crisis, a move away from coal mining to clean energy, and economic globalization have all disproportionately impacted rural communities. Additionally, the **out-migration** of younger populations, many of whom leave their small towns for jobs or educational opportunities and never return—referred to as depopulation—is outpacing natural population growth, resulting in many small towns experiencing a slow and painful death. While these population trends are mediated somewhat by in-migration (the return of former residents), out-migration in many small towns is having a devastating effect on the vitality and growth of the community (Reichert, Cromartie, & Arthun, 2014).

Overall, the rural poor fare far worse in a number of life domains compared to those living in poverty in urban communities. Rural populations tend to have worse health outcomes than those living in urban communities, and as referenced earlier, many people in rural communities experience a higher than average rate of chronic diseases, many of which are directly related to obesity and other lifestyle choices—eating unhealthy foods, a lack of exercise, smoking, and excessive alcohol consumption (Befort, Nazir, & Perri, 2012). Research has found correlations between poverty, food access, and health, which in a rural context can be explained by **food deserts**—regions where healthy food is a scarcity. Food deserts are quite common in rural communities where large grocery stores have either closed or never existed. A lack of reliable transportation (private and public) can also create barriers to accessing healthy foods (Canto, Brown, & Deller, 2014). Without access to healthy food options and education about what constitutes a healthy diet, many people living in geographically isolated communities rely on junk food, which is cheap and filling but rarely nutritious.

Many members of poor rural communities suffer in some manner, although various demographic groups are impacted differentially depending on the nature of the community, and the impact of the various social problems on its residents. In many rural communities, women are more likely to be employed than men but at significantly lower wages (Albrecht, Albrecht, & Murguia, 2005), a trend leading to many men feeling displaced. This dynamic has increased rural men's risk for a range of psychosocial and physical problems, such as substance abuse, depression, and suicide (Hirsch & Cukrowicz, 2014; Singh & Siahpush, 2014).

There has also been a steady rise in female single heads of households and **multi-partner fertility** in rural areas, which increases social isolation and financial stress, and which has implications for the entire family structure since rural communities are often geographically cut off from necessary resources, such as prenatal care (Daley, 2015; USDA, 2015). For instance, a 2015 study found that pregnant women living in rural communities had to travel very long distances for their prenatal care (one to two hours each way), which was particularly challenging during the winter months (Gjesfjeld, Weaver, & Schommer, 2015). The study also found that there were few child care options in rural communities. This situation has been made worse by the decline of manufacturing jobs, which offered regular, set hours, and a move toward service sector jobs, which often involve erratic hours and little opportunity for advancement (Smith & Tickamyer, 2011). As a consequence, many women believe they cannot afford to work outside the home, and thus rely on informal employment and government assistance (Gjesfjeld, Weaver, & Schommer, 2015).

Children are among the most vulnerable members of poor rural communities. More than half of all rural children live in low-income families, many of which live far below the federal poverty line (compared to about one-third of urban children). The economic situations in many rural communities began to improve in 2014, except for child poverty, which increased by almost 25 percent since the 2007 recession (USDA, 2015). Research has shown strong links between poverty and delays in child development, including low educational attainment, social skills deficits, and other challenges that can have long-lasting consequences for children and their families (Vernon-Feagans & Cox, 2013).

The Poorest Regions in Rural America

Some of the poorest rural communities are in the South. Geographically isolated and economically depressed parts of the Mississippi Delta, the Southern Black Belt, and the Appalachia region rank among the poorest regions in the entire country (Ulrich & Staley, 2011). **The Mississippi Delta** is known for its serene and beautiful farmland as well as its shameful and violent history of slavery, longstanding racial segregation, and deep and chronic poverty, much of which is rooted in decades of institutionalized racism, such as post-slavery era **Jim Crow laws**. For instance, although **sharecropping**, which replaced slavery, permitted some African Americans to purchase land, most later lost their investments due to overt exploitation and inequity and, because of Jim Crow laws, there was little recourse for exploited families.

Today, the Mississippi Delta is considered the poorest area in the nation's poorest state and is an example of rural depopulation. The first wave of depopulation occurred during the height of the Civil Rights movement in the 1950s and '60s, when Caucasians left the Delta in droves, a process that sociologists refer to as **white flight**. This was followed by a second wave of depopulation in the 1960s and '70s, called **black flight**, when thousands of African Americans migrated north to cities such as Chicago, Philadelphia, and Detroit in search of jobs and better economic opportunities. Those who have remained in the Delta are either too poor to leave, have no place to go, or don't want to leave their families behind (University of Georgia. (n.d.).

Poverty remains high in the Delta, particularly in the Lower Mississippi Delta, where infrastructure is poor, and despite various discussions about community investment, very little economic restructuring has been accomplished. The remaining residents in this area either commute long distances for jobs in one of the few remaining factories, or survive on government assistance and the charity of family and friends. Among the many social ills gripping the Delta, alcoholism has been a growing problem for the past few decades. As grocery stores and other industries have closed, liquor stores have opened, and alcoholism among the communities' remaining residents has taken hold (Rodd, 2015).

The Southern Black Belt is an almost all rural region in the southern United States, which includes 11 states that contain counties with high black populations as

Watch the video on the life of Tammy and her children, living in a rural community, struggling with poverty. What role do you believe human service providers can play in addressing the intergenerational poverty and enduring despair experienced by many single-parent rural families living in geographically remote areas?

ENHANCEDetext *video example 14.2*

www.youtube.com/watch?v=cqs4_Zs2Gvl&list=PLC6D871A2A8C3C8EF&index=11

well as extremely high poverty rates. The states included in the Southern Black Belt are Alabama, Arkansas, Florida, Louisiana, Mississippi, North Carolina, South Carolina, Tennessee, Texas, and Virginia. The Southern Black Belt was originally named for the color of the fertile soil where slaves worked—a rich black velvet—but the term became known for the demographic makeup of the area when Booker T. Washington, author and leader in the African American community, used the term in reference to states where the black population was higher than the white. The states of Louisiana and Mississippi have the highest rates of poverty (about 20 percent) and Virginia has the lowest (about 9 percent). The Southern Black Belt suffers from many of the same social problems as other poor rural regions—chronic and persistent poverty, high unemployment rates with poor employment prospects, low educational attainment, higher than average infant mortality, and higher than average government dependence (Harris, 2013).

One of the poorest areas in the United States is the Appalachian Region, a large geographical area (about 205,000 square miles) extending through 13 states, from northern Mississippi to southern New York, along the Appalachian mountain range. The Appalachian Region includes all of West Virginia and parts of Mississippi, Alabama, Tennessee, Georgia, South Carolina, North Carolina, Kentucky, Virginia, Ohio, Maryland, Pennsylvania, and New York.

The Appalachian Regional Commission (ARC), an economic development agency established by Congress and led by the governors of the 13 Appalachian states, ranks each county in the region by economic status. The goal of the ARC is to facilitate economic development in each county within the Appalachian Region through a range of economic stimulating activities and the investment in infrastructure. Counties are ranked each fiscal year on a five-level ranking system, with "Distressed" being the lowest ranking and "Attainment" being the highest ranking. Figure 14.1 shows the economic status of the 420 counties in the region in the recent years. Note how most counties in the Appalachian Region have not economically recovered from the 2007 recession. The counties with the most economic distress are located in central and eastern Kentucky, eastern Tennessee, West Virginia, southeastern Ohio, and northeastern Mississippi, right along the spine of the Appalachian mountain range.

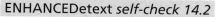

ENHANCEDetext *self-check 14.2*

POPULATIONS WARRANTING SPECIAL ATTENTION

Many communities within the Appalachian Region are considered food deserts, requiring local residents to depend on charitable food banks, such as this one in McArthur, Ohio

While everyone who experiences poverty in rural communities warrants attention from human service professionals, there are certain longstanding and more recent trends among specific populations that warrant particular attention. Many ethnic minority populations in the United States have a long history of challenges, particularly in rural communities. For instance, rural minorities experience some of the highest rates of

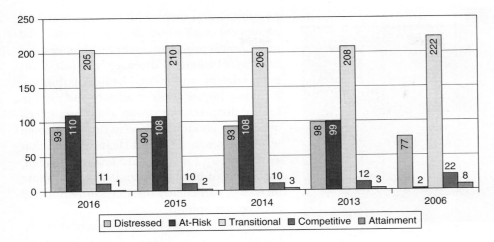

Figure 14.1
ARC Economic Rating of Appalachian Counties
Source: http://www.arc.gov/research/MapsofAppalachia.asp?F_CATEGORY_ID=1

poverty in the entire nation, more than twice that of rural Caucasians, and tend to be highly segregated, even if they aren't living in poverty (Lichter, Parisi, & Taquino, 2012).

The majority of African Americans in the United States live in rural communities in the South, in high-poverty counties. While Caucasians have the highest rates of poverty in numbers, African Americans have the highest rates of poverty relative to their proportion of the population (Lichter, Parisi, & Taquino, 2012). Poverty rates for rural black children reached about 45 percent in 2007 and surpassed 50 percent in 2014, reflecting a concerning backward trend (USDA, 2015). Rural African Americans also experience significantly higher rates of obesity, heart diseases, hypertension, and diabetes (Befort, Nazir, & Perri, 2012) and as a consequence have generally lower life expectancies than rural Caucasians and affluent African Americans living in suburban and urban communities (Murray et al., 2006; Singh & Siahpush, 2014). Most ethnic minority populations experienced increased poverty rates during the 2007–2009 recession, but almost all have since returned to pre-recession rates, except rural African Americans (USDA, 2015).

Another rural population warranting special attention is a rather surprising one to many social scientists—middle-aged Caucasians (Davis, & Enjoli, 2011). This is surprising because for generations Caucasians have experienced disproportionately better outcomes on virtually all indicators compared to other demographic groups—psychosocial, educational attainment, mental health, physical health, and life expectancy. Data revealing that this group in particular was struggling were discovered somewhat inadvertently, when two researchers, Anne Case and Angus Deaton, were reviewing census data and noted an unexpected trend: while all other demographic groups were experiencing gains in **longevity**, middle-aged Caucasians were heading in the wrong direction—dying younger than in previous generations (Case & Deaton, 2015).

They wondered what could be causing this disturbing trend. After some further exploration Case and Deaton discovered several alarming dynamics. Death rates for middle-aged Caucasian Americans had risen about 22 percent, but only for those with lower levels of education—as education levels rose, so did longevity. They

© MARIO TAMA / GETTY IMAGES

A mom stands in her trailer as her daughter looks out the window, in Fluker, Louisiana. The highly impoverished rural town has very few jobs and no mayor. The recession has hit many Americans hard, but the rural Lower Mississippi Delta region has had some of the nation's worst poverty for decades. The mechanization of agriculture and movement of textile plants out of the country has left the region's economy in tatters, leaving generational poverty in its wake. Louisiana's poverty rate is 19.2 percent, the second highest rate in the nation behind Mississippi

Watch the video featuring an interview with researchers Case and Deaton. If you were researching why the death rate was rising among middle-aged Caucasians, what would you focus on in follow-up studies?
ENHANCEDetext *video example 14.3*

www.youtube.com/
watch?v=78ntgGOiW8A

also found that those with lower educational attainment (high school degree and lower) had more health problems, including higher rates of musculoskeletal diseases, chronic joint pain, sciatica, and mental health disabilities, including higher levels of anxiety and psychological distress. This group also experienced on average about a 20 percent drop in income in recent years. Case and Deaton noted that as this group's income and health declined, their rates of alcoholism and substance abuse increased, particularly the abuse of heroin and prescription **opioids**.

They also found an even more disturbing trend—an "epidemic" of suicides among middle-aged Caucasians that corresponded with increasingly poor mental and physical health and worsening financial situations. Their research discovered that the mortality rate from alcohol and drug poisoning quadrupled for middle-aged Caucasians with only a high school degree, and deaths from chronic liver disease, such as **cirrhosis of the liver** (caused by excessive alcohol consumption), rose by 50 percent. Case and Deaton noted that the spike in early deaths among middle-aged Caucasians from alcoholism, drug abuse, and suicide was so dramatic that it was reminiscent of the AIDS epidemic just a few decades ago. They concluded that today's middle-aged Caucasians living in the United States may just be a "lost generation."

Case and Deaton's research also found that the pattern of early deaths due to unhealthy lifestyle choices was higher in states with high levels of poverty, low levels of educational attainment, and weak health care systems. Thus, while these dynamics apply to urban, suburban, and rural communities, middle-aged Caucasians living in rural communities are at far higher risk. Additionally, while both middle-aged men and women struggle, there is considerable evidence that women are particularly vulnerable to the struggles noted in Case and Deaton's research. For instance, the National Center for Health Statistics recently reported that suicide rates for women between the ages of 45 and 64 increased 63 percent between 1999 and 2014 (Curtin, Warner, & Hedegaard, 2016). Men have always had higher suicide rates than women, but the incidence of suicides among middle-aged men has not been rising, at least not to the extent experienced in the female population. The question human service professionals need to be ask is "why?". Why when just about every other demographic group is making at least some headway on a range of social, psychological, and medical indicators are middle-aged Caucasians, particularly those in rural communities, declining in virtually all of them? A review of some recent Gallup well-being surveys may provide some clues, at least with regard to women.

The Gallup-Healthways Well-Being Index releases several reports each year on a range of well-being indicators, such as the impact of caregiving on well-being and the impact of aging on well-being. The Gallup-Healthways and Well-Being Indexes are based on the compilation of six different indexes focusing on a range of dynamics that when evaluated collectively reflect general well-being of various populations and within various contexts (see Table 14.1).

Table 14.1   Gallup-Healthways Well-Being™ Index: Methodology Report for Indexes

Life Evaluation Index	Includes the evaluation of one's present life situation with one's anticipated life situation in five years (based on Cantril's Self-Anchored Striving Scale)
Emotional Health Index	Evaluates the daily affective experiences of survey respondents, as well as evaluating any prior history of diagnosed depression
Physical Health Index	Measures both acute and chronic diseases as well as physical limitations, obesity, and energy level
Healthy Behavior Index	Evaluates lifestyle habits that affect health including smoking, healthy diet, fruit and vegetable intake, and exercise
Work Environment Index	Measures workers' feelings and perceptions about their work environment, including job satisfaction
Basic Access Index	Measures access to basic needs including food, shelter, and healthcare, a safe and satisfying place to live, and perceptions of the community

Source: Gallup-Healthways Well-Being Index: Methodology Report for Indexes. Available at: http://wbi.meyouhealth.com/files/GallupHealthwaysWBI-Methodology.pdf

A 2010 Gallup-Healthways and Well-Being Index exploring well-being through the life course, involving 350,000 respondents, including 152,298 midlifers between the ages of 44 and 64 years of age, found that well-being is at its lowest in middle age, compared to younger and older age groups (Coughlin, 2010). A 2011 Gallup-Healthways and Well-Being Index on American women and well-being, involving 1.3 million female respondents between the ages 45 and 64 years of age, found that women approaching midlife had the highest levels of stress among all age groups and genders, as well as all previous generations of women. Specifically, the study found that most of the women surveyed had multiple caregiving roles, including caring for children and aging parents. In addition, most of the respondents were working (often full-time) and were also responsible for much of the household responsibilities, including caring for husbands or partners. The survey revealed that a majority of the respondents experienced significant stress and anxiety, with about 44 percent experiencing significant daily stress and about 20 percent experiencing depression.

Overall the women surveyed were not well rested and lacked sufficient energy to manage all of their responsibilities. As a result, they were not engaging in healthy behaviors, such as daily exercise and making healthy food choices, instead resorting to unhealthy behaviors as coping mechanisms. The study also found that despite the heavy load placed on middle-aged American women, many felt a profound sense of guilt—no matter how much caring, giving, and sacrificing they engaged in, they rarely felt as though they were doing enough—there was always more they believed they should be doing. As a result, most of these women put themselves last and rarely did anything for themselves.

Another recent study examining the impact of aging on middle-aged American women's self-esteem found that among thousands of women surveyed, the majority began feeling invisible and dismissed in society by the time they were 50 years of age. Among the thousands of women surveyed, 75 percent felt ignored by men when they walked into a crowded room, 50 percent felt as if they'd been "left on a shelf" and were judged negatively because of their age, 60 percent felt that society was geared toward younger women, and 50 percent wished there was more focus on the plight of older women. Only 15 percent of the women surveyed reported feeling confident in any area of their life (Cooney, 2014).

Since virtually all of the risk factors noted in these studies are more prevalent in rural communities—psychological distress, poverty, social isolation, lower educational attainment, poor medical care—and most rural communities have far fewer available resources to address these problems, it makes sense that rural middle-aged Caucasians, particularly women, would have the greatest risk of experiencing the range of challenges noted in these studies and surveys. Questions still remain though regarding why middle-aged Caucasians appear to be more significantly impacted by these dynamics compared to other ethnic groups, and why they are more impacted now versus a decade ago.

While additional research in this area is important in that it can help us better understand causal relationships and correlates, thus filling in the gaps, hearing from those who are living these realities is equally important. An April 2016 article in the Washington Post provides a personal glimpse into the lives of middle-aged Caucasians living in rural Oklahoma (Saslow, 2016). The article explores the life of recently deceased Anna Marrie Jones. Anna died at the age of 54 of cirrhosis of the liver after years of alcohol abuse. The author writes a story of heartache and challenges, of never-ending financial hardship, of multiple friends lost to an equally hard lifestyle, including Jones' best friend and fiancé, both who died during middle age, also from cirrhosis. The author then asks a question similar to that I have posed: What is happening to middle-aged Caucasian women? Why in the last eight years alone have over 300,000 women died of alcohol poisoning? The conclusion of Anna's family and friends? Life just gets to be too much sometimes.

ENHANCEDetext *self-check 14.3*

WORKING WITH RURAL POPULATIONS

There is a shortage of human service providers working in rural communities. There are many reasons for this shortage, including a lack of awareness of this practice area on the part of providers, as well as the fact that most educational programs are located in urban areas, which creates challenges for those living in rural communities wishing to enter the field. Many rural human service providers have limited education, with few opportunities to advance their educational status. Rural human service providers also face challenges with networking for themselves and their clients. The closest psychiatrist or treatment center may be hundreds of miles away. There may be no children's counseling center within a day's drive and the closest battered women's shelter may be several counties away. This can leave many rural human service providers feeling cut off from the broader profession, as there are few opportunities for referrals and collaboration and few opportunities for advancement (Daley, 2015). As with other professions, when rural youth desiring a career in the human services leave their communities to attend college, many fail to return, opting instead to seek positions with advancement opportunities in more urban areas.

Rural **itinerant human service providers** often have difficulty making strong connections to their clients because they are perceived as outsiders, and their services are often stigmatized (Daley, 2015). Domestic violence intervention in rural communities is an example of stigmatized services that not only place clients at risk of gossip, but also can place them in danger due to the lack of anonymity in many rural communities, as well as their tight-knit natures. In some rural communities, victims of domestic violence are hesitant to report violence and seek services because they know that their husbands or partners can rely on a network of other males for protection, including members of law enforcement (DeKeseredy & Schwartz, 2008; Rennison, Dragiewicz, & DeKeseredy, 2013). Agencies providing domestic violence services must be creative in how they conduct outreach, as well as how they provide counseling and advocacy, because exposing a victim's involvement with a human service agency can increase the risk of violence and marginalization within their extended families and community.

Technology can help with some of these challenges, particularly with a lack of access and anonymity. E-counseling, telephone sessions, and email can increase the frequency of provider contact and enable clients to seek services without having their car spotted in the only counseling center in town, although in many rural communities, Internet access is still spotty, and low-income clients may not have Internet access in their homes. Additionally, while technology is a valuable tool for rural human service providers and their clients, it can also create additional challenges, especially in cases of violence, where abusive parents, partners, or classmates can use technology to inflict abuse on others, such as is the case with cyberbullying and cyberstalking.

The reality is that many of the human service professions, including counseling and social work, were developed within urban communities with urban problems in mind; thus many of the treatment models that are taught in educational programs and relied on in field placement settings are urban-based and will not necessarily work in a rural environment (Daley, 2015). This places rural human service providers in a position of having to be very creative, perhaps even engaging in community development to create the services that the community members need, rather than applying an urban template to a rural environment. Rural human services may involve solely direct practice, but often there are elements of community development that occur right alongside counseling, focusing on the needs of the population being served. Examples of community development efforts include organizing health drives, school supply giveaways, educational programs, and parenting classes. Thus rural human service providers must be able to wear many hats.

Rural Culture Competence

There is a distinct culture that exists within rural communities that human service providers must be aware of to be effective in their service delivery. Sociologists refer to rural culture as **rurality**. According to Daley (2015), rural culture, while varied depending upon age cohort, race, and location, is often based on shared interests, social interaction, and behavior patterns. More specifically, people living in rural communities tend to have a stronger attachment to their land and community than their urban counterparts. There tends to be far less mobility in rural communities, and rural people will often cite the importance of remaining in a region where their families have been for generations. Rural communities also tend to be close-knit and the lives of community residents are often highly intertwined. Rural people tend to have a more personal style of communication and social interaction, and they have more natural and

Watch the video produced by Every Woman's House about domestic violence in rural areas. What are some of the challenges associated with providing services to rural victims of domestic violence?

ENHANCEDetext *video example 14.4*

www.youtube.com/
watch?v=N23UpigoouA

© KAREN KASMAUSKI / CORBIS DOCUMENTARY/
GETTY IMAGES

The Little Red School Bus, sponsored by the Christian Appalachian Project, helps Floyd county residents prepare for high school equivalency certificates and a better chance of finding a job

informal helping networks. Religious faith tends to be important to people living in rural communities, and rural populations tend to be more conservative and traditional in lifestyle and beliefs (Daley, 2015).

How these aspects of rural living manifest are often the foundation of many of the negative stigmas associated with rural communities. For instance, Daley notes that couches and other living room furniture on porches or in yards are often perceived as trashy by urbanites, but when evaluated through the lens of rurality, such practices are seen as a way of extending the inside out, allowing residents to connect with their neighbors and friends. A couch in a yard is an invitation for someone to sit and visit, a core component of a rural way of life. In a similar vein, rural communities, particularly those in the southern part of the country, tend to be more collective in nature than individualistic. Extended "kin" is important—reflected in a form of **familism**, defined as family loyalty, interconnectedness, and interdependence. Family members are encouraged to rely on one another, and decisions are made with family in mind.

Human service providers working in rural communities must develop rural cultural competence, which begins with a willingness and ability to move beyond the myths and negative stereotypes often associated with a rural way of life. Unfortunately, there is a lack of information about the complexity of rural life, particularly what has happened in the wake of deindustrialization and depopulation (Pugh, 2003). Human service professionals must be willing to invest in the rural communities they serve and take time in getting to know the broader and more contextual cultures, including similarities and differences between rural and urban societies.

Understanding that the lack of formal resources has caused many people within rural communities to resist outside help, or to turn to natural helpers (e.g., family, friends, paraprofessionals) (Waltman, 2011), can help human service professionals recognize the value of these informal resources, rather than negating them. Taking a strengths-based approach can assist human service providers recognize that much of rural culture has evolved in response to generations of struggles, resulting in resiliency, compromise, and ongoing adaptation.

Ethical Standards in a Rural Context

Rural human service providers often face challenges in adhering to some of the ethical standards foundational to the human service profession, particularly the admonition against having **dual relationships** with clients, and remaining detached and professional within the context of their work. Challenges are particularly common if rural human service providers live in the communities they serve (Pugh, 2007). Brocious et al. (2013) refer to this as the *rural reality*—many rural communities are so small and interconnected that dual relationships are unavoidable.

In a recent study exploring the experiences of human service providers in rural and remote communities, providers expressed their experiences with attempting to maintain professional boundaries and personas, as well as avoiding dual relationships. Many of the providers expressed feeling personally isolated and at times going so far as to not engage in the community at all (i.e., avoiding going to bars or parties) in order to avoid dual relationships and appearing unprofessional. They also discussed the challenges associated with overlapping roles and relationships because their communities were so small. Some respondents noted how various friends, family, and others in the community would often ask them service-related questions, and that they felt it would be rude not to answer, as informality, friendliness, and helpful attitudes were so integral to rural culture. They also cited their difficulty with ethical mandates against accepting gifts, since gift-giving was a part of rural culture (Brownlee, Halverson, & Chassie, 2015).

Several respondents also shared their struggles with how to handle thirdhand knowledge and community gossip, which they noted was very common in small towns and rural communities. They described how living in a rural community was like living in a fishbowl, and when they learned information about their clients from thirdhand sources, they weren't sure how to respond (Brownlee, Halverson, & Chassie, 2015). According to Pugh (2007), gossip in rural communities creates unique ethical dilemmas not addressed in most professional ethical codes. Pugh questions whether at times it is more ethical to violate confidentiality to set the record straight and quash damaging rumors about clients that could significantly harm them.

Brocious et al. (2013) also question whether ethical standards developed with urban communities in mind are applicable to rural contexts. For instance, they note that some dual relationships can be beneficial to clients. They recommend using a strengths-based approach to this and similar challenges, balancing the establishment of good boundaries with rural realities. Brocious et al. (2013) assert that, with advanced training, rural human service providers can manage complex situations, such as negotiating dual relationships, in a way that does not harm clients, but enhances the provider–client relationship.

ENHANCEDetext *self-check 14.4*

CONCLUSION

Rural human services has existed for decades or longer, but has gained recent attention because of the increase in social problems plaguing many rural communities. Rural human services is a vibrant practice area providing human service providers with opportunities to engage in micro and macro practice with populations that are in dire need of assistance. Many of the challenges noted in the literature associated with reaching remote communities can be addressed with the development of creative solutions, such as the development of interagency coalitions, community development, and the integration of various types of technology into practice. Educational institutions can also play an active role in addressing many of these challenges by offering coursework in rural practice and developing field placement sites in much the same way they would develop international placements—with consistent outreach and flexible and creative placement options, such as block placements with subsidized housing.

Although there are similarities between urban and rural human services, there are enough differences to warrant increased attention in the areas of rural practice, in research, within educational institutions, and among human service providers. Developing effective intervention strategies designed for rural contexts on a micro and macro level may provide some of the best opportunities for reversing many of the alarming trends currently experienced within rural populations.

SUMMARY

- Current issues and trends in rural communities are identified. The current state of rural communities, including many of the challenges facing rural populations, such as deindustrialization, high poverty, low educational attainment, high unemployment and underemployment, limited formal services, and geographic isolation, are examined.
- Urban and rural poverty are compared and contrasted. The nature of rural poverty, including an examination of ways that rural poverty differs from urban poverty. Some of the poorest rural regions in the United States are explored, including the Mississippi Delta, the Southern Black Belt, and the Appalachia region, with an examination of the history of these areas, and the rea-sons why they are facing economic challenges.
- The needs of populations warranting intervention in rural communities are identified. The nature of human service assistance for people living in rural communities who are in particular need, such as ethnic minority populations living in the South, and middle-aged Caucasians, particularly women, is examined. Issues such as poor health, psychological distress, increasing alcohol and substance abuse, and increasing mortality rates, particularly among middle-aged Caucasians are explored.
- Important factors associated with working with rural populations are examined. The nature of rural human services is explored. Issues such as rural culture and the importance of rural cultural competence are examined. Common ethical dilemmas, such as dual relationships and maintaining professional distance, are explored within a rural context.

Internet Resources

Learn more about the Appalachian Region by conducting an Internet search for "A Fresh Look at Appalachia—50 Years after the War on Poverty, and then click on the "Looking at Appalachia" link.

Conduct an Internet search for Rural Health Information Hub, and then search for "20 Years of Rural Voices."

Conduct an Internet search for the U.S. Department of Agriculture, and then click on Topics, and then on Rural Economy Population, and then Rural Poverty and Well-Being.

Conduct an Internet search for "Walk Your Camera," and then click on Appalachian Photo Book Friday—Expanded.

Conduct an Internet search for Housing Assistance Council, and then click on Initiatives, and then click on High Needs Regions and Vulnerable Populations.

References

Albrecht, D. E., Albrecht, C. M., & Murguia, E. (2005). Minority concentration, disadvantage, and inequality in the nonmetropolitan United States. *Sociological Quarterly, 46,* 503–523.

Appalachian Regional Commission (2016). County Economic Status by in Appalachia. Retrieved online from https://www.arc.gov/research/mapsofappalachia.asp?F_CATEGORY_ID=1.

Befort, C. A., Nazir, N., & Perri, M. G. (2012). Prevalence of obesity among adults from rural and urban areas of the United States: Findings from NHANES (2005–2008). *Journal of Rural Health, 28,* 392–397.

Brocious, H., Eisenberg, J., York, J., Shepard, H., Clayton, S., & Van Sickle, B. (2013). The strengths of rural social workers: Perspectives on managing dual relationships in small Alaskan communities. *Journal of Family Social Work, 16*(1), 4–19.

Brownlee, K., Halverson, G., & Chassie, A. (2015). Multiple relationships: maintaining professional identity in rural social work practice. *Journal of Comparative Social Work, 7*(1).

Burton, L. M., Lichter, D. T., Baker, R. S., & Eason, J. M. (2013). Inequality, family processes, and health in the "new" rural America. *American Behavioral Scientist,* 0002764213487348.

Canto, A., Brown, L. E., & Deller, S. C. (2014). Rural poverty, food access, and public health outcomes. *Choices, 29*(2), 1–5.

Case, A., & Deaton, A. (2015). Rising morbidity and mortality in midlife among white non-Hispanic Americans in the 21st century. *Proceedings of the National Academy of Sciences, 112*(49), 15078–15083.

Conway, P., BigFoot, D. S., & Sandler, E. P. (2011). Resiliency and behavioral health challenges among American Indians and Alaska natives in rural communities. In L. Ginsberg (Ed.), *Social work in rural communities* (5th ed., pp. 249–269). Alexandria, VA: Council on Social Work Education.

Cooney, A. (2014). Past 50, menopausal and invisible? [Press Release]. Retrieved May 19, 2016, from

Coughlin, J. (2010). *Facets of well-being across the age spectrum in the American population.* Center for Health Research, Healthways, Inc.

Curtin, S. C., Warner, M., & Hedegaard, H. (2016). Increase in suicide in the United States, 1999–2014. *NCHS Data Brief,* (241).

Daley, M. R. (2015). *Rural social work in the 21st century* Chicago, IL: Lyceum Books.

Davis, L., & Enjoli Fancis, E. (2011, July 27). "Most stressed out" in U.S.? Middle-aged women have lowest well-being, study finds. Available at http://abcnews.go.com/Health/MindMoodNews/stressed-us-middle-age-women-lowest-study-finds/story?id=14174138

DeKeseredy, W. S., & Schwartz, M. D. (2008). Separation/divorce sexual assault in rural Ohio: Survivors' perceptions. *Journal of Prevention & Intervention in the Community, 36,* 105–120.

DeNavas-Walt, C., Proctor, B. D., & Smith, J. C. (2013). Income, poverty, and health insurance Coverage in the United States: 2010. 2011. *Washington, DC: US Government Printing Office Google Scholar.*

Foulkes, M., & Newbold, K. B. (2008). Poverty catchments: Migration, residential mobility, and population turnover in impoverished rural Illinois communities. *Rural Sociology, 60,* 181–201.

Gjesfjeld, C. D., Weaver, A., & Schommer, K. (2015). Qualitative experiences of rural postpartum women and implications for rural social work. *Contemporary Rural Social Work, 7*(2), 115–126.

Harris, R. (2013). Community-University partnerships for change in the Black Belt south. *Professional Agricultural Workers Journal, 1*(1), 4.

Hirsch, J. K., & Cukrowicz, K. C. (2014). Suicide in rural areas: An updated review of the literature. *Journal of Rural Mental Health, 38*(2), 65.

Housing Assistance Council (HAC). (2011). Rurality in America. Retrieved online at http://www.ruralhome.org/storage/research_notes/Rural_Research_Note_Rurality_web.pdf

Housing Assistance Council (HAC). (2012). Poverty in rural America. Rural Research Brief. Retrieved online at http://www.ruralhome.org/storage/research_notes/rrn_poverty.pdf

Kusmin, L. (2016, January). Rural America at a Glance 2015 Edition. USDA, Economic Information Bulletin 145. Retrieved online http://www.ers.usda.gov/media/1952235/eib145.pdf

Lichter, D. T., Parisi, D., & Taquino, M. C. (2012). The geography of exclusion: Race, segregation, and concentrated poverty. *Social Problems, 59*(3), 364–388.

Lichter, D. T., & Johnson, K. M. (2007). The changing spatial concentration of America's rural poor population. *Rural Sociology, 72*(3), 331–358.

Martinez-Brawley, E. E. (2000). *Close to home: Human services and the small community.* NASW Press.

Moreland, J. J., Raup-Krieger, J. L., Hecht, M. L., & Miller-Day, M. M. (2013). The conceptualization and communication of risk among rural Appalachian adolescents. *Journal of Health Communication, 18*(6), 668–685.

Murray, C. J., Kulkarni, S. C., Michaud, C., et al. (2006). Eight Americas: Investigating mortality disparities across races, counties, and race-counties in the United States. *PLoS Med, 3,* e260.

Office of Rural Health Policy, U.S. Department of Health Resources and Services Administration. (2011). *Rural behavioral health programs and promising practices.* Retrieved from http://www.hrsa.gov/rural health/pdf/ruralbehavioralmanual05312011.pdf

Pugh, R. (2003). Considering the countryside: Is there a case for rural social work? *British Journal of Social Work, 33*(1), 67–85.

Reichert, C., Cromartie, J. B., & Arthun, R. O. (2014). Impacts of return migration on rural US communities. *Rural Sociology, 79*(2), 200–226.

Rennison, C. M., DeKeseredy, W. S., & Dragiewicz, M. (2013). Intimate relationship status variations in violence against women urban, suburban, and rural differences. *Violence against Women,* 1077801213514487.

Rennison, C. M., Dragiewicz, M., & DeKeseredy, W. S. (2013). Context matters: Violence against women and reporting to police in rural, suburban and urban areas. *American Journal of Criminal Justice, 38*(1), 141–159.

Rodd, S. (2015). The depths of poverty in the Deep South. Think Progress. Retrieved online May 16, 2016, from http://thinkprogress.org/economy/2015/06/15/3669553/tchula-mississippi/

Saslow, E. (2016, April). We don't know why it came to this. *The Washington Post*. Retrieved online April 12, 2016, from http://www.washingtonpost.com/sf/national/2016/04/08/we-dont-know-why-it-came-to-this/.

Singh, G. K., & Siahpush, M. (2014). Widening rural–urban disparities in life expectancy, US, 1969–2009. *American Journal of Preventive Medicine, 46*(2), e19–e29.

Smith, K., & Tickamyer, A. R. (Eds.). (2011). *Economic restructuring and family well-being in rural America*. University Park, PA: Pennsylvania State University Press.

Ulrich, J. D., & Stanley, M. J. (2011). *Rural Americans in chronically poor places report less access to health services than other rural Americans* (Carsey Brief, Fall 2011). Durham, NH: The Carsey Institute, University of New Hampshire.

University of Georgia. (n.d.). Black Belt FAQ. Initiative on the economy and poverty. Retrieved online May 16, 2016, from http://www.poverty.uga.edu/stats/faq.php

Van Gundy, K. (2006). *Substance abuse in rural and small town America*. A Carsey Institute Report on Rural America. Durham, NH: Carsey Institute.

Vernon-Feagans, L., & Cox, M. (2013). Poverty, rurality, parenting, and risk: An introduction. *Monographs of the Society for Research in Child Development, 78*(5), 1–23.

Waltman, G. (2011). Reflections on rural social work. *Families in Society: The Journal of Contemporary Social Services, 92*(2), 236–239.

15

International Human Services

© HIKRCN/SHUTTERSTOCK

There is a movement for all professionals in the human services to become more engaged in global issues, even if they do not plan to travel internationally or directly engage in global practice. For instance, Chi-Ying Chung (2005) made several recommendations to professional counselors to get involved in international human rights work, suggesting they apply their training in multicultural counseling and competencies to the international arena to combat human rights abuses. In fact, most, if not all of the human services professions are encouraging increased international awareness and engagement, at least on some level.

Although the human services profession exists worldwide, and concerns about specific social issues such as gender-based violence and children's rights are shared among all countries, the nature of the social issues and the function and role of the human service professional will vary depending on the political and economic conditions unique to each country. Human service professionals around the globe have many shared values but also have differences in values. For instance, in the United States, self-determination is highly valued in all the human services, particularly the social work profession, but in many countries in Asia, Africa, and Eastern Europe, not only is self-determination not considered a core value of the profession but also the concept of self-determination is considered either unimportant or dangerous, as it detracts from the value of community and cooperation (Weiss, 2005).

Human service professionals in virtually every country place a high value on the protection of human rights, social justice, and the end to human oppression in whatever form it might manifest within a particular region. For instance, in many regions of the world certain groups of individuals are oppressed due to their ethnic background, religious heritage, or their **caste system** level, and as a consequence they typically have little to no political power and are subject to mistreatment and exploitation. A primary concern of human service professionals in South Africa relates to issues of race left over from its former system of apartheid, and school social workers are commonly used to teach positive race relations among the students in South African public schools. Race issues take on a different form in the United States related to its history of slavery and mass immigration.

THE IMPACT OF GLOBALIZATION

Many professionals working in the human services fields have long wanted to venture into the area of international work, but haven't had either the opportunity or ability. Without strong connections in the world of global advocacy, it has historically been very difficult to break into the field of international work. But the world is getting smaller, not in terms of population, but in terms of its interconnectedness. This is making it far easier to gain knowledge about what is going on in other parts of the world and to make worldwide connections with other practitioners and advocates. The increased international connectedness among all countries, and consequently, all people, is called **globalization**.

No longer are countries completely isolated either in their financial economy or political climate. In the world's newest wave of globalization, countries are connected to others through the development of a global economy (e.g., international financial interdependence, mutual trade, and financial influence), increased international migration, and increased ease in communication, most notably, the Internet. All of these forces combine to create situations where the cultural, economic, and political states of one country influence the cultural, economic, and political states of others (Ahmadi, 2003).

One of the positive impacts of a shrinking world is the increased awareness, communication, and cooperation among social advocates around the world. In fact, social reform on a global level is now more possible than ever before. Consider the impact the Internet has had on the exchange of information between relatively remote communities, and especially oppressive countries with closed communication. Although limits can be placed on information exchange, the Internet has made the global exchange of information about social issues as easy as pressing a few buttons. Of course that is a somewhat simplistic statement, but the importance of the Internet and computer-mediated communication, both in regard to direct communication and the global awareness of social issues, cannot be understated.

Watch this video on globalization and poverty. What are the positive and negative impacts of globalization on various social systems? ENHANCEDetext *video example 15.1*

www.youtube.com/watch?v=dlldvz0jygE

Human rights organizations that track social issues around the globe have a far broader reach now that they are able to communicate so quickly and directly with their support base. Consider Amnesty International, a human rights and advocacy organization with a website that includes a comprehensive list of human rights abuses and concerns occurring throughout the world. With an Internet connection and a few clicks, individuals can obtain detailed information on the types of abuses and targeted population, as well as instructions on how to take steps to assist in the global campaign to address these concerns. We can also learn real-time information from the informational websites of **non-governmental organizations** (NGO) and can watch documentaries for free and direct eyewitness reports on YouTube.

The increased ease in global communication has meant that human service professionals in one part of the world can quickly communicate with human service professionals in another part of the world—through email; texting apps, such as WhatsApp and Telegram; voice-over-Internet communication programs and apps, such as Skype and Viber; and social media sites, such as Facebook and Twitter—sharing valuable information and coordinating efforts and services. In fact, there are several international organizations that exist for this very purpose—facilitating global collaboration.

The International Federation of Social Workers (IFSW) is an international organization founded in 1956 that works with a broad range of human service organizations and NGOs, encouraging international cooperation and communication among human service professionals around the globe. The IFSW has members from 80 different countries, including countries in Africa, Asia, Europe, Latin America, and North America. The International Association of Schools of Social Work (IASSW) is a support organization and information clearinghouse that promotes high standards in education, research, and scholarship, with a focus on well-being around the globe. The IASSW also supports an exchange of information and expertise between social work educational programs. Both the IFSW and the IASSW have ethical standards setting the bar for practice, knowledge, and cultural competence.

The International Council on Social Welfare (ICSW) is an independent organization founded in 1928 in Paris, which is committed to social development. The ICSW works with the United Nations on matters related to social development, social welfare, and social justice throughout the world. The work of the ICSW is an excellent example of community development at work using networking and international liaisons with other organizations to achieve its goals. The ICSW mission captures the way that macro practice occurs through a comprehensive network of agencies and organizations on all levels of society to achieve the global mission of eliminating social injustice.

The International Consortium for Social Development (ICSD) is an organization dedicated to economic and social development, facilitated by practitioners, scholars, and students in the human services. The ICSD's primary goal is to confront social and economic injustice by increasing individual and community capacity and sustainable economic structures. The ICSD provides opportunities for collaboration among professionals, academics, and researchers, as well as government organizations such as the United Nations, the World Bank, and NGOs. It serves a as an information clearinghouse, a source for experts in a range of areas pertinent to economic and social development, and facilitates an annual symposium attended by academics and practitioners from around the world.

In the next several sections I will be exploring examples of international social issues, including human rights violations, as well as some strategies for combating social problems on a global level, including global poverty, female genital mutilation, child labor, human sex trafficking, global human rights violations against indigenous populations, lesbian, gay, bisexual and transgender (LGBT) populations, refugees and migrants, rape as a weapon of war, and genocide. While this certainly is not an exhaustive list, my goal is to provide readers with a summary of some of the more serious global social problems occurring around the world while providing readers with some guidance and insights on how human service professionals work, either from home or abroad, to make the world a better, safer, and more equitable place.

Global Poverty and Social Exclusion

Watch this video on the challenges of global poverty. What are some of the causes of uneven growth in economies around the globe?
ENHANCEDetext *video example 15.2*

www.youtube.com/
watch?v=9UABa09QsvM

A common theme underlying virtually all types of disadvantage, often fueled by globalization, is poverty because it leads to and results from various types of oppression and injustice. Somewhere between one-fourth and one-half of the world's population suffers from poverty, meaning that they do not have enough money for their basic sustenance. While global poverty has been declining in recent years, determining actual progress across the globe is complex, with some countries' economies growing and others not growing.

The process of accurately framing the poverty condition is a challenging one due to its complex nature. There is no universally applied concept of poverty (Lister, 2004). Perceptions of poverty (and its causes) are often framed ideologically and politically which then often dictates policy directing the societal distribution of goods and resources. Thus, arriving at a universally agreed-upon definition of poverty and method of measuring poverty is challenging at least in part due to the politically laden "call of action" such definitions often require. Any definition of poverty must effectively capture the full effect and manifestation of poverty, as well as accurately reflect the reciprocal relationship between the poverty condition and other related forms of disadvantage (Martin, 2014).

Traditionally poverty has been defined (and then measured) in either absolute or relative terms. **Absolute poverty** uses a poverty threshold (or reasonable standard of living) where individuals who fall below the established minimum standard of living threshold are considered to be living in poverty (Gordon, 2000; Townsend, 1979). The World Bank's definition of extreme poverty of living on less than one dollar per day is another example of poverty being defined in absolute terms (Ravallion, 1998). These narrower and concrete definitions of poverty use income and resources as tools with which to define and describe poverty (Lister, 2004).

The absolute threshold does not vary from country to country and does not take time or living standards into consideration (Simler & Arndt, 2007; Lister, 2004). While defining poverty in absolute terms has some advantages (such as comparing levels of poverty between countries), absolute definitions are often criticized for being arbitrary. This is because the amount of money that is determined to be required to live "adequately" differs widely from community to community, yet is set at a static level when using the absolute poverty threshold (Marx & van dan Bosch, 2007; Townsend, 1979). Poverty in developing countries is often reflected in absolute terms, primarily because poverty in many regions of the world, such as sub-Saharan Africa, is extreme.

Another way of defining poverty is in relative terms, where the poverty threshold is set relative to the standard of living within a particular community (Simler & Arndt, 2007). Relative measures of poverty recognize that evaluating poverty in relation to a standard of living is more meaningful (Callan & Nolan, 1991). An advantage of considering poverty in relative terms is that inequality and the level of relative deprivation can be more easily explored, which more accurately reflects the complicated nature of poverty

(Alcock, 2006; Lister, 2004). Additionally, when poverty is measured in relative terms and within context, complexities of differing financial markets, varying lifestyles, and the ease (or challenge) of social mobility are considered. Most European countries use **relative poverty** measures where poverty is measured based upon economic distance from the median income level.

Poverty is almost always considered along with the concept of **social exclusion**, a form of deprivation that involves the **marginalization** and consequent exclusion of vulnerable groups from various domains within society such as employment, education, and housing (Lessof & Jowell, 2000; Lee & Murie, 1999). Individuals can be said to be living in poverty when they lack the resources to eat sufficiently, participate in the mainstream activities (such as working and voting), and lack the living conditions and amenities customary for their culture (Townsend, 1979). In other words, poverty is not just a lack of money. Rather, poverty is a holistic condition that involves deprivation on multiple levels.

Global poverty is a multi-dimensional social problem with complex causes and manifestations. The roots of poverty in many countries, particularly countries with **developing economies** and **least developed countries** (LDCs) (as defined by the United Nations), are deep, often rooted in histories of Colonialism and a world economic order that favors some countries, while crippling others with unfair labor practices and large debt (Polack, 2004). According to United Nations, women bear the brunt of global poverty, primarily due to discrimination they face in multiple sectors of society, including the labor market, education, and the health care sector. Additionally, in many parts of the world, woman lack the ability to own and maintain control of their assets.

Poverty, particularly extreme poverty, is often considered a human rights issue because it intersects with other social problems that make it difficult, if not impossible, for women to remain safe and live optimal lives. Women living in extreme poverty often do not have access to clean drinking water, sufficient food, adequate health care (including family planning), education, and suitable sustainable employment, and often cannot protect themselves and their and children from violence and other forms of exploitation (Martin, 2014).

Women living in LDCs are at increased risk of poverty because the majority of women live in rural areas and are dependent on agriculture for their livelihood. There are approximately 48 countries that are considered LDCs, many of which are located in Africa and Asia. Over 70 percent of the population in all LDCs live in rural areas, where agriculture is the main source of employment and food insecurity is a daily event (United Nations Women, 2011). While both men and women experience food shortages in rural areas in LDCs, women who work in agriculture are particularly vulnerable because they have less access than men to economic opportunities and resources, get paid less than men, are often excluded from the lending and credit market, and work in informal or undocumented work such as domestic work, which can be unstable and insecure (United Nations Women, n.d.).

Many global lending practices are an example of economic policies that can hit

Pushkar, India, November 3, 2014: A poor women draws water from the well and takes it to her tent

© YAVUZ SARIYILDIZ / SHUTTERSTOCK

women hard. Many economic policies in LDCs are not designed with women in mind, and whether intended or unintended, women are often the most significantly affected by policies that are economically unjust. Polack (2004) discusses the impact of hundreds of billions of dollars in loans made to countries in the **Global South** (South America, South Asia, and Sub-Saharan Africa) by countries in the **Global North** (UK, Spain, France, the United States, etc.). The cumulative impact of these loans to some of the poorest countries in the world has been devastating to the most economically vulnerable members, many of whom are women. Additionally, very little if any of the loan money has benefited women in LDCs; in fact, in many cases it has harmed them by increasing the poverty within the already devastatingly poor regions. In an attempt to repay this debt, many countries in the Global South exploit their own workers, many of whom are women, forcing them to work long hours, under extremely harsh conditions, for very little pay.

The remedies to global poverty are as complex as the problem. Many NGOs believe that community development programs coupled with humanitarian relief are the best approaches to reducing poverty. The United Nations and world leaders made a commitment in 2000 to significantly reduce extreme poverty by half and address related social problems by 2015. The result of this project was the development of eight goals, called the **Millennium Development Goals** (MDG):

1. Eradicate extreme hunger and poverty
2. Achieve universal primary education
3. Promote gender equality and empowerment
4. Reduce child mortality
5. Improve maternal health
6. Combat HIV/AIDS, malaria, and other diseases
7. Ensure environmental sustainability
8. Develop a global partnership for development

Each goal had a target(s), indicators reflecting progress and success. For instance, Target 1 for eradicating extreme poverty was to cut poverty in half between 1990 and 2015 for those people who earned less than $1 a day, as indicated by World Bank population statistics, the poverty gap ratio, and the percentage of the poorest quintile in national consumption. Target 2 for eradicating extreme hunger was to cut the proportion of people suffering from hunger by half from 1990 to 2015. The indicators for this target were the prevalence of underweight children under five and the proportion of the population below the minimum level of dietary consumption (United Nations Development Program, 2000).

The Millennium Project, an independent advisory board, was commissioned by the U.N. Secretary General in 2002 and charged with the responsibility of developing an action plan to help the United Nations and world leaders achieve the MDGs by 2015. The final report of the Millennium Project, *Investing In Development: A Practical Plan to Achieve The Millennium Development Goals* (2005) made 10 core recommendations for all country leaders, a summary of which included:

1. the development of bold MDG-based poverty reduction strategies in a transparent and inclusive process by 2006;
2. developed and developing countries jointly initiating a rapid response to crisis situations (called Quick Wins), including mass distribution of malaria bed-nets,

increasing the availability of antiretroviral treatment for AIDS patients, and the massive training of community-based workers;

3. increased donor support for regional projects, such as the building of roads and railways;

4. an increase in assistance from high-income governments (as defined by the United Nations);

5. and an increase in support for global scientific research and development addressing the needs of the poor.

While this summary provides only a brief synopsis of the comprehensive recommendations, it reflects the report's focus on development and governance (from the top down and bottom up) as key strategies for combating extreme poverty and its correlates (e.g., hunger, child mortality, and health pandemics).

In 2015 the United Nations announced that significant progress was made in meeting the MDGs. In a summit held in September of 2015, the U.N. General Assembly launched a post-MDG campaign, which focused on sustaining progress and achieving what wasn't achieved during the MDG campaign. The summit report, "Transforming Our World: The 2030 Agenda for Sustainable Development," outlines 17 Sustainable Development Goals (SDGs) (see Table 15.1) and 169 indicators, which were adopted during the Summit and came into full force in January of 2016. World leaders have agreed to take all

Table 15.1   Sustainable Development Goals

Goal 1	End poverty in all its forms everywhere
Goal 2	End hunger, achieve food security and improved nutrition, and promote sustainable agriculture
Goal 3	Ensure healthy lives and promote well-being for all at all ages
Goal 4	Ensure inclusive and equitable quality education and promote lifelong learning opportunities for all
Goal 5	Achieve gender equality and empower all women and girls
Goal 6	Ensure availability and sustainable management of water and sanitation for all
Goal 7	Ensure access to affordable, reliable, sustainable, and modern energy for all
Goal 8	Promote sustained, inclusive, and sustainable economic growth, full and productive employment, and decent work for all
Goal 9	Build resilient infrastructure, promote inclusive and sustainable industrialization, and foster innovation
Goal 10	Reduce inequality within and among countries
Goal 11	Make cities and human settlements inclusive, safe, resilient, and sustainable
Goal 12	Ensure sustainable consumption and production patterns
Goal 13	Take urgent action to combat climate change and its impacts
Goal 14	Conserve and sustainably use the oceans, seas, and marine resources for sustainable development
Goal 15	Protect, restore, and promote sustainable use of terrestrial ecosystems, sustainably manage forests, combat desertification, and halt and reverse land degradation and halt biodiversity loss
Goal 16	Promote peaceful and inclusive societies for sustainable development, provide access to justice for all, and build effective, accountable, and inclusive institutions at all levels
Goal 17	Strengthen the means of implementation and revitalize the global partnership for sustainable development

Source: http://www.un.org/sustainabledevelopment/

necessary measures to achieve these goals by 2030. The SDGs build on the MDGs, focusing on strategies that encourage economical growth and address areas that are known to combat poverty and other social problems, such as education, health, peace, and job opportunities, while also addressing global problems related to climate change and protecting the environment.

ENHANCEDetext *self-check 15.1*

HEALTH PANDEMICS AND MAJOR PUBLIC HEALTH CONCERNS

Major **health pandemics** occur worldwide, but they have a disproportionate effect on people living in developing countries and LDCs. Among those most significantly affected by major health pandemics, women and children are impacted the most severely due to their vulnerable status in many parts of the world. HIV/AIDS, malaria, Ebola, and other health crises put everyone at risk, but those living in LDCs are impacted the most because of increased prevalence and often marginal health care.

HIV/AIDS, Malaria, and Ebola Virus Disease

AIDS is a life-threatening disease that has had a devastating impact on families, particularly children, in many parts of the world, but especially in sub-Saharan Africa. The life expectancy in many African countries has dropped from 61 to 35 years of age, and resulted in millions of children being orphaned. For instance, as of 2015, of the approximately 17.8 million children estimated to have been orphaned by the AIDS epidemic, 85 percent live in sub-Saharan Africa (UNAIDS, 2008; UNICEF, 2004). This represents an increase over prior years despite the fact that adult HIV-infection rates have declined in recent years, and use of antiviral medications have become increasingly available in several sub-Saharan African countries (UNAIDS, 2008). But progress is being made, in large part due to the health programs and treatment protocols initiated in coordination with the MDGs.

Another serious health concern impacting many countries in the Global South is malaria, a disease caused by a parasite transmitted by mosquitos. Humans can be infected if they are bitten by a female mosquito that has the parasite. It is a serious health problem that infects over 262 million people a year, and over one million deaths, primarily in sub-Saharan Africa. Women and children are at particular risk of fatality. Although visitors to high-risk regions can take antiviral medication (such as Malarone) to prevent malaria, long-term use carries certain health risks, leaving those who live in moderate and high-risk areas vulnerable to infection. Although malaria deaths have decreased by about 50 percent in most regions, malaria remains a very serious health risk, particularly for women and children living in rural areas, which tend to have higher malaria risks, and lower prevention protocol and compliance (WHO, 2015).

The Roll Back Malaria Partnership (RBM) is a large consortium consisting of over 500 partners around the globe, initiated in 1998 by the World Health Organization (WHO), UNICEF, UNDP, and the World Bank. The ultimate RBM operates in conjunction with the MDGs and SDGs, with the ultimate goal of reducing malaria by 90 percent by 2030. RBM's Global Malaria Action Plan (GMAP) for a malaria-free world was initiated in 2008 (2008–2015), with a recommitment in 2016 (2016–2030). The plan to reduce

Watch this video on Hlengiwe "Leo" Mchunu's personal crusade against AIDS and her support of AIDS orphans. What are some ways in which human services professionals in the United States could coordinate with her to provide support and assistance?

ENHANCEDetext *video example 15.3*

www.youtube.com/
watch?v=gtqNwu0yfXc

malaria involves a wide range of responses, including vector control, wide dissemination of insecticide-treated nets, rapid treatment using antiviral drugs, and research (Whittaker, Dean, & Chancellor, 2014).

Ebola virus disease (EVD) is another deadly disease affecting primarily people in Western Africa (Guinea and Liberia), even though the first outbreaks of EVD were in the Central African countries of Democratic Republic of the Congo (DRC) and South Sudan. According to the WHO (2016) EVD is transmitted to humans from dead animals (e.g., chimpanzees, gorillas, fruit bats), as well as from human-to-human contact. The fatality rates of EVD are extremely high, ranging from 50 to 90 percent.

The symptoms of EVD are painful and gruesome, beginning with flu-like symptoms, and evolving to diarrhea, vomiting, and internal and external bleeding. EVD is highly contagious, and people remain contagious even after their deaths, which has made it challenging to contain. In fact, one of the methods for rapid transmission through entire villages was infections through funeral attendance, where villagers would pay their respects to one who died of the disease, and in the process of touching the body, become infected with EVD. Health care workers are also at high risk of infection. A health care worker that is exposed to the body fluids of an infected person transferred from an item, such as a hospital gown, can be infected (WHO, 2016).

While there is no vaccine for EVD, there are two experimental vaccines currently being tested. Treatment at this point is focused primarily on prevention and psychosocial assistance for family members who have been decimated by this disease. One area where human service professionals can respond to the EVD crisis and other major public health emergencies is by responding to the devastating impact on families and communities, including the intense fear many people feel when an outbreak occurs. Psychosocial support of affected communities involves case management, accurate information dissemination, and training and assistance (WHO, 2016).

Female Genital Mutilation

Another issue confronting women and girls throughout sub-Saharan Africa and Arab countries is female genital mutilation (FGM) (also called female circumcision), where historical tradition and tribal culture prescribes that a girl's external genitalia, typically her labia and clitoris, be cut away in a rite of passage ceremony marking her entry into her womanhood (see Table 15.2). WHO estimates that between 100 and 200 million girls have undergone FGM. The prevailing belief in cultures that practice FGM is that female circumcision is necessary to ensure a woman's purity, to control her sexual behavior, and to ensure her compliance and obedience while married. Depending on the country and specific cultural traditions, FGM is typically performed on girls 10 and older, but in some countries it may be performed on girls much younger (WHO, 1998).

The most serious type of FGM is Type 3, which includes the cutting away of the labia minora and the sewing together of the labia majora (the outer vaginal lips), which then creates a seal with only a small opening for the passing of menstrual blood and urine. The vaginal seal is intended to keep the women in the tribe from having sexual relations before marriage. It is literally torn open during the woman's first sexual encounter with her husband, which not only causes extreme pain but also has serious health consequences such as bleeding and possible infection. In some cultures, the torn pieces of labia are actually sewn together again if the woman becomes pregnant and are then torn open again during childbirth.

Table 15.2   Types of Female Genital Mutilation

Type	Name	Description
1	Clitoridectomy	The partial or total removal of the clitoris and, in very rare cases, only the prepuce (the fold of skin surrounding the clitoris).
2	Excision	The partial or total removal of the clitoris and the labia minora, with or without excision of the labia majora.
3	Infibulation	The scraping away of the inner labia (labia minora). The outer labia (labia majora) is then sewn together to cover the wound and create a vaginal "seal" leaving only a small opening for the passage of menstrual blood and urine. This "seal" is intended to keep the girl or woman from having sex prior to marriage. It is often torn open when the woman has sex with her husband the first time. In some cultures the torn pieces of labia are then sewn back together, and must be torn open again for childbirth.
4	Other	All other harmful procedures to the female genitalia for non-medical purposes such as pricking, piercing, stretching, incising, scraping, and cauterizing the genital area.

FGM can cause serious health risks including lifelong pain, infertility, and death (World Health Organization, 1998). FGM is rarely performed by a physician, but is frequently conducted by a village leader with no pain medication. Girls are often tied down and subjected to this surgery, which is intended to ensure chastity and purity. Clitorectomies are most common in African countries, with infibulation being most popular in Islamic cultures, although most Muslim countries do not practice FGM (Lightfoot-Klein, 1991).

The origins of FGM are difficult to trace, but there are some indications that this practice can be traced back to Arab and Ethiopian cultures in the fifth century BC, or perhaps even earlier. There are indications that it was practiced in ancient Rome and Egypt as well (Lightfoot-Klein, 1991). The reasons for FGM are similar, but vary somewhat. Most cultures practicing FGM connect female circumcision to purity, cleanliness, modesty, and sexual restraint. Currently, FGM is practiced in several Central, Eastern, and Northern African countries, as well as countries in the Middle East and some Asian countries. Somalia is one of the worst offenders, with 98 percent of women having undergone FGM by the age of 12 (Mitike & Deressa, 2009). Although FGM is believed to be primarily culturally rooted, some people in Muslim countries cite the practice as a religious one (UNFPA, 2009).

In general, the practice has its origin in the cultural belief that the clitoris is dirty, dangerous, and will lead to sexual promiscuity. Girls who refuse to undergo FGM are not considered marriageable and often treated with scorn and experience social isolation. In a 2010 report on FGM prepared by Human Rights Watch (HRW) detailing the extent of FGM in Iraqi Kurdistan, advocates emphasized that most girls are forced to undergo FGM by loving mothers and aunts who believe this is the only way to ensure their daughters or loved ones are marriageable, and in a culture where there are few other options for girls, hanny away from this long-practiced cultural tradition is not easy (Human, 2010a).

Hanny Lightfoot-Klein, a noted expert on the practice of FGM, conducted field research in Sudan, Kenya, and Egypt and wrote four books based on her years of research within each of these countries. In her first book, published in 1989, she describes some common perceptions in Sudan of the woman's clitoris, which reflects why changing attitudes in traditional cultures are so challenging. She cites a prevalent belief in Sudan that if the clitoris is not cut, it will grow into a penis. Sudanese men are so anxious about this possibility that most would never marry a woman who wasn't circumcised, and those girls who refuse to undergo the procedure for whatever reason are considered "unclean" and are shunned from society.

FGM is typically conducted by a community or tribal healer, such as a midwife, in a non-medical setting. The instruments used include unsterilized razors or scalpels, and ashes are often used as a healing agent. Women and girls who have undergone FGM share stories of being told they are going to see a friend, then being held down, and beaten if they resist. With their legs forced open, they are then compelled to endure the cutting of their labia and/or clitoris without pain medication. Many girls have shared stories of being in immense pain, sometimes for more than a month, sometimes for life (HRW, 2010a).

Maasai tribe elders and women in Shompole, Kenya, gather for a forum organized by AMREF, and geared at sensitizing the elders and women towards an alternative rights of passage for young girls, that would stop female circumcision

© JONATHAN TORGOVNIK/GETTY IMAGES

There are numerous health risks associated with FGM, including immense pain (some women reported being immobile for up to a month), infection, scar tissue that interferes with sexual intercourse and childbirth, urinary problems, infertility, cysts, and reinjury. When women undergo infibulation and have sex the first time, their vaginal opening is torn open, and must be kept open so that the wound does not heal and close the vagina again. This practice is particularly painful as the raw and bleeding remnants of the labia may take months to heal (WHO, 2011).

There has been a strong international response to the practice of FGM, starting in the early 1990s with numerous U.N. international treaties referencing FGM, calling it a human rights violation against women and girls, and identifying this practice as a form of gender-based discrimination. For instance, in 1990 the Committee for the U.N. Treaty *The Convention on the Elimination of All Forms of Discrimination* (CEDAW) adopted a general recommendation calling on all state parties to develop health policies that incorporate measures to eradicate the practice of FGM. In 2002, the United Nations General Assembly (UNGA) passed a resolution urging all nation states to enact national legislation to abolish FGM. In 2008 numerous U.N. agencies, such as WHO, UNICEF, UNFPA, UNAIDS, and UNHCR (to name a few), issued a joint statement on FGM in a report that included increased information about the extent of the practice as well as the severity of the consequences. Three of the U.N. MDGs also directly addressed FGM by focusing on women's health.

Community-based approaches that can build upon international pressure will have the greatest likelihood of successfully eradicating FGM (Lexow, Berggrav, & Taraldsen, 2009; UNICEF, 2004). There has been a recent surge in grassroots efforts to eradicate FGM in response to a backlash among local women, particularly in African countries, such as Kenya and Nigeria. Such grassroots efforts address FGM from multiple perspectives, including training tribal leaders about the true origins of FGM, highlighting the physical risks as well as the effect on girls' self-esteem. Educational campaigns also help men better understand the female anatomy, confronting myths (such as the clitoris becoming a penis if left uncut) and explaining how their marital relationships would likely improve if their wives experienced increased sexual pleasure (Martin, 2014).

In 2012 I had the opportunity to visit Dr. Sr. Ephigenia Gachiri, a Loreto sister in Nairobi, Kenya, who has been engaging in a grassroots effort to stamp out FGM in Kenya for the last two decades, particularly in the Maasai tribe, through her organization Stop FGM. Dr. Gachiri explained to me that when a girl (or her family) refuses to undergo FGM, she isn't just risking her ability to marry, she's risking her entire future. Maasai culture promotes the belief that if a woman does not undergo FGM she will become promiscuous and will not remain faithful to her husband, choosing instead to have sex with many men.

The Maasai (like many other cultures) also believe that uncircumcised women not only bring shame on their families but also will cause their deaths. Uncircumcised women are treated as social outcasts and are not allowed to interact with others in their community—eating communally or even gathering water with the other women. They are not allowed to attend school, and of course, they are not permitted to marry. Since FGM is the rite of passage to womanhood, uncircumcised women have virtually no authority in their communities, and are considered children, with less authority than a young girl who has had FGM.

Uncircumcised Maasai girls (and girls from other traditional tribes across Kenya) typically have only two options available to them—becoming a nun or a prostitute, and according to Dr. Gachiri, the latter is far more common. The irony of this dynamic is that a justification village leaders use in support of FGM is that women will become promiscuous if they aren't circumcised. Yet the primary reason why uncircumcised women in the Maasai and other tribes in Kenya resort to prostitution is because they were shunned.

Dr. Gachiri works closely with Maasai leaders, because despite Kenya outlawing FGM in 2011, the practice is entrenched in their culture and changing culture is a very slow process. Dr. Gachiri has developed a new ceremonial rite of passage that she hopes ultimately replaces FGM. She has also developed an educational curriculum that is shown in many schools, educating teachers and students on the nature and risks of FGM. She also works directly with tribal chiefs and elders, educating them about the myths of FGM. While FGM is perceived as a human rights violation against women, Dr. Gachiri points out that it is often the women in the village who force girls to undergo the ritual, and women are often the circumcisers. In addition, sometimes uncircumcised women seek out FGM, despite their families' objections. Thus, Dr. Gachiri works with the women in the tribes as well, providing workshops and educational resources.

Dr. Gachiri's work is an example of the bottom-up approach—advocacy and community development initiated within communities by community members, where advocacy leaders have more legitimacy because they're seen as a part of the community, rather than as outsiders imposing change. Not only is Dr. Gachiri a native Kenyan (she is from the Kikuyu tribe), she also spent months getting to know the girls who had undergone FGM, and sought permission from elders before doing so. She was perceived as having legitimacy because she was viewed as "one of them." She also collaborates with national and international partners, who provide funding, technical support, and guidance, when needed. Dr. Gachiri's approach to addressing FGM can be used as a model for similar advocacy efforts.

ENHANCEDetext *self-check 15.2*

HUMAN TRAFFICKING

Trafficking in persons is a multi-billion-dollar criminal enterprise involving modern forced slavery, and includes sex trafficking, child sex trafficking, forced labor, forced child labor, domestic servitude and bonded labor, and unlawful recruitment and use of child soldiers. It's impossible to know how many people are victims of trafficking, but the latest estimate from International Labor Organization (ILO) places the number at 20.9 million (adults and children)—14.2 million in private industry forced labor (e.g., agriculture, domestic work, sweatshops), 2.2 million in state-sanctioned forced labor (e.g., prisons), and 4.5 million in sex trafficking (ILO, 2012). See Figure 15.1.

Forced Labor

Forced labor involves compelling someone to work through coercion or manipulation. Labor traffickers may use physical threats or may use psychological coercion and deception to force someone to work for them. Examples include luring someone to work in a different country with promises of high pay and good working conditions, and then once they arrive, compelling them to work under harsh conditions for little or no money, and not allowing them to leave through threats of violence (ILO, 2012).

Forced labor can also include bonded debt, where an individual is either forced to work as repayment for a debt or inherits a family member's debt. The majority of victims of bonded labor are men. A common scenario involves a man who borrows money to support his family, with the agreement that he will work off the debt for a certain amount of time. But the terms of the work agreement always benefit the employer, and often the debt grows in time, rather than decreases. Bonded labor is particularly common in South Asian countries, such as India and Pakistan. The industries where bonded labor is practiced the most include the agricultural sectors, bricklaying, mining, stonecutting, and carpet weaving (Premchander, Prameela, & Chidambaranathan, 2015).

Forced Child Labor

The ILO estimates that approximately 30 percent of forced labor involves children, totaling about 5.5 million children who are exploited in some form of forced labor: 21 percent in sex labor (sex trafficking), 27 percent in the private sector labor force (factories,

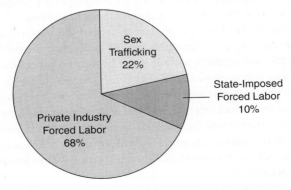

Figure 15.1
Trafficking in persons by type
Source: International Labour Office [ILO], 2012

A child worker sits working precariously perched on a high wooden hanger, the addan, 20 meters high from the ground, on January 10, 2007 at a textile dyeing factory in Rajasthan, India

agriculture, domestic servitude), and 33 percent in state-imposed labor (ILO, 2012). If children between 16 and 18 are included, the number of children forced into full-time labor jumps to 120 million, 61 percent in Asia, 32 percent in Africa, and 7 percent in Latin America (HRW, 2004).

Child labor is a social justice issue across the globe, but is a particular concern in Asian, African, and Latin American countries, where children as young as four years old are required to work up to 12 hours per day in jobs that put them in both physical and psychological danger. Child labor abuses include children in India who plunge their hands into boiling water while making silk thread and children as young as four years in Asia who are tied to rug looms for many hours a day and forced to make rugs. International human rights organizations such as HRW, Amnesty International, and UNICEF work diligently to protect children's rights, including lobbying of international policies and legislation that protect children as well as funding human rights efforts in specific countries allowing for intervention at the local level. But the problem of child labor, particularly in sweatshops in the Global South (Central and South America, Southeast Asia, India, and the Southern region of Africa), remains a serious problem impacting the entire world both socially and economically.

For instance, Polack (2004) discussed the impact of hundreds of billions of dollars in loans made to countries in the Global South by countries in the North (England, Spain, France, the United States, etc.). Polack argued that the cumulative impact of these loans to some of the poorest countries in the world has been devastating to the poorest members of these countries because these loans (1) financed large-scale projects, such as hydroelectric plants, that either benefited the North or displaced literally millions of people, pushing them even further into poverty, (2) financed military armaments for government regimes that oppressed the countries' most vulnerable and poorest residents, or (3) lined the pockets of corrupt leaders of many countries in the Global South, resulting in increased oppression of the country's least-privileged members.

Very little if any of this loan money has benefited the majority of the citizens of these countries; rather, it has harmed them and in fact continues to harm them by increasing the poverty within these already devastatingly poor regions. In an attempt to repay this debt, many countries of the Global South exploit their own workers to make loan payments. For example, countries in South America have sold sections of rainforest formerly farmed by local residents to Northern timber companies, and other countries have been forced to privatize and then sell utility services formerly provided by the government, resulting in dramatic increases in the cost of utilities. These developments have resulted in many Northern companies making millions of dollars literally at the expense of the poorest residents of these debt-ridden countries.

One of the most devastating impacts of what has now evolved into trillions of dollars of debt for these Southern countries is the evolution of the sweatshop industry, large-scale factories that develop goods exported to the North. Some of the poorest people in the world, including children, work in sweatshops throughout Asia, India, and Southern Africa, where horrific abuses abound. This occurs legally in many of these countries because in a desperate attempt to attract export contracts, many countries in Asia, including India, created "free-trade" agreements or free-trade zones for Western corporations, allowing them to circumvent local trade regulations, such as minimum wage, working hour limits, and child labor laws, if they would open factories in their impoverished countries.

Polack (2004) suggests that literally every major retail supplier in the United States benefits from sweatshop conditions such as extremely low wages, extremely poor working conditions, physical and sexual exploitation without retribution, excessively long working hours (sometimes in excess of 12 hours per day with no days off for weeks at a time), and severe retribution such as immediate termination for complaints or requests for better working conditions. Child labor is the norm in these sweatshops, with most sweatshop owners preferring adolescent girls as employees because they tend to be more compliant and are more easily exploited.

Although local and international human service professionals work diligently to change these working conditions, at the root of the problem of child exploitation is economic injustice rooted in generations of intercountry exploitation. Thus, there is significant complexity not easily confronted without government involvement, which is often slow in coming when large corporations are making millions of dollars with the system as it currently operates. For instance, as labor unions have become the norm in the United States, many companies such as Nike and Wal-Mart moved their factories to Asia and Central and South America, where millions of dollars can be saved in wages and benefits cuts. Addressing the issue of child labor and economic injustice will take the lobbying efforts of many international human rights organizations working with the media to create public awareness, where buying power is often the only tool powerful enough to influence sweatshop owners and large retail establishments.

Human Sex Trafficking

While the gender breakdown in forced labor is about equal, the ILO estimates that 98 percent of sex trafficking involves female victims. In fact, younger women and girls are the most sought after targets of large criminal organizations that are in the business of trafficking human beings. Human sex trafficking may comprise a smaller portion of all trafficking incidences per year, but its consequences are severe and long-lasting.

Women and girls are often sold into sex slavery by family members in need of money, are kidnapped, or are lured into the sex trade with promises of modeling contracts or domestic work in other countries. Many of these girls are kept in inhumane living conditions where they are forced to have sex with between 10 and 25 men a day. Many contract the HIV/AIDS virus and are cast out onto the street once they become too sick to be useful (Martin, 2014; U.S. Department of State, 2010).

Much of the effort of human service professionals in countries with high rates of human trafficking, including India, Burma, Thailand, and Sri Lanka, is focused on rescuing these women and children and ensuring that they are delivered to safe communities where they will not be exploited again. Complicating intervention strategies is the fact that many government officials in many high-risk countries either look the other way when confronted with the illegal sex trade or openly contribute to it by protecting

Watch this UN video on survivors of human trafficking. What can human service providers do to support this population?
ENHANCEDetext *video example 15.4*

www.youtube.com/ watch?v=W5u2IUF8JUw

criminal organizations responsible for human trafficking. Human rights organizations have reported that many police officers, members of the military, and other government officials often arrest victims who attempt to flee, putting them in prison on charges of prostitution, a clear act of retaliation, rather than helping them to escape (HRW, 2004).

Efforts to confront trafficking are being fought on the legislative level as well. In 2000 the U.S. government passed the *Trafficking Victims Protection Act* (TVPA), which sets forth guidelines for how trafficking should be addressed on a national and global level. As a part of the legislation, the U.S. State Department releases an annual report entitled the *Trafficking in Persons Report* (TIP), which provides an update and analysis on the status of trafficking conditions worldwide. The report also ranks each country based on actions, such as the governments' actions in combating trafficking.

The ranking system—called the Watch List—consists of three tiers, with Tier 1 being the highest and reserved for those countries that are in compliance with the minimum standards set forth in the TVPA. Countries that are not in compliance with the TVPA but are making progress are ranked at Tier 2, and countries that do not meet the minimum standard and are not taking sufficient steps toward doing so are ranked at Tier 3. Summaries are included on the status of every country, including the country's tier, its annual accomplishments, and areas in need of improvement. Countries are assessed on their effectiveness in targeting and then prosecuting traffickers, as well as the level of services provided to victims.

ENHANCEDetext *self-check 15.3*

MISTREATMENT OF INDIGENOUS PEOPLE AND REFUGEES

Protecting the rights of **indigenous people** is a common concern of human service professionals practicing in countries such as the United States, Australia, and many Central and South American countries. Indigenous populations are often forced to engage in harsh and dangerous labor practices, such as working in fields sprayed with insecticides, transporting supplies on their person, or begging, in order to survive.

The human rights issues pertaining to indigenous peoples of Australia, primarily comprised of Aborigines, are similar in nature to those in the United States, where the historic immigration of Europeans displaced the indigenous tribal communities. In addition, both countries engaged in an official campaign of discrimination and cultural annihilation as indigenous tribes were forced off their lands and onto restricted areas, where they were unable to practice traditional methods of self-support. Both indigenous populations in the United States and Aborigines in Australia were subject to the mass forced removal of children, who were mandated to attend schools where they were forced to abandon their cultural heritage and native language. The 36-year civil war in Guatemala, which ended in 1996, involved what many human rights organizations consider the genocide of indigenous populations, or what is commonly referred to as the "disappearance" of indigenous populations. The U.N. Truth and Reconciliation Committee estimates that up to 200,000 people were killed by government forces (HRW, 2008).

In response to the intergenerational trauma that has resulted from physical and cultural genocide, many indigenous people, including Native Americans, Native Hawaiians and Pacific Islanders, and Alaskan Natives, have experienced a decimation of their population, as well as extreme poverty, forced migration, and marginalization, often manifesting in physical and mental health problems. Human service professionals work with indigenous people in reconciliation efforts to restore them to a level of self-sufficiency and cultural pride. Several movements are underway within indigenous tribal communities intended to move them toward wholeness and a life without substance abuse, depression, and the brokenness in families that has so often been the result of social ills.

One program within one Native American community was developed by a tribal member who suffered from alcoholism for years and who received inspiration and input from tribal elders who shared wisdom regarding traditional cultural laws for authentic change. The four laws of change became known as the *Healing Forest Model*, which is based on the philosophy of the Medicine Wheel, a Native American concept that addresses the interconnectedness of everything in life. According to the teachings of the Medicine Wheel, the pain of one person creates pain for the entire community, and thus there are no individual issues or concerns. This community concept of healing is very consistent with a model of macro practice, which posits that there are no such things as individual problems; instead because people make up communities, all individual problems become community problems. This philosophy may be counterintuitive to North Americans, who as a society place an exceedingly high value on individuality, oftentimes at the cost of community. Yet many believe that the key to reclaiming physical and mental health in indigenous culture is through such a community practice approach (Coyhis & Simonelli, 2005).

According to the Office of the United Nations High Commissioner for Refugees (UNHCR) there are approximately 42 million displaced people who have been forcibly removed from their homes and communities due to civil war, conflict, political and cultural persecution, natural disaster, ethnic cleansing, and genocide. Individuals may become refugees through a variety of circumstances. In the last two decades there have been between 17 and 33 armed civil conflicts at any one time, leading to civil unrest and instability in several developing countries and LCDs. In the midst of a civil war, innocent civilians are often forced to flee in search of safety, a phenomenon referred to as **forced migration**.

If civilians flee but do not cross international boundaries, they are referred to as internally displaced persons (IDPs), but if they are forced to flee into another country, then they often receive the legal designation of refugee. When refugees live secretly in a country with closed borders, they are considered by the host country as illegal immigrants. Life as an illegal immigrant is lived on the fringes, in constant fear of detection, detainment, and repatriation. In other situations, refugees are warehoused in refugee settlements or camps.

In many refugee camps, refugees are not allowed to leave and are often considered a serious risk to the host country. Most refugee camps are established in "border" regions and may remain in close proximity to the war that caused the displacement in the first place. **Protracted refugee situations** foster a sense of significant despair, as most protracted situations linger for generations. Those refugees fortunate enough to be selected for resettlement in the United States or another developed country often face years of challenges as they struggle to survive in a complex society, often underemployed and socially isolated (Hollenbach, 2008; Loescher, Milner, & Troeller, 2008).

Human service professionals often work with refugees in a variety of practice settings, including refugee resettlement agencies (contracted with the U.S. Department of

Watch this UNHCR video on the plight of refugees. What do you think are some durable solutions to the world's refugee crisis?

ENHANCEDetext *video example 15.5*

www.youtube.com/
watch?v=UrSQcEcs8KM

State), schools, and mental health agencies. It is for this reason that human service providers should have awareness of global dynamics, even if they never intend to practice abroad. Many clients in need of human services have emigrated from countries where they were victims of oppression and human rights violations. Working with populations that have a history of oppression and marginalization requires an understanding of the wide range of global abuses related to social injustice and human rights violations, as well as recognizing how these abuses have implications on direct practice with individual clients.

ENHANCEDetext *self-check 15.4*

HUMAN RIGHTS VIOLATIONS AGAINST LGBT POPULATIONS

Watch this film on the treatment of LGBT populations in Iraq. Write down three ways in which the international community should respond to the treatment of LGBT populations in Iraq and similar countries. What role does the human services profession have in your suggestions?
ENHANCEDetext *video example 15.6*

https://www.youtube.com/
watch?v=-miF7F8oPv4

The plight of lesbian, gay, bisexual, transgender (LGBT) populations, as well as those whose sexuality is questioned, is quite bleak in many regions of the world. In many developing countries and LDCs, same-sex relationships are illegal, with punishments ranging from prison to death. Harassment and abuse of LGBT populations, sometimes even by police or others in positions of power, are not uncommon. For instance, in Iran having a same-sex relationship is punishable by death (HRW, 2010b). In Senegal "homosexual conduct" is punishable by a minimum of five years in prison (HRW, 2010c).

A recent report by HRW on crimes against the LGBT population in Iraq detailed the death squads that combed the country in 2009 searching for men who appeared gay. In what HRW describes as a "killing campaign," bands of armed men barged into private homes and abducted men who were perceived as gay, often for no reason other than they did not appear manly enough. Abducted men were murdered and their dead bodies discarded, leaving evidence of gruesome torture, including having their genitals cut off and having glue injected into their anuses. HRW was informed that most of the death squads were from a militia group that espouses the threat of effeminate men, and considers the killing of men perceived as gay as "social cleansing" (HRW, 2009, p. 4). Although the militia were from militant Islamic groups and may have been acting in response to a cleric's fatwa (order), neither the Iraqi government nor the Iraqi police investigated the killings or made any arrests, leading HRW and other advocacy organizations to believe that the Iraqi government is not concerned about these death squads, perhaps because they are targeting an undesirable and unsympathetic group (Martin, 2014).

South Africa is another country known for excessively high rates of violence, particularly against women. According to advocacy organizations, about half of all women in South Africa are victims of sexual assault (HRW, 2011). In fact, in a recent study about one-quarter of South African men surveyed admitted to having raped a woman, and many of them admitted to committing rape in gangs (Jewkes, Sikweyiya, Morrell, & Dunkle, 2009). Many of these rapes were called "corrective rape," where women whose gender expression is perceived as too masculine are raped to teach them how to be women. Often these rapes are particularly brutal, involving numerous men, who beat the women while calling them derogatory names. South African men who rape lesbians or women with more masculine gender expression often do so with complete impunity, confident they will not be arrested.

Advocacy organizations around the world confront these injustices in a variety of ways, including through education and awareness, legal remedies, and seeking U.N. remedies through the human rights treaty system. Advocacy on a legal level includes attempts to change U.S. asylum laws, making it easier for applications based on persecution due to sexual orientation to be accepted by immigration judges. Currently, despite the fact that many people around the globe are highly persecuted based on their sexual identity and/or sexual conduct, current U.S. asylum laws make it difficult for LGBT populations to be granted asylum because the legal test for persecution based on the membership in a social group doesn't allow for the contextual reality of gays and lesbians, who are forced to hide who they are, or fear imprisonment or death (Sridharan, 2008).

London, December 9, 2015: Gay rights activists take part in a protest outside the Ugandan High Commission urging the president of Uganda to not sign the anti-gay The Non-Governmental Organisations Bill, 2015

ENHANCEDetext *self-check 15.5*

GENOCIDE AND RAPE AS A WEAPON OF WAR

The 1948 U.N. Convention on the Prevention and Punishment of the Crime of Genocide defines genocide as any act committed with the intention to destroy, in whole or in part, a national ethnic, racial, or religious group: killing members of the group; causing serious bodily or mental harm to members of the group; deliberately inflicting on the group conditions of life calculated to bring about its physical destruction in whole or in part; imposing measures intended to prevent births within the group; and forcibly transferring children of the group to another group (U.N. General Assembly, 1948).

Genocides typically occur within a broader armed civil or international conflict. Thus, determining whether civilian deaths in conflict rise to the level of genocide can be quite political in nature. A determination of genocide can be made by any country that is a signatory of the 1945 U.N. Genocide Convention, as well as by the General Assembly of the United Nations. Yet it is important to note that just because an incident of civilian killings is not deemed to be genocide by the international community does not mean that genocide has not occurred, as there may be political reasons why the United Nations does not level charges of genocide against a particular government or group.

There have been several genocides in the world's recent history, each one seemingly more gruesome than the next. The U.S. genocide of Native Americans during the 1700s through the 1800s and Turkey's genocide of the Armenians in 1917 are examples of genocides that have never been officially recognized by the international community. More recent genocides include the Nazi Holocaust against the Jews in Europe during World War II, the Serbian genocide against the Bosnians in 1992 through 1994, and the Rwandan genocide against the Tutsi in 1994.

March 31, 2004: Jean Claude Gassira, 38, stands up to an accusation at a Gacaca court hearing (literally, justice on the grass), a traditional restorative justice model that is designed to lead to community healing

Each of these genocides also involved **rape as a weapon of war**—the raping of women of the targeted ethnic or religious group in the midst of civil conflict. Rape as a weapon of war is a systematic tactic used in armed conflict targeting the civilian population (primarily women and girls) involving sexual violence in an officially orchestrated manner and as a purposeful policy to humiliate, intimidate, and instill fear in a community or ethnic group (Buss, 2009; HRW, 1996). Thus, rape during wartime is not a by-product of armed conflict, but an instrument of it (Buss, 2009). For instance, in Rwanda, the Habyarimana government's armed forces, government-sponsored militia groups called Interahamwe, and Hutu civilians not only used machetes to kill and maim hundreds of thousands of Tutsi but also subjected hundreds of thousands of Tutsi women to sexual violence with the goal of impregnating them as well as infecting them with HIV (Buss, 2009; Cohen et al., 2009; Des Forges, 1999; HRW, 1996).

In June of 2008 the United Nations Security Council adopted Resolution 1820, which recognizes rape as a weapon of war and establishes a commitment to addressing sexual violence in conflict, including punishing perpetrators (U.N. Security Council, 2008). This resolution became an important part of convictions by international criminal tribunals in response to genocides in former Yugoslavia (the ICTY), Rwanda (the ICTR), and in the United Nations–backed Special Court for Sierra Leone (SCSL) (UNDPKO, 2010).

In addition to international legal remedies, there are several advocacy and human service agencies that work with survivors of genocide and rape as a weapon of war. For survivors who have immigrated to a different country, culturally adapted trauma counseling can be very effective. For survivors remaining in their home country, indigenous healing approaches are often used based on a **restorative justice model**. Additionally, many human service professionals, such as social workers and psychologists from the United States and Europe, have partnered with agencies in Rwanda. Using a train-the-trainer model, these professionals train counselors in Rwanda to provide trauma-informed therapy to survivors, often merging Western approaches with indigenous ones.

ENHANCEDetext *self-check 15.6*

CONCLUSION

As the world shrinks due to globalization, people are becoming more aware of human rights violations committed against vulnerable populations. Poverty is an underlying factor in virtually all global social problems, both with regard to who is affected and how governments and the international community respond. Human service professionals along with social justice advocates work on multiple levels to address a range of global social problems—health pandemics; human trafficking; the treatment of indigenous people; migrants and refugees; mistreatment of LGBT populations; and genocide—using culturally adapted intervention strategies on micro and macro levels.

SUMMARY

- The nature of globalization and its impact on advocacy and global poverty are explored. The nature of globalization on various systems is explored, including how the globalization of communication, such as the Internet, has made international human services more possible than it was in the past. Global poverty and social exclusion are also explored with a focus on how these conditions undercut the majority of social problems and human rights violations in the world, particularly those in developing economies and least developed countries. Efforts to address poverty are explored, including the U.N. Millennium Development Goals and the Strategic Development Goals.

- Major global health pandemics and other public health concerns, and the international community's response, are identified. Global health pandemics, such as HIV/AIDS, and other public health crises, such as malaria and the Ebola virus, are examined, with a particular focus on vulnerable populations. Female genital mutilation is also explored, tracing its historic roots to current practice throughout sub-Saharan Africa, South Asia, and Middle Eastern states. International initiatives and collaborative efforts are explored, including the role of human service professionals working on a global level.

- The nature of forced labor, including sex trafficking and child labor, is explored. Various forms of human trafficking, including forced labor, bonded labor, and human sex trafficking impacting both adults and children, are discussed. Global initiatives focused on legal remedies as well as advocacy efforts on micro and macro levels are explored, highlighting the role of human service providers facilitating direct services and macro-level advocacy.

- The ways in which indigenous populations and refugees have been mistreated and marginalized and how human service professionals can respond are examined. Historic and current mistreatment of indigenous populations within the context of culturally adapted intervention strategies is explored. The plight of the world's refugees is also explored, including forced migration and protracted refugee situations. Advocacy efforts focusing on trauma, resettlement, and repatriation are also explored.

- The range of global human rights violations committed against lesbian, gay, bisexual, and transgender populations, and ways that human service professionals can respond, are identified. The nature and types of human rights violations committed against LGBT populations and those with nonconforming gender expression including the nature of treatment of LGBT populations in particular countries are discussed. Advocacy efforts and challenges are explored, including the role of human service providers.

- The nature of genocide and rape as a weapon of war and the role of human service providers working with survivors is examined. The human impact of genocide on survivors and the path toward healing are explored. Rape as a weapon of war is explored, including the conditions under which it is committed, as well as ways that advocates and human service professionals can respond on a micro and macro level.

Internet Resources

Conduct an Internet search for Amnesty International, and then click on Our Work.

Conduct an Internet search for the International Federation of Social Workers, and then click on Statement of Ethical Principles.

Conduct an Internet search for the International Association of Schools of Social Work, and then click on Global Standards for Social Work Education and Training.

Conduct an Internet search for the International Council on Social Welfare, and then click on Activities, and then on the Global Agenda.

Conduct an Internet search for the United Nations, and then click on What We Do, and then click on Protect Human Rights.

Conduct an Internet search for the World Bank, and then click on About, and then click on What We Do.

Conduct an Internet search for the United Nations Millennium Development Goals.

Conduct an Internet search for the Roll Back Malaria Partnership, and then click on News & Events.

Conduct an Internet search for StopFGM Kenya, and then click on About Us.

Conduct an Internet search for International Labor Organization, and then click on Topics, and then click on Forced Labor, Sex Trafficking and Slavery.

Conduct an Internet search for UNHCR, and then click on About Us, and then click on Figures at a Glance.

Conduct an Internet search for Polaris Project, and then click on Menu, and then click on Human Trafficking.

Conduct an Internet search for Human Rights Watch, and then click on Topics, and then click on LGBT Rights.

References

Ahmadi, N. (2003). Globalisation of consciousness and new challenges for international social work. *International Journal of Social Welfare, 12*, 14–23.

Alcock, P. (2006). *Understanding poverty.* Basingstoke: Palgrave Macmillan.

Buss, D. E. (2009). Rethinking "rape as a weapon of war." *Feminist Legal Studies, 17*(2), 145–163.

Callan, T., Nolan, B. and Whelan, C. (1993), Resources, Deprivation and the Measurement of Poverty. *Journal of Social Policy, 22*, 141–172.

Chi-Ying Chung, R. (2005). Women, human rights & counseling: Crossing international borders. *Journal of Counseling and Development, 83*, 262–268.

Cohen, M. H., Fabri, M., Cai, X., Shi, Q., Hoover, D. R., Binagwaho, A., & Anastos, K. (2009). Prevalence and predictors of post-traumatic stress disorder and depression in HIV-infected and at-risk Rwandan women. *Journal of Women's Health, 18*(11), 1783–1791.

Coyhis, D., & Simonelli, R. (2005). Rebuilding Native American communities. *Child Welfare, 84*(2), 323–336.

Des Forges, A. (1999). Leave none to tell the story. New York, NY: Human Rights Watch. Retrieved from http://www.hrw.org/legacy/reports/1999/rwanda/rwanda0399.htm

Gettleman, J. (2010, January 4). *Americans' role seen in Uganda anti-gay push.* New York Times. Retrieved from http://www.nytimes.com/2010/01/04/world/africa/04uganda.html

Gordon, D. (2000). *Breadline Europe: The measurement of poverty.* Policy Press.

Hollenbach, D. (2008). *Refugee rights: Ethics, advocacy and Africa.* Washington, DC: Georgetown University Press.

Human Rights Watch. (1996). *Shattered lives: Sexual violence during the Rwandan genocide and its aftermath.* New York, NY: Human Rights Watch.

Human Rights Watch. (2004). *All Jamaicans are threatened by a culture of homophobia.* Retrieved from http://hrw.org/english/docs/2004/11/23/jamaic9716.htm

Human Rights Watch. (2008). *Guatemala: World Report 2009.* Retrieved from http://www.hrw.org/en/node/79213

Human Rights Watch. (2009). *Uganda: "anti-homosexuality" bill threatens liberties and human rights defenders proposed provisions illegal, ominous, and unnecessary.* Retrieved from http://www.hrw.org/en/news/2009/10/15/uganda-anti-homosexuality-bill-threatens-liberties-and-human-rights-defenders

Human Rights Watch. (2010a). "They Took Me and Told Me Nothing" Female Genital Mutilation in Iraqi Kurdistan. Retrieved from https://www.hrw.org/report/2010/06/16/they-took-me-and-told-me-nothing/female-genital-mutilation-iraqi-kurdistan

Human Rights Watch. (2010b, December 15). We are a buried generation: Discrimination and violence against

sexual minorities in Iran. Retrieved from http://www
.hrw.org/node/94978.

Human Rights Watch. (2010c, November 30). Fear for
life: Violence against gay men and men perceived as
gay in Senegal. Retrieved from http://www.hrw.org/
reports/2010/11/30/fear-life.

International Council on Social Welfare. (n.d.). What is
our mission? Retrieved from http://www.icsw.org/
intro/missione.htm

International Labour Office [ILO]. (2012). ILO Global
Estimates of Forced Labor: Results and Methodology.
Retrieved online from http://www.ilo.org/wcmsp5/
groups/public/---ed_norm/---declaration/documents/
publication/wcms_182004.pdf

ILO. (2012). ILO Global Estimate of Forced Labour: Results
and methodology. ILO Publications.

Jewkes, R., Sikweyiya, Y., Morrell, R., & Dunkle, K.
(2009). Understanding Men's Health and Use of
Violence: Interface of Rape and HIV in South Africa.
Retrieved from http://www.mrc.ac.za/gender/
violence_hiv.pdf

Lee, P. and Murie, A. (1999). Spatial and social divisions
within British cities: beyond residualisation. Housing
Studies, 14(5), 635–640.

Lexow, J. Berggrav, M. Taraldsen, S. (2009). Prevention and
eradication of Female Genital Mutilation (FGM) and
other Harmful Traditional Practices (HTPs). Norad
Collected Reviews. Retrieved from http://www
.norad.no/en/Tools+and+publications/Publications/
Publication+Page?key=125122

Lessoj, C. and Jowell, R. (2000). Measuring Social Exclusion.
Working paper, No. 84, Centre for Research into Elections and Social Trends (CREST), University of Oxford.

Lightfoot-Klein, H. (1991). Prisoners of ritual: Some contemporary developments in the history of Female Genital Mutilation. Presented at the Second International
Symposium on Circumcision in San Francisco,
Apr. 30–May 3, 1991.

Lister, R. (2004). Poverty. Cambridge: Polity. Applied ethics
and social problems, 715–728.

Loescher, L., Milner, J., & Troeller, G. (2008). Protracted refugee
situations: Political, human rights and security implications.
New York, NY: United Nations University Press.

Martin, M. E. (2014). Advocacy for social justice: A global
perspective. Upper Saddle River, NJ: Pearson Publishing.

Marx, I., & K. van den Bosch. (September 2007). How
poverty differs from inequality. On poverty measurement
in an enlarged EU context: conventional and alternative
approaches. Paper presented at the 34th CEIES Seminar,
Helsinki.

Millennium Project. (2005). Investing in development: A practical
plan to achieve the Millennium Development Goals. Report to

the UN Secretary General. Retrieved from http://www.
unmillenniumproject.org/reports/index_overview.htm

Mitike, G., & Deressa, W. (2009). Prevalence and associated factors of female genital mutilation among Somali
refugees in eastern Ethiopia: A cross-sectional study.
BMC Public Health, 9(1), 1.

Polack, R. (2004). Social justice and the global economy:
New challenges for social work in the 21st century.
Social Work, 49(2), 281–290.

Premchander, S., Prameela, V., & Chidambaranathan, M.
(2015). Prevention and elimination of bonded labour: The
potential and limits of microfinance-led approaches. International Labor Organization [ILO]. Retrieved online
from http://www.ilo.org/wcmsp5/groups/public/-
--ed_norm/---declaration/documents/publication/
wcms_334875.pdf

Ravallion, M. (1998). Poverty lines in theory and practice:
Living standards measurement study. (Working Paper
133)., World Bank, Washington DC.

Ryan, C., & Rivers, I. (2003). Lesbian, gay, bisexual and
transgender youth: Victimization and its correlates
in the U.S. and U.K. Culture, Health and Sexuality, 5(2),
103–119.

Simler. K. R. & Arndt, C., 2006. Poverty comparisons
with absolute poverty lines estimated from survey
data. FCND discussion papers 211, International Food
Policy Research Institute (IFPRI).

Sridharan, S. (2008). The difficulties of U.S. asylum claims
based on sexual orientation. Migration Information
Source. Retrieved from http://www.migrationpolicy.
org/article/difficulties-us-asylum-claims-based-sexual-
orientation

Townsend, P. (1979). Poverty in the United Kingdom: A survey
of household resources and standards of living. Univ of
California Press.

UNAIDS. (2008). 2008 report on the global AIDS epidemic.
Geneva, Switzerland: UNAIDS. Available at: www
.unaids.org

United Nations Children's Fund [UNICEF], U.S. Agency
for International Development. (2004). Children on the
brink 2004: A joint report of new orphan estimates and
a framework for action. The Joint United Nations Programme on HIV/AIDS. New York, NY: United Nations
Children's Fund.

United Nations Development Program. (2000). Millennium development goals. Retrieved from http://www.
undp.org/mdg/basics.shtml.

United Nations, Department of Peacekeeping Operations
[UNDPKO]. (2010). Review of the sexual violence elements of the judgments of the international criminal
tribunal for the former Yugoslavia, the International
Criminal Tribunal for Rwanda, and the special court

for Sierra Leone in the light of Security Council Resolution 1820. Retrieved from http://www.unrol.org/files/32914_Review%20of%20the%20Sexual%20Violence%20Elements%20in%20the%20Light%20of%20the%20Security-Council%20resolution%201820.pdf

United Nations Population Fund (UNFPA). (2009). The end is in sight: Moving toward the abandonment of female genital mutilation/cutting. Annual Report 2009. UNFPA/UNICEF Joint Programme.

United Nations General Assembly. *Prevention and punishment of the crime of genocide, 9 December 1948, A/RES/260.* Retrieved from http://www.unhcr.org/refworld/docid/3b00f0873.html [accessed 5 November 2012].

United Nations Security Council, 5916th Meeting. (2008). Resolution 1820 [sexual violence as a war tactic] 19 June 2008 (pp. 51–52). In *Resolutions and Decisions of the Security Council 2008* (S/RES/1820). Official Record. New York.

United Nations Women. (n.d.). Women, Poverty & Economics. Retrieved from http://www.unifem.org/gender_issues/women_poverty_economics/.

United Nations Women. (2011). Fourth United Nations Conference on the Least Developed Countries. Retrieved from http://www.unwomen.org/wp-content/uploads/2011/05/UNWomen-LDC-Key-Messages.pdf.

U.S. Department of State. (2001). *Afghanistan: Country reports on Human Rights Practices, Bureau of Democracy, Human Rights, and Labor.* Retrieved from http://www.state.gov/g/drl/rls/hrrpt/2000/sa/721.htm

Weiss, I. (2005). Is there a global common core to social work? A cross-national comparative study of BSW graduate students. *Social Work, 50*(2), 102–110.

Whittaker, M. A., Dean, A. J., & Chancellor, A. (2014). Advocating for malaria elimination—learning from the successes of other infectious disease elimination programmes. *Malaria Journal, 13,* 221.

World Health Organization [WHO]. (1998). *Female genital mutilation—an overview.* Geneva, Switzerland: Author.

World Health Organization [WHO]. (2016). Ebola virus disease. Fact Sheet No 103. Geneva, Switzerland: Author.

World Health Organization [WHO]. (2016). Achieving the Malaria MDG Target: Reversing the Incidence of Malaria 2000-2015. Retrieved from http://www.unicef.org/publications/files/Achieving_the_Malaria_MDG_Target.pdf.

The Future of Human Services: New Opportunities

The human services profession exists to help people meet their basic needs. One of its strengths is its multidisciplinary approach, wherein individuals with education and training in various disciplines—including human services, social work, and counseling—work side by side, addressing the barriers to self-sufficiency and optimal living. Unlike many other mental health disciplines, human service professionals are true generalists, and those who specialize are less often focused on a particular psychological disorder than on a particular social problem or practice setting, such as interfamily violence or child welfare.

The passion to create meaningful change in the lives of others creates a drive in many human service professionals that may compensate for the relatively low pay and often less-than-ideal working conditions. It would be incorrect to assume, however, that just because one enters the human services field, he or she cannot earn a decent living—creative opportunities are plentiful for those with an entrepreneurial spirit and the willingness to accept new challenges. Nonetheless, it is this drive and passion to make the world a better place that pushes so many individuals forward in a career that does not have particularly high status but affords the unique experience of making a significant difference in the lives of others. We do this by reminding people of their worth, holding the hand of the dying, assuring a grieving child that there is still hope, or standing with survivors of violence who are facing their attackers in court. This is an empowering career that changes with every new client.

Human services is a unique career in that it can often lead to other opportunities including a career in academia, writing, public speaking, policy analysis, advocacy, or international human rights work. Additionally, a career track that leads to clinical private practice can remain exciting and varied if the human service professional remains committed to social justice and advocacy.

THE IMPORTANCE OF SELF-CARE

As wonderful as this career is, it is also wrought with stress, crises, and significant burnout potential if human service providers aren't proactive in their self-care. Among the many ways to avoid burnout are developing mental paradigms that help professionals avoid becoming overinvolved in the lives of their clients, and taking action to meet one's personal needs within a variety of domains. One paradigm that can benefit human service professionals is to recognize that their clients are on a life journey—*their own* journey—and the role of the human service provider is to assist the client on a small portion of this journey. Many human service professionals experience professional burnout because they take too much responsibility for the lives of their clients. This is a natural temptation. We care, and therefore we want to do as much as we can to ensure our clients are living their lives at the optimum level. Yet, understanding that our clients are on their own journey, not ours, and trusting in their ultimate ability to navigate their own lives are vitally important for the provider and the client. Human service providers are counselors, mentors, advocates, and guides. We come along in our clients' lives to help them during a particular time period, and we must believe that other helpers have contributed before us and more will arrive after us. This paradigm puts the clinician–client relationship into a healthy perspective and can assist human service providers in not overfunctioning.

Self-care for human service professionals also involves taking concrete steps to ensure that we are getting our own needs met, that we are taking time for ourselves, that we have good boundaries, and that our lives are in balance. This may seem like a pipe dream for the overworked and too-often underpaid human service provider, but it's vitally important to take good care of ourselves. If we are out of balance, then we aren't going to be of much help to our clients. Examples of getting our needs met include making sure that we're getting enough sleep, we're eating nutritiously (minimizing those quick meals of processed, high-fat foods), we are exercising on a regular basis, we have social lives that feed us emotionally, and we are allowing for time away from work so that we can engage in fulfilling activities.

New research is revealing the devastating impact stress has on our bodies, minds, and general well-being. Unchecked stress, particularly due to stressful workplace environments, can lead to a host of problems beyond mere burnout, such as depression and anxiety, and a range of stress-related physical ailments. Those professionals who accept the stress as a normal part of their jobs may fare worse than those who are able to set reasonable boundaries (Reid & Ramarajan, 2016). Chronic stress floods our bodies with the hormone cortisol, keeping us in a constant state of "fight or flight," which eventually takes a toll on the body. Human service providers suffering from professional burnout often experience an emotional shutdown, where they no longer accept input, feel unappreciated and overworked, experience irritability and unprovoked anger, and, as a consequence, have lower productivity and far less satisfaction (Smullens, 2015).

I went to a conference recently on self-care where a speaker described human needs within various domains: emotional, physical, spiritual, and sexual. I hadn't expected that last one! But her explanation made sense—when we're living lives out of balance, that is, when we aren't getting our emotional, physical, spiritual, or sexual needs met outside of work, we're more likely to commit an ethical breach by falling to the temptation of getting our needs met through our clients. Someone who for the most part has a robust social life, is healthy physically, is fulfilled spiritually in the way that makes sense to him or her, and is getting his or her intimacy needs met will be far less likely to respond inappropriately to a client who, for example, develops a crush. It is often the lonely provider who steps over the line, who is inappropriately flattered by a client's attention, and who loses perspective and allows professional boundaries to be crossed.

I know what it feels like, though, to be exceedingly busy attempting to meet the needs of clients in an environment that is understaffed and underfunded. And I know what it feels like to be underpaid, underappreciated, and unsupported. When I heard about the importance of self-care earlier in my career, I almost scoffed. "Sure! Talk to me about self-care while you're giving me far more cases than any human being can handle! And while I'm at it, I'll just hop on a plane and take a little vacation in Hawaii, or perhaps a cruise! Oh wait, that's right, I can barely pay my rent." So I get it—we can talk about self-care all day long, but when we're all so overworked, and often underpaid, we may feel as though we have very few options.

The good news is that positive self-care often doesn't require an exotic vacation (although that would be nice) or days spent in an expensive spa. Often, self-care is a mind-set—a well-formed attitude that values setting limits and saying no, even when doing so may feel scary, or make us feel guilty. Good self-care can involve setting aside technology whenever possible and taking a walk. It involves spending time with friends and family who offer us relationship reciprocity. Good self-care means we eat nutritious foods, get plenty of sleep, and don't distract ourselves with unhealthy lifestyle choices. Respectfully articulating our needs to our supervisors may be far easier than we imagine ("I'm feeling professionally burned out and need to take a day off"). We all know what healthy living looks like, but sometimes it just feels easier to make the unhealthy choices—emotional eating, surrounding ourselves with negativity, never taking a day off, and so on. Again, balance is the key, as is living within the margins and not becoming emotionally and/or physically overdrawn.

HUMAN SERVICES AND TECHNOLOGY

Technology has changed the world; the human services profession has been slow in making use of technological changes but in many ways has recently caught up. E-counseling is gaining in popularity, and recent legislation, such as the January 1, 2014 federal mandate that all health care providers utilize technology in recordkeeping (electronic medical records), has resulted in many human service providers becoming technologically adept. Technology, despite its challenges, enhances the profession by increasing efficiency and supplying providers and clients with increased tools. Consider the fact that most human services organizations, government assistance programs, and various grant-giving agencies provide valuable information on their Websites as well as an expedited application process for services.

The Internet can be tremendously useful for human service providers who want to coordinate services with other professionals or obtain information on a particular issue. Technology is also being used to facilitate various types of testing, including personality and career assessments, ADHD (attention deficit/hyperactivity disorder) evaluations, and adaptive functioning evaluations. Advocacy efforts have also been made easier through the Internet—legislation can be researched online and a virtual letter-writing campaign can be conducted in minutes. Social media can allow the isolated to feel connected, providing online support for those who are reluctant (or unable) to seek assistance outside of their homes. But social media can also be a source of difficulty, as cyberbullying and cyberstalking allow abuse to come into the homes of clients through their personal electronic devices. Human service providers must be up-to-date on the latest trends in social media apps and usage, so that they may be better informed about the various benefits and stressors impacting the lives of clients who are social media users. Imagine a human service provider working in a school who is unaware of the benefits and risks of Snapchat, the social media app that allows users to send photos and videos to online friends, which then disappear within seconds. Snapchat can be fun when used appropriately, but when it's used to disseminate sexual content, particularly among teens, it can be very harmful. Human service providers can guide their clients of all ages on how to effectively use social media in a way that enhances their lives, while avoiding the pitfalls of overuse and the dangers of posting unsecured information. Some providers may even be able to offer guidance on how to manage potential dangers, such as being in contact with those who use the Internet as a tool for exploitation and abuse.

Despite the concerns about the risks, the Internet can be empowering for clients, enabling them to be more self-sufficient in finding resources, including housing, job opportunities, and child care. In addition, resources are available for homebound individuals who might not be able to benefit from an on-site support group but can garner some of the same benefits from online support groups or bulletin boards. Whether the Internet is used as a beneficial tool or as a portal for danger is completely dependent on the sophistication of the user, and technologically adept human service providers can be effective guides in assisting their clients in this regard.

GLOBALIZATION

Our world is shrinking due to a variety of domains becoming "globalized," a trend that is having a dramatic impact on the world and how it functions. The globalization of world market economies means that if one region experiences an economic crisis, several other regions will likely follow. If a civil war rages in a far-off country, the ripple effect will be felt worldwide, whether through forced migration and refugee flow or international community involvement. The globalization of communication technologies means that we can switch on our televisions, laptops, or smartphones and know instantly what is happening thousands of miles away. We can text or video chat friends and family across the globe, and make connections with old friends from elementary school and new friends in foreign countries through Facebook, Twitter, WhatsApp, or Skype. These are exciting times for communication, but such rapid technological developments create both positive and negative consequences. Migrants can remain connected to their homelands on a daily basis (good), but terrorists intending to commit violent acts against governments can use the Internet to recruit (bad). Child pornography is rampant online (bad), but law enforcement can use virtual online stings to catch producers and consumers of child pornography (good).

The human services profession has no doubt been affected by the globalization of technology because our clients have been. Those in the human services field are committed to addressing problems in society, often before those within society are prepared to admit that such problems even exist. Human service professionals are consistently on the frontlines of social problems, creating change in the lives of individuals and communities, on a local, national, and global level. Society is constantly evolving, which can create negative by-products of conflict, complexity, and challenges for many. It is for this reason that human service professionals will always be needed to recognize and confront human problems, helping society's most vulnerable members meet their basic emotional, physical, and spiritual needs.

This is an exciting time in human services. We are coming out of a long period of economic decline, and many agencies are experiencing an increase in funding for the first time in years. While this isn't the case for all regions or practice settings, things do seem to be getting better, which has a positive impact on agencies and the client populations they serve. Increased opportunities for human service professionals exist in both employment and education. As the profession continues to develop, even more opportunities will be created, particularly with the guidance and support of professional organizations, such as the National Organization for Human Services (NOHS) and the Council for Standards in Human Service Education (CSHSE). Today is a great time to enter this profession, and it is my hope that reading this text helps to both inform and guide you on your path.

THE 2016 PRESIDENTIAL ELECTION

I completed this book just before businessman and reality television star Donald Trump was elected as the 45th president of the United States. Many believe that the future of human services may be significantly impacted if Trump's campaign promises come to fruition. His election sent shockwaves through human services and social justice advocate communities because of the various and numerous ways he negatively targeted the very populations human service providers strive to protect. While it's too soon to determine the impact on human service clients, at-risk communities, and on the profession itself, most of us believe that the human, social, and environmental cost of this election will be great.

The question that many people are asking is how the polls and political pundits could have been so wrong. The answers to the "why" and "how" questions are complex and lie in economic and social dynamics addressed throughout this book, especially in the chapter on rural human services. According to many postelection articles and commentary, Trump's team identified a struggling demographic that had been largely ignored: middle-aged white working-class voters who lived in small towns, rural communities, and blue-collar regions, such as the Rust Belt—areas most impacted by deindustrialization. Trump's promise to bring back manufacturing jobs and revive the coal and steel industries resonated within these communities, and they came out to vote in droves (Cohn, 2016; Zitner & Overberg, 2016).

The Southern Law Poverty Center (2016) has reported bias-based bullying incidences and hate crimes occurring across the country in the days following Trump's election—racially charged slurs and beatings, hijabs getting ripped off of women's heads, gays and lesbians being accosted verbally and physically, and Ku Klux Khan literature being distributed throughout communities. In fact, the increase in bias-based bullying has been so significant during the presidential campaign that many media outlets termed the phenomenon the "Trump Effect" (Klein, 2016).

By the time this book is published and in your hands, we will know Trump's cabinet selections and policy commitments, and human service professionals will have a much better idea of where we need to focus our individual and collective action. Reproductive rights and women's health, protection of religious minorities, migrant and refugee rights, indigenous rights, environmental protection, economic regulation, poverty alleviation, LGBTQ+ rights, and gender equity (to name a few) are areas that may require increased attention and advocacy.

This election has in a very short time created a groundswell of grassroots organizing and social action. People who are committed to social justice causes are connecting all across the country, initiated primarily through online social networking, and then extending to offline social action. For instance, the organization Pantsuit Nation, a secret Facebook group created by Libby Chamberlain a few weeks before the election to support Hillary Clinton, exploded to over 3.4 million members within two days of the election and to 4 million a few weeks later. Pantsuit Nation primarily serves as a safe space for storytelling, but even that is a form of social action, as telling one's story of marginalization, displacement, oppression, and discrimination can be quite empowering. By providing a voice for those who may not have a forum for expression anywhere else in their lives, Pantsuit Nation and other online social networking groups effect change through the facilitation of increased awareness, engagement, and social connection.

How we, as human service professionals, respond to ideological, political, and economic demands placed on service delivery systems, increased barriers to at-risk clients' self-sufficiency, and threats to human rights is anchored in our profession's values. The foundational principles of the human services inform us that all people have human rights simply because they are human; that just because someone lacks resources doesn't mean they lack value; that health care and mental health care are human rights, not privileged rights; that immigration reform should be compassionate and honor our country's history of purposefully porous borders; that climate change is real and the environment is worth protecting; and that this country belongs to all of us: people of color, immigrants, indigenous people, women, men, religious minorities, and LGBTQ+ people—all of us. We can then ask ourselves this question: What would Jane Addams do?

References

Cohn, N. (2016). Why Trump won: Working class whites. Retrieved from http://www.nytimes.com/2016/11/10/upshot/why-trump-won-working-class-whites.html

Cook, N., & Restuccia, A. (2016). Meet Trump's cabinet-in-waiting. *Politico*. Retrieved from http://www.politico.com/story/2016/11/who-is-in-president-trump-cabinet-231071

Klein, A. (2016). 'Rash of hate crimes' reported day after Trump's election. *NBC New York*. http://www.nbcnewyork.com/news/national-international/Array-of-Hate-Crimes-Reported-Day-After-Trumps-Election-400711591.html

Markoe, L. (2016). White evangelicals, Catholics and Mormons carried Trump. *Religious news service*. Retrieved from https://www.ncronline.org/news/politics/white-evangelicals-catholics-and-mormons-carried-trump

Murphy, T. (2016). Trump's cabinet is going to be as bonkers as you thought. *Mother Jones*. Retrieved from http://www.motherjones.com/politics/2016/10/what-donald-trumps-cabinet-might-look-like

Reid, E., & Ramarajan, L. (2016). Managing the high-intensity workplace. *Harvard Business Review*. Retrieved from http://www.iconnectsxm.com/files/2016/05/HBR-managing-the-high-intensity-workplace.pdf

Smullens, S. K. (2015). *Burnout and self-care in social work: A guidebook for students and those in mental health and related professions*. Washington, DC: NASW Press.

Southern Law Poverty Center. (2016). The Trump effect: The impact of the presidential campaign on our public schools. Retrieved from https://www.splcenter.org/20160413/trump-effect-impact-presidential-campaign-our-nations-schools

Zitner, A., & Overberg, P. (2016). Rural vote fuels Trump; Clinton loses urban grip. *The Wall Street Journal*. Retrieved from http://www.wsj.com/articles/rural-vote-helps-donald-trump-as-hillary-clinton-holds-cities-1478664251

Glossary

Ableism   discrimination in favor of able-bodied people.

Abrahamic religions   a religion whose people believe that Abraham and his descendants hold an important role in human spiritual development. Judaism, Christianity, and Islam are Abrahamic religions.

Absolute poverty   a set standard that is the same in all countries and which does not change over time. An income-related example would be living on less than $X per day.

Abstinence-only program   sex education programs that focus solely on encouraging students not to have sexual relations, compared to prevention programs that explore birth control, empowerment, and sexual health.

Abstract reasoning ability   the ability to use critical thinking in cognitive processing.

Acting out behavior   a term often used to describe rebellious behavior within the adolescent population.

Active aging   potential, well-being, and active participation in all life has to offer within a range of domains, including social, economic, cultural, spiritual, and civic domains.

Active listening skills   the ability to attend to the speaker fully, without distraction, without preconceived notions of what the speaker is saying, and without being distracted by thoughts of what one wants to say in response.

Activities of daily living   daily self-care activities that healthy people can perform without assistance, such as walking, bathing, dressing, toileting, brushing teeth, and eating.

Administration on Aging   the primary agency of the U.S Department of Health and Human Services designated to carry out the provisions of the Older Americans Act of 1965.

Adult Protective Services Agency   agencies that provide services to abused, neglected, or exploited older adults and adults with disabilities. APS is typically administered by local or state departments and provide investigative services as well as other support services.

Advance directives   a written statement of a person's wishes regarding medical treatment, often including a living will, made to ensure those wishes are carried out should the person be unable to communicate them to a doctor.

Affective flattening   A lack of emotional expressiveness. Also called blunted emotions.

Affordable Care Act   The Patient Protection and Affordable Care Act (ACA), commonly called the Obamacare, is a U.S. federal statute signed into law on March 23, 2010, that significantly overhauled the U.S. health care system.

Affordable housing   housing costs (including utility costs) that make up no more than 30 percent of a household's income.

Ageism   discrimination based on age.

Aid to Families With Dependent Children   an entitlement program passed as a part of the Social Security Act of 1935 that provided economic assistance to mothers and their children. AFDC was replaced with the passage of PRWORA 1996 and TANF.

AIDS cocktail   A variety of antiretroviral drug therapies used to treat HIV-infected patients to prevent the virus from replicating. In many cases the combination of drugs can restore the patient's T-cell counts, thus improving the quality and longevity of life.

Alaska Natives   indigenous peoples of Alaska, United States, including the Iñupiat, Yupik, Aleut, Eyak, Tlingit, Haida, Tsimshian, and a number of Northern Athabaskan cultures.

Allah   refers to the God in Abrahamic religions. A term used by Muslims to refer to their God.

Appalachian Region   a 205,000-square-mile region that follows the spine of the Appalachian Mountains from southern New York to northern Mississippi. Known for high rates of poverty, particularly among Caucasians.

Alzheimer's disease   progressive, degenerative disorder that attacks the brain's nerve cells, or neurons, resulting in loss of memory, thinking and language skills, and behavioral changes.

Anger management   a structured set of classes or program that focus on strategies designed to assist individuals in managing their anger more effectively.

Annual Homeless Assessment Reports (AHAR)   uses collective Homeless Management Information System (HMIS) data from communities across the country, as well as the CoC applications, to produce an annual report presented to U.S. Congress on the extent and nature of homelessness. AHAR reports provide nationwide estimates of homelessness, including information about the demographic characteristics of homeless persons.

Apprenticeship   a labor system involving the legal binding of an individual, including children, through indenture to a master craftsman in order to learn a trade.

Area Agencies on Aging   a nationwide network of programs created in response to the Older Americans Act of 1965, providing an array of services for the older adult population.

Atypical antipsychotic drugs   second generation antipsychotics used to treat psychiatric disorders.

Authorization to release information   a signed voluntary agreement between a client and service provider granting permission to the provider to release certain privileged communication.

Baby boomers   an age cohort of people born between 1946 (just after World War II) and 1964. The age cohort is important demographically because it was large and therefore has been a powerful lobby. The baby boomers are currently between the ages of about 53 and 72 years of age, and thus are an important factor in the growing older adult population.

Behaviorism   a theory used to explain human behavior. Behaviorists believe that behavior is learned through conditioning (reward and punishment), and not due to feelings and emotions.

Best interest of the child doctrine   a court's determinations involving child welfare cases that are determined to serve the best interest of the child.

Bias-based bullying   harassment, intimidation, or bullying based on a person's gender, race, ethnicity, perceived sexual orientation, religion, age, familial status, or mental, physical, or sensory handicap.

Bind out   a historic labor system that connected host families with poor children, usually boys, for the purposes of coerced labor.

Biopsychosocial model   an approach that recognizes the reciprocal involvement of biological psychological, and social factors in human functioning.

Black flight   the large-scale out-migration of African Americans from black or mixed areas with the goal of seeking better economic opportunities, safer communities, newer housing, and better schools.

Bridge employment   a job between full-time work and retirement. Many people will engage in bridge employment when they're approaching retirement age, but aren't quite ready to retire, either for emotional or financial reasons.

Caregiver respite   a service provided for family caregivers (often spouses) of older adults with dementia, providing the family caregiver with a temporary break from caregiving responsibilities. Respite services can be provided in the home or in an adult day care setting.

Case management   a collaborative process involving the coordination of services with a client's service providers, including the assessment, planning, evaluation, and treatment to meet a client's psychosocial needs.

Caste system   a class structure that is determined by birth. In some societies with little social mobility, an individual is destined to remain in the caste within which they are born throughout their life.

Catatonic behavior   a symptom of psychosis involving repetitive behaviors or the lack of movement, such as remaining frozen for long periods of time.

Charity Organization Society   A movement in the late 1800s that had as its goal the organization and centralizing of poor relief, based on the belief that outdoor relief created dependency, and that the poor were better helped through the diagnosis of the causes of poverty by friendly visitors, and the development of a case plan that focused on behavioral reform. The approach of the

Charity Organization Society movement is considered the origin of case management.

Child bonded servants children who were bonded out for labor in early America.

Child labor children involved in the labor force, often on a coerced basis by the government or parents, often due to the child's orphan status and/or social position within society.

Child Protective Services government agencies charged with the legal responsibility for the protection of minor children.

Christian right a social and political movement espousing traditional values and a return to "traditional America," composed of a number of groups from various conservative Christian denominations, most principally evangelicalism and fundamentalism. Also referred to as the conservative right and the hard right.

Chronically homeless an individual or family who has either been continuously homeless for a year or more or has had at least four episodes of homelessness in the past three years.

Cirrhosis of the liver a slowly progressing disease in which healthy liver tissue is replaced with scar tissue, eventually preventing the liver from functioning properly. Caused by hepatitis C, a fatty liver from obesity and diabetes, and alcoholism.

Class conflict the tension or antagonism that exists in society due to competing socioeconomic interests and desires between people of different socioeconomic classes. Also referred to as class warfare or class struggle.

Cognitive symptoms a collection of symptoms associated with schizophrenia involving cognitive processes, including neurocognitive deficits, such as issues with memory, attention, and social skills.

Cognitive theory a theory used to explain mental processing involving thinking and learning, often applied to human behavior. Cognitive theorists believe that behavior is influenced by an individual's thoughts.

Colonial America a period of time in the history of the United States between 1492 and 1763 when it was still under the control of England, prior to independence.

Comorbidity the simultaneous presence of two chronic diseases or conditions in a patient. Often used in reference to a client who is diagnosed with a mental disorder and also has an addiction to alcohol or another substance.

Compulsory education laws state laws that require children to attend school. The first state to pass a compulsory education law was Massachusetts in 1852, and the last state to pass a compulsory education law was Alaska in 1929. The majority of states passed laws between 1870 and 1915. The lower age limit for attendance ranges between 5 and 7 years of age, and the upper age limit ranges between 16 and 18 years of age.

Conservative Christians a term used to describe identified Christians who tend to follow conservative values. Evangelicals, fundamentalists, and some Pentecostal faith traditions are considered conservative Christians. Also associated with the "Christian Right," a conservative religious movement that advocates for traditional family values.

Contemplative practice practices that cultivate an accepting awareness and enhanced attention to present moment experiences, and a belief that with this experience, a sense of interconnectedness to everything else emerges on its own. Also referred to as the mindfulness movement.

Continuum of Care (CoC) program An organization of service providers established by the Department of Housing and Urban Development (HUD) to oversee community planning around homelessness. Also refers to HUD's federal funding program.

Counter-transference the alternate process associated with transference—the process of a client transferring his or her emotions onto a therapist. Countertransference involves the same process, but the therapist transfers emotions onto the client. The concepts of transference and countertransference were originally defined and explored by theorist and psychoanalyst Sigmund Freud.

Court-appointed special advocates CASA workers are court-appointed volunteers who provide advocacy services for children involved in the child welfare system.

Crowdfunding funding a project or venture by raising many small amounts of money from a large number of people, typically via the Internet, on sites such as GoFundMe.com and Kickstarter.com.

Cultural competence the ability to work effectively with people of color and minority populations by being sensitive to their needs and recognizing their unique experiences within society, both historically and culturally.

Curative treatment medical care focused on curing a patient's illness.

Cyberactivism civic, social, and political advocacy that occurs online, particularly via social media.

Cyberbullying the use of electronic communication to bully a person, typically by sending messages of an intimidating or threatening nature, usually via social media.

Cyberstalking the repeated use of electronic communications to harass or frighten someone, for example, by sending threatening emails or stalking someone online.

Cycle of Poverty a phenomenon where poor families remain impoverished because they have no ancestors who can transmit the intellectual, social, and cultural resources necessary to lift them out of poverty.

Cycle of violence Drawn from the work of Lenore Walker, who theorized that domestic violence occurred most often in repeated cycles, beginning with a honeymooning phase, followed by a tension phase, and culminating in an explosion phase, which then led back to another honeymoon phase, repeating the cycle.

Deindustrialization a process of economic change caused by the reduction of industry, such as manufacturing, in a geographical region.

Deinstitutionalization movement The process of transitioning from an institutionalized system of mental health care to a community-based mental health model. Often criticized due to a lack of funding that resulted in erratic and inefficient care for the seriously mentally ill.

Delusions strongly held false beliefs or misperceptions that are not consistent with the person's culture, many of which could not possibly be true.

Dementia a chronic and degenerative brain disease, primarily experienced in old age, marked by memory disorders, personality changes, impaired reasoning, and the eventual shutting down of all bodily systems.

Developing economies a term typically used to describe governments with capitalist societies and democratic governments. The term is criticized by some for implying that other types of economies are inferior to capitalistic ones.

Digital abuse the use of technologies such as texting and social networking to bully, harass, stalk, or intimidate another person, most often a partner. Similar to cyberstalking.

Direct practice counseling practice with individuals.

Discrimination is the behavior or actions, usually negative, toward an individual or group of people, especially on the basis of a unique and defining characteristic, such as gender, race, nationality status, sexual orientation, ability status, social class and age.

Disenfranchised populations a group of people often considered to lack power in society, with no political voice. Examples include refugees, some immigrant groups, and other populations that have experienced social exclusion.

Disorganized speech speech often reflects thinking that makes no sense, with frequent trailing off into incoherent talk.

Disproportionality (child welfare system) a term used to describe the overrepresentation of children of color within the child welfare system.

Domestic sex trafficking The process of forcing an individual to engage in sexual acts for payment against their will. Domestic trafficking involves activities that originate within the United States.

Domestic violence shelters housing and support services for survivors leaving a domestic violence relationship. Services are typically provided to women and children.

Don't Ask, Don't Tell (DADT) the official U.S. policy on service by gays and lesbians in the military. DADT was instituted by President Bill Clinton on February 28, 1994, in response to an attempt to lessen the punitive measures taken when a member of the military was determined to be gay or lesbian. DADT ended on September 20, 2011.

Do-not-resuscitate (DNR) a medical order written by a doctor at a patient (or patient's family's) request instructing health care providers to not do cardiopulmonary resuscitation (CPR) if a patient's breathing stops or if the patient's heart stops beating. Usually used in cases where the patient is terminally ill.

Doubling-up living with family and friends for economic reasons, also called "couch surfing." Considered a part of the hidden homeless.

Dual Relationships a term used in the mental health field to refer to multiple roles held by the mental health provider, such as counselor and friend, or counselor and teacher. Such relationships can lead to ethical dilemmas.

Duty-to-protect a mental health provider's legal obligation to determine that his or her client presents a serious danger of violence to himself or herself, or another human being, and to then take necessary and reasonable steps to protect the client or intended victim against danger.

Duty-to-warn a legal obligation of mental health providers to verbally tell a potential victim that there is a foreseeable danger of violence.

Eastern religious philosophies religions originating from Eastern and Southeastern Asian countries, such as India, China, and Japan. Some Eastern religious philosophies include Taoism.

Ecological model a theory in the social sciences that describes dynamic interrelations among and between personal and environmental factors, for example, Urie Bronfenbrenner's Ecological Framework for Human Development.

Economic injustice disparity within economic distribution with regard to individuals' economic positions, often related to certain characteristics, such as ethnic background, gender, geographic location, and family socioeconomic status.

Elizabethan Poor Laws of 1601 The Act for the Relief of the Poor 1601, popularly known as the Elizabethan Poor Law, was a collection of laws passed in 1601 creating a national poor law system for England and Wales. This legislation effectively formalized previous poor relief legislation and policies.

Emergency shelters supervised sheltering programs that provide beds, a hot meal, drinking water, and restroom facilities. Most emergency shelters include time limits for stays ranging from 30 to 120 days, and offer basic services, such as case management.

Emotional regulation the ability to control one's emotions.

Empowerment theory a multi-dimensional social process that helps people gain control over their own lives.

Empty nesting a stage in the family' life cycle when the children have grown up and moved out of the parental home. This stage can be particularly difficult for some parents, particularly women who may grieve the loss of their daily parenting responsibilities, compelling them to renegotiate their identity, and develop new interests.

Enmeshment a Western concept introduced by Salvador Minuchin to describe families where personal boundaries are undifferentiated, leading to a loss of autonomous development.

Ethical dilemmas refers to situations where there is a choice to be made between two or more options, where none of the options appear to clearly resolve the situation in an ethically acceptable fashion. No clear right or wrong answer, or an argument could be made for each option as being the moral one.

Ethical standards pertaining to conduct in accordance with the rules (or standards) of correct conduct, especially the standards of a profession.

Ethical values determine what is right and what is wrong, behaviorally. To behave ethically means to behave in a manner that is morally correct.

Ethnicity cultural factors, including nationality, regional culture, ancestry, and language.

Ethnic cleansing the mass expulsion or killing of members of an unwanted ethnic or religious group within a society.

Ethics moral principles that govern an individual's or group's behavior.

Eurocentric focusing on European culture or history as preeminent and "normal," to the exclusion of a wider view of the world.

Euthanasia The practice of intentionally ending a life in order to relieve pain and suffering. Illegal in most countries due to ethical issues, including the active role a physician takes in ending a life.

Exclusion from the labor market the systematic process of excluding a subpopulation from employment.

Familism a social structure where the needs of the family are more important and take precedence over the needs of any of the family members.

Family continuity stability along various domains, such as emotional, psychological, and financial, within a family system.

Family genogram a pictorial representation of a person's family tree used in Murray Bowen's family systems theory, highlighting communication styles and other psychosocial dynamics, and focusing on the intergenerational transmission of relational patterns.

Family preservation programs   a movement designed to keep children at home with their biological families rather remove and place them in foster homes or institutions.

Family reunification   the process of reunifying children who have been placed in foster care and returning them to their biological parent(s).

Feeble-minded   an outdated term used during the visiting teacher movement in reference to children with intellectual and cognitive disabilities.

Feudalism   the primary system structure in medieval Europe, where the nobility controlled the monarchy's land in exchange for military service, while the peasants or serfs worked the land in exchange for housing, a share of the produce, and protection.

Food deserts   a low-income region where a substantial number of residents have limited access to a supermarket or large grocery store.

Forced migration   the coerced movement of a person or persons away from their home or home region.

Forensic interviewing techniques   an evidence-based and developmentally sensitive method of obtaining factual information in cases involving abuse or violence. Interviewing techniques involve open-ended questions and forced-choice questions that are not leading in nature.

Friendly visitor   a volunteer working for a charity organization society who visited clients to assess the nature of their problems and offer support and guidance.

Gay-straight alliance clubs (GSAs)   A gay-straight alliance (GSA) is a student-run club in a high school or middle school that brings together LGBTQ and straight students to support each other, provide a safe place to socialize, and create a platform for activism to fight homophobia and transphobia.

Gender nonconforming populations   An umbrella term that refers to people who do not follow other people's ideas or stereotypes about how they should look or act based on the female or male sex they were assigned at birth.

Genderqueer   a person who does not subscribe to conventional gender distinctions but identifies with neither, both, or a combination of male and female genders.

Generalist practice model   a model of working with people in a helping capacity that focuses on basic skills involved in the helping process.

Generalist skill set   the use of a wide range of professional roles, approaches, and skills in a planned change process in diverse settings.

Gerotranscendence   the process of transcending the material aspects of life and moving toward a more existential existence.

Globalization   a process of increasingly interrelated interactions among people, organizations, governments, and systems, including communication that has essentially made the world smaller and more closely connected.

Global North   United States, Canada, Western Europe, and developed parts of East Asia. A preferred term to "Western." Typically references a socioeconomic and political divide.

Global South   Africa, Latin America, and developing Asia including the Middle East. A preferred term to "eastern countries" or "non-Western" countries.

Go viral   related to how communication occurs on the web, specifically when computer mediated communication (CMC) becomes very popular as evidenced by the number of views. What grabs the attention of the online public is of interest to social scientists, who study how a post or video goes from relative obscurity to millions of views, often in a very short time.

Graying of America   a term used to describe the growing aging population.

Great Recession of 2007   one of the terms used to describe a major recession that began in December 2007 in response to the bursting of the real estate bubble, in large part due to predatory lending practices. The recession quickly became a global crisis because of the globalization of market economies, and although the recession officially ended in June of 2009, many economists believe the country is still in recovery.

Great Society programs   the poverty alleviation programs that were developed in response to President Lyndon B. Johnson's war on poverty legislation.

Grief   an emotional reaction, such as deep sorrow, in response to a significant loss, such as a death.

Halakhah   the totality of Jewish law.

Hallucinations   sensations that are experienced as real, but are not, such as hearing voices, seeing things that are not there, smelling smells that do not exist, or feeling sensations when nothing is present.

Health insurance marketplace   A resource (website) where individuals, families, and small businesses can learn about their health coverage options; compare health insurance plans based on costs, benefits, and other important features; choose a plan; and enroll in coverage. Also called the Exchange.

Health pandemic   a global disease outbreak.

Hidden homeless   Although there is not one definition of the hidden homeless, the term typically refers to those individuals who are homeless but not living in shelters or on the streets. Rather they may be "couch surfing," living temporarily with friends or family and not paying rent, or they may be institutionalized, or may be living in a motel not paid for by a government program. This population is considered "hidden" because they usually do not access homeless supports and services even though they are improperly or inadequately housed. Because they do not access services, they do not show up on standard statistics regarding homelessness.

Higher power   A term used to refer a deity. An alternate term used for God that doesn't refer to a specific denomination.

HIPAA Privacy Rule   the first national standards to protect patients' personal health information (PHI).

Historic marginalization   the process of marginalizing population-based identifiable and commonly immutable characteristics, such as race, on a historic (intergenerational) basis.

Historically oppressed and marginalized groups groups of individuals who have experienced intergenerational oppression, often due to some defining characteristic because of race, gender, age, social status, and so forth and are then excluded from the activities and benefits of mainstream society.

HIV/AIDS   HIV stands for human immunodeficiency virus. If left untreated, HIV can lead to the disease AIDS (acquired immunodeficiency syndrome).

HIV-positive status   Being diagnosed with HIV means that an individual has been infected with the human immunodeficiency virus (HIV) and that two HIV tests—a preliminary test and a confirmatory test—have both come back positive.

Holistic   interconnectedness, such as seeing an individual as a whole and not in a compartmentalized fashion.

Holistic health   an ancient approach to health that considers the whole person with an emphasis on the connection between mind, body, and spirit.

Homeless Emergency Assistance and Rapid Transition to Housing (HEARTH) Act   reauthorized HUD's McKinney-Vento Homeless Act Assistance programs under the Obama administration in 2009. The HEARTH Act consolidates three of the separate homeless assistance programs administered by HUD under the McKinney-Vento Homeless Assistance Act into a single grant program, and revises the Emergency Shelter Grants program and renames it the Emergency Solutions Grants (ESG) program. The HEARTH Act also codifies in law the Continuum of Care planning process. The HEARTH Act enhanced the definition of homelessness.

Homophobia   the irrational fear of, aversion to, or discrimination against "homosexuality" or "homosexuals." Note: the term homosexual and homosexuality is now considered an offensive term, which is why these terms are reflected in singular quotation marks.

Housing projects   a euphemism for 1960 congregated housing subsidized by the government through HUD. Also called "the projects."

Imam   a title of various Muslim leaders, including the person who leads prayers in a mosque.

Implicit bias   bias in judgment and/or behavior that results from subtle cognitive processes, such as attitudes and belief in stereotypes, that often occur below a conscious level of awareness.

Impulse control   the ability to control one's emotional impulses, usually anger.

Incapacitated sex   sexual activity engaged in when a party is too intoxicated on drugs and/or alcohol to consent.

Indentured servitude   a labor system commonly employed in the 18th century in North America, where people paid for their passage by working for an employer for a set amount of years. The system was often a source of exploitation of the poor, particularly immigrants.

Indigenous people   people defined in international or national legislation as having a set of specific rights based on their historical ties to a particular territory, and their cultural or historical distinctiveness from other populations that are often politically dominant.

Indigenous populations   groups with historical ties to a particular territory that culturally distinct from other populations. Indigenous populations are often protected in international or national legislation.

Individualized Education Plan (IEP)   a plan or program developed to ensure that a child who has a disability identified under the law and is attending an elementary or secondary school receives necessary instruction specialized for the student.

Indoor Relief   social welfare assistance under England's poor laws and later America's early social welfare system, consisting of recipients being required to enter a workhouse or poorhouse. Indoor relief was typically reserved for those deemed the unworthy poor.

Informed consent   a written document that informs clients of the purpose of the services, related risks, limits to services, and clients' right to refuse services or withdraw consent, and the time frame covered by the consent.

Insight therapy   refers to a range of psychological therapies that have as their goal the increase of personal insight into clients' feelings, behaviors, and motives.

Institutionalized racism   a form of racism expressed in the practice of social and political institutions.

Interfaith   an organization that is comprised of different faith traditions working together for some cause.

Interparental violence   violence occurring between parents in a family structure.

Intersectionality   the interconnected nature of social categorizations such as race, class, and gender, as they apply to a given individual or group, regarded as creating overlapping and interdependent systems of discrimination or disadvantage.

Intrafamilial homicides   the homicide of an individual by a family member, such as when one spouse kills the other, or when a child kills a parent (also called parenticide).

Islamophobia   dislike of or prejudice against Islam or Muslims, especially as a political force.

Itinerant human service providers   human service providers responsible for a large geographical area, who visit communities on a monthly or bimonthly basis.

Jim Crow laws   state and local laws enforcing racial segregation in the Southern United States until 1965. Among other restrictions, Jim Crow laws mandated the segregation of public schools, public places, and public transportation, including restrooms, restaurants, and drinking fountains for whites and blacks. Many believe that Jim Crow laws picked up where slavery left off, leaving African Americans with minimal protections and civil rights.

Judeo-Christian   refers to the common roots of the Jewish and Christian religions. Also refers to an ethical system.

Kaposi's sarcoma (KS)   a cancer that develops from the cells that line lymph or blood vessels. KS is considered an "AIDS defining" illness, thus when KS occurs in someone infected with HIV, that person officially has AIDS.

Kinship care   the raising of children by family members, usually grandparents, because the biological parents are unwilling or unable to do so. Often used in reference to child welfare placements as an alternative to traditional foster care.

Learned helplessness   a condition in which a person suffers from a sense of powerlessness caused by repeated trauma where they initially have no possibility of escape (or perceive they have no control). Individuals who struggle with learned helplessness often continue to feel and act helpless long after their circumstances change and they have power to change their situation.

Least developed countries   a group of countries that have been classified by the UN as "least developed" in terms of their low gross national income (GNI), their weak human assets, and their high degree of economic vulnerability.

Least restricted environment   a requirement of federal law that students with disabilities must receive their education with nondisabled peers, to the maximum extent appropriate and that special education students are not removed from regular classes unless, even with supplemental aids and services, education in regular classes cannot be achieved satisfactorily.

LGBTQ + populations   an acronym for lesbian, gay, bisexual, transgender, queer/questioning, and others, a population of people united by having gender identities or sexual orientations that differ from the heterosexual and the gender majority.

Licensed clinical social worker (LCSW)   the professional license obtained by social workers who have an MSW and complete 3,000 hours of practice work supervised by an LCSW.

Linear stage theory   theories of development that posit that people proceed through a set of sequential stages, with earlier stages serving as a foundation for successive stages.

Limits of confidentiality   legal limitations of clients' right to confidentiality, including a provider's duty to protect and duty to warn.

Living will   a written, legal document that spells out medical treatments you would and would not want to be used to keep you alive, as well as other decisions such as pain management or organ donation.

Longevity   length of life.

Macro level   practice on a societal level.

Macro practice   practice on a broad level, with organizations, communities, or on a policy level.

Macrosystems   in ecological systems theory describing the culture in which individuals live.

Maladaptive behavior   behavior that interferes with an individual's functioning within a range of domains of life.

Mandated clients   Clients who enter treatment under the coercion of a legal body such as a court order, a probation department, or child protective services. Also called involuntary clients.

Mandated reporters   the legal obligation of professionals who regularly engage with children to report cases of suspected abuse to the appropriate legal authorities.

Marginalization   a concept used to describe a contemporary form of social disadvantage and relegation to the fringe of society. Subpopulations with stigmatizing characteristics related to race, sexual orientation, gender, age, religion, immigration status, nationality, and socioeconomic status are often marginalized by more privileged and powerful members of society.

Mass urbanization   a population shift from rural to urban, often in response to a changing economy.

Medical power of attorney   a type of advance directive in which you name a person to make decisions for you when you are unable to do so. In some states this directive may also be called a durable power of attorney for health care or a health care proxy.

Mental Health Courts Program   A Bureau of Justice Assistance (BJA) program designed as an alternative court system for adult mentally ill nonviolent felony defendants with the goal of diverting offenders with a diagnosed mental illness from the criminal justice system to the mental health system. Services include counseling, employment, housing, and support services.

Mental health parity   a term used to describe mental health conditions and substance use disorders being treated equally to physical health disorders by insurance companies.

Men who have sex with men (MSM)   a term used to categorize males who engage in sexual activity with other males, regardless of whether they identify themselves as gay or straight.

Meta-theories   a theory whose subject matter is broad and perceived universal.

Mezzo level   counseling practice with groups.

Micro-aggressions   everyday verbal and nonverbal slights, snubs, or insults, whether intentional or unintentional, which communicate hostile, derogatory, or negative messages to target persons based solely upon their marginalized group membership. Often used in reference to disparate treatment of certain ethnic minority populations and other marginalized groups.

Micro level   practice with individuals.

Micro practice   counseling practice with individuals, also called direct practice.

Microsystems   the institutions and groups that most immediately and directly impact the child's development, including family, school, religious institutions, neighborhood, and peers.

Middle Ages   the period of European history from the fall of the Roman Empire in the West (5th century) to the fall of Constantinople (1453), or, more narrowly, from circa 1100 to 1453.

Midlife crisis   a term used to describe an experience that some individuals have in middle age when they reach the midpoint in their lives and realize they have more time behind them than ahead of them. Although there is no empirical support for the uniformity of the midlife crisis, contemporary folklore posits that people in a midlife crisis are prone to behave irrationally in an attempt to regain their lost youth, such as buying a sports car, quitting their job, or having an extramarital affair.

Millennium Development Goals   eight international development goals designed to better the lives of the world's poorest people. They were established following the Millennium Summit of the United Nations in 2000.

Mindfulness Movement   a broad term used to describe a practice that helps individuals develop a sense of awareness and presence in their daily life.

Mission statement   a formal summary of the goals and values of a company or organization.

The Mississippi Delta   a 200-mile long and 70-mile wide (at its widest point) of the northwest section of the state of Mississippi between the Mississippi and Yazoo Rivers. Known for its unique history, including its history of slavery, as well as for high rates of poverty.

Mood symptoms   a collection of symptoms associated with schizophrenia involving alterations in mood, typically including excessive happiness or sadness.

Morality   principles concerning the distinction between right and wrong or good and bad behavior.

Moral treatment movement   an approach to mental disorder based on humane psychosocial care that emerged in the 18th and 19th centuries in response to systemic abuses of the mentally ill.

Motivational interviewing (MI)   a method that works on facilitating and engaging intrinsic motivation within the client in order to change behavior.

Mourn   the process one undertakes to psychologically deal with a significant loss, such as a death.

Multi-infarct dementia   multiple strokes in the brain that cause memory loss and other cognitive impairments.

Multi-partner fertility   parents who have children with more than one partner.

Muslims   a follower of the religion of Islam.

Native American   a member of any of the indigenous populations of America, but often excluding those of Hawaiian, Pacific Islander, or Alaskan origin, who have their own distinct designations.

Native-born   born in a particular country. Often used in the context of native-born citizen, indicating that an individual gained citizenship by being born in a country, compared to naturalized citizenship granted to a foreign-born citizen.

Native Hawaiians and Other Pacific Islanders   the indigenous peoples of Hawaii, Guam, Samoa, or other Pacific Islands.

Nativism   the policy of protecting the interests of native-born or established inhabitants against those of immigrants.

Negative symptoms   a collection of symptoms associated with schizophrenia involving a lack of feelings or behaviors that are present in the normal population. For example, the loss of interest in everyday activities. Associated with psychotic disorders, such as schizophrenia.

Neoliberal philosophies   political philosophies that support laissez-faire economic liberalism, including privatization, deregulation, free trade and smaller government. There is considerable debate surrounding whether neoliberalism benefits all members of society or principally the more wealthy. The term has its origins in 1930s Europe but experienced a resurgence in the 1980s to reflect a more radical form of capitalism that advocates for a significant reduction in government involvement.

New Age spirituality   a term applied to a range of spiritual or religious beliefs and practices that share a belief in a holistic and universal divinity. The New Age movement is comprised of a loose network of organizations that became popular in Western countries in the 1970s and 1980s that believe in mysticism and universalism, a holistic approach to the divine where all is one.

New Deal programs   a series of domestic programs enacted by Congress and executive order by President Franklin D. Roosevelt in the United States between 1933 and 1938, in response to the Great Depression. The New Deal Programs focused on the "Three R's": Relief, Recovery, and Reform.

No Child Left Behind Act   federal legislation focusing on standards-based educational reform. Reauthorized as the Every Student Succeeds Act, which in response to intense criticism about NCLB's national mandates, returned primary control for curriculum development to the states.

Non-governmental organizations   an organization or charity that is not a part of a government or a for-profit business.

Observation skills   the ability of a counselor to observe all aspects of clients' demeanor during sessions, including their words, eyes, and body language.

Older Americans Act   the first federal law, passed in 1965, that provided comprehensive services for older adults.

Open-ended questions   questions that do not allow respondents to answer "yes" or "no" and permit them the scope to answer in a way they believe is appropriate.

Opioids   Opioids are medications that reduce pain by lowering the intensity of pain signals reaching the brain. Opioids also control emotion. Common opioids include Vicodin, OxyContin, Percocet, morphine, and codeine. Opioids can be highly addictive.

Orphans   a child with no parents, either through death or abandonment. May also include children with only one parent, or unaccompanied children.

Orphan trains   a movement in the late 19th and early 20th centuries started by Rev. Loring Brace that involved sending street orphans from New York and other large urban centers on trains to reside with farming families in the west who were willing to care for them.

Outdoor Relief   social welfare assistance under England's poor laws and later America's early social welfare system, consisting of money, food, clothing, or goods without the requirement that the recipient enter an institution.

Outlaw motorcycle gang (OMG)   A group of motorcycle owners who band together and agree to disobey society's laws, typically for monetary gain and to increase power and terror. The Hells Angels is considered an outlaw motorcycle gang.

Out-migration   the process of leaving one community to settle in another. It is usually widespread, as seen in population movements that are economically driven.

Palliative care   specialized medical care for people with serious and/or life threatening illnesses that focuses on providing patients with relief from the symptoms and stress of a serious illness, including pain. The goal is to improve quality of life for both the patient and the family.

Parachurch organizations   Faith-based organizations that work outside of a specific church to engage in human services and evangelism.

Parenting classes   a structured set of classes or program that focus on parenting training, including normative child development and best practice in regard to parenting styles and techniques. Often required for biological parents involved in the child welfare system.

Patient Protection and Affordable Care Act   a U.S. federal statute signed into law by President Barack Obama on March 23, 2010. Also referred to as the Affordable Care Act (ACA) or colloquially Obamacare. Considered a significant overhaul of the U.S. health care system, with the goals of increasing the quality and affordability of health insurance, and reducing the costs of health care for individuals and the government.

Patriarchy   a hierarchical political and social system that privileged males, where men as a group have more power and control women as a group, both structurally and ideologically.

Permanency plan   a report prepared by child welfare workers involving a plan regarding children having removed from their homes and biological parents and placed in the custody of the child welfare system.

Permanent housing programs   supportive housing programs that offer subsidized housing on a permanent basis, typically government subsidized through HUD.

Person-in-environment approach   a practice-guiding principle in social work that highlights the importance of understanding an individual within the context of the environmental contexts in which that person lives and acts.

Personal Responsibility and Work Opportunity Act   social welfare legislation passed in 1996 that ended the former entitlement social welfare program, ushering in a welfare-to-work philosophy.

Physician aid-in-dying (PAD)   a practice in which a physician provides a competent, terminally ill patient with a prescription for a lethal dose of medication, upon the patient's request, which the patient intends to use to end his or her own life. This newer approach to assisted dying is believed to be easier for the physician ethically since the physician does not take as active an approach as with euthanasia.

Plea arrangement   an agreement in a criminal case between the prosecutor and defendant where the defendant agrees to plead guilty to a particular charge in return for some concession from the prosecutor. Also called a plea bargain and plea deal.

Pneumocystis carinii pneumonia (PCP)   A lung infection caused by the fungus *Pneumocystis jirovecii*. PCP occurs in people with weakened immune systems, including people with HIV. The first signs of infection are difficulty breathing, high fever, and dry cough.

Point-in-time (PIT) counts   (as defined by HUD) is a snapshot of the homeless population taken on a given day. It provides a count of sheltered and unsheltered homeless persons from either the last biennial count or a more recent annual count. This count includes a street count in addition to a count of all clients in emergency and transitional beds.

Policy advocacy   a form of macro advocacy that is facilitated on a policy level in an attempt to change government policies and legislation to benefit human services clients.

Post-traumatic stress disorder   a psychological disorder involving a set of symptoms commonly experienced by individuals after experiencing a traumatic event or experience.

Post-traumatic stress disorder (PTSD)   a clinical disorder that involves a collection of symptoms in response to the exposure of a traumatic event, including intrusive memories, hyperarousal, and efforts to avoid emotional triggers.

Positive identity   a positive appraisal of one's personality and strengths.

Positive symptoms   a collection of symptoms associated with schizophrenia involving a presence of thoughts, behaviors, and sensory perceptions, not present in the normal population.

Prejudice   an unjustified or incorrect attitude (usually negative) toward an individual based solely on the individual's membership in a social group.

Privileged communication   a client's legal right barring having their disclosures to certain professionals revealed during legal proceedings or other communication, without their informed consent.

Prohibition era   the period from 1920 to 1933 when the sale of alcohol beverages became illegal in the United States through a constitutional amendment.

Proselytizing   the process of converting or attempting to convert (someone) from one religion, belief, or opinion to another.

Protestant work ethic   a term originally coined by Max Weber emphasizing that hard work and frugality are a result of a person's status of salvation in the Protestant faith, particularly in Calvinism (also referred to as the Puritan work ethic).

Protracted refugee situations   The Office of the United Nations High Commissioner for Refugees (UNHCR) defines protracted refugee situations as those "in which refugees find themselves in a long-lasting and intractable state of limbo. Their lives may not be at risk, but their basic rights and essential economic, social, and psychological needs remain unfulfilled after years in exile."

Psychoeducational approaches   an intervention strategy that combines counseling with education about psychosocial dynamics and other relevant phenomena.

Psychosocial assessment   a comprehensive evaluation prepared by many mental health providers upon intake of a client's mental health, social status, and functioning level and capacity.

Psychosocial risk factors   psychological, emotional, and social factors in an individual's life that increase their risk for a range of problems.

Qur'an   the Islamic sacred book, believed to be the word of God as dictated to Muhammad by the archangel Gabriel and written down in Arabic. Also spelled Koran.

Race   a person's physical characteristics, such as bone structure and skin, hair, or eye color.

Racialized others   a sociological term referring to the process of ascribing ethnic or racial identities to a group that did not identify itself as such.

Rape as a weapon of war   wartime sexual violence involving rape, gang rape, and any type of sexual violence by combatants during armed conflict.

Rape Trauma Syndrome   the psychological trauma experienced by a rape victim, which includes disruptions to normal physical, emotional, cognitive, and interpersonal thinking and behavior.

Rapid rehousing   Continuum of Care funds may provide supportive services, and/or short-term (up to three months) and/or medium-term (for 3 to 24 months) tenant-based rental assistance as necessary to help a homeless individual or family, with or without disabilities, move as quickly as possible into permanent housing and achieve stability in that housing. Assistance must include case management services.

Relative moral principles   the view that ethical standards and morality (principles of right or wrong) are culturally determined and thus subject to a person's individual perspectives, worldview, and choice. Also referred to as moral relativism.

Relative poverty   a standard for defining poverty in terms of the society in which an individual lives and which therefore differs between countries and over time.

Religion   a social or cultural experience grounded in a religious tradition.

Resilience   a person's ability to recover quickly from challenges and difficult times.

Restorative justice model   a model for handling crime that is based not on punitive measures, but on bringing the victim, offender, and community together, where all parties have equal parts in repairing the relationships destroyed by crime.

Restraint   physical restraint that immobilizes or reduces the ability of a student to move. Physical restraint does not include actions taken to break up a fight, comfort a student, or actions taken to prevent a student's impulsive act to injure him or herself.

Rural depopulation   decreasing populations of remote and economically depressed rural communities.

Rural enclaves   rural areas within a larger geographic community.

Rurality   a sociological term defining what is rural.

Section 8 Housing   a HUD subsidized housing program for the general population.

Section 811 Housing   a HUD subsidized housing program for adults with disabilities, including mental illness.

Seclusion   the involuntary isolation of a student in a room, enclosure, or space from which the student is isolated from others.

Self-appraisal   the evaluation of one's own strengths and deficits.

Self-assessment   the evaluation of oneself, including one's actions, attitudes, and performance, most commonly in comparison to an objective standard.

Self-efficacy   a concept originally coined by social psychologist Albert Bandura referring to an individual's belief in his or her competence in completing tasks successfully.

Self-fulfilling prophecy   a prediction that directly or indirectly causes itself to become true.

Self-injury   the act of injuring oneself intentionally without meaning to commit suicide.

Self-knowledge   understanding of oneself and one's motives.

Serious mental illness   any mental, behavioral, or emotional disorder that significantly interferes with their life activities, such as their relationships, employment, parenting, or personal life management skills.

Settlement houses   social service residential organizations in large urban centers that provided a home and services to primarily newly arrived and non-English-speaking immigrants who were often exploited in factories. The settlement house movement was initiated in the United States by Jane Addams.

Settlement house movement   a reformist social movement (1880–1920) initiated in England and then the United States that established interdependent communities of middle class and poor (especially immigrants) with the goal of creating community through the sharing knowledge and culture in order to alleviate poverty and social exclusion. The settlement houses provided advocacy, child care, housing, and classes.

Sharecropping   a system of agriculture in which a landowner allows a tenant to use the land in return for a share of the crops produced on their portion of land. Similar to Feudalism in the Middle Ages. Sharecropping was practiced after the end of slavery, but few blacks had any legal protection because despite working a piece of land for generations, the sale of a property, or upon the whim of a landowner, black sharecropping families could be evicted from the land with little notice and no recourse.

Single room occupancy   the SRO Program provides rental assistance for homeless persons in connection with the moderate rehabilitation of SRO dwellings. SRO housing contains units for occupancy by one person.

Skid Row   a section in downtown Los Angeles that contains one of the country's most stable homeless population (between 3,000 and 6,000 people). Skid row has become a euphemism for the stereotypical homeless man of color who abuses alcohol and drugs.

Smart mobs   Internet-driven mass mobilization.

Social change   change affected on a social level involving social justice and human rights.

Social Darwinism   a concept referring to the application of the biological principles of natural selection and survival of the fittest to the social and political realms.

Social diagnosis   a concept created by Mary Richmond, an early COS leader, involving the search for the cause of poverty by examining the interaction between the poor and their environment.

Social exclusion   often considered in relation to poverty, referring to the overt or covert exclusion of segments of society from the benefits of mainstream society, including political activities (e.g., the limiting of voting rights), social activities (e.g., through the barring of church attendance or club memberships), and economic activities.

Social gospel A Protestant religious movement in the United States in the late 19th century that had the goal of compelling the Christian church to be more responsive to social problems, such as poverty and social reform.

Social learning theory explains how people learn new behaviors, values, and attitudes through watching others and modeling after their behavior.

Social mores acceptable customs, norms, and behaviors in a particular society or social group.

Social oppression a concept that describes a relationship of dominance and subordination between categories of people in which one benefits from the systematic abuse, exploitation, and injustice directed toward the other.

The Southern Black Belt a group of counties containing higher than average percentages of black residents, stretching through parts of Virginia, the Carolinas, Georgia, Florida, Alabama, Mississippi, Tennessee, Louisiana, Arkansas, and Texas. Known for high poverty rates, particularly among African Americans.

Social problems a social issue, such as poverty, that negatively impacts segments of society (often more vulnerable members of society).

Spirituality the experience of having an independent relationship with a deity, involving a search for the sacred—a process that involves seeking out that which is considered holy or the divine.

Statement of faith a creed summarizing the core tenets of a religious community.

Strengths-based approach a practice perspective used initially in social work, developed by David Saleebey, that focuses on finding strengths in client and communities, rather than focusing on deficits. Saleebey believed that clients have the ability to be resourceful and resilient in the face of adversity, and that by using a strengths-based perspective with any counseling model, a social worker could tap into these strengths to assist clients and client systems in more effectively managing challenges.

Student services team a multidisciplinary team of professionals that support students in a range of ways. Most student services teams include school social workers, school counselors, school psychologists, as well as speech/language therapists, learning specialists, and school administrators.

Successful aging a term used to describe aging well psychologically, socially, and biologically.

Suicidal gesture a suicidal attempt that does not result in death.

Suicidal ideation the process of thinking about committing suicide, without actually doing so.

Survival of the fittest a term coined by Herbert Spencer, a British philosopher, referring to the application of the biological principles of natural selection to the social world. Survival of the fittest implies that only the stronger members of society are destined to survive, thus charity and other means to intervene in the natural order will only serve to weaken society.

Swarming a strategy used by cyberactivists that organizes multiple groups in the engagement of simultaneous political activities, made to appear as though their actions were independent and unrelated.

Sweatshop conditions any working environment, but particularly factories, that does not employ labor laws and compels workers to work in harsh conditions, such as long hours, unsafe working conditions, and perhaps even emotional and physical abuse.

Schizophrenia an incurable and chronic brain disorder that impacts how people think, feel, and behave. Characterized by hallucinations, delusions in thinking, as well as other profoundly debilitating symptoms.

Tanakh The Jewish scriptures, which consist of three divisions, the Torah, the Prophets, and the Writings.

Temporary Assistance for Needy Families (TANF) the public assistance program in the United States that replaced Aid to Families With Dependent Children (AFDC). The social welfare program developed in response to PRWORA of 1996 legislation.

Thanatologist an individual who practices the scientific study of death and the practices associated with it, including the study of the needs of the terminally ill and their families.

Therapeutic foster care intensive, individualized mental health services provided to children within specialized foster care placement.

Three-strikes law a law that significantly increases the prison sentences of persons convicted of a felony who have been previously convicted of two or more violent crimes or serious felonies. Three strikes laws often result in individuals receiving an automatic sentence of life for their third qualifying felony. Often criticized by human rights advocates due to the harsh nature of the law, including what qualifies as a serious felony (e.g., drug offenses) and the age of those being charged (youth or young adults).

Throw-away youth   Youth who have been asked, told, or forced to leave home by parents or caregivers with no alternate care arranged.

Torah   the law of God as revealed to Moses and recorded in the first five books of the Hebrew scriptures, also called the Pentateuch.

Transitional housing programs   temporary housing programs that offer housing and associated services for up to 24 months.

Transitional shelter   A long-term shelter for female survivors of intimate partner violence focusing on gaining self-sufficiency and autonomy.

Transracial adoption   the placement of a child of one race or ethnic group with adoptive parents of another race or ethnic group.

Trauma-informed therapy   an organizational structure and treatment framework that involves understanding, recognizing, and responding to all types of traumatic experiences.

Treatment modalities   a therapeutic approach including treatment intervention strategies used with individual clients or within a mental health program.

Tudor Poor Laws   poor relief laws in England during the Tudor period (1485–1603). These laws were replaced with the passage of the Elizabethan Poor Laws of 1601.

Tzedakah   the religious obligation to do what is right and just for the poor and needy.

U.S. Housing and Urban Development (HUD) The U.S. Department of Housing and Urban Development (HUD) is a department in the executive branch of the U.S. federal government. HUD's mission is to create strong, sustainable, inclusive communities and quality affordable homes for all.

Ungame   a non-competitive learning and communication board game that fosters listening skills and prosocial communication skills.

Universal moral principles   the view that ethics and morals are universal for all people in similar situations, regardless of culture, race, sex, religion, nationality, sexual orientation, or any other distinguishing feature. Also referred to as moral universalism.

Vagrancy   a term used in early America and England to describe an idle homeless person, typically a man. The term was often used as a pejorative.

Vicarious trauma   the impact on a trauma worker or helper that results from empathic engagement with traumatized clients and their reports of traumatic experiences.

Visiting Teacher Movement (1906–1940)   visiting teachers were social workers who worked at settlement houses in large urban centers and volunteered to work in public schools to help immigrants, children with disabilities, and maladjusted children. The focus of the visiting teacher movement was on creating stronger connections between home and school and encouraging children to attend school.

War on Poverty   the unofficial name for legislation introduced by President Lyndon B. Johnson during his State of the Union address on January 8, 1964, in response to an unprecedentedly high national poverty rate.

Watergate scandal   a major political scandal that occurred in the United States in the 1970s following a break-in at the Democratic National Committee (DNC) headquarters at the Watergate office complex in Washington, D.C., and President Richard Nixon's administration's attempted cover-up of its involvement. President Nixon resigned in response to the scandal.

Welfare queen   a pejorative phrase used in the United States to refer to people, usually women of color, who are accused of fraudulently collecting welfare benefits because they do not want to work. Most historians and social policy experts now deem the welfare queen a myth created and used by politicians to manipulate the public into supporting reductions in social welfare spending.

Western society   There are many different definitions, but most often in social and political discourse, "western" society, culture, or civilization refers to developed countries that share certain fundamental political ideologies, including those of liberal democracy, the rule of law, human rights, and gender equality. Western versus Eastern (or the "West versus the rest") and developed versus undeveloped is increasingly considered culturally insensitive, thus the terms *Global North* and *Global South* are often the preferred terminology when attempting to describe the nature of societies.

The Worthy and the Unworthy Poor   Under England's earliest poor laws the poor were categorized as either worthy or unworthy. Worthy poor included those dependent persons who were poor through no fault of their own—principally, orphans, widows, the handicapped, and older adults were considered the worthy poor. Dependent persons who were perceived as having caused their own poverty—principally those who were vagrants, drunkards, lazy and immoral, and refused to work, were considered the unworthy poor. Many social welfare experts believe that elements of these sentiments remain in contemporary social welfare policy.

White flight   the large-scale out-migration of middle-class Caucasians from racially mixed urban regions to more racially homogeneous suburban or exurban regions. Sociologists believe that when a neighborhood reaches approximately 30 percent racially mixed, Caucasians will begin to leave.

White privilege   societal privileges that benefit white people (often from European descent), unavailable to non-white people under the same social, political, or economic circumstances.

Women's shelter   A temporary shelter for women and their children escaping a domestic violence relationship. Also called a battered women's shelter.

Women's suffrage   women's right to vote.

Word salad   a symptom of schizophrenia involving disorganized speech and incoherent talk

Wraparound services   an approach to human services that provides intensive, individualized, and holistic care to individuals in need.

Xenophobia   an intense or irrational dislike or fear of people from other countries.

Text Credits

Chapter 1

p. 7: Michelle E. Martin, Introduction to Human Services: Through the Eyes of Practice Settings, 4E, © 2018, Pearson Education, Inc., New York, NY; p. 13: Michelle E. Martin, Introduction to Human Services: Through the Eyes of Practice Settings, 4E, © 2018, Pearson Education, Inc., New York, NY.

Chapter 2

p. 37: From "GLAAD Media Reference Guide" by GLAAD. Published by Gay & Lesbian Alliance Against Defamation, Inc. © 2010.

Chapter 3

p. 52: Michelle E. Martin, Introduction to Human Services: Through the Eyes of Practice Settings, 4E, © 2018, Pearson Education, Inc., New York, NY.

Chapter 4

pp. 78–79: Michelle E. Martin, Introduction to Human Services: Through the Eyes of Practice Settings, 4E, © 2018, Pearson Education, Inc., New York, NY.

Chapter 5

p. 109: Michelle E. Martin, Introduction to Human Services: Through the Eyes of Practice Settings, 4E, © 2018, Pearson Education, Inc., New York, NY.

Chapter 6

p. 136: From "Adolescence: Its Psychology and Its Relations to Physiology, Anthropology, Sociology, Sex, Crime, Religion and Education." by G. Stanley Hall, published 1904 by D. Appleton & Company.

Chapter 8

p. 192: Michelle E. Martin, Introduction to Human Services: Through the Eyes of Practice Settings, 4E, © 2018, Pearson Education, Inc., New York, NY.

Chapter 9

p. 209: Michelle E. Martin, Introduction to Human Services: Through the Eyes of Practice Settings, 4E, © 2018, Pearson Education, Inc., New York, NY.

Chapter 12

p. 292: Matthew 25:35–36; p. 297: Qur'an 70:24–25.

Chapter 14

p. 345: Based on Appalachian Regional Commission; p. 347: Based on Gallup-Healthways Well-Being™ Index: Methodology Report for Indexes. Published by MeYou Health, LLC.

Chapter 15

p. 361: From "Road to Dignity by 2030: UN chief launches blueprint towards sustainable development." By United Nations Development Programme. Used by permission of the United Nations Development Programme © 2014; p. 364: Michelle E. Martin, Introduction to Human Services: Through the Eyes of Practice Settings, 4E, © 2018, Pearson Education, Inc., New York, NY; p. 367: Based on "ILO Global Estimate of Forced Labour". Published by International Labour Organization © 2012.

Index

Note: Page numbers followed by an *f* refer to figures. Page numbers followed by a *ph* refer to photographs. Page numbers followed by *t* refer to tables.